D1188036

Quaker Constitutionalism and the Political Thought of John Dickinson

In the late seventeenth century, Quakers originated a unique strain of constitutionalism, based on their theology and ecclesiology, that emphasized constitutional perpetuity and radical change through popular peaceful protest. While Whigs could imagine no other means of drastic constitutional reform except revolution, Quakers denied this as a legitimate option to halt governmental abuse of authority and advocated instead civil disobedience. This theory of a perpetual yet amendable constitution and its concomitant idea of popular sovereignty are things that most scholars believe did not exist until the American Founding. The most notable advocate of this theory was Founding Father John Dickinson, champion of American rights, but not revolution. His thought and action have been misunderstood until now, when they are placed within the Quaker tradition. This theory of Quaker constitutionalism can be traced in a clear and direct line from early Quakers through Dickinson to Martin Luther King, Jr.

Jane E. Calvert received her Ph.D. from the University of Chicago in 2003 and is currently assistant professor of history at the University of Kentucky. Her articles and reviews have been published in *History of Political Thought, Pennsylvania Magazine of History and Biography, History Compass, Annali di storia dell' esegesi, Quaker Religious Thought, Journal of Religion, Quaker History*, and *Pennsylvania History*. She has also received fellowships and grants from the University of Chicago (1996–99, 1999, 2001, 2002); Haverford College (2000); the Library Company of Philadelphia/Historical Society of Pennsylvania (2002); the Newberry Library (2005); the National Endowment for the Humanities (2005); the American Philosophical Society (2006); the Huntington Library (2006); and the David Library of the American Revolution (2007). She is currently working on an edited volume of John Dickinson's political writings.

Quaker Constitutionalism and the Political Thought of John Dickinson

JANE E. CALVERT
University of Kentucky

CAMBRIDGE
UNIVERSITY PRESS

CAMBRIDGE UNIVERSITY PRESS
Cambridge, New York, Melbourne, Madrid, Cape Town, Singapore, São Paulo, Delhi

Cambridge University Press
32 Avenue of the Americas, New York, NY 10013-2473, USA

www.cambridge.org
Information on this title: www.cambridge.org/9780521884365

First published 2009

Printed in the United States of America

A catalog record for this publication is available from the British Library.

Library of Congress Cataloging in Publication Data

Calvert, Jane E., 1970–
Quaker constitutionalism and the political thought of John Dickinson / Jane E. Calvert.
     p.   cm.
Includes bibliographical references and index.
ISBN 978-0-521-88436-5 (hbk.)
1. Dickinson, John, 1732–1810 – Political and social views.   2. Quakers – United
States – Political activity – History – 18th century.   3. Constitutional history – United States.
4. Political science – United States – History – 18th century.   5. United States – Politics and
government – 1775–1783.   6. United States – Politics and government – 1783–1809.
7. Pennsylvania – Politics and government – 1775–1865.   8. Delaware – Politics and
government – 1775–1865.   9. Legislators – United States – Biography.   10. Quakers –
Pennsylvania – Biography.   I. Title.
E302.6.D5C34   2009
973.3'092–dc22   2008029668

ISBN   978-0-521-88436-5 hardback

For Eric

Contents

Acknowledgments

Looking back, I imagine I can see the beginnings of this book in my first year of college – at a Quaker school, reading Aristotle's *Nichomachean Ethics*, and being entranced with his description of moderated political participation as the highest good. By graduation I had a growing collection of questions that needed answering – about Americans and how they relate to one another and their government and about Quakerism. Beginning this project as my master's thesis at the University of Chicago was a first attempt to find answers.

As the study progressed through the dissertation and into this final form, teachers, mentors, colleagues, and friends shaped it and helped bring it forth with their own questions and observations. I can trace the birth of specific themes back to their words. Tom Hamm asked me what I thought of Quaker quietism. Martin Marty talked with me about the "leaky Quakers," with their porous and fluid community. Catherine Brekus pushed me to think about whether Quakers were simply radical Puritans. Pauline Maier and Ethan Shagan thought with me about whether Quakers, as pacifists, could be considered Whigs. And, in a question that turned the dissertation toward a book, Cass Sunstein asked whether Quakers considered the constitution sacrosanct. While these snippets are hardly the only guidance I received, they are the moments that stand out in my mind as turning points in the development of my thesis. I hope my responses do justice to their queries.

Many others were helpful in equally important ways. Mark Noll served as my constant optimistic skeptic, always challenging, rarely convinced in the early stages, but always encouraging. Matt Cohen described, in terms that are still beyond me, why my project was worthwhile. Paul Rahe and Kenneth Bowling had, among much sage advice, the foresight to know that I was writing a book about John Dickinson years before I did. It was my good fortune that Jim Green at the Library Company of Philadelphia directed me their way. The kind folks at the Friends Library of Swarthmore College were always ready with bountiful resources, reliable assistance, and donations to the Calvert library. Georg Mauerhoff at Readex gave me access to *Archive of Americana*, without which I would have been at a loss. Lisa Clark Diller provided me with among the most thoughtful comments on an early draft. My student assistants, Peter Regan and Karl Alexander, worked long hours with messy early footnotes. The RHCP were ever present with their spicy soul food for the heart and mind, which sustained me in ways nothing else could. Lew Bateman, my editor at Cambridge, was as patient as he could be with this simultaneously picky and ignorant first-time author. And the Friends of the John Dickinson Mansion have been as enthusiastic an audience as a scholar can hope to have. My heartfelt appreciation to each and all.

Fellowships and grants from a number of institutions were also crucial for the completion of the project. Most important was the Newberry Library (Monticello College Foundation Fellowship), where, with the gifts of six months without teaching and a lively and supportive intellectual community, the dissertation transformed, seemingly on its own, into a book. Those were, without a doubt, the most fulfilling months of my professional life. An NEH "We the People" Summer Stipend and the administration of St. Mary's College of Maryland contributed to this scholarly getaway. The support of the Library Company of Philadelphia and the Historical Society of Pennsylvania (Andrew W. Mellon Foundation Fellowship), often embodied in the person of librarian Connie King, allowed me access to the seminal resources on Dickinson. The American Philosophical Society (Library Residence Research Fellowship), the Haverford College Quaker Collection (Gest Fellowship), and the Huntington Library (Robert L. Middlekauff Fellowship) offered unique and indispensable resources and support in spectacular environs. The bucolic, if not rabbit-friendly, environment of the David Library of the American Revolution (Library Fellowship) was the fulfillment of a dream – twenty-four-hour library access to everything a girl could desire on the War of Independence. Conversations with the staffs and scholars I have met at these places enriched and complicated my ideas. I am grateful to all of them.

Acknowledgment is also due to several journals for allowing me to reprint portions of articles in this study: "The Quaker Theory of a Civil Constitution," *History of Political Thought* vol. 27, no. 4 (2006), 586–619; "America's Forgotten Founder: John Dickinson and the American Revolution," *History Compass*, 5/3 (May 2007), 1001–11, DOI 10.1111/j.1478–0542.2007.00424.x; and "Liberty without Tumult: Understanding the Politics of John Dickinson," *Pennsylvania Magazine of History and Biography* vol. 132, no. 3 (2007), 233–62. The readers at these journals, as well as those at Cambridge University Press, offered wonderful encouragement and suggestions.

My deepest appreciation goes to my family. My mother, Jenifer Patterson, was a constant, without whom I would not have even made it through graduate school. I am sure the political theory genes I inherited from my father-professor, Robert Calvert, as well as the decades of ideas he exposed me to, are the reason I had any questions to begin with. And my brother, Edward Calvert, was always interested in and appreciative of my progress.

Above all, however, this project would not have emerged from the dark recesses without my husband, Eric Kiltinen. The questions he asked, drawing it out, and the hours he spent (often trapped in a moving car) listening to my inchoate musings cannot be enumerated. He has been an invaluable sounding-board, a learned theologian, a meticulous editor and index-helper, a competent computer-fixer, a reliable and loving cat- and horse-sitter, a steady Baconbringenhomer, cook, carpenter, and all-around Hausmann, and my friend. If there is anything worthy about this book, I owe it to him, because it could not have been written without him.

Lexington, Kentucky
June 2008

Abbreviations

APS	American Philosophical Society
Delegates	*Letters from the Delegates to Congress, 1774–1789.* Paul Hubert Smith, ed. 25 vols. Summerfield, FL: Historical Database, 1995.
DPA	Delaware Public Archives
FHL	Friends Historical Library, Swarthmore College
HSP	Historical Society of Pennsylvania
HQC	Haverford College Quaker Collection
Friends' Library	*The Friends' Library: comprises journals, doctrinal treatises, and other writings of the Religious Society of Friends.* William Evans and Thomas Evans, eds. 14 vols. Philadelphia: J. Rakestraw, 1837–50.
JCC	*Journals of the Continental Congress, 1774–1789.* Worthington C. Ford et al., eds. Washington, DC, 1904–37.
JDP/LCP	John Dickinson Papers, Library Company of Philadelphia
LL	*Lawmaking and Legislators in Pennsylvania: A Biographical Dictionary, 1682–1709.* Craig Horle et al., eds. 3 vols. Philadelphia: University of Pennsylvania Press, 1991–2005.
LCP	Library Company of Philadelphia
Letters	John Dickinson, *Letters from a Farmer in Pennsylvania, To the Inhabitants of the British Colonies* (1767–68) in Forrest McDonald, ed., *Empire and Nation: Letters from a Farmer in Pennsylvania (John Dickinson); Letters from a Federal Farmer (Richard Henry Lee)*, 2nd ed. (Indianapolis: The Liberty Fund, 1999).

"Notes"   John Dickinson, handwritten notes on his copy of
                 *The Constitution of the Common-Wealth of
                 Pennsylvania* (Philadelphia, 1776), 5–9, located
                 in the Library Company of Philadelphia.

Resolutions   Resolutions from the "Meeting in the State-House
                 Yard" in Peter Force, ed., *American Archives.*
                 ser. 5 (Washington, DC, 1837–53), 1149–52.
                 Published in the *Pennsylvania Gazette*, Oct. 23,
                 1776.

RRL/HSP   R. R. Logan Collection, Historical Society of
                 Pennsylvania

PA   *Pennsylvania Archives, Eighth Series: Votes and
                 Proceedings of the House of Representatives of
                 the Province of Pennsylvania.* Gertrude
                 MacKinney, ed. 7 vols. Philadelphia: Franklin
                 and Hall, 1931.

Penn-Logan Corresp.   *Correspondence between William Penn and James
                 Logan, Secretary of the Province and Others.*
                 Edward Armstrong, ed. 2 vols. Philadelphia:
                 Historical Society of Pennsylvania, 1870–72.

PMHB   *Pennsylvania Magazine of History and Biography*

PWP   *The Papers of William Penn.* Richards. Dunn and
                 Mary Maples Dunn, eds. 5 vols. Philadelphia:
                 University of Pennsylvania Press, 1981–86.

PYM   Philadelphia Yearly Meeting

Statutes   *Statutes-at-Large of Pennsylvania from 1682–1801.*
                 James T. Mitchell and Henry Flanders, eds. 15
                 vols. Harrisburg, PA: Clarence M. Busch, State
                 Printer of Pennsylvania, 1896–1911.

WMQ   *The William and Mary Quarterly*

Introduction

Few religious groups in America have provoked such mixed and extreme reactions as the Religious Society of Friends. Commonly known as Quakers, since their inception in the 1650s and their energetic pursuit of dissenters' rights, they have been scorned and celebrated by popular and scholarly observers alike. While some commentators have derided them for arrogance, hypocrisy, and the subversion of social and political institutions, others go as far as to say that the Quakers "invented" America and credit them with originating much of what is right and just in this country.[1] Interestingly, others still have dismissed them as irrelevant to the larger questions of American political life or simply taken no notice.

Yet as anyone with a passing familiarity with American history might observe, in one way or another, for better or worse, Quakers have been an important force. They were ubiquitous and "peculiar," as they described themselves, in the seventeenth and eighteenth centuries; it is well-known that Quakers caused significant difficulties for Massachusetts Puritans and that Pennsylvania was a Quaker colony. Although they blended into American culture more in the nineteenth and twentieth centuries, very little probing of the more recent past reveals them to be equally present; many, for example, are aware that Friends had a prominent role in the social reform movements of the Antebellum period. Beyond that, at the very least, it would be hard to find an American today unfamiliar with the Quaker Oats man, contrived image though it is.

But even with this significant presence, few scholarly works have undertaken to show precisely what Quakers have contributed to American political culture and how they accomplished it. Despite the grandiose claims, both negative and

[1] See, for example, Joseph Smith, *Bibliotheca Anti-Quakeriana: A Catalogue of Books Adverse to the Society of Friends* (London, 1873; rpt. New York: Kraus, 1963). In the twentieth century, commentary has tended toward the other direction. See, most recently, David Yount, *How Quakers Invented America* (Lanham, MD: Rowman & Littlefield Publishers, 2007). A fuller discussion of the popular reception of Quakerism appears in the following chapters.

positive, there has been at the same time a curious neglect of the intricacies of Quaker theologico-political thought that has kept many of the arguments superficial, implausible, or merely limited.

That Quaker constitutionalism is the subject of a formal analysis challenges conventional approaches to the study of Quakerism and Anglo-American political history. In the first instance, a common anachronism committed by contemporary scholars, and what has undoubtedly contributed to the absence of Quakerism from the political historiography, is to consider religion and politics as though they were separate and distinct realms of thought and action. In discussing Quaker thought, I borrow the term "theologico-political" from Spinoza. This term signifies the interrelatedness of the religious and the political that has shaped Anglo-American thinking even beyond the First Amendment. When Spinoza wrote his *Theologico-Political Treatise* (1670), he did so as an objection to this relationship. This has led some scholars to argue that he was the first liberal democrat.[2] Whatever Spinoza might have been, his treatise is not best viewed whiggishly as a harbinger of things to come, but rather for what it was, a commentary on his present, in which few could conceive of a secular political world. It is only in this context that we can understand how Quakers and other men of their time understood theology and ecclesiology as largely indistinguishable from political theory and civil structures. While at times throughout this study I speak of them separately, this is an artificial device used for the sake of a comprehendible discussion and does not reflect the actual way people of the time thought. Quaker theories on church and state emerged simultaneously. The only sense in which religion preceded politics occurred when they looked for the ultimate justification for their political theory; then they turned to God.

Among scholars sensitive to the historical relationship between religion and politics, the neglect of Quakerism stems from another source – confusion about the genealogy of Quakerism. There has been a largely unarticulated tension in the literature about whether they were Anabaptists or reformed Calvinists; or, rather, toward which side of their family tree they tended.[3] For different reasons, placing them too firmly on one branch or the other has had the consequence of making them appear irrelevant to political history.

When scholars have considered Quakerism as a variation of Anabaptism, they have cultivated a myth that that they were quietists. Some claim that, after a period of enthusiastic proselytizing in their founding years, the Society retreated inward and disengaged from the world. Quaker historians, such as W. C. Braithwaite, have argued that, after their initial intensity, there was eventually an "indifference to public life which persecution and nonconformity with

---

[2] Hillel G. Fradkin, "The 'Separation' of Religion and Politics: The Paradoxes of Spinoza," *The Review of Politics* vol. 50, no. 4, Fiftieth Anniversary Issue: Religion and Politics (1988), 603–27.

[3] The only work that confronts this problem head on is Melvin B. Endy's "Puritanism, Spiritualism, and Quakerism," in Mary Maples Dunn and Richard Dunn, eds., *The World of William Penn* (Philadelphia: University of Pennsylvania Press, 1986), 281–301.

the practices of the world gradually fostered."[4] Following them, others such as Christopher Hill maintain that after 1660, "[t]he Quakers turned pacifist and abandoned any attempt to bring about by political means a better world on earth."[5] This alleged quietism has not been seriously examined since by most political historians who usually consider Quakers as a whole to be, as Garry Wills has categorized them, "withdrawers" from government and civil society – a corporately exclusive sectarian group that shuns engagement with the world to preserve its own purity.[6] Until relatively recently, the perception of Quakers as apolitical has discouraged attempts to investigate their political theory. Naturally, a quietist group would have no need to formulate a theory of a civil constitution or civic engagement. In her seminal work on Anglo-American political thought, therefore, Caroline Robbins writes that Quakers can be "safely neglected" in the study of constitutionalism. "Their continued existence," she says, "was a reminder of a demand for greater liberty, but they took no great part in political agitations of any kind."[7] Most subsequent

[4] William C. Braithwaite, *The Beginnings of Quakerism* (Cambridge: Cambridge University Press, 1955), 314; Hugh Barbour, *The Quakers in Puritan England* (New Haven, CT: Yale University Press, 1964), 251; W. C. Braithwaite, *The Second Period of Quakerism* (London: Macmillan and Co., 1919), 179; H. Larry Ingle, "Richard Hubberthorne and History: The Crisis of 1659," *Journal of the Friends' Historical Society* vol. 56, no. 3 (1992), 189–200, 197.
[5] Christopher Hill, *The Religion of Gerrard Winstanley* (Oxford: The Past and Present Society, 1978), 55; also see Christopher Hill, *Experience of Defeat: Milton and Some Contemporaries* (New York: Viking, 1984), 130. Daniel Boorstin, *The Americans: The Colonial Experience* (New York: Vintage Books, 1958), 68; Blanche Weisen Cook, et al., eds., *Peace Projects of the Seventeenth Century* (New York: Garland Publishing, 1972), 15. A sort of quietism was certainly an important aspect of Quaker thinking, but explaining it simply as withdrawal does not take into account the political expressions of this stance. Nor was this stance ubiquitous throughout the Society of Friends in the eighteenth century. Richard Bauman describes three main modes of Quaker political behavior that existed – sometimes in tension with one another – in mid-eighteenth century Pennsylvania: religious reformers, worldly politicians, and "politiques," those who were a mixture of both. He emphasizes the importance of understanding the so-called quietists as political leaders on their own terms. Although Quakers participated in politics in diverse ways, Bauman's analysis presupposes an underlying unity that is important for the purposes here – the idea of a government and society based on Quaker principles. They simply took different approaches to reforming civil society in different periods. See Richard Bauman, *For the Reputation of Truth: Politics, Religion, and Conflict among the Pennsylvania Quakers, 1750–1800* (Baltimore: Johns Hopkins University Press, 1971).
[6] For more on the category of "withdrawer," see Garry Wills, *A Necessary Evil: A History of the American Distrust of Government* (New York: Simon & Schuster, 1999). There was a point at which some Quakers did indeed withdraw from office holding; however, this fact does not define all Quakers or their entire relationship to government and politics.
[7] Caroline Robbins, *The Eighteenth-Century Commonwealthman: Studies in the Transmission, Development and Circumstance of English Liberal Thought from the Restoration of Charles II until the War with the Thirteen Colonies* (Cambridge, MA: Harvard University Press, 1961), 222. This statement may not be representative of her later thought. In 1979 she contributed a brief essay to discussion on the *West Jersey Concessions and Agreements* of 1676/77, the first Quaker constitution, in which she wrote that the *Concessions* "naturally reflected Quaker ideology" and remains "the clearest expression of the liberal aspirations of mid-century revolutionaries" (Caroline Robbins, "William Penn, Edward Byllynge and the Concessions of 1677," in *The*

work on early modern politics has followed this assumption. Although there
are many studies of the influence of the political world on Quakerism and their
practical politics in Pennsylvania,[8] there are few studies on the relationship
of Quaker theology to their political thought,[9] fewer still on the significance
of their thought and practice for the American polity,[10] and none on their
collective understanding of a constitution.[11]

West Jersey Concessions and Agreements of 1676/77: A Roundtable of Historians, Occasional
Papers No. 1 [Trenton, NJ: New Jersey Historical Commission, 1979], 17–23. 19, 23). Those
following her earlier thought include Christopher Hill, *The World Turned Upside Down:
Radical Ideas during the English Revolution* (New York: The Viking Press, 1972), 327; Boorstin,
The Americans, 68; J. G. A Pocock, "Interregnum and Restoration," in *The Varieties of British
Political Thought, 1500–1800* (New York: Cambridge University Press, 1993), 155; Wills, *A
Necessary Evil*.

[8] Frederick B. Tolles, *Meeting House and Counting House: The Quaker Merchants of Colonial
Pennsylvania, 1682–1763* (New York: W. W. Norton, 1948); Gary B. Nash, *Quakers and Politics: Pennsylvania, 1681–1726* (Princeton, 1968; rpt. Boston: Northeastern University Press,
1993); James H. Hutson, *Pennsylvania Politics, 1740–1770: The Movement for Royal Government and Its Consequences* (Princeton, NJ: Princeton University Press, 1972); Alan Tully,
*Forming American Politics: Ideals, Interests, and Institutions in Colonial New York and Penn-
sylvania* (Baltimore: Johns Hopkins University Press, 1994); and Tully, *William Penn's Legacy:
Politics and Social Structure in Provincial Pennsylvania, 1726–1755* (Baltimore: Johns Hopkins
University Press, 1977).

[9] A useful work by Herman Wellenreuther discusses of the influence of Quaker theology and
ecclesiology in Pennsylvania government: *Glaube und Politik in Pennsylvania, 1681–1776:
Die Wandlungen der Obrigkeitsdoktrin und des Peace Testimony der Quäker* (Köln: Böhlau,
1972). This study presents in impressive detail the difficulties Quakers confronted in reconciling
their political authority with their peace testimony. Richard Bauman gives an analysis of various
forms of Quaker political engagement in Pennsylvania as based on their different understandings
and expressions of Quaker principles in *For the Reputation of Truth*. Other studies examine
the political thought of William Penn, but with little or no attention to his Quakerism. See
Edwin Corbyn Obert Beatty, *William Penn as Social Philosopher* (New York: Columbia University Press, 1939); Mary Maples Dunn, "William Penn, Classical Republican," *PMHB* vol. 81
(1957), 138–56 and *William Penn: Politics and Conscience* (Princeton, NJ: Princeton University
Press, 1967). A work that begins to address the religious aspects of Penn's political thought is
Melvin B. Endy, *William Penn and Early Quakerism* (Princeton, NJ: Princeton University Press,
1973).

[10] The only work on this is Tully's *Forming American Politics: Ideals, Interests, and Institutions
in Colonial New York and Pennsylvania* (Baltimore: Johns Hopkins University Press, 1977).
A work that seems as though it will engage a discussion of Quaker political theory and its
implications for America is E. Digby Baltzell's *Puritan Boston and Quaker Philadelphia: Two
Protestant Ethics and the Spirit of Class Authority and Leadership* (New York: The Free Press,
1979). However, he purports to analyze Quaker conceptions of government by saying that theirs
were purely negative and therefore made no substantive contribution to American political
culture. A brief but important corrective to this thesis is put forth by Stephen A. Kent and
James V. Spickerd, "The 'Other' Civil Religion and the Tradition of Radical Quaker Politics,"
Journal of Church and State vol. 36, no. 2 (1994), 374–87. This piece addresses a few of the
constitutional innovations of Quakers and the importance of Quaker antiauthoritarianism for
American political culture.

[11] Richard Alan Ryerson gives us a glimpse into William Penn's constitutional thought, but he
not does extend his analysis to the rest of the Society, nor does he address the theological

Robbins's assertion that Quakers can be neglected depends, of course, on how one defines "political agitations." If they are understood exclusively as armed revolts or violent riots, then she is correct. For most of their existence, Quakers have been pacifists, refusing to engage in armed warfare even to defend their own colony of Pennsylvania. It is likely that one of the main reasons for their exclusion from American political historiography is their stance as conscientious objectors in the Revolution and the specter of Loyalism this conjured up in the minds of their critics then and since. But, as we shall see, although revolution, mob action, and other sorts of violent behavior were an important part of early modern political culture, they were not the only extra-legal mode of redressing grievances.[12]

Ironically, despite the assumption of Quaker quietism, another common misunderstanding of Quakerism is that it is simply a radical form of Puritanism.[13] Among early modern religions, Puritanism has received the most attention from political historians. To be sure, Quakerism arose during the Puritan Revolution, and there are some important theological and temperamental characteristics that Quakers shared with Puritans. The most important trait for this study is political aggression, a quality wholly lacking in most expressions of Anabaptism. Because so much attention has gone to the political influences of reformed Calvinism on Western political thought, it then seems that, by extension, Quakerism has also been treated. But when scholars define Quakerism in this way, they obscure any separate contribution. Although this study does not

---

underpinnings. See Ryerson, "William Penn's Gentry Commonwealth: An Interpretation of the Constitutional History of Early Pennsylvania," *Pennsylvania History* vol. 61, no. 4 (1994), 393–428. Only once have I come across the term *Quaker constitutionalism* outside of my own work. In less than three pages on the theological foundations of Pennsylvania, Barbara Allen describes with remarkable accuracy – although perhaps attributing too much to Penn – several of the fundamental premises of Quaker theologico-political thought. See Barbara Allen, *Tocqueville, Covenant, and the Democratic Revolution: Harmonizing Earth with Heaven* (Lanham, MD: Lexington Books of Rowman & Littlefield Publishers, 2005), 51–53.

12 Most studies of dissent and protest in America, especially early America, focus on the violent expressions of mobbing and rioting. See, for example, William Pencak, Matthew Dennis, and Simon P. Newman, eds., *Riot and Revelry in Early America* (University Park: Penn State University Press, 2003); Wayne E. Lee, *Crowds and Soldiers in Revolutionary North Carolina: The Culture of Violence in Riot and War* (Gainesville: University Press of Florida, 2001); Paul A. Gilje, *Rioting in America*, Interdisciplinary Studies in History (Bloomington and Indianapolis: Indiana University Press, 1996); John Phillip Reid, *In a Rebellious Spirit: The Argument of Facts, the Liberty Riot, and the Coming of the American Revolution* (University Park: Penn State University Press, 1979); Pauline Maier, *From Resistance to Revolution: Colonial Radicals and the Development of the American Opposition to Britain, 1765–1776* (New York: W. W. Norton & Co., 1991).

13 Many major works, both by Quakers and non-Quakers, have put forth this interpretation. See, for example, Sydney E. Ahlstrom, *A Religious History of the American People* (New Haven, CT: Yale University Press, 1972), 130, 134, 177–78, 208–09; and, among others, the most influential study of early Quakerism, Barbour's *The Quakers in Puritan England*, 2, passim. See also James F. Maclear, "Quakerism and the End of the Interregnum: A Chapter in the Domestication of Radical Puritanism," *Church History* vol. 19 (1950), 240–70. For a detailed refutation of this interpretation, see Melvin B. Endy, "Puritanism, Spiritualism, and Quakerism."

undertake a detailed comparison of Quakerism and Puritanism, it demonstrates that on several key points, Quaker theology and practice were importantly different from reformed Calvinism. Insofar as these two religious systems differed, so did the political theories and institutions that grew from them.

Quakers were therefore neither Anabaptists nor reformed Calvinists. They were torn between their Anabaptist roots, which inclined them to reject government, office holding, civic engagement, and war, and the Calvinism at their nascence that drove them into the political arena. This dualism in Quakerism is something that Friends have always tried with varied success to balance. Consequently, there is a certain schizophrenia about Quakerism – a people militant at times in their insistence on peace and extreme in their moderation. Throughout this study we see Quakers both as individuals and as a body struggling to reconcile this and other competing and sometimes-contradictory aspects of their identity.

This study has three overarching purposes – to describe Quaker constitutional theory; to identify the practical expressions of this theory; and to explain the thought and action of Founding Father John Dickinson within this tradition, using him as the best, though imperfect exemplar of it in early America.

In the late-seventeenth century, the Religious Society of Friends originated a unique theory of a civil constitution and a philosophy of civic engagement that they practiced and actively disseminated beyond their Society for the next three hundred years. Their political thought and action was inextricably connected to their theology, the form and function of their ecclesiastical constitution, and appropriate behavior within their faith community, all of which this study will engage in detail. The most important practical expression of this theory was peaceful resistance to government to effect constitutional change. Of the possible methods of peaceful protest, civil disobedience was the most extreme. It is thus a main theme of this work. The study follows the development and use of this method and others by Quakers in Interregnum and Restoration England, through the American Revolution with Dickinson as its foremost advocate, and, in an epilogue, up to its articulation by Martin Luther King, Jr., in the Civil Rights Movement of the 1960s. In doing so, it offers the first exposition of Quaker constitutional thought, the first discussion of the Quaker foundations of American civil disobedience, and the first coherent analysis of John Dickinson's political thought.

The most familiar concept in this study, civil disobedience, warrants some attention at the outset. Although since the 1960s it has become a widely accepted form of civic engagement, it is often misunderstood. Scholars and the public alike confuse it with other modes of dissent, both violent and nonviolent, which is not surprising, since the various forms of resistance overlap. Thus a few words by way of definition of civil disobedience and a brief overview of its relationship to Quaker constitutional theory are in order.

Although the definition of civil disobedience has been in contention over the years, it is most generally accepted to be a public, nonviolent, submissive transgression of law. This is to say, it is an act performed out in the open; it does neither physical nor mental harm to people or property; and the actor accepts the punishment for the act. Breaking the law in this case must also be intentional, not inadvertent. Finally, it must be committed with the intent to educate and persuade the general public to the position of the disobedient. The figures whom scholars consider to be the major thinkers on the matter and who have received almost exclusive attention, Gandhi and Martin Luther King, Jr., concurred with this definition.[14] Civil disobedience also presumes a number of other political requisites. There must be a democratic element of the system that assumes the people have a say in the laws. The act must be for the public good rather than private or sectarian interests. There also must be a substantial degree of stability in the polity. And, most importantly, for it to be legitimate, there must be a sense of moral obligation to the constitution and government. There is, in other words, no basis for dissent in anarchy.

There are also other forms of political resistance that are similar to, but not the same as, civil disobedience. Many of these have aspects in common with civil disobedience, but they leave out some elements. They include actions or nonactions that range from legal and peaceful to overtly violent and illegal, such as obstructionism, evasion, nonresistance, and revolution. Some specific examples are voting, disseminating political literature, boycotts, sit-ins and marches, rioting, tax evasion, manipulation of the legal system, withdrawal of financial or other assistance, bombing of public buildings, and overthrow of the government. For reasons that are fairly clear, these actions usually do not meet the criteria for civil disobedience – some of them break no laws,[15] some are violent and destructive, some are clandestine, and some show no sense of political obligation.

Civil disobedience can also be exercised by various means. It can be direct or nondirect action, persuasive or coercive. In direct action, the disobedient breaks the specific law he believes to be unjust. In nondirect action, he breaks laws that are not directly related to the specific injustice he is protesting, except perhaps symbolically, in order to disrupt the system and bring attention to his cause. Also, civil disobedience is a form of pressure, but that pressure can be manifested in different ways. It can be gently educative or persuasive when it seeks to convert the community to the position of the disobedient; or it can be coercive when it uses the body of the disobedient as a means to make people behave contrary to their inclinations. It cannot be violent. But, as will become clear, violence is a concept that can be broadly construed.[16]

[14] This definition describes the theory and action of King and Gandhi, but not, for reasons I explain in the epilogue, Henry David Thoreau. The classic statement is from Martin Luther King, Jr., *Letter from a Birmingham City Jail* (Philadelphia: American Friends Service Committee, 1963).
[15] This is to say that they do not break contemporary American laws. In seventeenth-century England or other countries today with fewer civil liberties, many of these nonviolent forms of protest might have been or may be illegal, which would then allow them to fit into the category of civil disobedience.
[16] James F. Childress, *Civil Disobedience and Political Obligation: A Study in Christian Social Ethics* (New Haven, CT: Yale University Press, 1971), 27–32.

The scholarship on civil disobedience, most of which was produced in the late 1960s and early 1970s in the wake of the Civil Rights Movement, usually begins with Thoreau and ends with King.[17] Much of it takes little account of religion in general or, if so, demonstrates a serious ignorance of the history of peace churches and the origins of pacifism in America; and the scholarship is decidedly anemic without Quakerism.[18] It was Quakers who were the first practitioners of this technique. Rather than follow the lead of their Puritan cousins in challenging the government, Quakers took another tack and became more than just the mild-mannered advocates of religious liberty that they have been portrayed to be, but something other than revolutionaries. Since their beginning, they were among the most radical and best organized political groups in Interregnum and Restoration England. Not only did they take part in political agitations, but they were, as far as their contemporaries were concerned, a menace to civil government to rival any – even Ranters and Catholics. They are proof against J. G. A. Pocock's claim that there was a "disappearance of sectarian radical culture" after the Interregnum.[19] Moreover, they were among the

---

[17] For a fuller analysis of the tenets of civil disobedience, as well as the debate over the definition, see Harry Prosch, "Toward an Ethic of Civil Disobedience," *Ethics* vol. 77, no. 3. (1967), 176–192; Wilson Carey McWilliams, "Civil Disobedience and Contemporary Constitutionalism: The American Case," *Comparative Politics* vol. 1, no. 2 (1969), 211–27; Hugo Adam Bedau, ed., *Civil Disobedience: Theory and Practice* (New York: Pegasus, 1968); Howard Zinn, *Disobedience and Democracy: Nine Fallacies on Law and Order* (New York: Vintage Books, 1968); Childress, *Civil Disobedience*; Marshall Cohen, "Liberalism and Civil Disobedience," *Philosophy and Public Affairs* vol. 1, no. 3 (1972), 283–314; John Rawls, *A Theory of Justice* (Cambridge, MA: Harvard University Press, 1971), 322; Hugo Adam Bedau, *Civil Disobedience in Focus* (New York: Routledge, 1991). See also the American Philosophical Association Eastern Division Symposium on Political Obligation and Civil Disobedience, Fifty-Eighth Annual Meeting, Atlantic City, NJ, December 27–29, 1961, the papers from which are: Richard A. Wasserstrom, "Disobeying the Law," *The Journal of Philosophy* vol. 58, no. 21(Oct. 12, 1961), 641–53; Hugo A. Bedau, "On Civil Disobedience," *The Journal of Philosophy* vol. 58, no. 21 (Oct. 12, 1961), 653–65; Stuart M. Brown, Jr., "Civil Disobedience," *The Journal of Philosophy* vol. 58, no. 22 (Oct. 26, 1961), 669–81. Many other works purportedly on the topic take an uncomplicated approach and, without setting forth a definition, mistakenly treat any sort of resistance to government as civil disobedience. One example is Mary K. Bonsteel Tachau, "The Whiskey Rebellion in Kentucky: A Forgotten Episode of Civil Disobedience," *Journal of the Early Republic* vol. 2, no. 3 (1982), 239–59.
[18] In *Advocates of Peace in Antebellum America* (Bloomington: Indiana University Press, 1992), Valeri Zigler explores the pacifist movement in Antebellum America, but without attention to its Quaker roots. Maurice Isserman finds that "American pacifism was largely an offshoot of evangelical Protestantism." *If I Had a Hammer...The Death of the Old Left and the Birth of the New Left* (New York: Basic Books, 1987), 127. Although he is right to argue that the peace movement of the early nineteenth century had a significant evangelical component, its progenitors acknowledged their debt to the two-hundred years of Quaker pacifism that had come before. See Peter Brock, *Radical Pacifists in Antebellum America* (Princeton, NJ: Princeton University Press, 1968). Of the few works that recognize Quakers, two are by Straughton Lynd, including *Nonviolence in America: A Documentary History* (Indianapolis: Bobbs-Merrill, 1966); and *Intellectual Origins of American Radicalism* (New York: Pantheon Books, 1968).
[19] J. G. A. Pocock, "Radical Criticisms of the Whig Order in the Age between Revolutions," in Margaret Jacobs and James Jacobs, eds., *The Origins of Anglo-American Radicalism* (London: George Allen & Unwin, 1984), 33–57, 33.

leaders in the early resistance movement against Britain in the Revolution. But they agitated without violence. They were *pacifists*, but by no means *passive*; as John Dickinson put it, they were turbulent, but pacific. In their own peculiar way, they instigated a most significant and effective kind of political agitation and were the first contributors to a distinctive mode of thought and behavior within the Anglo-American dissenting tradition. A Milton scholar writing in 1896 also noted this Quaker contribution and found that it "has never been sufficiently acknowledged."[20] His observation holds true still.

If Quakers were quietists or self-interested sectarians, their exclusion from this historiography on this subject would be warranted. But their protest always had a political purpose. The main form of protest with which Quakers are associated is conscientious objection, a form of dissent that is usually distinguished from civil disobedience. Scholars rightly argue that in order for protest to be properly defined as civil disobedience, the goal of the disobedient must be not only for the protection and salvation of his own soul but also for the well-being and reform of the political society in which he lives. They make a distinction between civil disobedience as a political protest and conscientious objection, or resistance required by faith.[21] About religious conscientious objectors, writes James Childress, "the agent is not trying to effect general social change, but rather to 'witness' to his personal values and perhaps to secure a personal exemption for himself. There is no effort at persuasion or coercion."[22] But of course, "witnessing" requires an audience – or a jury. In all their protests, Quakers witnessed before the court of public opinion with the intent to persuade non-Quakers to their position. It was a form of proselytizing. To be sure, they wanted to absolve themselves from any implication in ungodly activity; but at the same time their goal was to set an example for others to follow, to testify for God's law through social and political reform. This study will show that the Quakers' intentions were far from merely self-interested, either personally or for their Society – they were for the public welfare. Indeed, throughout much of American history, most outsiders were fully aware of the Quakers' intentions and bristled at them.[23]

In each phase of their incarnation – from "grassroots" activists in England, to politicians in colonial Pennsylvania, and back to activists after the American Revolution – Quakers expressed all forms of nonviolent resistance with varying

[20] David Masson, *The Life of John Milton: Narrated in Connexion with the Political, Ecclesiastical, and Literary History of His Time* (1896; rpt. New York: Peter Smith, 1945), 6: 587–88.
[21] See, for example, Rawls, *A Theory of Justice*, in his definition of civil disobedience and conscientious refusal, 319–26.
[22] Childress, *Civil Disobedience*, 24.
[23] Indeed, Childress's statement should be qualified in a significant way. There are certainly some religious sects, including many of those who are in the Anabaptist tradition such as the Amish and Mennonites who fit this description. Like the Quakers, most conscientious objectors from the early Christians onward have used their position as a means of publicizing their convictions and converting others to their stance. Such is the fundamental proselytizing impulse in pacifism itself. See Devere Allen, ed., *Pacifism in the Modern World* (New York: Garland Publishing, 1972) and Peter Brock, *Pacifism in Europe to 1914* (Princeton, NJ: Princeton University Press, 1972).

emphasis on each tactic depending on the tenor of the situation. Sometimes the lines between their tactics blurred. It was not unusual that they used various techniques simultaneously, and it is sometimes difficult to distinguish one form from another. Their spheres of action – social, religious, economic, and political – were also conflated. This is especially true where civil laws were either unclearly defined or undistinguished from social norms and customs. Beyond their political resistance, then, Quakers engaged in social resistance in which they did not necessarily break any laws but rather challenged entrenched behaviors and institutions. The punishments for these actions were often as bloody as those meted out by the state for civil disobedience, and Quakers embraced their martyrdom enthusiastically.

Thus, far from being "withdrawers" from political society, Quakers traditionally sought to make their religious convictions public in order to convince, or coerce when necessary and possible, non-Quakers to share their vision of the world and their mode of engagement with it.[24] Because of this concern for missionizing, Friends were also very savvy about how to use various media at their disposal to shape their perception by non-Friends. Accordingly, an important subtheme of this study is the Quakers' public image. We will see how Quakers manipulated their image and how, with the changing sociopolitical climate, the public perception of them evolved – albeit unevenly – from extremely negative to very positive. I argue that the shift in the public image of Quakerism indicates a degree of success in their missionizing.

Because political obligation, a commitment to preserving the constituted polity, is the foundation on which civil disobedience rests, the analysis here necessarily focuses on the Quaker understanding of a civil constitution.[25] The Quaker theory of a civil constitution demands respect for the constituted polity and its founding principles. The respect is premised on a belief that the power in the polity resides with the people – all the people – and that they are bound to participate in it according to the rule of law; that is to say, individuals should be governed by a process that is internalized in the individual, but might be enforced from without if necessary. They must contribute to the welfare of the polity through word and deed, and do so in a way that will preserve the harmony in the polity while furthering its ends. The Quaker theory is a mode of constitutional interpretation that values original intent and requires written codification of them, but recognizes that a paper constitution is merely an

---

[24] Throughout I will make a distinction between what I call *traditional* Quaker thought and activism and newer modes that did not comport with Quakers' historical behavior and theology as it arose in the mid-seventeenth century.

[25] A good deal of the work on political obligation was produced alongside the literature on civil disobedience. A few of these are Michael Walzer, *Obligations: Essays on Disobedience, War, and Citizenship* (New York: Simon and Schuster, 1971); Rawls, *A Theory of Justice*; Bently LeBaron, "Three Components of Political Obligation," *Canadian Journal of Political Science / Revue canadienne de science politique* vol. 6, no. 3 (1973), 478–93; Karen Johnson, "Perspectives on Political Obligation: A Critique and a Proposal," *The Western Political Quarterly* vol. 27, no. 3 (1974), 520–35.

expression of the founding ideals of liberty, unity, and peace. The constitution is a representation of the polity itself, which is a living entity. The theory therefore presumes the need for evolution in a constant process of realizing the founding ideals. The people individually and collectively assume their imperfection while striving for perfection.

Not surprisingly considering the peculiarity of religious Quakerism, the action that grew from this theologico-political theory was something strange in the early modern period. Though many "Quaker" political goals were the same as those of other Englishmen of the seventeenth and eighteenth centuries – security of civil liberties, a limited, constitutional government, a measure of popular participation, and a peaceful and moral society – Quakers' means to these ends differed markedly from others and signified priorities not shared by most Englishmen. Moreover, the means were often more important than the ends. If incorrect means – such as violence, which could mean even excessively disruptive words – were used, not only would the results be illegitimate, the polity might be fatally destabilized by them.

The hallmark of Quaker constitutionalism that gave rise to civil disobedience was a twin emphasis on constitutional unity and perpetuity and a peaceful process of rights advocacy and reform. Such was the Quaker sense of political obligation that their dissent was carefully undertaken with meticulous attention to the stability of the polity. For Quakers, the unity of a constituted polity, ecclesiastical or civil, was sacred; but so was dissent. How they balanced these two seemingly irreconcilable imperatives forms a main theme of this study. Quakers were cautious in their advocacy even of peaceful dissent. They knew that civil disobedience itself was a powerful tool that could lead to violent action by those uncommitted to pacifism and could threaten the stability of the government. Quaker action was situated on a continuum of nonviolent protest, and their mantra was moderation.[26] Their protest techniques ranged from less to more disruptive depending on how stable the state was and the extent of their own power in relation to it. They tempered their civil disobedience accordingly with other modes of nonviolent resistance to remain moderate in action even as they made radical demands for individual liberties. In no case was violent disruption of the existing system through rioting, rebellion, or regicide ever acceptable. Unlike their Puritan counterparts, Quakers denied the legitimacy of any theory of revolution. Conversion (or "convincement," as Quakers would say) and persuasion were always the way, although the exact meaning of these terms in the Quaker application of them is relative, and sometimes they crossed the line into coercion. Theoretically, at least, they desired to apply the

---

[26] Political moderation has a long history with many sources. Robert M. Calhoon's broad discussion in *Political Moderation in America's First Two Centuries* (New York: Cambridge University Press, 2008) investigates many of them. As perhaps the most thorough work on Anglo-American moderation, it serves well as a companion to the present study, which highlights only one strain. Calhoon identifies this particular brand of moderation as based on the concept of love in the late-seventeenth century.

minimum amount of pressure with the end goal always to effect a voluntary and permanent change in the worldview of non-Quakers. This way they would achieve both reform and the preservation of the constitutional government.

In this "Quaker process," as Friends call it today, they had a distinct use and understanding of language and speech. They self-consciously used particular words and the very act of speaking (or not speaking) itself to order their polity, define their political procedures, and effect change in the world around them. For Quakers, theory and practice were not separate; theirs was a theory of action. And in this theory, practice, process, language, and the act of speaking were the same.[27] Their theory was about a constant process of creating and recreating the constitution – both the composition of the body politic and the written document – of a polity through what they termed "conversation" and "walking" – words and deeds that were "peaceable," "holy," and "orderly." Speech-acts in effect created the polity. Because of the Quaker emphasis on action, it is crucial to note at the outset of this study that the theory being explored here is not found exclusively in written texts.

With their emphasis on process, it is useful to consider Quakers as very effective bureaucrats in their religious meetings and civil government. Drawing on Weberian theories of political authority – particularly the legal-rational and charismatic models – the analysis deals with how they used their process for balancing both their ecclesiastical and civil polities. It was a form of authority used to contain the libertine, dissenting elements in the meeting and keep it unified, and also a means for manipulating the legal and political systems of the state to secure more liberties for themselves and others. They became experts at exploiting the very mechanisms of state oppression to achieve their ends.

By engaging with the polity in this manner with the intent to effect drastic systemic change, Friends thus challenged conventional understandings of a constitution that held it to be either static or dispensable. And they pioneered a mode of political engagement unlike anything their contemporaries had seen. They gave the people a role in the legal process that preserved the sanctity of the government while effectively limiting its reach. But there is a distinctly problematic aspect of this theory as it was translated into practice. Once such a dissenting theory has been disseminated and implemented, how can radicalism or anarchy be prevented? What if those who adopted the dissenting aspects of Quaker theory did not also employ the process that demanded a conciliatory posture toward government? This was a perennial problem Quakers faced both in- and outside of their Society, and Martin Luther King and Gandhi had their own difficulties as well in this regard. On the other hand, in containing the dangers of a dissenting theology, how is tyranny prevented? Exploration of the question of political balance in the context of Quaker theologico-politics is thus another important theme of this study.

---

[27] See J. L. Austin, *How to Do Things with Words*, 2nd ed. (Cambridge, MA: Harvard University Press, 1975).

In the following pages, I use the early modern nautical metaphor of the "trimmer" to describe Quakers' relation to the polity. Two opposing meanings of the term were employed in the seventeenth and eighteenth centuries to describe political actors. The first and more common was derogatory and referred to trimming the sails to steer the course of the ship with the prevailing winds. In other words, these trimmers allied themselves opportunistically with one faction or another, privileging self-preservation over principle. Today we call them "centrists" and "flip-floppers." But the second meaning, used most notably by George Savile in 1688, was laudatory.[28] It referred to one whose duty it is to strategically place the cargo or ballast on a ship to keep it stable and afloat.[29] Trimmers such as these acted on principle, espousing moderation and eschewing self-interest. The story of a principled trimmer – as opposed to an opportunistic one – is complicated. This sort of trimmer functions both relative to his immediate environment and apart from it. His job is to keep the ship of state from listing right or left on a straight and true course to the desired destination. Because of this, something of an optical illusion occurs: The trimmer is fixed in relation to the destination, which gives him the appearance of sometimes-drastic movement in relation to his immediate surroundings. It is true that he adjusts his position slightly, but only for the sake of staying straight and balanced. He is not static; but neither is he changeable. He does not ally himself too closely with one side or another to protect his own interests as an opportunistic trimmer would. Rather, he remains independently in the middle with a view to the object beyond himself. Those short-sighted people on either extreme who do not understand the trimmer accuse him of cowardice or rashness, indecision or haste, and, invariably, duplicity and self-interest. If he is weighty, they resent the fact he does not side with them, and they label him "trimmer" in the first sense of the term.

One of the consequences of the historic misunderstanding of Quaker theologico-politics has been the omission of Quakerism from the study of political history. A second is the corresponding neglect of an important figure at the American Founding, John Dickinson. Of the Founders, none has confounded scholars more. Because of his simultaneous call for colonial rights and opposition to the Declaration of Independence, historians have labeled his

---

[28] See George Savile, *The Character of a Trimmer* (1688).

[29] In "On Political Moderation," *The Journal of the Historical Society* vol. 6, no. 2 (June 2006), 275–95, Robert M. Calhoon adheres to the negative sense of the term *trimmer* (275). He makes a distinction between trimming and moderation and mediation, defined as "*civic action intentionally undertaken at some significant risk or cost to mediate conflicts, conciliate antagonisms, or find middle ground*" (276). Yet the second sense of the term *trimmer* expresses his meaning perfectly. This sort of trimming, I argue, is precisely what Quakers and their followers practiced in pursuit of religious and civil rights and preservation of the civil constitution. An excellent work to pair with the present study is Andrew R. Murphy, *Conscience and Community: Revisiting Toleration and Religious Dissent in Early Modern England and America* (University Park: Pennsylvania State University Press, 2001). He discusses early modern advocates of religious toleration, including Quakers, as seeking a *modus vivendi*, "a way of living together without descending into the bloodshed that had traditionally settled religious differences" (4).

political stance a "perplexing conservatism," and he himself "a conservative sort of rebel" and a "negative-minded agrarian."[30] Because of this confusion, Dickinson has received relatively little attention when compared to the volumes of work on the other Founders. Edwin Wolf 2nd rightly called him the "forgotten patriot," "doomed to limbo in the popular mind."[31] Most ironically, however, many historians have also labeled him "the Penman of the Revolution"[32] – he who *opposed* the Revolution. Dickinson's contemporaries, says Milton E. Flower, "were unable to comprehend the direction and rationale of the straight course Dickinson pursued, as he fearlessly continued to protest against every action of Britain that infringed on the liberties of the colonists and joined with military preparedness in case of armed struggle, yet remained loath to face the question of independence."[33] It would seem that this lack of understanding has been on our part as well.

Considering his achievements, Dickinson's absence from the historiography on the Revolution is striking. Throughout the creation of the Republic, he was among the most active and prolific leaders from the onset of the tensions to the solidification of the Union. Before and during the Revolution, he was an important figure in the Stamp Act Congress; member of the First and Second Continental Congresses, and the Confederation Congress, as well as many of the committees within those bodies; author of, in addition to many other public and official documents, the Resolutions of the Stamp Act Congress (1765), *Letters from a Farmer in Pennsylvania* (1767–68), the First Petition to the King (1774), *An Address from Congress to the Inhabitants of Quebec* (1774), the Olive Branch Petition (1775), the Declaration for Taking Up Arms (1775), and the first draft of the Articles of Confederation (1776).[34] He was also a colonel in the Pennsylvania militia and first a private soldier and then a brigadier general in the Delaware militia. After the War he was president of Delaware, Pennsylvania, and the Annapolis Convention. He was an important presence at the Constitutional Convention and author of the *Fabius Letters*

---

[30] H. Trevor Colbourn, "John Dickinson, Historical Revolutionary," *PMHB* vol. 83 (1959), 271, 272; and Forrest McDonald, "Introduction," in Forrest McDonald, ed., *Empire and Nation: Letters from a Farmer in Pennsylvania (John Dickinson); Letters from a Federal Farmer (Richard Henry Lee)*, 2nd ed. (Indianapolis: The Liberty Fund, 1999), ix.

[31] Edwin Wolf 2nd, *John Dickinson: Forgotten Patriot* (Wilmington: n.p., 1967), 6.

[32] Dickinson is most generally known by this designation. It was probably used for the first time in Charles J. Stillé and Paul Leicester Ford, eds., *The Life and Writings of John Dickinson*, 2 vols. (Philadelphia, Historical Society of Pennsylvania, 1891–95), 2: ix; and the label, as well as the misconception behind it, has been perpetuated by almost all of the few scholars who have dealt with Dickinson since. The confusion on this point reaches far back. As early as 1787, Thomas Jefferson felt compelled to correct the editor of the *Journal de Paris*, which published an article crediting Dickinson with effecting American independence. See Pauline Maier, *American Scripture: Making the Declaration of Independence* (New York: Alfred A. Knopf, 1997), 169.

[33] Milton E. Flower, *John Dickinson, Conservative Revolutionary* (Charlottesville: University Press of Virginia, 1976), 146.

[34] Although earlier versions of the Articles had been written, because Dickinson's was the one debated in Congress, his is considered the first draft.

(1788) to advocate ratification. In retirement, he was a generous philanthropist, supporting causes such as education, prison reform, and abolitionism. In short, he was the "man of preeminence" who E. Digby Baltzell denies Pennsylvania ever produced.[35]

The confusion over Dickinson's politics hinges on two seminal and apparently contradictory moments – the publication of the *Farmer's Letters* and his absence from the vote on the Declaration of Independence. It is clear that the *Letters* had the result scholars have claimed – they certainly helped prepare the colonists for revolt. But after painting him as the "Penman of the Revolution," scholars then find themselves at a loss to explain Dickinson's stance on the Declaration. If one takes their interpretation of the *Farmer's Letters* as accurate, Dickinson's behavior does indeed seem erratic and contradictory – flip-flopping even. David L. Jacobson, the author of the only scholarly monograph on Dickinson's politics, writes that in 1776 his opinions were "a hodgepodge of contradictory ideas."[36] For centuries, historians have been trying to make sense of his seemingly inscrutable opposition to the Declaration, but they have given only vague, speculative, and unsatisfactory explanations for it, many of which paint him in an unfavorable light.[37]

Yet Dickinson was hardly a "timorous rebel," "irresolute," a mere pedant, or an idealist with no practical sense of how the colonists should achieve their ends. Indeed, he counseled the colonies in their most effective resistance and negotiations until the day before the vote on independence and then was one of a minority of congressional delegates to take up arms for the cause, serving, among other campaigns, at the Battle of Brandywine. His continued press for reconciliation even as he joined the militia and hostilities with Britain turned violent in 1775 undoubtedly seems a species of naïveté or hypocrisy; however, as we shall see, he had a theory and precedents for success on his side. His position, as will be argued here, was largely an ideological one, a principled stance for reconciliation. There is, however, certainly more than a grain of truth in the argument that Dickinson had pragmatic concerns about independence as well. As a lawyer, he would have been distinctly aware of the legal and political benefits of pursuing reconciliation as far as possible as a protection against charges of treason from the British government. Dickinson himself

---

[35] E. Digby Baltzell, *Puritan Boston and Quaker Philadelphia*, 38. Dickinson was not originally from Pennsylvania – he was born in Maryland and raised in Delaware – but he spent much of his life in Pennsylvania and the preponderance of his career there.

[36] David L. Jacobson, *John Dickinson and the Revolution in Pennsylvania, 1764–1776* (Berkeley: University of California Press, 1965), 115. An article that offers brief analysis that begins to approach some of the findings here, though without the religious emphasis, is M. E. Bradford, "A Better Guide Than Reason: The Politics of John Dickinson," *Modern Age* vol. 21, no. 1 (1977), 39–49. A brief study that presents a "scientific theory" of Dickinson's political ideas is M. Susan Power, "John Dickinson: Freedom, Protest, and Change," *Susquehanna Studies* vol. 9, no. 2 (1972), 99–121.

[37] The negative histories began with David Ramsay in *The History of the American Revolution* (Philadelphia, 1789) and reached their apex with George Bancroft in *History of the United States, from the Discovery of the Continent* (New York: D. Appleton and Co., 1912).

claimed that timing was his reason[38] – America had no central government yet and, he believed, too little foreign support, and Pennsylvania, itself on the verge of a revolution, had no settled government. But this still does not explain completely the tenor of Dickinson's career or this particular conundrum.

Milton Flower, his only modern biographer, explains Dickinson's seemingly contradictory political positions in terms of "radical," "moderate," and "conservative." Others have similarly observed that he "was always an intense conservative, and that he had a horror of any changes brought about by revolutionary means."[39] But Dickinson's aversion to riots and tumults was more than merely a reactionary conservatism or a "temperamental revulsion to mass violence."[40] Moreover, situating his views along the continuum of conventional political ideology neither does justice to their complexity nor explains how these apparently disparate views and actions harmonized in one man's thought. In what is perhaps the most intellectually honest comment on the enigma, J. H. Powell wrote in frustration, "Where in hell did Dickinson learn the complicated wway [sic] of politics he tried to put into practice?"[41]

Scholars have been confused about Dickinson's position because they have not placed his thinking in what Sheldon Wolin calls its "connotative context."[42] In other words, what most analyses fail to take seriously is the religious climate in which Dickinson lived and worked as well as his personal religious belief.[43] Although Dickinson rejected formal affiliation with any religious group, his sociopolitical environment and his faith were predominantly Quaker. Interestingly, many scholars have noted the Quaker influence in his life, often mistaking him for a member of the Religious Society of Friends.[44] Bernhard Knollenberg posits that Dickinson "may have been influenced by his family and other Quaker connections."[45] Forrest McDonald and Ellen Shapiro

---

[38] See John Dickinson, Defense of Actions before the Council of Safety, 1777, Ser. I. b. Political, 1774–1807, n.d., RRL/HSP.

[39] Stillé and Ford, *Life and Writings*, 1: 43.

[40] Flower, *John Dickinson, Conservative Revolutionary*, ix.

[41] J. H. Powell, notes for Dickinson biography, May 26, 1955, John Dickinson Materials, John Harvey Powell Papers, APS.

[42] Sheldon Wolin, "Political Theory as a Vocation," *The American Political Science Review* vol. 63, no. 4. (1969), 1062–82, 1070–71.

[43] Those who do seriously consider his religion muddle the conversation further by conflating Quakerism with Puritanism. See M. Susan Power, "John Dickinson After 1776: The Fabius Letters," *Modern Age* vol. 16, no. 4 (1972), 387–97, 391. The same is true for J. H. Powell in "John Dickinson and the Constitution," *PMHB* vol. 60, no. 1 (1936), 1–14. He finds Dickinson's politics to be the "most vigorous expression" of Puritanism of his generation (13).

[44] One of the earliest incidents of this mistake appearing in the historiography is in William Wade Hinshaw, *The Encyclopedia of American Quaker Genealogy* (Ann Arbor, MI: Edward Brothers, 1938), 505. Bernhard Knollenberg corrects this misperception in "John Dickinson vs. John Adams: 1774–1776," *Proceedings of the American Philosophical Society*, Philadelphia (1963), 142.

[45] Knollenberg, "John Dickinson vs. John Adams," 142.

McDonald note that his "orientation was toward Quakerism."[46] Despite this, Frederick Tolles explains that "no one has ever tried to say with exactness just what that Quaker influence was or just how it expressed itself in his thought and action."[47] In political history, a field that has not always been receptive to religious interpretations, some would likely agree with the McDonalds that his reliance on Christian language was little more than a "rhetorical strategy."[48] Although strategy may have played a role, it does not preclude sincere belief on Dickinson's part, nor does it take seriously the power and uniqueness of this tradition. As this study describes, his theory and the actions they prompted were predominantly Quaker. It is no coincidence that most of his political expressions had, as Powell writes, "the reinforcing agreement of the Society of Friends."[49] Without an understanding of Quaker political and constitutional theory, however, scholars have attempted to force Dickinson into the limited and ill-fitting traditions that they have previously identified, most significantly, Whiggism.

This work is intended neither as a comprehensive analysis of Quaker thought nor an enumeration of all of its contributions to American political culture. It concentrates on a few seminal ideas and traces them with broad strokes over the period in question. It therefore omits detailed discussion of many particulars of Quaker history and thought that have been treated in depth elsewhere or that may be the subject of future studies. For example, there is little mention of the economic factors that influenced or arose from their thought, although it is a rich vein to mine. Similarly, it focuses on the thought of individuals as they represent the Society and does not deal with the myriad Quaker voluntary organizations that have existed in each century. Further, this study assumes that there was a measure of consensus and continuity on some fundamental points of Quaker thought, even if sometimes this continuity only persisted in a few individuals. While neither religious nor political Quakerism was static over time or uniform among members of the Society, there are nonetheless significant aspects on which there was enough agreement among most members so that no great or permanent schism occurred until the early nineteenth century. Even then, there were still Quakers who adhered to what I will define as the traditional thought. It is these most important aspects of Quaker constitutionalism that this study addresses, with due attention to the most significant divergences.

---

[46] Forrest McDonald and Ellen Shapiro McDonald, "John Dickinson, Founding Father," *Delaware History* vol. 23, no. 1 (1988), 24–38, 28.

[47] Frederick B. Tolles, "John Dickinson and the Quakers," *"John and Mary's College": The Boyd Lee Spahr Lectures in Americana* (Carlisle, PA: Fleming H. Revell Co., 1951–56), 67.

[48] McDonald and McDonald, "John Dickinson, Founding Father," 38. For example, Thomas Pangle betrays a presentist cynicism about religion when he asks, "Was Christianity the dominant or defining element in [the Founders'] thinking? Or were they not rather engaged in an attempt to exploit and transform Christianity in the direction of a liberal rationalism?" (21).

[49] Powell, "John Dickinson and the Constitution," 11.

Moreover, there are, to be sure, many areas of overlap between Quaker thought and other sources, most notably reformed Calvinism, but also secular thought such as classical liberalism and republicanism and Scottish common sense philosophy. Any claims to uniqueness of Quaker theologico-politics are therefore limited and based exclusively on their distinctive theology and ecclesiology. There is likewise no claim that Dickinson was animated by only Quaker theory; rather, his thought is representative of the ecumenicism possible in political Quakerism. What we find in Quakerism and Dickinson is a strain of thought that defies categorization in any previously identified tradition or language.[50] It is neither Whig nor Tory, liberal nor republican; it is a bit of all with something other. The main intent of the study is to bring Quaker history into dialogue with American political history, to situate Quaker thought and practice in the broader stream of the Anglo-American dissenting tradition, while at the same time differentiating it from other ideologies. As will become clear, just as religious Quakerism was an anomaly among early modern religious groups, so was political Quakerism rife with seeming paradoxes that they reconciled in their thought – antiauthoritarianism without antigovernmentalism; a permanent yet changeable constitution; government that was neither absolute nor limited; divine right that was not of kings; liberty of conscience in a theocracy; the centrality of a written constitution without it being the foundation of government; political radicalism that was peaceful; pacifism that was not passive; bureaucracy in the service of liberty.

The study takes a dual theoretical and historical approach. Part I discusses Quaker constitutional theory and practice in England and Pennsylvania, and Part II describes how the theory was expressed in word and deed by John Dickinson during the Founding. In the first part, Chapters 1 and 2 describe the foundations of Quaker theologico-political thought in England. They deal with a thirty-year period of intense creativity from roughly 1652 to 1682. During this era, Quakers were absorbed in the business of formulating their theology and political theory, as well as creating both ecclesiastical and civil governments. These chapters present a view of Quaker constitutionalism from two angles – the religious and the civil, respectively. They follow the creation myth of government to consider Quaker theories of government and the "Quaker process" that animated their polities: how the governments were originally

---

[50] It is debatable whether Quaker constitutionalism is best considered a tradition or a language. Following Glenn Burgess's discussion of these descriptors in *The Politics of the Ancient Constitution: An Introduction to English Political Thought, 1603–1642* (University Park: Pennsylvania State University Press, 1993, 116–17), it seems reasonable to suggest that it might have been both at various times. As the present study will show, early on, political Quakerism was very much a *mentalité* transmitted through speech to the outside world; but, as it became more respectable, it was also a tradition that was self-consciously handed down, accepted, and further transmitted by non-Quakers. And even at later dates, the unique linguistic element has persisted among practitioners of civil disobedience. I perhaps use the term *tradition* more often; however, the linguistic component of their theologico-politics will be clear.

constituted, how fundamental law is discerned, what a constitution is, the pur-pose of government, how government should be structured (i.e., where power should lie), how decisions are made, and what remedies exist if the constitu-tion or government are flawed in some way. They draw mainly on religious and political treatises, but also on the Quakers' conflict with the English and Mas-sachusetts governments over liberty of conscience, and identify the origins of both the persuasive and coercive techniques Friends used to mold their Society and shape public opinion, which in these early days was deeply negative. These chapters lay the theoretical foundations for Quakers' subsequent experiments in civil government.

Chapters 3 through 5 cover the familiar ground of Pennsylvania Quakerism cast in the new light of the preceding discussion on their theologico-politics. They treat the practical expressions of Quaker theory in West Jersey and Penn-sylvania, but mainly the latter, from the late-seventeenth century to just before the American Revolution. They show how Quakers defined the legitimacy of their own civil government and moved from persuasion to coercion in their efforts to promote this definition. Chapter 3 describes how Quakers dealt with the ideological differences amongst themselves during the establishment of their civil governments in America. In the main, they agreed on the fundamen-tal points of their theory except how the government should be structured to situate authority in the proper place. The West Jersey experiment failed when two competing versions of Quaker thought struggled for dominance and in short order cost Friends control of the government. It is an informative pro-logue to the same problem in Pennsylvania. A similar contest over structure and power ensued there, but in this instance, Quakers' consensus on the process of constitutional change allowed them to pursue drastic reform without losing their colony or having to resort to violence or threat of violence. The result was one of the seminal moments in Quaker constitutional history, the creation of the 1701 Charter of Privileges. Not only did the colony remain united under Quaker control with this Charter, but once the internal problems were resolved, it allowed Friends to conduct their "holy experiment" without reserve.

The fourth chapter then describes Quaker rule in mid-eighteenth century Pennsylvania, the political culture it engendered, and the polarized reception of political Quakerism by inhabitants and observers of the colony. It argues that they created a theocracy with a coercive bent in which they attempted to disseminate their twin constitutional tenets of unity and dissent. The discus-sion centers on an examination of the formal and informal techniques they used to proselytize to the non-Quaker inhabitants and challenges the scholar-ship that has interpreted Quaker laws such as liberty of conscience as "liberal" or "negative liberties." It argues, rather, that their laws and policies are rightly understood as positive liberties, designed to guide Pennsylvanians to the "civil Quakerism," as Alan Tully terms it, that would sustain their theocracy. Friends were only partially successful in that some Pennsylvanians adopted their whole outlook, while others chose what they liked and rejected the rest, with conse-quences Quakers neither foresaw nor sanctioned.

Chapter 5 concentrates on a second important constitutional moment in Pennsylvania history, the so-called campaign for royal government, and introduces the primary figure in the study, John Dickinson. Through this episode, it describes how the unintended consequence of Quaker political proselytization led to the evolution of three amorphous factions based on differing interpretations and uses of their seminal theological tenet, the peace testimony. Here we see the beginnings of divisions that would deepen during the Revolution: Some Friends retreated from formal politics, some Friends and Quakerized non-Friends disregarded the peace testimony and became radicalized, and still others adhered to a traditional strain of thought that espoused peaceful engagement. The radicalized politicians, led by Benjamin Franklin and Joseph Galloway, attempted to abolish the Quaker constitution, while the more traditional faction of the Quaker Party, led by John Dickinson, a "Quaker" politician, though not a Quaker, fought to preserve it. Out of this controversy Dickinson emerged as the most important advocate of Quaker political thought and leading figure in Pennsylvania and American politics through and beyond the Revolution. The remainder of the book explains Dickinson's thought and behavior in light of Quaker constitutionalism.

Part II, covering the years from 1763 to 1789, explores how Dickinson actively and self-consciously offered Friendly theories and processes to Americans as a means of constitutional reform for rights and unity. Chapter 6 describes how in the Revolution, Dickinson acted as the Quakers' spokesman and advocated resistance to Britain through distinctively Quaker means. As the tensions increased, however, Friends shifted their considerable weight to protect the constitutional unity with Britain and their unique Charter, first advocating reform over revolution and then retreating into neutrality. This shift was a move away from their traditional activism and caused their temporary alienation from American society and their permanent self-exile as a body from participation in government at the highest levels; however, in the short term, their resistance to independence constituted a significant threat to the American cause. Throughout the contest, Dickinson's aim, in keeping with traditional Quaker political theory, was not only to preserve the constitutional relationship with Britain but also to support the American cause. This interpretation of Dickinson's thought and action up to the point of independence situates him in the tradition of Gandhi and King as the first advocate and, to the extent Americans heeded his advice, leader of a national peaceful protest movement.

The seventh chapter continues the discussion of the Revolution with an examination of the Critical Period in Pennsylvania. During this chaotic time, the radical Quaker element that was budding during the campaign for royal government blossomed and joined with the radical revolutionary movement, headed largely by Presbyterians disgruntled by the Quaker government. With the climate in Pennsylvania hostile to dissent of any sort from the American cause (as defined by the radicals), and especially Quaker pacifism, Dickinson worked to created both national and state constitutions that would protect the rights of dissenters. This chapter chronicles his efforts from his drafting of the first version of the Articles of Confederation through his presidency of Pennsylvania and the Annapolis Convention, and it describes the troubles he and Quakers confronted as they fell through the constitutional gaps at the state and national levels.

In Chapter 8, we see Dickinson's constitutional thought in its maturity. It revisits the creation myth used in the first two chapters to demonstrate how his perspective on the creation of the U.S. Constitution was an expression of Quaker constitutionalism. He saw the Constitution as a sacred and perpetual, yet flexible and amendable document that was perfectible through a process of peaceful dissent and cooperative negotiations among the members of the polity. The chapter also discusses how Dickinson's conceptions of federalism and democratic process were largely a product both of his Quaker beliefs and his experiences in the Pennsylvania government. His contributions at the Constitutional Convention modeled Quaker concerns for moderation, reconciliation, and unity and dissent, while balancing between extremes that could lead to anarchy or tyranny. Dickinson's thought gives us a new interpretation of the Constitution – one that is religious, but neither reformed Calvinist nor Unitarian; one that allows for negotiation, but is not based on contract theory; one that advocates factions, but not Madisonian-style competition; one that encourages individual liberties, but not individualism; and one that values the intent of the framers, but also assumes and encourages change.

Finally, an epilogue surveys expressions of traditional Quaker constitutionalism since Dickinson. With the Hicksite Separation of the Society of Friends in 1827–29, Quaker theologico-politics also splintered. In the Antebellum reform movements, the best-known Quaker activists and those who followed their teachings abandoned the balance earlier Quaker rights advocates struck between unity and dissent. On the extremes they approached tyranny or anarchy in their constitutional thought. Few advocated or practiced civil disobedience as the term has been defined in this study. The epilogue notes the variations of the theologico-political thought and also discusses a few thinkers who did adhere to traditional Quaker theologico-politics, such as Jonathan Dymond in the early nineteenth century and Alice Paul and Bayard Rustin in the twentieth century. It also discusses the dramatic shift in the public perception of Quakerism during this period to overwhelmingly positive. The study concludes with a discussion of the Quaker influences on the thought and practice of Martin Luther King, Jr., whose theories of pacifism and civil disobedience were shaped and encouraged by individual Quakers and Quaker organizations.

Quakerism was an important force in the formation of American political culture, but it is indeed true that the winners write the history. By concentrating on the strain of thought that led to the Revolution, historians have undervalued a competing strain that prevailed after it. That since the ratification of the Constitution, revolution has been little more than a theory, and civil disobedience has become a widely, if not universally accepted means of protest is evidence that something more or other than a Lockean or secularized Puritan understanding of government and citizenship has become a significant part of American political culture. This is not to say that after the Revolution all Americans became Quaker anymore than one might argue that all Americans who advocated revolution were Puritans. The point is that there was a current of thought that was so widely promulgated that it lost its sectarian color and became a feature of the American political consciousness. This particular divergent political current, which became mainstream, deserves closer analysis.

I

QUAKER CONSTITUTIONALISM IN THEORY AND PRACTICE, c. 1652–1763

I

Bureaucratic Libertines

The Origins of Quaker Constitutionalism and Civil Dissent

The Quakers' conception of a political constitution and their understanding of acceptable forms of civil dissent were based on their theology, ecclesiology, and experiences with the English and Massachusetts governments during the Interregnum and Restoration. This chapter gives an overview of the religious structures and processes that were evolving in Quaker society in the mid-1650s through the 1670s and that informed their political thought.

The Quaker ecclesiastical polity was animated by a bureaucratic process that determined how the members of the meeting related to each other and to the world outside their Society. If we think of their authority and their modus operandi in Weberian terms – legal-rational, traditional, or charismatic – it does not fit into any one of these categories; rather it rejected the second and is an amalgam of the first and the third.[1] It was not a category Weber envisioned, and it can be described most simply as a "legal-charismatic" model.[2] It was based on the "rule of law," but instead of being rooted in rationality, as Weber's model is, it was based on charisma. Further, rather than this charisma being unique to one individual, it was found in each member of the group.[3] There was a paradox in Quaker theologico-political thought and expression that is captured in the name "bureaucratic libertines." Their bureaucratic process was designed to produce charismatically based unity and dissent in the ecclesiastical

---

[1] Max Weber, *Economy and Society: An Outline of Interpretive Sociology*, G. Roth and C. Wittich, eds. (Berkeley: University of California Press, 1978). See Chapter 3, "The Types of Legitimate Domination," 1: 212–301.

[2] Weber finds that the legal model has a charismatic element only "in the negative sense" that the lack of it could pave the way for a "charismatic revolution" (*Economy and Society*, 1: 263).

[3] There is, however, a similarity between the Quaker structure and one of Weber's models, discussed in "The Transformation of Charisma in a Democratic Direction," *Economy and Society*, 1: 266–71.

and civil polities, and with both of these things aimed at the same purpose – discovering God's law.[4]

What follows is a sketch of the rise and settlement of the Quaker church, or "meeting," and an analysis of the theological foundations and assumptions underlying the decisions Friends made in trying to realize their priorities and stabilize their polity.[5] The narrative structure follows the creation mythology of political society that Hobbes, Locke, Rousseau, and others used to discuss the origins of government. In other words, it describes the origins of the Quaker religious society, the process by which the members related to one another to discern the fundamental law, the purpose for the establishment of the ecclesiastical polity, and the creation of the ecclesiastical constitution. Finally, the discussion turns to show how Quakers related to the civil governments of Britain and Massachusetts. The theology and practice they developed and the ecclesiastical government they founded would serve as a blueprint for their civil governments.

The Origins of the Meeting for Worship

The Religious Society of Friends constituted itself before it established a "formal" church government.[6] Unlike other religious groups of the time, its members did not leave as one from an already established church. It was rather a movement that grew organically and spontaneously out of the chaos of the Interregnum – a state of nature of sorts. Although George Fox is generally acknowledged to be the founder of Quakerism, he was only the most prominent of several early ministers, known as the Valiant Sixty, who proselytized on behalf of what would become the Religious Society of Friends. Fox took the lead early on, and in later years served as the unifying force of the meeting. The movement developed in several areas of England – although mostly in the north – and absorbed many people who had belonged to earlier radical groups that were now dying out, such as the Ranters, Levellers, and others who were

---

[4] In *Let Your Words Be Few: Symbolism of Speaking and Silence among Seventeenth-Century Quakers* (Cambridge: Cambridge University Press, 1983), Richard Bauman gives a much fuller analysis of Quaker charismatic authority in Weberian terms than appears here. He also approaches it through their linguistic and performative process, and goes further to discuss the routinization of the charisma (Weber, *Economy and Society*, 246–54; and fn. 25 in this chapter) in this process. My argument agrees with his in its fundamental elements.

[5] For simplicity's sake, throughout this study I will frequently use the word *church* to refer to the ecclesiastical structure of the Society of Friends. Early Friends used *church* much more broadly than this to mean the universal body of people who followed the Light Within, regardless of whether they had heard of Christ or belonged to a specific denomination. See Thomas D. Hamm, *The Transformation of American Quakerism: Orthodox Friends, 1800–1907* (Bloomington: Indiana University Press, 1988), 9.

[6] I use the word *formal* advisedly because Quakers considered themselves opponents of religious "formality" and believed that the true Church of Christ did not consist of man-made structures and rituals, which only detracted from worship and obedience. As we shall see, however, structure of a sort became an integral element of Quakerism.

generally seeking an alternative to the existing systems of faith and politics.[7] As Fox and others traveled and missionized, a growing number of people began to cohere loosely and call themselves by the same name.[8] By 1660, there were around 60,000 Quakers in England.[9] It is not quite accurate to say, however, that they were organized.

In its first few years, Quakerism existed without formal processes or structures – no instituted church government. The meeting, Quakers held, was originally constituted and governed by God directly through the individual believers. Quakers modeled themselves on the ancient or primitive Church,[10] in which man needed no human contrivances to know and obey God; law and order were known inwardly by the believer. William Penn described this informal community as a "Scripture-Church," that is, "*A Company or Society of People, believing, professing, and practicing according to the Doctrine and Example of Christ Jesus and his Apostles,* and not according to the *Scribes and Pharisies,* that *taught for Doctrine the Tracitisms of Men.*"[11] The meetings for worship occurred spontaneously, whenever and wherever individuals felt moved by the spirit to come together. Because of this organic development, it is difficult to date the exact beginning of Quakerism. Scholars have generally settled on the year 1652 as when the Society coalesced.

As contradictory as it may appear on the surface, this lack of formal structure was a key element in the Quaker understanding of ecclesiastical order. Unplanned and "unprogrammed" meetings were, they believed, an expression of God's law and order known intuitively by man.[12] Friends rejected formal religious arrangements because they were seen as representing only the "dead letter" of God's law in the form of man-made sacraments, rituals, and dogma. With only informal, inward processes and structures to guide them, Friends believed they were following the living spirit of God.

This divine law and order, what Friends now call "Quaker process," regulated the posture of the individual toward God in his internal communion with him and externally in his interactions with the outside world. Correct process

---

[7] See Hill, *The World Turned Upside Down*; David R. Como's *Blown by the Spirit: Puritanism and the Emergence of an Antinomian Underground in Pre-Civil War England* (Stanford, CA: Stanford University Press, 2004) details the emergence of competing factions of religious radicals in the Puritan Revolution. Unfortunately, he has little to say about Quakers in particular. Rather he categorizes them as "antinomians," something, as we shall presently see, they were not in the usual sense of the word.

[8] At first, they called themselves "The Children of Light" or "The Children of God." They later settled on The Religious Society of Friends. The importance of the name *Quaker* is discussed later.

[9] Phyllis Mack, *Visionary Women: Ecstatic Prophesy in Seventeenth-Century England* (Berkeley: University of California Press, 1992), 1.

[10] This period spans from the death of Jesus in 29 A.D. to the conversion of Constantine to Christianity in 313. During this period, Jesus' followers held closely to the teachings of the New Testament.

[11] William Penn, *The Continued Cry of the Oppressed for Justice* (London, 1675), 23.

[12] An unprogrammed meeting has no minister or liturgy.

was conducted through perlocutionary speech-acts.[13] Quakers described it as "conversation" and "walking" – words and deeds that were simultaneously a means of engaging on appropriate terms with God in oneself and with other men, and a signifier of the spiritual status of the Walker, who should serve as an example to the unconvinced. The process was enacted on three levels, which will be dealt with in turn: the individual and his relationship with God; the decision-making process within the ecclesiastical polity; and the relation of the meeting to the larger society.

Individual Communion

The first step in Quaker process was an inward one. The foundational premise of Quaker theology was that all individuals had the capacity to experience a direct relationship with God and that the individual must freely abandon himself to God's law. He must voluntarily consent to be governed by nothing but that higher law. This began the process of internal communion. He must purify himself of all man-made traditions and ordinances, including his own reason and will. Liberty of conscience was thus a necessary precondition for the would-be Quaker. It was impossible, they believed, to come to and accept God if one was being coerced by outside forces or otherwise inhibited from discovering and following divine injunction. Once he had liberated himself from these obstacles and waited in patient and submissive silence, man would find God's Light in his conscience. This Light in the conscience – not the conscience itself, which is of man and but a vehicle for the Light – was his direct knowledge of divine will. This was the primary way of knowing. All other ways were creations of man, and thus secondary. These included Scripture, history, tradition and custom, and reason. Ideally, these things should comport with the Light – they should be based on it – but because they were of man, they could be fallible, corrupted, and contradictory. In other words, the spirit was never contradictory, but man's interpretation of it could be.[14] Thus, secondary guides should be tested against the Light, and if a discrepancy existed between them, the Light was to be obeyed.[15]

For the same reasons – informality, purity, and accurate discernment – Quakers did not believe in adhering to a written theology or creed. They even denied that they had a theology at all. Faith was rather a living thing that should grow and be flexible as man moved closer to God.[16] Importantly, however,

---

[13] Austin, *How to Do Things with Words.*

[14] See Robert Barclay, *An Apology for the True Christian Divinity* [1676] (New York: Samuel Woods and Sons, 1827), 18–19; and William Penn, *A Discourse of the General Rule of Faith and Practice* (London, 1699).

[15] This formula varied among different groups of Quakers and over time. Although most Friends agreed they should not contradict one another, sometimes the Light was privileged over Scripture, and sometimes the other way around. This caused a great deal of tension at various points in Quaker history and ultimately led to the Hicksite Separation of 1827–29.

[16] Braithwaite, *The Beginnings of Quakerism*, 515.

God did not reveal his will to man all at once; revelation was progressive.[17] Thus man must be prepared to receive new information that might change his understanding of the world and command of him different behavior. A written theology followed too closely would encourage dependence on empty rituals and man-made forms that would restrict his understanding of God.[18] The closest thing Quakers have to a written theology is Robert Barclay's *Apology for the True Christian Divinity* (1675), which was composed not primarily as a guide for Quakers (although it was certainly used as such), but as an explanation and justification of their faith to their persecutors, as well as a vehicle to convince non-Quakers of the Truth. When man had purged himself of all inward and outward earthly guides, he cast himself into a posture of humility, submissiveness, and receptiveness to God's will. He would then be in a state to understand God within and follow his directives.

Quakers believed that when man followed this inward process and adhered faithfully to God's law, he would achieve perfection. He could become "free from actual Sinning, and transgressing of the Law of God."[19] But despite this potential perfection, they also believed that "after having tasted of the Heavenly Gift [of grace], and been made Partakers of the Holy Ghost," man might still "again fall away."[20] The dual possibility of sin and salvation in the individual's life meant that there were no certain outcomes, no predestined fate of salvation or damnation. Achieving grace was a process that sometimes included regression. Barclay wrote, even "doth Perfection still admit of a Growth" in that there "remaineth a Possibility of Sinning."[21] Man's relationship with God was in a continual state of flux that, they hoped, was progressing toward grace.

Because of the emphasis on the individual's connection with God, many people, Quakers and some scholars of Quakerism, have misunderstood Quakerism as a predominantly individualistic and quietistic faith.[22] But the relationship of

---

[17] Rufus M. Jones, *The Quakers in the American Colonies* (New York: W.W. Norton and Co., 1966), xxi–xxii. See also Hill on "continuous revelation" (*The World Turned Upside Down*, 366–7). On this point, there are both striking similarities and differences between Quaker and Puritan theology. For the Puritan side, see Perry Miller, "The Marrow of Puritan Divinity," in *Errand into the Wilderness* (Cambridge: Belknap Press, Harvard University, 1956), 48–98.

[18] It is one of the apparent contradictions of Quakerism that, although Quakers scorned a written theology as a guide for belief, they placed extraordinary emphasis on the written word for more worldly, utilitarian purposes, and in ways that were different from most of their contemporaries. In *Print Culture and the Early Quakers* (Cambridge: Cambridge University Press, 2005), Kate Peters shows how Friends developed a complex and unique print culture that served to cultivate a unified Quaker identity, solidify the authority structure within the meeting, proselytize, and combat their opponents. As I will argue in the following chapters, they used the written word for unique legal-political purposes as well.

[19] Barclay, *Apology*, 9.

[20] Ibid., 10.

[21] Ibid., 9.

[22] For example, Patricia Bonomi calls the Light within "a private source of law" in *Under the Cope of Heaven: Religion, Society, and Politics in Colonial America* (New York: Oxford University Press, 1986), 25. Likewise, Sally Schwartz writes that among Quakers, "[k]nowledge of God

the individual to God – the inward posture of silent and submissive waiting – was only the first step in the process of legal discernment. There were also powerful communal components.[23]

The next phase in the process was collective. The individual received only a "measure of the spirit," not a complete understanding of it. Like a jigsaw puzzle, each individual piece must be combined properly with the others to form a coherent picture. Quakers were thus compelled to seek each other out and worship as a unified group. This unity in the Light was a sacred bond that constituted the meeting. Knowing God in one's conscience changed individuals and how they related to one another. The same spirit working in all members created a whole that was more than merely the aggregate sum of the individual parts.[24] The body of the meeting was an entity unto itself. The communal aspect of Quakerism was thus as important, if not more so, as the individual aspect.

The Foundations and Purposes of the Ecclesiastical Polity

Just as there was a process for internal communion, there was also a distinct process to be followed in the context of the meeting for worship. In the early days of Quakerism, however, Friends had yet to come to consensus on exactly how that process should function. It took a degree of formality or, as Weber would put it, of routinization, to bring most Friends into agreement.[25]

There were several purposes for which God constituted the informal meeting. It was first for worship and the discernment of his law, but also to facilitate charity – so that man could express "Love and Compassion" for the unfortunate, for "the Care of the Poor, of Widows, and Orphans." This, said Barclay, is "one main End, do we meet together."[26] It was this same duty of benevolence that "gave the first Rise for this Order among the Apostles" and it "might have been among the first Occasions that gave the like among us." However, when Barclay composed his treatise on church government, *The Anarchy of the Ranters and other Libertines* (1676), he and other leading Quakers found

---

was individual and could not be judged by another" (*"A Mixed Multitude": The Struggle for Toleration in Colonial Pennsylvania* [New York: New York University Press, 1987], 13).

[23] Hill also notes the importance of corporate decision making among radical sectarians (*The World Turned Upside Down*, 368).

[24] Emerson Shideler, "The Concept of the Church in Seventeenth-Century Quakerism (Part I)," *The Bulletin of Friends Historical Association* vol. 45, no. 2 (1965), 67–81, 69.

[25] Weber, "The Genesis and Transformation of Charismatic Authority," in *Economy and Society* 2: 1121–57. For a succinct overview of the foundations of the Quaker polity, see Michael J. Sheeran, *Beyond Majority Rule: Voteless Decisions in the Religious Society of Friends* (Philadelphia: Philadelphia Yearly Meeting of the Religious Society of Friends, 1996), 30–35. For a more detailed discussion, see W. C. Braithwaite, *The Second Period of Quakerism*. There are subtle distinctions between the ways different Quaker leaders envisioned the ecclesiastical polity. Fox's was more experiential, while Barclay's was more institutional. See Shideler, "The Concept of the Church," 73–74.

[26] Barclay, *The Anarchy of the Ranters and other Libertines* (London, 1676), 37.

that though "they were [earlier] all filled with the Spirit, yet there was something wanting."[27] Therefore, "Jesus Christ, the King and Head of the Church, did appoint and ordain, that there should be Order and Government in it."[28] There should be a man-made church government that would organize, direct, and discipline the meeting in its charity work. This should not necessarily be seen as a failure on the part of man to fulfill God's will, but rather as part of a providential process. Government was not merely for the sinful – even *"the Apostles and Primitive Christians, when they were filled with the Holy Ghost, and immediately led by the Spirit of God, did practice and commend it."*[29] Just as there was an inward process of perfection, so was the creation of government an on-going process toward perfection of the meeting. Barclay explains that God "hath also gathered and *is gathering* us into the good Order, Discipline, and Government" of Christ.[30] The fundamental constitution and government are formed first by God and then, as the need inevitably arises, they are solidified in divinely ordained but man-made structures. Accordingly, in the late 1650s, Fox, along with other leaders, began to organize local meetings around England whose main purpose was to maintain unity and discipline among Friends.

The organization of charity and worship was one reason for which the Quaker leaders wanted a more formally constituted meeting structure, but Barclay hinted that there were others. There was, in fact, an urgent need for it. While Quakers were still functioning under the direct governance of God, without a formal church government, they soon encountered the problem of where authority lay. When all individuals had access to divine law through the Light within, was it primarily in the individual as such? Or was it in the group as a whole? In the early days, many Friends believed it was in the individuals. This was problematic because the first members of the Society of Friends were a zealous lot. They were convinced of the Truth and were ardent soldiers in what they called "the Lamb's War" – Christ's war against sin.[31] This enthusiasm led some early Friends to extreme behavior and divergent interpretations of the Light that threatened to disunite the meeting. They seemed unaware that the Light was – or was becoming – both a positive and a negative law; that is, both liberating and restrictive. As Friends grew in number, the problem increased. Individuals challenged what was becoming the standard interpretation of how the meeting should function and how Quakers should behave.[32]

---

[27] Ibid., 38.
[28] Ibid., 18–19.
[29] Ibid., 16.
[30] Ibid. Emphasis added.
[31] On "the Lamb's War," see Barbour, *The Quakers in Puritan England*, esp. 33–71.
[32] For example, the controversy surrounding Quaker leader James Nayler's behavior in 1656 in Bristol – reenacting Christ's arrival in Jerusalem on Palm Sunday – was an important catalyst for change in the Society. See Barbour's description of this incident, *The Quakers in Puritan England*, 62–64.

From Fox's perspective, and most Friends agreed, such organization of the church was not "a step back into earthly things, but a step up into the life and order of the gospel."[33] A small but vocal minority of Quakers, however, became increasingly uncomfortable with what they perceived as Fox's growing personal authority among Friends and his seeming wont to impose his vision for the Society on others. In 1675 a number of Friends, led by John Wilkinson and John Story, separated from the Society under protest that the new meetings were conducted under a spirit of outward (i.e., man-made) authority and that there was too much control over the behavior of individuals. The Wilkinson-Story Controversy was a major episode in the definition of Quakerism in that it brought to the fore the perennial question of authority in Quaker ecclesiastical and civil governments. It was a question, fundamentally, about who had the power to determine the law according to God.

The partisans of the Wilkinson-Story faction were not swayed by Barclay's argument for church government. Instead, they described the evolution of a more corporate Quakerism as an attempt "to deprive us of the law of the Spirit and to bring in a tyrannical government: it would lead us from the rule within to subject us to a rule without."[34] The most extensive denunciation of this "outward rule" came from William Rogers, spokesman for the Wilkinson-Story faction, in *The Christian-Quaker, Distinguished from the Apostate & Innovator* (1680). Here he disputed the legitimacy of the very idea of a church government among Quakers. The words "church government" itself, he argued, are "mostly used under the profession of *Christianity*, by those who have become Persecutors."[35] In no sense did Rogers accept Barclay's claim that government was necessary for Christian fellowship or innocuous to the Spirit. "*Government* over the *Consciences* of *Believers*," he argued, "we take to be contrary to the Principle of Truth and Liberty we have in Jesus Christ."[36] No kind of outward structure, guidance, or direction could force the conscience of the believer; Christ's Light alone must convince him. He objected to creation of the basic Quaker meeting structures, denying "that Monthly and Quarterly Meetings are called the Church, and ought to be submitted to."[37] It is not a stretch to call these Friends spiritual anarchists, as Barclay did.

But beyond simply objecting to having their inward lives regulated in any way, the Wilkinson-Story faction located the source of these "Evil Practices" in one man, the now-clear leader of the Society of Friends, George Fox. They were determined that the power of being the de facto spiritual leader of Friends had gone to his head, and he was seeking to glorify his own ambitions for greatness by making all Quakers his disciples. Accordingly, Rogers disputed the implication, as he understood it, of the progovernment Friends "that the

[33] George Fox quoted in Braithwaite, *The Second Period of Quakerism*, 252.
[34] Ibid., 292.
[35] William Rogers, *The Christian-Quaker, Distinguished from the Apostate & Innovator* (London, 1680), 45.
[36] Ibid., 48.
[37] Ibid., 11.

Lord hath ordained G[eorge] F[ox] to be in that place amongst the Children of Light in this our Day, as *Moses* was among the children of *Israel* in his day."[38] Rather, they saw Fox as someone who was "over-driving, imposing, lording over Mens Consciences, setting up in the Church another government then that of the Spirit."[39]

It was the rise of threats to the survival of the meeting from within that prompted Barclay to write his treatise on church government. Barclay explained that

some are so great Pretenders to Inward Motions and Revelations of the Spirit, that there are no Extravagances so wild, which they will not cloak with it; and so much are they for every one's following their own Mind, as can admit of no Christian Fellowship and Community, nor that of good Order and Discipline, which the Church of Christ never was, nor can ever be without; this gives an open Door to all *Libertinism*, and brings great reproach to the *Christian-faith*.[40]

Quaker leaders feared that individuals' departure from the fundamental principles that initially brought Quakers together and united them would cause the disintegration of the sacred body.

There was therefore an individualistic, democratic, and informal element of Quakerism that was important for Quaker process, but dangerous, tending as it did to encourage libertinism. Thus Fox and other leading Friends moved to establish a church government through new structures, those monthly and quarterly meetings to which the Wilkinson-Story faction objected, as well as a strong central government, London Yearly Meeting. They argued that government as such not only was ordained by God but was the form it should take and the processes by which it should function, the "order" and "method."

"Order" and "Method" in the Quaker Society

Quakers considered the order and method of governance, the authority structure and the decision-making process, to be among the most important components of their faith. Because of this, Quakers were quintessential bureaucrats. They believed that a particular collective process must be followed if God's Truth were to be accurately discerned. The means by which Quakers worshipped – when worship is defined as legal discernment – were more important than the ends. Indeed, as we shall see, the means were almost an end in themselves.

The goal of each meeting was accurate discernment and eventual consensus or unity in the spirit. The outward or visible process of collective interaction in which Quakers engaged to achieve these goals was characterized by the speech-action of its members – when members should speak, who should speak,

[38] Ibid., 10.
[39] Ibid., preface.
[40] Barclay, *Anarchy*, 6.

how they should speak, and what they spoke. Each of these rules of speaking grew out of the inward communion with God, and thus the beginning point of every meeting was silence. Just as the individual waited in silence for the spirit, so did the entire meeting. Discernment and achieving consensus were not a deliberative process in the usual sense, with debate and argumentation; that would be to employ reason in the wrong capacity. Rather, the meeting was based on knowing God through quiet introspection and contemplation.[41] Members were admonished not to speak unless they could improve upon the silence, and as John Burnyeat, convinced of Quakerism in 1653, described a meeting, "we met together and waited together in silence; it may be sometimes not a word in our meetings for months; but everyone that was faithful waited upon the living word in our own hearts."[42] Indeed, the absence of speaking could be as profound a spiritual experience as speaking. Neither were there outward rituals to follow. The members simply waited on God and spoke whenever they were moved to do so by the spirit. And when they were moved, they were obliged to speak, regardless of whether they wanted to or not. It was, in fact, a sin and denial of God's will to refuse to deliver his Word. Of course, as the meeting grew and individual members had variant interpretations of the Inner Light, disagreement became more frequent, as the Wilkinson-Story Controversy demonstrated.

Accordingly, an important feature of the discernment process was not just when to speak or to remain silent, but who had authority to speak. An authority structure began to evolve that was a sort of democracy, although different in several ways from what we might suppose.[43] It was based on a fundamental degree of spiritual egalitarianism. All men (i.e., all *people*) were created (spiritually) equal in that all had the equal opportunity to receive, discern, and express God's Light in their consciences.[44] But all men did not receive equal measures of the Light, nor did they have equal powers of discernment or facility of expression. Thus, while every member of the meeting had a voice, not all voices had equal weight. Barclay explained that God gives "unto ever member a measure of the same Spirit, yet divers, according to the Operation, for the Edification of the Body."[45] There was a delicate balance to maintain so that

---

[41] But, in a sense, neither are these words accurate. They imply a greater role for human will and reason than Quakers allowed. Waiting for and receiving God was a passive act that required a cleansing, opening, and emptying of the conscience of human influences.

[42] John Burnyeat quoted in Howard H. Brinton, *Quaker Journals: Varieties of Religious Experience among Friends* (Wallingford, PA: Pendle Hill, 1972), 30.

[43] Their religious organization notwithstanding, Quakers, like most other men of their time, were decidedly hostile to the idea of political democracy. See George Fox, *A Few Plain Words to be considered by those of the Army, or others that would have a parliament that is chosen by the voices of the people, to govern three nations. Wherein is shewn unto them according to the Scripture of Truth, that a parliament so chosen are not likely to govern for God and the good of his people* (London, 1660).

[44] It is important to note that this spiritual equality did not translate into civil or social equality until, one might argue, the late-eighteenth or early nineteenth century.

[45] Barclay, *Anarchy*, 10.

the right people spoke at the right moment, while others were appropriately limited. They also sought a balance between looking to the group for guidance and acting on immediate individual leadings. As minister Job Scott explained in the late-eighteenth century, members of the meeting "were advised to keep their own gifts, and not depend upon one another, to the neglect of occupying their own talents; lest they as individuals, and the meeting at large, suffer loss thereby."[46]

How members spoke – the words they used and the physical manner in which they were delivered – was indicative of the Speaker's spiritual weight and facilitated the discernment-consensus process. Indeed, the process was fulfilled *through* speech-action. As described previously, speaking was necessarily preceded by silent waiting for guidance. In the early years of the Society, it was also preceded by quaking. When God's light illuminated the soul, the individual was so appalled at the sight of his own sins that he quaked with fear. Similarly, when many Friends were led to testify before the meeting, the prospect of speaking before the group was frightening enough – especially for women, who were forbidden to preach by other religions – to make them tremble. Such preliminary physical actions lent authority to the words that followed because they indicated the submission of the individual's will to the divine spirit; God was flowing through that individual contrary to the will of that person.

The particular choice of words that the preacher – for to speak in meeting was to preach – used was of the utmost significance. Quakers self-consciously redefined and manipulated words unlike any other early modern group. It was, as they intended, one of the things for which they were best known. In 1788 Brissot remarked, "The Quakers, of all others, have a language of their own, which cannot be easily understood, without having read some of their books, such as Barclay's Apology, with a great deal of attention."[47] Indeed even today, books about Quakers written with the expectation of a non-Quaker audience often include a lexicon to explain their unusual terms and word usage. As when any particular language is used, it signifies the speaker's unity with the group.[48]

The most widely known way Quakers differed from others in their speech was by using the "plain speech" – addressing people using the informal singular *thee* and *thou* rather than the formal plural *you*. They did this to indicate their belief in spiritual equality and to reject the formality and vanity of the world's customs. For example, they also used the word "convince" where most Christians said "convert." When someone is *convinced* of Christ, it signifies an inward, voluntary change by the individual, whereas when someone is *converted*, it is something happening to the person from the outside. All speech

---

[46] Job Scott, *Journal of the Life, Travels, and Gospel Labours of that Faithful Servant and Minister of Christ, Job Scott* (London, 1815), 124.

[47] Jean-Paul Brissot de Warville, *A Critical Examination of the Marquis de Chatellux's Travels in North America in a Letter Addressed to the Marquis; Principally Intended as a Refutation of his Opinions Concerning the Quakers, the Negroes, the People, and Mankind* (Philadelphia, 1788), 25.

[48] On the uniformity of Quaker language, see Peters, *Print Culture and the Early Quakers*, 171.

should, of course, be "holy conversation" as opposed to "carnal talk."[49] Similarly, what they did not say was significant. They did not use salutations or season's greetings, nor would they swear oaths to the government. Their unorthodox use of speech is more apparent in their interactions with non-Quakers, and will be discussed shortly.

In addition to the timing of speech, and the words used, the physical manner in which the words were delivered was also important and lent authority to the speaker.[50] Quaker women, for example, demonstrated their submission to divine direction, and thereby their spiritual authority, by preaching in a "sing-song" manner unlike male preaching in either Quaker or non-Quaker societies.[51] We can see the importance this manner of preaching held in the fact that renowned Hicksite minister Lucretia Mott undermined her authority with more traditional Quakers by not using this style.[52] The speech-acts of individual members could either facilitate or fundamentally disrupt the discernment process and corporate unity on which achieving consensus depended.

Determining exactly where the weight lay in the meeting based on speech-acts was a delicate balancing act. Everyone had to assume his or her divinely ordained role or there was the risk that "some forward spirits be pushed forward into too great activity, in a formal manner, by the backwardness and withholding of others."[53] The principle that guided Friends in seeking this balance was their most important testimony, the peace testimony.[54] Although some of the earliest Friends held to peaceful principles, pacifism was not a defining feature of the group until 1660 when George Fox was led to declare his testimony on this law.[55] Very generally speaking, the peace testimony was a nonviolent

---

[49] For a discussion of conversation in the context of the family, see Barry Levy, "'Tender Plants': Quaker Farmers and Children in the Delaware Valley, 1681–1735," *Journal of Family History* vol. 3, no. 2 (1978), 116–35.

[50] See also Mack, *Visionary Women*, 151–52.

[51] On "sing-song" preaching, see Kenneth Carroll, "Singing in the Spirit in Early Quakerism," *Quaker History* vol. 73 (1984), 1–13, esp. 10–13. On speaking as a demonstration of political authority, see Maurice Bloch, ed., *Political Language and Oratory in Traditional Society* (New York: Academic Press, 1975).

[52] Nancy Isenberg, "'Pillars in the Same Temple and Priests of the Same Worship': Women's Rights and the Politics of Church and State in Antebellum America," *The Journal of American History* vol. 85, no. 1 (1998), 98–128, 120.

[53] Scott, *Journal of the Life, Travels, and Gospel Labours*, 124.

[54] For thorough discussions of the peace testimony, see Peter Brock, *Pioneers of the Peaceable Kingdom* (Princeton, NJ: Princeton University Press, 1970); Peter Brock, *The Quaker Peace Testimony 1660 to 1914* (Syracuse, NY: Syracuse University Press, 1990); and Meredith Baldwin Weddle, *Walking in the Way of Peace: Quaker Pacifism in the Seventeenth Century* (New York: Oxford University Press, 2001).

[55] As Weddle points out, some Quakers did, even after the advent of their peace testimony, take up arms on occasion. However, by the mid-eighteenth century, those who did so were read out of their meetings. On the institution of the peace testimony, see George Fox, *A Declaration from the Harmles & Innocent People of GOD called Quakers. Against all Plotters and Fighters in the World* (1660). Interestingly, the first line of the book reads: "Our Principle is, and our Practices *have always been* to seek peace, and ensue it" (emphasis added). Another tract admits

stance in relation to God's creations. Historians have usually considered its application to war and the treatment of men.[56] But this testimony had a much wider sphere than we might suppose. As nineteenth-century Quaker Thomas Clarkson put it, Quakers adopted a "larger interpretation of the words in the sermon upon the Mount" than most.[57] It applied not simply to war and killing but also to mundane interactions with all God's creations. Within the ecclesiastical polity, God's creation of the individual conscience must be respected. Similarly, speech-action as a divine creation also fell under the purview of the testimony. Most importantly, however, preservation of God's creation of the constituted body was paramount. Within the meeting, then, conversation and walking must be holy, orderly, and peaceable.

Because the discernment of Truth was a communal effort, it was inextricably bound with the preservation of corporate unity. Quakers thus had a sense of communal and ecclesiastical obligation of the highest order. As Barclay asserted, those who "study to make Rents and Divisions" are "prostrating the Reputation and Honour of the Truth."[58] Moreover, their safety, their protection from sin, and their persecution from the outside world lay in their unity. Barclay explained that to preserve the uniqueness that bound them together, "certain Practices and Performances, by which we are come to be separated and distinguished from others, so as to meet apart, and also to suffer deeply for our Joint-Testimony; there are, and must of Necessity be as in the Gathering of us, so in the Preserving of us while gathered, Diversities of Gifts and Operations for the Edifying of the whole Body."[59] The unifying uniqueness of the body was based on the acts of its members – the *practices*, *performances*, and *operations*.

In spite of the importance of unity, because of the individual's access to the Light, dissent was a critical element of the discernment process as a way to the Truth. For Quakers, bringing the Light of Truth to their community through dissent was a form of proselytization. As indicated previously, there was a special commission placed with the individual to follow Christ's example

---

that, although Quakers once bore arms against the king, "[y]et being now altered and turned in their judgement to the contrary, and that it is not lawful (in the Administration of the Gospel) to fight against, or go to war with Carnal Weapons in any wise, there is no danger of us on [this] count." P. H., *The Quakers Plea, answering all Objections, and they proved to be no way dangerous, but Friends to the King: And may be tollerated in their Religion, with safety to the Kingdom* (1661), 4–5, in *Quaker Tracts* 9 vols. [1658–76] (London, 1661), 4: 923–36.

[56] The exact definition and applicability of the peace testimony remained unsettled for Friends for almost another century, and even after that, warm adherence to causes such as American liberties in 1776 or abolitionism in 1861 led some Quakers into battle. It was the cause of many of the biggest controversies within and outside of their Society when they controlled the Pennsylvania government.

[57] Thomas Clarkson, *A Portraiture of Quakerism. Taken from a View of the Education and Discipline, Social Manners, Civil and Political Economy, Religious Principles and Character of the Society of Friends,* 3 vols. (New York: George Forman, 1806), 3: 29.

[58] Barclay, *Anarchy*, 25.

[59] Ibid., 34.

and "[give] Witness to the Dispensation of the Gospel."[60] A crucial and indispensable part of this witnessing was that conscientious believers should be "Discerners of Evils" who have a duty to "reprove" and "warn" the meeting; they ought not to remain silent.[61] The Truth might be "divers in its Appearance," and if the dissent "layeth not a real Ground for Division or Dissension of Spirit, Fellow Members ought not only to bear one another, but strengthen one another in them."[62] The Truths that dissenting members brought to their meetings were their "testimonies" for God to man.

As important as individual Truth-seeking was, however, it was not more important than the unity and harmony of the meeting. Because of the imperative to preserve unity, although it was incumbent upon the majority to hear dissent as a way to the Truth, the dissenter was equally obliged to follow a prescribed method in bringing his testimony to the meeting to preserve the constituted ecclesiastical polity. "For there is no greater Property of the Church of Christ," said Barclay, "then pure Unity in the Spirit that is a consenting and oneness in Judgment and Practices in Matters of Faith and Worship (which yet admits of different Measures, Growths and Motions, but never contrary and contradictory Ones)."[63] In other words, contradiction and disunity come from man and his misinterpretation of the Gospel, not from contradictions in the Gospel itself. In order to dissent correctly, the dissenter must first engage in the process of communion with God – purify himself of his own selfish motives and approach the meeting in humility as Christ's agent. If, however, the meeting does not hear him at first, he must then exercise "Forbearance in Things wherein [the others] have not yet attained, yet . . . [the dissenter] must walk so, as they have him for an Example."[64]

This idea of walking as an example was drawn directly from primitive Christianity and was a refrain throughout Quakerism. As Christ's way of walking was a model for Quakers, so their "walking in the way of Christ" was a model for one another and non-Quakers. They believed that although some individuals may have had a more advanced understanding than the group, in time God would eventually reveal the Truth to all. There was, in other words, an idea of progressive revelation for the group as well as the individual. If still there was no unified sense, the matter must be put aside for the time being so as not to jeopardize the fundamental unity and harmony of the meeting. Dissent thus should be a slow process of persuasion, convincement, and gradual revelation, not coercion. In theory, there was no elitist tyranny or democratic despotism in a Quaker meeting. But difficulties could develop in two ways – if the dissenters did not respect the process and asserted their interpretation of the Truth in a disruptive way; or, if the body tried to repress the voice of the

---

[60] Ibid., 9.
[61] Ibid., 57.
[62] Ibid., 58.
[63] Ibid., 54.
[64] Ibid., 55.

dissenter. In other words, there was a constant danger of anarchy on the one hand or tyranny on the other if the peace testimony were not observed.

The clearest example of Quaker process at work is in the origins of the antislavery testimony in the mid-eighteenth century. Although isolated concerns had been raised about the divine lawfulness of slavery as early as 1675, still by the late 1730s, there were few Friends who saw it as a pressing concern for the Society as a whole.[65] Benjamin Lay, predating the famous abolitionists, John Woolman and Anthony Benezet, was one of the first to come forward with the testimony of abolitionism. But at the time, the Society was neither ready for his message nor appreciative of how he delivered it. Not only did Lay expect Friends to manumit their slaves immediately, he employed shock tactics to make his point. In 1737 he published a broadside entitled, *All Slave-Keepers That Keep the Innocent in Bondage, Apostates Pretending to lay Claim to the Pure & Holy Christian Religion.* He also once kidnapped the child of a fellow Quaker so he would know how slaves felt to have their children sold away. But the meeting for worship was the main forum for the expression of his testimony. He was known during the winter to stand in the doorway of the meetinghouse with one shod foot inside and one bare foot outside in the snow to symbolize the slaves who had no shoes. His final act was much more dramatic. He arrived at meeting in a cloak that concealed a military uniform and a Bible, hollowed out and filled with a bladder of red liquid. At a crucial moment in the meeting, he rose, threw off his cloak, and stabbed the Bible with a sword to symbolize that slavery is a bloody act of war against mankind. For this aggressively provocative expression of disunity with Friends, Lay was disowned in 1738.[66]

Only a few years later in the 1740s, John Woolman approached Friends with exactly the same testimony, but with a very different delivery. Rather than shocking them and denouncing them as apostates for holding slaves, he delivered "hints" and "soft persuasion," preaching gently to them, urging them to examine their ways.[67] In sharp contrast to Lay's tone and language, Woolman compared his fellow Quakers with biblical figures, writing, "It appears by Holy Record that men under high favours have been apt to err."[68] He even went so far as to assure them, "I do not believe that all who have kept slaves have therefore been chargeable with guilt. If their motives thereto were free from selfishness and their slaves content."[69] Also, to ensure the receptiveness

---

[65] The first Friend to denounce slavery was, according to Barbour, William Edmondson in 1675 (*The Quakers in Puritan England*, 242).

[66] Gary B. Nash and Jean Soderlund, *Freedom by Degrees: Emancipation in Pennsylvania and Its Aftermath* (New York: Oxford University Press, 1991), 49.

[67] Michael Alan Heller, "Soft Persuasion: A Rhetorical Analysis of John Woolman's Essays and 'Journal,'" (Ph.D. Diss., Arizona State University, 1989).

[68] John Woolman, "Some Considerations on the Keeping of Negroes," in Phillips P. Moulton, ed., *The Journal and Major Essays of John Woolman* (Richmond, IN: Friends United Press, 1989), 201.

[69] Ibid., 211.

of the meeting to his testimony, Woolman waited almost twenty years for the right time to present it, after many weighty Quaker slave owners had died. His testimony was then heard willingly by Friends and adopted by most of the Society in 1758. Later slave ownership became a cause for disownment from the meeting.

Clearly, then, it was not Lay's testimony as much as it was his conversation and walking that displeased Friends. It was accusatory and disruptive. His actions seemed as calculated to sow discord as they were to abolish slavery. He did not heed Barclay's advice that "some [dissenters are] behoved to submit, else [the group] should never have agreed."[70] Woolman, on the other hand, waited patiently and approached the meeting in a spirit of love. It was Woolman's manner of walking that Quakers hoped to encourage when they constituted their government.

Constituting the Quaker Meeting

Because of the libertinism of some members, Fox and other leaders found it necessary to bring the Society of Friends into the Gospel order by establishing a governmental structure that would provide a framework to facilitate correct process. It became clear early on that there were some Friends who spoke better on behalf of the Truth than others. The preponderance of the power to decide the direction of the meeting thus lay with the "weighty Friends." These Friends were ordinary people who would make their spiritual gifts known to the meeting by their peaceable conversation and orderly walking. It would be clear to all that they, regardless of gender, age, social status or other worldly quality, had been called by God to minister to the group. Once God had ordained them, they were then approved by the meeting to travel as ministers. This was the extent of the procedure. Not all individuals whose voices carried weight became "public Friends," as they were called. Some remained at home and served as elders or overseers of their meetings.

The structure that resulted from the identification of weighty Friends was to be a sort of federal system with governing bodies organized hierarchically and geographically – preparative weekly meetings, regional meetings that met monthly and quarterly, which were themselves governed by a strong central body that met annually. Representatives to these bodies emerged organically from the meetings with their spiritual authority established by the speech-act process. "[I]n every particular meeting of Friends," explained William Dewsbury, "there be chosen from among you, one or two who are most grown in the power and life, and in discernment in the truth, to take care and charge over the flock of God in that place." They should also serve as "examples to the flock."[71] There was no single pastor of the meeting.

---

[70] Barclay, *Anarchy*, 22.
[71] William Dewsbury, "The Life of William Dewsbury," in William Evans and Thomas Evans, eds., *The Friends' Library: Comprises Journals, Doctrinal Treatises, and Other Writings of the*

The business of establishing the order of church government began in the 1650s at the local level. The institution of the central government was most difficult; it took around ten years, from the late 1660s to the late 1670s, for it to take hold. The federal system was a departure from earlier Quaker process in that it took some of the decision-making power out of the hands of individuals, especially at the local levels. In the years before the central government was established, most Quakers believed that a unified decision at the local level equaled an infallible decision; in this new federal structure, although the local meetings retained a degree of autonomy, the only decisions considered to be infallible were those made at the higher levels of the quarterly and yearly meetings of elders and ministers. The individual, then, had to submit his or her will to the meeting as it was guided by the body of the meeting.[72] "Every [member]," wrote John Banks, "ought to be subject and condescending one unto another, in things which are already settled and established as to church-order; and not any one say to this or the other, I would be left to my freedom and liberty."[73]

Quaker government was, then, a representative democracy with what we might call a spiritual aristocracy of leadership. But even with this rule by the holy, in theory, there was no oligarchy. Barclay wrote: "That God hath ordinarily, in the communicating of his Will under his Gospel, imployed such whom he hath made Use of in gathering of his Church, and in feeding and watching over them, though *not excluding others*."[74] All members, therefore, had a role in choosing representatives and all were allowed to attend the "meeting for business."[75] There was a popular sovereignty in the Quaker meeting that was more than the theoretical popular sovereignty that existed in the British government. Because God might give any individual member, no matter that member's standing in human society, a clearness he has not bestowed on the others, all voices need to be reckoned with on an individual basis according to their weight. Appropriate to this group process, there was no head of the church to act as leader. The closest Quakers came to having such a figure was the clerk of the meeting. But his was more a bureaucratic office than a position of leadership. It was the clerk's job to discern the "sense of the

---

Religious Society of Friends (Philadelphia: J. Rakestraw, 1837–50), 2: 213–310, 233. (Hereafter referred to *Friends' Library.)*

[72] Sheeran, *Beyond Majority Rule*, 30–35.

[73] John Banks, "Dear Friends and Brethren, unto whom the salutation of my love reacheth" (1684) in *Friends' Library*, 1: 55.

[74] Barclay, *Anarchy*, 68.

[75] "Institution of the Discipline," *Friends' Library*, 1: 109–41, 112. There were "meetings for worship" and "meetings for business." The latter was the political assembly of the church and dealt with the governmental issues within the Society. About the meeting structure and representation within it, Bauman notes that all members were in theory allowed to attend meetings at any level, but in practice only the most active attended the Quarterly and Yearly Meetings. Also, the number of representatives was fairly small. In Philadelphia Yearly Meeting, for example, during the first half of the eighteenth century, the number of representatives was around 1 percent of the total membership (*For the Reputation of Truth*, 65–66).

meeting," that is, the collective feeling of the group about which direction to proceed. The clerk must do this by taking into account what is said, what is not said, and the weight of the individuals who did or did not speak, and then combine these communications to determine if there is consensus or whether to wait until God has "opened the way" further. Contemporary Quakers liken the difficult job of the clerk to herding cats – guiding the individuals in the same direction must be done by persuasive suggestions rather than coercive measures, and it must take into account the idiosyncrasies of each member.

If the process of discernment demonstrated in the Woolman example was the ideal, there was always a fundamental and perennial tension between persuasive efforts Friends might employ and coercive ones that were out of keeping with the peace testimony. This tension naturally turned on the issue of where power resided in the body of the meeting – with those who had or who sought power. As the church government was being established, coercive power lay with the leaders. In accordance with good church order, they argued, if anyone contradicts the "fundamental Truth" that brought "a People" together, that person should be cast out. The problem, of course, is when all have the ability to discern God's Truth at least to some degree, the "Truth" may be hard to define. Although most Quakers held that the Truth was ultimately decided by the group, for detractors of the new church government this raised the difficult question of how far the positive law of the meeting would extend to regulate the conscience and behavior of the individual. Barclay was unwavering on this point: The church had authority over matters of the conscience and the power to discipline members for transgression of divine order. "*That any particular Persons de Facto, or effectually giving out a positive Judgment, is not Incroaching nor Imposing upon their Brethren's Consciences*," he claimed.[76] The proof for Barclay about the true meaning of the Light was not only that the weightiest Friends discerned the need for church government, but also that Scripture and reason were on their side. The church government, these sources all agreed, could denounce any doctrine that is contrary to the bonds that held them together, "the original Constitution," as he called it.[77] And "Whatsoever tendeth to break that Bond of Love and Peace," proclaimed Barclay, "must be testified against."[78] In the early years, the preponderance of power and the use of coercion resided with the minority of de facto leaders of the meeting.

A point that should be kept in mind is that, although the positive law was powerful, the exercise of it was relatively mild for a church government so adamant about its understanding of Truth. Disciplinary measures and punishments were meted out firmly but gently, and with continued concern for the spiritual well-being of the transgressor. If there were a dissenter who persisted in expressing himself in a disruptive way, thus threatening the harmony of the meeting, the meeting had the latitude – the responsibility even – to exclude that person, to "disown" him. The way Quakers understood it, because such

[76] Ibid., 73.
[77] As opposed to the written constitution.
[78] Barclay, *Anarchy*, 57.

a dissenter was following his own will rather than that of God, "[b]y refusing to hear the Judgment of the Church, or the whole Assembly, he doth thereby exclude himself, and shut out himself from being a Member."[79] Yet the Quaker belief in perfectionism conditioned how the transgressor was dealt with. Thus the meeting should not entirely exclude a transgressor from contact with the faithful and continued spiritual guidance. "[W]e also meet together," Barclay explained, "that we may receive an opportunity to understand if any have fallen under [the Enemy's] Temptations that we may restore them again."[80] There was always hope of repairing the relationship and saving a soul. The responsibility for identifying and dealing with disorderly walkers lay not exclusively with the elders, ministers, and overseers of the body, but "with any other who discerns them, and is moved to speak to them."[81] In the disciplinary process, the individual was first dealt with privately. The transgressor was then brought before a judicial body, and if he was still unrepentant, he was then disowned. Even after this, however, representatives from the meeting retained contact with him and extended the opportunity for him to repent before the meeting and be restored as a member. And the only way this restoration was possible was if there were order in a church government that could facilitate and approve it.[82] While this was a gentle means of discipline, there is a kind of force and tenacity about it that should not be overlooked. Quakers were determined not just to make converts but to keep people within their fold using all the power allowed them. They ought to be "a body fitly framed together in unity."[83]

The Creation of a Written Constitution

In 1669 Quakers codified their laws and institutions in a written document.[84] The Quakers' government and their implementation of the law was based previously on a practice akin, but not identical, to the British common law tradition. According to Friends, the meeting was constituted before the formal Discipline was established. As they explained it,

it may be safely asserted, that there was never a period in the Society when . . . that order and subjection which may be said to constitute a *discipline* did not exist. But as the number of members increased, those mutual helps and guards which had been, in great measure spontaneously afforded, were found to require some regular arrangements for the preserving of order in the church.[85]

---

[79] Ibid., 14.
[80] Ibid., 46.
[81] Dewsbury, "The Life of William Dewsbury," 2: 234.
[82] On this disciplinary process, see Braithwaite, *The Second Period of Quakerism*, 258–59. For a contemporary description, see Dewsbury, "The Life of Dewsbury," 2: 233–34; and Joseph Pike, "Some Account of the Life of Joseph Pike," *Friends' Library*, 2: 374–75.
[83] Banks, "Dear Friends and Brethren . . . ," in *Friends' Library*, 1: 56.
[84] An extensive discussion of the Discipline is "Institution of the Discipline" in *Friends' Library*, 1:109–41.
[85] The Book of Extracts from London Yearly Meeting, quoted in *Friends' Library*, 1: 114.

In the earliest meetings for business, Quakers took detailed minutes of the proceedings that described the issues and concerns raised by members and how they were resolved. The implementation of the law was then based on these records that grew organically from the meetings, which were founded on Friends' discernment of the Light, Scripture, reason, and history. For Quakers, Scripture was the most important history book. It was "A faithful Historical Account of the Actings of God's People in divers Ages."[86] The origin of historic precedent was vital. Tradition and custom not based on the Light, on the other hand, were invalid. In that Quakers identified with the primitive church and saw themselves as acting in the same spirit, apostolic precedent was the most trustworthy. Barclay wrote,

[W]e are greatly confirmed, strengthened and comforted in the joint Testimony of our Brethren, the Apostles and Disciples of Christ, who by the Revelation of the same Spirit in the Days of Old believed, and have left upon Record the same Truths; *so we having the same Spirit of Faith*, according as it is written, *I believe, and therefore I have spoken*; we also believe, and therefore we speak.[87]

Quakers' own experiences and actions were valid precedents as well, as long as they were in keeping with earlier precedents enacted in the living spirit of Christ. Because precedents were so important for establishing and further developing their legal code, Friends examined their origins very closely and tended toward conservatism. They naturally distrusted "Innovators" who were "given to change, and introducing new Doctrines and Practices, not only differing, but contrary to what was already delivered in the Beginning; making Parties, causing Divisions and Rents."[88] A precedent enacted in the wrong spirit could harm the meeting for years to come.[89] Importantly, however, change was not rejected out of hand. A theory of change formed part of their theology and ecclesiology and was built into their written constitution.

In 1669 as the leaders worked to establish the central church government, Fox, acting as a representative of the body, drew up the first Discipline of the unified meeting. The Discipline was the Quakers' ecclesiastical constitution. Its title was *Canons and Institutions drawn up and agreed upon by the General Assembly or Meeting of the Heads of the Quakers from all parts of the kingdom...January 1668/9, George Fox being their president.* Even from the language in the title, we can see that this document looked very much like the civil constitutions that were being written at this time; it was a statement of the origins and purpose of the Quaker meeting and codification of the law Friends had discerned through their consciences and transcribed thus far. It dealt with laws that governed Quakers in relation to one another and, to a degree, to the outside world. Among the topics covered are the representatives

---

[86] Barclay, *Apology*, 3.

[87] Barclay, *Anarchy*, 25.

[88] Ibid., 9.

[89] On the tension between precedent and established conviction in the meeting, see Bauman, *For the Reputation of Truth*, 55.

chosen to attend the "General Meetings" to report on needs of the unfortunate and the transgressions of members; appropriate timing and places for the General Meeting; guidelines for proper deportment among members, including peaceable conversation; the education of children; choosing burial places; and recording important events such as births, deaths, and the persecution of Friends by the civil government.[90]

According to Friends, this constitution was, because of its origins in a collective process of discernment, perfect in its fundamental elements and therefore sacred and perpetual. The creation of the Discipline was a case in which "the Judgment of a certain Person or Persons in certain Cases . . . is infallible" and for this reason, it was appropriate for the General Assembly to "pronounce it as obligatory upon others." But here Barclay made a point that was crucial for the survival of both the written constitution and the ecclesiastical polity. The infallibility of this judgment "is not because [these men] are infallible, but because in these Things & at that Time they were *led by the infallible Spirit.*"[91] Insofar as the written constitution was in keeping with the spirit, it was perfect and perpetual. If aspects of it were not discerned in the right spirit, however, they would not be binding. This meant that the written constitution, like the constituted body, was not a static thing. On the contrary, because Quakers believed in adhering to the "living spirit" as opposed to the "dead letter," they left the form, function, and laws of their government open to change. The written constitution was a living entity, flexible and amendable to remain in keeping with the spirit. "Seasons and Times," explained Barclay, "do not alter the Nature and Substance of Things in themselves; though it may cause Things to alter, as to the Usefulness, or not Usefulness of them."[92] In other words, although the fundamental law embodied in the constitution was eternal, changes in the written document might be necessary in order to apply the law as times changed and as God gave man greater clearness of his will. A constitution, like a man, was imperfect, yet perfectible.

This idea of creating and amending ideas and texts was based on a belief in progressive revelation in individuals and the community. Quakers therefore exhibited the same attitude toward the interpretation of all of their theologico-political texts as they did their constitution. In 1672 they established an "editorial committee" that would screen and approve all works printed under the auspices of the Society.[93] In the reprinted edition of the works of Quaker political theorist Isaac Penington, for example, they edited his work not strictly according to a standard of original intent of the author in keeping with his historical circumstances, but rather according to the eternal Truth as they had come to understand it. Accordingly, with due respect to the author's abilities

[90] A more detailed discussion of this constitution can be found in Braithwaite, *The Second Period of Quakerism*, 256–60.

[91] Barclay, *Anarchy*, 67.

[92] Ibid., 24.

[93] Rebecca Larson, *Daughters of Light: Quaker Women Preaching and Prophesying in the Colonies and Abroad, 1700–1775* (New York: Alfred A. Knopf, 1999), 36.

of discernment, they deleted passages that they found to be out of keeping with the Spirit and retained the ones that agreed with it.[94]

The flexibility of the Quaker ecclesiastical constitution is evidenced in its evolution from the seventeenth to the late-eighteenth century. The 1669 Discipline is sixteen pages long; the 1798 Discipline is 135 pages. Over the years it was rewritten and expanded, and it evolved to include a preamble that stated more clearly the purpose of the Quaker meeting, new laws that governed the meeting, clarification or amendment of old laws, and features to make it more useful as a reference tool for members, such as a table of contents and an index. The document was printed in limited numbers and then circulated among the members who then transcribed it for their own use.[95] But, as evidence of their confidence in the infallibility of the spirit leading the original General Assembly, the essence of it remained the same, including the very language they used. There were also some administrative changes. These were the creation of a system of elders as additional authority structure in 1727 and the institution of birthright membership around 1737.[96] As will be explored in later chapters, there was also a change in the peace testimony in the mid-eighteenth century. Other than these, the basic theology and ecclesiology remained the same among all Friends' meetings until the Hicksite Separation in 1827–29.

Barclay's treatise on church government, *The Anarchy of the Ranters*, written after the *Canons and Institutions*, but before the settlement of London Yearly Meeting, served a similar function as *The Federalist Papers* (1787–88) did in the American founding. It was to clarify the basic principles of the polity; explain and justify the new, strong central government; and convince the informally constituted body to accept it in order to make the unity formal. Also like the implementation of the U.S. Constitution, the structure was imposed on those who may not have been fully persuaded of its legitimacy.

The constitution of the church, the fundamental law that governed it, and the structural order it prescribed were all thus divinely ordained antecedents to the written constitution and the formal structures of government implemented by man. The man-made document and structures were handed down directly from God and were merely carried out by man as best he could. Because the church government, the structures it created, and the processes it prescribed were all ordained by God, they were sacred and perpetual. But because man

---

[94] D. F. McKenzie, *The London Book Trade in the Later Seventeenth Century* (Unpublished manuscript, Cambridge University: Sandars Lectures, 1976), 33. I am grateful to Stephen Foster for bringing this manuscript to my attention at a Newberry Library seminar.

[95] See the Philadelphia Yearly Meeting, Books of Discipline, HQC. See Michael Warner, "Textuality and Legitimacy in the Printed Constitution" in *The Letters of the Republic: Publication and the Public Sphere in Eighteenth-Century America* (Cambridge, MA: Harvard University Press, 1990), 97–117. Warner describes the origin, form, and function of a constitution in very similar ways to this. The constitution is formed through a collective effort and legitimized by its distribution among and use by the members of the polity. But he dates the origins of this theory and process at the American Revolutionary period.

[96] Braithwaite, *The Second Period of Quakerism*, 542, 459.

was fallible, and because God did not give man "clearness" of his will all at once but rather revealed it as he saw fit, they were also flexible and amendable.

By modern categorizations, Quakers were thus bureaucrats of a very peculiar sort. Theirs was a collective, informal, legal-charismatic authority. In some important ways, it was opposite from Weber's legal-rational model and his charismatic model, although it shared some similarities with both. It was legal in the sense that it followed the rule of law, but it rejected rationalism as its foundation. It was charismatic in the sense that authority was perceived to come from a divine source, but unlike Weber's charismatic authority, the authority of the Light was not in a single individual leader, but rather was embodied in the collective. It was also informal in that the process was, at least in theory, internalized, thus rendering formal structures unnecessary. On the other hand, the Quaker model does comport with charismatic leadership in the sense that the process had to become routinized for the group to survive. But the collective nature of the charisma kept it from dissipating, as does charismatic power in individuals. Thus Quaker bureaucracy combined elements of authority that are contradictory in the usual models.

Quakers used this bureaucratic authority – their process of walking and conversation – for two related purposes: first, as described previously, they turned it inward upon their members to preserve the unity of the group by controlling the individualizing aspects of the Inward Light; and second, they turned it outward toward civil society and government. But in the latter case, it was to expand rather than limit individual liberty.

Quaker Civil Disobedience: Preaching by Example

The Quakers' legal discernment process began as an individual and collective quietism, or inward withdrawal, and resulted in outward activity.[97] In other words, they looked inward for God's mandates, which directed them to engage intensively in the world. The main reasons Quakers organized themselves and established church government were to worship God properly, organize charity efforts, and to ensure unity in the meeting. There was another reason, however, that prompted Friends to organize – public relations. They needed both to facilitate their proselytizing and to combat the resulting persecution from the civil government.

As noted earlier, in the years before the establishment of the Discipline, Quakers were a much more enthusiastic group than they would later become. As is true of many new movements with powerful ideological momentum

---

[97] Quietism in general, as well as Quaker quietism in particular, is a complex of theological ideas. Inward seeking, bodily and spiritual stillness, and a distrust of human abilities are among the things that characterize Quaker quietism. For a thorough discussion, see Rufus Jones, "Quietism in the Society of Friends," *The Later Periods of Quakerism* (Westport, CT: Greenwood Press, 1970), 1: 57–103. The mistake has been when scholars have interpreted Quaker quietism to mean a complete and permanent, rather than temporary withdrawal from the world.

and charismatic members, it was seeking converts. Early Friends were thus ardent proselytizers. One of the names they called themselves was the "First Publishers of Truth," where "to publish" means "to make public" through all media. They saw themselves like the Apostles, "Instruments" sent by God to go "forth and [preach] the Gospel in the Evidence and Demonstration of the Spirit, not in the Enticing Words of man's Wisdom; but in Appearance, as Fools and mad to those that judged according to Man."⁹⁸ The goal of early Quakers was to convince the entire world of Quakerism.⁹⁹ In the civil polity as in the ecclesiastical, for Quakers, to dissent was to proselytize. They hoped that "their Words and Testimony pierced through into the inner Man in the heart, and reached to that part of God in the Conscience."¹⁰⁰ Accordingly, they traveled as missionaries and public Friends and sent epistles around the world – to the sultan of Turkey, the emperor of China, and the pope in Rome. And, moreover, to be true to historical precedent, they did so "in Appearance as" fools and the insane. These early Friends set out to provoke, to disrupt, and to become martyrs for the Truth.

The basis of their aggressive campaign was their understanding of God's law and the process by which they brought it to the public. Members were continually "put in mind of the necessity of trying to be good examples to others, in bearing a faithful testimony for the truth."¹⁰¹ In setting an example for the Truth, Friends acted upon their testimonies – that is, fundamental points on which divine law and human law and conventions disagreed and which inhibited liberty of conscience. In following God's law above human law, Quakers were giving their testimony on a range of issues that challenged civil, ecclesiastical, and social order. They took the initiative as individuals to confront the law.¹⁰² In this sense, they were like the antinomians who rejected the prevailing legal order and followed their own instead.¹⁰³ But they were not identical; their law was not purely inward.

⁹⁸ Barclay, *Anarchy*, 12. See Hill on "radical madness" (*The World Turned Upside Down*, 277–84). He finds that "[s]uch actions were also a deliberate form of advertisement for the cause" (280).
⁹⁹ Barbour, *The Quakers in Puritan England*, 127.
¹⁰⁰ Barclay, *Anarchy*, 12.
¹⁰¹ George Churchman, 2nd mo. 5th day, 1781, *The Journal of George Churchman, 1759–1813*, 8: 22. HQC.
¹⁰² It is very difficult, if not impossible in the context of the English legal system, to determine exactly what laws Quakers were breaking. What seem like minor infractions of social custom to us were serious offenses in a society in which customs were the law. See Glenn Burgess's discussion of legal customs in *The Politics of the Ancient Constitution*. He describes the common law as "the practices that held society together as a whole" (35). For example, today not doffing one's hat to one's social superior may seem relatively innocuous, but such an omission would have signaled the breakdown of the entire social order to a seventeenth-century Englishman.
¹⁰³ On the definition and description of antinomianism, see Como, "The Sinews of the Antinomian Underground," in *Blown by the Spirit*, 33–72.

In the process of civil dissent, speech-action was as important as it was in the meeting, and for the same reasons.[104] As they accessed God through the Light in the conscience, and he led them to speak, they believed their words to be directly from God. The power they believed was behind the words thus drove them to extreme public acts and an equally shocking disregard for the opinions of mere men, especially ministers of other persuasions, whom they believed to be speaking only the "dead letter." In this case, in the reverse of the way in which they used Quaker process as a political structure in their meeting, the speech-acts in the civil sphere were intended to break down illegitimate structures and replace them with constitutional (i.e., godly) ones.

Quaker speech-acts were a form of political theater.[105] They were intended to be provocative, a spectacle in the public arena. More than this even, they were participatory, encouraging audiences of potential converts to join the Quaker movement.[106] And early on they were not peaceable and persuasive, but aggressively confrontational and coercive to the point of hostility. In the beginning, they identified themselves defiantly by embracing, adopting, and publicizing the derogatory name given to them by their enemies and referring to themselves as "the people in scorn called Quakers."[107] In this and other ways, Friends seemed to challenge all the fundamental structures of English society. Their conversation and walking were political acts of "leveling." With their spiritual egalitarianism, they wanted to level the patriarchal authority of church, state, and society and replace corrupt laws with godly ones. As one non-Quaker explained, they "shew contempt" through "theire gestures & behavior" without even using words. For example, they would simply stare at people without speaking to make them uncomfortable.[108] They also went to opposite extremes by shouting down Puritan ministers in their own churches, running naked through the streets to symbolize the spiritual nakedness of the unconvinced, letting women travel alone and preach, refusing to engage in polite and subservient behavior with social betters, refusing to use the pagan names for days and months, refusing to attend Church of England services, refusing to swear oaths, and carrying out other measures that signified an alternate understanding of the Word and world. Their dramatic speech-acts were designed to be shocking and thus memorable. All of these things were to advocate liberty of conscience, God's law, and spiritual equality. They sought to make all men equally humble before God.

---

[104] Jane Kamensky treats Quaker speech in *Governing the Tongue: The Politics of Speech in Early New England* (New York: Oxford University Press, 1997), esp. 117–126.

[105] Ibid., 120.

[106] Peters explains that one of the Quakers' aims in proselytizing through print was "involvement of the audience" (*Print Culture and the Early Quakers*, 166–67).

[107] Peters discusses the formation of the Quaker identity through not just the appropriation of this name from their detractors, but more importantly their own cultivation and dissemination of it. See Chapter 4, "'The Quakers Quaking': The Printed Identity of the Movement," 91–123.

[108] Quoted in Kamensky, *Governing the Tongue*, 121.

As indicated previously, not just Quaker men participated in the disruption; women and children did their part as well. Women especially were a threat. Although the testimonies of Quaker women were not substantively different from those of men, they were disruptive on a much deeper level. Not only did women break most of the same laws and customs as men by adhering to their testimonies, but they defied many other conventions by doing these things *as* women. Moreover, they took their dissent into the innermost sanctums of their private lives to challenge the patriarchal bonds of family and matrimony. Adhering to their testimonies often meant disobeying not just the authority of the state, but also the authority of their husbands and fathers.[109]

The radicalism of Quakers caused them, as they hoped, to be branded very quickly as lunatics, heretics, and a threat to the civil government. Their behavior reminded contemporaries variously of the dangers of radical Anabaptism of the sort that dominated Münster from 1534 to 1536, radical Puritanism that fomented the Civil War, Ranterism that sought to democratize England, and, worst of all, the ever-present threat of popery. To many Englishmen, the Quakers followed the Inner Light as slavishly as papists followed the pope. And the Quakers' "Pope within" was just as subversive as the one in Rome.[110] The fear on the part of their contemporaries was that they would succeed in their missionizing efforts. Quaker opponent Francis Bugg worried that their meetings were not merely about worship; "they Debate and Treat of other Matters, which may tend to the Promoting of *Quakerism*, and agree upon such Measures, and give such Orders for the Executing of them, as tend exceedingly to the Weakening [of] the Public Interest."[111] Quakers' opponents rightly recognized that Quakers did not meet exclusively for worship, but also for the business of coordinating their resistance to the civil authorities. "The Quakers Synod" (Figure 1) is a depiction of how "the Quakers hold a General Synod every

---

[109] See, for example, Elizabeth Ashbridge, "Some Account of the forepart of the life of Elizabeth Ashbridge" (1713–55), FHL. There is a substantial literature on Quaker women. See Isabel Ross, *Margaret Fell, Mother of Quakerism,* 2nd ed. (York: William Sessions Book Trust, 1984); Bonnelyn Young Kunze, *Margaret Fell and the Rise of Quakerism* (Stanford, CA: Stanford University Press, 1994); Mack, *Visionary Women*; Larson, *Daughters of Light*; Peters, *Print Culture and the Early Quakers.* Peters notes that, although Quakers supported their female members in their activities and defended them publicly, they had concerns that women might be a substantially disruptive force within and without the meeting and thus tried to limit their expressions (147–49). Although women's preaching and printing contributed much to the solidity of the early movement, curtailing passionate outbursts by women in the early years of the movement, Peters argues, was also a major part of the developing Discipline.

[110] John Faldo, *Quakerism no Christianity: Or, a Thorow Quaker no Christian proved by the Quakers Principles, detected out of their chief Writers . . . with . . . an Account of their Foundation laid in Popery* (London, 1675), 120.

[111] Francis Bugg, *Quakerism Anatomized, and Finally Dissected: Shewing, from Plain Fact, that a Rigid Quaker is a Cruel Persecutor* (London, 1709), 423. It should be noted that Bugg was a former Quaker himself who left the meeting on extremely bad terms. His observations, therefore, should be understood in light of both the experience he gained as a Quaker but also his vindictiveness toward Friends.

FIGURE 1. A seventeenth-century depiction of a "Quakers Synod" with Quaker leaders presiding. William Penn says, "Call over ye List, Are none of Truths enemies here?" George Whitehead asks, "Are the doors shut?" William Bingley replies, "Yea the doors are lockt." The Journal of George Fox is on the table to be pitted against the Church Canons. (Francis Bugg, *The Pilgrim's Progress, from Quakerism to Christianity* [London. 1698; rpt. 1700], inserted between pages 108 and 109. FHL.)

Whitsontide, with Doors Lock'd, Bar'd, Bolted, or else Guarded by Stout Fellows, that no Body may inspect their Proceedings; against the known Law."[112]

The consequences of Friends' transgressions from English and early American law and custom were severe, and Friends were well aware of them as they published their testimonies.[113] In *A Collection of Sufferings of the People Called Quakers for the Testimony of a Good Conscience* (1753), Joseph Besse estimated that between 1650 and 1689, there were 20,721 Quakers in England and America who had encounters with the law, and 450 died as a result, mostly in prison. Beyond the officially imposed punishments, the physical violence that Quakers endured at the hands of soldiers, mobs of teenage boys, and others, all tacitly or openly encouraged by the religious and civil authorities was severe; there were beatings and mutilations of elderly men, young children, and pregnant women that often led to death or disfiguration. Some of this was clearly prompted by Quakers' refusal to obey laws and customs, but much of it was provoked by things as seemingly innocuous as difference in dress and can be attributed to simple bigotry and xenophobia. Quakers were convenient targets for the intolerant and sadistic.[114] The most extreme example of Quaker persecution in the seventeenth century is the execution by hanging of four Quakers, including Mary Dyer, on Boston Common in 1660. Significantly, Quaker agitation during this period gained them more followers as witnesses to their suffering were convinced of Friends' salvation.[115]

During the 1660s and 1670s, the simultaneous development of the church government and the peace testimony tempered and shaped the quality, though not the quantity, of their dissent. Fox eventually convinced most Friends that peace and nonviolent resistance was the essence of true Quakerism. As Friends came to believe, God ordained that man should not destroy divine creation, which included both other men but also government, ecclesiastical *and* civil. Barclay wrote that, in the recent past, struggles for liberty of conscience had been good, "albeit always wrong in the manner by which they took to accomplish it, *viz.* by Carnal Weapons."[116] The Quakers' new understanding of the sanctity of a civil constitution was in part a result of the creation of their own ecclesiastical constitution. And a similar sense of political obligation existed

---

[112] Ibid., 422.

[113] Most works of Quaker history address the topic. In addition to the sources cited below, for discussions of persecution of Quakers in America see Jonathan Chu, *Neighbors, Friends, or Madmen: The Puritan Adjustment to Quakerism in Seventeenth-Century Massachusetts Bay* (Westport, CT: Greenwood Press, 1985) and George A. Selleck, *The Quakers in Boston, 1656–1964: Three Centuries of Friends in Boston and Cambridge* (Friends Meeting at Cambridge, 1976); also see Jones, *The Quakers in the American Colonies*, especially Book 1, Chapter 4, "The Martyrs."

[114] Craig W. Horle, *Quakers and the English Legal System, 1660–1688* (Philadelphia: University of Pennsylvania Press, 1988) provides graphic examples of physical abuse of Quakers, 125–30, and statistics on sufferings from 1660 to 1688 in Appendix One, 279–84.

[115] Chu, *Neighbors, Friends, or Madmen*, 46.

[116] Barclay, *Apology*, iii.

in both areas. The same principles that applied to dissent in the meeting were thus applied to dissent in the civil polity.

The peace testimony had a significant effect on Quaker proselytizing. Some historians have posited that at the time it was instituted, Quakers turned quietist or toned down their enthusiasm in order to lessen their persecution.[117] Although there was certainly a change in behavior, there was not such a drastic change in Friends' attitude as has been maintained. It is true that a portion of the Society did exhibit quietistic tendencies, but the term has often been inaccurately applied to Quakers to mean a group that has withdrawn from the world into sectarian isolation. The urge to "conquer" the world did indeed fade, but the urge to change it did not. Writing about one of the defining characteristics of the Quaker church, Barclay explained that they were a people who

have not been wanting with the Hazard of our Lives to seek the scattered ones, holding forth the Living and Sure Foundation, and inviting and perswading all to *obey the Gospel of Christ*, and to take Notice of his Reproofs, as he makes himself manifest by *his Light* in their Hearts; so our Care and Travail is and hath been towards those that are without, that we may bring them into the Fellowship of the Saints in Light; and towards those that are brought in, that they may not be led out again, or drawn aside.[118]

It would seem rather that Quakers were less afraid of persecution than they were the possibility of their mission failing. If their Society disintegrated under the pressure of persecution, they would fail in their divinely appointed commission to secure liberty of conscience for all and open the way for the world to become Quaker. Thus they also tempered their goal of convincement to something more realistic and one that relied more on gentle persuasion than aggressive and overtly disruptive tactics. Missionizing was, if not as aggressive or obvious as in early Quakerism, still very much a compelling force among Friends.

Therefore, while the intensity and aggression of the Lamb's War tapered off in the second generation of Quakerism, its overarching goal did not disappear. It has persisted into the twenty-first century as Quakers have engaged in a variety of social reform efforts that have grown out of their ancient and new religious testimonies. The persistence of this missionizing and purifying mentality is present in numerous Quaker writings. After a particularly satisfying meeting in 1804, for example, George Churchman noted in his journal that he looked forward to "a prospect of things rising into more clearness or of a season when Sluggards & dwarfish persons will be hunted out of their holes, or lurking-Places."[119] Although the vocabulary of war is missing from this glimpse into the Quaker mentality at the turn of the nineteenth century, this expression is only a few degrees milder than the language of the Lamb's

---

[117] See, for example, Barbour, *The Quakers in Puritan England*, 251; Braithwaite, *The Beginnings of Quakerism*, 525; Braithwaite, *The Second Period of Quakerism*, 179; also Boorstin, *The Americans*, 68. Most subsequent histories have accepted this assumption.

[118] Barclay, *Anarchy*, 33–34.

[119] Journal of George Churchman, 5th mo. 23rd day, 1804, 8: 80, HQC.

War, and the sentiment is the same – there should be a sustained and vigorous effort to assure that the cause of Truth is promulgated.

It is also true that Quaker testimonies became less a means of aggressive confrontation and more a mark of their uniqueness, but uniqueness in itself was a way of missionizing. Their conversation became more peaceable, but no less peculiar. This new conversation was due in part to changes in the world around them, some of which their agitations had engendered. Massachusetts Puritans, for example, eventually decided that toleration of Quakers was preferable to the discord created by the persecution; and William Penn managed to secure a measure of legal toleration from James II in the form of the 1687 Declaration of Indulgence, authored by Penn himself. By 1689 when the Act of Toleration was passed, instigated largely by Quakers, the worst of the persecution was over.[120] But the new truce between Quakers and the civil authorities was also due to the evolution in Quaker public relations. Their new tack involved a reinvention of the Quaker image. Quakers were what we would today call "media savvy." They understood intuitively the subtleties of "publishing" from many angles and with many media, which was precisely why their opponents feared them. In the 1650s, it was the individual Quaker who controlled and shaped the spoken word. But as their central government formed, it was the group that regulated the speech-action of the individual. They limited physical expressions of enthusiasm and overtly subversive preaching.[121] They renovated their public image to be something less threatening and more attractive. Although not yet quite "respectable" in the late-seventeenth century,[122] over the centuries, they managed to shape the connotation of the name "Quaker" in the popular mind from a detestable and offensive misfit to a virtuous, pious, and trusted citizen. Today most of us imagine the Quaker in the person of the Quaker Oats man, whom we can hardly imagine shouting at anyone, let alone running naked through the streets.

In spite of the new corporate structure, it is easy to see why historians have mistaken Quakerism for an individualistic faith; they always took the initiative to proselytize as individuals. What began to change with the institution of church government was not the individual initiative but rather the regulation of that initiative by the Society. Now the body must give its "approbation" for a Friend to travel in the ministry.[123] Preaching, however, was still founded on individual initiative; meetings did not "send" missionaries. But as the persecution heated up, the body supported individuals more in their endeavors. The meeting thus had both positive and negative roles to play in relation to

[120] See Ethyn Williams Kirby, "The Quakers' Efforts to Secure Civil and Religious Liberty, 1660–96," *The Journal of Modern History* vol. 7, no. 4 (1935), 401–21.

[121] Mack explains that by the 1670s, members – women in particular – who preached or wrote against the government in regards to war were censored (*Visionary Women*, 365, 368). Censorship on this topic also gives us a clear indication that the peace testimony was not used, as it would become by the late-eighteenth century, against state-sponsored war.

[122] Hill, *The World Turned Upside Down*, 359.

[123] William Reckitt, "The Life of William Reckitt," in *Friends' Library*, 9: 54.

the individual – to facilitate piety and proselytizing, though not to compel, and also to regulate the interpretation and expression of the religious impulses.

Thus although their testimonies of dress and speech became pleasingly quaint, amusing, or inspirational to outsiders instead of offensive, they continued to function much as they did before, merely more subtly. As Friends saw it, their testimonies acted as both a hedge and a Light – a hedge to keep out sin and a Light as a beacon to the unconvinced. A Friend was to set an example of piety in every way. James Bringhurst, a respected Philadelphia Friend, expressed sentiments common to Quakers in the early nineteenth century:

> We, who are not called, or at least are not engaged in the line of the ministry, may be very usefully exercised in our respective allotments, and may sometimes preach to others, either by example, or by the distribution of good books, or in some way or other, by which we may promote the benefit of individuals and the welfare of society at large.[124]

Everyone, then, was a sort of minister. Certainly when compared to George Fox's admonition to Friends that their lives and words should be "a Terrour to all that speak not Truth," Bringhurst's words signify that Quakerism had indeed evolved into a gentler religion. But this desire to influence people to Quakerly ways, expressed time and again in eighteenth- and nineteenth-century Quaker writings, is no less ardent or sincere. Bringhurst was always hopeful that the efforts of Quakers would "open the way in the minds of the people towards Friends" and was pleased to note that "those of other [religious] societies are frequently seen attending Friends' meetings with much solidarity. There are many," he concluded, "looking towards Friends in various parts of this continent."[125] A Society that opened its meetings for worship to the general public and regularly had more observers of their peculiar practice in attendance than members must have been at least as concerned with missionizing as purity.

The goal for Friends was always the transformation of the world, but now this regeneration no longer had to come from each person being convinced to become a member of the Society of Friends. The hope of most Friends was not that everyone in the world would *become* Quaker in name, only that they would *act like* Quakers. Theirs became a missionizing movement with an ecumenical bent. The name of a believer's sect was less important than the substance of his belief; the Quakers' universalism let them believe that all had the capacity to recognize and follow the Inner Light. Their movement and its effect thus had a greater potential to be both broader and deeper than that of many other religions.

From their understanding of how a closer knowledge of God's law is gained in meeting through a process of dissent – that is, calm and respectful of the corporate unity – they knew that it must function the same way in the state: Some

[124] John Murray, Jr., to James Bringhurst, 1st mo. 21st day 1805. Bringhurst Letters, FHL.
[125] James Bringhurst to John Dickinson, 1st mo. 22nd day, 1802; and James Bringhurst to Moses Brown, 2nd mo. 25th day, 1802. Bringhurst Letters, FHL.

members will understand the true law earlier, and it is incumbent upon these visionaries to convince the others gently, even if that means waiting patiently for years for God to give them clearness. Thus, for Quakers, adherence to God's law – the higher law – meant breaking ungodly human laws, but they were obliged to do so peacefully, according to the same order and method that God prescribed for the church. In other words, they had to preserve the divinely ordained civil government by working within the existing system.

So seminal is the peace testimony still to Quakerism that one could argue that it has led to a clouding of Quaker history. Most histories of the Society of Friends (which, until recently, were written mainly by Friends) emphasize the sufferings of Friends and encourage a misperception about the Society's collective response to persecution. The myth is that they suffered their punishments without complaint and without resistance. "Where we cannot obey," wrote William Penn somewhat misleadingly, "we patiently suffer."[126] According to their beliefs, they were to accept both their punishments and the oppressive government that inflicted them peacefully and with love. While imprisoned, Isaac Penington wrote,

The Lord hath made my bonds pleasant to me, and my noisom Prison (enough to have destroyed my weakly and tenderly-educated nature) a place of pleasure and delight, where I was comforted by my God night and day. And filled with Prayers for his People, as also with love to and Prayers for those who had been the means of outwardly-afflicting me and others upon the Lord's account.[127]

While it is certainly true that Friends accepted their punishments, and did so "lovingly," it is not the case that they continued to "suffer patiently" or quietly; they were by no means passive. For Friends, religious quietism did not equate with political quietism.[128] The case is, in fact, the opposite. Retreating inward to worship and discover God's law then compelled them to go forth and, as Tocqueville says, "to *harmonize* earth with heaven."[129]

Thus persecution is only part of the story of Quakers in their early years. It was merely the catalyst for Quakers to develop their process of civil dissent. Friends were not content merely to suffer the unjust punishments doled out to them by the government; instead, they established themselves as a formidable force for legal and political reform in early modern England.[130] Although they used many tactics, some of which were the typical means Englishmen protested governmental oppression, the most significant was the new practice of civil disobedience.

---

[126] William Penn quoted in Isaac Sharpless, *A Quaker Experiment in Government: History of Quaker Government in Pennsylvania, 1682–1783* (Philadelphia: Ferris and Leach, 1902), 15.

[127] Isaac Penington, "Three Queries Propounded to the King and Parliament . . ." in *Penington's Works* (London, 1680), 406.

[128] Weddle, *Walking in the Way of Peace*, 10.

[129] Alexis de Tocqueville, *Democracy in America*, J. P. Mayer, ed. (New York: HarperPerenial, 1988), 287.

[130] Horle's, *Quakers and the English Legal System* is the definitive work on this topic.

Quaker civil disobedience followed a distinct process that met the criteria laid out in the Introduction for true civil disobedience and foreshadowed the process articulated later by reformers such as Martin Luther King, Jr. It was a nonviolent, public protest against unjust laws with the intent to educate for change. The first step was to purify the conscience in communion with God. Next, one discerned the fundamental law through inward searching and outward testing. God's law was then compared with the civil law. When the two conflicted, testifying for the true law began. In this part of the process, a key component of Quaker dissent was testifying – publishing the Truth – openly. In spite of the grim punishments that awaited Friends for challenging the laws of England and the American colonies, they nevertheless resigned themselves – often jubilantly – to their status as criminals and did not hesitate to break the law repeatedly. On the matter of oath taking, for example, Barclay was decisive: "Neither is it lawful for them to be unfaithful in this, that they may please others, or that they may avoid their hurt: for thus the primitive Christians for some ages remained faithful."[131] One relatively unusual pamphlet on early Quakerism comments favorably on Friends' constant dissent. This anonymous Anglican admired the fact that a Quaker

could never be Tempted by Interest, or even the Preservation of his Property, to Act contrary; and often has rather chose to suffer by ill Men, even to the entire Ruin of his Family, rather than offend his Conscience: So no Interest or Preferment could ever Tempt him to any *Occasional Conformity* to the Church or Government.[132]

A Friend, it was generally recognized, was, for better or worse, more concerned about the state of his soul than any bodily or other punishments that could be inflicted by man. "I went [by the justices] in fear," says Thomas Ellwood, "not of what they could or would have done to me . . . but lest I should be surprised, and drawn unwarily into that which I was to keep out of."[133]

Friends, when faithfully following the Inward Light, rarely avoided conflict over their testimonies. When acting in Truth, they were bound by conscience to reveal themselves as Friends, although it oftentimes would have been much more convenient to hide the fact. But openness was more than just a testimony. This practice was calculated both to send a message that Friends were confident in their faith and mission and also to establish a good relationship with the civil authorities. Although Friends actively sought conflict with the government over what they perceived as unjust and ungodly laws, their main goal was not simply to anger government officials. Ultimately, they were trying to convince them, if not of the truth of Quaker ways, then to allow Quakers and others to pursue their ways unmolested. They had an interest in dealing forthrightly with the government as the most effective means of achieving their ends. In his

[131] Barclay, *Apology*, 553.
[132] G. D. *The Quaker No Occasional Conformist, but a Sincere Christian in his Life* (London, 1703), 5–6.
[133] Thomas Ellwood, *The History of the Life of Thomas Ellwood* (Philadelphia, 1865), 36.

Apology, Barclay reminded Charles II of the Quakers' openness in their civil disobedience:

> In the hottest times of persecution and the most violent persecution of those laws made against meetings, being clothed with innocency, [Friends] have boldly stood to their testimony for God, without creeping into holes or corners, or once hiding themselves, as all other Dissenters have done; but daily met, according to their custom, in the public places appointed for that end; so that none of thy officers can say of them that they have surprised them in a corner, or overtaken them in a private conventicle, or catched them lurking in their secret chambers; nor needed they to send out spies to get them, whom they were surely daily to find in their open assemblies, testifying for God and his truth.[134]

This kind of openness was in keeping with other Quaker testimonies of plainness, such as those of deportment or speech.

Quakers then disobeyed a range of laws that were passed against religious dissenters in general, and them in particular. In both England and America, for example, they broke laws that required attendance at the state-established church or prohibited dissenters from holding their own public meetings, which were seen as conspiratorial against the state and encouraging of religious schism in the Church of England.[135] The First and Second Conventicle Acts of 1664 and 1670 made attendance at any other religious meeting outside the Church of England punishable by imprisonment, stiff fines, or banishment.[136] Friends met anyway. Also, despite the fact that Quakers often met in complete silence and bodily stillness, they were harassed by officials for rioting. They continued, however, to meet openly in spite of being fined, imprisoned, beaten, and physically expelled from their meetinghouses.[137] In 1665 Parliament passed the Five Mile Act, in part to curb Quaker public preaching. This law prohibited individuals who had been convicted of preaching in the past, and who refused to swear oaths of loyalty to the government, from coming within five miles of any borough sending burgesses to Parliament. Infractions against the act could earn an offender a fine and six months in prison without a trial.[138] Quakers, of course, still preached.

The next step in their civil disobedience was to accept the inevitable punishments willingly and with love. As suggested previously, not only were early Friends willing to accept their penalties, they were eager. "And if by [testifying against unjust laws] our sufferings be continued," explained Robert Smith, "we shall not rise up with carnal Weapons to work out our own deliverance, but

---

[134] Barclay, *Apology*, iv.

[135] Horle, 46.

[136] Hugh Barbour and J. William Frost, *The Quakers* (New York: Greenwood Press, 1988), 66.

[137] Thomas Ellwood, *A discourse concerning riots: occasioned by some of the people called Quakers, being imprisoned and indicted for a riot, for only being at a peaceable meeting to worship God* (London, 1683), passim.

[138] Horle, *Quakers and the English Legal System*, 51.

patiently endure what may be further laid upon us for the Truth's sake."[139] Martyrdom was an extremely important component of Quaker dissent. What distinguished early Quakers from other dissenters in the eyes of their contemporaries was their zeal in seeking out conflict with authorities. Moreover, they reveled in their punishments, embracing their martyrdom as a sign of their righteousness and salvation and earning converts in the process. The more extreme the punishment, the more certainty of righteousness and the great possibility of a convincement

But ideally, of course, Friends were not seeking persecution but reform and liberty. Thus their process continued. The next step was not to retreat, but to engage more intimately with their persecutors. They did this by organizing themselves and going to law. Early Friends had a justifiable distrust of the law and lawyers. It was, after all, English law that gave their oppressors license to abuse them; and it was the lawyers who exploited their need for assistance, charging exorbitant fees for often-ineffectual counsel. Despite the fact that many Quakers would later become great lawyers themselves, the sentiment among Friends that lawyers were "terrible and lawless" persisted into the nineteenth century.[140] Although Fox had been making regular appeals for justice to the government since the 1650s, by the 1670s, Friends were beginning to establish a system of their own for achieving liberty of conscience. They evolved from a people who seemed to reject the laws of the polity completely to one that defined itself based on a similar kind of legal structure and process and employed this process to strike at their oppressors.[141] When faced with oppression, then, Friends' alternative to violent resistance was exploitation of the existing legal system.

Friends seemed to know instinctively that, for direct action against the government to be effective, they must organize. At the same time they were founding the church government, they were also forming committees and meetings to deal with civil matters through their process. One of the earliest and broadest groups organized by early Friends was called the Meeting for Sufferings. Established in 1676 this meeting was convened in order to document the religious persecutions inflicted on Friends. The institution of this meeting was crucial to Friends as a legal weapon against the English government.[142] Under the auspices of the Meeting for Sufferings, Friends collected, recorded, and published their persecution. It became the first-ever lobbying group in England as members took the recorded sufferings and presented them to justices and members of Parliament.[143] It acted also as a legal advocacy group for individual Friends.

---

[139] Robert Smith, *A Cry against Oppression and Cruelty* [1663], 3, in *Quaker Tracts*, vol. 6 (London, 1663–64).

[140] Edward Byllynge, *A Word of Reproof, and Advice* (London, 1659), 20. See also Journal of George Churchman, esp. 1794, 3rd mo., 7: 11, HQC.

[141] Horle, *Quakers and the English Legal System*, 162.

[142] Ibid.

[143] Frederick Tolles, *Quakers and the Atlantic Culture* (New York: Macmillan, 1960), 44. Also, Mary Maples Dunn, *Politics and Conscience*, 23; and Kirby, "Quakers' Efforts."

Members of the meeting traveled around the English countryside, informing Friends in remote locations of their legal rights, should unscrupulous officials attempt to confiscate their goods or fine them.

The purpose of collecting facts at this point was to determine whether or not injustice existed. But it was also to assemble the evidence, mobilize the efforts, and prepare for the next phase of the nonviolent campaign: engagement with the system. From the 1670s on, Friends devoted themselves to peaceful reform, using every legal strategy available to them, as well as creating new ones and recreating old ones. "[N]o people upon the Earth," complained Francis Bugg, "seek more to the Higher Powers [the civil government], than they do; it would be too tedious to recite the many Petitions, and Addresses to the Parliament, from the beginning for This, That, and the Other Favour, to settle and establish them."[144] Their tactics ranged from the straightforward, such as engaging legal counsel, keeping detailed records of all proceedings against them, and gathering and presenting evidence, to more complex maneuvers such as extensive appealing and officially discrediting informants. Some of their activities also helped reform unfair or corrupt judicial and law enforcement systems.[145] They insisted, for example, that in order for each person to understand and address the judicial system, all laws and customs should be printed and they also should be "pleaded, showed, and defended, answered, debated, and judged in the English tongue in all courts."[146] They also argued in favor of expanding the role of juries and not allowing anyone to be tried except by a jury of his or her peers.[147]

Friends also engaged in some tactics that cannot be classified as civil disobedience, but they were nonetheless forms of nonviolent resistance. With remarkable dexterity, they manipulated the bureaucracy of the English legal system. They found ways to circumvent unfair laws through legal loopholes. One example of this was placing a poor Friend in a meetinghouse as a tenant,

---

[144] Francis Bugg, *A Retrospective-Glass for the Quakers* (1710) republished in *A Finishing Stroke: Or, Some Gleanings, Collected out of the Quakers Books... Whereby The Great Mystery of the Little Whore is farther Unfolded* (London, 1712), 490.

[145] See Horle, *Quakers and the English Legal System*, specifically the chapters "The Lamb's War," 161–86, and "Quaker Legal Defense," 187–253.

[146] Richard Farnworth, *The Liberty of the Subject by Magna Carta* (1664), 12, quoted in Horle, *Quakers and the English Legal System*, 167. Horle notes that the complaint of court cases being conducted in Latin was a common one during this period, but we should remember that plainness of communication and speaking directly at all times was a particular concern of Quakers (183).

[147] Ibid., 169. For commentary on *Bushell's Case*, usually cited for its importance for trial by jury, see Simon Stern, "Between Local Knowledge and National Politics: Debating Rationales for Jury Nullification after *Bushell's Case*," *Yale Law Journal* vol. 111, no. 7 (May 2002), 1815–59; Thomas A. Green, *Verdict according to Conscience: Perspectives on the English Criminal Jury Trial, 1200–1800* (Chicago: University of Chicago, 1985). Green's work demonstrates that "at the hands of the Quakers" the practice of legal review by juries based on freedom of conscience became "a staple of post-Restoration pro-jury argument" (160; see esp. Chapter 6, "The Principle of Non-Coercion: The Contest over the Role of the Jury in the Restoration," 200–64).

thereby avoiding high fines that would otherwise have been imposed on the owner of the house.[148] They also used noncooperation and obstructionism to frustrate legal procedure that they could not control to their advantage. They refused to recognize laws passed against them without necessarily challenging them publicly. They delayed legal proceedings by traversing indictments and demanding changes of venue, and generally harrying their would-be prosecutors with their meticulous attention to legal minutia and technical error.[149]

At the outset of a trial, Quakers would always plead "not Guilty" before the court. Their plea was based not on man's law but God's. They would admit to breaking "unfounded Law"[150] but would claim that they "had transgressed no just Law."[151] Thenceforth, they did not, as one might assume, simply claim knowledge of the divine and let that stand as their defense. The approach of Quakers' legal argumentation was rather to appeal to reason as a tool to articulate the teachings of the Light. Although Quakers based their defense in court on God's law known through the Light within, their argumentation was nothing if not meticulously logical. They challenged the judges, magistrates, and the very law itself on their own terms, using the very reason these men held in esteem to dispute the charges against them. Robert Smith frustrated a judge over the matter of wearing his hat in court. In this exchange, Smith mixed religious and civil issues:

Judge. *What is the reason you appear thus contemptuously before the Court with your Hat on?*

R.S. My Hat is my own, and I came truly by him, and it is not in contempt I wear him.

Judge. *By it you contemn the Authority and Laws of this Kingdom.*

R.S. Where is that Law that forbiddeth a man to wear his own Hat? Instance it.

Judge. *It is a custom in England to shew their subjection to Authority by putting off their Hats.*

R.S. It is a custom in England for men to wear, or to come before Courts with Coats or Cloaks, and I am here without either; and is not the one as much a contempt as the other?

Judge. *Fine him five pounds, and record it, and now take off his Hat.* Which the Gaoler did accordingly.[152]

Smith continued in the same vein concerning oaths and whether the Doctrine of Christ contradicted the Doctrine of the Law, with similar responses from the judge. Here he accomplished two things. First, his primary goal was to testify on the issue of spiritual equality by leaving his hat on. And second, he denied

---

[148] Ibid., 188.

[149] Ibid., 208, 215.

[150] Smith, *A Cry against Oppression and Cruelty*, 7.

[151] W. S. *A True, Short, Impartial Relation Containing the Substance of the Proceedings at the Assize held the 12th and 13th day of the Moneth called August, 1664*, 1, in *Quaker Tracts*, vol. 6 (London, 1663–64).

[152] Smith, *A Cry against Oppression and Cruelty*, 4.

the legitimacy of customary law in two ways by arguing first that it is unwritten and second that it is inconsistent and unreasonable. Smith's civil disobedience thus arose from the Light and was defended by reason.[153]

Quakers could and did use arguments based on reason and natural law to appeal to the conscience – proceedings as those just discussed were deemed by them to be "*contrary to all equity and reason*" – but if that failed or when it suited their cause better, they could argue that God's law *seemed* unreasonable because it was not what people expected. When men would not "hear Reason," the defendant should rather "remain Silent" and leave the decision to the "Jury-mens Consciences."[154]

Their efforts eventually bore fruit. The Quakers, wrote Francis Bugg contemptuously, "[r]epeal, not verbally, yet virtually, so far as their Power reaches, all Acts of Parliament which suit not their *Light Within*."[155] But Bugg did not take his criticisms far enough. Over many decades, Quakers did, in fact, succeed in *actually* repealing many of the laws that did not agree with their Inward Light.[156] And when they were not immediately successful in England, they applied their skills to colonial American governments, where they eventually, one way or another, usually achieved their goals. This peaceful outlet for frustrations with government, exploiting the existing machinery, would be the Quakers' most significant contribution to the American dissenting tradition. Out of their process would grow new forms of constitutionalism and civic engagement.

Quaker thought and practice was an apparent contradiction for their contemporaries. They simply could not categorize Friends because they had never seen anything like them before. They did not understand the meaning of a people who in the same stroke of the pen could write to the king that "[Quakers] never sought to detract from thee, or to render thee and thy Government odious to the people" and yet that "it is not lawful for any whatsoever, by virtue of any authority or principality they bear in the government of this world, to force the consciences of others."[157] This was a new understanding of government and civic engagement, and it was premised on a comparatively modern understanding of political arrangements.[158] In the traditional legal understandings, peace

---

[153] A much more extensive example of Quakers' legal reasoning against their judges can be found in W. S., *A True, Short, Impartial Relation*, 1; and *A Second Relation from Hertford* [1664], *Quaker Tracts*, vol. 6 (London, 1663–64). In the first tract the author describes in detail the trial of some Friends for unlawful assembly, using extensive notes to refute each illogical turn in the proceedings. The second is a transcription of the trial in which the Quakers harried the court with their arguments. Numerous other tracts of the same sort are extant.

[154] *A Brief Relation of the Proceedings, &c.*, 19. in *Quaker Tracts*, vol. 5 (London, 1662).

[155] Francis Bugg, *The Pilgrim's Progress from Quakerism to Christianity* (London, 1698), 38.

[156] Isaac Sharpless, *Political Leaders of Provincial Pennsylvania* (New York: Macmillan, 1919), 232.

[157] Barclay, *Apology*, xxii. See also William Penn, *England's Present Interest Discovered* (London, 1675), 35.

[158] By "arrangements," I mean the structures and processes only, which can be secularized, not the motivation behind them, which was religious.

had no firm place. Quakers continually pointed out that that they broke the law in peace. According to English law, however, to break the law at all was always to do so "by force of arms." "Force of arms" was a "form of law," as a judge explained. If several men should break the law by meeting together, "although they have no visible weapons with them, yet their so meeting together is by force of Arms, because it is contrary to the Laws; and if they do but disturb the peace, it is by force of arms, expressed in all indictments."[159] Hence, despite the fact they sat in silence and refused to bear arms, Quaker religious meetings were considered "Riotous," "Tumultuous," and a "terrour of the People, and to the evil example of all others."[160]

Conclusion

Quakers needed to have a tremendous amount of faith in the English constitution and its prescribed legal system for them to have embraced it so. Indeed, they believed that the Magna Carta was rightly constructed and was a resource to be drawn upon for the defense of their liberties.[161] They somehow knew that the remedy of the ills came from the same source as the cause. The constitution merely needed reform. Their detractors did not yet understand that civil disobedience, as disruptive as it can be, is based on a strong sense of political obligation and a deep respect for the constitution of the state. Quakers were not antinomians of the usual definition.

The advent of the peace testimony served to lessen persecution, but it also enabled Friends to achieve liberty in such a way that it would be permanent. While religious discrimination and persecution did not halt entirely, Quaker activism embedded the ideal of religious liberty – or at least toleration – in the political consciousness, conscience, and laws of the nation. Religious persecution, as Isaac Penington knew, "will always be committed in nations and governments, until the proper right and just liberty of men's consciences be discerned, acknowledged and allowed."[162] In discussing popular liberties, Charles McIlwain describes the development of the modern constitution as a process whereby a more distinct line was drawn between the *gubernaculum* and *jurisdictio*, the power of the government in relation to the rights of the people. It is clear that this line was darkened by religious dissenters who drew the limits of *gubernaculum* where God's jurisdiction began – in the realm of the conscience. And in subsequent years, the line surrounding conscience was secularized and applied in a broader range of conflicts. As John Dickinson would write in 1774,

---

[159] Smith, *A Cry against Oppression and Cruelty*, 11. Smith's response in writing was: "Now let it be considered how that form of Law can be good and just, wherein things are expressed otherwise then it is, as so to say the People are met together by force of Arms, when the least appearance of such a thing cannot be found amongst them."

[160] *A Brief Relation of the Proceedings, &c.*, 3.

[161] *The Liberty of the Subject by Magna Carta* [1664] in *Quaker Tracts*, vol. 6 (London, 1663–64). Also in the same volume, see *Christian Tolleration*.

[162] Isaac Penington, *Concerning Persecution* . . . (London, 1661), title page.

"Whatever difficulty may occur in tracing that line, yet we contend, that by the laws of God, and by the laws of the constitution, a line there must be, beyond which [the government's] authority cannot extend."[163] How these slippery limits – slippery because the bounds of the conscience could change depending on the individual interpretation of God's will – were enforced by the people, however, was as important as defining them. In their nonviolent protest, Quakers reinforced the fundamental legitimacy of the government even as they limited its scope and redefined its role.

As Quakers were developing their principles and process and enacting them in their ecclesiastical polity, they were also beginning to imagine how their process would function on a much larger scale. When they began writing political theory and implementing civil constitutions of their own, they applied the lessons learned from their own efforts at establishing church government.

---

[163] John Dickinson, *An Essay on the Constitutional Power of Great-Britain over the Colonies in America* (Philadelphia, 1774), 34.

2

A Sacred Institution

The Quaker Theory of a Civil Constitution

The late-seventeenth century was an intensely creative period in Quaker political thought. Between 1669 and 1701, members of the Society wrote and implemented at least seven constitutions both ecclesiastical and civil. Yet the idea of Quaker constitutionalism is oxymoronic to many political historians, who have considered Quakers to be quietistic "withdrawers" from civic life; this is despite the fact there is a substantial body of literature that attests to their political activities. But while scholars have undertaken important examinations of the political philosophy of William Penn and studies of practical politics in Pennsylvania, few have attempted to explore the thought of Quakers as a body in detail and with consideration of their theology.[1] Moreover, those who address the topic of their theory disagree on how to classify it. Some situate them in the Whig tradition; others count them as Tories during the American Revolution; and others simply deny that specific principles of theirs are whiggish, but do not offer much beyond that.[2] But to categorize them within any single early modern tradition or language causes us to imagine affinities where

[1] A work that treats Penn's constitutional thought is Richard Alan Ryerson, "William Penn's Gentry Commonwealth." He notes the main influences on Penn of the usual early modern traditions, as he terms them, "radical dissenter-Leveller, Commonwealth(man), Whig, and Tory-patriarchal" (395). Although he writes that there were "distinctive . . . radical Quaker additions" to Penn's constitutions, he does not examine the underlying theologico-political thought (403).

[2] For works on Quaker politics, see the Introduction, fn. 9. Dunn counts Quakers as Whigs (Penn repudiated Whiggism in 1680. See "Persuasives to Moderation," in *Politics and Conscience*, 132–61), as do Bauman in *For the Reputation of Truth* and Fredrick Tolles in *Meeting House and Counting House*, passim. Endy also included Penn in this faction, noting the same limitations as Dunn (*William Penn and Early Quakerism*, 342). From Beatty's analysis of Penn's thought, we can infer that he would agree with this assessment. See Edward Corbyn Obert Beatty, *William Penn as Social Philosopher*. More recent is Andrew R. Murphy, *Conscience and Community*, 170. Others, including Alan Tully in *Forming American Politics* and Gary Nash in *Quakers and Politics*, disagree with this characterization and note some departures in Quaker thinking from conventional Whig thought. See "Understanding Quaker Pennsylvania," Chapter 7 and passim, in Tully *Forming American Politics*; and Nash, *Quakers and Politics*, 46.

none exist and to ignore important variations. As Quakers themselves said, "neither are we for one party or another."[3] An exegesis of their theory on its own terms is long overdue. Their ideas overlapped in some significant ways with other thought of the seventeenth and eighteenth centuries, but they came to them often through unique routes and for peculiarly Quaker ends. Moreover, the differences between Quakerism and Whiggism, or any other strain of thought at their time, put them decidedly out of step with their contemporaries in fascinating and important ways.

In many ways, Quakers most closely resemble Whigs, which is not surprising. They had many of the same concerns, and they drew on the same classical and contemporary sources. The key to the differences lies in religious influences. In the last few decades, scholars have explored the contribution of religion to Anglo-American political thought and constitutional development. They have focused on reformed Calvinism, and their work has revealed it to be an important influence. The republican ideology at the American Founding, they argue, is a sort of secularized Puritanism.[4] But, because Puritanism proper had long since vanished by this period, to use this idea as a means of interpreting theories at the Founding necessitates an abstraction of Puritanism – there were no Puritan governments in the late-eighteenth century, and what remained of Puritan thought was much altered and diluted from its original form.

There was, however, at least one functional Quaker government at the Founding and an active, living theology. And importantly, Quakerism is not a branch of reformed Calvinism. It grew out of the Puritan Revolution and thus shares with Puritanism some important theological tenets such as the importance of the individual's relationship with God; the idea of a voluntary relationship between God, the individual, and the faith community; and a distrust of hierarchy and ritual. But Quaker theology differed in significant ways from Puritanism, most notably in Friends' belief in the possibility of universal salvation, the peace testimony, a much greater degree of spiritual egalitarianism, the authority of immediate revelation equal to or above Scripture, and the possibility for human perfection. The virulent animosity of Puritans toward Quakers tells us clearly they did not see their faiths as the same. Insofar as

---

[3] Edward Burrough, quoted in Braithwaite, *The Beginnings of Quakerism*, 466.

[4] Gordon S. Wood, *The Creation of the American Republic, 1776–1789* (New York: W. W. Norton, 1972), 418. Perry Miller is responsible for bringing American Puritanism to the attention of political scholars. Some have broadened the topic to include pietistic Calvinism in the mid-eighteenth century. See, among others, the work of Patricia Bonomi, John Patrick Diggins, Daniel Elazar, Nathan O. Hatch, Alan Heimert, James H. Hutson, Donald S. Lutz, Wilson Carey McWilliams, Sydney Mead, Edmund Morgan, Mark A. Noll, Ellis Sandoz, Harry S. Stout, and Michael P. Zuckert. Specifically, on Puritan covenantal theology as a basis for American constitutionalism, see Lutz, "Religious Dimensions in the Development of American Constitutionalism," *Emory Law Journal* vol. 31, no. 1 (1990), 21–40. For the influence of Calvinism on Locke, see John Dunn, *The Political Thought of John Locke: An Historical Account of the Argument of "The Two Treatises of Government"* (Cambridge: Cambridge University Press, 1969; rpt. 1995), 188–89.

their theologies differed, so did the political theories and practices that arose from them. Moreover, and very importantly, Quaker political ideas in the late-eighteenth century were far from "secularized." Although there were people who extracted certain Quaker ideas and used them in a secular way, Quakers themselves were a powerful political force as a religious body. Thus Quaker thought emerged and continued as a divergent strain from that of Puritan-informed Whiggism, yet one that comported less perfectly with Toryism. Also, it had powerful elements of what we might term classical liberalism and republicanism, as well as significant influence from the British common law tradition, but neither can it be described using only these traditions.

Quaker theory comes into partial focus with the writings of a few leading seventeenth-century Quakers.[5] Their political treatises as well as the constitutions they drafted for West Jersey and Pennsylvania in the latter decades of the seventeenth century give a political form to the faith and practice established by their religious Society. The following is not an examination of all the sources that combined to make up Quaker political thought.[6] Rather it undertakes to show how their political theory was informed by their theology and ecclesiology. In the first instance, it will explain the Quakers' epistemology of fundamental law, which is the basis for their political theory. Their

---

[5] The analysis concentrates on the works of Isaac Penington and William Penn, two Quakers who can rightly be called political philosophers. It is safe to assume, however, that their views in this early stage of the formation of their theory were representative of the body of the Society of Friends. When the Quaker church government was established in the 1660s and 1670s, everything that was published by Quakers had to be critiqued and approved by the church to ensure that Friends were in unity with it before it was released to the public.

An argument might be made for considering Gerrard Winstanley a Quaker political theorist. Many tenets of his philosophy are the same or strikingly similar to the articulations of Penn and Penington. Moreover, there is circumstantial evidence that Winstanley became a Quaker later in life. But I have chosen to leave him aside in this discussion because, although many of his ideas during his Digger phase were the same as Quakers', there were others that differed significantly. And although the evidence of his later Quakerism is convincing, it is ultimately not fully conclusive. Finally, unlike Penington, who also wrote many of his treatises before he turned Quaker, Quakers never claimed Winstanley and his writings the way they did Penington and his work. On Winstanley and his thought, see mainly the work of Christopher Hill; also James Alsop, "Gerrard Winstanley's Later Life," *Past and Present* no. 82 (1979), 73–81. John Lilburne was another radical theorist who ended his life a Quaker, but whose thinking before then was more Calvinist. See Diane Parkin-Speer, "John Lilburne: A Revolutionary Interprets Statute and Common Law Due Process," *Law and History Review* vol. 1, no. 2 (1983), 276–96.

[6] I am referring here to the secular influences on Quaker constitutionalism. There is strong evidence that they drew on the ideas of Bacon, Harrington, and Milton, among many others whose ideas were compatible with their theology and practice. The works cited earlier on the thought of Penn cover some of this.

The following discussion has much in common with Larry D. Kramer's *The People Themselves: Popular Constitutionalism and Judicial Review* (New York: Oxford University Press, 2004). Kramer traces the early modern understanding of a constitution as something shaped, reviewed, and amended by the people. Yet, though his topic is the same, his focus is on the American Founding and adheres to Whig thought. It does not deal with the question of civil disobedience.

unconventional mode of legal discernment and decision making conditioned their understanding of what was contained in a constitution, how political arrangements should be constructed, and, most importantly, what should be done if the government overstepped its limits or flaws were perceived in the constitution. These theories were political versions of their religious understandings and arrangements. Thus, although they shared many political goals with their contemporaries, their ideology and their methods for achieving these ends were as peculiar as their religious doctrines and institutions.

Discernment of Fundamental Law

The singularity of Quaker constitutionalism lies in its casuistic epistemology of fundamental law. As many other Englishmen, Quakers believed that there was a fundamental, higher law that came from God. For most, God planted the law of nature in man, and man accessed it through his own reason.[7] Quakers, by contrast, believed that the fundamental law came directly to man through God and was immediately discernable through what William Penn called "*Synteresis.*"[8] The concept of synteresis is an old and confusing one, and there does not appear to have been any more agreement on the definition of the term over the centuries than there was on the meaning of fundamental law. It can, however, be understood loosely as using one's conscience as a guide to follow the divine will. Before Penn, philosophers and theologians from Plato to Aquinas to William Ames debated the subtleties of the term. Many cited Scripture and described it as "the Lord's Candle" in the conscience. Penn described it as "That Great *Synteresis*, so much renowned by *Phylosophers* and *Civilians*, learns Mankind, *to do as they would be done to.*"[9] But as often,

---

[7] On the origins of and interpretation fundamental law, see, in addition to Kramer, J. W. Gough, *Fundamental Law in English Constitutional History* (Oxford: Oxford University Press, 1955); Charles Howard McIlwain, *The High Court of Parliament and Its Supremacy* (New Haven, CT: Yale University Press, 1910); Edward S. Corwin, "'Higher Law' Background of American Constitutional Law," in *Corwin on the Constitution:* Volume One: *The Foundations of American Constitutional Political Thought, the Powers of Congress, and the President's Power of Removal* (Ithaca, NY: Cornell University Press, 1981), 79–139; B. Behrens, "The Whig Theory of the Constitution in the Reign of Charles II," *Cambridge Historical Journal* vol. 7, no. 1 (1941), 42–71; Martyn P. Thompson, "The History of Fundamental Law in Political Thought from the French Wars of Religion to the American Revolution," *The American Historical Review* vol. 91, no. 5 (1986), 1103–28; Michael Zuckert, *Natural Rights and the New Republicanism* (Princeton, NJ: Princeton University Press, 1994).

[8] Penn, *England's Present Interest Discovered*, 1.

[9] William Penn, *The Great Case of Liberty of Conscience* (London, 1670), 23. It is unclear exactly what part of speech Penn and others considered "synteresis" to be – whether it was a thing or a process. Earlier theologians seemed to use it as a noun such as "light," "conscience," or "reason." Penn used it this way as well, but the suffix *-sis* indicates that it was a process as well – a process of looking inward to find the light or reason. The Oxford English Dictionary defines it as "A name for that function or department of conscience which serves as a guide for conduct; conscience as directive of one's actions." In this context, it makes sense to consider it more of a "function" than a thing; more a way of discerning the Light than the Light itself.

earlier thinkers equated this Light with the light of reason. Although aspects of the idea of synteresis had become an accepted part of English thought, the word synteresis itself had become obsolete by Penn's time. Some of its meaning, however, was transferred into the terms "instinct" and the "spark of knowledge" that man knows through nature.[10]

While on the surface, the distinction between the natural law "promulgated and made known by reason only"[11] and synteresis may seem negligible – and may in fact have been for some thinkers – it was significant for Quakers.[12] Reason and Light for Quakers were distinctly separate things. Reason, which was of man, was corrupt and unreliable.[13] In his *Apology*, Robert Barclay asserted that when man is fallen, he is "deprived the Sensation (or feeling) of this Inward Testimony, or *Seed of God* and is subject unto the Power, Nature, and Seed of the Serpent, which he sows in Men's Hearts, while they abide in this Natural and Corrupted State." "Man therefore, as he is in this State, can know nothing aright," explained Barclay, "until he be ... united to the *Divine Light* ... Hence are rejected the *Socinian* and *Pelagian* Errors, in exalting a Natural Light."[14] Reason could interfere with an accurate understanding of the divine will and direct man to act in his own self-interest. Thus the Light and reason as ways of knowing were not interchangeable for Quakers and, when in conflict, the former superseded the latter. It is important to note, however, that Penn affirms that the "Eternal Principle of Truth and Sapience" which are the "Corner-Stones of Human Structure, the Basis of reasonable Societies," and which are discovered through synteresis, should be "agreeable

[10] Good brief discussions on the origins and use of the word are in Robert A. Greene, "Synderesis, the Spark of Conscience, in the English Renaissance," *Journal of the History of Ideas* vol. 52, no. 2 (1991), 195–219 and "Instinct of Nature: Natural Law, Synderesis, and the Moral Sense," *Journal of the History of Ideas* vol. 58, no. 2 (1997), 173–98. A more detailed analysis is Timothy C. Potts, *Conscience in Medieval Philosophy* (Cambridge: Cambridge University Press, 1980). Potts notes that Philip, Bonaventure, and Aquinas understood the conscience and light to be two distinct things, which was also how Quakers understood it. An analysis of casuistry that explains synteresis as a subversive force is in Lowell Gallagher's *Medusa's Gaze: Casuistry and Conscience in the Renaissance* (Stanford, CA: Stanford University Press, 1991). See also Michael C. Baylor, *Action and Person: Conscience in Late Scholasticism and the Young Luther* (Leiden: E. J. Brill, 1977); and Lynne Courter Boughton, "Choice and Action: William Ames's Conception of the Mind's Operation in Moral Decisions," *Church History* vol. 56, no. 2 (1987), 188–203.

[11] John Locke, *The Second Treatise of Civil Government*, sect. 57.

[12] Melvin Endy is the only author of whom I am aware who discusses Penn's use of the word "synteresis." He equates this in Penn's mind with the phrase "Universal Reason," describing it as the combined "divine-natural law" (*William Penn and Early Quakerism*, 339). The description is useful, and I agree with this equation where Penn is concerned; but, for reasons stated here, I believe this formulation would not necessarily have been the general understanding among Friends.

[13] Perry Miller notes that Puritans "also held that these remains [of the divine image in man], in the form of natural reason or 'the light of nature,' were exceedingly unreliable, but they had rescued them from the rubbish heap where Calvin had cast them" ("The Marrow of Puritan Divinity," 74).

[14] Barclay, *Apology*, 5–6.

with right reason."[15] There were also other guides for knowing the law. These were the same sort that Quakers used in their worship and religious business – Scripture, learned thinkers, and historic and apostolic precedent. In the civil realm, however, they also used the precedent of statute law, as long as it was in keeping with divine fundamental law.[16] Custom, on the other hand, which was also of man, was suspect because it was often not strictly based on divine law, but on human habits much like the rituals of the Roman Church. Moreover, it was unwritten, and thus arbitrary.

The Quaker process of understanding God's law, then, was not the deliberative, discursive process we imagine when we think of a body meeting to establish government or decide on laws. Rather, it was something akin to intuition, a nondeliberative process – the same process they used in religious worship to know God.[17] Penn's use of the word "synteresis" must have been an intentional evocation of an earlier understanding of the term, and one related more directly to immediate revelation, that would thus distinguish their thought from a range of other contemporary ideas. Advocates of natural law theory objected to the irrationality of the process and the wrong use of religion in politics[18]; and those of less enthusiastic religious convictions were uncomfortable with the antinomian implications of it. Penn's principle of synteresis is clearly the political equivalent of the religious doctrine of the Inward Light – in both religious and political terminology, the conscience is the medium through which God reveals his law to men. "[T]he Light of [God's] Son," said Penn, "shines in Man's Conscience; Therefore the *Light* of Christ in the Conscience must needs have been the *General Rule*"; and "That no Man can know what is agreeable to God, *except a Man hear God himself*, and that must be within."[19]

The Quaker way was thus not a process of "reasoning" or noetic intelligence but spiritual discernment.[20] In his *Essays on the Law of Nature* (c. 1663–64), Locke derided the Quaker way of knowing the law. "We do not maintain," he said, "that this law of nature . . . lies open in our hearts, and that as soon as some inward light comes near it . . . it is read, perceived, and noted by the rays of that light."[21] Likewise, Cato wrote that "There is no government now

---

[15] Penn, *England's Present Interest Discovered*, 6; and Penn, "Fundamentall Constitution of Pennsylvania," in Mary Maples Dunn and Richard Dunn, eds., *The Papers of William Penn* (Philadelphia: University of Pennsylvania Press, 1981–87), 2: 142.

[16] Penn, *England's Present Interest Discovered*, 6.

[17] Greene, "Synderesis," 198.

[18] See Ellis Sandoz on Locke's distinction between intuition or "inward" knowledge and reason (65); and his rejection of enthusiasm (73). Ellis Sandoz, *A Government of Laws: Political Theory, Religion, and the American Founding* (Baton Rouge: Louisiana State University Press, 1990).

[19] Penn, *Discourse of the General Rule*, 4–5.

[20] Sandoz, *A Government of Laws,* 63. Sandoz makes a distinction between Aristotle's understanding of noetic, as "the divine something in man," and Locke's, which is removed from God who is not knowable through "direct intuitive evidence" (66–67).

[21] John Locke, *Essays on the Law of Nature,* in Paul E. Sigmund, ed., *The Selected Political Writings of John Locke* (New York: W. W. Norton & Co.), 173. He reiterates this assertion

upon earth, which owes its formation or beginning to the immediate revelation of God."[22] Quakers were undoubtedly foremost among the sectarian radicals from whom Locke and Hobbes were trying to preserve the English polity.[23]

Despite their advocacy of synteresis or the Light, as we have seen in Chapter 1, Quakers were not hostile to reason, but they were highly suspicious of it when it was divorced from the Light. The earliest and most devout Quakers distrusted it most, but there were always some, such as Penn, who placed significant emphasis on it and did not shy away from using the language of natural rights.[24] As Quakerism evolved through the eighteenth century and into the nineteenth, the ideas of Light and reason gradually merged to become synonymous for some Quakers.[25] But before this, the way in which Quakers balanced the two allowed them to embrace the scientific rationalism of the Enlightenment without the paganism, and made them, without contradiction, among the most serious Christians as well as the greatest scientists and supporters of science in the eighteenth century.[26] Their approach to scientific inquiry was very much like that of Newton, who believed that it was done for the glory of God, and with his help. There was a revelatory quality of Newtonianism that was similar to Quaker "seeking" in that God revealed the secrets of nature to the scientist in his own time. The laws of nature, Newton said, "will be discovered to us" and we will then be "allowed to penetrate to the first cause [i.e., God] himself, and see the whole scheme of his works as they are really derived from

---

in *Essay Concerning Human Understanding* (1689) and in the *Two Treatises of Government* (1689). Interestingly, however, John Dunn argues that in *The Reasonableness of Christianity* (1695), Locke comes to "a sort of fedeist voluntarism" in his religious thought (*The Political Thought of John Locke: An Historical Account of the Argument of "The Two Treatises of Government"* [Cambridge, Cambridge University Press, 1969; rpt. 1995], 188–98).

[22] John Trenchard and Thomas Gordon, Letter No. 60, in Ronald Hamowy, ed., *Cato's Letters, or Essays on Liberty, Civil and Religious, and Other Important Subjects* (Indianapolis: Liberty Fund, 1995), 1: 413–20. 413.

[23] See also Thomas Pangle's discussion of reason versus revelation in Chapter 17, "The Divine and Human Supports for Justice," in *The Spirit of Modern Republicanism: The Moral Vision of the Founding Fathers and the Philosophy of John Locke* (Chicago: University of Chicago Press, 1988), 198–229; Paul A. Rahe, *Republics Ancient and Modern:* Volume Two: *New Modes & Orders in Early Modern Political Thought* (Chapel Hill: University of North Carolina Press, 1994), 266–67; as well as Rahe on Locke's distinction between "the God of revelation" and "nature's God" (252–63).

[24] Indeed, as Hugh Barbour notes in *The Quakers in Puritan England*, Penn was unusual among Quakers in that he did not make stark a distinction between Light and reason (244–45). But, as we shall see, this was not the only area in which Penn's political philosophy departed from that of the majority of Quakers.

[25] Thomas D. Hamm, "The Problem of the Inner Light in Nineteenth-Century Quakerism," in M. L. Birkel and J. W. Newman, eds., *The Lamb's War: Quaker Essays to Honor of Hugh Barbour* (Richmond, IN: Earlham College Press, 1992), 101–17.

[26] Tolles, *Meeting House and Counting House*, esp. 205–29. Brooke Hindle, "The Quaker Background and Science in Colonial Philadelphia," *Isis* vol. 46, no. 3 (1955), 243–50. Geoffrey Cantor, *Quakers, Jews, and Science: Religious Responses to Modernity and the Sciences, 1650–1900* (Oxford: Oxford University Press, 2005); Matthew Stanley, *Practical Mystic: Religion, Science, and A.S. Eddington* (Chicago: University of Chicago Press, 2007).

him, when our imperfect philosophy shall be completed."[27] This was also the Quaker view of how man would come to understand the fundamental laws of the polity.

The Civil Constitution and Its Components: The Basis for Political Obligation

The Quaker belief that the fundamental law was discerned through synteresis conditioned their understanding of the origin of the civil constitution, the structure of the government and the positive laws, and the process by which man governed. Because their epistemology of law was different from most, their constitutional theory does not conform entirely to the usual understanding of the "ancient constitution" or a "modern" idea of it.[28] Very generally, the notion of the ancient constitution is that a civil constitution is comprised of all aspects of government and laws – the fundamental law; positive laws (both written and *jus non scriptum*); and the institutions, customs, and structure of government.[29] Conversely, the principles of the constitution are embodied in all these things. In contrast to this ancient notion was a modern view that separated the constitution from the government: The people were first constituted as a body. They then created a written constitution that embodied fundamental law and limited the government.[30] A nation's government is, by extension, only a creation of the constitution and any acts of government to which the people consent are subordinate to that constitution. Consequently, in the modern view there is a disjuncture between the constitution, on the one hand, and the governmental structures, institutions, and laws on the other. The important difference between these two models for our purposes, and what will be explored subsequently, is in the notion of change – whether change is acceptable, under what circumstances, and to what degree.

[27] Colin Maclaurin, *An Account of Sir Isaac Newton's Philosophical Discoveries* (1748), 23, quoted in Robbins, *The Eighteenth Century Commonwealthman*, 71.

[28] This brief definition draws on Charles McIlwain, *Constitutionalism Ancient and Modern* (Ithaca, NY: Cornell University Press, 1947), 1–22.

[29] These words – *constitution, government, law, polity*, etc. – are problematic because of their various and overlapping meanings in different time periods. In this study, I often use the words *constitution* and *government* interchangeably, as did thinkers in the seventeenth and eighteenth centuries. These words also had broader meanings than they do today. For example, *constitution* meant a written document, but also – and more usually – the composition of a polity. I try to distinguish between these two meanings as I use them. Similarly, *government* meant, among other things, constitution, but also a geographic area controlled by a particular regime, such as a colony. For a discussion of their meaning in historical context, see Gerald Stourzh, "*Constitution*: Changing Meaning of the Term," in Terrence Ball and J. G. A. Pocock, eds., *Conceptual Change and the Constitution* (Lawrence: University Press of Kansas, 1988), 35–54.

[30] Endy makes brief note of the priority that William Penn placed on fundamental law and the primary role it should play in limiting both kings and magistrates (*William Penn and Early Quakerism*, 338–39).

Quaker constitutional thought was an amalgam of both of these understand-ings of a constitution with some differences from each. According to Quaker thought and practice, man originally lived without formal government. This time was man's state before the fall, similar, but not quite identical to what Lockeans would have identified as the state of nature. It was, as Penn wrote in his *First Frame of Government* for Pennsylvania (1682), a time in which "[t]here was no need of Coercive or Compulsive means; the Precept of Divine Love and Truth, in his own Bosom was the Guide and Keeper of his Inno-cency."[31] In this pure condition, man was governed by the "general rule" of God's Light.[32] But according to God's plan, for a number of reasons, prelap-sarian man had need of civil government as well. The rest of the political arrangements then followed – written constitution, government, positive law. In this sense, Quaker constitutionalism was like the modern. But unlike the modern understanding and more like the ancient, not only was the fundamen-tal law embodied in the constitution, so too was the civil government and the laws it created and implemented. Quakers' was a variation of divine right theory.[33]

Similar to most Englishmen, Quakers held that man was obliged to obey and maintain government because it was ordained by God. In his *First Frame*, Penn quoted Romans 13 that "The Powers that be are ordained by God: Whosoever resisteth the Power, resisteth the Ordinance of God." But more than this, even, Penn wrote that "*Government* seems to me a part of *Religion* itself, a thing Sacred in its *Institution* and *End*."[34] According to Friends, there were several reasons for this sacred institution. These are, in the main, similar to the reasons given by Whigs for why man created government – to maintain peace and punish the wicked. But there were some significantly different emphases on these things for Quakers that in turn reveal other purposes and priorities for government. Quaker political theory embodied an optimism about man's potential for good that is absent from most other thought at the time. As with the ecclesiastical polity, the main reason for the ordination of the civil polity was to facilitate charity and free worship. While charity was an important aspect in the thought of many seventeenth-century philosophers, most also held that government was instituted mainly for the purpose of controlling man's baser impulses and punishing his transgressions. Hobbes is the most extreme example of this, but even Locke, for whom peace with minimal interference from government was paramount, was most concerned with man's propensity for bad. Locke's optimism (expressed in the idea of the consent of the governed) notwithstanding, most early modern political thought held that government is

[31] William Penn, *First Frame of Government*, PWP, 2: 212.
[32] Penn, *Discourse of the General Rule*.
[33] To be clear, it was a theory of the divine right of government – the belief that government was created by God – as opposed to the divine right of kings.
[34] Penn, *First Frame*, 212.

founded on force and, often, violence.[35] Paine summarized the idea when he said that "government is but a necessary evil."[36] But Quakers held that there was more possibility for the good in man to prevail. They did not believe that man's purity was ultimately lost. They did not believe in original sin. Barclay wrote that "the Seed [of evil] is not imputed to Infants, until by Transgression they actually join themselves therewith." Man will inevitably sin, they believed, but because of the availability of the Light to all people, there was the possibility of attaining perfection in spite of inevitable transgressions.[37] Their theology thus tempered and amended the more pessimistic understanding of man's sinful nature, and their institutions were organized accordingly.

Thus Quaker civil government, like their ecclesiastical government, was not instituted by God primarily for coercing and punishing man. On the contrary, civil government was "as capable of *Kindness, Goodness,* and *Charity* as a more private Society." And though one of the purposes was certainly "To Terrifie Evil-doers," Penn asserted, "They weakly Err, that think there is no other use for *Government,* than *Correction,* which is the coarsest part of it: Daily experience tells us, that the Care and Regulation of many other Affairs, more soft and daily necessary make up the greatest part of *Government.*"[38] While there were others with ideas such as this, they never put them into effect in English politics.[39] The Quakers, on the other hand, did in their utopian "holy experiment" in Pennsylvania.[40]

Of course, even Quakers knew that most men had not purified themselves enough to follow God's law and were far from perfect. Therefore, Penn said, "we must recur to some lower but true Principle" – "Civil Interest."[41] The

---

[35] See Paul A. Rahe, *Republics Ancient and Modern: Volume Three: Inventions of Prudence: Constituting the American Regime* (Chapel Hill: University of North Carolina Press, 1994), 32–33.

[36] Thomas Paine, *Common Sense* (Philadelphia, 1776), 1.

[37] Beatty notes that, among other inconsistencies in Penn's thought, his sense of man's goodness seems to have changed in later years, as exemplified in his tract *An Essay towards the Present and Future Peace of Europe* (London, 1693), which depicts a state of nature resembling that of Hobbes more than Locke or Rousseau. By 1693, Penn was already embittered by difficulties with Pennsylvania. His Quaker brethren in the Pennsylvania Assembly had given him trouble from the beginning, and at the time, he had been deprived of his government by the crown. It would not be surprising if his faith in mankind failed. To understand the general Quaker view of the purpose of government, therefore, we can safely refer to their theology.

[38] Penn, *First Frame,* 212. See also John Crook, *An Apology for the Quakers Wherein is shewed How they Answer the Chief Principles of the Law, and the Main Ends of Government* [1662], in *Quaker Tracts,* vol. 5 (London, 1662).

[39] Robbins notes that "[t]hough Cumberland propounded no political plan for an egalitarian utopia, he provided almost as an essential part of the philosophical presuppositions of the reformers as his contemporaries, John Locke and Isaac Newton" (*The Eighteenth-Century Commonwealthman,* 78).

[40] For more on Penn's optimism about the ends government and its consensual functioning, see Endy, *William Penn and Early Quakerism,* 354.

[41] William Penn, *One Project for the Good of England: That is, Our Civil Union is Our Civil Safety* (London, 1679), 1.

nation's survival would be secured by a civil government that protects the people's most basic civil right, the "free Exercise of their Worship to Almighty God."[42] Government, he explained, "was an "Emanation of the same *Divine Power* that is both the *Author* and *Object* of *Pure Religion*," and as such, it was also a coercive power to restrain and punish.[43] But still Penn believed that this lower order was ultimately benevolent and, most significantly, for divine ends. It existed to protect all individuals so that they would be free of earthly coercion and free to find God for themselves.[44] The worst civil injustice as far as seventeenth-century Quakers were concerned was religious persecution. With Penn in the lead, their crusade was to assert liberty of conscience as a part of the fundamental law, the ancient constitution, and to secure it as part of current legal practice. In this, Quakers faced two main challenges: jurists who could easily deny the existence of this liberty in the common law; and the great diversity of religious groups in England, each seeking to impose its faith on others. "No sooner one Opinion prevails upon another," said Penn, "(though all hold the *Text* to be sacred) but *Human Society* is *shaken*, and the *Civil Government* must receive and suffer a *Revolution*."[45]

The one recourse of a people was to unite on the basis of this "lower principle" rather than a common understanding of God. "Our Civil Union is our Civil Safety," he said. Unity in the civil polity was for Quakers as important as in the ecclesiastical polity and for similar reasons – to protect the body from disintegration by either atomizing or domineering forces from within and to be a refuge from coercive powers from without, such as the Roman Church. Safety in union meant liberty; and union would be preserved through religious liberty.[46] Everyone must agree to unite, not on the basis of one imposed understanding of religion, but on the basis of their all being Protestant dissenters. And as dissenters, they must avoid popery by securing the one means – liberty of conscience – that would allow people to find the true religion. Unlike most republican thinkers who believed that political opinion must be homogenous, Penn argued that "*Unity* (not as the least but greatest End of Government) is lost for by seeking an Unity of Opinion (by [coercion])

---

[42] Ibid., 5. See also Andrew R. Murphy, *Conscience and Community*.

[43] Penn, *First Frame*, 212.

[44] We should understand that there is really no equivalent in the ecclesiastical polity of this lower civil principle. As Barclay made clear in *The Anarchy of the Ranters*, the church government had the power to extend positive law to regulate the conscience of the believer (47–65, 73).

[45] Penn, *One Project*, 1.

[46] This equation of union, security, and religious liberty by Quakers complicates John Phillip Reid's discussion of liberty and security. He finds, convincingly, that the concepts of liberty and security of property were interchangeable. But while Quakers shared this concern for protection for property, and also related it to liberty in the ways Reid argues, it is not clear that this was their only or primary understanding of the concepts of liberty and security. It seems, rather, that union was held above property as the guarantor of liberty, and religious liberty was, in turn, the guarantor of union. Property, as is discussed later, was primarily a tool for proselytization. See John Phillip Reid, *The Concept of Liberty in the Age of the American Revolution* (Chicago: University of Chicago Press, 1988), 71–73.

the Unity requisite to uphold us, as a *Civil Society*, will be quite destroy'd. And such as relinquish *that*, to get the *other* (besides that they are Unwise) *will infallibly lose both in the end.*"[47]

The image one gets of Penn's ideal political society is one in which individuals might, as he did, stand on the street corner hawking their religious wares. If the Truth is allowed expression, he believed, the people will find their way to it. In this way, Quakers had a view of politics and civic engagement that approximated modern understandings. They did not believe, as did many Englishmen, that political differences and potential conflict were inevitably problematic. Similar to Machiavelli, theirs was rather a philosophy – religious and political – that depended on an amount of disagreement, dissent, and competition of ideas in order to flourish, so long as there was always the fundamental agreement that the unity of the body was paramount. In their way, Quakers promoted debate, deliberation, and the search for truth among the people at a time when many did not believe that popular discourse was possible or relevant.[48]

While the Quaker idea of toleration seems to be similar, if not identical to Locke's, their ideas are distinct on two levels.[49] First, as we have seen, the bases are different in that Locke expected that man should resort to his reason as a means to political virtue (to the extent that virtue was necessary), and thus leave his religion at the door to the state house. Quakers, by contrast, expected that freedom to worship would bring man closer to God and thus make his civil behavior an expression of Christian love. Second, although their conceptions of toleration looked much the same in theory, they could be quite different in practice. Locke asserted that the civil government had no role in coercing the conscience of the individual. He also granted, as did all Englishmen, that "obedience is due in the first place to God, and afterwards to the laws" and that disobedience was acceptable if the civil government tried to force the conscience.[50] But for Locke, there were limits to toleration that potentially conflicted with Quaker thought and practice. In his *Letter*

---

[47] Penn, *Great Case*, 29. For one of the best succinct discussions of Penn's ideas of religious liberty, see Schwartz, "*A Mixed Multitude*," 12–35. For a longer discussion, with which this study sometimes disagrees, see J. William Frost, *A Perfect Freedom: Religious Liberty in Pennsylvania* (New York: Cambridge University Press, 1990). On the issue of toleration as *modus vivendi* and the subject of toleration in general reconsidered in historical and contemporary context, see Murphy, *Conscience and Community*.

[48] This is also Alan Tully's argument in *Forming American Politics* about the main contribution of Quakers to American political culture. He finds that their mode of political engagement in Pennsylvania with its contentious partisanship was the precursor of the First Party System. Seventeenth-century Trimmers were another group that anticipated the modern idea of politics as a forum for disagreement. See James Conniff, "The Politics of Trimming: Halifax and the Acceptance of Political Controversy," *The Journal of Politics* vol. 34, no. 4 (1972), 1172–1202.

[49] It is necessary here to make a distinction between religious *toleration* and religious *liberty*. Although the two terms are often used interchangeably today, as the following discussing demonstrates, the first is more limited than the latter. In their advocacy of religious rights, Quakers often settled temporarily for toleration even as they continued to press for liberty.

[50] John Locke, *A Letter concerning Toleration* (London, 1689), 61.

concerning Toleration (1689), he discussed four grounds on which toleration should be suspended: beliefs or practices that conflict with the civil peace; violation of civil oaths; the idea that political power was based on grace; and if the faith encouraged loyalty to a foreign government.[51] But Quakers defined the realm of conscience and faith to include civil, ecclesiastical, and social institutions and customs. They were seeking not mere toleration, but liberty. With their radical and public expressions of dissent, it is clear how critics could argue that their behavior conflicted with matters purely civil or social. At one time or another they were accused of transgressing each of Locke's articles, in which case, they had "no right to be tolerated by the magistrate."[52] Locke believed that Quakers were one of the sorts of antinomians who inappropriately mixed religion and politics.

Once a people has come together under this lower principle of civil interest, they must discern and codify the fundamental law into a written document. The constitution was an expression of God's law. The Magna Carta, explained Penn, is "not the *Original* Establishment, but a *Declaration and Confirmation* of that Establishment."[53] This language clearly reflects the Quakers' understanding that a civil constitution is in its way like Scripture, which they described as "a Declaration of the *Fountain* but not the *Fountain* it self," or like their Discipline, the paper constitution that followed the assembly of the religious body.[54] Moreover, the constitution, like Scripture or the Discipline, is not man-made in the usual sense of the term. It was a collaboration between God and man.

Although Penn advised his children not to be "meddlers in Government," if he meant to convey an image of quietism, it was likely part of the Quakers' campaign to dispel perceptions of them as seditious and destructive of civil government. But Penn qualified his statement, saying that man should not work in government "Unless God requires it of you."[55] And what God sometimes required of man was that he act as a vehicle for the transmission of his law to the rest of mankind.[56] A civil constitution, then, was not man-made per se, but was rather created by God and then discerned through synteresis and transcribed by men.[57] It was like any other divinely ordained guide executed by man such as the Scriptures, apostolic precedent, or legal precedent that was in keeping with the spirit of the divine law. Moreover, because it came from God,

---

[51] Ibid., esp. 62–67.

[52] Locke, *Letter concerning Toleration*, 65.

[53] Penn, *England's Present Interest Discovered*, 29.

[54] Barclay, *Apology*, 5

[55] William Penn quoted in Isaac Sharpless, *Quakerism and Politics* (Philadelphia: Ferris & Leach, 1905), 79.

[56] Beatty would agree with this interpretation. "A Quaker," he says, "could believe in God as the source of society and in the human race as the means chosen by Divinity to work out his plans" (*William Penn as Social Philosopher*, 20).

[57] See Zuckert on government as a man-made artifact (*Natural Rights*, 9–10).

it was sacred. There was, therefore, a powerful sense of political obligation for Friends.

Political Arrangements

Another basis for political obligation was in the structural arrangements dictated by the civil constitution. In Quaker thought, the fundamental law came directly from God, who ordained both a written constitution and civil government. The political arrangements – the "order" (the structure of government) and the "method" (the decision-making process) – were also ordained as part of the constitution. If liberty was safety, safety came through the order and method of government. At first glance, because of discrepancies between early theory and practice, it appears uncertain what form of government Quakers preferred. In the preface to his *First Frame*, Penn was intentionally vague on this topic, writing "For particular Frames and Models, it will become me to say little; and comparatively I will say nothing." His reasons were several, but the most important were that the age was "too nice and difficult" and that while all agreed that happiness was the end of government, most people did not know the right way to use "Light and Knowledge" to achieve that end. Quakers themselves wrangled about this issue amongst themselves for several decades as governors of their own colonies. But all things considered, from the Quakers' theory, their own frames of government, and their actual political arrangements, it is clear that most Friends would eventually agree that there was one true way in which government should be structured. "Any *Government* is **Free** to the People under it (what-ever be the Frame) **where the Laws Rule**," wrote Penn, "**and the People are a party to those Laws.**"[58]

Early in his thinking, Quaker political theorist Isaac Penington began to hint about the ideal form of government. Like Penn, his future son-in-law, Penington favored a strong central government for the sake of unity. In 1653 he articulated something that sounds much like Plato's theory of divine competence.[59] If there existed a single ruler who embodied divine will and exercised his power in strict keeping with God's law, this would be the best form of rule – a benevolent despotism. Penington tentatively agreed that "*Absoluteness* is best in itself." But because no such individual existed, "limitations are safest for the present condition of man." Likely with both the divine right of kings and the chaos of the Interregnum in mind, however, he continued, "[b]ut what if God (from whom both these had their being, continuation and blessing) be striking at the root of both Absoluteness and Limitedness, shewing the weakness and insufficiency of both, and turning them upside down as fast as he discovereth it?" Penington did not venture a direct answer. Because God had not spoken to him on these matters, he desired rather "to be silent... not only outwardly

---

[58] Penn, *First Frame*, 213.
[59] J. B. Skemp, trans., *Statesman: A Translation of the Politicus of Plato* (New Haven, CT: Yale, 1952). See also McIlwain, *Constitutionalism*, 50.

before men, but even inwardly in mine own Soul." But he did offer some advice to the governors and the governed that gives us a hint of his ideas. "The governor," he counseled, needs to remain humble and not "bring forth that which is not in them." In the recent revolution, it was Parliament, he said, that "seemed to spring up with a more excellent spirit, undertaking to rectify that which was crooked in the foregoing Government, but did they indeed and in truth effect it?" Penington's advice to the governed then was "[e]xpect not that fruit from your Governors, the root whereof is not in them." Neither, recent history suggested, should the people look to themselves alone because their own limits might be faulty "(for man himself knoweth neither his own heart nor ways, seldom being what he still taketh himself to be)." They should look elsewhere. "He who is of counsel with the Lord, may know what he intends."[60] This is to say, whether absolute or limited, government by man instead of by God is always corrupt and oppressive.

A strong central government might come in many forms, but for Quakers it seems, one was preferable. In most Quaker thought, the strength did not arise from the top of the political authority structure – from an executive or a parliament. Contrary to the usual understanding of divine right theory that placed right in the hands of a king and obligation on the people, "The Fundamental Right, Liberty and Safety of the People," said Penington, "is radically in themselves, derivatively in Parliament, their Substitutes or Representatives." He wrote these lines some thirty years before Sidney wrote the same in his *Discourses concerning Government* (1698), the "textbook" to the American Revolutionaries.[61] This right, safety, and liberty "lieth chiefly in these three things," wrote Penington, "in their *Choyce* of their Government and Governors, in the *Establishment* of that Government and those Governors which they shall chuse, and in the *Alteration* of either as they find cause."[62] The last point is an important one, and one to which we will return in a moment. Penn agreed in 1675 that "the People" must have "a Share in Judgment, that is, in the Application, as well as in the making of the Law."[63] He explained that the English people had at once time exercised a direct control over the government and had themselves handed it over to their representatives when the population grew too large.[64] In a clear equation of political practices with those of his religion, he tacitly accused the government of popery because it had divested the people of their rightful power, lodging it instead with the representatives. In

[60] Isaac Penington, *A Considerable Question about Government* (London, 1653), 5–7.

[61] Caroline Robbins, "Algernon Sidney's *Discourses on Government*: A Textbook of Revolution," *WMQ* 3rd ser., vol. 4, no. 3 (1947), 267–96. Sidney wrote his *Discourses* shortly before his execution in 1683, but they were first published in 1698.

[62] Isaac Penington, *The Fundamental Right, Safety and Liberty of the People* (London, 1651), 1.

[63] Penn, *England's Present Interest Discovered*, 23.

[64] William Penn quoted in Edmund S. Morgan, *Inventing the People: The Rise of Popular Sovereignty in England and America* (New York: W. W. Norton & Company, 1988), 210–11.

the ideal constitution, he wrote, there is "no *Transessentiating* or *Transubstan-tiation* of Being from People to Representatives."[65] We might understand this as the problem of virtual, as opposed to actual representation. Christ and his power are with the people, Penn clarified, not the representatives. The poten-tial for Light in all men meant the political responsibility was on individuals to participate in some capacity.[66] Accordingly, in the first two civil constitutions that Quakers drafted, most if not all of the legislative powers were given to the people.[67]

If this were all Quakers told us, we would know very little about their ideal form of government and only that Quakers agreed with other Whigs that some element of popular participation was necessary for the legitimacy of a govern-ment. But the way they envisioned this engagement tells us more about their ideal structure of government and the role of the people. For Quakers, pop-ular participation in a civil or ecclesiastical polity was a process of collective discernment through synteresis. They must combine their understanding of the Light with those of others to get a complete understanding of God's will.[68] Penington advised the governed that they should not look to their governors for guidance. If they were oppressed they must instead look to God in them-selves. "Be still, be quiet," wrote Penington, "and ye shall see that the Lord will deal with those that oppress you."[69] In a pamphlet addressed to the King and Parliament, Penington explained further that those seeking a true under-standing of the law should free themselves from the "eye which cannot see the things of God" and the "heart also which is insensible and so runs into the pit." Instead, they should seek recourse in the "eye, to which God giveth the true sight, which foreseeth the evil and seeking an hiding place; and an heart which feareth its Maker, and waiteth on him for counsel, distrusting its own under-standing, which it feeleth shallow and apt to err."[70] As in a religious meet-ing, to understand God the people would use the means typical of Whigs – history, legal precedent, experience, and reason. But primarily, they should first look, as Penn did, for "God's evidence in my own Conscience" in their relations with government and only then confirm it with "the Judgment and Example of other Times."[71] Insofar as the discernment of the law was a collective process,

---

[65] Ibid., 22.
[66] See also Endy, *William Penn and Early Quakerism*, 343.
[67] See Chapter 4 in this book.
[68] This process is not entirely dissimilar from Edward Coke's understanding of how reason forms the common law – as a collective endeavor whose product is greater than any single man could create. "The commentator's reason," writes James R. Stoner, "evidently performs the work of collection, silently discovering order in multiplicity but making no independent claims." Reason was used as a means of interpreting the law as well as a measure of consistency and accuracy in the development of the law. James R. Stoner, *Common Law & Liberal Theory: Coke, Hobbes, & the Origins of American Constitutionalism* (Lawrence: University Press of Kansas, 1992), 24.
[69] Penington, *A Considerable Question*, 5–7.
[70] Isaac Penington, *Three Queries Propounded to the King and Parliament* (London, 1662), 1.
[71] Penn, *England's Present Interest Discovered*, 35.

the divine competence was thus in the people collectively – a divine sovereignty by proxy.[72] In Quaker theory, the power was in *the people* like never before because God was – or could be – in all people. In theory at least, there was no difference between "the people" and the entire population. Here was an equality and popular political agency that scholars generally do not find until the American Founding.[73]

The first two constitutions written by Quakers reflect this concern for popular sovereignty – the *West Jersey Concessions and Agreements* (1676/77) and the "Fundamentall Constitutions of Pennsilvania" (c. 1681). Both were created in a similar process – a collective effort of leading Friends, using advice from other non-Quakers as well, and with one individual as primary draftsman.[74] The authorship of the *Concessions* is uncertain, but there is good evidence that its primary draftsman was elder Friend Edward Byllynge; the draftsman of the Pennsylvania constitution was Penn.[75] Scholars have identified the New Jersey constitution as "one of the most politically innovative documents of the seventeenth century," and the Pennsylvania constitution was "the most liberal plan of government for Pennsylvania."[76] In addition to other characteristics,

---

[72] As in their religious polity, this idea of popular sovereignty did not translate into egalitarianism or democracy. For a discussion on Penn's ideas of social hierarchy, see Endy, *William Penn and Early Quakerism*, 356–59.

[73] Hill's work shows how the democratic thinking of Quakers at this time was common among many radical groups, but he also claims that none of these groups, Quakers included, had a lasting affect on English or American politics (*The World Turned Upside Down*, 381). Following Hill, Morgan finds that "[t]he decline of social status as a force in ecclesiastical polity seems to have preceded, and may have contributed to, its decline in civil polity" (*Inventing the People*, 300). Of course, as we have seen, social status was not a determinant of leadership in the ideal Quaker community. Rather than Quakerism as a leveling force in early America, however, Morgan finds that the rise of pietism in the First Great Awakening was the greatest religious element in the development of equality and popular sovereignty in America (295–300). Of course, pietism, as its adherents and opponents recognized, drew much from Quakerism.

[74] This practice departs from the common understanding of the day that the best governments are created by one man. See Harrington, *Oceana* and Machiavelli, *Discourses*. Mary Maples Dunn argues to the contrary in *Politics and Conscience* that Penn followed these examples and took the opportunity to act alone. In their commentary on the "Fundamentall Constitutions" in *The Papers of William Penn*, Dunn and Dunn likewise find that Penn was in favor of drafting alone (2: 145, n. 6). But it is not clear how they came to this conclusion. They and others have noted that when Quakers drafted their constitutions, although one man may have taken the lead in the transcription, it was submitted for review to a number of other people whose changes were often adopted. They note that there is no evidence that "Fundamentall Constitutions" was not submitted to "adventurers or settlers" of Pennsylvania for their approval (*PWP*, 2: 153 n. 1), but it did undergo a review process by "a range of people" from weighty Friends to non-Quaker lawyers and political thinkers (*PWP*, 2: 137). This process is very similar to the one that Michael Warner claims originated in the American constitutional era in "Textuality and Legitimacy in the Printed Constitution," in *The Letters of the Republic: Publication and the Public Sphere in Eighteenth-Century America* (Cambridge, MA: Harvard University Press, 1990), 97–117.

[75] Mary Maples Dunn, "Did Penn Write the Concessions," in *West New Jersey* and *The West Jersey Concessions and Agreements of 1676/77: A Roundtable of Historians*, Occasional Papers, no. 1 (Trenton, NJ: New Jersey Historical Commission, 1979), 24–28.

[76] *PWP*, 1: 387; and 2: 140.

a common feature of both was the popular control of the legislative process. In both constitutions, the legislature was the dominant branch of government, and the executive wielded very little power. Inhabitants of the colonies were also accorded significant liberties, such as liberty of conscience, universal manhood suffrage in New Jersey, suffrage for all freeholders in Pennsylvania, and trial by jury. Neither of these constitutions was successful. The *Concessions* failed, and the "Fundamentall Constitutions" was never implemented. As we shall see presently, Quaker theory and practice were not always in harmony.

The laws were made binding through collective discernment, agreement by consensus, and submission by consent. "The collective body of people agreed to" the "Fundamental points of English-Law Doctrine," and this was "the most solid Basis, [on which] our *secondary Legislative Power*, as well as our Executive is built."[77] The points of fundamental law to which the people agreed in the Quaker colonies were much the same as any Whig's, but with subtle and significant differences. "We are a *Free People* by the *Creation* of God," said Penn.[78] In treatises and constitutions, he outlined the fundamental laws ordained by God. The most important were the right to property, the vote and a share in the judiciary powers for the people, and liberty of conscience.[79] The first and the last of these are related in a way that demonstrates the religious priorities of Quakers.

Protection of property was basic for all Whigs, but for Quakers, as for other religious groups such as Puritans, it was used not as a means to worldly status or creature comforts but as a way to express faith in and obedience to God.[80] As Frederick Tolles has shown, for the Quakers, earning more money allowed them to do more of God's work – charity was one of the primary reasons both the ecclesiastical and civil governments were established. But with plainness and simplicity in attire and worldly possessions, Quakers did not, as Puritans, see material wealth as a sign of spiritual status; it was to raise other members of the community both in- and outside their Society by meeting their basic material needs.[81] One cannot find God, they knew, if one were distracted by lack of basic necessities such as food, shelter, and education. Thus when the civil government persecuted Quakers by fining them and confiscating their goods, it was interfering with their religious duty to God and man. Civil punishments for religious expression were, according to Penn, the "enemy of Grace."[82] Thus government was established so that man could "*enjoy Property* with

---

[77] Penn, *Great Case*, 29.

[78] Penn, *England's Present Interest Discovered*, 32.

[79] For a discussion of Penn's views on these fundamental laws see Winthrop Hudson, "William Penn's English Liberties: Tract for Several Times," *WMQ* 3rd ser., vol. 26, no. 4 (1969), 578–85.

[80] Max Weber, *The Protestant Ethic and the Spirit of Capitalism* (New York: Charles Scribner's Sons, 1958).

[81] This, of course, was the ideal. Tolles mentioned how many Quakers fell away from this ideal in the midst of their prosperity in eighteenth-century Pennsylvania (*Meeting House and Counting House*, 140–43).

[82] Penn, *England's Present Interest Discovered*, 3–4.

Conscience that promoted it."[83] This understanding of the purpose of property made Quakers exemplars of the so-called Protestant work ethic, which in turn caused their ideas of property to evolve in advance of their non-Quaker counterparts. While relationship of land-ownership to civil liberty was still under debate in England,[84] Quakers were establishing what would become the most powerful colony economically and themselves as one of the most influential political groups through trade.

In sum, Quaker political obligation rested on three related features of their political thought – first, that the constitution and the government it created were sacred and perpetual; second, that a process of popular participation was ordained by God to determine the laws of the polity; and third, that the polity should maintain a basis of unity. These features provided a basis for a theory of constitutional change and legitimate civil dissent.

A Theory of Constitutional Change

Of all the peculiarities of the Quakers' political thought, their idea of constitutional change distinguished them most visibly from their contemporaries. The recognition of governmental corruption, the dangers of an unlimited government, and the risks of legal innovation were the cornerstone of both Quaker and Whig thinking. For Whigs, what to do about them was a perennial problem. Whigs, regardless of whether they adhered to the ancient conception of a constitution or a "modern" understanding, had no satisfying solution or functional process for how to change government. The problem was the common law itself.[85]

---

[83] Ibid., 32.

[84] Pocock, "Radical Criticisms," 38.

[85] The following discussion of the aspects of the ancient constitution and constitutional change draws on several sources. See J. G. A. Pocock, *The Ancient Constitution and the Feudal Law: A Study of English Historical Thought in the Seventeenth Century* (Cambridge: Cambridge University Press, 1957). Working mainly with the thought of Coke, Pocock considers the common law a "paradox" – as something common lawyers perceived as immemorial, that is, immutable, but always changing. In a 1987 reissue of his work, Pocock undertakes to clarify misinterpretations of his argument. Here he maintains that it was not the law itself that was immemorial but rather the juridical process. "[T]he notion of refinement and reform," he says, "was inherent in common-law ways of thinking." Glenn Burgess, seeking to explain the "Janus-faced" (Pocock, 275) quality of the common-law mind – in being able, without contradiction, to believe in stasis and change simultaneously – expands Pocock's analysis beyond Coke to highlight the singularity of Coke's thinking in this regard. He posits that most common lawyers believed the ancient constitution to be ever-changing and changeable, but that they advised against "innovation" (Burgess, *The Politics of the Ancient Constitution*, 55). In *Common Law & Liberal Theory*, Stoner finds an early precedent for judicial review in Coke's interpretation of *Doctor Bonham's Case* and thereby makes an argument for the compatibility of change with the common law tradition. However, like Pocock, Burgess, and McIlwain, Stoner does not find evidence of a formal mechanism for change during this period. On more general aspects of early modern Anglo-American constitutionalism, see also Thomas C. Grey, "Origins of the Unwritten Constitution: Fundamental Law in American Revolutionary Thought," *Stanford Law Review* vol. 30, no. 5 (1978), 843–93; Gordon Wood, "State Constitution-Making in the American Revolution," *Rutgers Law Journal* vol. 24 (1993), 911–26; Zuckert, *Natural Rights*.

The common law was, in the first place, unwritten in its entirety. Second, it was divided into essentially three sections: the fundamental law, only some of which was written in the Magna Carta; statute law, which was written, but not collected in one place or catalogued; and custom, which was entirely unwritten. All the laws were said to be based on one of two kinds of reason – artificial or practical. The former, the basis of statute law, must be obtained by arduous study and was thus comprehendible only to the preeminent legal scholars. The latter, known in general, was the traditions and customs that had developed in the populace over centuries and had proven reasonable over the course of history. The problems were several: First, no one could possibly know exactly what the law was at any given time or place. Second, given these characteristics of the common law, there could be no formal mechanism for change. This is not to say, however, that change did not happen. All common lawyers acknowledged that it did. But those adhering to the ancient model of the constitution agreed that change was dangerous and should be avoided. The law could be formally changed by enacting statutes or through the courts – the artificial perfection of reason – but this was dangerous in two ways.[86] First, it was too easy; it could potentially happen so quickly – at the whim of an individual or individuals – that there was a tremendous risk of instability.[87] Second, even if new statutes were enacted, this would not necessarily change the law in practice – people's habits change only very gradually. In essence, moreover, change is meaningless – or, at best, a "legal fiction" – unless it is somewhere transcribed and legitimized so it can be recognized by all and obeyed.[88] And finally, because of the danger in changing laws, precedents were extremely important. Once established, however bad, the law was thus legitimized and could remain in place for decades, if not centuries, doing irreparable harm to the polity. The response of those adhering to the ancient constitution, then, was to avoid change; and their caution was virtually paralyzing.[89] It was better, the common lawyers believed, to endure bad laws rather than to risk chaos by trying to change the old ones.[90]

Thus change to resist oppression under this rubric was limited and problematic. Ultimately, most Englishmen believed as Quakers did, that the government was ordained by God, and thus irresistible. Therefore, although it was bad if the government, either the king or Parliament, overstepped its constitutional bounds, this did not negate the right of the government to do so.

---

[86] See John Underwood Lewis, "Sir Edward Coke (1552–1633): His Theory of 'Artificial Reason' as a Context for Modern Basic Legal Theory," *Law Quarterly Review* vol. 84 (1968), 330–42.

[87] McIlwain explains that early in England's legal history, law was "judge-made." Then, "[m]agistrates could stretch it to cover new circumstances by an untrue assumption of fact which no one was permitted to disprove" (*Constitutionalism*, 54). Legal change later became part of the legislative process.

[88] Ibid., 53–55.

[89] See McIlwain's discussion of *stasis* as the result of the fear of revolution (ibid., 38–39).

[90] See also Kramer, *The People Themselves*, 16.

There was little distinction between the fundamental principles of the unwritten constitution and the positive law, which in turn made it difficult to draw the boundaries of the resistance. Although a limited amount of resistance was practiced, the possibility for change was restricted. Petitioning, nonresistance, suffering under the oppression, and continued deference to the civil authorities were usually thought to be the appropriate responses to governmental oppression.[91] Many writers agreed that, in theory, constitutional limitation through peaceful means to secure a balanced government was both possible and desirable. Neville, Harrington, and Ludlow suggested that government ought to be limited and changeable. Most significantly, Ludlow suggested the idea of a supreme court.[92] Still, Englishmen generally believed that preserving traditional liberties meant preserving the constitution in its entirety.[93]

The "modern" view of a constitution is equally problematic in regard to change, although the solution was much simpler. It was like the ancient constitution in that there was no solution to the problem of a parliamentary despotism or the tyranny of a divine right monarch, but with one exception.[94] It held that when a government oversteps its bounds, it acts unconstitutionally and thus forfeits its right to any obedience. In the view of authors such as Locke, Tyrrell, Sidney, Trenchard, Molesworth, and American Whigs, the entire government may then be legitimately overthrown by revolution.[95] It was a contractual relationship between ruler and ruled, which was broken if either party reneged on its obligation. Some, such as Cato, suggested ways to limit the government such as frequent elections, term limits, or the exclusion from office of MPs who had court employment, but there was a disjuncture between the fundamental principles, the constitution, and the government that made the latter two dispensable.

The main question that remained unanswered until popular sovereignty became an accepted idea was whether any government could be legally limited by something other than force.[96] How could a constitution be both permanent

---

[91] McIlwain, *Constitutionalism*, 3–6.

[92] Robbins, "Algernon Sidney's *Discourses on Government*," 48.

[93] McIlwain, *Constitutionalism*, 12. See also Burgess on avoiding deliberate change (*The Politics of the Ancient Constitution*, 68–69).

[94] Charles McIlwain, *The American Revolution: A Constitutional Interpretation* (Ithaca, NY: Cornell University Press, 1966), 160.

[95] This theory of revolution embraced by most Whigs grew mainly from reformed Calvinism. The most thorough discussion of the Puritan theory of revolution is Michael Walzer's *Revolution of the Saints: A Study in the Origins of Radical Politics* (New York: Atheneum, 1976). In *The Foundations of Modern Political Thought: Volume Two: The Age of Reformation* (Cambridge: Cambridge University Press, 1978), Quentin Skinner disagrees with Walzer to some extent and complicates the argument, writing that "the main foundations of the Calvinist theory of revolution were in fact constructed entirely by their catholic adversaries" (321). Nevertheless, he does agree that the right to resist was "Calvinist in its later development" (347). Kramer agrees that the popular will to effect change was expressed through violence or threat of violence (*The People Themselves*, 15).

[96] McIlwain, *Constitutionalism*, 9.

and amendable?There was no means to stop the abuse, nor mechanism to institute change.[97] In the Glorious Revolution, for example, some agreed with Locke that the English constitution had been abolished, while others tried to legitimize the Revolution within the confines of the ancient constitution and preserve it in toto.[98] Quakers would have agreed with both positions, but only in part. The ancient constitution would remain, and significant reform and renewal would take place within its framework.

For Quakers, legal change was the logical and inevitable result of their discernment process. Using Light instead of reason as the basis for their laws – both fundamental and positive – allowed them, unlike other Englishmen, to believe change was not only inevitable, but also desirable as man strove for perfection. The Light was a perfect guide. "The laws of this Kingdom," said Isaac Penington, "are given forth in the Kingdom from the Covenant of life, which is made there in Christ... There sin is reproved, and everlasting Righteousness manifested, in the Light which cannot deceive."[99] In other words, God's Light is always consistent and true. To this point, there is not much practical difference with the common lawyers who believed in the difference in a fundamental immutable law that came from reason and the changeable law that came from reasonable custom. The key difference was this: Man, Quakers believed, was fallible in his abilities to understand and follow the divine fundamental law. They would agree with Newton who wrote, "The errors are not in the art but in the artificers."[100] If they followed their reason alone, or even reasonable custom that has allegedly proved the rightness of the law, "Men many times," warned Penington, "make Laws in their own will, and according to their own wisdom (now the wisdom of the world is corrupt, and hath erred from the guidance of God) and are not free from self-ends and interests."[101] Quaker John Crook explained that "outward Authority" was exercised properly when "the Principle of Reason [was] subordinate and subjected to the Principle of Life, and did not take upon itself to govern without or against it."[102]

Of utmost importance was that God did not reveal his whole law to man at once, but rather unfolded it in progressive revelation. Penington explained that "He who is of counsel with the Lord, may know what he intends."[103] He summarized the Quaker position on man in relation to the law in a 1661

[97] Ibid., 4; and B. Behrens, "The Whig Theory of the Constitution," 43.

[98] Pocock, "Radical Criticisms," 34–35.

[99] Isaac Penington, *The Consideration of a Position Concerning the Book of Prayer... Likewise a few Words concerning the Kingdom, Laws and Government of Christ in the Heart and Conscience; it's [sic] Inoffensiveness to all Just Laws and Governments of the Kingdoms of Men* (1660), 27.

[100] Colin Maclurin, *An Account of Sir Isaac Newton's Philosophical Discoveries* (1748), cited in Robbins, "Algernon Sidney's *Discourses on Government*," 71.

[101] Penington, *Consideration of a Position*, 28.

[102] Crook, *An Apology for the Quakers*, 8.

[103] Penington, *A Considerable Question*, 5–6.

tract entitled *A Brief Account of What the People Called Quakers Desire in Reference to Civil Government*. They wanted

[t]hat no Laws formerly made, contrary to the Principle of equity and righteousness in man, may remain in force; nor no new ones be made, but what are manifestly agreeable thereunto. All just Laws, say the Lawyers, have their foundation in right reason, and must agree with, and proceed from it, if they be properly good for and rightly serviceable to Mankind. Now man hath a corrupt and carnal reason, which sways him aside from Integrity and Righteousness, towards the favoring of himself and his own party: And whatever party is uppermost, they are apt to make such new laws as they frame, and also the interpretation of the old ones, bent towards the favour of their own party. Therefore we would have every man in Authority wait, in the fear of God, to have that Principle of God raised up in him, which is for righteousness, and not selfish; and watch to be guided by that in all he does, either in making Laws for Government, or in governing by Laws already made.[104]

In waiting on God, an individual might at any moment receive a revelation about the law that is entirely new and *nonrational*, but that could be seen by most as *irrational*.

An account of a trial of thirty-two Quakers *"for unlawfully and tumultuously gathering and assembling our selves together, by Force and Arms, &c. under pretense of performing Religious Worship, &c."* exemplifies this doctrine of change. In challenging the statute upon which they were indicted, the defendants proclaimed that not only did the statute "take counsel against the Lord," but also that "it was made in a time of ignorance, when that people were newly stept out of Popery, but now there was more knowledge."[105] The law was thus meant to be changed based on new discoveries of God's will.

The best example for Quakers of an ungodly law that had been accepted as reasonable for centuries was the mixing of church and state. Penn's revelation said the combination of the two was unconstitutional, and his reason agreed. For him, their separation was not only necessary, it was in keeping with divine law and therefore with the fundamental constitution of England. *"Religion,"* he insisted, "under any Modification is not part of the old *English Government.*" He argued that mixing church law and civil law and making property holding a means of maintaining religious conformity are "an Alteration of old English Tenure" and a most dangerous innovation.[106] Nonetheless it had become an

---

[104] Isaac Penington, "A Brief Account of What the People Called Quakers Desire in Reference to Civil Government" (1661), in *Pennington's Works* (London, 1680), 327.
[105] John Chandler, *A True Relation of the Unjust Proceedings, Verdict (so called) & Sentence of the Court of Sessions, at Margaret's Hill in Southwark . . .* [1662], 3, 5, in *Quaker Tracts*, vol. 5 (London, 1662).
[106] Penn, *England's Present Interest Discovered*, 31–32, 37. It was Penn's tenacious advocacy of liberty of that led his former Whig allies to suspect him of popery and Jacobitism at the Glorious Revolution. While it does seem on the surface contradictory that such a zealous supporter of rights and constitutionalism would collaborate with a papist, it is in keeping with the Quaker agenda. Although Penn was a radical Protestant and supporter of the Whig cause, he was also a politician who had James II's ear. Penn was not a supporter of James himself, and

accepted part of English custom and law. Following from this, although toleration was generally professed to be an ideal for England, most Englishmen also believed that uniformity in opinion – and hence an established church – was the only way to preserve the state. Conformity to the Church was enforced by various means, both by statute and custom, by officials and commoners. Quakers, who challenged the statutes and the practices, were considered to be insane and subversive of government. Not only were they persecuted, but more laws were passed on the same basis with the aim of eradicating them entirely. Because of the divine revelation that religious dissent was constitutional, if not legal, Quakers were keenly aware of the need for change in both laws and customs and were especially suspicious of the latter, which was more nebulous and evolved more slowly than legislation. In response to the reaction of non-Quakers to the apparent irrationality of Quaker demands, Penington counseled, "Therefore all people be still and quiet in your minds, and wait for righteousness, for that is it which the Lord is making way for in this Nation, and which he will set up therein; and he whose desire is not after that, and whose interest lies not there, will find himself disappointed, and *at unawares surprised with what he expects not.*"[107] In other words, do not expect God to conform to human reasoning.

In addition to this rejection of reason as the basis for law, which itself was seen as a serious challenge to the government, Quakers' use of language was also troubling to contemporaries. As we have explored in the first chapter, they used it to challenge civil society in numerous ways. Their refusal to use conventional speech or ideas when discussing law itself amounted to subversion. Glenn Burgess explains that the common law was a "structure of discourse," and that it possessed "hegemonic status. It defined the appropriate sphere within which other languages operated."[108] Although this hegemony had been fundamentally undermined in 1649 with the execution of King Charles I, it was not yet destroyed.[109] In the Quakers' refusal to use the language of natural law, as well as the more obvious use of plain language, including not just *thee* and *thou*, but also their advocacy of English rather than Latin in the laws and courts, made contemporaries aware of their intention to establish an alternate legal paradigm and that they were undertaking a well-organized campaign to actualize it.

Through their theology and practice, then, Quakers found a way to contextualize changes, evaluate them for soundness, and accept them – or not – as an

---

thus not a Jacobite, but rather he was in favor of what James could do and how he would do it. Quakers were opportunists to a certain extent and would befriend even apparent enemies if they believed it would help them achieve their primary end – liberty through constitutional means. Dunn presents a similar opinion in a discussion of Penn's thought during this period and his relationship to James II (Dunn, *Politics and Conscience*, 132–61).

[107] Penington, "What Quakers Desire," 15. Emphasis added.

[108] Burgess, *The Politics of the Ancient Constitution*, 212.

[109] Ibid., 223–24. Burgess goes on to discuss the Levellers' rejection of the common-law language of reason in favor of the more "abstract" basis of the Gospel (228–29).

integral part of their political theory and a valid part of the legal and political process. They believed that man was born innocent and was capable of perfection, but he was also capable of mistakes, sins, and transgressions of the law. He might misstep when transcribing God's law into a written constitution or statutes. But in his relationship with God, he was never irredeemable. He may change himself and return to the proper path. Just as the individual is salvageable, neither are his efforts at political arrangements hopelessly flawed. "There is hardly one Frame of Government in the World so ill designed by its first Founders," wrote Penn, "that in *good hands* would not do well enough."[110] Therefore, man may also change his political arrangements while retaining the constitution. On framing a government, Penington said, "That which is well done will endure a review; and that which is ill done doth deserve a review, that it might be amended: yea that which is of very great consequence may in equity require a review."[111] With God's guidance, man may recognize both what is accurate and what is flawed in his interpretation. The laws, said Penn, "are resolvable into two *Series* or Heads, *Of Laws Fundamental, which are indispensable and Immutable: And Laws Superficial, which are Temporary.*" The former, of course must be adhered to and executed in a "punctual" manner. The latter are "consequently alterable."[112] He told his Provincial Council in Pennsylvania, "If in the constitution . . . there be anie thing that jars, alter itt."[113] If Bacon and Descartes liberated man from the superstitions of the Church and began to formulate a doctrine of human progress based on reason, Quakers, as they understood themselves, liberated man from his reason to allow a doctrine of not just spiritual, but sociopolitical progress.[114]

The relationship between the people and the government was therefore not the same kind of contract as envisioned by Locke and others. The people consented to be governed and thereby entered a contract, but the contract could never be broken. The contract was rather in a continual process of negotiation.[115] It is no surprise then that we find little language of covenant in Quaker religious or political writings.[116] There was a vaguely Hobbsian

---

[110] Penn, *First Frame*, PWP, 2: 213.

[111] Penington, *Right, Safety and Liberty*, 32.

[112] Penn, *England's Present Interest Discovered*, 6. Gordon S. Wood notes that Americans did not see this distinction until they began writing their state and federal constitutions. See *The Creation of the American Republic*, 261–65.

[113] William Penn, "Speech to the Provincial Council," April 1, 1700. PWP, 3: 591.

[114] See J. B. Bury, *The Idea of Progress: An Inquiry into Its Growth and Origin* (New York: Dover Publications, 1932).

[115] See Zuckert: "[I]f political life is understood as derived from God or nature that suggests a limit to what can be done with it" (*Natural Rights*, 10). See also John Dunn, *The Political Thought of John Locke*, 68. For most Englishmen, the laws and government were sacred. The argument here is that the meaning of "sacred" was different for non-Quakers and Quakers. For non-Quakers, this meant unchangeable; for Quakers, it meant evolving.

[116] This is not to say that they never used the language of covenant or the word *contract* in their political treatises, merely that the meaning was different from the manner in which it was used by their contemporaries. Andrew Murphy also notes the difference between Penn's

quality to the absoluteness of the Quaker arrangement and therefore little need to discuss an unbreakable bond.

In contrast to both the ancient and modern theories, then, Quakers related all parts of a fundamental law, constitution, government, and its structures and laws inextricably to one another; but they qualified that relationship so that there was a flexibility that the ancient constitution lacked and a permanence that the "modern" constitution had not yet developed. There was a sort of relativism in Quaker thought that held the fundamental law to be unalterable, but interpretation of it may change depending on who discerned it, when, and how. Evolution was therefore allowed – encouraged, even – and piecemeal changes could be made as necessary but without the same risks. The people would comply with the laws because they had created and approved them; instability would be even less of a danger because change could still happen cautiously, but through an established process, and it would be documented for reference. Penn could therefore observe without trepidation: "I do not find a Model in the World, that Time, Place and some singular emergency have not necessarily altered."[117]

Despite the fact that Quakers were intent on preserving the ancient constitution, we should not make the mistake of thinking that they were champions of the common law tradition. The common law was useful and important as a tool, a well of information, but only God was absolute. The common law was suspect whether it was based on reason, custom, or, insofar as they were often considered essentially the same thing, a mixture of both. In their defense, in court they quoted St. Germain's *Doctor and Student* (c. 1531) to prove that "According to the Law of God, *Prescription*, *Statute*, nor *Custome*, ought not to have prevailed" in their trials.[118] The trial of William Penn and William Mead, known as *Bushell's Case*, exemplifies the Quaker position when Penn, accused of disturbing the peace by public preaching, demanded of the court, "unless you shew me, and the People, the Law you ground your Indictment upon, I shall take it for granted that your proceedings are merely arbitrary . . . It is too general and imperfect an Answer, to say it is the Common-Law, unless we knew both where, and what is it; For where there is no Law, there is no Transgression; and that Law, which is not in being, is so far from Common, that it is no Law at all."[119] Custom was therefore not good enough evidence of the constitutionality of a law.

Friends were unequivocal on the matter of the necessity of a legitimately established written law and its accessibility to ordinary people.[120] Laws that

---

contractarianism and Puritan covenant theology, although he finds Penn to be functioning only within a more typically English tradition than Puritans rather than anything specifically Quaker (*Conscience and Community*, 171–73).

[117] Penn, *First Frame*, 213.

[118] *A Brief Relation of the Proceedings, &c.*, 31, in *Quaker Tracts* vol. 5 (London, 1662).

[119] *The Peoples Ancient and Just Liberties Asserted in the Tryal of* William Penn, *and* William Mead (London, 1670), 8–9.

[120] Horle, *Quakers and the English Legal System*, 167.

could not be easily traced both to their divine origins and their placement in a written document were null and void. As Edward Byllynge wrote, "let the Law be printed, that everyone may know that Law, which he is subject to, to the intent that no man may be condemned by a Law which he neither knowes, nor ever heard of, nor understands; neither indeed can he, when as it lyes the brest other men."[121] A Quaker arrested for testifying against sin at a public fair said impertinently to the magistrate, "Shew me what law I have broken . . . I shall not believe thee now, except thou reade the Law to me." He chastised the judge, "[T]hou ought to have such things ready when men are brought before thee."[122]

Thus, by adhering to the Light instead of reason, secular history, or custom, Quakers avoided two problems of the common law advocates – misreading the present laws into the past and the "idealization of custom."[123] The Quaker theory of the permanent yet changeable constitution had the adaptability of the common law tradition without the drawback of harmful "innovations" becoming permanently institutionalized. The Quaker process of discernment of a higher law along with other guides that were complementary but subordinate resolved the common law dilemma of whether to adhere to history (custom) or reason as the basis for legal decisions. By contrast, Whigs were uninterested in explaining how the laws had come into existence.[124] Quakers took a more critical view of history in that they could acknowledge the failure of man's reason and the subsequent development of corrupted custom. For Quakers, the fundamental law was immutable, and the positive law was perfect *until* God gave them more clearness, which he inevitably would in his own time. Knowledge of their own inevitable fallibility along with the possibility of perfection let Quakers avoid the complacency, paradox, and hubris of the common lawyers who could, with confidence, believe not only that the common law was infinitely changeable, adaptable, and perfect, while also remaining always the same in its fundamentals, but also that they had discerned it correctly.

---

[121] Edward Byllynge, *A Mite of Affection* (London, 1659), 3. See also *A Brief Relation of the Proceedings, &c.*, which says that "E. Burroughs spoke again to the Court and told them, That this common Law (which they had said was not written) but lay in the Breasts of the Judges (this was said both then and the Sessions before) he was not well knowing in, neither the extent of it, nor the Penalties of it" (14). A discussion that highlights the importance of process in Quaker law is in Bradley Chapin, "Written Rights: Puritan and Quaker Procedural Guarantees," *PMHB* vol. 114, no. 3 (1990), 323–48. See Bernard Bailyn, *Ideological Origins of the American Revolution* (Cambridge, MA: Belknap Press, Harvard University, 1967), 189–93. Bailyn explains that before the American constitutional period, no writers saw the need for their fundamental laws and principles to be codified and actually objected to it. It was not until the mid-1770s, he argues, that this idea became commonplace in American thinking.

[122] Solomon Eccles, *Signs are from the Lord to a People or Nation to forewarn them of some eminent Judgment near at hand* [1663] in *Quaker Tracts* vol. 6 (London, 1663–64). This item is a foldout in the middle of the book with no page number.

[123] Pocock, *Ancient Constitution*, 31, 34.

[124] See Martyn P. Thompson, "A Note on 'Reason' and 'History' in Late Seventeenth Century Political Thought," *Political Theory* vol. 4, no. 4 (1976), 491–504. 499. Also see Behrens, "The Whig Theory of the Constitution."

The Quakers' acceptance of change led them to view a return to first principles as a salutary endeavor. It was man's duty to create a constitution based
on first principles and then engage in a continual process of review to see that
the laws never strayed from them. If they did, there must be a return. This
marks another departure of Quaker thought from others of the day. Most
seventeenth-century theorists rejected with horror the idea of the sort of return
to first principles that Machiavelli advocated. It was, as far as they were concerned, a necessarily violent and destructive endeavor that would return society
to the chaotic state of nature.[125] Quakers, on the other hand, believed that a
return to first principles was not only necessary but desirable. Isaac Penington
argued that "[a]ll things by degrees gather corruption."[126] The people must
"search out and discover things from their first rise," but which "from suc-
ceeding *Principles* or *Practices* . . . may easily decline awry and cover the true
knowledge and intent of things."[127] But the change could not come from the
top down. The "Superstructure" of government, Penn explained, the "visible
Authority," cannot invalidate any of the fundamental laws without "a clear
overthrow of its own Constitution of Government, and so to reduce them to
their . . . first principles."[128] This was a clear distinction between the outward
power of the government from above against the power of the people collectively as they derive it from God. Divine sovereignty by proxy established government, and the same force had the power to change it. "When [the people],"
said Penington, "find [their government] either burdensome or inconvenient
they may lay it aside, and place what else they judg lighter, fitter or better in
the stead of it."[129] This was because, agreed Penn, "those things that are abro-
gable or abrogated in the *great Charter*, were never a Part of the Fundamentals,
but hedg'd in then for present Emergency or Conveniency."[130] Thus while a
return to first principles did destroy the corrupt aspects of the government,
the fundamental constitution of the people remained intact and the power to
reconstitute the government lay with them. It was this supposedly new principle
of "constituent sovereignty" that brought the U.S. Constitution into being.[131]

---

[125] *Republics Ancient and Modern*, 2: 36, 195, 201, 248, 298–305. Also Samuel H. Beer, *To Make
a Nation: The Rediscovery of American Federalism* (Cambridge, MA: Belknap Press, Harvard
University, 1993), 204.

[126] Penington, *Right, Safety and Liberty*, 7.

[127] Ibid., 15.

[128] Penn, *Great Case*, 30

[129] Penington, *Right, Safety and Liberty*, 3.

[130] Penn, *England's Present Interest Discovered*, 29.

[131] Beer explains the principle: "Given this concept of popular sovereignty, the Americans necessarily conceived of two sorts of human law: on the one hand, a fundamental law made by the
sovereign people which authorized government and defined individual rights and, on the other
hand, another sort of law made by bodies authorized by this fundamental law. Needless to
say, if the rules made by such inferior law-making bodies breached the fundamental law, these
rules were invalid not merely morally but legally, since the law giving these bodies authority at
the same time limited that authority. Above these inferior law-making bodies was a sovereign

In 1728, however, in defense of the Pennsylvania constitution, Quaker speaker of the Assembly David Lloyd wrote that legislative acts, "together with the [constitution], must be binding upon the People and their Delegates, until they are regularly altered or repealed, by and Authority, at least equal to that which First enacted them."[132]

Like Levellers who decried the "Norman Yoke," Penn differentiated between the "Lawful" and the "Unlawful" civil laws in arguing that not all laws enacted, though legal, are constitutional – that one is mistaken to think that "the enacting of *any-thing* can make *it* lawful."[133] But Penn did not reject the common law in its entirety or the ancient constitution. So how, then, should constitutional change take place practically? There were two ways, both of which were in keeping with divine law. One used the existing governmental structures; the other employed extra-legal means. The first way, which was preferable, but also only theoretical in Britain, was to build a process for change into the constitution. In a momentous occasion in constitutional history, Penn wrote the first amendment clause into his *First Frame of Government* for Pennsylvania.[134] Article XXIII begins in the negative with "No *Act*, *Law* or *Ordinance* whatsoever, shall at any time hereafter be made or done by the **Governour**, or by the **Free-men** in the **Provincial Council**, or the **General Assembly**, to *Alter*, *Change* or *Diminish* the *Form* or *Effect* of this **Charter**, or any *Part* or *Clause* thereof, or contrary to the true Intent and Meaning thereof." This restriction is, no doubt, Penn's answer to the problematic history of the common law tradition when unwritten laws accrued over time and were not traceable to first principles. But the clause continues, specifying that changes could be made with "*the Consent of the* **Governour**, *his Heirs* or *Assigns, and Six Parts of Seven of the said* **Free-men** *in* **Provincial Council** and **General Assembly**." As novel as this provision was, another leading Quaker, Benjamin Furly criticized the

power which had authorized them and which watched over them and could intervene to correct them. To appeal to this superior authority against transgressions of the fundamental law did not disrupt the social order or send society back into the state of nature but rather called into action the sovereign law-making power, the people" (*To Make a Nation*, 152). Although God has been excised from this process, it is clear where the divinity would be in the Quaker model. It would be in the people.

[132] David Lloyd, *A Defence of the Legislative Constitution of the Province of Pennsylvania as it now stands Confirmed and Established, by Law and Charter*, (Philadelphia, 1728), 4.

[133] Penn, *Great Case*, 35. Wood finds this distinction first at the American Revolution: "[I]t was precisely this distinction between 'legal' and 'unconstitutional' that the Americans and British constitutional traditions most obviously diverged" ("State Constitution-Making," 920). Most religious groups made distinctions between what was lawful and unlawful, where man's law did not correspond with God's. But because Quakers believed God's law was embodied in the civil constitution, thus conflating civil law and divine law, "unlawful" and "unconstitutional" were the same things.

[134] Benjamin F. Wright, Jr., "The Early History of Written Constitutions in America," in *Essays in History and Political Theory in Honor of Charles Howard McIlwain* (New York: Russell & Russell, 1964), 344–71, 357. Here Wright also finds that this *Frame* "reflects a more mature conception of fundamental law than any other of the seventeenth century."

clause for being too restrictive in favor of the governor and not open enough to a popular process.[135]

Beyond this, however, there was no formal process for constitutional change – no such thing as judicial review was built into the Pennsylvania government. But Quakers already had a process for legal review and peaceful change that made use of the existing system – nonviolent protest of various sorts, including civil disobedience, and then legal reform. If a law was found to be unconstitutional, Penn said, it might be necessary "that the Law should be broke."[136] As Quakers demonstrated in England and the American colonies, "If the enacting of *any-thing* can make it lawful, then we [have disobeyed the law]." They must do so because they are "commanded by God."[137] And Penington affirmed, "Now that which is of God cannot bow to any thing which is corrupt in man: it can lye down and suffer . . . but it cannot act that which is against its life."[138] But the uniqueness in Quaker practice was more than simply *that* they should disobey, but also *how.*

They followed the process that we have seen in their ecclesiastical polity. According to their peace testimony, they were commanded by God not to destroy his creations, including the constitution.[139] From the beginnings of their Society, Quakers had been taking their religious commission to testify for God's law into civil society to secure liberty of conscience. They were the only radicals to survive the Interregnum and continue to "publish" their understanding of God's law. They did this by developing a systematic process of civil disobedience, the first in Anglo-American history. "We do own and acknowledge *Magistracy* to be an Ordinance of God, instituted of him,"

---

[135] *PWP*, 2: 227.

[136] Penn, *Great Case*, 25. Almost thirty years after Quakers began practicing civil disobedience, Locke came to agree with the appropriateness of their actions to gain toleration, writing in his *Letter concerning Toleration* (1689) that if a magistrate enacts anything that goes against the conscience of the individual, "such a private Person is to abstain from the Action which he judges unlawful, and he is to undergo the Punishment which it is not unlawful for him to bear" (57). This is, of course, in marked change from his earlier position against toleration as expressed in the *Two Tracts of Government* (1660–c.1662). Given that the Quakers were the only remaining radical sect engaging in the public sphere during the Restoration and practicing this form of dissent, they must have been a factor in Locke's changed thinking.

[137] Ibid., 35.

[138] Penington, *Consideration of a Position*, 29.

[139] This is a vast simplification of this very complex theological doctrine. The peace testimony was neither uniform nor codified in the Discipline until decades after the seventeenth century. As Meredith Baldwin Weddle points out in *Walking in the Way of Peace*, individual Quakers interpreted the testimony differently at this point, and for some, violence or killing under certain circumstances was acceptable. And as for the duties of the government in this regard, Quakers generally distinguished between the civil and temporal realms and agreed that the government had a right to impose capital punishment for crimes such as treason. But another point of agreement was on the sanctity of the government, for which, of course, executions for treason were necessary. Contrary to Weddle's claim that there was no consensus on how to apply the testimony, all evidence in Quaker political philosophy and most practice points to the fact that they believed the constitution to be inviolable by man.

explained Edward Burrough, and "that we are subject by *doing* or *suffering*, to whatsoever Authority the Lord is pleased to set over us, without Rebellion, Sedition, Plotting, or making War against any Government or Governors." In a rightly constituted government, he continued, "We are, and do engage to be subject thereunto all the Commands and Injunctions of such *Authority* and *Government* whose Laws, Ordinances, and Commandments are grounded upon right Reason, Equity, which leadeth to *do unto all men as we would be done unto*." And their duty was likewise "patient suffering under all Penalties inflicted for *disobedience* to the Commands which we cannot perform by Obedience for Conscience sake."[140] They broke laws that restricted their religious practice peacefully, openly, and submitted to the resulting brutal punishments to bring attention to the injustice and effect reform in the system. But more than that, as discussed in Chapter 1, they organized themselves to confront the government from within. They established the first lobbying group in England and mastered the law to the extent that they baffled the very system that was oppressing them.[141]

Unlike resistance theory from Duplessis-Mornay's in *Vindicæ Contra Tyrannos* (1579) to the practice of American mobs before the Revolution, Quakers advocated resistance by individuals. As far as resistance to government was allowed by thinkers such as Sidney, Locke, and Hoadly, they agreed that it must be undertaken by the "whole people who are the Publick" or their representatives, not private individuals.[142] Quakers, on the other hand, not only encouraged individuals to follow their inner "leadings" against the government but often preferred this mode instead of protesting en masse, which they believed could be too disruptive.

Quaker thought and practice was an apparent contradiction for their contemporaries. Friends' actions caused most to believe that "the Quakers deny Magistracy and Government as such."[143] Without precedent, Quakers were uncategorizable. Non-Quakers did not understand the meaning of a people who could in the same breath proclaim loyalty to the king while breaking the laws he passed. This was a new understanding of government and civic engagement. And it was premised on a comparatively modern understanding of

[140] Edward Burrough, *A Vindication of the People Called Quakers* (n.d.), 22–23, in *Quaker Tracts*, vol. 4 (London, 1661), 466–88.

[141] On Quaker interactions with the government, see Horle, *Quakers and the English Legal System*. Their establishment of an organization that would approach the government on behalf of Friends was likely an inheritance from their Puritan predecessors, who "explored the techniques of lobbying" less formally (Walzer, *Revolution of the Saints*, 129).

[142] Pauline Maier, *From Resistance to Revolution: Colonial Radicals and the Development of American Opposition to Britain, 1765–1776* (New York: W. W. Norton & Co., 1972, 1991), 33–36. As indicated in fn. 136 in this chapter, however, Locke seemed to come around to accepting the propriety of individual resistance, at least where religion was concerned.

[143] Francis Bugg, *Hidden Things brought to Light. Whereby The Fox is Unkennel'd: And the Bowells of Quakerism Ript up, laid open, and expos'd to Publick View; by a Dialogue Tripartite. Whereby the Quakers Inside (to speak Figuratively) is turn'd Outward; and the Great Mystery of the Little Whore Farther Unfolded* (London, 1707), 162.

political arrangements. Quakers needed to have a tremendous amount of faith in the English constitution and its prescribed legal system to have embraced it so. They knew that the remedy for the ills came from the same source as the cause; the constitution merely needed reform. Their detractors did not yet understand that civil disobedience, as disruptive as it could be, is based on a strong sense of political obligation and a deep respect for the constitution of the state. They were right, however, when they wrote that Quakers "Repeal, not verbally, yet virtually, so far as their Power reaches, all Acts of Parliament which suit not their *Light Within*."[144] Moreover, Quakerism necessitated a greater degree of popular power than existed in any established group for the legal discernment and action to grow organically.

When they wrote their political treatises, they made peaceful reform a fundamental principle of their political theory not just for the sake of liberty of conscience, but for civil liberty and limitation of the government in general. Penington wrote, emphasizing their process, that "the right *Constitution* and orderly motion of them is of the greatest consequence that can be, there being so much embarqued in this *Vessel*."[145] Likewise, in a treatise considered by some historians to be one of the earliest definitive statements of Whig political philosophy, Penn expressed a belief atypical of subsequent Whig tracts: "The *Weapons* of [Christ's] warfare were not *Carnal, but Spiritual*."[146] He also expanded their action beyond liberty of conscience: "Nor is there any Interest so inconsistent with *Peace* and *Unity*, as that which dare not rely upon the Power of *Persuasion*."[147] Thus Quakers could in good conscience advocate a return to first principles because they had a process by which it could be done peacefully, constitutionally, without overthrow of the government. This was how, as Penington hinted, God would work through the people to alleviate their oppression. In Quaker theologico-politics, no theory of revolution was ever legitimate. So important was this right of civil disobedience that it was codified in the "Fundamentall Constitutions" of Pennsylvania. Penn wrote that if a governor or his deputy "by the evill insinuations and pernicious Councells of some in powr or esteem, with him of or from his mistakeing the true extent of his Authority . . . command or require the offi[c]ers or Magistrates in this Province . . . to do a thing that is Contrary to thes Fundamentalls . . . every such officer or Magistrate, shall be surely oblieged to reject the same & follow the tenure of thes Fundamentalls."[148] Thus the laws were subject to interpretation

[144] Francis Bugg, *Pilgrim's Progress*, 38.

[145] Penington, *Right, Safety and Liberty*, 7.

[146] William Penn, *England's Great Interest in the Choice of this New Parliament* (London, 1678/79), 4. David Ogg in *England in the Reign of Charles II* (Oxford: Oxford University Press, 1955) and Mary Maples Dunn in *Politics and Conscience* have identified this tract as such. For another reference to "spiritual weapons," see also Penn's "Fundamentall Constitutions," *PWP*, 2: 143. For the earliest and most thorough analysis to date of the role of pacifism in Quaker political thought, see Wellenreuther, *Glaube und Politik*.

[147] Penn, *England's Present Interest Discovered*, 32.

[148] Penn, "Fundamentall Constitutions," *PWP*, 2: 152.

by the people and civil disobedience was identified as a fundamental right.[149] This demand by Quakers to determine collectively the validity of the law shattered the traditional hierarchy and undermined both divine right of kings and the forthcoming theory of parliamentary sovereignty.

It was this pacifism and desire for genuine and substantial reform, not revolution, that was at the core of Quaker political thought; and this is what makes their theory unique in the seventeenth and eighteenth centuries. They were radicals, but not revolutionaries.[150] Certainly Whig political thought had a significant element of moderation. The Whiggism of the American Revolutionaries, drawn from the likes of Sidney, Locke, Hutcheson, and Cato, was concerned at least as much with preserving laws, government, and peace as it was with resisting oppression through revolution. There was a strong propensity for first attempting peaceful means through resistance of specific unjust laws before resorting to revolution. But in spite of the pronounced Whig conservatism during the Restoration and the continued preference for peace in the eighteenth century, Whigs were ultimately willing to resort to violence. At bottom, they could and did justify revolution, but Quakers could not. Whiggism was an "oppositional" ideology; Quakerism was conciliatory. Furthermore, while it is clear that there was a whiggish theory of peaceful resistance, it is not clear that it developed independently of the Quaker theories on government and their methods of resistance that were being articulated and practiced at the same time. Penn moved in the same circles and exchanged ideas with the most prominent Whig thinkers, including Locke. Moreover, in England and America, the Quakers were practicing peaceful resistance more staunchly and more visibly than any other group. Other Englishmen certainly looked to constitutions, bills, and petitions as guarantors of their rights, they appealed to fundamental principles, and they tried to reform with moderation; but in their impatience, they knew no way to effect major reform without destroying the constitution through revolution.[151] As Thomas Paine explained in his appendix to *Common Sense* (1776), "having no defense for ourselves in the civil law; [we] are obliged to punish [the British] by the military one and apply the sword."[152]

In some ways, we can understand civil disobedience as the primitive precursor of judicial review.[153] It is a way to check the power of the government

---

[149] To be sure, the idea of disobedience was current in many forms of religious thought, both Catholic and Protestant. But in this context, with Quakers' theological imperative to publish the truth through civil disobedience if necessary, we can assume that this clause would have been understood as giving official sanction of this practice.

[150] Hill hints at this when he writes that "In the last resort, perhaps, Quakers did not want to overturn the world" (*The World Turned Upside Down*, 374).

[151] On Whig resistance in general, as well as their inclinations for peace, see Maier, *From Resistance to Revolution*, esp. 28 and 42.

[152] Thomas Paine, *Common Sense* (1776), 92.

[153] It is not altogether certain that Quakers would have approved of judicial review had the idea been in circulation, and likely for the same reasons that the thinkers at the American Founding

and change the laws without violence. In judicial review, guardians of the constitution on behalf of the people test the positive law against the fundamental principles of the constitution and then, if necessary, repeal the ones that are unconstitutional.[154] Civil disobedience is a process of judicial review in which the people themselves are the judges.[155] They repeal laws virtually before they are formally abrogated. A point to remember is that, for Quakers, the process was as important as the result. The means were not just tools, they were an integral part of Truth-seeking, and adhering to them correctly was an end in itself. Thus what historians have found to be an innovation of the American Founding – the idea and creation of a sacred and perpetual yet amendable constitution that is formed through a sort of democratic process[156] – was envisioned and enacted by Quakers one hundred years earlier.

Conclusion

In a sense, Quakers were a sort of "trimmer." Describing the character of a Trimmer, a faction of moderates during the Glorious Revolution, George Savile wrote that "This innocent word *Trimmer* signifies no more than this, That if Men are together in a Boat, and one part of the Company would weigh it down on one side, another would make it lean as much to the contrary, it happens there is a third Opinion of those who conceive it would do as well, if the Boat went even, without endangering the Passengers."[157] Quakers, like Savile's Trimmers, returned repeatedly to the theme of a balanced vessel. Penington wrote in 1651 that "it becometh everyone (both in reference to himself and the whole) to contribute his utmost towards the right steering of *this Vessel*, towards the preserving of it both in its state and motions."[158]

---

expressed. See Kramer, *The People Themselves*; Tom Paine and Robin West, "Tom Paine's Constitutionalism," *Virginia Law Review* vol. 89, no. 6, *Marbury v. Madison*: A Bicentennial Symposium (2003), 1413–61. And note as well that Paine was raised a Quaker. See Eric Foner, *Tom Paine and Revolutionary America* (New York: Oxford University Press, 1976), 3.

[154] Wood calls them "agents of the people" in "State Constitution-Making," 925.

[155] See also Kramer, *The People Themselves*.

[156] Ibid., 917. It was the framers, says Wood, who "showed the world how written constitutions could be made truly fundamental and distinguishable from ordinary legislation, and how such constitutions could be interpreted on a regular basis and altered when necessary." Likewise, Willi Paul Adams writes that "[t]he Americans went beyond Locke and Blackstone in 1776 ... by institutionalizing peaceful means of making and amending constitutions" (*The First American Constitutions: Republican Ideology and the Making of State Constitutions in Revolutionary America* [Chapel Hill: University of North Carolina Press, 1979], 139). Jack Rakove finds that "the resort to popular sovereignty in 1778–88 marked the point where the distinction between a constitution and ordinary law became the fundamental doctrine of American political thinking" (*Original Meanings: Politics and Ideas in the Making of the Constitution* [New York: Vintage Books, 1997], 130). Beer and Zuckert also follow this interpretation. Kramer, it seems, would date this development latter, in the 1820s and 1930s with the establishment of judicial review.

[157] Savile, *The Character of a Trimmer*, preface.

[158] Penington, *Right, Safety and Liberty*, 7.

Similarly, in justifying the establishment of the Quaker ecclesiastical polity, Barclay explained in *Anarchy of the Ranters* that the problem of establishing a church government was that man is "inclinable to lean either to the right Hand or to the left." The goal, of course, is to keep it somewhere in the middle. In their politics, therefore, Quakers resisted party affiliations in favor in maintaining their agenda of moderation to preserve the constitution and gain or retain rightful liberties. This is not to say they did not make temporary alliances on one side or the other to achieve these ends – they were as ecumenical in their politics as they were in their religion. It was not the name that mattered but the principles, which caused Friends to choose seemingly strange traveling companions, such as James II. But those who espoused moderation, especially when they were perceived as radicals, were attacked from all sides. "[I]t so happens," explains Savile, "that the poor *Trimmer* hath all the Powder spent on him alone . . . there is no danger now to the state . . . but from the Beast called a *Trimmer*."[159] Barclay found the same problem for those who sought to establish church government: "If through the power of God they be kept faithful and stable, then they are calumniated on both Sides; each likening or comparing them to the worst of their Enemies."[160] But although Savile's Trimmers preferred balance, when revolution took place, they were content to stand aside and let it run its course.[161] The struggle for a balanced and lasting constitution recurred in all the Quakers' relationships with government, regardless of whether they played the role of dissenter or politician. And unlike Trimmers, Whigs, or Tories, traditional Quakers held steadfast to their convictions about peaceful dissent, unity, and rights even in the worst storm. Their practical politics in Pennsylvania show us their political philosophy in action.

[159] Savile, *The Character of a Trimmer*, preface.
[160] Barclay, *Anarchy*, iii.
[161] Robbins, *The Eighteenth-Century Commonwealthman*, 57. On the Trimmer position see also Behrens, "The Whig Theory of the Constitution," 70–71, and Conniff, "The Politics of Trimming," who would add that Trimmers had a darker view of the nature of man that made his dissent aggressively competitive rather than cooperative.

3

"Dissenters in Our Own Country"

Constituting a Quaker Government in Pennsylvania

The transition from political theory to practice in the Quaker colonies was a difficult one. The same problems plagued them in their early years as troubled the Quaker ecclesiastical polity at its founding. How would a people whose theologico-political thought was based on apparently irreconcilable tenets of unity and dissent, of bureaucracy and liberty, settle the question of authority amongst themselves? In the church, they had decided the issue in favor of a representative spiritual democracy with elders and ministers bearing most of the weight of legal discernment and governance. The balance in a civil polity, however, was not so easily achieved. The Quaker theory of a civil government, like their theology, suggested a strong popular element. But leading Friends were all too aware that the libertinism that necessitated a powerful central government in their church could surface in their new civil polities, West Jersey and Pennsylvania. Although Quakers could not agree at first on what balance should look like in these polities, they concurred on their other basic principles – that the polity was sacred and perpetual, and that change must be made within the existing framework and without violence. Unlike the church government, in the early years of these civil experiments, we see the balance of power shift from the elite few to the popular majority. The following discussion concerns the internal struggles of the Quaker government in Pennsylvania during the first twenty years,[1] from 1681 to 1701, and how these struggles followed a similar pattern and exemplified similar difficulties as in the ecclesiastical polity.[2]

---

[1] Therefore, when I use the term *popular* or *elite*, I am speaking about factions within the General Assembly and not the entire population.

[2] The standard work on this period is Gary B. Nash, *Quakers and Politics*. The difficulty with this otherwise important work is that, while Nash acknowledges the importance of theology as a foundation for Friends' politics (338–39), he finds that self-interested financial gain is their primary motivator (79). See also Edwin B. Bronner, *William Penn's Holy Experiment: The Founding of Pennsylvania, 1681–1701* (New York: Temple University Publications; distributed by Columbia University Press, 1962).

In particular, this chapter explores the process of constitutional reform at the highest level of the polity, with the polity being understood by Quakers as the meeting writ large. What we find here is an internal dissent and reform process that reveals how Quakers imagined their civil constitution (meaning primarily the unity of the people, a written document as a safeguard and guide, and the ensuing structures) as something sacred that must evolve while remaining intact. This aspect of their thought and practice was unique in this time period. While other colonies were certainly changing their governments and evolving as well, there was not yet a thought amongst them about either codifying their fundamental principles in a written document or a theory that would allow for a methodical change of the system.[3]

Holy Politics in West Jersey

Before we turn to Pennsylvania, the early history of West Jersey can serve as a brief and helpful prologue.[4] *West Jersey Concessions and Agreements* (1676/77) is indicative of a Quaker understanding of a rightly ordered government; but there were departures from the ideals as well.[5] Its draftsman, Edward Byllynge, in consultation with other Friends, seems to have created it to be in keeping with the Friendly ideal that the body of the meeting should have the responsibility of discerning and creating the law. A provision for dissent was built into it: "every respective member hath Liberty of speech" so that he could "enter his protests and reasons of protestations." Accordingly, not only did the constitution allow universal manhood suffrage, it placed the legislative power in the hands of the Assembly. The people also had direct access to the legislative process in that they "have Liberty to come in to hear and be witnesses of the voate[s] and the inclinations of the persons voating." Another distinctive point of the *Concessions* was its prescription for how to handle civil and criminal cases. There was no imprisonment for debt or jail fees, and there was to be a collective process of decision making in which a jury, "in whom only the Judgment resides," will "direct" the verdict of the justices. Further, plaintiffs "have full power to forgive and remit the person or persons offending against him or her selfe," whether before or after the judgment of the court. Such a process that emphasizes collective judgment on the one hand and leniency on

---

[3] Bailyn, *The Ideological Origins of the American Revolution*, 189–93.

[4] The Quaker experiment in New Jersey was quite short-lived, lasting only ten years before it passed into non-Quaker hands. There is very little written on West Jersey. John E. Pomfret has published most widely on it with: *The New Jersey Proprietors and Their Lands, 1634–1776* (Princeton, NJ: Van Nostrand, 1964); *Colonial New Jersey: A History* (New York: Scribner, 1973); *The Province of West New Jersey, 1609–1702: A History of the Origins of an American Colony* (New York: Octagon Books, 1976). See also the collection of essays *The West Jersey Concessions and Agreements of 1676/77: A Roundtable of Historians*, Occasional Papers, No 1 (Trenton, NJ: New Jersey Historical Commission, 1979).

[5] *West Jersey Concessions and Agreements* (1676/77), *PWP*, 1: 387–410.

the other reflects Quaker priorities and their preference for arbitration over litigation.[6] On the other hand, in a departure from Quaker political theory, the *Concessions* initially had no provision for amendment.

Problems developed in the practical application of the constitution. Although several issues arose, the most relevant for our concerns are Byllynge's actions in relation to the legislature. Most likely motivated by economic concerns, Byllynge immediately tried to override the constitution and assert his will as executive on the inhabitants. The Quaker assembly resisted this imposition and took measures to secure its power. First, members appealed to the British government, but they later acquiesced to Byllynge's request to use Quaker arbitration procedures instead. It was, after all, stipulated in the Quaker Discipline that disputes among Friends should be resolved among Friends. In 1684 the council of elder Friends that presided over the dispute, which included George Fox, favored Byllynge in their verdict.[7] This is hardly surprising since during this time leading Friends had just fought their own struggle against much radical resistance to establish a strong ecclesiastical government, and now, dissenters and other "libertines" within the meeting were kept under close watch. As Byllynge and other leading Friends, including Penn, wrote the *West Jersey Concessions* in 1676/77, Robert Barclay had just published *The Anarchy of the Ranters* (1676), which justified the Quaker system of representatives and reprimanded "disorderly walkers" in the meeting. He wrote that God "imployed such whom he that made use of in gathering of his Church" as governors of the church.[8] In other words, those who founded the colony should lead the colony. The leaders of the New Jersey assembly, however, more or less rejected the verdict and continued, without violence, to resist Byllynge and appeal to Friends for understanding. Nevertheless, the original intent of the *Concessions* was ultimately compromised as, among other things, the Assembly was compelled to accept a governor and upper house, and power remained in the hands of the few. Significantly, however, despite the stipulation that the *Concessions* could not be changed, the Assembly gave itself the power of amendment and then proceeded to change, or neglect to implement those aspects of the constitution they deemed inconsistent with the fundamental law.[9] But ultimately, this first Quaker experiment in government failed as it gradually came under the control of people indifferent to Quaker interests.

[6] Paul G. E. Clemmens, "The *Concessions* in Relation to Other Seventeenth-Century Colonial Charters," in *Roundtable*, 29–33, 31.

[7] On the controversy, see *The Case Put and Decided by George Fox, George Whitehead, Stephen Crisp, and other* [of] *the most Ancient & Eminent Quakers, between Edward Billing on the One Part, and some West-Jersians, headed by Samuell Jennings on the other Part...* (London, 1699); and Samuel Jennings, *Truth Rescued from Falsehood, being and answer to a Late Scurrilous Piece Entituled,* The Case Put and Decided... (London, 1699).

[8] Barclay, *Anarchy*, 70.

[9] Ibid., 36.

The Pennsylvania Experiment

The West Jersey dispute demonstrates on a small scale what was to happen in Pennsylvania, but with the important difference being that Pennsylvania survived the turmoil of its early years and remained a Quaker colony. Because the purpose here is to show the Quakers' internal process of change and reconciliation, the focus of the present discussion is the struggle of Quakers against one another rather than Quakers against the crown or other forces outside the immediate circle of politicians in the government. Contrary to their detractors' claims that Quakers principles were hostile to government, and Quakers themselves ungovernable, Pennsylvania survived not in spite of, but because it was a Quaker colony.[10]

Contrary to expectations, the first forty years of Pennsylvania government were characterized by raucous factionalism and antiauthoritarianism at all levels, which seems to us, as well as people of the time, atypical of the allegedly quiet and quietistic Quakers. After the king granted Penn his original charter in 1681, there were three different paper constitutions, and a period of time when there was none, before Friends codified their understanding of the law in the 1701 Charter of Privileges. During this time, all branches within Pennsylvania government vied for power amongst themselves and created alliances of convenience to combat the greatest perceived threat from the top. Whichever individual or elite group seemed to possess the most authority at any given moment was challenged by an ad hoc alliance from those below who claimed to be oppressed. The overarching trend, however, was the popular Assembly seeking to co-opt the legislative powers of both Penn (or the governors, whether royal or provincial) and the Provincial Council, while Penn and his supporters tried to curb the Assembly in its grasping for power. Quaker John Pearson observed with dismay in 1686 that

[i]t may be cause of wonder that this people that came out together in the Light and Unity of the one Spirit, and have stood together ... against the many Heads and Horns that have pushed at them, and have been struck at more or less, under every Government that hath been since they were a People, and none has been able to break them; but all has tended to their Encrease and Stability ... that such should now, when their outward Ease comes to be enlarged, fall at Odds and Difference amongst themselves, apparently as some may expect, to the great Damage, if not the Ruin of them.[11]

---

[10] My claim on this point differs from other scholars of Pennsylvania who have found the colony to be a failure as a Quaker experiment. See, for example, Edwin B. Bronner, "The Failure of the 'Holy Experiment' in Pennsylvania, 1684–1699," *Pennsylvania History* vol. 21 (1954), 93–108; and Endy, *William Penn and Early Quakerism*, 348–77, 367. Although it is true, as we will see in the next chapters, that as the eighteenth century progressed, Quakers had to compromise their principles in order to govern the colony, they never really lost control and succeeded in retaining much of what they believed to be important in a polity.

[11] John Pearson writing about the Wilkinson-Story Controversy in *Anti-Christian Treachery Discover'd and Its Way Block'd Up* ... (London, 1686), preface.

Pearson was referring to the Wilkinson-Story Controversy that threatened to destroy the Quaker ecclesiastical polity even before it could take root. And now Friends seemed to be following the same path in their civil government.

But the disunity among Friends was only temporary and relatively superficial in that there was no schism that permanently separated the Society. Further, there was a great sense of purpose behind the contention. As Pennsylvania Quakers explained, "wee are a Quiet people and Inclined to peace, and to fall out now is a thing by us abominated and obhorred; but in Conscience wee are bound to Doe our utmost to preserve the Rights of our Selves and posterity."[12] Now that liberty of conscience was relatively secure (although only as secure as their government was stable and controlled by Quakers), the main right that concerned them was legal and political self-determination.

Beneath the turmoil of these first years, there was a process of reform at work to constitute Pennsylvania as a truly godly polity. As in England, Quakers used their expertise in bureaucratic process and civil dissent to resist the authorities and press for greater liberties. Each successive written constitution wrested a little more power away from the proprietor and his elite council and placed it in the hands of the people (that is to say, the representative branch of the government). It is important to reiterate that all the American colonies were undergoing upheavals and changes similar to those in Pennsylvania. They were all striving for greater popular power at the expense of the other branches. Thus it was not so much what the Quakers were doing that was unique, although arguably they took their quest to a further extreme than most to create the most powerful popular legislature.[13] Rather, it was how they did it that is important. This turnover of constitutions, the constant pressing for more popular power, the insistence on rights, the contentious negotiating over the dynamics of political power, and finally, the essentially peaceful way in which they achieved reform, was exemplary of Quaker process. When we note the struggles for change in other colonies, we should also observe that Pennsylvania was the only colony to make such drastic transformation in their government in the seventeenth century without force of arms and with a theory and process animating their actions.[14] What they were doing was

---

[12] The Provincial Council and Assembly to Penn, 18th of the 3rd mo. 1691. *PWP*, 3: 318.

[13] On the lower houses' rise to power, see Jack P. Greene, "The Role of the Lower Houses of Assembly in Eighteenth-Century Politics," in *Negotiated Authorities: Essays in Colonial Political and Constitutional History* (Charlottesville: University Press of Virginia, 1994), 163–84. He notes Pennsylvania and Massachusetts as the colonies with the most powerful legislatures (166).

[14] Timothy H. Breen and Stephen Foster, "The Puritans' Greatest Achievement: A Study of Social Cohesion in Seventeenth-Century Massachusetts," *Journal of American History* vol. 60, no. 1 (1973), 5–22. The major incidents in each major colony were Leisler's Rebellion in New York (1689); Bacon's Rebellion in Virginia (1676); the Protestant Revolution in Maryland (1689); Governor Andros of Massachusetts forced from office by rebels (1689). Very early in Massachusetts history, significant changes took place in the government peacefully through a reinterpretation of the original charter. These were initiated from the top by John Winthrop himself, and although they undoubtedly went farther than he intended, he put up no resistance

not necessarily legal by the terms of Pennsylvania's *First Frame of Government* or in accord with Penn's wishes. But it was, according to a significant number of Friends, constitutional. Quakers took the theory of Penington and Penn seriously. Penington had important duties in mind for a representative assembly: "Parliaments have a difficult piece of work, *viz. to chastise the greatest Oppressors, and to strike at the very root of oppression.*" Furthermore, "unless they have Power answerable they cannot possibly go through with it."[15] They demonstrated they agreed with Penn when he wrote in the *Frame* that "I do not find a Model in the World, that Time, Place and some singular emergency have not necessarily altered."[16] The following pages chronicle the struggles of the Pennsylvania Assembly to realize Quaker political principles according to Quaker process.

It cannot be overemphasized that from its inception to the Revolution, Pennsylvania was self-consciously Quaker in its origins, identity, goals, structures, and internal processes. "We are a Quaker Colony, it was so intended," affirmed Penn in 1701.[17] And Friends had come there for distinctly Quaker reasons – to establish and maintain a Quaker government. Penn wrote,

The Govermt was our greatest inducement, & upon that public[k] faith, wee have buried our blood & bones as well as estates to make it wht it is, for being Dissenters, we therefore came that we might enjoye that so farr of wch would not be allowed us any share of att home, & wch we so much needed to our security and happiness abroad.[18]

The composition of the government reflected their priorities. It was conceived in the spirit of the Quaker meeting for business, the administrative assembly of the ecclesiastical polity.[19] Indeed, in translating Scripture, Quakers noted that, while the Greek word εκκλησία (*ekklēsia*) was translated as "church" in the English version, it also had strong political connotations that may or may

that would have tested the commitment of the Puritans to peace. For a succinct narrative of this episode, see Edmund Morgan, *The Puritan Dilemma: The Story of John Winthrop* (New York: HarperCollins Publisher, 1958), 84–114.

[15] Penington, *Right, Safety and Liberty*, 38.

[16] Penn, *First Frame*, *PWP*, 2: 213. By contrast, Greene notes that "imperial authorities persisted in the views that colonial constitutions were static and that the lower houses were subordinate governmental agencies with only temporary and limited lawmaking powers." He explains that most colonial legislatures scoffed at such views and did not shy away from innovations. On the other hand, he does not suggest that the lower houses had a philosophy or established method for change beyond piecemeal or ad hoc innovations. Rather, he explains that they applied the same principle of the English common law tradition to their own constitutions. That is to say, change inevitably happened and was validated by precedent, but there was no established process, nor were changes necessarily codified in a written document ("Lower Houses," 463–66).

[17] Penn to William Penn, Jr., 2 January 1701. *PWP*, 4: 27.

[18] Ibid.

[19] Allan Tully calls the Assembly the "analogue of the meeting." Tully, *Forming American Politics*, 274. Bronner notes the provisions Friends made in their statutory laws for Quaker priorities such as their unorthodox marriage practices and arbitrators in the courts (*Holy Experiment*, 55). Laws will be discussed in greater detail in the following chapter.

not have had religious implications.[20] Considering themselves, as they did, to be like the primitive Christians, they interpreted the word as it was used in Jesus' day, in political terms, as a popular assembly convened to deliberate on public matters. There was thus very little distinction made between church and state. In the Quaker mind, then, only a certain kind of man could govern with authority – a Christian and, more specifically, a Quaker.

Religion was not only important in the private lives of the Assemblymen; it was a crucial element of their public lives as well. With Quakers always comprising at least half of the House and sometimes as much as 80 percent, Quakerism was a significant political interest.[21] Many active politicians in this early period were also considered "devout Quakers" or "weighty Friends," active not just in the General Assembly, but also in their monthly meetings and Philadelphia Yearly Meeting as clerks, elders, ministers, and authors of epistles. Isaac Penington expressed the common Quaker position on what a politician should be: "only such as can clear the derivacy of it from Christ to them, such as are fitted and appointed by [Christ] to be under him in his own seat and place of Government." But beyond this, it was not just what a man professed, but how he actualized his faith in the government that was important: "Nor," as Penington wrote, "are they to govern as men; by outward force; but as Christians, by spiritual virtue and efficacy upon the Conscience, the seat of Christ in man, so that it appear that not they, but the *Spirit of Christ, the Spirit in Christ* doth rule and govern."[22] God was to govern through each politician and, in according to Quakerism, peaceful process, "orderly walking," would rule.

One of the most important men in Pennsylvania government in its formative years was Thomas Lloyd. A minister himself, he wrote to Penn in 1684 of Pennsylvanians: "We are glad to See the faces of serviceable Friends here, who Come in God's freedom, who are persons of a Good Understanding & Conversation: & Will Discharge Their Stations Religiously; Such will be a Blessing to The Province."[23] If they do not, Penn wrote, they "*shall be reputed and Marked as breakers as the Fundamentall Constitutions of the Country, and therein as well as publique enemies to God as the people, and never to bare office till they have given good Testimony of their repentance.*"[24] Friends in office were thus on guard about transgression from the fundamental law, and they were prepared to defy those who disagreed with it.

The "Fundamentall Constitutions" of Pennsylvania was the first constitution for the colony. Like the West Jersey *Concessions*, historians have called it "innovative."[25] In this original plan Penn gave the people the power to elect and

[20] Barclay, *Anarchy*, 32.
[21] Craig Horle, et al., eds., *Lawmaking and Legislators in Pennsylvania: A Biographical Dictionary, 1682–1709* (Philadelphia: University of Pennsylvania Press, 1991), 1: 115. (Hereafter referred to as *LL*)
[22] Penington, *Right, Safety and Liberty*, 43.
[23] Thomas Lloyd to Penn, November 2, 1684, Howland Collection, HQC.
[24] Penn, "Fundamentall Constitutions," *PWP*, 2: 143.
[25] *PWP*, 1: 387.

instruct their representatives, who, in turn, would chose a Council from their own members and instruct it and the governor. In this model, in keeping with Quaker theory, a popular assembly was the dominant branch of government. Moreover, this plan was liberal compared to the charter Charles II granted Penn, which conferred almost all powers in the colonial government on Penn, making him the virtual king of his own land.[26] Penn instead allotted only a slight power to himself alone as the governor of the colony. "I propose that wch is extreordinary," he said, "& to leave myselfe & successors noe powr of doeing mischief, that the will of one man may not hinder the good of an whole Country."[27]

The 1682 *Frame of Government*

This plan would have been eminently agreeable to Friends. But Penn did not institute the "Fundamentall Constitutions." Instead he drafted the *First Frame of Government* (1682) and installed it as the first constitution of Pennsylvania.[28] The official structure of Pennsylvania government that he laid out was a three-part system consisting of the proprietor (Penn) or a governor as the executive and two elected branches – an elite Provincial Council as the legislative branch and an Assembly as the representative branch, which had a voice, but no legislative power. All of these branches worked together as a unified body called the General Assembly. Although in keeping with the British system, his structure stands in contrast to most other expressions of Quaker political thought, and it departs significantly from earlier versions of Penn's civil constitutions. Perhaps trying to save himself the trouble that Byllynge experienced with his colonists, the *Frame* abandoned the original scheme of the "Fundamentall Constitutions" by significantly restricting the popular element. Instead Penn placed most of the authority with the Provincial Council, leaving the popular Assembly with only the power to suggest amendments to legislation. Moreover, in a change that Quakers resented for a long time to come, Penn reneged on his earlier promise to restrict executive power and instead conferred upon himself a treble vote in the General Assembly.[29] The representative Assembly – the most important branch as far as most Quakers were concerned – was virtually impotent. For many reasons, including the unrealistic number of representatives that Penn thought would be available for governmental duty, it became clear very

---

[26] William Penn, "The Charter of Pennsylvania," in Jean Soderlund, ed., *William Penn and the Founding of Pennsylvania, 1680–1684: A Documentary History* (Philadelphia: University of Pennsylvania Press, 1983), 39–50.

[27] Penn to Robert Turner, Anthony Sharp, and Roger Roberts, 12th of the 2nd mo. [April 16], 81. *PWP*, 2: 89.

[28] A further discussion of the practical provisions of this *Frame*, as well as many of its ideological elements, can be found in Endy, "The Kingdom Come: Pennsylvania" in *William Penn and Early Quakerism*, 348–77. This chapter also includes discussion of the objections of Friends to the new *Frame*.

[29] See Nash, *Quakers and Politics*, 71; and From the Assembly to William Penn, 25 August 1704, *PWP*, 4: 296.

quickly after the founding of the colony that this organization of government was hopelessly unstable. And many Friends' dissatisfaction with the balance of power gave them no great incentive to try to preserve the existing *Frame*.

Even before the 1682 *Frame* was enacted, a number of prominent thinkers, some of them Quakers, criticized Penn harshly for straying from his values. They too believed he had shifted the weight too far in favor of the executive. Algernon Sidney proclaimed the *Frame* "the basest laws in the world, and not to be endured or lived under."[30] Quaker Benjamin Furly wrote to Penn, giving him a line-by-line critique of his *Frame* in comparison to his earlier constitution. The "Fundamentall Constitutions," he wrote, "is much more fair and equal, in my mind, than...the new Frame, which take from the General Assembly the whole faculty of proposing any bills, and lodges it solely in the Provincial Council, which seems to be a divesting of the people's representatives (in time to come) of the greatest right they have."[31] It is clear that Furly thought that Penn's earlier attempt at constitutional discernment was more accurate than his later one. But even more striking than his concern for popular legislative power, however, is Furly's foresight as to the consequences of the 1682 *Frame* for the political climate in the Quaker colony. He anticipated the difficulties that would arise in Pennsylvania almost immediately and plague the government for the next twenty years. The structure of the *Frame*, he tried to convince Penn, "will lay morally a certain foundation of dissension amongst our successors, and render the patronizers of this new Frame obnoxious to future parliaments." He concluded with a plea to Penn to "let the General Assembly be restored to those powers and privileges which thy first Constitutions do give it."[32] But Penn left it as it was and assumed that the Assembly would simply meet and approve the *Frame*. It did not. What it did instead was assume the role of trimmer and undertake a twenty-year process of revision to balance the ship of state according to the earlier, more accurate constitution.[33]

The Assembly's efforts exemplify Pennsylvania's identity as a Quaker colony concerned with rights advocacy and systemic reform. The way they enacted their role as trimmers was to adhere to the Quaker process of reform that was based on their understanding of a sacred constitution. They carried over the "order and method" of the ecclesiastical polity into the political assemblies and used synteresis to gain "clearness" about how to amend their faulty constitution. As in their religious business, they began by waiting in silence at the start of the meeting in order to reach a state of inward silence and hear more clearly

---

[30] Algernon Sidney quoted in William I. Hull, *William Penn: A Topical Biography* (London: Oxford University Press, 1937), 229.
[31] Benjamin Furly, "Benjamin Furly's Criticism of *The Frame of Government*" in Soderlund, *William Penn and the Founding of Pennsylvania*, 137.
[32] Ibid.
[33] Alan Tully writes suggestively of Quakers' conception of balance – that it was unbalanced in a traditional, Lockean sense, but balanced in another way. "Pennsylvanians," he explains, "primarily concerned themselves with the balance of power between the legislative and executive branches of government" (*Forming American Politics*, 284).

the voice of God in their consciences. In 1687 Penn advised his deputies to "be most Just as in the sight of the allseeing allsearching God, and before you lett your spirits into an affaire, retire to him... that he may give you a good understanding & govermt of your selves in the management thereof... lett the People Learn by your example as well as by your powr the happy life of Concord."[34] As late as the middle of the next century the Assembly could still be observed "to sit in silence awhile, like solemn worship, before they proceed to do business."[35] After this period of productive silence, the governor or speaker of the house would often begin the meeting for government by giving "religious and wholesome Council to the Members of the House."[36] Next, "The Governor having assum'd his Seat of Authority," describes minutes from the colonial Assembly, "makes his Address to the General Assembly in the Way of Christian Council and Exhortation, advising the Members of Assembly to look unto 'God in all their Proceedings.'"[37] In contrast to a process of debate and argumentation, synteresis was naturally very slow and cautious. Moreover, because they were concerned that "great Inconveniences doe oftner arise from hasty than deliberate Councels... unless it be in a Case of Immanent and Immediate danger" they preferred that "no business of state in Assembly or Counc{e}ll shall be resolved the day it is proposed, to end, time may be given to learn all that may be known or said about the matter in hand, in order to a Cleer and Safe Detirmination" of God's law.[38] These practices continued in the latter half of the eighteenth century as well, when Quaker legislators would end sessions by calling for the "sense of the House" instead of a vote.[39] This reflects exactly the procedure in religious business when the clerk would take the "sense of the meeting" from the unified group to determine what direction to take. The clerk, the weightiest office in the meeting, had to make his decisions based on what he gleaned from both the vocal and the silent members, while also taking into account the measure of Light from each person.[40] Finally, a meeting of the Assembly would end with more "religious Counsel."[41] The goal in all this was to accurately discern God's law, which could only be accomplished by a group effort at synteresis.

The troubles for the colony began when the Assembly's efforts at discernment did not agree with Penn's. In addition to their theories of change, they also had some more concrete tools available to them to remedy the defects they

---

[34] Penn to the Commissioners of State, 1 February 1687. *PWP*, 3: 145.
[35] John Churchman, *An Account of the Gospel Labours and Christian Experiences of a Faithful Minister of Christ* (Philadelphia, 1779), 96–98.
[36] Gertrude MacKinney, ed., *Pennsylvania Archives, Eighth Series: Votes and Proceedings of the House of Representatives of the Province of Pennsylvania* (Philadelphia: Franklin and Hall, 1931), 1: 44. (Hereafter referred to as *PA*)
[37] Ibid., 1: 47.
[38] "Fundamentall Constitutions," *PWP*, 2: 147.
[39] Tully, *Forming American Politics*, 274.
[40] For a concise historical and contemporary analysis of this aspect of Quaker process, see Michael J. Sheeran, *Beyond Majority Rule*, 95–97.
[41] *PA*, 1: 11.

found. As noted in the previous chapter, Penn had included a novelty in the *Frame*. But if that were insufficient for the drastic changes Quakers hoped to make, they could resort to their informal process, which at one time Penn had considered constitutional. In a clause from the "Fundamentall Constitutions" that did not make it into the *First Frame*, Penn wrote that if a governor or his deputy oversteps his bounds, "every such officer or Magistrate, shall be surely oblieged to reject the same & follow the tenure of thes Fundamentalls."[42] Thus Penn acknowledged the laws were subject to interpretation and the constitutionality of resistance was identified as a fundamental obligation. Quaker politicians took these clauses seriously.

When the Assembly met to implement the *First Frame*, they did not simply approve it as Penn had anticipated. Instead, they began their process of reform. But the process, it should be noted, was not identical to that which they used in their religious meeting. It was not "peaceable conversation" in the sense that they spoke to one another with calm reserve. This was, rather, political conversation – it was peaceful in the sense that no one took up arms. But inflammatory rhetoric became a hallmark of the Quaker Assembly. Accordingly, they began by casting "undeserving Reflections and Aspersions upon the Governor."[43] They accused Penn of hoarding power and worried that if more control were not given to the Assembly, the colony might fall into the hands of non-Quakers as had happened in West Jersey.[44] They desired, as Penn had said, that "God's power among honest Friends, should have Rule & Dominion."[45] Penn disagreed that his treble vote should amount to much among so many representatives, but the issue was more than that for him. He argued that God had tested him and then put this amount of power into his hands, and he had a duty to exercise it. "My God hath given it me in the face of the Worl[d] {& it is} to hold it in true Judgment as Reward of my Sufferings." He had paid for it, it was his, so he admonished grasping Friends to "keep [ye?] in thy place; I am in mine."[46] This, however, was not a sufficient rationale for Friends, and his claims to such authority may have provoked them further. They immediately tried to step beyond what the *Frame* allowed, asserting "the ancient and undoubted rights and privileges of the people."[47]

The 1683 *Frame of Government*

Thus the meeting to approve the *Frame* became instead a meeting to amend it. They produced first the 1683 Act of Settlement. This act was originally intended as an amendment to the *Frame* to make it more workable. It reduced the number of Council- and Assemblymen and made a number of other mechanical

---

[42] "Fundamentall Constitutions," *PWP*, 2: 152.
[43] *PA*, 1:18.
[44] *PWP*, 2: 346.
[45] William Penn to Jasper Blatt, February 5, 1683, *PWP*, 2: 347.
[46] Ibid.
[47] *PA*, 1:18.

adjustments to the *Frame*. But this was not enough as far as the Assembly was concerned. They were interested in expanding their law-making powers. After they allegedly spread "wicked lying reports"[48] against Penn, in 1683 all agreed the entire *Frame* of 1682 was unworkable, and a new frame was established. At this time, the Assembly resolved that they "might be allowed the Privilege of proposing to [the governor and Council] such Things as might tend to the Benefit of the Province."[49] But they were refused. Instead, the Council and the governor believed that "the House presuming to take that Power [of debating proposed laws], seemed too much to infringe upon the Governor's Privileges, and Royalties."[50] The new 1683 *Frame*, written by Penn, was intended to keep popular powers in check and decreed that only the governor and the Council could propose laws. Penn did relent a bit, however, and allowed the Assembly the "Liberty to consult amongst themselves, touching such Proposals...as might tend to the Benefit of the Province."[51] This small concession, however, only encouraged the Assembly to struggle harder against his authority. In defiance of Penn, they proceeded to pass laws anyway, one of which was a bill stating that no one could interfere with them in their political duties. With the explicit aim "to inviolaby [*sic*] keep the and preserve all the Articles of the Charter," the Assembly proclaimed that "it is their undoubted Privilege to proceed upon reading, debating, and concluding upon the promulgated Bills by Vote, in order to pass them into Laws, without any the least Restriction by the Council to hinder them from so doing."[52] The new *Frame* not only abolished Penn's treble vote, it stated that he was to act "with the Advice and Consent of the Provincial Council" in "any publick Act of State whatsoever that shall or may relate unto the Justice, Trade, Treasury, or Safety of the Province and Territorries."[53] Thus from the very infancy of Pennsylvania, Quakers were resisting the established authorities and claiming popular authority to discern the law.

In the first decade of Pennsylvania politics, the antiauthoritarianism of the Quakers in the Assembly was not directed at Penn per se. Friends still revered him very much as their spiritual and political leader. In these early years, most Quakers not only had no desire to remove Penn, they were, despite their antagonism, even supportive of the proprietary government itself. Penn himself remarked that he "was receiv'd...wth much Kindness & respect" by the denizens of Pennsylvania.[54] But before long, Penn's assessment of his treatment by Pennsylvanians would change dramatically.

---

[48] James Claypoole to William Penn, April 1683, *PWP*, 2: 396.

[49] *PA*, 1: 14.

[50] Ibid., 1: 15.

[51] Ibid., 1: 46.

[52] Ibid., 1: 62, 63.

[53] See Sister Joan de Lourdes Leonard, "The Organization and Procedure of the Pennsylvania Assembly," *PMHB* vol. 72 (1948), 376–412, 387–88.

[54] William Penn to the Earl of Arran, January 9, 1684, *PWP*, 2: 512.

At first, most resistance by the Assembly was directed at the nearest, most obvious threat – the Provincial Council. In the first decade of the colony, the Assembly pursued a campaign to remove legislative rights from the Council. By 1684, it became clear that whatever harmony there was in the colony was due only to Penn's presence. As soon as he left the colony for England, acrimony between the Assembly and the Council became open. Until 1688, the main focus of the Assembly's resistance was the Council and its leader, Thomas Lloyd. A well-to-do Quaker merchant and minister, Lloyd was quickly becoming the most powerful man in the colony, holding many offices and controlling as much or more of the government than Penn ever did. He was at once president of Council (and hence chief officer of province) until 1688, keeper of the seal, master of the rolls, and member of the Board of Propriety. Beyond this, even, in 1685 he led the Council in co-opting Penn's power of judicial appointment in county courts and then in the provincial court.[55] To the Assembly, Lloyd embodied the unbalance in the government and the threat this posed to their popular rights.

Penn was distressed in these years as his brethren bickered in office. He clearly hoped that his government would resemble the meeting more closely in its mode of conversation. "I am sorry at heart for yr Anemositys," he wrote. "Cannot more friendly & private Courses be taken to sett matters at right in an infant province[?] . . . for the love of God, me & the poor Country, be not so Governmentish, so Noisy & open in yr dissatisfactions."[56] But to express dissatisfactions was the Quaker way in religion; and so was it in politics, although louder. Penn, always keeping in mind the Quaker goal to set an example to the world of godly behavior, reminded the politicians in Pennsylvania repeatedly that "[m]any eyes are Upon you of all sorts"[57] and "that the Province is sufficiently watcht by friends & foes; & it much depends upon thos in powr."[58] He appealed to them as Friends not to "debase [their] Noble calling[s] by a low, mean & partial behaviour: neither lett any privat concerns defraud the public of your care." And, "Remember that your station obliges you to be the light & Salt of the Province; to direct & season thos that are under you, by your good example." Penn was always hopeful "that by a conscientious discharge of your duty to god and man, you may provoke others to do the like."[59] It is clear from this and other expressions of shock by observers of the Assembly that they expected Quakers to be as placid as they were in their religious meetings. Instead, the Assembly in these early years reproduced the radicalism during the establishment of their ecclesiastical polity.

But Penn's admonitions went unheeded as the Assembly continued to attack the Council, and by 1686, it had gained some ground in establishing both a

---

[55] *LL*, 1: 505–17.

[56] Penn to Thomas Lloyd et al., 17th of the 6th mo. 1685. *PWP*, 3: 50.

[57] Penn to the Provincial Council, 24th of the 2nd mo. 1686. *PWP*, 3: 88.

[58] Ibid., c. June 1686. *PWP*, 3:93–96. See also Penn to Thomas Lloyd, et al., 17th of the 6th mo. 1685; Penn to Thos. Lloyd, 21 Sept. 1686, *PWP*, 3: 117.

[59] Penn to the Provincial Council, c. June 1686. *PWP*, 3: 93–96.

larger scope of power and a separate identity from the Council. It had already begun to propose and debate legislation; it was beginning to determine for itself the duration of their sessions; and it was beginning to refuse to continue laws from one session to the next, which infringed upon the legislative authority of the Council.[60] Assemblymen were taking seriously Isaac Penington's idea that "A *Parliament* have . . . a right and power conferred upon them by the people, to *order, settle, amend,* or (if need be) *new-make* the Government for themselves and the people."[61] William Markham, a close advisor to Penn who reported the activities of the Assembly in anxious detail, wrote "they had severall Conferences between the whole Councill and the Assembly . . . I Feare it will prove an Ill president . . . their Subject was the privilidg of the people, a Dangerous thing to Dispute in the Face of such a Congregation." At this time the Assembly also challenged the authority of the Council by suggesting the repeal of some laws and proposing a limit to the duration of other laws, which would have forced the Council to agree with the Assembly before passing any future legislative package.[62] The Council, of course, refused these demands. Markham expressed his opinion on the matter to Penn that "if such Disputes be allowed it will hazard the overthrow of the Governmt, For what ever privelidg you once grant you must never think to Recall without being Reflected on and Counted a great oppressor."[63] The non-Quaker Markham was learning very quickly about Quaker politics.

And it was a very real risk indeed that Penn could be seen as a "great oppressor." The proprietor's two-year absence had begun to take its toll on the disposition of the colonists. The next years, so soon after the founding of the colony, would prove to be a turning point for Penn's influence. As the Assembly and the Council struggled with one another, confidence in Penn was waning. Because of serious mismanagement of the colony and an ensuing lack of trust from his colonists, Penn was gradually becoming the object of resentment by both the Assembly and the Council.[64] Penn noted in 1686/87 that his "lettrs to the P[rovincial] councel are so slightly regarded." He further complained that "I have with a religious minde consecrated my paines in a prudent frame [of government], but I see it is not valued, understood, or kept."[65] Rather, Friends were adhering to their own understanding of a legitimate constitution.

Friends' disappointment at Penn's long absence, the postponement of legislation, and the miscommunication that transpired from erratic transatlantic messages all conspired to encourage not just antiproprietary sentiment in general, but anti-Penn feeling in particular. Penn's apparent neglect of his own colony, combined with his abilities to insulate the colony from the centralizing effects of the English government, allowed the colonists to develop a unity

[60] Markham to Penn, 22 August 1686. *PWP*, 3: 99.
[61] Penington, *Right, Safety and Liberty*, 40.
[62] Markham to Penn, 22 August 1686. *PWP*, 3: 99, 109.
[63] Ibid., 99.
[64] Nash, *Quakers and Politics*, 97.
[65] Penn to James Harrison, 28th of the 11th mo., 1686-87, *PWP*, 3: 137.

amongst themselves as a people and practice and polish their own govern-ing style.[66] The situation was a sort of the "salutary neglect" that Edmund Burke described in America as a whole in the years preceding the Revolution, when Americans learned to govern themselves and became suspicious of any intervention by remote powers. Similarly, as Penn became more remote from his brethren, he quickly became the target of their suspicions.[67] His authority would be gradually and irrevocably undermined; he would never regain power as the political leader of the colony, nor full respect as a political and spiritual leader in his lifetime.

Contrary to the perceptions of the Assembly, as far as Penn and his closest advisors were concerned, he had very little actual power. On the one hand, Penn asserted confidently that "[the General Assembly] has no Powr but wt is derived by me, as myn is from the King... I see I am to lett them know that tis yet in my powr to make them need me."[68] On the other, Penn wrote numerous letters to his confidants, lamenting his weakened condition as leader of his own colony, and foretelling danger for those who would undermine his authority: "I hope some of thos that once feared I had too much powr will now see I have not enough, & that excess of powr does not the mischief that Licentiousness does to a state, for tho the one oppresses the pocket, the other turns all to confusion."[69] But Penn's hopes were futile. Thomas Holme, a fellow Quaker and devoted friend to Penn, wrote to him soon after that "one of the Generall Assembly had the confidence or rather impudence publiquely to say amongst them, he would or could give $\frac{1}{2}$ his estate, that the Govr had not so much power as he hath, & this by a Q[uaker]." He warned Penn that "[u]nless thou hast more power, this Government will not thrive as it might."[70] In an ominous expression of frustration, Penn wrote: "It almost tempts me to deliver up to the K[ing] & lett a mercenary Goverr have the taming of them."[71] Little did Friends know how close Penn was to acting on this impulse.

Quite apart from the practical implications of a disorderly and fractious gov-ernment, Penn was very much concerned with the colonists' spiritual welfare. He was distressed by reports from his agents about their allegedly un-Quakerly behavior and the corresponding judgment that Friends as a group were funda-mentally "litigious & brutish."[72] Thomas Holme felt in a position to comment candidly to Penn on the shortcomings of Friends in office. Not surprisingly, his appraisal of the Quaker attitude toward government and authority are strongly reminiscent of Massachusetts Puritans' criticisms of Quakers, of the Anglicans' in England, and of leading Friends' during the Wilkinson-Story Controversy.

---

[66] *LL*, 1: 39.

[67] Clearly, as Tolles notes, this behavior bears a strong resemblance to Whig opposition (*Meeting House and Counting House*, 14).

[68] Penn to James Harrison, 28th of the 11th mo., 1686-87, *PWP*, 3: 137.

[69] Penn to Thos. Lloyd, 17th of the 9th mo. 1686, *PWP*, 3: 129.

[70] Holme to Penn, 25th of the 9th mo. 1686, *PWP*, 3: 131.

[71] Penn to Thos. Lloyd, 17th of the 9th mo. 1686, *PWP*, 3:129.

[72] Ibid., 128.

"The want of veneration," he observed, "to Magistracy, & Courts kept in due order, & respect to them, is not the least cause of reproaches among us, & many disorders and confusions ensue." To Holme, the reason for this was increasingly clear: "truly as things are here, makes me think sometimes, these peopl are not worthy of such a Govr and Governt, nor fitted to rule themselfes, or be ruled by a friend thats a Govr."[73] Quakers and governing, he concluded, do not mix.

Some Quakers, including Penn, believed that the problem was that too many Friends had forgotten the conciliatory principles in Quakerism, and that the principles of the peace testimony should extend to everyday behavior and not just the issue of war. They were hopeful that if these Quaker principles were observed more carefully, the situation might improve. Penn hoped for a revival of the restrictive aspects of Quaker process. If a few "weighty men mett apart & waited on god for his minde & wisdom & in the sense & authority," he said, they might better be able to check the behavior of the unruly ones.[74] But the other Quaker principle of concern for individual rights and privileges, and a willingness to suffer for them – the libertine part of the process – was, from the perspective of some, superseding the desire for peaceable conversation. Penn's concerns grew and in 1686 he wrote, "I am very much afflicted in my Spirit that no Care is taken by those that have a Concern for the Lord's Name & Truth, by Perswasion or Authority to stop these scurvy Quarrels, that break out, to the Disgrace of the Provinces." Almost worse was that this contentious behavior was taking its toll on the reputation of Pennsylvania. "There is nothing but Good said of the Place, and little thats Good said of the People," Penn complained.[75] Further, not only were Penn and other elite members of the Quaker government concerned with their reputation in England, but it had begun to occur to them that the Pennsylvania government acted much differently than the governments of surrounding colonies. They began to compare themselves unfavorably with their neighbors. The leaders of Pennsylvania felt themselves in an unfortunately unique dilemma. William Markham wrote to Penn that members of the Assembly "took large liberty with Goverrs, wch I thought was not usual any where but here."[76]

In 1687 in a desperate attempt to bring order to the colony in his absence, Penn appointed five men – the Commissioners of State – to act collectively as governor in his absence and gave explicit instructions "to suffer noe disorder in Council nor the Council and Assembly or either of them to intrench upon the powrs & Priviledges remaining yet in me."[77] Penn's seeming partisanship caused "much dissatisfaction" in the Assembly and instigated another confrontation. The Commissioners of State met with the Assembly which "Stood

[73] Holme to Penn, 25th of the 9th mo. 1686, *PWP*, 3: 131.
[74] Penn to Thos. Lloyd, 17th of the 9th mo. 1686, *PWP*, 3: 129.
[75] Penn to James Harrison, November 20, 1686, Penn Papers, Domestic and Miscellaneous Letters, 31, HSP.
[76] Markham to Penn, May 2, 1688, *PWP*, 3: 186–87.
[77] Penn to the Commissioners of State, February 1, 1687, *PWP*, 3: 145.

Stiff For their Supposed previliges." The next day they reconvened and again "Fell into a Dispute of their priviliges," which included confronting the Commissioners with a number of demands: to "see by what war[an]t they Could pass Laws"; to view the original charter and an accurate record of the laws; and to arrange a convenient and dignified place they could meet with the Council where they could sit, "For they looked upon it as a great Indignity to Stand when they Came to the Councill."[78]

As far as Penn and the Council were concerned, the Assembly was pushing beyond all reasonable boundaries and "touching upon many things not belonging to them to {meddle wth}." Markham described what he considered the proper relationship of the Assembly to the Council. It was the same relationship as Fox and the other leaders had with the Society of Friends as a body. They are "Brethren and Representatives of one body, only with {this} Difference that wee [the Council] may very well have the Elder Brothers place."[79] As far as he was concerned, the Assembly was stepping out of the place ascribed to them by God. "I Look upon the Councill and Assembly to be one Generall assembly," he explained, "and it were monstrous if it should be other wise as much as one body have two heads or any other monstrous thing in Nature."[80] In most of their demands in this confrontation, Markham notes, the Assembly "were Knock'd Downe rather then {gently} laid."[81] One can only speculate about the quality of the conversation that flowed from the members of the Council towards those of the Assembly.

By 1688, Pennsylvania government had become so factionalized, and Penn felt his loss of control in the colony so acutely, that he committed what Friends must have perceived as the ultimate betrayal. In a letter to his Commissioners of State, he informed them of his appointment of John Blackwell, a Puritan military man, to the position of governor of the colony. "For your ease," he wrote reassuringly, "[I] have appointed one, that is not a Friend, but a grave sober wise man to be Goverr in my absence . . . I have ordered him to confer in private with you, & square himself by your advice; but bear down with a visible authority vice & faction, that it may not look a partiality in Frds to act as they have done." In other words, Penn told them that a man representing all that Quakers had rejected would arrive and punish them all, regardless of their previous good or bad behavior, and restore order with a heavy hand. And in a most telling plea, signifying the depths to which this was a peculiarly Quaker problem in Pennsylvania, Penn urged Quakers to "use his not being a Friend, to Friends advantage."[82] As far as Penn was concerned, the problem in Pennsylvania was a problem with Quakers, and, worst of all, they needed the help of a Puritan to solve it.

---

[78] Markham to Penn, July 21, 1688, *PWP*, 3: 196.
[79] Ibid.
[80] Ibid., 3: 197.
[81] Ibid., 3: 196.
[82] Penn to the Commissioners of State, 18th of the 7th mo. 1688, *PWP*, 3: 209–10.

In hoping a firm hand would restore order to his General Assembly, Penn was blinded to how this appointment would affect Friends. It is clear that Penn was privileging unity over dissent and popular power when he brought in a Quaker arch-enemy to govern a self-consciously Quaker colony; but it is hard to imagine his lack of foresight as to the animosity this would cause. With Friends' persecution at the hands of Massachusetts Puritans only a few years behind them, and their disavowal of all things military, the decision was disastrous to his relationship with them. Ironically, however, Penn's ill-conceived appointment achieved in part the result he sought. It caused the previously bickering Quaker factions to unite firmly – but against him.

He may not have anticipated the new unity of the Assembly, but he was not completely ignorant of the how they would react. Knowing full well the propensity of the Assembly for resistance to authority, and in anticipation of their dislike of Blackwell, Penn attempted to lay down the law. Prior to Blackwell's appointment, he delineated more clearly than ever his view of the improper behavior of the Assembly, and outlined its proper sphere of activity.

[T]he Assembly, as they call themselves, is not so, without Govr & P[rovincial] councel & that noe speaker, clark or book belong to them. that the people have their representatives in the Pro. Councell . . . & the Assembly as it is called, has only the power of I or no, yea or nay. If they turn debators, or Judges, or complainers, you overthrow your charter quite, in the very root of the constitution of it. for that is to usurp the P. councels part in the cha[rter] & to forfit the charter it self . . . the Negative voice is by that in them, & that is not a debateing, mending, altering, but an accepting or rejecting powr.[83]

Clearly Penn believed that the actions of the Assembly were revolutionary and out of keeping with Quaker political theory. But the Assembly had Quaker process, theory, and history on their side.

Penn's admonition did nothing to help Blackwell or curb the Assembly. The Puritan governor's tribulations with the Pennsylvania government is one of the most colorful episodes of Quaker dissent during this period. Not only did Blackwell's appointment tarnish Penn's reputation with his colonists, Blackwell himself had a miserable time trying to fulfill his appointment. By his own allowance, he was wholly unprepared to govern a colony of Quakers, admitting his "unworthiness to manage so great trust and power over a people of so different perswasions, and . . . principles from me."[84]

Little did he realize how right he was. Penn's letter to Friends informing them of the appointment only meant they were forearmed in their battle against Blackwell. They began their peaceful but vigorous resistance even before his arrival. First, they ignored his letters announcing himself. Then, upon his arrival at Penn's home north of Philadelphia, he had no one to receive him but the gardener, who "courteously intertayned" him. Once in Philadelphia as well, he

[83] Ibid.
[84] John Blackwell to Penn, January 25, 1689, *PWP*, 3: 218.

was ignored and avoided. All the Quaker politicians had mysteriously left town, and Blackwell found himself standing alone in the street in front of William Markham's house – the usual meeting place of the Council – and taunted by a large group of boys. When he finally gained admittance to the meeting room, it was deserted and dusty. But determined in his business, he "resolved [he] would publish my Commission there before [he] removed, & that if no others came [he] would call in the boys [from the street] to be witness of it." When some members of government finally did arrive, Blackwell still received no words of greeting, no offer to sit down, and, in short, no acknowledgment that he had any business at all in their colony. Instead, they chided him for accosting them with his business "in this publique and unusual manner," suggesting it would have been more appropriate to first pay them all a "friendly visit."[85]

After this introduction to the Quaker political style, Blackwell was in for more trouble. Friends blackballed him and did everything they could through-out his tenure to inhibit his attempts to reform their government; but never with the faintest threat of violence. In a very long and embittered letter to Penn, Blackwell described the tactics of Friends in office in great detail and leveled at them serious charges of corruption, deceit, evasion of duty, and malfeasance. In specific, one man seemed to lead the charge against Blackwell – Thomas Lloyd. Weighty Friend and president of the Council, Lloyd was for-merly a loyal supporter of Penn and advocate of his interests. Now, however, his main interest was in thwarting Blackwell. Blackwell wrote to Penn that Lloyd "tould me, he did not apprehend that my Commission from you gave me sufficient authority to direct the setting of the great seal to any Commissions (and yet at other times asserted he had authority to do it by his Commission as Keeper [of the seal])."[86] With this, and other manipulative tactics, Lloyd was "indeavoring to keep all your affayrs in the same posture of Laxness and confusion, whereby into his managemt most of them are reduced."[87]

In general, Friends were quite capable of effectively shutting down the gov-ernment when it served them to do so. Their adept use of bureaucratic tactics and nonattendance at government meetings "cloggs the wheels of indeavors for your Service," wrote Blackwell to Penn.[88] Moreover, from their feigned ignorance of procedure and demonstrated unwillingness to serve as provincial officials, Blackwell concluded that "the matter of Magistracy & Governmt begins to be burthensome to some friends."[89] In sum, Blackwell observed that "[t]he affayrs of your Province not only in the Generall, but most particu-lars . . . are in a most confused frame and posture." His assessment was that some of the fault lay with Penn himself, for being too pacific as a governor. "Instead of yielding obedience, in some things, there are [those] that support

[85] Ibid., 3: 218–20.
[86] Ibid., 3: 223.
[87] Ibid., 3: 231.
[88] Ibid., 3: 225.
[89] Ibid., 3: 227.

their unfriendliness towards you by the Honey of your concessions, having tasted too much of it; more indeed than their stomachs can beare."[90] In the final grim analysis, Blackwell wrote, "The truth is, I find divers not only so slothfull, but so opinionated of themselves, as, it's difficult to advise them than to do many a businesses a man's selfe."[91] Penn could not have received a stronger recommendation to return to his colony and resume his place as active governor.

The Assembly, however, was anything but disorganized. The chaotic appearance they presented to Blackwell belied the process beneath it. They responded to Blackwell's charges in a wounded tone. A petition came to Penn jointly from the Provincial Council and the Assembly, which at this point presented a united front against both Blackwell and Penn. In the petition, they pled innocently, "Wee know not that wee have givin any Just occasion of offence." On the contrary, they insisted they had been "the more Cautious & Circumspect" since his appointment. The fault was rather Blackwell's for being distrustful of them and anticipating misbehavior. "He hath rather watched {us} for Evill," they claimed, "and takes downe every word wee Say in short hand whereby to Insnare {or over awe or both} us." The Assembly eventually decided that Blackwell was an enemy of Quakerism. He was unsympathetic to the concerns and processes that characterized the Quaker government and was determined to undermine them. Thus they complained:

For want of true love to us & our Principle, he acts allmost in all things against us . . . and Renders us . . . in the most odious terms as Factious, Mutinous, Seditious, turbulent & the like For noe Just occasion given as wee know of, unlesse it be For our asserting {in moderation & Soberness} our Just rights & libertyes and appearing unanimously in Choice of our Representatives, & our Standing together as agst our knowne enimyes wth Cautiousness & watchfullnesse and our unanimous resolvednesse as men & Christians not to Suffer an Invasion upon our Charter & laws, wherein wee hope wee have discharged a good Conscience to God.[92]

According to the General Assembly, they were merely trying to be good Quaker governors, something Blackwell could not hope to understand.

And Friends were not wrong in their assessment of why Blackwell had difficulties. He confirmed it himself. In a revealing statement to Penn, Blackwell summarized the underlying reason for his conflict with the Quakers: "I meddle not with their Religeous but civill polity; though I could draw a parallel thence." Quaker religious practices and principles were the foundation of their political structure. And this phenomenon, Blackwell believed, was already apparent to Penn. "I doubt not but your piercing eye discerns it," he wrote.[93] Ultimately, Blackwell too judged the Quakers to be ungovernable. "Your people & tenents pretend to so high privileges from their charter & Laws" that they

[90] Ibid., 3: 226.
[91] Ibid., 3: 233.
[92] Provincial Council to Penn, 9th of the 2nd mo. 1689. *PWP*, 3: 238.
[93] Blackwell to Penn, 1 May 1689. *PWP*, 3: 243.

were unmanageable.[94] In his letter of resignation to Penn, he concluded that it was impossible "To govern a people who have not the principles of governmt amongst them, nor will be informed." Furthermore, nothing about Pennsylvania suited him. "Besides," he continued, "the Climate is over-hott, ... the hosts of Musqueetos are worse than of armed men," and, in a final jab at the Quakers and their pacifist – yet aggressive – principles, he finished, "the men without Armes worse than [the Musqueetos]."[95]

In another act of desperation – or resignation – Penn removed Blackwell and threw nearly the entire government into the hands of the Council. They could pass their own laws, Penn allowed ("hold so long only as I shall not declare my dissent"); choose their own deputy governor; and remember only to "avoide factions & partys, whisperings & reportings, & all animositys."[96] Penn himself was gradually being reduced to the status he had originally given the Assembly. In theory, he still retained a small amount of power. Rather than conforming to Penn's request for a deputy governor, however, in Quaker form, the deputy governorship was assumed collectively by the Council.[97] Soon Penn would be entirely aware of the ultimate goals of his brethren in office. "Doe you think," he asked, "I am not sensible that all such would if they durst or could, say, Away wth the Governor too?"[98] They were intent on governing themselves without interference from higher temporal authority.

With free rein given them, the Assembly was not at all worried about Penn and his feeble protests from across the ocean. In vain he hoped that since they could not seem to understand what it meant to bow to governmental authority on their own, they should find a model to follow. "Let the Govmt know that they are to follow the example of Maryland, and the other Provinces in reference to their submission to Authority in all cases of governmt."[99] But neither did this have any effect. Penn's Quakers proceeded to disregard him more than ever before, and shut him out almost completely from the workings of the government. About the affairs of his own province he wrote, "I am wholly in the dark."[100] He complained that he had little idea even about the laws of the colony, since he had "long writt for a book of the Laws butt no body has yet been pleased to send me one throughout the divers forms of Government & administracion."[101] He was reduced to obtaining his information about the activities of the General Assembly by word of mouth and then sending his belated objections: "I hear the Assembly [is able] to exercise the power of a Cort of Record And to debate & Contest with you upon occasion. Surely you doe not consider how great a violation this is of the Charter that it is a usurpation

[94] Ibid., 3: 244.
[95] Ibid., 3: 252–53.
[96] Penn to the Provincial Council, 12th of the 6th mo. 1689. *PWP*, 3: 253.
[97] Blackwell to Penn, May 15, 1690, *PWP*, 3: 279.
[98] Penn to the Provincial Council, 11th of the 9th mo. 1690, *PWP*, 3: 285.
[99] Instructions to Blackwell, 25th Sept. 1689, *PWP*, 3: 262, n 20.
[100] Penn to the Provincial Council, 15th of the 7th mo. 1690, *PWP*, 3: 284.
[101] Ibid., 11th of the 9th mo. 1690, *PWP*, 3: 286.

upon other parts of the government."[102] By this time, he too had begun to compare his situation as Pennsylvania's proprietor to that of the governors and proprietors of neighboring colonies. "I cannot finde," he wrote bitterly, "that either doctor cox [governor of West New Jersey] or l[or]d Baltimore [of Maryland], are so used."[103]

The General Assembly at this time was in their strongest position ever in relation to Penn. They took this opportunity to caution Penn not to believe "Misrepresentations" of their behavior and to remind him sternly about what they believed was the true role of the Assembly and the powers that it should have, and, as far as they were concerned, had always been a part of their fundamental constitution. "No thing novell hath been introduced" since the founding of the province, they argued. Not only did they outline the role of the Assembly, they made it clear that they viewed Penn's role as governor as quite circumscribed.

We insist on those priveledges which thou hast Declared to be the undoubted rights of the free borne English, which are not Cancelled by Coming hither, nor can be Lawfully Denied by thee, or abdicated and Dissolved by Us . . . Certainly the King our Soveraigne Intends not that a Subject Shall Exercise greater power over his people in a forraign plantation, then he Doth himself at home in parliaments . . . do thou take what is thine, Suffering the people to take and Enjoy what is theirs according to what thou thy Self hast published to the World.[104]

In what must have been a shock to Penn – but hardly a surprise – Friends also clearly delineated where their loyalties lay. They informed Penn in no uncertain terms that obedience to him was not their top priority. "Surely, Governr, our fidellity to thee is not native but Dative, not Universall but Locall." With this powerful assertion of their loyalty to Penn being but a gift given at their pleasure, they fell back on their Quaker identity and principles in which God and conscientious adherence to his law came before all.

The Keithian Controversy of 1690–1692 and Its Political Implications

During the first ten years of Pennsylvania government, it grew increasingly clear that there were two groups of Quakers with opposing political views, emphasizing different aspects of the Quaker understanding of government. There were those who generally followed Penn and subscribed to the model of Quaker ecclesiastical hierarchy and those who dissented from and opposed his – or anyone's – authority over them. Although these lines occasionally

---

[102] Ibid.
[103] Ibid., 15th of the 7th mo. 1690, *PWP*, 3: 284. Perhaps Penn chose a most convenient comparison and was intentionally blind to the behavior of most other colonial governments. Interestingly, according to Jack Greene, Maryland was one of the colonies whose popular Assembly made the least amount of progress toward achieving independence from the executive or proprietors. See Greene, *Negotiated Authorities*, 168–69.
[104] The Provincial Council and Assembly to Penn, 18th of the 3rd mo. 1691, *PWP*, 3: 316–18.

blurred, this remained the general dynamic during the first years of the colony. The differences between these factions, however, were more than just political. They were differences that had always been present among Friends as a religious body as well. The Keithian Controversy over theology and ecclesiastical power in 1690 marked a decisive shift in political power from the elite leaders in Pennsylvania government to the popular majority.[105]

In their first 180 years, Friends around the Atlantic world had a more or less stable agreement on the fundamentals of theology and organization of the religion with two exceptions – the Keithian Controversy and, later, the separation of the "Free Quakers" in the Revolution. Except for these, Quakers retained enough uniformity on basic principles of faith and practice to keep them together. From his experience in America during the 1770s, Crèvecœur observed, "The Quakers are the only people who retain a fondness for their own mode of worship; for, be they ever so far separated from each other, they hold a sort of communion with the society, and seldom depart from its rules, at least in this country."[106] Similarly, in 1788 Pennsylvania Friend James Bringhurst confirmed this earlier observation, writing, "I expect the practices of Friends in different places to be nearly the same in most respects."[107]

The Keithian Controversy was named for George Keith, a long-time Friend, minister, and one of the few Quakers who can rightly be called a theologian. This controversy was a complicated internal dispute fueled initially by theological challenges put forth by Keith to the leaders of the Society, but perpetuated by political discontent among Pennsylvania Friends. It was the eruption of a latent theological dispute that had been a cause of the political tensions in Pennsylvania government over the preceding ten years. Now it manifested itself in the political forum.[108]

---

[105] Without minimizing the importance of this event in Quaker history, I have chosen to use the word *controversy* rather than *schism* to describe this episode because, although a number of Friends either left voluntarily or were disowned by PYM, a separate branch of Quakerism did not arise as a result.

[106] J. Hector St. John de Crèvecœur, *Letters from an American Farmer* (New York: Oxford University Press, 1997), 50.

[107] James Bringhurst to William Almy, 12th mo. 24th day 1788, Bringhurst Papers, FHL.

[108] For a summary of the controversy, see J. William Frost's introduction to *The Keithian Controversy in Early Pennsylvania* (Norwood, PA: Norwood, 1980). Gary Nash was one of the first to argue that this controversy had a significant effect on the political climate of the colony. But he considered the motives of the historical actors to be primarily economic (Nash, *Quakers and Politics,* 144–160). According to Nash, the Keithian Controversy was essentially a political and economic struggle that expressed itself in religious terms. In an important corrective, Jon Butler put forth another claim that "it was precisely because the schism was rooted in religion that it disrupted Pennsylvania's politics" (Jon Butler, "'Gospel Order Improved': The Keithian Schism and the Exercise of Quaker Ministerial Authority in Pennsylvania," *WMQ* vol. 31, no. 3 [1974]: 431–452, 432). Nash's position has merit, but the matter cannot be understood that simply. It makes more sense to follow Butler. For an alternate, yet complementary perspective on the Controversy to the one put forth here, see Andrew Murphy, *Conscience and Community,* 187–207.

During the first decade of the province, Friends were thrown into a new situation that tested their convictions. Almost overnight they went from being despised and disenfranchised dissenters to politicians at the highest rank of government. Being forced so suddenly to act on their principles brought crucial differences among them to the fore. There had always been tensions in Quakerism between those who wanted freedom to follow divine revelation and those who wanted more structure imposed on the individual and church. It is not surprising that these two old competing strains would surface in this new and challenging environment.[109] These two conceptions of Quakerism were represented by the competing factions in the Pennsylvania government. While the Assembly practiced a popular, egalitarian Quakerism, the proprietary and members of the elite Council advocated a more hierarchical version.

The Keithian Controversy unfolded along similar lines as the Wilkinson-Story Controversy of the 1670s, but with some important digressions. Just as John Wilkinson and John Story criticized and eventually separated from Friends in England whom they believed were distorting the true spirit of Quakerism, the Keithian Controversy grew from similar threats to success of the Quaker experiment in America.[110] Both controversies grew out of concerns that some Friends had gained positions of power and were using that power to coerce the consciences of other Friends. The dissenting Friends in both situations also believed that the spiritual egalitarianism that was fundamental to Quakerism was being undermined. Interestingly, the difference between these two dissenting groups is an odd twist. Whereas Wilkinson and Story believed there was too much structure imposed on Friends and not enough Light, Keith believed there was too little structure and too much dependence on only the Light. From their respective positions, both emphasized the potential for tyranny by the other side.

The essence of Keith's concern was that some Friends – namely, supporters of the proprietary – were placing too much emphasis on the Inward Light, which caused them to deny the significance of Christ himself. Keith had an understanding of Quaker theology from the earliest days – he was present when the church government was established and the Discipline written. Early Friends, we should remember, tested their understanding of the Light against Scripture and emphasized the importance of Christ as a human being and his presence through the Holy Spirit. This understanding alone, rather than any man-made religious institution, defined the doctrine of the Inward Light. When the ecclesiastical government was established in the 1670s, it respected this understanding of the Light (though not according to Wilkinson and Story), while providing the additional guiding structure that came from a corporate community.

---

[109] In a later essay, Butler notes that criticism of elite Friends was known prior to and independently of Keith's. See "Into Pennsylvania's Spiritual Abyss: The Rise and Fall of the Later Keithians, 1693–1703," *PMHB* vol. 101 (1977), 151–70.

[110] Butler, "Gospel Order," 433.

Although some have seen Keith as hyper-intellectual and fundamentally misguided when it came to Quaker theology, it seems, rather, that Keith was more in keeping with the Quakerism of the Friends' early years than most of his contemporaries.[111] Many of the points Quakers have used to prove that Keith was out of step with Friends in general – including his intellectual approach to Quakerism, his interest in Jewish mysticism, and his familiarity with German mysticism – actually show him to have had even stronger similarities with esteemed Quaker leaders such as Fox and Barclay.[112] In fact, in Keith's brief, unpublished tract, "Gospel Order Improved," his purpose was to rekindle an understanding among Friends of the aims and standards of these early Friends, not to create some new form of Quakerism.[113]

Keith's understanding of Quakerism clearly contrasted with that of many of the elite Quaker members of the General Assembly. Some Pennsylvania Friends had moved away from what had become the orthodox Quakerism of the 1670s and had begun to insist *"That the Light is sufficient without anything else*, thereby excluding the *Man Christ Jesus without us*, and his *Death & Sufferings, Resurrection, Ascension, Mediation & Intercession for us in Heaven*, from having any part or share in our Salvation; and thereby making him only a Titular, but no real Saviour."[114] According to Keith, this was a dangerous assertion. It essentially separated the guiding principles of history, Scripture, and community from the Light and allowed the individual to interpret the Light freely to his own advantage. The result, he believed, was that some Friends in high places claimed to be able to understand the leadings of the Light through their own abilities entirely. It became very easy, then, for ministers and elders to place themselves above the body of Friends and bear rule over them by claiming a higher understanding of God's law. These ministers, he charged, "uphold and defend [the elders] in their Tyrannical Usurpation over your Consciences, as if ye were only to see with their Eyes, and hear with their Ears, and not with your own, and that ye were to take all things without all due Examination and Tryal, by implicit Faith, *Papist*-like, from them."[115] The government of the Yearly Meeting in Philadelphia, Keith charged, had become a dictatorship of sorts, rather than a unified fellowship of believers deciding their path as one. The Yearly Meeting, he wrote, was "not any true Representative of the Body [of Friends]...but a Party or Faction of people...against the Truth"[116] The problem was, as always, where authority lay.

Accordingly, Keith proposed a new organization for church government. His vision of it had more structure – a stronger, more imposing Discipline

---

[111] Ethyn Williams Kirby, *George Keith, 1636–1716* (New York: D. Appleton-Century Company, 1942).

[112] Butler, "Gospel Order," 432–33, 435.

[113] Ibid., 436.

[114] George Keith, *An Appeal from the Twenty Eight Judges to the Spirit of Truth & True Judgment in all Faithful Friends, called Quakers* (Philadelphia, 1692), 5.

[115] Ibid., 2.

[116] Ibid.

and more dependence on knowledge and interpretation of Scripture – but was fundamentally more egalitarian and designed expressly to keep individuals from claiming absolute power based on an irrefutable understanding of the Light.

Although at first Keith confined his criticisms to the religious sector, it was not long, considering how closely they were connected, for civil crimes before he extended them to the political. The fact that he was put on trial by Thomas Lloyd, his main adversary in the dispute, must have encouraged this extension.[117] In *An Appeal from the Twenty Eight Judges* (1692), Keith accused Quaker magistrates loyal to Penn of betraying their religious principles while in office. Not only, Keith charged, had tyrannical ministers threatened believers by dominating processes within the church government, but they had encroached upon the civil government in a manner most inappropriate to Friends. Much like William Penn who challenged the English government on its mixing of church and state, he asked "[w]hether there is any Example or [Precedent] for it [in] Scripture, or in all *Christendom*, that Ministers should eagress [*sic*] the Worldly Government, as they do here? which hath proved of a very evil Tendency."[118] As if this were not bad enough, church government, Keith argued, was coming to resemble the civil government – authority from the top down. The Keithian Controversy revealed that Quaker church government, as Quaker civil government, had strayed from the original balance that it had as a representative democracy and was becoming an oligarchy – or perhaps a dictatorship.

Keith was disowned by the meeting, but interestingly, it is not clear that it was because of his theological assertions. It seems, rather, that it was his "walking" that was the problem. He was warned about his deportment, but he scorned descriptions of his "rude and unchristian-like behavior."[119] He minimized such charges, attacked his opponents on doctrinal grounds, and, adding abuse onto abuse, claimed that calling them "ignorant Heathens" was not "railing or ungodly speech."[120] He accused them of prioritizing process above Truth when he said they cared more that members "come to Meetings, and use plain Language and plain Habit" than about what they believed. While dissent was vital to the Quaker meeting, Friends were as concerned with the process of dissent – how one dissented – as the ends. It may have been Keith's delivery of the message as much as the message itself that was offensive to Friends.

Thus, although Keith's remedy for the church government was rejected by London Yearly Meeting, and Keith himself was disowned, a change in civil government was on the way.[121]

---

[117] *PWP*, 3: 375, n. 6.

[118] Keith, *Appeal*, 7.

[119] Minutes from the Meeting of Ministers, March 5, 1692, in Frost, *Keithian Controversy*, 140.

[120] George Keith, *The plea of the innocent against the false judgment of the guilty* . . . (Philadelphia, 1692), 7.

[121] At this point in time, Philadelphia Yearly Meeting still generally deferred to the sense of London Yearly Meeting.

The 1696 *Frame of Government*

The largest effect of the Keithian Controversy was still a few years away. In the immediate future, great changes in the political situation in England were about to affect Pennsylvania. By 1692, after the Glorious Revolution, William and Mary were on the throne, and Penn was under suspicion of treason for his former dealings with James II. It did not help matters for Penn that Pennsylvania had gained a reputation as a disruptive, disorderly, and disobedient colony. Not only did the Pennsylvania government ignore Penn's laws and directives, it also defied the crown on a number of issues, including evading the laws in the Navigation Acts, refusing to support the crown in its war with France, and resisting to take or administer oaths.

Because of these circumstances, in 1692 William and Mary deprived Penn of his government in Pennsylvania. Once he was removed, in 1693 Pennsylvania was annexed to New York with Benjamin Fletcher, an Anglican military man, as governor of both. Fletcher's appointment was perceived as a threat by some Quakers but a boon by others. Penn's objection to Fletcher stemmed from his concern that Quakers remain autonomous from the crown and preserve their unique liberties, but other Friends – those who had been swayed by Keith's arguments – welcomed him as a reprieve from Penn and the domination of the Council.

With Fletcher's arrival in Pennsylvania, two parallel oppositional campaigns were launched, both using established methods of Quaker resistance. First, and most apparently, the Quaker elite – Penn's supporters – embarked on a program of obstruction against Fletcher.[122] As they had with Blackwell, they thwarted every attempt Fletcher made to achieve his political ends. Only this time, Penn encouraged them. Since he was denied any part in his own government by the crown, Penn reasoned that the remaining Quakers "must have the part alone . . . to [stand] upon their Patent agst the commission of the Gov. of N. York." In an interesting twist in colonial governance in general, yet in true Quaker form, Penn led the resistance against the governor, outlining the legal steps they were to take should Fletcher threaten their interests: "draw up yr exceptions descreetly & fully & Lay them before the Lords of Plantation here, & frds concerned in the Province here will appear for the Prov. & if that dont do, Westminster Hall, & if that fail, the hous of Lords will do us right."[123] Although Penn did not write a public letter, preferring to "whisper it to you by one of you," Fletcher discovered a copy of a letter with similar advice and was therefore well aware of these Quakers' stance against him.[124] According to Fletcher, they followed Penn's instructions and did "as much in theire [power] . . . to baffell my endeaviors . . . for theire Majesties service."[125]

---

[122] Nash, *Quakers and Politics*, 186.
[123] Penn to Robert Turner, 29th of the 9th mo. 1692, *PWP*, 3: 356–57.
[124] *PWP*, 3: 358, n.20, 377, n.5.
[125] Benjamin Fletcher to Secretary of State, Aug. 18, 1693, quoted in Nash, *Quakers and Politics*, 186–87.

The second oppositional campaign was the old familiar one. Members of the Assembly had dismissed Penn as a threat and they continued their resistance to him and the Council. This time, however, they had a sense of unity following the Keithian Controversy. They also saw the opportunity for an ally in their cause. Seeing a possibility of achieving otherwise-unreachable ends through Fletcher, members of the Assembly (composed at this time of Keithian Quakers and malcontented non-Quakers) had welcomed him to Philadelphia.[126] Not surprisingly then, as Fletcher went about the task of trying to govern the colony, he favored the Assembly. In this way, Penn unwittingly played into the hands of these radical Friends by instructing his supporters to resist Fletcher's rule – elite Quakers shunned the official positions Fletcher offered them, leaving Fletcher little choice but to bestow more power on the Assembly. Furthermore, Friends who were once Council members retreated, taking up positions in the Assembly, and thereby strengthening it. Fletcher all but disbanded the Provincial Council and gave the Assembly the power to make legislation. Penn, realizing his mistake, remarked on this most recent turn of events to his supporters that "the advantage the disafected [am]ong us make by [the Keithian Controversy] ag[ainst un]ity, against Frds haveing power, [against] me, & [you] in perticular are great & Lamentable... Oh! Sorrowfull Conclusion of 8 or nine years Governmt."[127]

In the summer of 1694, Penn reestablished good relations with the crown and was reinstated as proprietor of the colony. William Markham, now deputy governor, had the onerous task of trying to bring the colony back under proprietary control. He attempted to reinstate the 1683 *Frame* that Fletcher had abolished, but to no avail. By this time the Assembly was strong enough so as to be nearly unstoppable in its progress toward complete control of the government. They wrote of the 1683 *Frame* that it "is not deemed in all Respects Sutably Accomodated to our present Circumstances."[128] Instead, David Lloyd, kinsman of Thomas Lloyd and speaker of the Assembly, argued for a "new modelling" of government that officially put almost the whole government into the control of the Assembly.[129] This was the most overt challenge to Penn's authority.[130] But it was nothing new for the Assembly.[131] During the Fletcher years as the elite councilmen had joined the Assembly, they realized that their best chance for provincial autonomy from royal or proprietary control was a strong lower house.[132] They accordingly took steps to secure their new-found strength.

---

[126] See *The Address of some of the Peaceable and Well Affected Freeholders and Inhabitants of the Town and County of Philadelphia* (Philadelphia, 1693).

[127] Penn to Friends in Pennsylvania, 11th of the 10th mo. 1693, *PWP*, 3: 383.

[128] 1696 Frame of Government, *PWP*, 3: 458.

[129] See Norris Papers, Family Letters, I, 122. HSP.

[130] *PWP*, 3:456.

[131] See Nash, *Quakers and Politics*. He argues that it was "strikingly different" than other challenges (200).

[132] Ibid., 201.

The 1696 *Frame*, while retaining some of the provisions from the 1683 *Frame*, made changes in Pennsylvania's power structure. The most notable of these was that the Assembly could now make laws. The new *Frame* decreed that "the Representatives of the Freemen when mett in Assembly Shall have power to prepare and propose to the Governour and Council all such Bills as the Majour part of them shall at any time see needful to be past into Lawes." The role left to the governor and Council was "recommending to the Assembly all such Bills as they shall think fitt to be past into Lawes." But the Assembly will only meet and confer with the Council on these matters "when desired" by the Assembly.[133] The popular Assembly finally had in its grasp the power and liberty it had been struggling for since the founding of the province – almost. It was still not official.

Meanwhile, Penn, distracted by deaths in his family, embattled by politics in England, and fully aware of the fruitlessness of asserting his will – or his version of God's will – in Pennsylvania, did not do anything actively to resist this new move. Though he did not reject the 1696 *Frame* outright, neither did he sanction it. His only existing reference to it on record is vague. In a letter to some leading Friends in office, he reasserted somewhat feebly that making a charter was his "own peculier prerogative, devolved thereby from the Crown upon" him in order to keep provincial laws "as neer as may be to those in Eng[land]." The only concern he made plain was that Pennsylvania's laws were "too remote from wt other Colonys are in their Constitution[s]" and that this might "furnish our enimys wth a weapon to wound us."[134] Quaker governance was dangerous and unbalanced according to those of a Whiggish bent. Finally, the 1696 *Frame* was instituted when Friends compelled Markham to accept it by threatening to withhold funds to aid in the defense of New York – a directive from the crown – if he did not. They did this by claiming that, because the 1683 *Frame* was invalid, they were not properly constituted as a body and needed to be reconstituted to vote to give funds for New York.[135] Markham refused their conditions and neither passed the new constitution nor delivered funds to New York.

The late 1690s in Pennsylvania government were by no means quiet or harmonious. The same struggles for power among Friends continued and were complicated by an influx of non-Quakers into the province, many of whom sided with the "radical" faction of Friends. Increasingly, in these years as the Assembly wrangled for its prerogatives, one man was coming to the fore as its leader – David Lloyd. Lloyd came to Pennsylvania in 1687 from Wales as Penn's trusted attorney general. In his forty-four-year career in Pennsylvania government, he was the most important and certainly most controversial political figure.[136] In 1691 he became convinced of Quakerism, and would later

---

[133] 1696 Frame of Government, *PWP*, 3: 462.
[134] William Penn to Samuel Carpenter and Others, 1st of the 10th mo. 1697, *PWP*, 3: 531.
[135] *LL*, 1: 528–29.
[136] Ibid., 1: 490. See also Roy N. Lokken, *David Lloyd: Colonial Lawmaker* (Seattle: University of Washington Press, 1959); H. Frank Eshleman, *The Constructive Genius of David Lloyd in*

be described by some as a "rigid Quaker."[137] During the early years of the province as he was still defining his political character, he played a crucial role in government by supporting the Assembly in their bids for power and actively aiding them by, among other things, writing the 1696 *Frame of Government*. At this point in time, however, his biographers believe he "had shown little indication of opposition to the proprietor or to the Quaker leadership."[138] Penn himself described Lloyd in glowing terms as "an honest man & the Ablest Lawyer in that province, & a zealous Man for the Government."[139]

Lloyd's knowledge and skill as a lawyer both helped and hurt his advancement in the province. It caused him to rise to great heights in the Pennsylvania government. By virtue of being one of the few Quaker lawyers, and having an aptitude for law and tenacious personality, Lloyd had made himself indispensable to the colonial legislative process. But this zeal and success also attracted the notice of the English government in unfavorable ways. In disputes with the crown over the regulation of trade, Lloyd championed colonists' rights and won great popularity among them. But he angered the Board of Trade, which became intent not just on enforcing the law, but on removing Lloyd from the scene. Penn found himself in an awkward position between the authority of the crown and the rights and interests of his colonists as represented by Lloyd. In 1699 the Board of Trade demanded that Penn remove him "not only from the Place of Attorney General . . . but from all other publick Imployments whatsoever."[140]

Whether or not Penn could have prevented Lloyd's removal is debatable. What can hardly be disputed, however, is that he executed the removal with very little tact, and furthermore, appeared to betray Lloyd in his attempt to appease the Board. Not only did he remove Lloyd from all his appointed offices, but in an un-Quakerly motion, he proceeded to prosecute him, making no allowances for Lloyd to defend himself. Adding insult to injury, Penn then removed Lloyd from his position on the Provincial Council and delegated the job of informing him to Lloyd's father-in-law.[141] Among the many unwise moves Penn made as proprietor, his treatment of David Lloyd in particular would shape the future of the colony in ways he did not intend. What Penn failed to consider was that, although he could officially strip Lloyd of his titles, Lloyd's qualification as the most able legal mind in the province guaranteed him a role in the government and a hand in the creation of future legislation.

Early Colonial Pennsylvania Legislation and Jurisprudence, 1686–1731 (Philadelphia: Pennsylvania Bar Association, 1910); Burton Alva Konkle, "David Lloyd, Penn's Great Lawmaker," *Pennsylvania History* vol. 4, no. 3 (1937), 153–56.

[137] *LL*, 1: 492.
[138] Ibid.
[139] William Penn to the House of Lords, 1 March 1697, *PWP*, 3: 486.
[140] The Board of Trade to Penn, *PWP*, 3: 577.
[141] *LL*, 1: 1: 493.

The 1701 Charter of Privileges

By 1701, the political events had conspired to create a very precarious situation for Penn. His neglect of the colony, the appointment of foreign governors, the Keithian Controversy, and his mistreatment of the foremost legal figure in the province all contributed to his loss of control of the government. Meanwhile, since the founding of the colony, Quakers had been practicing self-government, angling for ever-greater popular power, and exercising their unique process of dissent and reform. This was the situation in Pennsylvania on the eve of the creation of the Charter of Privileges, the Quakers' sacred institution that would be the foundation of the colony for the next seventy-five years.

In 1699, after a fifteen-year absence, Penn returned to America. He planned to spend several years restoring order to the colony and faith in his leadership. But even if the developments of the last decades had not already converged to make his job nearly impossible, new circumstances arising in England did. The English government had begun aggressive action to take colonies away from proprietors. The Reunification Bill, which was intended not to void the colonial charters (as some Anglicans had wanted) but simply to remove all rights of a proprietary governor, was introduced to the House of Lords in 1701. The Quaker legal advocacy group in England, the Meeting for Sufferings, lobbied against it and informed Penn of the danger.[142] Although Penn had planned on remaining in the colony for some time, he realized soon after his arrival that he would need to sail for England as soon as possible. His concern was to preserve his Quaker colony and the privileges to which the inhabitants had become accustomed, most importantly, liberty of conscience. Penn wrote: "Can it enter the head of any man of Common Sence knowing any thing of America that wee came hither to be under a Kings Governour that is Mercenary[?]...are wee come 3000 Miles into a Desart of only wild people as well as wild Beasts...to have only the same priviledges wee had at home?"[143]

Penn saw this move by the English government as a direct, deliberate, and specific attack on the colonies of religious dissenters in America. "The Design," he explained, "seems to Lye against Proprietary Govmts upon the foot of Dissent in Religion." He argued, "[f]or Except for Carolina they were all granted to Non Conformists and then the meaning is that no Dissenters Even in a Wilderness at 3000 Miles Distance & at the other End of the world shall Enjoy the powers first granted them for their Incouragement & Security in their Hasardous & most Expensive Enterprises." Furthermore, he believed that if other dissenters in America, especially the Baptists and Independent Presbyterians suspected this, they would unite and "make a bold Appearance & stand both within doors & without agst the progress of such a Bill."[144]

---

[142] *PWP*, 4: 64.
[143] Penn to Charlwood Lawton, 18th of the 6th mo. 1701, *PWP*, 4:67.
[144] Ibid., 4: 73.

In Pennsylvania the matter seemed dire. The threat from England necessitated more stability in the colony than had ever existed and, most importantly, a legitimate, functional constitution. By 1699 the colony had been without an approved, written constitution for seven years since the 1683 *Frame* was discarded and not replaced with any that satisfied Penn. If Penn would have a chance of securing the colony's political privileges against the crown, a new charter would have to be drawn up in the two months before he left for England. Penn was then caught in a difficult position. He had come with the aim of restoring his authority in the province, but since 1693 the Assembly had had virtual control over the colony. Friends had gotten a taste of sovereignty and were not about to relinquish it.

In relation to his colonists, where William Penn found himself in 1701 was exactly the position in which George Fox found himself a few decades earlier during the Wilkinson-Story Controversy – distrusted and resisted by Friends intent on not being oppressed. In the first twenty years of Pennsylvania government, Penn had attempted to realize his vision for the province, with himself as its leader. From the beginning, the question of where authority lay for Penn was clear. He had put the power to make laws and regulations in the hands of an elite few and expected the people to disregard their God-given powers of legal discernment and simply obey. Perhaps he should have known better than to think a colony of Quakers would be so easily led. These people had contested this kind of "top-down" delegation of power in their religious lives, and it surely would not be tolerated in any holy political experiment. In the eyes of his co-religionists, Penn had ceased to be a revered leader, and instead took the shape of a tyrannical ruler. That he too was a Quaker mattered less than that he was the one who wielded authority over them. Authority by any human was to be questioned, and weighed against the authority of God within.

With his authority threatened both from above by the English government and from below by his colonists, Penn did not have much time before he left Pennsylvania to work out a plan that would balance his rights, interests, and authority as the proprietor with those of his colonists, and at the same time preserve the rights of the Quaker colony in the face of a royal threat. Just over a year earlier, he had recognized that "Tho' this be a Colonie of 19 years standing . . . we have yet much to do to establish its constitution . . . there are in it Some Laws obsolete others hurtfull, others imperfect that will need Improvement & it will be requisite to make some new ones . . . If . . . there be anie thing that jars, alter itt."[145] Now his decision was to give the job to the lesser of his adversaries – his brethren in the Assembly. In a hurried address to the General Assembly, Penn gave them carte blanche to write up whatever sort of charter they liked. He told them to draft "some suitable expedient and Provision for your safety, as well in your Privileges as Property, and you will

---

[145] William Penn, "Speech to the Provincial Council," April 1, 1700, *PWP*, 3: 590–91.

find me ready to Comply with whatsoever may render us happy, by a nearer Union of our Interest."[146] But those who had the future of Pennsylvania in their hands were hardly concerned with Penn's interests. They took him at his word and, given this golden opportunity, they made the most it.

At this moment, all the factors of Pennsylvania's short history converged – the colonists' discontent, their suspicion of authority, the religious differences among Friends, and Penn's mishandling of David Lloyd's dismissal. With the dissatisfied Keithians behind him, as well as most other Friends in office, Lloyd drafted a charter that was radically different from Penn's last constitution, the 1683 *Frame*, and even more favorable to the Assembly than the 1696 *Frame*. This new charter codified the powers they had been exercising and the arrangements they had established in recent years. In addition to securing religious liberty in Pennsylvania once and for all, it abolished the Provincial Council altogether as part of the legislative process, relegating it to being merely an advisory body to the governor, and granted power to the Assembly, with gubernatorial ascent, to make laws. Although there were still those loyal to Penn in government at this time who might have looked out for his interests, these Friends, like Penn, were concerned about the possibility of falling under royal government and losing their liberty of conscience. The legacy of Fletcher's governorship and the current tense situation between proprietors and the crown convinced them to go along with Lloyd and the "radical" faction in pushing for this new charter. The Lloydians were mainly interested in a government that would be out of Penn's control. As James Logan, Penn's loyal secretary characterized it, "David [Lloyd] professes so much zeal for the public good that . . . he has gained too great ascendant over the honest country members to let thy interest be considered as it ought."[147]

Very soon it became apparent to Penn that he had made himself extremely vulnerable. As the Charter was being drawn up, Penn caught wind of rumors about "wht D[avid] L[loyd] has declared as to my powrs in proprietary matters, by wch I perceive tis publick." On this point, he instructed James Logan to "let [Lloyd] know my minde (occasionally) . . . while he is [on the] draught of that scheam."[148] Further, he hoped Logan would "Ply David Lloyd discreetly; dispose him to a proprietary plan, and the privileges requisite for the people's and Friends' security."[149] But Logan must have had a more realistic sense of the situation. He explained to Penn that the Provincial Council was helpless to protect Penn's interests "for they are looked upon as ill here as the Court party [in England]."[150]

---

[146] *Minutes of the Provincial Council of the Province of Pennsylvania from the Organization to the Termination of the Proprietary Government*, vols. 1–4 (Philadelphia: Jo. Severn, 1852), 2: 35.

[147] Logan to Penn, 28th of the 7th mo. 1704, *Penn-Logan Corresp.*, 1: 316.

[148] Penn to Logan, 8 Sept. 1701, *PWP*, 4: 88.

[149] Ibid., 6th of the 7th mo. 1701, *Penn-Logan Corresp.*, 1: 52.

[150] Logan to Penn, 3rd of the 8th mo. 1704, *Penn-Logan Corresp.*, 1: 321.

Lloyd's biographers believe that it is difficult to know his deepest motives for how and why he drafted the Charter as he did.[151] Penn's supporters believed that Lloyd was driven by a deep-seated grudge against Penn for the rough treatment he had received a few years earlier.[152] While it seems this was certainly a factor considering the vehement and calculated opposition Penn met from Lloyd since his dismissal, it should not be forgotten that Lloyd had a history of writing radical legislation that furthered popular rights. Although the grudge he bore toward Penn may have focused his efforts, it cannot be considered his only motive for leading the movement for popular government.

Regardless of Lloyd's motives, Penn had been manipulated into acquiescence to the Assembly's will. Under pressure from all sides, Penn grudgingly signed the Charter into law – a decision he and his closest advisors would soon regret. In what can only be called a peaceful coup d'etat, these dissenters among Friends wrested all legislative prerogative away from the Provincial Council and placed it squarely – and legally – in the hands of the popular Assembly. To do this, they employed the same peaceful process that their brethren in England had been using to resist unjust rulers and their laws. They did not overthrow the government Penn had founded, they merely reorganized it; likewise, they did not remove Penn, they simply made him irrelevant. And neither, as in most other colonies, did these dissenters ever take up arms against their government. At the moment the Charter was put in place, it became not just one of the most significant examples of Quaker political ideals and process but also a vehicle for promoting them until the American Revolution. Shortly after his return to England, Penn wrote to James Logan, "I wish now I had never past it . . . when my hasty goeing for wt obliged yt motion was unforeseen, when those Laws & yt c[h]arter received their sanction from me."[153] He complained to his confidant, "Let these ungrateful men see what I suffer for them . . . they may meet with their match after a while that they have so basely treated me – unworthy spirits!"[154] At this point, the table had been fully turned, and now William Penn and his ally against the radicals in the Assembly, Isaac Norris, Sr., lamented that they were "Dissenters in our own country."[155] But of course, all Friends might have described themselves thus.

Although hardly what Penn had in mind for his Quaker political experiment, the polity that this charter constituted was more Quakerly than anything he could have achieved by his own design. The distinctive character of Pennsylvania politics that would define the colony depended on two clauses in the Charter, only one of which Penn had intended – liberty of conscience and popular control of the legislative process. Aside from the implications these things

---

[151] *LL*, 1: 494. Although authorship of the charter has not been established definitively, it seems clear that Lloyd had a great part in writing it. In 1704, Logan informed Penn that "bills are all drawn by David Lloyd," 28th of the 7th mo., *Penn-Logan Corresp.*, 1: 316.

[152] Ibid.

[153] Penn to Logan, "Notes and Queries," *PMHB*, vol. 7 (1883), 228–36.

[154] Penn to Logan, 21st of the 4th mo. 1702, *Penn-Logan Corresp.*, 1: 111.

[155] Isaac Norris to Penn, 23rd of the 9th mo. 1710, *Penn-Logan Corresp.*, 2: 431.

might have had for later constitutional thought, they were immensely important for the immediate purposes of the Quaker government. The first clause
allowed inhabitants of the colony to be Quakers; the second allowed them to
act like Quakers in political office. The Charter, in other words, allowed political legitimacy to be defined in good measure by Quaker faith and practice. It
redefined the very government itself. There would be no top-down imposition
of authority from remote rulers; legislation would evolve from the sense of the
Assembly, not the dictates of a governor or proprietor; each individual would
be allowed to follow instead the leadings of his conscience in matters of religion and politics; and peace, not war, would be pursued as a matter of policy.
Beyond strictly governmental activities, the Charter also allowed Friends to
determine to a great degree the civil law, social policies, and civic culture of
the province according to their theology and thereby minimize the influence
of other non-Quaker groups and regulate individual behavior in the polity.
Friends in office were able to establish a political culture that was, according
to their opponents, *Quakerized.*[156]

Conclusion

The Charter was not fully "settled" for another twenty-five years. The factions
that had existed before it was implemented, led by Lloyd and Logan, revived
after 1701 and struggled over whose interpretation of the Charter would prevail. David Lloyd wrote to Penn that "I hold my self Obliged in Conscience"
to defend his views on the Charter.[157] But by 1728, the Lloydian faction
had finally adopted a more moderate tone and preached Quaker process and
unity to their opponents in their disputes. They argued that "all the proper
means for a Reconciliation were used by Us, and rejected by our Brethren
with Contempt," and that "the Supporters of this Difference never intended
to redress our Grievances, by desiring Us to joyn them; but wanted our Con-
currence, only to reinstate themselves in a Capacity of Acting." The Lloydians
finally "appealed to our Brethren" and proved that "[w]e are not singular in
Our interpretation of the Law."[158] The interpretation of this constitution was
finally set.

The Charter of Privileges was a unique document in colonial American government. It was not exceptional simply because it created the only major colonial government with a unicameral legislature, thus granting more power to its
popular representatives than any other colonial charter; nor was it extraordinary merely because it was the only colonial constitution with clauses guaranteeing religious liberty and constitutional amendment; nor was it remarkable
only for its longevity – lasting seventy-five years intact as the constitution
of Pennsylvania. It was also unique because it was a quintessentially Quaker

[156] Jones, *The Quakers in the American Colonies*, 287.
[157] David Lloyd to Penn, 19th of the 5th mo. 1705, *PWP* 4: 373.
[158] David Lloyd, *Defence of the Legislative Constitution*, 7.

achievement. What makes the 1701 Charter a Quaker constitution – and distinguishes it from other colonial constitutions – is that it grew out of an established process of peaceful dissent and resistance within the Society of Friends. The process by which it came into being, how it was used once in place, and what its advocates achieved for the province made manifest the internal procedures, experiences, and theology of the Society of Friends in the seventeenth and eighteenth centuries. The 1701 Charter was the culmination of a twenty-year period of constitutional turmoil, and an even longer period of practiced resistance to authority by members of the Society of Friends. In pushing for a constitution that effectively placed power in the hands of the people and alienated their leader, Quakers were repeating a pattern of behavior learned and practiced in the earliest years of their existence in England.

This constitutional moment prepared and enabled Quakers to create a truly Quaker colony. Over the next seventy-five years, they expand their process and principles with remarkable success to the entire province. How one defines success, is, of course, relative.

4

Civil Unity and "Seeds of Dissention" in the Golden Age of Quaker Theocracy

Quakers in Pennsylvania spent their first forty years from the 1680s to the 1720s struggling among themselves to realize the ideal structure of a Quaker civil government. As in the establishment of their ecclesiastical polity, there were competing visions for how it should function. And as always, Friends were attempting to determine the extent of popular participation and where the locus of authority should be – in the hands of the people themselves or with their spiritually and politically elite representatives. The dispute within the civil government, as we have seen, resolved itself in favor of the popular branch. The Assembly united against Penn and his agents, considering them an oppressive force, and effectively wrote them out of the constitution as lawmakers.

Until this point, we have considered the difficulties of applying Quaker theologico-political theory at the highest levels of government. But Friends did not confine themselves to shaping merely the government, narrowly construed. They were naturally concerned with the entire polity, which was increasingly non-Quaker. The question now at hand is: What does a political theory that mixes unity and dissent that was originated by a group on the fringes of political power look like when it is subsequently established as the basis of a political system – when the group moves from challenging the state to controlling the state? The short answer seems contradictory: It was at once coercive and antiauthoritarian. While their theory maintained the delicate balance between anarchy and tyranny, dissent and conformity, working it out in practice was more difficult.[1]

---

[1] This chapter might well be paired with Richard R. Beeman's Chapter 8, "The Paradox of Popular and Oligarchic Behavior in Colonial Pennsylvania," in *The Varieties of Political Experience in Eighteenth-Century America* (Philadelphia: University of Pennsylvania Press, 2005), 204–42. The argument here accords with Beeman's in identifying a "paradox" of Quaker Pennsylvania. But this discussion is cast and elucidated differently. Beeman takes a more technical approach in examining the dual oligarchic and popular political culture by dealing with such issues as elections and governmental structures, whereas the present argument focuses on explaining how

Now, as they controlled their own civil government, we must consider Quaker theologico-political behavior from two perspectives – first in the relation of Friends to the inhabitants of Pennsylvania and, second, in their relationship to the political authorities above them, the proprietary and the crown. In the first instance, in question are the policies, regulatory laws, and practices that Friends implemented to create Quakerly unity in the colony.[2] In the second, the discussion will treat how Quakers modeled their own behavior for their constituents in their relationship with the proprietors of the colony. Friends attempted to create Pennsylvania as a larger version of their own ecclesiastical polity, governed by the same bureaucratic-libertine process. Because the major events of Pennsylvania history have been treated in detail elsewhere, this discussion will paint with broad strokes and touch on a few familiar and some lesser known events in Pennsylvania history that exemplify the Quaker culture and the tension in the different aspects of their theory and practice. The discussion will turn on their public policy, both formal and informal.

Alan Tully has examined well the phenomenon of Quaker political culture in Pennsylvania. He argues in *Forming American Politics* that Friends developed a political language and unique culture all their own, which he calls "civil Quakerism." He defines the components of civil Quakerism as "a deep appreciation of Pennsylvania's unique constitution, liberty of conscience, provincial prosperity, loosely defined pacifism, rejection of a militia, and resistance to the arbitrary powers of proprietors." "Friends," he writes, "developed civil Quakerism into a unique language of politics – a provincial dialect as it were."[3] My argument follows his – that Quakers actively disseminated this culture beyond the bounds of their immediate Society and compelled conformity to it. But I take the discussion a bit further and in a different direction in this and the next chapters to explore some further implications of this missionizing for Pennsylvanian and American politics.

More than simply describing the Quakers' behavior and efforts at governing, this chapter will also deal with the response of non-Quaker observers of their government and religion.[4] Because, as we have seen, one of the Quakers' goals was convincing people of the Truth of Quakerism, their public image was crucial. As the Society coalesced in the mid-seventeenth century and developed into the early eighteenth, public opinion about Friends was predominantly

---

Quaker theology was expressed and received to create simultaneous, and ultimately, conflicting cultures of unity and dissent.

[2] A work that deals extensively with this topic is Jack D. Marietta and G. S. Rowe, *A Troubled Experiment: Crime and Justice in Pennsylvania, 1682–1800* (Philadelphia: University of Pennsylvania Press, 2006). A discussion of the principles of ecclesiastical unity and decision making translated into Pennsylvania political culture is in Herman Wellenreuther, "The Quest for Harmony in a Turbulent World: The Principle of 'Love and Unity' in Colonial Pennsylvania Politics," *PMHB* vol. 108 (1983), 537–76.

[3] Tully, *Forming American Politics*, 258.

[4] See also Rebecca Larson, "From 'Witches' to 'Celebrated Preachers': The Non-Quaker Response to the Women Ministers," in *Daughters of Light*, 232–95.

negative. Quaker detractors recognized the dualism in Quaker thought and action and demanded that members of the Society explain it. Robert Barclay wrote his treatise on church government in part to answer those "that accuse [Quakers] of Disorder and Confusion on the one hand, and from such as Calumniate them with Tyranny and Imposition on the other."[5] By the mid-eighteenth century, this dualism remained, but now, because of changes in Quakerism and the world around them, opinion was polarized. Their governing style and policy continued to evoke similar harsh criticisms, but, as the transatlantic intellectual climate evolved into the Enlightenment, a new and extremely positive view emerged based on many of the exact same practices that continued to elicit condemnation. As we shall see, Quakers were a polarizing force in proportion to the degree of influence they exercised over Pennsylvania civil society. And the more extreme the views, the more difficult it is to tell whether observers were commenting on reality or a "mirage."[6] It was likely both when they noted – and exaggerated – those defining and seemingly contradictory features of theologico-political Quakerism – unity and tyranny, dissent and anarchy, and the distinctive testimonies that continued to provoke animosity, and now also admiration. Either way, Quakerism was a force that demanded recognition and, for the inhabitants of Pennsylvania, adaptation.

Quakers as Political Elders

Despite the struggle among Friends to decide the locus of power among themselves, there was no question in their minds about the role they would play in relation to the general population, which was growing quickly to make Quakers the minority in their own colony.[7] An observer of Quakers and their experiment in Pennsylvania found that "the change of *the Climate* [from England to America], has in no wise changed the *Spirit of Quakerism*."[8] Insofar as they considered the civil polity to be the ecclesiastical polity writ large, the goal for Pennsylvania was the same as the goal of any Quaker meeting – to achieve a perfectly united godly society. Accordingly, Quakers, as the most spiritually weighty in the province, were the appropriate leaders. As Tully put it, "Quaker legislators accumulated [power] to prevent its abuse."[9] Thus

---

[5] Barclay, *Anarchy*, title page.
[6] Durand Echeverria, *Mirage in the West: A History of the French View of American Society to 1815* (Princeton, NJ: Princeton University Press, 1968).
[7] The massive influx of immigrants was the cause of the Quakers' minority. See Sally Schwartz, *"A Mixed Multitude"*; Tully, *Forming American Politics*, 257. By contrast, according to *LL*, the majority of the Assembly was clearly Quaker from the founding at least until 1756 (1: 801–06; 2: 1123–27). By 1750, Quakers were the third largest religious body in the colonies, exceeded only by Anglicans and Congregationalists for number of churches. See Edwin Scott Gaustad, *Historical Atlas of Religion in America* (New York: Harper and Row, 1962), 21–25, 92–96, 167, 169.
[8] Edward Cockson, *Rigid Quaker, Cruel Persecutor* (London, 1705), 36.
[9] Tully, *Forming American Politics*, 339.

although all freemen in Pennsylvania had a vote, only a few had divine competence to rule.[10] In the civil polity, as in the ecclesiastical, they believed that "[God] hath laid Care upon some beyond others, *who watch for Souls of their Brethren, as they, that must give Account.*"[11] The Quaker Assembly cast itself in relation to the populace the way the elite Provincial Council had to the Assembly, before the Assembly nullified it – as elders: They were collectively "Brethren and Representatives of one body, only with {this} Difference that wee may very well have the Elder Brothers place."[12] And their role was clear: In 1658 Edward Burrough explained that lawmakers should behave so that "the people may receive examples of righteousness, and holy and lawfull walking from their Conversations."[13] They must not act "contrary to the light in [their] own conscience[s]."[14] In 1687 Penn attempted to actualize this ideal when he wrote to the Assembly, "lett the People Learn by your *example* as well as by your *powr* the happy life of Concord."[15] As elders and ministers to the polity, the Assembly thus had direction from Penn to use both persuasion ("example") and coercion ("powr") for the development and security of the colony.

As discussed in Chapter 1, one of the prevailing concerns that shaped Quaker behavior in the seventeenth century and that they carried to Pennsylvania was the missionizing spirit. The Quaker impulse to reform and regulate the society according to their religious principles was as old as Quakerism itself. But missionizing took on a new form in Pennsylvania, in keeping with the Quakers' different worldly status as political insiders. It was no longer a "grassroots" effort; it was institutionalized. Therefore, although not as apparent in the usual ways, missionizing certainly was not gone. It had, on the contrary, become so blatant that historians have not recognized it as such. Indeed, the Quaker government was the largest missionizing effort in American history.[16] Similar to the Puritan Massachusetts "city on a hill" mission, the Quakers came to America for a religious purpose – to found a Christian colony and, more specifically, a *Quaker* colony. Unlike the Puritan experiment, however, Quakers sought

---

[10] On the matter of voting, Quakers displayed the same penchant for encouraging individual leadings and transparency through documentation as they did in other aspects of their religious and political processes. Beeman explains that "the most notable feature of Pennsylvania election laws . . . was the provision for written ballots" (209). Having the ballots in writing gave voters a chance to reflect on their choices and "an opportunity to exercise political judgments free from outside pressure" (ibid.).

[11] Barclay, *Anarchy*, 9.

[12] William Markham to William Penn, 21 July 1688, *PWP*, 3:196.

[13] Edward Burrough, *A Message for Instruction to all the Rulers, Judges, and Magistrates . . .* (1658), 1.

[14] Ibid., 2.

[15] Penn to the Commissioners of State, Feb. 1, 1687, *PWP*, 3: 145. Emphasis added.

[16] Not only was Pennsylvania the largest colony, its efforts may have been significantly scaled back from the Quakers' original plans. According to John Pomfret, initially Pennsylvania was merely part of a "grand strategy" by Friends to control a significant portion of America, from New York to Maryland and west to the Ohio River. See John E. Pomfret, "The Proprietors of the Province of West New Jersey, 1674–1702," *PMHB* vol. 75 (1951), 117–46.

not to expel those who disagreed with them but rather to embrace and absorb them. Moreover, they came not with an eye cast back to England with the intent to reform a corrupt church, but rather on the future of their own province and beyond.[17] Compared to the Puritan endeavor, Quakers were more persistent and energetic proselytizers. Their initial object was not simply to achieve conformity in action, but in conviction as well. Such an object was enabled by the fact that they believed in universal salvation and human perfection, which made many more people eligible to be Quakers than otherwise. Moreover, their goals for convincing the world of Quakerism had changed since the seventeenth century. They always believed that the Light was universally accessible, and now, regardless of an individual's profession, they believed he could find the Light within without necessarily being a member of the Society of Friends. Now they were less concerned that people *be* Quakers, as long as they *acted* like Quakers. In other words, Friends believed that it was how one moved in the world rather than the name of one's sect that mattered. One disapproving Frenchman claimed that "[t]his is their secret for one day becoming the masters of the world."[18]

One of the biggest misconceptions of Pennsylvania in our day is that it was a bastion of separation of church and state and unfettered religious liberty. It was, rather, in spite of the fact there was no officially established church, a powerful theocracy.[19] While Puritan Massachusetts is usually what comes to mind when we think of an early America theocracy, in that colony, in some ways, there was a more distinct separation of church and state than in Pennsylvania. Puritan leaders were clear that the religious ministers should not also be political ministers.[20] Most Quaker politicians, on the other hand,

---

[17] Perry Miller, "Errand into the Wilderness," in *Errand into the Wilderness* (Cambridge, MA: Belknap Press, Harvard University, 1956), 1–15. On Penn's "peaceable imperialism" in the New World, see Fred Anderson and Andrew Cayton, *Dominion of War: Empire and Liberty in North America, 1500–2000* (New York: Viking, 2005), 54–103.

[18] Gabriel Naudé, *Histoire abrégée de la naissance et du progrès du Kouakerisme avec celle ses dogmas* (1692) quoted in Edith Philips, *The Good Quaker in French Legend* (Philadelphia: University of Pennsylvania Press, 1932), 29.

[19] Tully argues that there was no separation of church and state. He finds, however, that there was less coercion than is suggested in the following argument (*Forming American Politics*, 115–16). Some historians who have claimed that there was separation of church and state in Pennsylvania are Sally Schwartz, "A Mixed Multitude," 8, 22; John M. Murrin, "Religion and Politics from the First Settlements to the Civil War," in Mark A. Noll, ed., *Religion and American Politics: From the Colonial Period to the 1980s* (New York: Oxford University Press, 1990), 19–43. 33; J. William Frost, *A Perfect Freedom*, passim. Another favorite claim of these and many other studies is that Pennsylvania is a "microcosm of the story of religion in America" (Robert T. Handy, "The Contribution of Pennsylvania to the Rise of Religious Liberty in America," in E. Otto Reimherr, ed., *Quest for Freedom: Aspects of Pennsylvania's Religious Experience* [Selinsgrove: Susquehanna University, 1987], 19–37, 20). The argument here agrees more with Glenn T. Miller who speaks of the "informal establishment" in *Religious Liberty in America: History and Prospects* (Philadelphia: Westminster Press, 1976), 52.

[20] Perry Miller, "The Puritan State and Puritan Society," in *Errand into the Wilderness* (Cambridge, MA; Belknap Press, Harvard University, 1956), 148–52, 150; Morgan, *The Puritan Dilemma*, 95–96.

assumed that there would be a tight, instrumental connection between the governing structure of the meeting and that of the colony. It was the only major colony in which the same people who held the leading positions in the ecclesiastical polity also held the highest posts in the civil polity.[21] The government was essentially run by the meeting, with a built-in hierarchical structure of monthly, quarterly, and yearly meetings to allow the theologico-political leaders to percolate to the top. Throughout most of the eighteenth century, Quaker candidates for the Assembly were selected by the religious meeting.[22] As the century progressed, the influence of the meeting on the political process became more blatant, causing one critic to remark that "the yearly and monthly Meetings of leading *Quakers* in this Province are not entirely for *spiritual* Purposes; but that they are degenerated into political Cabals, held the Week before our annual Election, to fix the Choice of Assembly-men, and issue out their *Edicts* to the several Meetings in the Province."[23] Indeed, in 1710, Philadelphia Yearly Meeting, the central Quaker governing structure in the colonies, issued an epistle directing members to vote only for other Quakers.[24]

William Penn was in the minority when he disagreed with the mixing of church and state. Early in Pennsylvania's history, he expressed concern at this trend of Quaker domination of the government. "We should look selfish," he said, "& do that, wch we have cry'd out upon others for, namely, letting no body touch wth Governmt but those of their own way."[25] The extent of Friends' domination of the government can be ascertained from concerns expressed by non-Quakers very early in the experiment. "There are grudges in some," wrote a devotee of Penn's, "that none are put in places of power but friends."[26] Almost seventy years later a non-Friend complained that still "a great Majority of one particular Persuasion, who are scarce a Fifth of the People of this Province, and by their religious Principles unqualified for Government, are kept in the Assembly, by the influence of the aforesaid *Cabal*, to the exclusion of Men of superior Property and Qualifications."[27] These people worried about "confusion and sad events" that might ensue if the proper "bounds and limits of Ch[urch] and state" were not observed.[28] Writing to William Penn in 1710, Isaac Norris, Sr., summarized the dilemma of Quakers in government:

We are a mixed people, who all claim a right to use their own way. We say our principles are not destructive or repugnant to Civil Government, and will admit of free liberty of

---

[21] Rhode Island and New Jersey, also governed by Quakers, had similar overlap between ministers and magistrates.
[22] On the meeting structure and its relationship to the government, see *LL*, 2: 24.
[23] William Smith, *A Brief View of the Conduct of Pennsylvania* (Philadelphia, 1755), 21.
[24] Ibid., 23–24.
[25] William Penn to Jasper Blatt, February 5, 1683, *PWP*, 2: 347.
[26] Holme to Penn, 25th of the 9th mo. 1686. *PWP*, 3: 131.
[27] Smith, *A Brief View of the Conduct of Pennsylvania*, 19.
[28] Holme to Penn, 25th of the 9th mo. 1686, *PWP*, 3: 131.

conscience to all; yet to me it appears . . . we must be either independent or entirely by ourselves; or, if mixed, partial to our own opinion, and not allow liberty to others.[29]

But most Quakers did not see this dilemma. In some important ways, being partial to their own opinions and not allowing liberty to others *was* the Quaker agenda. Well before Pennsylvania was founded, Isaac Penington reminded his readers of the purpose of government, writing, "remember this Word, *Be sure you smite none for Obedience to God. Limit not His holy Spirit in His People, but limit the unclean and evil Spirit in those who manifest themselves not to be his People.* This is the true intent of Government."[30] What developed during this period was a system that was, contrary to the Quaker theory of an ideal government, not a spiritual aristocracy, but an oligarchy.[31]

The policy the Assembly pursued vis-à-vis its constituents has evoked widely varied commentary from historians and contemporaries alike that reveals the complexity of the Quaker approach to government. On the one hand, there were those who criticized the Holy Experiment for exactly the same reasons they did the Society of Friends. They were "cruel persecutors" in the eyes of many, conducting their government as they did their religious meeting, by imposing a severe discipline on all. And as their power stabilized and expanded, they were charged with "priestcraft" by political opponents. Francis Bugg claimed that the dominant Quaker faction was "Guilty of that Persecution which they have condemn'd in others."[32] Similarly, Edward Cockson spoke directly to the Quakers, arguing that "your Party have exceeded *all Mankind in the Extensions of their Persecutions.*"[33] Bugg claimed to see through the surface image:

their Pretense, of *Mercy, Justice, Peace, Freedom, Goodness, Righteousness, Meekness, Temperance, Unity, Humility, Soberness, Constancy to Good Principles,* &c. is nothing but an Amusement, Deceit, Hypocrisy, and Gross Dissimulation; with a Design to Engross and Translate the Government into their own Hands, and then to Exercise both Cruelty and Injustice, Partiality and Persecution.[34]

But Quakers had partisans of their own. In the mid-eighteenth century, they gained a mythical status among some observers of the colony. Their biggest fans

---

[29] Isaac Norris to Penn, 23rd of the 9th mo. 1710, in Edward Armstrong, ed., *Correspondence between William Penn and James Logan, Secretary of the Province and Others* (Philadelphia, 1870–72), 2: 431.

[30] Isaac Penington, *The Way of Life and Death Made Manifest, and Set Before Men* (London, 1680), part I, 294.

[31] On the Quaker oligarchy, see Tully, *William Penn's Legacy,* and Richard Alan Ryerson, "Portrait of a Colonial Oligarchy: The Quaker Elite in the Pennsylvania Assembly, 1729–1776," in Bruce C. Daniels, ed., *Power and Status: Office Holding in Colonial America* (Middletown, CT: Wesleyan University Press, 1986), 106–35.

[32] Bugg, *Hidden Things,* 184.

[33] Cockson, *Rigid Quaker, Cruel Persecutor,* 35.

[34] Bugg, *Quakerism Anatomized,* 443.

were the French *philosophes*, for whom the Holy Experiment became a touch-stone for the ideals of the Enlightenment.[35] Historians of American politics, even those who emphasize the influence of the *philosophes* on the American political ideas, seem to have overlooked their obsession with Quakerism.[36] Yet French anglophilia manifested itself most acutely in their interest in Quakers. From the earliest days of the Society in the 1650s, the French had taken notice – and Quakers had encouraged their notice – of their peculiar breed of radical-ism, which by the middle of the next century had blossomed into a tradition of commentary that lasted into the twentieth century and spread well beyond France.

The *philosophes* praised Quaker Pennsylvania for embodying the Enlight-enment. Quakers, it seemed, had invented the perfect civil society – one that would promote republican virtues of frugality, simplicity, equality, and peace. Among the numerous French authors who wrote positively about *les Trem-bleurs* are some of the best known, including Voltaire, Montesquieu, Bris-sot, and Crèvecœur. Voltaire began the trend when he wrote in his *Lettres Philosophique* that "William Penn might glory in having brought down upon earth the so much boasted golden age, which in all probability never existed but in Pensilvania."[37] The Encylopedists promoted Friends in several articles, and Brissot championed them as "republicans" and "pure moralists," writing, "[t]his then is the sect for those States which would banish despotism, and all other political crimes. It is the sect for republics; It is the sect for monarchies; In a word, it is the sect for humanity. Since if Quakerism were universal, all mankind would form but one loving and harmonious family."[38] In *Letters from an American Farmer*, Crèvecœur discoursed on the idyllic homestead of "enlightened botanist" John Bartram – the pleasing simplicity of his speech and manner, his kind treatment of his servants, and the profundity of a meet-ing for worship with both silence and a female minister (Figure 2).[39] Like the Quakers' opponents, the *philosophes* had their own agenda to promote and Quakers seemed the best agents.

In answers to the charges of inappropriate mixing of religion and politics, Quakers reconciled the dilemma of their authority in their own way. In a 1725 pamphlet, the Quaker author claimed, "I meddle not with Society: I only desire

35 Isaac Hunt, *A Looking-Glass for Presbyterians. Or A brief examination of their loyalty, merit, and other qualifications for government. With some animadversions on the Quaker unmask'd. Humbly addres'd to the consideration of the loyal freemen of Pennsylvania* (Philadelphia, 1764), 3.

36 There is only one monograph devoted entirely to the topic, Philips, *The Good Quaker*. See also, Echeverria, *Mirage in the West*; Larson, *Daughters of Light*, 249–51; Bernard Faÿ, *The Revolutionary Spirit in France and America*, trans. Ramon Guthrie (New York: Harcourt, 1927); William Pencak, "In Search of the American Character: French Travelers in Eighteenth-Century Pennsylvania," *Pennsylvania History* vol. 55, no. 1 (1988), 2–30.

37 Voltaire, *Letters Concerning the English Nation* (London, 1733), 30.

38 Jean-Paul Brissot de Warville, *A Critical Examination*, 14, 48.

39 J. Hector St. John Crèvecœur, *Letters from an American Farmer*, 197.

FIGURE 2. "Quaqueresse." (FHL)

its protection."[40] But the meaning of his statement depends on how one defines "meddle" and "protection."

Liberty of Conscience as an Instrument of Proselytization

As we have seen, for Penn, protection came from civil unity, which was based on liberty of conscience. This liberty was something in which all Christians could unite and thus prevent the destruction of civil society through religious wars and persecution. In short, the freedom of particular religious bodies depended on the stability of civil government. Quakers generally agreed that civil union equaled civil safety. And they all agreed that liberty of conscience was the means. But there was a subtle yet important difference between how Penn understood liberty of conscience and how Quaker politicians thought it should function to produce unity. Penn believed that it would mean negative liberty for all – freedom from coercion. Through this liberty, Truth would naturally find its way. In some ways, this was also the view that Quaker politicians held.

---

[40] *Conference Between a Parish-Priest and a Quaker; Published for the preventing (if possible) the vile deceits of priestcraft in America* (Philadelphia, 1725), 26. In *The Beginnings of Quakerism*, Quaker historian Braithwaite also claims that "The Quakers resolutely excluded compulsion from the scheme of the Kingdom of God" (484).

But because Pennsylvania civil government was the *ekklēsia*, they believed as well that they should help people along on the way to Truth. They would accomplish this "Concord" in two ways, as Penn said, though "example" and "power" – missionizing and regulation. The first way was persuasive, the other coercive; and the line between the two methods was by no means distinct.

In order to "protect" the inhabitants of the colony and guide them along the right path toward unity and Truth, Quakers needed to impose a number of theological imperatives on the polity. These imperatives followed the Quaker religious Discipline and were intended to create "holy conversation," a society of "orderly walkers." They believed that the Assembly, as the elders, "may and hath Power . . . to pronounce a positive Judgment, which no doubt will be found obligatory upon all such who have Sense and Feeling of the mind of the Spirit, though rejected by such as are not watchful, and so are out of the Feeling and Unity of Life."[41] In short, they imposed their religious testimonies on civil society. Because liberty of conscience was the first principle of the ecclesiastical polity, so was it the most basic principle codified in the Quaker constitution. And it served the same purpose – to allow people to become Quakers. The hope that lay behind liberty of conscience was that individuals, once freed from the obligations of a state church, would eventually find their way to Quakerism.

Certainly Pennsylvania was in important ways the most ambitious experiment in religious liberty in the world at the time.[42] The diversity of the population, its relative harmony, and the entire lack of persecution of dissenters either by the government or the inhabitants was noted by most who visited the colony.[43] Attending as many churches as possible while in Philadelphia was a common pastime of tourists. William Black, a Scotsman visiting the colonies in 1744, took the opportunity while in Philadelphia to attend the services of Anglicans, Moravians, Presbyterians, "New Lights," several Quaker meetings, and a sermon by Gilbert Tennant. His experience was a positive one, and he remarked that "I found everything come up to, or rather exceed the Character I had often heard of Philadelphia."[44] In mid-century, Lawrence Washington commented that Pennsylvania "has flourished under that delightful liberty [of conscience], so as to become the admiration of every man, who considers the short time it has been settled."[45] For the *philosophes*, religious liberty was the crowning glory of Pennsylvania. They saw it as a place not only without the oppression of religion but, some believed, without theology at all. They

---

[41] Barclay, *Anarchy*, 53.

[42] It may be objected that Rhode Island was as free as Pennsylvania, but, of course, shortly after Roger Williams founded it, it was taken over and dominated by Quakers until the end of the colonial period.

[43] See, for example, Andrew Burnaby, *Travels through the Middle Settlements in North-America in the years 1759 and 1760 with Observations upon the State of the Colonies* (Ithaca, NY: Cornell University Press, 1963), 58.

[44] William Black, "The Journal of William Black," *PMHB* vol. 1, no. 3 (1877), 233–49.

[45] Lawrence Washington to John Hanbury, in *The Writings of George Washington*. Jared Sparks, ed., (Boston: American Stationers' Co., 1838), 2: 481.

celebrated the lack of priests or dogma of any kind, and there were no tithes, no enforced church attendance, and no restrictions on any religious practice. Some equated Quakerism with deism.

But as genuine as this religious liberty was, it was in some ways a superficial quality of the colony; there was much more going on beneath the surface. Pennsylvania was in reality far from "laissez-faire," "complaisant," or "less concerned with religious structures" than its neighbors, as some historians have described it.[46] Frank Lambert has noted that Adam Smith himself found Pennsylvania to be a religious model for his free market economic system; but neither Smith nor the Quakers believed that "free" meant "unregulated."[47] The mistake scholars have made is in viewing Quaker liberty of conscience through the lens of modern liberalism and assuming that it was legislated purely as a negative freedom, in other words, that the Quaker government would leave everyone alone to pursue his or her own religious course unguided. Even William James was beguiled by what he imagined to be the modern, individualistic sensibilities of Friends. In *Varieties of Religious Experience* he wrote, "[S]o far as our Christian sects today are evolving into liberality, they are simply reverting in essence to the position which Fox and the early Quakers long ago assumed." Quakerism, he concluded, was "impossible to overpraise."[48]

But even the French did not find a separation of church and state – they just happened to approve of the religion they found there, which seemed to them a kind of civil religion. Truth was not relative to Quakers; and if the conscience could not be mastered, Quakers believed that it at least could be directed. Thus liberty of conscience was understood by Quakers to be both a negative liberty – the freedom from obstacles to the Truth – but also a positive liberty, an opportunity for the individual to be guided toward Quakerism. Liberty of conscience was only a part of the Quakers' plan and only the first step

---

[46] Most recently, see Marietta and Rowe, *A Troubled Experiment*, passim. Also see Benjamin Hart, *Faith and Freedom: The Christian Roots of American Liberty* (San Bernardino: Here's Life Publishers, 1988), 197–206; Bonomi, *Under the Cope of Heaven*, 35; Daniel J. Elazar, *American Federalism: A View from the States*, 3rd ed. (New York: Harper and Row, 1984), 115–17; and Donald S. Lutz, following Elazar in *The Origins of the American Constitutionalism* (Baton Rouge: University of Louisiana Press, 1988), 54–56.

[47] Frank Lambert, *The Founding Fathers and the Place of Religion in America* (Princeton, NJ: Princeton University Press, 2003), 10, passim. For the same analogy, see, Bonomi, *Under the Cope of Heaven*, 81.

[48] William James, *Varieties of Religious Experience* (New York: Modern Library 1936), 7. Although James and others who find a modern form of liberalism in Quakerism are mistaken, it is clear that many of the "liberal" aspects of Quakerism were adopted by non-Quakers. A concrete example is in their penology, which is discussed later in this chapter. While Quakers did not institute lenient penal codes for humanitarian reasons, it is hard to conclude otherwise than with Harry Elmer Barnes that "it is probable that the influence of these Quaker laws and theories did more than anything else to promote that movement for the liberalizing and humanizing of the criminal codes in this country, which began immediately after the Revolution and spread from Philadelphia throughout the United States." Harry Elmer Barnes, *The Evolution of Penology in Pennsylvania* (Indianapolis: Bobbs-Merrill, 1927), 27–28.

toward what their opponents called the "Quakerization" of Pennsylvania.[49] In their own way, in the early years of the colony, Quakers established their church de facto every bit as much as the Anglicans in Virginia or the Puritans in Massachusetts established theirs de jure. It just so happened that liberty of conscience was one of their most fundamental theological premises – a gateway belief, of sorts, and the most important proselytizing tool. In 1769 the *Pennsylvania Chronicle* claimed approvingly that William Penn had said that "liberty of conscience is the first step to *have* a religion."[50]

This Quakerization was effected at all levels of the polity, beginning among the ranks of the politicians. If Quakers knew that they needed Friends in the Assembly, they also knew that they could not completely exclude people of other persuasions. But they did need to weed out the un-Quakerly from the Quakerly. Early on Penn objected to such practices and denied the legitimacy of Friends' use of their tenets as criteria to filter or recruit rulers. He wrote, "for that Right [to participate in government] is founded [upon] Civil & not Spiritual Freedom."[51] But that is exactly the basis on which Friends defined eligibility for office – at least unofficially. Politicians did not even have as much constitutional religious liberty as others in Pennsylvania. All inhabitants were granted liberty of conscience under the first four *Frames of Government*, but in the 1701 Charter, liberty of conscience was changed to religious toleration where public officials were concerned. It stipulated that only Christians could hold office.[52]

Despite the accolades bestowed by many visitors on the colony for the liberty of conscience, others found it troubling as they recognized the advantage this gave Quakers in winning converts to both their religious and their political cause. One detractor claimed that "[b]y discouraging regular Ministers [of other denominations], it gives the Quakers an Opportunity of making more Proselytes."[53] "[I]t is a very great misfortune to us," remarked an Anglican clergyman in 1749, "that many of our people, having been born in the place & converse always with Quakers, are so much tainted with their way of thinking as to have very slight notions of an outward Visible Church & Sacraments which gives ye Minister very great Trouble in many respects."[54] Another wrote

---

49 Richard Peters quoted in Tully, *Forming American Politics*, 274.

50 *The Pennsylvania Chronicle; and Universal Advertiser*, Monday, August 21, to Monday, August 28, vol. 3, no. 31 (1769), 256.

51 Schwartz, "*A Mixed Multitude*," 30.

52 The charters can be found in the volumes 2–4 of *The Papers of William Penn*. See also Schwartz, "*A Mixed Multitude*," 32–33. Although there were very few non-Christians in the colonies, and Quakers preferred to pass no laws against them, the crown compelled Pennsylvania to pass laws banning Catholics, Jews, and atheists from full citizenship. These laws were not enforced. See Bonomi, *Under the Cope of Heaven*, 36.

53 William Smith, *A Brief State of the Province of Pennsylvania... In a Letter from a Gentleman who has resided many Years in Pennsylvania to his Friend in London* (London, 1755), 35.

54 Edgar L. Pennington, "The Work of the Bray Associates in Pennsylvania," *PMHB* vol. 58, no. 1 (1934), 1–25, 5.

that Quakers "were a Dread to all Christians, besides those of their own Party."[55]

Convincement through Benevolence

Liberty of conscience was the most important law that would "open the way" for a unified, Quakerized populace, but it was not the only apparently negative liberty intended for this purpose. There were other legal tools that Friends used to bring people to Quakerism. These also understandably strike the modern mind as liberal, and so they were in one respect. They were designed to free the individual from worldly oppressions by providing the basic necessities for freedom – food, shelter, clothing, education, sobriety, mental and physical health, piety, and civic virtue. As similar as they appear to modern liberalism on the surface, however, these were not humanitarian efforts; they were tools of convincement.[56] All of these liberating laws and policies were based solidly on the Quaker ecclesiastical constitution, the Discipline. They dealt with, among other things, how the state managed criminals, slaves, Indians, and the sick-poor.

The early penal codes and Quaker penology reflected both the Quakers' collective experiences in the English and Massachusetts prisons and their own treatment of members who had transgressed the religious Discipline in meeting. They were forgiving and aimed more at rehabilitation – a new concept in the Western world – than punishment. But, properly speaking, they were not so much for *rehabilitation* as they were for *regeneration*. They were intended to be more effective that the brutal punishments handed down by non-Quaker authorities in other colonies. They worked on the conscience rather than the body. In the Quaker meeting, for example, when an individual transgressed the Discipline and was disowned, the meeting still retained ties with him and attempted to "tender" his conscience to bring him back into membership. They never gave up hope that the person might be truly and permanently convinced of Quakerism. In the 1719 version of their ecclesiastical constitution, they wrote, "[t]his is called our Discipline in the exercise whereof Persuasion and gentle dealing is and ought to be our practice."[57] The same principle held in Quaker civil society. Hardly a man was beyond hope for rejoining society. Permanently banishing someone or killing him shut the door on any possible

---

[55] Bugg, *Quakerism Anatomized*, 442.

[56] As Sydney V. James argues, "[I]n the first century of Quakerism there was little evidence of humanitarianism, apart from the desire to convert people... In modern usage, conferring the benefit of one's religion is not defined as humanitarian charity." James, *A People among Peoples: Quaker Benevolence in Eighteenth-Century America* (Cambridge, MA: Harvard University Press, 1963), 317. To be clear, this social control was not primarily a means to political power; or, if so, the goal of political power was for the security of an overarching religious purpose. For the debate on whether the benevolence of various religious dominations was from humanitarian, religious, or self-interested motives, see Lois W. Banner, "Religious Benevolence as Social Control: A Critique of an Interpretation," *Journal of American History* vol. 60, no. 1 (1973), 23–41.

[57] Philadelphia Yearly Meeting, *Book of Discipline* (1719), HQC.

spiritual convincement. There was no "warning out" of undesirables as there was in Massachusetts.[58] And although banishment was the punishment for some crimes, it was not as harsh as in England, where the criminal must leave or face death. Rather, it was in effect a pardon for a crime, with the provision the individual must quit the colony.[59] Thus Quaker penalties were lenient and aimed at regeneration of the individual rather than his exclusion from society. In contrast to Massachusetts' sixteen capital crimes, Pennsylvania only had one, for murder (although treason remained punishable by death under English common law), and, rather surprisingly, there were only two capital punishments carried out in the first thirty-six years of Pennsylvania government.[60] The reason for this was that Friends believed that if they killed a man, "he would have no time to repent."[61] Late in the eighteenth century, Quaker prisons gained an international reputation for, among other innovations, their rejection of corporal punishment, and their efforts to transform criminals into good citizens. The Philadelphia Prison is the best example of Quaker proselytizing through prison reform. Quaker principles and practices were in plain view to visitors, who remarked on the benevolence of the unarmed guards, the industrious and well-mannered inmates, the use of silence as an organizing principle, and the Quaker invention of solitary confinement as a time for inmates to retreat inward to find the Light of God in their consciences.[62] For Quakers, "Emulation [was] a principle, and often an only incentive to a moral conduct."[63]

While punishments in Pennsylvania always remained more lenient than those in England or other colonies, they were not always as "easie" as they were in the first few decades.[64] When Pennsylvania was under the control of the royal governor, Benjamin Fletcher, many of the laws were found to be too much out of keeping with English laws. Then, and also later when Penn was afraid of losing his government again in 1700, punishments became harsher. The pivotal

[58] In Massachusetts, paupers and other suspicious individuals who wandered into towns were warned by town leaders to leave or face imprisonment, forcible expulsion, or worse. See Ruth Wallis Herndon, *Unwelcome Americans: Living on the Margin in Early New England* (Philadelphia: University of Pennsylvania Press, 2001).

[59] Herbert William Keith Fitzroy, "The Punishment of Crime in Provincial Pennsylvania," *PMHB* vol. 60, no. 3 (1936), 242–269, 259–60.

[60] Marietta and Rowe, *A Troubled Experiment*, 12, 35.

[61] Thomas Chalkley, "The Journal of Thomas Chalkley," *Friends' Library*, 6: 73. See also John Bellers, "Some Reasons Against Putting Felons to Death" in *Essays about the poor, manufactures, trade, plantations, & immorality* (London, 1699), 17–20.

[62] Robert Turnbull, *A Visit to the Philadelphia Prison; Being an accurate and particular account of the wise and humane administration adopted in every part of that building; containing also an account of the Gradual Reformation, and Present Improved State, of the Penal Laws of Pennsylvania: with observations on the impolicy and injustice of capital punishments. In a Letter to a Friend* (Philadelphia, 1796). It is probable that Turnbull's account is somewhat embellished, but the fundamentals are credible. On Quaker penal codes, penology, and prisons, see Barnes, *The Evolution of Penology in Pennsylvania*.

[63] Turnbull, *A Visit to a Philadelphia Prison*, 44.

[64] Marietta and Rowe, *A Troubled Experiment*, passim.

moment in the penal code was the passage of the "Act for the advancement of justice and the more certain administration thereof" in 1718. Twelve new capital crimes were added, and punishments generally became more physically severe, with an aim more toward deterring and punishing crimes than rehabilitating criminals. It is apparent why scholars of the Pennsylvania penal code consider that the Quaker experiment failed in this regard.[65]

The Pennsylvania laws protecting non-whites were a product of the Quaker missionizing impulse as well. Laws pertaining to Indian relations aimed at convincement and were reproduced exactly from the religious Discipline.[66] Friends had always sought good relations with Indians, and their interactions are well documented in the primary literature.[67] They also expected the same good relations to exist between Indians and denizens of Pennsylvania – whether Quakers or not. Accordingly, in 1705–06 they instituted "[a]n act for the better improving a good correspondence with the Indians."[68] It was important, they believed, "that a friendship be cultivated between [the Queen's] subjects and the native Indians, the first possessors of these lands."[69] In 1685 they wrote one of their earliest religious testimonies for the benefit of the Indians in the minutes of PYM. "This Meeting doth unanimously agree, & give as their Judgment," Friends wrote, "that it is not Consistent with the Honour of Truth, for any that makes Profession thereof, to sell Rum or other strong Liquors to the Indians, because they use them not to moderation, but to Excess & Drunkenness."[70] In 1701 the Assembly then codified this testimony into civil law as "[a]n act against selling rum and other strong liquors to the Indians." This law spells out even more fully than the meeting minutes the purpose and intent of the regulation. Quakers were concerned for the welfare of the Indians over economic gain for Anglo-Americans. The Indians, they explained, were "not yet able to govern themselves in the use" of alcohol, "as by sad experience is too well known . . . whereby they are not only liable to be cheated, and reduced to great poverty and want, but sometimes inflamed to destroy themselves and one

---

[65] Ibid., 248–53. But it is important to note that Friends did not cease to be concerned about religion or to encourage non-Quakers toward Quakerly behavior. It is, however, an indication that they were willing to forego some aspects of the Discipline to secure others. It is an indication of a compromise with reality. While it is true that Quakers gave up on controlling the now-diverse population to the extent they desired, this did not mean that they then reversed themselves entirely and adopted a policy of laissez-faire.

[66] On meeting discipline pertaining to Indians, see Philadelphia Yearly Meeting, Minutes, 1682–1746, FHL.

[67] For such a rich topic, there are surprisingly few scholarly monographs that deal with it in detail, especially in the colonial period. However, almost all works on Quakers discuss their relations with Indians. For a recent brief discussion of the relationship of Friends to Indians, see Anderson and Cayton, *Dominion of War*, 54–103.

[68] James T. Mitchell and Henry Flanders, eds., *Statutes-at-Large of Pennsylvania from 1682–1801* (Harrisburg, PA: Clarence M. Busch, State Printer of Pennsylvania, 1896–1911), 2: 229. (Hereafter referred to as *Statutes*.)

[69] Ibid.

[70] Philadelphia Yearly Meeting, Minutes, 1682–1746, FHL.

another."[71] But equally important to Friends was that the Indians' alcoholism inhibited their acceptance of and adherence to Quakerism. Penn, his governors, and the popular representatives of the colony were "desirous to induce the Indian nations to the love of the Christian religion, by the gentle, sober and just manners of professed Christians (under this government) towards them." A main concern of Quaker politicians that they noted in the act itself was that the Indians "be induced as much as may be by a kind and obliging treatment to embrace the Christian religion."[72] Missionizing was thus, in a sense, a legal obligation.

Quakers also embraced Indians as part of their civil society as no other governments did. Should any person commit bodily injury against an Indian, the Indian was to be considered the same as "a natural-born subject of England" and the perpetrator punished accordingly.[73] Moreover, it was a crime to "[spread] false news or stories as may alienate the minds of Indians or any of them from this government."[74] They allowed them to serve as witnesses in court in the second instance and considered in general that, as part of Quaker civil society, their bad behavior would reflect on the colony as a whole. In specific, their abuse of alcohol and the ensuing unchristian acts would "plainly tend to the great dishonor of God, scandal of the Christian religion, and hindrance to the embracing thereof, as well as drawing the judgments of God upon the country."[75] The public, in short, was charged in several ways with promoting the welfare of the Indians, even to the extent of a tax being levied for maintaining the good relations in the form of treaties and gifts.[76] Friendly relations with Indians continued and grew throughout the eighteenth century. Although *philosophes* found reason to rejoice at such amiable relations with the Natives, settlers on the frontier believed that the Quakers compromised their safety by engaging in "secret schemes" and "iniquitous practices" with Indians.[77]

Similar to the laws protecting Indians, there were relatively gentle slave codes and laws pertaining to free blacks in Pennsylvania. While the laws regulating the behavior of blacks and prescribing their punishments were undoubtedly severe by our standards, they were lenient and enlightened when compared with those of the Southern colonies. For example, in Pennsylvania slaves were classified as people, rather than property, and whites were subject to the same punishments for killing a slave as a white person. Furthermore, blacks in Pennsylvania could own property, be taught to read and write, hold any kind of job, and if they

[71] *Statutes*, 2: 168.

[72] Ibid., 2: 229.

[73] Ibid.

[74] Ibid.

[75] Ibid., 2: 168–69.

[76] Ibid., 2: 381.

[77] Hugh Williamson, *Plain Dealer: Or, a Few Remarks upon Quaker-Politicks, and their Attempts to Change the Government of Pennsylvania. With some Observations on the false and abusive Papers which they have lately published* (Philadelphia, 1764), 3: 10.

were freed, they did not have to leave the colony.[78] These laws were intended to alleviate the oppression of these groups so that they could find their way to Quakerism. It was in the mid-eighteenth century that Quakers began the abolitionist movement among themselves and then, by the end of the century, began to take their testimony to the public. They founded schools to educate blacks and encouraged them to meet for religious purposes. But while they were happy for the existence of black meetings, Friends were undecided whether they should allow blacks to worship in their midst.[79]

Quakers also concerned themselves much with the sick-poor of the colony (Figure 3). In the early decades of the eighteenth century, they directed their relief efforts mainly toward convinced members of the Society of Friends. But as the century and their proselytizing progressed, they expanded their concern to the colony in general. They instituted several almshouses and the Pennsylvania Hospital – the first hospital in the colonies. Like the prisons, these institutions were designed, when possible, to rehabilitate inmates and provide them the necessary means to raise themselves up to a higher station in life. They were provided food, shelter, clothing, and education and were taught skills that would allow them to find work on the outside. The laws they established enabled this regeneration both directly and indirectly. Funds raised from fines levied on individuals for breaking other laws – especially those concerning public morality – were directed toward charitable causes. The statutes specified that fines collected from those convicted of swearing were used "for the use of the poor."[80]

In addition to the preceding measures, Quaker Pennsylvania led other colonies in their organization of public efforts for reform and improvement. Along with their observation of the diverse religious climate, visitors to Pennsylvania also noted the remarkable number of voluntary associations. John Adams noted with envy that Quaker Philadelphia surpassed Boston in its "charitable, public foundations."[81] Likewise, Manasseh Cutler wrote, "Whatever may be said of the private benevolence of the Philadelphians, there is certainly a greater

---

[78] Nash and Soderlund, *Freedom by Degrees*, 12–13.

[79] An important point to note is that while Friends were undoubtedly concerned about the well-being of blacks for their sake, many were more concerned with the possibility of the necessary cruelty of slave ownership making members of the Society of Friends stray from their Quakerly principles of meekness, humility, and peaceful behavior. The mild slave codes and abolitionist principles of some Pennsylvania Quakers was as much for the preservation and advancement of Quakerism as for the well-being of blacks. On lenient slave codes in Pennsylvania, see Nash and Soderlund, *Freedom by Degrees*, 12–13; on tension within the Society over slavery, see David Brion Davis, *The Problem of Slavery in Western Culture* (Ithaca, NY: Cornell University Press, 1966); see also, Thomas E. Drake, *Quakers and Slavery in America* (New Haven, CT: Yale University Press, 1950); Jean Soderlund, *Quakers and Slavery: A Divided Spirit* (Princeton, NJ: Princeton University Press, 1985).

[80] *Statutes*, 2: 50.

[81] John Adams quoted in Carl Bridenbaugh and Jessica Bridenbaugh, *Rebels and Gentlemen: Philadelphia in the Age of Franklin* (New York: Oxford University Press, 1962), 229.

FIGURE 3. "Quakers Giving Charity." (In Edith Philips, *The Good Quaker in French Legend* [Philadelphia: University of Pennsylvania Press, 1932], facing page 98; incorrectly cited as appearing in Raynal's *Histoire philosophique et politique des etablissemens & du commerce des Européens dans les deux Indes* [1770].)

display of public charity here than in any other part of America."[82] While visiting the colonies, Brissot also observed that "'[u]pon an attentive examination of the contributions of their churches, schools, hospitals and other charitable institutions, there appears a degree of philanthropy that should disarm envy and ridicule.'"[83] Their efforts began in England and were continued in America.[84] The dozens of organizations they established and directed included libraries, schools, almshouses, learned societies, a hospital, fire companies, and societies to aid oppressed groups such as slaves, "distressed prisoners," and the poor and to improve relations with the Indians through "pacific measures." Many of these societies were the first of their kind in the colonies, many of them lasted well into the nineteenth century, and new ones were continually established.[85] Quakers set an example for their Evangelical counterparts who,

[82] "New York and Philadelphia in 1787," *PMHB* vol. 12, no. 1 (1888), 97–115, 114.
[83] Brissot de Warville quoting "a Pennsylvanian," in *A Critical Examination*, 49.
[84] On their seventeenth-century activities, see Mack, *Visionary Women*, 4.
[85] See James, *A People among Peoples*; Jean Barth Toll and Mildred S. Gillam, eds., *Invisible Philadelphia: Community through Voluntary Organizations* (Philadelphia: Atwater Kent Museum, 1995).

once mobilized in the early nineteenth century, took the lead in establishing reform societies of their own.

All of these laws and institutions demonstrate a sort of forgiveness and optimism that we do not see among other religious groups and governments. Because of Quakers' belief in the possibility of human perfection, but also the probability of imperfection, they were more inclined to see the unfortunate as truly unfortunate rather than sinful. This benevolence cannot rightly be called philanthropy, however, because it was not directed toward the man as a creature but rather the salvation of his soul. It was a subtle paternalism wielded by the elders of the meeting over their wayward brethren. The French did not recognize the distinctive practices of Friends for what they were – religious testimonies. They took them instead as ideal civic behavior. They projected rationalism onto Pennsylvania, which turned Quaker proselytizing into humanitarianism and spiritual egalitarianism into civil equality. Thus the "Good Quaker" was born.[86]

Legal and Moral Guides toward Quakerism

The image some political historians have presented of Pennsylvania has been through a lens distorted by modern priorities and understandings. Daniel Elazar, for example, describes Pennsylvania's as an "individualistic" political culture with a government established "for strictly utilitarian reasons" and with "no direct concern with questions of the good society."[87] Eighteenth-century idealists made a similar mistake when they found the Quakers were "without municipal government, without police, without any means of coercion for the administration of the state." But in this view it was not because they were unconcerned with creating a good society, but rather it was their "entirely moral" customs that naturally cultivated it.[88]

Yet if benevolence might be mistaken for liberalism, it would be hard to reconcile this interpretation of Pennsylvania with much of Quaker legal and cultural restriction. Pennsylvania's lenient stance on some issues was only one half of the equation for Quakerizing the colony. There was a manifestly paternalistic quality to Quaker rule. Friends were well aware that for every liberty granted, there was the potential of the abuse of that liberty[89] or, more specifically, the misperception that that liberty of conscience meant unfettered freedom to follow one's own interpretation of God's will. Barclay made it clear that the church had authority over matters of the conscience and the power to discipline members for transgression of divine order. He wrote, "*That any particular Persons* de facto *or effectually giving out a positive judgment, is not*

---

[86] Echeverria argues that "there is no evidence apart from the legend of the 'Good Quaker' that the Physiocratic or Rousseauistic idealization of the American was as yet a popular concept familiar to the general literate public" (*Mirage in the West,* 36).

[87] Elazar, *American Federalism,* 115–17.

[88] Brissot quoted in Philips, *The Good Quaker,* 121.

[89] See also Schwartz, *"A Mixed Multitude,"* 31.

Incroaching nor Imposing upon their Brethren's Consciences."[90] Friends under
the jurisdiction of PYM were reminded that "[t]he awful prudent and watchful
Conduct of our friends in early Days, did, and such always will, preach and
extend silently to the notice of all."[91] But in case this form of preaching by
example did not work on society at large, Friends would try another tack.

One highly visible way Pennsylvania took shape as a Quaker experiment
was in its regulatory laws. To counter the potential for licentiousness inherent
in their "liberal" policies, Friends in office attempted to regulate the polity the
way they regulated the meeting – by imposing a strict communal discipline.[92]
Pennsylvania civil society was thus characterized as much by its restrictions as
its liberties. Opponents condemned the government in Pennsylvania because
of "the Quakers Tyrannical Reign, and Arbitrary Government; together with
their Persecutions, and Partial Proceedings in their Courts of Judicature."[93]

Especially in the early part of the century, Friends concerned themselves
greatly with how people lived their lives down to the smallest detail of how they
entertained themselves, how they imbibed their drinks, how they conducted
themselves in the marketplace, how they dressed, and how they styled their
hair. Public morality was the subject of more than forty laws passed between
1682 and 1709.[94] While the crown did not legitimate all of these laws, nor were
they reinstated throughout the entire colonial period, the restrictions Quaker
law and culture placed on public morality in Philadelphia shaped the culture
of the city for the entire colonial period. It was only after the Quaker Party
was forced from office and the Charter of Privileges abolished in 1776 that the
Quaker grasp on the city was truly loosened, though not broken.

The "excellent legislation," as some saw it,[95] in Pennsylvania ranged from
minor Quaker idiosyncrasies, such as requiring recognition of the numerical
naming of dates, to the more stringent codes on public behavior. Almost all
of these laws are directly traceable to the Quaker religious Discipline.[96] Predictably, Quakers banned "rude or riotous sports, as prizes, stage-plays, masks,
revels, bull-baitings, cock-fightings, [and] bonfires."[97] A later rewrite of this law
added tennis to the litany of "riotous sports." Similarly, the Quakers' admonition to the members of their Society in 1722 to avoid "impudent noisy &
indecent behaviour in Markets and other publick places" was translated into
laws against swearing, scolding, smoking, and dueling. But more distinctly

[90] Barclay, *Anarchy*, 73.
[91] Philadelphia Yearly Meeting, Minutes, 1682–1746, FHL.
[92] Tolles, *Meeting House and Counting House*, 64.
[93] Bugg, *Quakerism Anatomized*, 443.
[94] *LL*, 1: 18. However, Marietta and Rowe demonstrate that the laws were largely unenforced in
the later period of Quaker rule.
[95] Raynal quoted in Philips, *The Good Quaker*, 100.
[96] For example, compare the religious rules in Philadelphia Yearly Meetings, Books of Discipline,
HQC, and Hugh Barbour and J. William Frost, "Chapter 10: A Disciplined Christian Life," in
The Quakers, 107–17 with the civil law in *Statutes* and *LL*.
[97] *Statutes*, 1: 5.

Quaker was their aversion to seemingly innocent activities such as toasting healths. A law stated that "every person that shall drink healths which shall promote excessive drinking" shall pay a fine and do hard labor.[98] Crèvecœur found it pleasing not to be subjected to the "irksome labour of toasts" in Bartram's home.[99] As the century progressed, Quakers also began to define the idea of gentility away from the culture of heavy drinking and began what would blossom into the temperance movement of the nineteenth century.[100]

Although some scholars now and then have considered Philadelphia to be "the most liberal and advanced city in the world before 1750, 'the city of firsts,'"[101] others see it as "backward" when compared with artistic expression in Massachusetts, New York, and Carolina. "Prior to the middle of the eighteenth century," writes an historian of music, "Quaker influences had been strong enough to repress almost wholly any public rendering of music outside the churches, even to discourage individual efforts in the homes of citizens."[102] A similar, though more stringent prohibition existed against the theater. In the religious discipline of Friends, it was written that none should "suffer Romances, play-books, or other vain or idle pamphlets in their house or families."[103] Friends included theater in this category and extended the restriction to the general public when they passed "[a]n act against riots, rioters, and riotous sports, plays and games" in 1710. Throughout their time in office, Friends battled aggressively against the theater, a crusade that continued into the nineteenth century.[104] A visitor to Philadelphia in 1825 remarked that "those [buildings] for public purposes are superior in any point of style, to any in the United States – excepting the Theatres."[105]

Interestingly, after the barrage of laws passed early on, historians have noted a surprising lack of legislation in the middle decades of the century.[106] They have suggested rightly that Friends expected regulation to come in other ways than outward, top-down coercion. The ideal was that individuals would be

---

[98] Ibid., 99.

[99] Crèvecœur, *Letters from an American Farmer,* 191.

[100] Peter Thompson, "'The Friendly Glass': Drink and Gentility in Colonial Philadelphia," *PMHB* vol. 113, no. 4 (1989), 549–73, 555. See also Thompson, *Rum Punch and Revolution: Taverngoing & Public Life in Eighteenth-Century Philadelphia* (Philadelphia: University of Pennsylvania Press, 1999).

[101] Thomas Clark Pollock, *The Philadelphia Theatre in the Eighteenth Century* (Philadelphia: University of Pennsylvania Press, 1933), xv.

[102] Harold D. Eberlein and Cortlandt Van Dyke Hubbard, "Music in the Early Federal Era," *PMHB* vol. 69, no. 2 (1945), 103–127, 105.

[103] Philadelphia Yearly Meeting, Minutes, 1682–1746, FHL.

[104] John P. Sheldon, "A Description of Philadelphia in 1825," *PMHB* vol. 60, no. 1 (1936), 74–76, 76. This is in contrast to several other colonies, including New York and Virginia, where plays were tolerated or encouraged as early as the seventeenth century. See George C. D. Odell, *Annals of the New York Stage* (New York: Columbia University, 1927–49), 1: 3–31.

[105] Sheldon, "A Description of Philadelphia," 76.

[106] Robert S. Hohwald, "The Structure of Pennsylvania Politics, 1739–1766" (Ph.D. Diss., Princeton University, 1978); Tully, *Forming American Politics,* 339; Beeman, *Varieties of Political Experience,* 214–15.

regulated by the Light. When that was unlikely, their preferred approach was rather the "soft persuasion" of the sort Woolman exhibited when dealing with slave owners; only, many people did not find it so soft or beneficent. Some Quaker testimonies, while not codified into law, were nonetheless enforced in public forums, and to the great consternation of some non-Quakers. Where Quakers were once excluded from participation in the political and judicial systems for not taking oaths, they now excluded non-Quakers who would not adopt this testimony. In 1740 future provincial secretary Richard Peters complained that the Quaker magistrates of Chester County "had the imprudence . . . to set a Juryman aside because he wou'd not take Affirmation (there being none present whose consciences as they say wou'd permit them to tender an Oath)." A prominent non-Quaker warned them "of the Illegality of their proceeding" and told "that by this means they took away the Security the Law had provided for the Preservation of mens Lives Liberties & Properties." It was the general belief at the time "that every Person who was to give Evidence in any cause should not be permitted to do so till he had given the highest Test he cou'd give of his Varacity." Anything less than an oath would not bind a man to honesty. The Quakers were accordingly "warned . . . in a very friendly manner of the ill use that People who are not of their Persuasion wou'd make of such an unjustifiable step at this time." But Friends paid no heed and instead dismissed the first man and "call'd another who wou'd take the Affirmation." It was this kind of behavior, this willful disregard of how their testimonies might be abused in the wrong hands, that caused Peters to believe that "[t]he Quakers in the Capacity of the Assemblymen have drawn the Eyes of Mankind upon them & made themselves liable to many disadvantageous Reflections."[107] It was one thing to not swear an oath as a Quaker; it was another to let non-Quakers go without swearing one. Expecting Quakerly honesty from non-Quakers was, contemporaries thought, clearly naïve at best, and legal malpractice at worst.[108]

As Quaker officials were vigorous in shaping early Pennsylvania from the top down, so were prominent Friends active in grassroots reform to mold the society in the image of the meeting. Historian of Quaker penology Harry Elmer Barnes notes that "the Quakers did not rely merely on legal regulation to secure a high degree of public morality, but resorted to an almost-Calvinistic type of inquisitorial supervision over the morality of private citizens."[109] Where the Quaker Discipline was not codified into law, individual Friends took it upon themselves to offer "close hints" to non-Friends about deportment, clothing, hairstyles, worldly possessions, pastimes, and other things that could, as far as Friends were concerned, inhibit a person's progress toward salvation.[110]

---

[107] Richard Peters Letterbook, 1739–41, 18, HSP.
[108] For Quakers in the Assembly reprimanded for administering oaths to non-Quakers, see *PA*, 5: 4021.
[109] Barnes, *The Evolution of Penology in Pennsylvania*, 32.
[110] In their journals and letters, many Quakers write about giving such "hints." See, for example, Journal of George Churchman, 1759–1813, passim, HQC.

George Churchman wrote in his journal about "a loving hint which I had to give to a young man... relating to his fashionable coat, was well taken, & I hope is likely to have some good effect." Similarly, Warner Mifflin "told a little Girl, perhaps 9 years old, about the uncomeliness of having a Roller put in her hair. Also to the mother he hinted the necessity of Care to direct the minds of her Children in the right way whilst they are young & tender."[111] Friends were not just concerned about spreading their message, however. They also monitored the reactions of the recipients of their hints to see what influence they might have had. In this particular case, Churchman noted with satisfaction that "this conversation appear'd to have some effect on the Child, so that when a young woman went to comb & dress her hair as usual... she refused to have the Roller put on, saying she did not want it anymore."[112]

For Quakers, of course, public morality and dissent were intimately connected. Dissent from ungodly behavior was, after all, a duty to the polity. This ethic is exhibited nowhere more clearly than in the Quaker practice of boycotting.[113] Friends were not just some of the most successful merchants in the colonies, they were also savvy consumers. They used their purchasing power as a proselytizing tool. John Woolman, Benjamin Lay, Anthony Benezet, and Joshua Evans were all prominent Friends who testified against such practices as using sugar and tea, wearing dyed clothing, eating meat, and riding in carriages to advocate frugality over luxury, abolitionism over slavery, and humane treatment of animals instead of abuse by refusing to spend their money on these things or otherwise perpetuate their existence through consumption.[114] In the 1730s, Benjamin Lay smashed his wife's tea set to protest the use of cane sugar produced with slave labor,[115] and later, toward the end of the century, Friends tried to cultivate substitutes such as maple sugar.[116] Joshua Evens also found "inconsistencies in the use of East India Tea, and that it sprang from an evil Root" in that poor people would sacrifice food for the sake of indulging in vain custom of tea drinking.[117] They did these things publicly, and often endured

[111] Journal of George Churchman, 7th mo. 27th day, 1806, 9: 69, HQC.
[112] Ibid., 7th mo. 24th day, 1781, 4: 86, HQC.
[113] There is no history of the boycott that treats pre-Revolutionary America. The most detailed study of the idea of the boycott in American history merely mentions that the Sons of Liberty used this resistance technique against the British. See Gary Minda, *Boycott in America: How Imagination and Ideology Shape the Legal Mind* (Carbondale: Southern Illinois University Press, 1999), 33–34. In "Narrative of Commercial Life: Consumption, Ideology, and Community on the Eve of the American Revolution," WMQ 3rd ser., vol. 50, no. 3 (1993), 471–501, T. H. Breen notes that American historians have accepted the boycotts during the Revolution as a matter of course. But, ignoring Quaker boycotts that began in the early eighteenth century, he errs on the other side by assuming "their utter novelty" at the Revolution (486).
[114] Nash and Soderlund, *Freedom by Degrees*; Phillips P. Moulton, ed., *The Journal and Major Essays of John Woolman* (Richmond, IN: Friends United Press, 1989); and Journal of Joshua Evans, FHL; Anthony Benezet, *Memoirs of the Life of Anthony Benezet,* Roberts Vaux, ed. (Philadelphia, 1817).
[115] Nash and Soderlund, *Freedom by Degrees,* 49.
[116] James Bringhurst to John Murray, 5th mo. 12th day 1790, Bringhurst Letters, FHL.
[117] Journal of Joshua Evans, 14, FHL.

the ridicule of not just non-Quakers, but some of their own brethren as well. Evans found that his principled vegetarianism caused his "chiefest friends to stand aloof from me," and that "the Cross in wearing white Cloths was more than I could bear."[118]

Abbé Raynal proclaimed that "[n]ever perhaps had virtue inspired legislation better designed to bring happiness to man."[119] For all this regulation, however, both official and informal, according to some Quakers, the Holy Experiment was not all that it could or should be where morality was concerned. There were many so-called "wet Quakers" – those who had become more concerned with their worldly than their spiritual lives – and a substantial population of non-Quakers whose consciences did not trouble them about drinking, dancing, or playing tennis.[120] In 1751 the minister Thomas Chalkley had a few complaints about the spiritual condition of the colony, and everyone from the most humble to the highest-ranking official bore responsibility for the depraved state of affairs. Kept awake one night because of his concerns, he wrote:

[T]he Lord was angry with the People of *Philadelphia* and *Pensylvania*, because of the great Sins and Wickedness which were committed by the Inhabitants, in Publick Houses, and elsewhere: and that the Lord was angry with the Magistrates also, because they use not their Power as they might do, in order to suppress Wickedness; and do not, so much as they ought, put the Laws already made in Execution against Prophaneness and Immorality: And the Lord is angry with the Representatives of the People of the Land, because they take not so much care to suppress Vice and Wickedness.[121]

Chalkley reminisced longingly of the days when politicians would prowl the streets, seeking out and admonishing transgressors of the civil and gospel order. "It is worthy of Commendation," he opined, "that our Governor, Thomas Lloyd, sometimes in the Evening, before he went to Rest, us'd to go in Person to Publick Houses, and order the People, he found there, to their own Houses, till, at length, he was instrumental to promote better Order, and did, in a great Measure, suppress Vice and Immorality in the City."[122]

From the comments of visitors to Philadelphia, however, the Quaker laws and customs were none too lax. They not only remarked on the religious diversity but also the plainness of the clothing; the lack of seasonal and daily greetings and polite customs such as removing the hat, the use of *thee* and *thou*, the strangeness of antitoasting laws, and the lack of the arts and entertainment.[123] The restrictions Quakers placed on the public culture shaped the province well

---

[118] Ibid., 17, 12.
[119] Raynal quoted in Echeverria, *Mirage in the West*, 73.
[120] On "wet Quakers," see Tolles, *Meeting House and Counting House*, 142.
[121] Chalkley, "The Journal of Thomas Chalkley," 203–4.
[122] Ibid., 204.
[123] An excellent source for observations on the Quakerization of Philadelphia is Paul Hubert Smith, ed., *Letters from the Delegates to Congress, 1774–1789*, 25 vols. (Summerfield, FL: Historical Database, 1995). (Hereafter referred to as *Delegates*.)

beyond the days when Quakers governed it. As late as the 1790s, a French-man visiting Philadelphia believed that the "melancholy customs of this city" were a Quaker legacy.[124] On the other hand, another visitor remarked in 1825 that "Philadelphia is fortunate in having for its citizens so many quakers their industry, sobriety, cleanliness, and steady habits, and honesty, are constantly before other classes of citizens as examples, and cannot fail to be, in some degree, contagious."[125] This contagion was exactly what Friends hoped for.

Institutionalized Dissent

Even as Quakers were imposing restrictions on Pennsylvania's inhabitants, they were teaching them Quakerly behavior in another way. Like the first years of the colony, the middle decades were characterized by continual battles between the Assembly and the proprietors and their deputies, which were increasingly hostile to Quaker interests. Now, however, not only were the proprietors no longer Quaker, they were Anglicans, and also the Quaker Assembly was now unified. Moreover, they were educating non-Quakers in their culture of dissent and enlisting them in their campaign of resistance. So successful were Friends in their attempts to excite partisanship that historians argue this period marks the beginning of the identification in the public mind of popular rights with the so-called "Quaker Party."[126] On the other hand, some scholars have claimed that Quaker Pennsylvania did not have a "strong dissenting tradition" when compared to Calvinist or Anglican colonies. While it is true that in some ways they did not "present as sharp a challenge to the established order," as the argument here will suggest, in other ways their dissent penetrated more deeply.[127]

The era began with a confluence of events. In the late 1730s, the Penn family was emerging from a difficult time financially and legally and refocusing its attention on Pennsylvania. Thomas Penn appointed George Thomas as lieutenant governor in 1738. No great supporter of the Quakers, Thomas became the first leader of the growing challenge to Quaker hegemony – the Proprietary Party.[128] Although Quakers had a long history of resisting proprietary

---

[124] Quoted in Kenneth and Anna M. Roberts, trans. and eds., *Moreau de St. Méry's American Journey, 1793–98* (Garden City, NJ: Doubleday, 1947), 280.

[125] Sheldon, "A Description of Philadelphia," 76.

[126] Tully, *Forming American Politics*, 408–10. The 1740s and 1750s were characterized by intense strife with the proprietary governors. A synopsis of all the gubernatorial administrations and the conflicts is in *LL*, 2: 57–70. Because of the "inexhaustible points of contention" between the two parties and the similar methods each used in all disputes to check one another's power, this discussion, for reasons explained later, focuses on the administration of George Thomas.

[127] Richard Alan Ryerson, "Political Mobilization and the American Revolution: The Resistance Movement in Philadelphia, 1765–1776," *WMQ* 3rd ser., vol. 31, no. 4 (1974), 556–588, 584.

[128] Beeman notes that the term *party* is not really applicable to those allied with the Proprietors because they never formed a coherent identity as did the Quakers (*Varieties of Political Experience*, 208). To use this term is, indeed, in a sense, the imposition of an anachronism; however, I will persist in using it as the actors used it themselves, as a synonym for *faction*.

authority, this new animosity was not between warring factions of Quaker politicians. The new Proprietary faction, while only a loose coalition, consisted of a good number of Presbyterians, Lutherans, and members of the German reformed church, none of whom shared Quakers' pacifist principles.

In addition to the challenge of the Proprietary faction, international tensions began to intrude on Pennsylvania. Shortly after Thomas's appointment, in 1739 the War of Jenkins's Ear began. The British sent orders for Pennsylvania to contribute to raising forces to be sent to the Spanish West Indies. Thomas responded by enlisting indentured servants belonging to prominent inhabitants, including members of the Assembly. Also, there was a demand for domestic forces as French and Spanish privateers began threatening the Pennsylvania coast, which necessitated some action on the part of the Assembly to call a militia or otherwise provide means for the defense of the colony.

But the most important development for the future of Quaker politics was the election of John Kinsey to the Assembly in 1739. Kinsey dominated public life in mid-century Pennsylvania.[129] Indeed, he embodied Quaker theocracy. In this one man, religion and politics converged and were used as means to the same ends – the political autonomy of the Quakers and the dissemination of their ethic. At one point or another, and often simultaneously, Kinsey held all the highest posts in both church and state. He was variously speaker of the Assembly, chief justice of the Pennsylvania Supreme Court, acting trustee of the General Loan Office, and provincial treasurer. But more than this, he was also by all accounts an active Quaker. As the clerk of PYM, he was the most prominent Quaker in the Delaware Valley. Significantly, he held the clerkship concurrently with the speakership of the Assembly, which allowed him to promote Quaker politics from every angle.[130] Kinsey was respected by even his non-Quaker opponents as "the Hinge on wch ye Quaker Politicks all turn."[131]

Provincial secretary Richard Peters observed that Kinsey "can influence [the Assembly] to do what he pleases." His power was due to his ability to use Quaker process to achieve political ends. Although Quakers had never disconnected religion and politics, Kinsey mixed them in a way that was different from before. He turned Quakerism into a powerful political force by using old modes of dissent and protest in new ways for the advantage of Quakers in office. Under Kinsey's tutelage, Quakers no longer used their testimonies merely to advocate and secure religious liberties, but also to increase and retain political power. The old testimonies were thus transformed as they became political tools in the hands of skilled dissenters. Peters saw Kinsey's ends clearly and knew that "[h]e will never promote an Agreemt with ye Govr. nor a Coalition of Parties."[132]

---

[129] For brief biographies of Kinsey, see Isaac Sharpless, *Political Leaders*, and LL, 2: 591–607.
[130] LL, 2: 593.
[131] Richard Peters Letterbook, 1739–43, 58–59, HSP.
[132] Ibid.

The Peace Testimony Reinvented

The most significant political move Kinsey made during his career was to appropriate the peace testimony for the purpose of retaining Quaker power over the colony. For a brief period, and out of keeping with Quaker tradition, Kinsey took this testimony to an extreme. Because it was at the heart of Quaker theologico-politics as the doctrine that preserved their constitutional unity, Kinsey's actions had monumental consequences both for the Society of Friends and the political culture of Pennsylvania.

Historically, Friends had two separate yet harmonious testimonies – those concerning peace on the one hand and one's obligation to civil government on the other.[133] In the seventeenth century and through at least half of the eighteenth, the peace testimony was a personal matter, not a matter of state. For example, although a good Quaker could not take up arms himself against his fellow man, he could, in good conscience, pay taxes for the necessary defense of the state. This distinction allowed Quaker politicians to separate their religious lives and their political lives to a certain degree, which in turn enabled them to fulfill a basic obligation to their constituents – protecting them and their property. In the earlier years of Pennsylvania government, Quakers gave money to either the crown or the governor to support defensive military measures, and their actions were in keeping with traditional Quaker practice.[134]

Governor Thomas set Friends against him immediately when he responded to the demands of the British government to raise a militia and meet the needs of the vulnerable Pennsylvania coastline. His enlistment of indentured servants angered the masters who saw it as an encroachment on their property rights. But the militia bill Thomas wrote to raise forces within the colony challenged Quaker power in more fundamental ways. It brought two important issues into question – the extent of the peace testimony and the extent of Quaker control over provincial affairs.

Friends moved aggressively to halt the progress of the bill. What was most important to Kinsey and the Quakers in the Assembly was not whether the colony should be defended from within, but who had the power to decide on policy inside the colony. In the past, Friends had looked to the crown to

---

[133] The following discussion draws on Herman Wellenreuther's "The Political Dilemma of the Quakers in Pennsylvania, 1681–1748," *PMHB* vol. 94 (1970), 135–72. See also Peter Brock, *Pioneers of the Peaceable Kingdom*, 97–99. Brock explains the following episode in Pennsylvania history as exemplifying "the basic difference of viewpoint between the two sides." He does not, as does Wellenreuther, identify the two conflicting testimonies. On the contrary, he explains how the Quakers made their cases for the consistency of their behavior with regard to giving money for "the king's use" in the past and finds that their argument "possessed greater validity than the governor was prepared to recognize." His discussion does not take into account any possible political motives for this apparent change in the use of the peace testimony. For more on the peace testimony during this period, see Jack D. Marietta, "Conscience, the Quaker Community, and the French and Indian War," *PMHB* vol. 95 (1971), 3–27.

[134] Wellenreuther, "The Political Dilemma of the Quakers," 172.

provide defense from threats outside the colony's borders, but when threats came from within, the Assemblymen wanted to reserve their right to determine how to react. But the peace testimony had put the Quaker Assemblymen in a bind. If they allowed the crown to come in to Pennsylvania and defend their colony, they would be relinquishing a significant degree of control. If, on the other hand, they did any more than give money to the king, they would be transgressing the peace testimony. Kinsey's solution was to redefine the testimony in hopes that their unity would result in a stronger Quaker position. In order to assert their legislative prerogative, then, Friends dissented from the governor's and proprietor's plans to prepare the colony for defense and disobeyed their demands for funds by adapting the testimony for their purposes. Now, for the first time, the peace testimony would preclude giving money for defense purposes.[135]

But first, in order to ensure that they would be able to use the peace testimony at all as a means of resistance, Kinsey had to make sure that enough Friends were in office. Accordingly, before the 1739 election, Kinsey rallied the forces with an epistle directing Friends to adhere steadfastly to the testimony as pressure mounted from the crown and the governor for Friends to defend Pennsylvania with military force.[136] Once Friends were securely in office for another term, they could then effect a transformation of the peace testimony from a personal religious testimony into a form of collective political resistance. No sooner had the Assembly convened for its first session than the disobedience began. In 1740, in response to Governor Thomas's request for the Assembly to impose a tax to support Britain's war with Spain, Quakers argued:

We have ever esteemed it our Duty to pay Tribute to Caesar, and yield Obedience to the Powers that God hath set over us, so far as our conscientious Perswasions will permit; but we cannot preserve good Consciences, and come into the Levying of Money, and appropriating it to the Uses recommended to us in the Governor's Speech, because it is repugnant to the religious Principles professed by the greater Number of the present Assembly, who are of the People called *Quakers*.[137]

Therefore, rather than relinquish control by allowing outsiders to dictate internal decisions, Friends pled conscience, and used their stance on peace as a tool to delineate the extent of their obedience. Now, for the first time, the testimony for peace became government policy, and the testimony for civil government fell by the wayside.[138]

---

[135] Ibid., 158.

[136] Ibid., 158–9; *LL*, 2: 593.

[137] *PA*, 3: 2593.

[138] Wellenreuther, "The Political Dilemma of the Quakers," 159. He explains that the constitutional principle involved, on which the Quakers rested their case in all disputes with the governor and the crown, was that only the representatives could decide on matters relating to affairs within the colony. If the Quaker representatives had extended their demand for defense by the crown to the area of Pennsylvania, then this would surely have affected the validity of their claim to speak and decide on provincial matters.

While the *philosophes* and others who were removed from the threat of attack in Pennsylvania praised Quaker pacifism, this new interpretation and use of the peace testimony was neither welcomed nor sanctioned by all inhabitants of Pennsylvania. In 1740 Thomas petitioned the Board of Trade to have Quakers removed from office, and in 1741 a group of prominent non-Quaker merchants petitioned the king to limit their power.[139] Significantly, there were also many Friends who disapproved of the new interpretation. Before long, weighty Friends levied criticisms against Kinsey for his "stubborn and provocative attitude" and his departure from the proper process of legal discernment. "For my own part," wrote Quaker Justice Samuel Chew, "I look upon this doctrine not only to be without warrant or colour, either from reason or revelation, but in its consequences pernicious to society, and entirely inconsistent with, and destructive of all civil government."[140] James Logan wrote a lengthy letter in a similar vein to Friends, reminding them that "friends have recommended themselves to ye Govt . . . by complying with its Demands, in chearfully contributing by ye paymt of their Taxes towds every War." Furthermore, he recommended that "all Such, who for Conscience Sake cannot joyn in a Law for Self-Defence, Should, not only decline standing Candidates at the ensuing Election for Representatives themselves, but also advise all others who are equally Scrupulous to do the Same."[141]

The extent to which Friends would go to preserve unity and power is evident in an incident in a meeting for business. One week before the general election in 1741, Logan presented PYM with an epistle on the defenselessness of the province. Instead of letting him read it, the Meeting formed a committee to see if the contents were appropriate for general consideration. After looking it over, the committee decided it was not and was ostensibly better suited for people who would understand the military and geographic issues it dealt with. One member, however, dissented. He stood and observed that since it was written by a weighty Friend and was meant "for the Good of the Society at these fickle & precarious Times," it should be considered by the whole group. But instead this Friend was rebuked and silenced. In the meeting, "Jonathan Bringhouse pluck'd him by the coat and told him with a sharp Tone of Voice, 'Sit thee down Robert, thou art single in that opinion.'"[142] Clearly some sorts of dissent were no longer acceptable.

The new interpretation and use of the peace testimony did not last in the short term. Within two years, the body of Friends reverted to their original position on it, objected strongly to Kinsey's actions, and the Assembly voted

---

[139] *LL*, 2: 65, 72–73.
[140] Samuel Chew, *The Speech of Samuel Chew, Esq. Chief Judge of the Counties of Newcastle, Kent, and Sussex on Delaware. On the Lawfulness of Defence against an Armed Enemy. Delivered from the Bench to the Grand Jury of the County of Newcastle, Nov. 21. 1741* (rpt., Philadelphia, 1775), 2.
[141] James Logan, September 22, 1741, American Friends Letters, HQC.
[142] Richard Peters Letterbook, 1739–1743, 33, HSP.

to give money for defense after all.[143] But Kinsey's politicking had planted seeds in a couple of fertile beds. First, his new version of the peace testimony would soon become the accepted interpretation of it. And second, his use of it set a powerful example for non-Quakers of how to dissent aggressively. But more than that, and much more problematic, was that this example of dissent expressed ambiguity – and perhaps ambivalence – about the testimony that preserved the unity of the polity. The message Quakers sent was that the testimony was something to be manipulated, and perhaps not taken seriously. Both of these seeds would bear fruit in the next two decades.

Charter Rights

What were ultimately at stake for the Quakers in their struggle with the proprietors were their constitutional rights as they were embodied in the 1701 Charter. Early in 1742 an apparently minor controversy arose that exemplifies the continuing pattern of Quaker resistance to government with the Charter at the center of it all. The specifics of the original cause of this particular controversy are relatively insignificant. They were instigated over who had the power to appoint doctors to meet ships arriving in port with potentially sick immigrants. The Assembly had replaced a doctor appointed by the governor with one of its own choosing. But the inflamed rhetoric and bitter acrimony of the debate indicated that the matter went much deeper than the mere appointment of a doctor. And eventually, in a heated exchange between Thomas and the Assembly, led by Kinsey, the issue boiled down to its essence. For the Assemblymen, at stake was the sanctity of the Charter of Privileges, the preservation of their liberties, and the definition of the legitimate boundaries of a potentially arbitrary power; for the governor, it was the containment of a radical group overstepping its proper bounds. Quakers saw it as maintaining constitutional balance and keeping power in the rightful hands.

Thomas began with the now-usual accusation of the Assembly that in appointing a different doctor they were trying to "seize all the Powers of Government into their own Hands."[144] Echoing Penn and his agents, he argued that the Assemblymen were "assuming to themselves a Power the Law hath not intrusted them with; is illegal and unwarrentable, a high Invasion of the Powers of Government; and a very dangerous Example."[145] But it was the governor's mistake if he thought he could make any headway with an argument based on the Charter. After having been in office only four years, he could not hope to know how to use the Charter as well as Friends, who had created it and used it for their advantage for nearly half a century; nor did he have their training in the dissenting process. In their response to the governor, Quakers claimed there was a "manifest design against the Liberties of the Freemen of

---

[143] Wellenreuther, "The Political Dilemma of the Quakers," 159.

[144] *PA*, 4: 2740.

[145] Ibid., 4: 2741.

this Province," enumerated at length their constitutional rights, and chastised him for his "unnatural Attack upon our Charter and Privileges."[146]

They charged the governor with "clandestinely attempting to deprive [them] of those religious and civil liberties which [he] had solemnly promised to support."[147] Meanwhile, as a petition was on its way to England, Richard Peters reported that "[the Quakers] are not ashamed openly to usurp Powers they have no Pretense of Claim to, & to endeavour without any regard to decency & manners to reduce another part of ye Legislature wch by ye Constitution is in all respects their equal & in many their super[ior]."[148] But what had made Thomas angry was that the Assembly had not been open in their protest either. Contrary to appropriate Quaker process, it was they who had acted surreptitiously; they had submitted their petition in secret and neglected to publish it in the official proceedings or to deliver a copy to the governor. Not surprisingly, Thomas denounced the petition as a "Stab in the Dark, which was intended both to Blast my Character and ruin my Fortune," and he insisted the Quakers' motives were merely to "prejudice [the Freemen of the Province] against me, the seeds of Dissention have been plentifully sown."[149] Peters echoed Thomas's sentiments, writing to England that the Quakers "must know ye Proprs. can't but see that they are attempting to strip their Govr. of ye most & essential Parts of Govmt. & ye Person of Coll. Thomas they are doing him all the Injury they possibly can."[150]

But Friends, unperturbed by the accusations, calmly replied that "the presenting of Petitions is the Right of every of the King's Subjects when they think themselves aggrieved . . . It was intended neither 'to Blast the Governor's Character,' nor 'ruin his Fortune' . . . but to obtain Justice."[151] The criticisms Thomas leveled at the Assembly sound the same as those always leveled at Quakers for their lack of deference to secular authority. "Your Language and Behaviour," he said, "shew a contempt of his Majesty's Sentiments, as well as a Departure from the Decencies Observed by all other publick Bodies towards Persons in Authority."[152] Clearly the Quakers' degree of antiauthoritarianism seemed to Thomas blatant and unusual in the context of colonial government. The Quakers, meanwhile, denied their behavior was anything but decent and proper and offered reasons for their actions: "People may, it is true, grow wanton with Liberty," Kinsey admitted. But he immediately turned the accusation back on the governor, adding, "and Governors may play the Wanton with the Liberties of the People." For Quakers in Pennsylvania, it was at least as much a function of their collective history as actual (or imagined) tyranny in their own government that prompted their behavior. "The Memory of what has

---

[146] Ibid., 4: 2752 and 2757.
[147] Ibid., 4: 2743.
[148] Richard Peters Letterbook, 1739–1743, 74, HSP.
[149] *PA*, 4: 2744.
[150] Richard Peters Letterbook, 1739–1743, 74, HSP.
[151] *PA*, 4: 2758.
[152] Ibid., 4: 2743.

passed in our own Time," he explains, "as well as History, afford us Examples of both; and perhaps the latter are the most numerous." Finally, to Thomas's complaint that he had been falsely charged with attempted tyranny, and that he "is as much a Friend to Liberty as the most zealous Assertor of it," the Quakers' flippant reply was, "Actions speak louder than Words."[153]

In this heated debate between the governor and the Assembly – ostensibly over the appointment of a doctor – Thomas cut to the quick, placing the Quaker assembly in a broader context and suggesting the underlying motive for their vehement protests:

Has the Honour of the Province been advanced ... by the distinguishing Behaviour of the Assembly here from all others in America? Have the odious Insinuations and bitter Invectives thrown out against me, been of Use to *convince the World* of your Meekness and Moderation, or have they been for the *Reputation* of the religious Society of which you call yourselves Members? Perhaps you will say, *it is enough to have opposed a designing and arbitrary Governor*: But this will be only calling Names without any Proof of my being such a Person.[154]

Here Thomas identified a twin Quaker concern – to resist authority and to cultivate a public image that would convince non-Friends to join their political cause, if not their religious society. His powers of observation about the Assembly were fairly on the mark. He was fully aware, as he put it, that "[t]he Interest of [the] Leaders ... depend[s] upon keeping alive a Spirit of Faction."[155] Quakers used their dissenting ethic to unite their supporters and pit them against their perceived oppressors. Thus, when the Assembly was full of one sort of people, it could easily dominate all the interests of the colony. To this end, public relations played a vital role in Friendly politics. Richard Peters made note of the Quakers' cultivation of partisanship as well: "Here they stick at nothing to preserve the Affections of ye People & by being a low weak sort of Men do strangely impose upon them, in short they have their Ear & can by that means give the best face to ye worst designs."[156]

With the extreme tension between the Assembly and the governor, the 1742 election was a pivotal one for both parties. Both used the best means at their disposal to win: The Quakers used their bureaucracy; the Proprietary, on the other hand, resorted to violence. As for the Quakers, in one of the most blatant examples of the use of his religious office for political ends, Kinsey functionally merged the meetinghouse with the state house. Again, Richard Peters reported that "[w]e have another Difficulty to cope with. It is yt a [Letter] is come from Friends in Britain to Friends here earnestly exhorting them to return none to the Assembly but contientious Friends who will be sure to support ye Cause of Truth agst the violent Attack made on it by ye Govr & [his] Friends." Such a directive from London Friends would have been newsworthy enough. But

[153] Ibid., 4: 2762.
[154] *PA*, 4: 2748. Emphasis added.
[155] Ibid., 4: 2769.
[156] Richard Peters Letterbook, 1739–43, 102, HSP.

it was *where* the letter was read that attracted the most attention. Peters was troubled "That this [Letter] came to Jon Kinsey as Clerk of ye yearly Meeting & that he open'd it and read it in ye Lobby of ye Assembly Room & that it was subscrib'd by a large number of Hands."[157] As far as Kinsey was concerned, the desired effect was achieved when Quakers were elected by a substantial margin over other candidates for the Assembly.

The election was itself an indicator of the climate in Pennsylvania, as the Proprietary faction took an even less honorable route to resist the Quakers' tactics. "On ye Morning of ye Election," wrote Richard Peters, "40 or 50 Sailors appear'd abt 7 a Clock at Andrew Hamilton's Warf with Clubbs in their Hands & s[aid]d to one another; Now my lads mind your mark, A plain coat & broad hat." They were warned by some Quakers "to disperse, & give no disturbance to Peoples Minds, who were going to do one of ye most important Things to the good of ye Publick that is to elect their Representatives, & yt if they came near ye place of Election they woud be committed to Jayle & severely punished." Before long, however, the sailors began beating people with their clubs. The sailors "promised to give up their Clubs & separate if he [Quaker Edward Shippen] wou'd give them a Drink." When no liquor was forthcoming, recounts Peters,

this enragd the Sailors to that degree yt they went to ye place of Election & in one Minute disper'd 500 Dutch & others, knock'd all down that were upon ye Stairs & laid abt 'em in ye most Shocking manner Eye ever beheld, it was realy a frightful sight & I expect numbers woud have been killd: for besides their Sticks ye Sailors threw whole Bricks at ye El[ec]t[ion] House Door where ye innocent Country People were giving in their Tickets, tho whether ye Sailors or ye Freeholders first threw Bricks is uncertain.

Peters concluded grimly that since the election riot was widely considered to have been orchestrated by supporters of the Proprietary, "it will turn greatly to ye prejudice of ye Publick" against them. "[F]or ye leading men in ye Assembly will think they are now more than ever at liberty to gratify their Resentmt agst ye Proprs & instead of doing ye Business of ye Country."[158] In confirmation of Peters's fears, Isaac Norris, Jr., prominent member of the Assembly, wrote in a letter four days later that

the Dangr. among our selves seems to be pretty much over for in our last Electn that party [the proprietary] has not only lost in every where to a prodigious dissproportn in all ye Counties . . . but have brot. such a reproach upon the heads of ye party as they will never clear themselves from and I think have effectually secured the Electn agt [them]selves for the future.[159]

---

[157] Ibid., 128. See also, Philadelphia Yearly Meeting, Minutes, 1739–41, HQC.

[158] Richard Peters Letterbook, 1739–1743, 134–38, HSP. It should be noted that in the heat of the moment, a few young Quakers forgot their testimony of peace and joined in beating the sailors – but only after the sailors had been safely apprehended by the authorities.

[159] Isaac Norris Letterbook, 1719–1756, November 21, 1742, HSP.

As Norris hoped and Peters feared, this incident settled the question of the Quaker Party's dominance in Pennsylvania for the remainder of the colonial period.[160] Peters cautioned the proprietors in 1742 that Friends were united amongst themselves, they had united the people, and they were busy using their bureaucratic skills for resistance and the security of their liberties. "They are contriving all sorts of Bills yt they think will give you uneasiness & they have by the impudence of ye last Election gain'd a deeper hold of ye common People than ever & can never be shaken unless they quarrel with one another.[161] From this point on until the eve of the American Revolution, their hegemony provoked frequent attacks, but these too only strengthened it.

Despite their dominance, Quakers continued to use their testimonies to resist the government and accrue more power. A seemingly insignificant testimony serves to illustrate the new lengths to which Quakers – and especially Kinsey – would go to use traditional Quaker means for new political ends. In 1745 Kinsey recounted a discussion with Isaac Norris about whether or not to remove their hats when meeting with Governor Thomas. "I said, in Effect, as follows: That our not putting off our hats to the Governor was not for want of true respect &c. to a Gentleman in his Station, but from principle." The principle at stake as far as Kinsey was concerned was not as it had been traditionally for Friends, spiritual equality. Rather, he believed that if the Quakers should be made by the governor to remove their hats in his presence, "such an act of [the governor] would be Affirming overall a power he had not." The principle was political power. Norris, on the other hand, was not entirely comfortable with Kinsey's testimony in this case and "seemed inclinable to permitt our hatts to be taken of[f]." In a more conciliatory vein, Norris argued: "That it might be said the law assumes no superiority, that [the governor] was bare himself and directing us to be Uncovered was putting up only in Equal condition with himself." But Kinsey would have none of it. As far as he was concerned, whether to remove their hats or not had to be their own free choice. If they were ordered to do it, all suggestion of equality of power would be destroyed. He asserted, "tho the Gov. himself might of shew make it his choice to be uncovered, yet as we were principally against it, and it could not be done with our consent, to suffer it to be done by order was plainly giving up the Equality we had a right to claim."[162]

Some historians have questioned the sincerity of Kinsey's hat testimony. The biographical dictionary *Lawmaking and Legislators*, for example, details a similar incident involving Kinsey and Governor William Keith in 1730. While

---

[160] Although Quakers dominated the Assembly for the entire life of the colony, during the 1740s it was almost complete when "Quaker majorities ranged as high as 90 percent." *LL*, Figure III. Religious Affiliation of Assemblymen by Assembly (1710–1756), 2: 132–33. See also Isaac Norris Letterbook, 1719–1756, HSP; Tully, *William Penn's Legacy*, 28–29; Pemberton Papers, 3:36, HSP; *PA*, 3: 2663; Richard Peters Letterbook, 1739–1743, HSP; Philadelphia Yearly Meeting, Minutes, 1741, HQC.

[161] Richard Peters, Letterbook, 1739–1743, 153, HSP.

[162] Journal of John Kinsey, FHL.

arguing a court case before Keith, Kinsey also refused to uncover his head and was forcibly removed from the court. In the wake of the incident, Quakers united behind Kinsey, and Philadelphia Quarterly Meeting condemned Keith for violating Kinsey's religious liberty. The editors of the volume speculate whether Kinsey was merely "grandstanding" for political purposes.[163] Whereas some see Quaker testimonies as insincere, others see them as too sincere. Daniel Boorstin argues that Friends adhered to their principles and testimonies too rigidly to be effective governors. "[T]he Quakers weakened themselves not by being false to their teachings, but by being too true to them," he says.[164]

But both of these assessments miss the point. What neither takes into account is the use and purpose of the testimonies for Friends. Boorstin believed that at this time "the Quaker's refusal to remove his hat became as arrogant and purposeless as the non-Quaker's insistence on hat-honor."[165] On the contrary, however, there was a great purpose behind it. Testimonies had always been a mode of dissent; they were the Quakers' traditional mode of political expression before they held office. They were a form of protest, a statement of justice, an indication of their antiauthoritarianism, and a statement of corporate solidarity. And then, during the mid-eighteenth century, they also became a tool for retaining and solidifying political unity and power. Kinsey's actions, admits the biographical dictionary, "enhanced [his] reputation among the Quakers and increased his notoriety in general" and furthered his political career.[166] How much Kinsey's actions were motivated by faith or mercurial ends it is impossible to determine.[167] There is no doubt, however, that he used the testimony to the political advantage of the Quaker Party. Quaker critics, at least, recognized it as such. Quakers, writes Bugg,

tell us that they were raised contrary to all Men, and as such **cannot seek to Authority.** But how their Practice gives the Lie to their Principles, I shall shew anon. You see also they stand in Opposition to Parliaments, Judges, and Courts of Judicature. That's true enough, They Teach also, That there are no Superior Orders of Men; this is a right levelling Principle, and they conform to it by their sturdy Practice of their Hats.[168]

On the eve of the French and Indian War in 1755, with tensions over defense high in Pennsylvania, a particularly virulent attack on Friends exemplifies both Quakers' political strategies and the security of their power. It came in the form of a pamphlet written by Anglican clergyman William Smith, and apparently commissioned by the Proprietary, called *A Brief State of the Province of Pennsylvania*. Smith was the Quakers' most vocal and vitriolic critic since

---

[163] *LL*, 2: 592.

[164] Boorstin, *The Americans*, 42.

[165] Ibid., 41.

[166] *LL*, 2: 592.

[167] In fact, there is good reason to believe that Kinsey's motives were self-interested. After his death, it was discovered that he embezzled a significant amount of money from the government. *LL*, 2: 604–05.

[168] Bugg, *Quaker Anatomized*, 390.

Francis Bugg at the turn of the century. In an attempt to persuade Pennsylvanians and the crown that Quakers were not fit to govern, he wrote *A Brief State* to expose their alleged political malfeasance: their failure to defend the colony from attacks by the French; their use of religion for political ends; their exploitation of the Germans to consolidate their power; and their inappropriate amount of legislative power. In addition to exemplifying one pole of the sentiment on Quakers, Smith's pamphlet, rather than proving the incompetence of Quaker politicians as he intended, instead gives us a view into the workings of the Quaker Party and an indication of the political aptitude of its members.

In the early years of Pennsylvania, Smith explained, the government, though run by Quakers, was "conducted with great Mildness and Prudence." The reason he gave for this was that they had not "as yet conceived any Thoughts of turning *Religion* into a *political scheme for Power.*"[169] Now, however, that they were "[p]ossessed of such unrestrained Powers and Privileges, they seem quite unrestrained; are factious, contentious, and disregard the Proprietors and their Governors. Nay, they seem even to claim a kind of Independence of their Mother-Country, despising the Orders of the Crown."[170] By this time, he claimed, "[t]he Powers they enjoy are extraordinary, and some of them so repugnant, that they are the Source of the greatest Confusion in the Government." "In some Instances," he clarified, referring to the unicameral system in Pennsylvania, "they have both a *legislative* and *executive* Power."[171] By now, of course, charges of political and religious impropriety were nothing new to Quaker politicians.

It was not only the fact that Quakers had this extraordinary power that antagonized Smith; it was also how they had gotten it. First, they made inappropriate use of their religion. Smith was fully convinced "that most of the *Quakers* without Doors" acted "from Conscience and their religious Tenets; but for those within Doors, I cannot but ascribe their Conduct rather to Interest than Conscience."[172] Commenting unfavorably on the overlap in Quaker Society between religion and politics, Smith also observed the convenient timing of PYM and the annual elections. He claimed that "they entered into Cabals in their yearly Meeting, which is convened just before the Election, and being composed of Deputies from all the monthly Meetings in the Province, is the finest Scheme that could possibly be projected, for conducting political Intrigues, under the mark of Religion."[173]

Second, Quakers made use of new and unorthodox techniques to sway the popular vote in their favor. "In order to keep their Seats in the Assembly," Smith complained, "they have not only corrupted the Principles of the Germans; but, to be consistent with their Interest, they must strive to keep these poor People in

---

[169] Smith, *Brief State*, 5.
[170] Ibid., 10.
[171] Ibid., 5.
[172] Ibid., 15.
[173] Ibid., 26.

The German bleeds & bears y.e Furs ⫶ Th' Hibernian frets with new Disaster ⫶ But help at hand Resolves to hold down
Of Quaker Lords & Savage Curs ⫶ And kicks to fling his broad brim'd Master ⫶ Th' Hiberman's Head or tumble all down

FIGURE 4. Quakers, allied with Indians, oppressing the German and Scotch-Irish settlers (1764). "The German bleeds & bears ye Furs/Of Quaker Lords & Savage Curs/Th' Hiberian frets with new Distaster/And kicks to fling his broadbrim'd Master/But help at hand Resolves to hold down/Th' Hiberian's Head or tumble all down." The scene shows a Quaker and an Indian riding a German and a Scotch-Irishman like horses. The Quaker is wearing spurs and the Indian's knapsack has the initials of Israel Pemberton on it, one of the most powerful Quaker merchants in the province. Another Quaker Party member, probably Benjamin Franklin, holds a paper saying: "Resolved, ye Propr[ietor] a knave & tyrant." (LCP)

the same dark State, into which they have endeavored to sink them."[174] Smith and others accused Quakers of lying to the Germans about the allegedly tyrannical intentions of the Proprietors. Similarly, another anti-Quaker pamphlet a few years later lamented that "the unhappy Germans... have been blindly led into your schemes, and patiently groan'd under the burthen"[175] (Figure 4).

Exactly how Quakers lured the unsuspecting Germans into a "cabal" with them seems to have been as much a source of admiration for Smith as something despicable. As in their early campaigns for liberty of conscience in England, Friends made ample use of printed materials to convince people to their way

[174] Ibid., 32.
[175] Williamson, *The Plain Dealer*, 1: 9.

of thinking. Smith focused on this as the most egregious – and ingenious – of the Quakers' schemes. The Quakers enlisted the help of a German printer to promote the Quaker Party position and gain votes among the German population of the colony. "In consequence of this, the *Germans*, who had hitherto continued peaceful, without meddling in Elections, came down in Shoals, and carried all before them. Near 1,800 of them voted in the County of *Philadelphia*, which threw the Balance on the side of the *Quakers*."[176] But Smith seemed perturbed because the Quakers had used a creative and aggressive technique for spreading political propaganda and mobilizing the popular vote, while the traditional techniques of the Proprietary Party had failed. "[I]t is by means of their hireling Printer, that they represent all regular Clergymen as Spies and Tools of State, telling the People that they must not regard any Thing their Ministers advise concerning Elections."[177] This, according to Smith, was "the evil Genius of the Quakers" in action.[178] "The *Quakers*, having found out this Secret, have ever since excluded all other Persuasions from the Assembly."[179]

But Quaker supporters would not take this criticism passively. In *An Answer to an Invidious Pamphlet*, an anonymous supporter of the Quakers responded to Smith's accusations predictably, claiming that "[his] scheme is altogether particular, and consists solely in . . . strip[ping] the Quakers of the rights and privileges, and submit[ting] them to the arbitrary will of their governors."[180] Furthermore, their unique privileges not only kept the proprietors at bay, but also distinguished Pennsylvania from her less-fortunate neighbors. "[H]ow necessary [these privileges] are to the well-being of the colony," concluded the author, "appears from the confusion and discontents which some neighboring provinces, at certain times, have laboured under for want of them."[181]

Shortly after the publication of Smith's invective, Isaac Norris was apparently unsurprised by the nature of the attack, centering as it did on the supposed insincerity of the religious principles of Quaker politicians. "The cloaking of our Parsimony under Disguises of Religious scruple," he wrote offhandedly in his letterbook, "has been ye General misrepresentation of us every where." Concerning the grounds on which Smith attacked them – for allegedly failing to provide funds for the defense of the colony – Norris responded with concrete figures: "[W]e have Evinced the Contrary at ye Expense of near 70,000 already seasonably applied & Extending for ye kings use. What more could be Expected from us[?]"[182]

Rather than address Smith's diatribe point by point, Norris seemed more interested in the potential damage – or lack of it – that Smith might do to the public reputation and efficacy of the Quaker Party. "[Y]e violent Spirit of

[176] Smith, *Brief State*, 27.
[177] Ibid., 33.
[178] Ibid., 32.
[179] Ibid., 28.
[180] *An Answer to an Invidious Pamphlet, intituled, A Brief State . . .* (London, 1755), 3.
[181] Ibid., 4.
[182] Isaac Norris Letterbook, 1719–1756, May 24, 1755, 76, HSP.

Smith's Pamphlet to ruin [the Quakers] at a blow is a scheme that has by no means been calmly considered or digested" by his readers.[183] Confident in the strength of his party, Norris concluded that Smith would be easily dismissed first as a "Tool [of the proprietors] to Propagate the Doctrine wherever he can here & in the neighboring Governmts." But also, his threat was minimal because "his Character with all here is at a low Ebb every way."[184] Such attacks, therefore, while calculated to undermine the strength and stability of the Quaker Party, instead had the opposite effect. When any "silly Parson Preaches against ye Quakers," he observed, "They are only Contemned for it by the Greater part of their Congregation." Because of this, he continued, the Quaker Party had been very successful in garnering support from other religious and ethnic groups in Pennsylvania: "[T]he Church of England & Quakers continue on very strong Terms of Union for ye Whole & themselves in Particular, without any formal Cabals for that Purpose. – And ye Dutch [Germans] joyn them in dread of an Arbitrary Govermt."[185]

After Smith's pamphlet in 1755, Norris elaborated: "I have an inclination . . . to explain our Parties here, if they can be called such, for I think I may say, ye Province was never more united . . . than at Present."[186] In response to Smith's charge that Quakers "out of doors" were of another mind from Quakers behind the State House doors, he continued: "Ye People are very unanimous without Doors and ye Assembly without any Dissenting Voices among Themselves."[187] Part of the reason for this unity had to do with the composition of the Assembly. "The Frontier of Lancaster, composed of all sorts of – Presbyterians & Independents, of all sorts of Germans & some Church of England – Elections have chosen all their Representatives out of ye Quakers, tho' there are scarcely One hundred of that Profession in the whole Country."[188] The sum of this great political unity for Norris was that now "[w]hatevr Opposit[ion] the Ass[embly] meet from the Govr & his advisors we have the [advantage] of being of one mind in almost all debates among ourselves."[189]

This unity of Quakers, both in and out of politics, and with other sects and ethnic groups, was essential to broaden their support and to secure their agenda. Norris considered it "Absolutely Necessary to keep ye Quakers as a Ballance here."[190] What he meant was that the Quaker Party was the balast, the trimmer, against the encroachments of the proprietors and the keepers of order. "I look upon ye Quaker System in Pensyl[vania] in a Political view," he explained, "wch if overturned, at least at presnt would introduce

---

[183] Ibid., April 29, 1755, 71.
[184] Ibid., May 18, 1755, 72.
[185] Ibid., April 29, 1755, 71.
[186] Ibid.
[187] Ibid., May 18, 1755, 72.
[188] Ibid., October 5, 1755, 83.
[189] Ibid., October 26, 1741, 10.
[190] Ibid., April 29, 1755, 71.

FIGURE 5. "Quiet Quaker Quashing Quarrelsome Quidnunc." (John Cowie and William Hammond, *Alliterative Anomalies for Infants and Invalids* [New York: Dodd, Mead & Co., 1913].)

violent Convulsions in this prov[ince] unless we are to be a Governmt of meer farce."[191] Norris continued, "this Colony (till it is out of their Power to help it) will not be Governed by Proprietary Instructions secreted from them with all ye arts of a Romish Inquisition & possibly almost as severe."[192] Norris made good use of Whig oppositional rhetoric – the threat from a remote power that is tinged with popery – with Quaker process and resistance techniques. It is not surprising that everything the opposition did to try to discredit the Quaker Party backfired and instead only made it stronger. Looking back on the colonial period, John Adams remarked, "I have witnessed a Quaker despotism in Pennsylvania."[193] By contrast, Frenchman Charles César Robin wrote that Pennsylvania was "the most virtuous colony that history had ever known."[194] The image that persisted in the American mind into the twentieth century seems to agree with both interpretations (Figure 5).

[191] Ibid., May 24, 1755, 75.
[192] Ibid.
[193] John Adams quoted in James H. Hutson, *The Founders on Religion: A Book of Quotations* (Princeton, NJ: Princeton University Press, 2005), 183.
[194] Charles César Robin quoted in Echeverria, *Mirage in the West*, 107.

Conclusion

By this period, Quakerism had moved beyond the bounds of the Society of Friends, and even the Quaker Assembly, to become something much broader. Isaac Norris summarized the Quaker theologico-political agenda at mid-century: "We have now very much thrown our Disputes from being a Quaker cause to a Cause of Liberty and the Rights derived to us by our Charter & our Laws."[195] But although the cause was broader, it was not less Quakerly. Each pole of the commentary, while too extreme to be trusted on its own, when paired with its opposite reveals some aspects of Quaker theologico-politics. Whether the comments were positive or negative, they demonstrate how the peculiar dualism in their theory was expressed practically and the deep impression their policies made on non-Quakers. The Holy Experiment was a test in balancing unity and dissent. Leaving judgment to their contemporaries as to the benefits or detriments of Quakerism for Pennsylvania society, it is probably fair to say that Quakers succeeded in their endeavor to achieve the balance – at least temporarily. They dominated the Assembly during this period and created a civic and political culture based on their principles. The balance was achieved, however, not by a meeting in the middle, but by significant weight on either extreme. How well they were able to preserve the unity and teach the dissent will become apparent in the next years.

[195] Isaac Norris Letterbook, 1719–1756, May 18, 1755, 73, HSP.

5

The Fruits of Quaker Dissent

Political Schism and the Rise of John Dickinson

During the heyday of Quakerism in the mid-eighteenth century, the practical necessities of governing began to challenge the applicability of Quaker theory. Even as their politicking was unifying the province, Quakers' own theologico-political cohesion was beginning to falter, and the dual ethic of unity and dissent that they had encouraged began to evolve in unexpected ways. Attributable mainly to John Kinsey's machinations in the 1740s, during the 1750s and 1760s, political Quakerism, or, more accurately at this point, Quaker-informed political behavior, began to separate into three roughly defined categories. These I will call "withdrawing,"[1] "radical," and "traditional." The main point of difference among them concerned the peace testimony in all its facets.

The withdrawers, whom most historians have taken to represent all of Quakerism from 1765 on, adopted Kinsey's restrictive interpretation of the peace testimony and, in what is known as the "Quaker Reformation," rejected any dealings with war.[2] Contrary to Kinsey's brand of politics, however, they went further and also rejected office-holding and civic agitation as incompatible with their principles. Far from being a "conservative" sort of Quakerism, as we might be tempted to call it, this was rather a new form that departed from the beliefs of the founders and historic theologico-politics of Quakers. In searching for a renewed purity in their Society, these Friends were coming to emphasize the unity of Quakerism against the outside world. They were a growing minority in PYM and their interpretation of Quakerism would eventually dominate the Society permanently, but not until after the Revolution. The leaders of this faction were men such as Israel Pemberton, clerk of the meeting.

The radical strain of Quaker-informed politics was, by contrast, in a sense a truly conservative one, albeit unconsciously. These Friends (still in good standing during this period) and their non-Quaker supporters seemed to revive

---

[1] Following Garry Wills in *A Necessary Evil*.

[2] For the most thorough discussion of this episode, see Jack D. Marietta, *The Reformation of American Quakerism, 1748–1783* (Philadelphia: University of Pennsylvania Press, 1984).

the earliest expression of Quakerism, before the peace testimony was adopted. They were more atomistic and contentious in the public sphere, and they had little use for the peace testimony in any of its expressions. They did not respect the sanctity of the constitution, nor would they eventually have qualms about taking up arms for their cause. Dissent characterized their behavior more than unity. Benjamin Franklin, himself not a Quaker, represented this faction. In the 1760s, Joseph Galloway also appeared to be a proponent of it.[3]

While both the withdrawers and radicals departed from how Quakerism had been expressed for the past ninety-some years, there also remained a traditional strain of Quaker-informed theory. Friends and their followers who exemplified this strain held to the pre-Kinseyan interpretation of the peace testimony and did not shun office holding or vigorous engagement in the public sphere; they tried to maintain the role of trimmer by respecting the sanctity of the constitution while also agitating peacefully for rights. Isaac Norris, Jr., now speaker of the Assembly, blended this and the radical strain without much difficulty. For a time in the 1770s, Joseph Galloway fit uncomfortably in this category. But the best, although imperfect, exemplar was John Dickinson. Though neither a Quaker nor ultimately a pacifist, he was nonetheless the most visible and articulate spokesman for the traditional theory and action from the 1760s through the Founding period.

These categorizations are admittedly inadequate tools intended to describe only generally the bent of each group. Moreover, they were hardly static, as adherents of each sometimes straddled the blurry lines. But the general contours hold and help explain the political developments in Pennsylvania and America at the end of the colonial period and into the early years of the Republic.[4] The following pages will describe how these three strains became distinct from one another beginning in the late 1750s, culminating in early 1760s with an incident known as the Campaign for Royal Government. Most importantly,

---

[3] Joseph Galloway is a complex character and one who deserves more attention than he will receive in this study. The scholarship on Galloway, now aged, gives unsatisfying analysis of his political theory. Some historians have identified his thought as Whiggish, which cannot explain his Loyalism in the Revolution. A lapsed Quaker, Galloway held some fundamental principles of traditional Quaker thinking, but rejected others. This and the next chapter will touch lightly on his stance in order to clarify the traditional Quaker position in the Revolutionary period. On Galloway, see Benjamin Newcomb, *Franklin and Galloway: A Political Partnership* (New Haven, CT: Yale University Press, 1972); Julian P. Boyd, *Anglo-American Union: Joseph Galloway's Plans to Preserve the British Empire, 1774–1788* (Philadelphia: University of Pennsylvania Press, 1941); John E. Ferling, *The Loyalist Mind: Joseph Galloway and the American Revolution* (University Park: Pennsylvania State University Press, 1977); and Robert M. Calhoon, "'I have Deduced Your Rights:' Joseph Galloway's Concept of His Role, 1774–1775," *The Loyalist Persuasion and Other Essays* (Columbia: University of South Carolina Press, 1989), 74–93.

[4] It is not the purpose of this study to define "true" Quakerism or to determine in each case who was a "real" Quaker and who was not. It is simply to identify and describe different modes of discourse that grew from Quakerism and discuss how they were manifest and by whom. Likewise, there is no intent to label participants beyond how they identified themselves or were viewed by their contemporaries.

they will serve as a prelude to the following chapters by chronicling the rise of John Dickinson to the leadership of the traditional faction of the Quaker Party.

Growing Tensions within Political Quakerism

The discomfort with politics of the Friends who would become the withdrawers began when John Kinsey was in office. Part of the problem was that Kinsey's tactics seemed too extreme – there was too much politicking. But taken in perspective, Kinsey was no more "Governmentish," as William Penn put it, than the Quakers who had established and settled the Charter of Privileges, although he may have been better at it. By the 1740s some adversaries were making a distinction among Quakers between "that People in General" and the "very small number of the most Zealous & bigoted" who were pushing the Quaker Party agenda.[5]

Kinsey's reading of the London Yearly Meeting epistle in the State House admonishing Friends to keep other Friends in power might have been a turning point for some. And opponents kept a close eye out for chinks in the Quaker armor. Richard Peters speculated that the incident "may perhaps startle several Quakers." Yet he was also fully aware of Kinsey's leverage in Quaker circles and suspected that there were those "who dislike ye present Set & woud lend an helping hand to remove them, but may be afraid to stir after such an Injunction."[6] Similarly, during the same few years when the Kinsey-led Assembly petitioned the king in secret for the removal of Governor Thomas, Peters observed that "[t]heir Report is so full of gross abuse & rude Invective[s] yt several of their staunch Friends blame them openly as a set of People who act from a Spirit of Resentment more than ye Publick Good: of this number are... men of considerable consequence in their respective Meetings."[7] William Smith agreed hopefully that the behavior of the Quaker politicians in Pennsylvania was causing a rift in the transatlantic unity of the Society. "[T]hus their whole Conduct has been of a piece in this Country," he wrote, "tho' I am well-assured it is very much disapproved of and condemned by their Brethren the *Quakers* in England."[8]

Isaac Norris, Jr., meanwhile, continued to justify the extreme actions of the Assembly on the grounds that they were preserving the principles embodied in the 1701 Charter of Privileges. "A Governmt founded on the Principle of Liberty," he explained, "seems to imply the Exercise of all the Powers necessary for the good of the Society, and it is allowed by great Authorities that the Crown

---

[5] John Dickinson, Manuscript Notes on Pennsylvania Law, 1766, vol. 29, RRL/HSP. This document is the transcript of the proceedings before the Board of Trade in London relating to the Quaker government of Pennsylvania copied by John Dickinson.

[6] Richard Peters Letterbook, 128, HSP.

[7] Ibid., 85.

[8] Smith, *Brief State*, 22.

in appointing Governors over his Colonies cannot divest them of it, much less can it be supposed that any inferior jurisdiction can do it."[9]

While the dualism of Quaker unity and dissent could be reconciled, albeit precariously, by the peace testimony, the separation of the groups resulted in the disconnection of these two ideological strains and would have major implications for the immediate safety of the Quaker constitution as well as longer-term effects on the broader political culture prior to the American Revolution.

The Continuing Dilemma of Pacifism

A continual point of contention both among Friends and non-Friends was the use, or, as some saw it, the abuse of the peace testimony for political purposes in the early 1740s in the War of Jenkins's Ear. If there was a single issue that caused the tension between Quakers in- and out-of-doors, it was this. This tension began to surface during the Kinsey administration as he manipulated the testimony aggressively for retaining Quaker power in the colony. At that time, however, Friends who were uncomfortable with the manipulation, but sincere about peace and political engagement, were not yet ready to give up control of the government. With Kinsey's death in 1750, Israel Pemberton inherited a considerable amount of power as clerk of PYM and put forth a new pacifist ticket to try to repopulate the Assembly with less disruptive Friends. He might have succeeded if he had also held, as Kinsey did, the speakership of the Assembly. But that position went to Isaac Norris, Jr., who also used Kinsey's methods.[10]

When the issue of war and defense surfaced again, it proved a breaking point for some Friends. In 1754 with the French and Indian War threatening Pennsylvania, the crown ordered the Assembly to provide funds for the defense of its province. This should not have caused a great problem for Quaker politicians; they had resumed giving money for the king's use. Rather than simply passing a bill to raise the money, they saw another political opportunity – to control the finances of the province completely. They wrote an appropriations bill to oblige the king, but included in it "self-serving" provisions that would allow them complete power for deciding how the money was spent. The plan was that the governor would be forced to pass the bill or appear to be disobeying the crown.[11] To the Assembly's surprise, however, Governor Hamilton vetoed the bill. In their indignation, the Assembly wrote another of their inflamed

---

[9] Isaac Norris Letterbook, May 25, 1755, 77, HQC.
[10] Bauman, *For the Reputation of Truth*, 11.
[11] Marietta, *The Reformation of American Quakerism*, 139. Common in other colonies as well, this tactic of trying to control the finances of the province through the passage of appropriations bills was nothing new. According to *Lawmaking and Legislators*, Friends had been using this technique to manipulate the governors and proprietor since the 1690s. Governor William Markham "was forced to accept the enactment of a new constitution, the Frame of Government of 1696, in order to obtain a grant of additional funds to aid in the defense of New York." *LL*, 2: 71.

petitions to the crown, insinuating that their civil and religious privileges were being trampled upon.[12] Then, in a move that was exactly the opposite of Kinsey's in the 1740s – refusing to give money at all and claiming pacifism as the reason – they established a committee themselves and, rather than giving the money to the king "for his purposes," they paid the committee directly to buy provisions for royal soldiers.[13] They did this in order to ingratiate themselves with the crown, and in doing so, they blatantly ignored the traditional distinctions Quakers had made between things belonging to Caesar and God. As Jack Marietta put it, "The assemblymen were not rendering to Caesar; they were Caesar."[14]

The actions of the Assembly highlighted the fundamental dilemma pacifists must face when they control a civil government – their duty to protect its inhabitants. Norris himself seemed genuinely to desire a world in which Quakerly peace would prevail. "Could the world be brought into a general System of Peace," he wrote, "the avowed Principles of this Colony would certainly be very agreeable to the Christian profession in its greater purity." Unfortunately, the reality of the situation was otherwise, and Norris explained that "as that prospect is very distant," the Assembly had a political obligation to uphold. "[W]hile we hold our share of Governmt," Norris explained, "it becomes necessary for our Assemblys whose immediate concern it is to Tax themselves and their Constituents, to contribute the means of supporting it in the best manner we can." But for the moment, in spite of the transgression of the historic interpretation of the peace testimony that was taking place, Norris was confident it was not a serious problem. "Some of our members at first hesitated upon the mode of [defending the colony] but," he said, "upon examination I presume all were made easy."[15]

The Political Schism

But Norris was mistaken about the ease with which his brethren accepted the decision of the Assembly on defense. They, in fact, did not. Whatever the motives of the Assembly, that they were transgressing the peace testimony while claiming that their religious rights were being violated by the governor made them hypocrites in the eyes of many, including their brethren.[16] This incident would become increasingly problematic for a number of members of the Society over the next few months. As far as they were concerned, Quakers in office were being too fractious and disrespectful both to the authorities and the Society. Accordingly, in May of 1756, PYM wrote an epistle to London Meeting for Sufferings concerning its position in relation to the political

---

[12] *PA*, 5: 3703–13.
[13] *PA*, 5: 3841, and Marietta, *The Reformation of American Quakerism*, 140.
[14] Marietta, *The Reformation of American Quakerism*, 141.
[15] Isaac Norris Letterbook, May 25, 1755, 77, HQC.
[16] Marietta, *The Reformation of American Quakerism*, 140.

situation in the province. It was a revealing document. Their first concern was "to give the Proprietaries some Assurance that whatever may be the Sentiments and Conduct of others, there is a considerable number of Friends who sincerely desire by following those Things which make for peace to revive and preserve our Friendship with them." This was a drastically new tone toward the Proprietary. Philadelphia Friends could be certain that their message would assure a sharp distinction between them and members of the Quaker Party. Second, they wanted "to avert the Consequences we apprehend from the Assembly's address to the King." They were afraid, they explained, that the London Meeting and the Proprietors "might be induced to judge the Sentiments of Friends here to be different from what we hope and believe they are." In other words, they did not want anyone to mistake what they wrote for "a vindication of the Conduct of the Assembly." Neither did they want the behavior of the Assembly construed as "being consonant to our religious Sentiments or agreeable to us in every Instance." But the most powerful statement in the epistle was yet to come. In a move calculated to seal the break between the Religious Society of Friends and the Quaker Party, they wrote:

[I]t hath been clear that human contrivances and policy have been too much depended on and such measures pursued as have ministered causes of real sorrow to the Faithful, so that we think it is necessary that the same distinction may be made among you and out to be here between the Acts and Resolutions of the Assembly of this Province tho' the majority of them are our Brethren in profession and our Acts as a Religious Society.[17]

To prove their sincerity, the truly faithful "appear by freely resigning or parting with these temporal Advantages and Privileges we have heretofore enjoyed, if they cannot be preserved without violation of that Testimony on the Faithful maintaining of which our true peace and Unity depends." This epistle was signed by some of the most prominent Quakers of the day, including Israel Pemberton and Anthony Benezet. In short, many Friends came to believe as Samuel Fothergill would put it later, that "[t]he Assembly have sold their testimony as Friends to the people's fears."[18]

The event that followed marked a significant moment in Quaker history, the "Quaker Reformation." It should be considered both a political and a religious event. In 1756 several Quaker members of the Assembly abdicated their seats in the House. Norris did not seem surprised when he recorded that "[s]ix of our Members of Assembly (all friends) have resigned their Seats in ye House, & I have this day Issued writs for a new Election." Eventually, ten Friends abdicated office that year. Norris, ever the politician, even claimed that the voluntary resignation of the Assemblymen could be considered a victory of sorts for the Quaker Party – it was proof against the governor's charge "that

[17] PYM to London Meeting for Sufferings, 5th mo. 1756, Philadelphia Yearly Meeting, Minutes, 1747–79, FHL.
[18] Samuel Fothergill, "The Life of Samuel Fothergill," *Friends' Library*, 9: 170.

[Quakers] use all arts to Possess and are tenacious of the Power they acquire by every stratagem & all ye Influence they are masters of." He concluded that "[s]uch facts [their] Resignation must confute with great force, for facts my frd are stubborn things."[19] Benjamin Franklin, a rising figure in Pennsylvania politics and one who had less regard for the peace testimony than Norris, wrote triumphantly that "[a]ll the Stiffrumps except One, that could be suspected of opposing the Service from religious Motives, have voluntarily quitted the Assembly."[20] But while Norris and others downplayed the turmoil caused by Friends leaving office, John Pemberton commented that the events "have produc'd a greater & more fatal change both with respect to our State of affairs in general & among us as a Society than Seventy preceding years."[21] The way events unfolded after the "Reformation," it would seem that Pemberton's assessment was the more accurate one.

Reflecting on his civic duty during this tumultuous time and comparing himself to his brethren, Norris wrote, "My own thoughts of the duties of a publick Character may probably be more enlarged than those of some of my very worthy Frds and Acquaintances." Taking what was considered a worldly path by many Friends, Norris explained that "[m]y own inclinations for many years have been strongly bent upon retreat and the publick station I suffer myself to hold arises from a Duty I apprehend every member of Society owes to the Publik when that Duty becomes binding upon him by the voluntary call of others."[22] This penchant for withdrawal from the public sphere for the sake of purity, while not historically an aspect of traditional Quaker behavior – as Penn had advised his children, they should assume office if God called them to – was nonetheless an inclination that many Quakers, even more aggressive politicians such as Norris, struggled against.[23] On the other hand, it must have been clear, even to Norris, that his Assembly had set a dangerous precedent in allowing

---

[19] Isaac Norris Letterbook, June 16, 1756, 100, HQC.

[20] Benjamin Franklin, quoted in *LL*, 2: 71. See also *PA*, 4: 565–66.

[21] John Pemberton to John Fothergill, November 27, 1755, Pemberton Papers, XI, 20, HSP. Scholars dispute the character of their withdrawal from government. Marietta writes that "these Friends did not espouse abandoning government in order to escape being tainted by the world beyond the Society of Friends. Instead, they had a vision that more might be done for society, or its suffering members, from a private station and in a philanthropic way" (*The Reformation of American Quakerism*, 136). It is no doubt true that Friends continued to work for the improvement of society out of office and to engage politically. In their own terms, however, it is hard to understand their withdrawal from government as anything but a protest against the political world and a quest for purity. Frederick Tolles finds that Friends left office because political power forced them to dilute their religious testimony. "The exercise of political power involved compromise," he writes, which in turn necessitated "some abatement of Quaker ideas" (Tolles, *Quakers and the Atlantic Culture*, 50).

[22] Isaac Norris Letterbook, May 25, 1755, 77, HQC.

[23] It is worth noting, however, that many gentlemen considered public service a burden of their rank in society, and something they performed only out of a sense of obligation to those beneath them. The desire to withdraw into private life, then, did not belong exclusively to Quakers. On the duty of gentlemen to hold office, see Gordon Wood, *The Radicalism of the American Revolution* (New York: Vintage Books, 1993), 77–92.

Friends to prepare actively for war. With their ascendance into a leadership role, navigating between extremes of quietism and violence was becoming more difficult for Quakers to maintain amongst themselves and enforce in their polity.

Dissemination of the Quaker Ethic of Dissent and the Rise of the Radicals

Those who abdicated might have been able to assuage their consciences and ensure their own purity by removing themselves from the corrupt atmosphere of the Assembly, but at that moment they also ceased to take responsibility for the culture of dissent that they had created. When the most pacific Friends left office, they took much of their peace testimony with them. As we have seen, this testimony was more than simply a stance against war; it was a code of behavior for Friends and restraining mechanism on the libertinism inherent in their theologico-political theory and practice. It circumscribed individuals' dealings with one another and helped preserve the unity of the polity. Historically, the peace testimony did not necessarily restrain Friends from enthusiastic politicking and sometimes vicious partisanship. But until now, it had served its purpose in preserving the fundamental constitution of the Quaker polity. From their earliest dealings with the civil governments of England, Massachusetts, and Pennsylvania, Quakers continually struggled against the authorities to secure their liberties and privileges. Yet, as we have seen, they restricted their behavior to include only reform of the government, not its overthrow. Although there was more turmoil and clamor for rights in the Pennsylvania government than might have been expected in a Quaker colony, it was also the colony with the strongest assembly, with the one of the oldest constitutions, and it was the only one of the major colonies in which political change through violence or threat of violence had not been attempted.[24] But now, in 1756, there was a fundamental change in Pennsylvania. Over the previous seventy years, Friends had created an extremely active culture of political dissent, and then in the space of two years, they suddenly removed the two biggest checks on it – the peace testimony and then themselves as models for and enforcers of the Quaker process of dissent. They left more hawkish Friends and their supporters to guide the polity.

Mistakes some scholars have made are assuming, first, that the Assemblymen who withdrew represented the predominant strain of Quakerism in government, and second, that the abdication of these Friends meant the end of all Quaker participation in politics and civic life. A number of Quaker politicians in good standing with PYM did continue to hold office and wield power after 1756, and many Friends continued their engagement in the civil sphere for political causes. Scholars have not considered the import of the political culture that survived the partial Quaker abdication. Not only did a distinctive culture

[24] Greene, "The Growth of Political Stability: An Interpretation of Political Development in the Anglo American Colonies, 1660–1760," in *Negotiated Authorities*, 131–62.

remain, it continued stronger than ever, but now trifurcated in traditional, radical, and withdrawing forms. It is the radical culture and the practices that we will turn to next. Grown from the dissenting culture of the previous decades, as evidenced by the Paxton Riot, it would ultimately be something against which the withdrawing Quakers would protest vehemently – the American Revolution.[25]

A perennial problem of Quakerism has always been how to keep people from adopting the liberating aspects of the doctrine of the Inward Light, while at the same time respecting the other fundamental aspects of Quakerism such as peace, unity, and ecclesiastical authority. Since the earliest days, Friends struggled to make people both in- and outside of their Society understand the true meaning of the Light. The Quaker process of discerning God's will through the Light was liberating, but also limiting. As individuals were freed from worldly authority, they were subject to God's law as it was interpreted by the body of the meeting. Even among Friends, however, this had not always been clear. Many of the first Friends were formerly Ranters and Levellers, who were seen as radical individualists with little sense of political obligation. William Penn chided the Ranters, saying, "They would have had every man independent, that as he had the [Light] in himself, he should stand and fall to that, and nobody else" and that they "weakly mistook good order in the government of church affairs for discipline in worship."[26] When too many people persisted in identifying Quakerism with Ranterism, Robert Barclay attempted to distance Friends from them and advocate a stronger church government in *The Anarchy of the Ranters*. More than a century later, one of the chief concerns of the prominent eighteenth-century minister George Churchman was that "those who are unfaithful to that which opens the inward eye, and discover what is necessary to be followed, are liable to start aside, grow unruly and testy."[27]

If it was difficult to make convinced Friends aware of the true meaning of the Inward Light with all its implications for the community, it was doubly hard to pass along this sense to non-Friends. Quakers continually confronted this problem in their proselytizing. Puritans in seventeenth-century New England, for example, misunderstood what Friends meant by the Light of Christ within. They were certain that Quakers considered themselves to *be* Christ and denounced them as heretics, and arrogant ones at that. At the turn of the nineteenth century, respected Friend James Bringhurst expressed his concern about non-Friends misunderstanding the Quaker message. "I find it is the case," he said, "that many [people] at times attend [meeting] who are afraid of the cross in being members and therefore can indulge in their own ways." And, he adds,

---

[25] Hutson, *Pennsylvania Politics*, 4. Beeman describes it not as a dissenting culture but as a "popular" culture. It appears we mean the same thing – the (inadvertent) cultivation by Quakers of a radical strain of behavior that challenged their hegemony. I find it useful to be more specific about the character of that culture to elucidate its connection to Quaker theologico-political practice.

[26] Hill, *The World Turned Upside Down*, 253.

[27] Journal of George Churchman, 7th mo. 23rd day, 1804. 8: 95, HQC.

these people have "brought Friends into disrepute."[28] For Bringhurst, what was important was not that the attenders were not becoming convinced Friends, but rather that they were adopting some aspects of Quakerism – the readily appealing ones – and leaving the burdensome ones behind. But many Quakers either did not acknowledge or recognize the relationship of their encouraging individuals to "follow the Truth in [one's] own heart" and the "grievous refractory libertine spirit" that resulted from it.[29] This same misappropriation of Quaker principles is evident in mid-eighteenth-century Pennsylvania politics.

The Quakers were more successful than they probably ever imagined at disseminating some of their principles and promoting their unique political style. "Civil Quakerism" was not just commented on by denizens of Pennsylvania, it was adopted. Early in the history of the province, Isaac Norris, Sr., identified a troubling attitude in the Assembly. He observed to Penn in 1709 that "a strange, unaccountable humour, [has] almost become a custom now, [of] straining and resenting everything, of creating monsters and then combating them."[30] By 1742, Governor Thomas noted during his battle with the Assembly that "the seeds of Dissention have been plentifully sown" by Quaker politicians.[31] By the late 1740s, they had blossomed. It was clear that the missionizing was working – at least in part. Observers noted that there were men "who call... [themselves] Quaker but hath not the least appearance of one of that Stamp either in Garb, Conversation, or Behaviour."[32] Likewise, historians have acknowledged this dissemination of the Quaker ethic of resistance and dissent in general, claiming that Quakerism was sometimes used as a "vehicle for rebellion" by women who wanted to "deny the male-dominated spiritual and civil regime" or by young men rebelling against parental authority.[33]

Quakers had perhaps not expected such a degree and kind of success; or, if they did, they had not prepared for it. During this period, the "seeds of Dissention" had sprouted and begun to bear fruit – or as a Quaker opponent described the Quakerized politicians, "[b]astards begot by the Quakers on the body politic."[34] In the government as well as in their religious meeting, they were aware that some of their doctrines were "rejected by such as are not watchful, and so [these people] are out of the Feeling and Unity of Life."[35] As the Quaker cause expanded beyond narrow Quaker interests to the "general cause of liberty," so were their cause, manner, and some of their

[28] James Bringhurst to Thomas Pole, 12th mo. 29th day 1802, Bringhurst Letters, FHL.

[29] William Reckitt, "Life of William Reckitt," *Friends' Library*, 9: 65 and 72.

[30] Isaac Norris to Penn, 2nd of the 10th mo., 1709, *Penn-Logan Corresp.*, 2: 417.

[31] *PA*, 4: 2744.

[32] Robert Jenney, October 1748, cited in Tully, *Forming American Politics*, 298.

[33] See Carla Gardina Pestana, "The City upon a Hill under Siege: The Puritan Perception of the Quaker Threat to Massachusetts Bay, 1656–1661," *The New England Quarterly* vol. 56, no. 3 (1983), 323–53, 348. Also, Hill, *The World Turned Upside Down*, 311.

[34] Lynford Lardner to Richard Penn, March 7, 1758, quoted in Tully, *Forming American Politics*, 157.

[35] Barclay, *Anarchy*, 53.

method adopted by broader interests out of keeping with Quakerism. Indeed, as Alan Tully has described, wherever the Quakers' opponents were successful in making head-way against them, it was because they had adopted the Quakers' modus operandi.[36] Clearly, Friends had limited control over who adopted their political ideology and style or how it was used once it left the immediate bounds of their Society. The solution was relatively simple in their religious polity: discipline or disown the person who "scattereth himself."[37] But they could not purify civil society by simply exiling undesirables as Puritans did. In the first place, this was not the Quaker way. In the second, the political culture was now replete with these scattering types who were impossible to extricate.

By the 1760s, even when many "Quaker" politicians were not actually Quakers, they were still persistently identified as such by their Proprietary opponents.[38] Evidence of the conflation of the Society of Friends with the Quaker Party can be seen clearly in the political fallout from the 1764 incident with the Paxton Boys, the only violent challenge to the Pennsylvania government. In the wake of the French and Indian War, tensions were high between Indians, who were frustrated by their treatment from the British, and frontiersmen, who were unprotected by the Assembly. These non-Quaker settlers believed the Assembly was giving preferential treatment to the Indians. The hostile Ottawa Tribe attacked the whites, and the frontiersmen took up arms to protect themselves. Ultimately, the colonists ended up slaughtering numerous members of the Conestoga Tribe, a peaceful group of Christian Indians whom they believed were spies for the hostile tribes. The Paxton Boys, as the rioters became known, then marched on Philadelphia, intent on overthrowing the Quaker regime. Then, in a response that only fueled the charges of hypocrisy against Friends, some radical Quakers and their supporters took up arms themselves, and prepared to meet the Paxtons in the city.[39]

The Paxton incident is significant in several ways. First, what it shows us immediately is the clear link in the public mind between members of the Society of Friends and the Quaker Party. Second, as will be discussed further later, the upheaval contributed to the growing rift between Quaker and non-Quaker factions within the Assembly. And third, as will be developed in the next chapters, this split metamorphosed into groups that would contend bitterly against each other during the Revolutionary period.

The pamphlet war and the series of political cartoons published after the incident show that there was no distinction made between the Quakers and the Quaker Party. In the cartoons, all of the peculiarities of dress and speech associated with Friends were portrayed in the caricatures of Quaker politicians engaging in illicit dealings with one another, heavy drinking, oppression of the

---

[36] Tully, *Forming American Politics*, 258.

[37] Barclay, *Anarchy*, 49.

[38] Richard Alan Ryerson finds that in 1764, 42 percent of the Assembly was Quaker. "Portrait of a Colonial Oligarchy," in *Power and Status*, 112.

[39] For a detailed account of the incident, see Brooke Hindle, "The March of the Paxton Boys," *WMQ* 3rd ser., vol. 3, no. 4 (1946), 461–86.

FIGURE 6. A 1764 political cartoon depicting the tensions between the Quaker government and the Paxton Boys. The Quakers (in broad-brimmed hats) are shown groping an Indian woman and arming themselves against the frontiersmen as Benjamin Franklin, one of the leaders of the Quaker Party, watches from behind the scenes. "An Indian Squaw King Wampum spies/Which makes his lustful passions rise./But while he doth a friendly Jobb, /She dives her hand into his Fob./And thence conveys as we are told;/His Watch whose Cases n'ere of Gold./When Dangers threaten tis mere nonsense:/To talk of such a thing as Conscience./To Arms to Arms with one Accord,/The Sword of Quakers and the Lord./Fill Bumpers then of Rum or Arrack:/We'll drink Success to the new Barrack./Fight Dog! Fight Bear! You're all my Friend[s]./By you I shall attain my Ends:/For I can never be content/Till I have got the Government./But if from this Attempt I fall,/Then let the Devil take you all." (LCP)

Germans, and lewd acts with a half-clad Indian woman (Figure 6). A similar conflation occurs in *The Quaker Unmask'd*, the most inflamed pamphlet on the Paxton incident. The pamphleteers did not even bother to use the name Quaker Party, and instead merely referred to the Quakers or the Society.[40] This confusion was no doubt compounded – and perhaps even cultivated – by one of the leaders of the Quaker Party at the time, Benjamin Franklin.

---

[40] For a discussion of the pamphlet war and the accompanying cartoons, see Alison Olson, "The Pamphlet War over the Paxton Boys," *PMHB* vol. 123, nos. 1/2 (1999), 31–55.

Though frequently mistaken in popular culture today for a Friend, Franklin was not. In fact, he disagreed with some of the most basic Quaker principles, most importantly, pacifism. Moreover, as we shall presently see, his political style put him at odds with many of the truly Quaker politicians. But he learned well from Quakers. His autobiography is rich with accounts of the Quaker influences on this thought and behavior. No doubt because of this influence, he was an excellent politician. When it served his purposes, he took what he needed from Quakerism and left the rest. The most obvious evidence of this is when he dressed and acted like a Quaker for calculated effect. During his travels to France as an ambassador for the American colonies in the 1770s, Franklin presented himself as a Quaker.[41] Designing to reap the advantages of the French obsession with Quakerism and their association of it with republican virtue, Franklin dressed in the plain Quaker costume, adopted the grave simplicity of Quaker manners (only to the extent that it would amuse the French court, that is), and made no efforts to correct misperceptions that he was not a member of the Society. "This Quaker wears the full costume of his sect," proclaimed one Frenchman.[42] With this sort of blatant manipulation of the Quaker image, Franklin was not beloved among Friends. It was he, partnered with Joseph Galloway, who would lead the Assembly into the controversy over royal government.

Yet even as Quaker-informed politics was splitting into the extremes of withdrawal and radicalism, we can see the persistence of a traditional strain of thought and behavior. There were a few men, who, although not necessarily formally affiliated with the Quaker religious Society, represented the historic Quaker cause more than many of their own members. The most important of these men for the next several decades was John Dickinson.

John Dickinson's Quaker Connections

Although John Dickinson was never a convinced member of the Society of Friends, he was what Quakers call a "fellow traveler." With both parents being Friends in good standing, he was born a "birthright Quaker" in 1732 and raised in a Quaker household. Although his father's relationship to the Society became remote, he was never disowned. His mother continued a devout Quaker her whole life. Dickinson himself was always very aware of and interested in his family heritage.[43] In 1770 he married into one of the most prominent Quaker families in the colonies. His wife, Mary (Polly) Norris, was the daughter of

---

[41] Franklin's Quaker persona in France is well-known. See, most recently, Gordon Wood, *The Americanization of Benjamin Franklin* (New York: Penguin, 2004), 180, 181. Also see Alfred Owen Aldridge, *Franklin and His Contemporaries* (New York: New York University Press, 1957), 59–60; Verner W. Crane, *Benjamin Franklin and a Rising People* (Boston: Little, Brown, 1954), 174; David Schoenbrun, *Triumph in Paris: The Exploits of Benjamin Franklin* (New York: Harper & Row, 1976), 95.

[42] Edward Everett Hale, *Franklin in France* (Boston: Roberts Bros., 1887–88), 90.

[43] Flower, *John Dickinson, Conservative Revolutionary*, 1.

Isaac Norris, Jr., and was herself a paragon of Quaker virtue. Dickinson's entire immediate family, his wife and two daughters, were much stricter Quakers than his parents had been.[44]

In his younger days, Dickinson's Quaker leanings were not as apparent or as fully developed as they would become in his later years. As a young man, he refused any affiliation with the Society of Friends, including marrying "under the care of the meeting," as Quaker Discipline dictated. His stubbornness on this point occasioned a rift between him and his bride-to-be that illuminates his thoughts about religion at the time. In a letter to his future sister-in-law, Dickinson spelled out his reasons for resisting the supervision of Friends and his views on organized religion. At first, he seemed to have a dislike of Quakerism in particular, writing that Mary "has been brought up, I fear, with such a Veneration for the Society of Friends, as teaches one to revere all its Rules as equally inviolable." Dickinson was troubled by his conviction that Mary's judgment had been skewed by not thinking for herself and rather, that "by always conversing with people who think & speak in one way," she had become complacent – and, in effect, brainwashed – by having "the same sentiments perpetually repeated to [her], & therefore believe[ing] them to be universally right." But as he explained his views further, it became clear that Dickinson was not objecting to the principles of Friends per se, but rather to conducting one's life according the "the Rules of a private Society" instead of a general understanding of "Virtue & Honor." "[I]f an Act is not contrary to the Laws of Virtue or of our Country," he asked, "can any Rule of a particular Society, however positive it may be, make that act improper or dishonourable?" Therefore, he reasoned, a civil marriage should be sufficient to satisfy Mary's sense of propriety. "Let her only determine to consider," Dickinson pleaded to her sister, "the Reason of any opinions inculcated by Education, and she will distinguish between those essential to Virtue & Piety, and those merely arbitrary & derived only from Rules of private Men."[45] Perhaps it was this argument to reject the "rules of men" in favor of a higher understanding of moral law gained from one's own or collective understanding – very Quakerly itself – that convinced Mary. She and John were eventually married in a civil ceremony (but with a Quaker-style marriage certificate[46]), for which she was disowned by her meeting. Not much later, however, Mary returned to her meeting and was reinstated after she formally apologized for her transgression from the Discipline.[47] From that point she remained a member in good standing.

But Dickinson's sympathy with Quakerism would emerge clearly over the years as he, according to one observer, "became much more of a Friend than

---

[44] Ibid., 148.

[45] Draft of letter from John Dickinson to Sarah (Sally) Norris [1769], Ser. I. a. Correspondence, 1762–1808, RRL/HSP.

[46] In the Maria Dickinson Logan Collection, HSP.

[47] Philadelphia Monthly Meeting Minutes, 12th mo, 28th day 1770, FHL.

formerly."[48] There was an evident progression in his thought and behavior from someone who functioned on the spiritual outskirts of the Society of Friends to a man who embraced Quakerism in almost every aspect of his life. So much of a Friend did he become that by 1789 a family acquaintance suspected that he would not approve of a non-Quaker husband for his daughter.[49] Not surprisingly, the turning point in his adherence to Quakerism seems to have been at the Revolution. Before the Revolution, for example, he saw a clear distinction between religion and politics, writing, "Religion and Government are certainly very different Things, instituted for different Ends" and they should be "kept distinct and apart."[50] After the war, and what must have been a traumatic time personally and professionally, he gradually accepted more Quaker tenets until he was among the most serious and publicly demonstrative among Friends. This in itself is telling, since, as we shall see, it was his Quakerism that caused much of his travail during this period. Nevertheless, he wrote after the Revolution that "[t]here is a Relation between the Principles of Religion and the Principles of Civil Society."[51]

Those unfamiliar with Quakerism find the idea of an "attender" or "fellow traveler" a perplexing one, and this lack of understanding of Quaker culture has occasioned much confusion on the part of scholars about Dickinson's religious proclivities, namely, whether he was a member of the Society of Friends.[52] He was not. He never joined the Quaker meeting. In 1807 he wrote to Reverend Samuel Miller, "I am not, and probably never shall be united to any religious Society, because each of them as a Society, hold principles which I cannot adopt."[53]

What is important in defining Dickinson's religion is that, unlike most religious groups, Quakers had a very fluid community in which individuals were accepted into their midst or rejected based on their behavior and beliefs more than their official status as recorded members. Friends and their friends moved constantly between grace and disgrace, and the line between who was and who

---

[48] Susanna Dillwyn to her father, September 20, 1789, quoted in Flower, *John Dickinson, Conservative Revolutionary*, 273.

[49] Ibid.

[50] Dickinson writing as "A. B." *Pennsylvania Journal*, May 12, 1768.

[51] John Dickinson, notes on government, n.d., Ser. I. b. Political, 1774–1807, n.d., RRL/HSP.

[52] Quakers and non-Quakers alike have perpetuated the myth of Dickinson as a convinced Friend for centuries. His contemporaries, including John Adams and Benjamin Rush, believed him to be a Friend. See Bernard Knollenberg, "John Dickinson vs. John Adams," 107; and Benjamin Rush to John Armstrong, March 19, 1783, in L. H. Butterfield, ed., *The Letters of Benjamin Rush* (Princeton, NJ: Princeton University Press, 1951), 1: 294–97. One of the earliest incidents of this mistake appearing in the historiography is in William Wade Hinshaw *The Encyclopedia of American Quaker Genealogy* (Ann Arbor, MI: Edwards Brothers, Inc, 1938), 505. Isaac Sharpless names him among the Quaker politicians in *Political Leaders*, 224–43. Bernhard Knollenberg corrects this misperception in "John Dickinson vs. John Adams," 142.

[53] John Dickinson to Samuel Miller, 8th mo. 10th day 1807, Ser I. a. Correspondence, 1762–1808, RRL/HSP.

was not a Quaker was decidedly blurry. James Bringhurst expressed a common understanding among Friends: "I am not for confining [all real Christian followers] within the limits of our Society[,] believing they are amongst various religious societies who endeavour to act consistent with all the knowledge receiv'd and so far I believe are right."[54] There was a formal membership procedure, but beyond that, there were no rituals performed on a daily basis that demarcated members from attenders of the meeting. When no records exist about the formal membership application of an individual, we can consult the minutes of the meeting for business, in which usually only full members were recorded. There were, however, many people such as Dickinson whose name never appeared in the minutes, but who were more Quakerly than many convinced members. These people, who adopted most theological tenets, customs, and principles of the Society without joining, were embraced by Quakers as one of their own. They were something less than full members, but something more than merely "ethnic Quakers." This is the mold into which Dickinson fit. True to all fellow travelers, as we shall see, he chose what he liked from Quakerism and rejected other aspects. For Dickinson, there was one main tenet he could not accept. As he wrote the year before his death, "I am on all proper occasions an advocate for the lawfulness of defensive war. This principle has prevented me from union with Friends."[55] We should note, however, that this was the same position held by a number of prominent Quakers when Dickinson entered Pennsylvania politics, including his father-in-law, Isaac Norris, Jr., who was never disowned by the meeting. And the peace testimony, as we have seen, encompassed much more than simply war. It was a way of moving in the world.

Without an understanding of the language and practice of Quakerism, it is difficult to recognize Dickinson's expression of them in his public political works, in which he was reserved (one might say politic); but it is hard to overlook his affinity for them in his private writings and personal deportment. His writings are suffused with religion as an organizing theme and a means for discerning the way to civil happiness. Although his interest in religion was ecumenical, his inclinations were not; they were mainly, though not exclusively, Quaker. He wrote about "the Light that Lighteth every Man that cometh into the World"; about being "holy in all manner of conversation"; and he collected newspapers clippings such as "*SOME REMARKS, On SILENT WORSHIP or DEVOTION; Seriously recommended to mankind universally for their most weighty consideration.*" He also demonstrated the unique ability of Quaker thinkers to combine an abiding piety with a fascination with and promotion of scientific enquiry. His essay *A Fragment*, published for "the religious instruction

---

[54] James Bringhurst to Jeremiah Wadsworth, 1st mo. 21st day 1801, Bringhurst Letters, FHL.
[55] John Dickinson to Tench Coxe, January 24, 1807, quoted in Flower, *John Dickinson, Conservative Revolutionary*, 301.

of youth," was steeped not only in Quakerly language but used religion to explain the latest and most important scientific principles.[56]

Over the years his outward behavior changed as well to mirror that of honored Friends, such as Anthony Benezet and the Pembertons. He adopted the testimony of plainness, including in his speech – using "thee" and "thou," taking an affirmation instead of an oath when he assumed the presidencies of Delaware and Pennsylvania, and using the traditional Quaker practice of naming the days and months by number – and thereby made a public statement of his affiliation.[57] James Bringhurst observed in 1799 that "he has now taken up the cross so far as to use the plain language to all people & is diligent in attending our religious Meetings for worship."[58] Indeed, Dickinson believed that although "Christianity is an active, affectionate, & social Religion," in order to fulfill our "Duties to our fellow creatures[, i]t therefore requires separation from them, tho enjoining 'that we be not conformable to the ~~vain fashions & Usages of the~~ World [Rom. 12.2.].'" Dickinson worried, however, that some Friends might have taken these testimonies too far: "In following [the testimonies]," he cautioned, "the utmost Attention is necessary, least distinction from others by plainness of Manners & Customs assume the place of Virtues, and become snares." Others too had made this criticism of Quakers throughout the decades. Yet he ultimately believed that Quaker testimonies "may be exceedingly beneficial, by promoting 'moderation' in ourselves and others, & especially in young persons."[59]

In addition to adopting the testimonies and attending meeting several times a week, he also assumed many of the main Quaker causes as his own, such as abolitionism, prison reform, education, and opposition to the establishment of theaters. For example, his "desire to prevent a continuance of slavery" was strong enough that in 1777 he provided for the manumission of his slaves. Recollecting the occasion, a witness noted that "his conviction of duty, on this subject, was so strong, that it seemed to him 'The recording Angel stood ready to make Record against him in Heaven, had he neglected it.'"[60] Bringhurst hoped that in this regard Dickinson would undertake "an exertion of his Talents & influence with others in high places in the World, such as General Washington, etc. who yet hold the black people as Slaves, as his own example would preach loudly to them."[61] And, indeed, as president of Delaware,

---

[56] John Dickinson, manuscript notes for *A Fragment* (1796), Ser. I. e. Miscellaneous, 1761–1804, n.d., RRL/HSP.

[57] Flower, *John Dickinson, Conservative Revolutionary,* 200–01.

[58] James Bringhurst to Thomas Pole, 26th of the 7th mo, 1799; and to Elizabeth Coggeshall, 8th of the 10th mo. 1799. Bringhurst Letters, FHL.

[59] John Dickinson, religious notes, n.d., Ser. I. e. Miscellaneous, 1761–1804, n.d. RRL/HSP. The crossed out portion is Dickinson's mistaken addition to Romans 12. 2. The language is typical of what is found in Quaker journals of the period.

[60] John Dickinson, May 12, 1777, Ser. I. e. Miscellaneous, 1761–1804, n.d., RRL/HSP.

[61] James Bringhurst to Thomas Pole, 26th of the 7th mo, 1799. Bringhurst Letters, FHL.

Dickinson drafted a bill for the gradual emancipation of slaves, and he protested it more vehemently than others in the Constitutional Convention.[62] Prominent Friend Warner Mifflin wrote approvingly to Dickinson in 1786, praising his testimony of plainness and affirming the Quaker belief that it is more important to act like a Quaker than to become one in name: "in as much as thou hast been favoured to do so much toward unfettering thy self from the delusive entanglements of Temporal and Uncertain Riches, may thou be strengthened and encouraged, (I don't mean to come to bear the name of a Quaker[;] this the least of my concern for thee)."[63] There were, of course, still some Friends who wistfully imagined what "a vigilant advancer of [Quaker causes] into execution" Dickinson would be "[i]f thou wast became a member of [the] Society."[64]

By the end of his life, Dickinson had begun to proselytize in the style – that is to say, cordially but firmly – of the most devout Quakers of his time such as George Churchman, Robert Pleasants, and James Bringhurst, who implored powerful figures including Thomas Jefferson, George Washington, and Patrick Henry to adopt Quaker concerns as an example to others. In an 1801 letter to Thomas Jefferson, for example, Dickinson wrote, "My Belief is unhesitating, that by his superintending Providence a Period greatly favorable is commencing in the destiny of the Human Race. That he may be pleased to honor thee as an Instrument for advancing his gracious purpose and that he may be thy Guide and Protector, is the ardent wish . . . of thy affectionate Friend."[65] When Dickinson died in 1808, he was buried in the cemetery of Wilmington Friends Meeting.[66]

In discussing Dickinson's political thought, there is no argument here that he adhered strictly to all tenets of traditional religious or political Quakerism,

---

[62] John Dickinson, "An Act for the gradual Abolition of Slavery," Logan Papers, n.d., vol. 30, HSP.

[63] Warner Mifflin to John Dickinson, 8th mo. 11th day 1786, Ser. I. a. Correspondence, 1762–1808, RRL/HSP.

[64] Ann Emlen, Jr., to John Dickinson, December 21, 1787, quoted in Sharpless, *Political Leaders*, 238–39.

[65] John Dickinson to Thomas Jefferson, 21st of the 2nd mo., 1801, Ser. I. a. Correspondence, 1762–1808, RRL/HSP.

[66] The work that describes Dickinson's Quaker connections most thoroughly and begins to make a case for the interpretation of his political thought as part of his Friendly beliefs is Frederick Tolles's "John Dickinson and the Quakers," 67–88. Although many cite the importance of Quakerism in Dickinson's life, says Tolles, "no one has ever tried to say with exactness just what that Quaker influence was or just how it expressed itself in his thought and action" (67). Tolles has made the best attempt to date to assess this influence, and my interpretation agrees with his; nevertheless, he did not venture to explore the deeper meaning of Quaker political thought that animated Dickinson's intellect. Only a few historians have followed in this vein – of identifying Dickinson's Quakerism but they too neglect analysis. In his *Pamphlets of the American Revolution, 1750–1776.* vol. 1 (Cambridge, MA: The Belkap Press of Harvard University, 1965), Bernard Bailyn cites Tolles, agreeing with him about the influence of Quakerism on Dickinson's thought, but then proceeds to analyze it strictly in terms of Whig republicanism (660–67).

especially in his early years. He was indeed "too large a man to be bound in his opinions by [Quaker] practices."[67] Likewise, many of his beliefs toward the end of his life were commensurate with those of the other Founders and not uniquely Quaker. There are, however, a number of principles and concerns he espoused that were found almost exclusively among Friends. But as much as the specific doctrines he held, what makes his political theory Quaker are the processes and methods he advocated and practiced. In most instances, even when he appeared to be spiritually distant from Friends, he nevertheless held to a traditional mode of Quaker political theory and practice that he had imbibed from the culture around him. During the 1760s, he would step to the fore of Pennsylvania and then national politics to become the Quakers' most visible spokesman for their political principles.

The Campaign for Royal Government

Since 1757 a controversy had been brewing between the Assembly and the Proprietary, one which would for the first time accentuate the three strains of Quaker-informed politics in Pennsylvania. Known as the campaign for royal government, for many reasons, this controversy would become more extreme than previous disputes.[68] Antagonism between the Proprietary and the Assembly had always been present and growing, especially in the late 1750s as defense and finance issues became more pressing. The immediate issue concerned the Assembly's contention that Thomas Penn's land should be taxed and that he should share the burden of the public revenue. Governor Andrew Hamilton insisted that he would approve no laws to that effect except by royal order. Meanwhile Penn, resentful of the Assembly's control of the provincial purse, instructed Hamilton to interfere with the Assembly's power to raise funds through taxes and interest on loans until the governor received a veto power over their expenditure of money. With its source of income gone, the Assembly's existing funds dried up quickly, and by 1763, Penn thought it would simply acquiesce to his demands. But it did not. Instead it launched its most vehement attack against the proprietor in Pennsylvania history. The Assembly's goal became not just to subvert the authority of the governor and manipulate the proprietor as in the past. This time it sought to overthrow the government entirely, abolish their charter, and replace them both with a royal government. The matter ultimately turned on a question that would come

---

[67] Stillé and Ford, *Life and Writings*, 1: 304.

[68] For the sake of focusing on the issue of constitutionalism and Dickinson's philosophy, what follows is a simplification of this episode in Pennsylvania history. The complexities of motive and action in both the Assembly and the electorate have been addressed in detail elsewhere. See James H. Hutson, "The Campaign to Make Pennsylvania a Royal Province, 1764–1770, Part I," *PMHB* vol. 94 (1970), 427–63; Hutson, *Pennsylvania Politics*; Marietta, *The Reformation of American Quakerism*; David L. Jacobson, "John Dickinson's Fight against Royal Government, 1964," *WMQ* 3rd ser., vol. 19, no. 1 (1962), 64–85, 64.

to the fore again during the Revolution – which constitution should Quakers privilege? Their local provincial constitution, or the Imperial British one?

Popular sentiment against the campaign and Quakerism, fueled in part by the Paxton incident, quickly heated up.[69] "Nothing else than a King's government will now suit the stomach of a Quaker politician," wrote an opponent of it. This author seems to have a fairly clear vision of the new radicalism of the Quaker Party:

Not that you love his Majesty neither . . . many who now push for a King's government, have never paid a farthing of a tax for the King's use . . . But whether it proceeds from a love to his Majesty, from a hatred of the Proprietor, from some hopes of keeping the people under a Quaker-yoke for ever by this scheme, or from a desire to throw down the whole fabric together, if you must fall, – whatever the motive, – you are determined on having a King's government.[70]

Other writers came out in defense of the plan. "The Quakers, when they found Life, Liberty and Property were no longer secure under a P——y Government, did, from a *perfect Confidence* in their *Sovereign*, unite in petitioning for a *Royal Government.*"[71] What neither side recognized was that the Society of Friends was not the originator of the campaign nor were most individual Friends proponents of it.

The campaign for royal government was, in fact, a significant departure from traditional Quaker political practice. At times when situations were tense, the idea of resorting to a royal government had been bantered about, but it was essentially empty talk. Friends had never seriously entertained the possibility of putting their fate into royal hands. On the contrary, for example, when word got out that Penn, in his frustration with the Assembly in 1704, was considering selling Pennsylvania to the crown, the idea was met with opposition from the Assembly.[72] Likewise, when later proprietary governors had ambitions toward a royal governorship in Pennsylvania, Quakers resisted.[73] They were afraid of losing their privileges under the crown, but it was more than that. The extent of Quaker resistance had always remained within the bounds of their own constitution. They confidently denied their proprietor his rights, evaded royal commands, and petitioned for the removal of their governors.[74] But it was not within their purview either ideologically or constitutionally to overthrow their entire government. Despite this tradition of privileging their

---

[69] See Beeman, *Varieties of Political Experience*, 241–42.

[70] Williamson, *The Plain Dealer*, 9–10.

[71] *An Address to the Rev. Alison, the Rev. Mr. Ewing, and others, Trustees of the Corporation for the Relief of Presbyterian Ministers, their Widows and Children: Being a Vindication of the Quakers from the Aspersions of the said Trustees in their Letter published in the London Chronicle, No. 1223,* By a Lover of Truth (Philadelphia, 1765), 15.

[72] See *PWP*, 4: 257, 381.

[73] Tully, *Forming American Politics*, 260–61.

[74] They attempted this most recently in 1742 and in 1755 Isaac Norris wrote in his letterbook that "nothing will unite ye different Branches of ye Legislature but a removal of [Governor Robert Hunter Morris]." Isaac Norris Letterbook, Nov. 27, 1755, 93, HSP.

local constitution, in the 1740s with Kinsey's extreme politics, Richard Peters could write prophetically: "It is my sincere opinion that the managers of the Opposition wou'd resign their All than give up their Power, & wou'd rather see the Governmt. in the Hands of the Crown than the Pro[prietors]. And on the other hand some People would rather give up the Constitution than have the Quakers in the Legislation."[75] In one stroke, Peters predicted the two biggest events in late-eighteenth century Pennsylvania constitutional history – the move for a royal government in 1764 and the abolishment of the Charter of Privileges, accomplished by Revolutionaries in 1776.

Despite popular conceptions and the continued Quaker domination of the Assembly, the Society of Friends as a body was moving farther away from the political scene. Beginning with that powerful epistle in 1756, they had attempted to dissociate themselves from the dissenting culture that it had created and that was now moving forward without it. The move for royal government was the most salient example of the dissemination of the Quaker ethic and the incident that accentuated a temporary break between the Society of Friends and the Quaker Party. The Party at this time was led by two men, Benjamin Franklin and lapsed Quaker Joseph Galloway.[76] The first man prominent Quaker Israel Pemberton considered to be a danger to Quakerism, and the second he called "a weak & bad man."[77] The move for a royal government was, in some ways, the logical culmination of Quaker dissent, but it was nothing most Quakers ultimately advocated.

Initially, however, there was a difference of opinion within the Society on which way to go – with the Quaker Party as it was now manifest or with a more traditional Quaker political practice. The split among Friends on this issue, both in and out of office, ran to a great degree along generational lines. Early on in the controversy, many older members, including weighty Friends on both sides of the Atlantic, took the traditional view of Quaker politics and opposed the petition. Among these were Isaac Norris, Israel Pemberton, John Fothergill, and David Barclay. So vehemently did Norris object to the petition that he resigned over it – twice. Meanwhile, similar to twenty years earlier when "the young fry of Quakers" were making "insolent rude Speeches . . . against all in Authority, the King not excepted," now a young "Set of Hotspurs" favored the petition.[78] It is important to note, however, that for a time many Quakers in good standing, tempted by the radicalism of the leaders, believed that a change of government was their best chance for securing religious liberty – always their main concern. At first, members of the Assembly found Franklin's proposal appealing.[79] Moreover, early on in the controversy, most Friends

---

75 Richard Peters Letterbook, 353–56, HSP.

76 Galloway was a birthright Friend but had left the Society and gravitated toward Anglicanism. See Newcomb, *Franklin and Galloway*, 22.

77 Hutson, *Pennsylvania Politics*, 166; Israel Pemberton quoted in Marietta, *The Reformation of American Quakerism*, 202.

78 Richard Peters Letterbook, 17, HSP; and Norris, quoted in Hutson, *Pennsylvania Politics*, 156.

79 Hutson, *Pennsylvania Politics*, 137.

understood that the issue was complex and they moderated their criticisms of Friends who disagreed with them.[80] Ultimately, however, PYM came out against the change, urging London Meeting for Sufferings not to support the petition either. Finally, most Friends rejected the Franklin-Galloway plan.[81]

A key figure in their decision was John Dickinson. In the debate, he was typical of the portion of the Assembly that opposed the petition with one notable exception – his age.[82] At age 32, Dickinson sided firmly with the traditional position held by older Friends. After 1766 he would take over as the new leader of the Quaker Party; but already in 1764, he stepped forward and advocated the traditional Quaker priorities of constitutional perpetuity and peaceful reform of injustice. On May 24, 1764, he made his case in *A Speech Delivered in the House of Assembly of the Province of Pennsylvania*.

In what one perplexed historian calls "an odd mixture of conservative maxims and radical political doctrines,"[83] Dickinson pled not just for the preservation of the 1701 Charter and traditional Pennsylvania Quaker liberties, but also for the continuance of the Quaker process of peaceful resistance to oppression rather than fundamental change. The mixture might have blended conservatism and radicalism, but it was not odd at all. He first laid out his view for orderly and peaceable walking, arguing that men in the throes of emotion cannot possibly govern effectively. He explained that "those who deliberate of public affairs, that their minds should be free from all violent passions."[84] Drawing on the Ancients (a neutral source) to make his case, he quoted Tacitus, reminding the Assembly "[w]hich misfortune hath happened to many good men, who despising those things which they might *slowly* and *safely* attain, seize them too hastily, and with fatal speed rush upon their own destruction."[85] He then proceeded to enumerate the many reasons why the change would not work to their advantage.

For Dickinson, as for most Quakers, the 1701 Charter of Privileges was the embodiment of Pennsylvania's unique liberties, especially in that it secured all of the Quakers' rights as a dissenting sect. He then proceeded to enumerate the privileges they had enjoyed, the first and most important being "*a perfect religious freedom.*" Giving voice to a perennial Quaker fear, Dickinson suggested the possibility of Pennsylvania losing its religious liberty. With the switch to a royal government, they could very well be taken over by the Church of England, which was eager to establish itself more firmly in America, "especially," he said, "in those colonies, where it is overborne, as it were, by dissenters."[86]

---

[80] Marietta, *The Reformation of American Quakerism*, 197.

[81] Ibid., 200.

[82] Hutson, *Pennsylvania Politics*, 156.

[83] Jacobson, "John Dickinson's Fight," 64.

[84] John Dickinson, *A Speech Delivered in the House of Assembly of the Province of Pennsylvania* (Philadelphia, 1764), 1.

[85] Ibid., 4–5.

[86] Ibid, 18. See also Richard J. Hooker, "John Dickinson on Church and State," *American Literature* vol. 16, no. 2 (1944), 82–98.

In Pennsylvania history, the crown had at times been as much of a threat to Quaker liberties as the proprietors. He reminded them of the privileges they currently enjoyed and how these contrasted with traditional English liberties and royal prerogatives: "Posts of honor or profit are unfettered with *oaths* or *tests*" and are open to men who pay "strict regard to their conscientious persuasion." "In what other *royal government* besides the Jerseys," he asked, "can a *Quaker* be a witness in criminal cases and bear offices? *In no other.*" And in New Jersey it was allowed only because at the founding of that colony there was an "ABSOLUTE NECESSITY, from the scarcity of other proper persons, to make use of the people called Quakers in public employment." That scarcity no longer existed either there or in Pennsylvania. Dickinson highlighted the fact that Quakers were no longer the majority in any colony, and thus needed to guard their rights even more closely. "Any body of men acting under a charter," he warned, "must surely tread on slippery ground, when they take a step that may be deemed a surrender of that charter."[87] He explained, in sum, how unreasonable it would be to think that their "extraordinary privileges" would be preserved in any change of government.[88]

After reminding the Assemblymen of their unique charter and privileges, Dickinson noted the distinction between the traditional British interpretation of the fundamental law and the divinely inspired laws of Quakers by writing, "how contradictory some of these privileges are to the most ancient principles of the English constitution, and how directly opposite others of them are to the settled prerogatives of the crown."[89] If they changed from the Charter of Privileges to a royal government, they would be in the untenable position of requesting more freedom for themselves than inhabitants of England possessed. "It will not be an easy task to convince [Parliament]," he argued, "that the people of *Pennsylvania* ought to be distinguished from all other subjects, under his Majesty's *immediate* government."[90] Moreover, it was unknown what ills might arise as a consequence of this change. In what would become a leitmotif of Dickinson's writings, the danger of precedent, he warned, "We may introduce the innovation [of a royal government], but we shall not be able to stop its progress. The precedent will be pernicious."[91] The solution, then, was to act slowly and cautiously. Appealing to the traditional way in which Quaker politicians had redressed their grievances and secured their rights, he suggested retaining the Charter, if at all possible, and seeking mediation. "Let us desire his Majesty's judgment on the point, that has occasioned this unhappy difference between [us]. This may be done without any violence, without any hazard to our constitution."[92]

[87] Dickinson, *A Speech*, 11.
[88] Ibid., 20.
[89] Ibid., 16.
[90] Ibid., 22.
[91] Ibid., 29.
[92] Ibid., 24.

Although at first glance, it would appear that Galloway, in his zeal to abolish the Charter, had none of the traditional Quaker respect for the constitution. But like Dickinson, Galloway also honored it; the two simply differed on *which* constitution. Like most convinced Quakers, Dickinson privileged the Pennsylvania constitution for what it gave Quakers; Galloway looked instead to the British, which may have protected their property rights against Penn, but, as Dickinson argued, would not guarantee their rights as Quakers. It was not just the rights embedded in the constitutions that were at stake; it was also the process by which they were advocated and secured. In addition to abandoning the Quaker constitution, Galloway also left behind other Quakerly concerns and practices, such as popular sovereignty. In advocating a royal government, Galloway claimed to be drawing on the proven ability and right of representatives to change the constitution. He cited the usual Quaker arguments for amendment: that "every government in the civilized world, has been changed"; Dickinson retorted, *"by force and injustice."* Galloway argued that "the first frame of our government was altered"; Dickinson expounded, *"being found impractical, and,"* repeating Galloway's point, *"its 'privileges could hardly be exercised or enjoyed.'"*[93] Quoting William Penn at length, Dickinson rejoined with the explanation of the Quaker understanding of a constitution, that the government is not a contract to be broken but a trust put in place for the good of the people and the trustees do not have the right to abandon their position. The trust, quoted Dickinson from Penn, "should not be invaded, but be inviolably preserved, according to the law of the land."[94] In other words, the constitution may allow amendment, but not the dissolution of itself. Moreover, Dickinson challenged Galloway's un-Quakerly suggestion that the representatives could change the government without the approval of the people. Drawing from Sully's *Memoirs*, he wrote that "no step should be taken, *without carefully and deliberately consulting the people* . . . who would be affected by their measures."[95] As if to punctuate his argument about popular consent, Dickinson took his concern to the public, and an election in the middle of the controversy decided it. The Franklin-Galloway contingent was firmly put down with Franklin and Galloway themselves removed from the Assembly. Thus the campaign for royal government failed. Before this point, Quaker behavior toward the British government might have led us to suspect that they preferred their own provincial constitution over the imperial one. With the controversy now resolved, it is clear that was the case.

Throughout the controversy, Dickinson advocated the traditional aims and principles of Quaker theologico-political thought. It is easy to see how his

[93] In this instance, we must understand here that there is a difference between "change" and "alter." Here "change" means abolition of one constitution and adoption of another; "alter" means adapting an existing constitution. Dickinson rejected change but approved of alteration.
[94] William Penn quoted in John Dickinson, *A Reply to a Piece called The speech of Joseph Galloway, Esquire* (Philadelphia, 1764), 30.
[95] Dickinson, quoting Maximilian of Béthune, Duke of Sully, *Memoirs*, in *A Reply to a Piece*, 30. Sully's *Memoirs* advocated a plan for peace in Europe through a federation of powers.

position was exemplary of some key aspects of "civil Quakerism" and why his argument for the Charter was ultimately successful.[96] Other historians' conclusions that Dickinson eventually "arrived on the side of the Proprietary Party," which, for obvious reasons, also opposed the campaign, are simply mistaken.[97] He was no more a supporter of Thomas Penn than the Quakers, who had always resisted the Proprietary, and who had also resisted the change in government. But this is the usual interpretation of Dickinson's role in this controversy, and one that has contributed to the confusion about his political thought in toto.[98] That the Proprietary Party celebrated and promoted Dickinson's speech is merely proof of their using his words for their political advantage, not proof of his allegiance. "No man," he assured his colleagues, "can be more clearly convinced than I am, of the inconveniencies arising from a strict adherence to proprietary instructions." He elaborated that the "distinct and partial mode of taxation" that the proprietors were imposing on the Province was "granted on all sides to be unequal." Furthermore, he affirmed that he was not in league with the proprietors, writing that despite his disagreement with the Assembly on this point, "I always receive satisfaction from being on [the Assembly's] side."[99] Years later he would add, "The proprietary People are known to be & to have been uniformly my deadly foes throughout my Life."[100] He admitted that simply agreeing with Franklin and Galloway "would have been the most *politic* part for me to have acted," but that he was bound to dissent from the majority and obey "the *unbiassed dictates* of my *reason* and *conscience*."[101] Both were aligned with the traditional balance of Quaker principles.[102]

Scholars sometimes misinterpret Dickinson's politics in another way in the wake of this controversy. The election that ousted Franklin and Galloway brought Dickinson to the fore of Pennsylvania politics. He was elected by a landslide in 1764, supported by the so-called New Ticket, which was composed of Presbyterians, who had always opposed the Quaker Party, and others against royal government. After so recently identifying Dickinson as a partisan of the Proprietary, now scholars consider him the leader of the Presbyterian Party.

---

[96] Tully makes this observation in *Forming American Politics*, 304.

[97] Flower, *John Dickinson, Conservative Revolutionary*, 36.

[98] See, for example, Theodore Thayer, *Pennsylvania Politics and the Growth of Democracy: 1740–1776* (Harrisburg: Pennsylvania Historical and Museum Commission, 1953), 94, 177; Jacobson, "John Dickinson's Fight"; G. B. Warden, "The Proprietary Group in Pennsylvania, 1754–1764," *WMQ* 3rd ser., vol. 21, no. 3. (1964), pp. 367–89, 368; Bernard Bailyn, ed., *Pamphlets of the American Revolution*, 660, 661; Flower, *John Dickinson, Conservative Revolutionary*, 36; and Arthur J. Mekeel, *The Relation of the Quakers to the American Revolution* (Washington, DC: University Press of America, 1979), 34.

[99] Dickinson, *A Speech*, 30.

[100] John Dickinson to unknown, August 25, 1774, Ser. I. a. Correspondence, 1762–1808, RRL/HSP.

[101] Dickinson, *A Speech*, 30–31.

[102] Marietta calls him a "kindred spirit" with Quakers (*The Reformation of American Quakerism*, 248).

But contrary to those who claim a "marriage" between the two, Dickinson was no partisan.[103] Like traditional Quakers, Dickinson was a trimmer in, I argue here and in the following chapters, the principled sense.

Conclusion

At heart, Dickinson was a "Quaker politician" and as ecumenical in politics as his Quaker forebears. They believed, as Penn wrote, that "[a] wise Neuter joins with neither [Party]; but uses both, as his honest Interest leads him."[104] They accordingly allied themselves with Whigs or King James II as it suited their cause. Likewise Dickinson pursued a middle way that was based not on party affiliation but on the principle of preserving charter liberties. With this destination in sight, he navigated a straight course by shifting slightly toward whatever side needed his weight. Rather than considering Dickinson as joining different parties, it is more accurate to say that parties gravitated toward him, as in the case of the Presbyterians. As we shall see, however, his political convictions denied him a home in any camp, and, in the rough political seas of the 1760s and 1770s, his principles soon became realigned, although not permanently or without tensions, with the Quaker Party.

As Quakers first entered politics in seventeenth-century England, they did so as martyrs for their theologico-political cause. The persecution they experienced was not only because they adhered to radical religious doctrines but also because they resisted permanent factional alliances. They were thus accused of Ranterism by one side and of popery by the other. When Dickinson's enthusiastic engagement with Pennsylvanian, and later American politics, earned him the same confused charges of partisanship, he reflected on his stance. He wrote that his "sentiments perhaps may prove destructive to one, who designs his reputation on the basis of a party – since it is highly improbable, that any man may be esteemed by a party, unless he is bound to it by PREJUDICES as well as by PRINCIPLES."[105] Dickinson's identification with the culture of martyrdom that pervaded Quakerism began to surface at this time. He was aware of the course he was taking by following his conscience. He wrote that "A good man *ought* to serve his country, even tho' she *resents* his services."[106] Several years later in the contest with Britain as he again found himself the advocate of unpopular causes, he reflected on his choices in life and his role in the royal government controversy:

---

[103] Hutson, *Pennsylvania Politics*, 212–13. On the contrary, in the previously cited letter from Dickinson to an unknown Presbyterian (fn. 100), he allays the concerns of his recipient that he might be biased *against* people of that religion, which indicates the perceptions of his contemporaries.

[104] William Penn, *Some Fruits of Solitude* (London, 1693; rpt. Richmond, IN: Friends United Press, 1978), 61.

[105] Dickinson, *A Reply*, 34–35.

[106] Ibid., 31.

I reconcile myself to my Lot the more easily perhaps, because, from my first outset in Life, I had laid down to Myself these maxims, to which, thro the Divine favor, I have, I think, invariably adhered throughout the part that is past... –"Never to sollicit or seek directly or indirectly any Post of Profit or Honor – In public affairs, to pursue solely the good of my Country, and *to defy the World*"... Is it possible for a Man to give greater proofs than have been given in other Instances that he is govern'd by the Dictates of his Conscience & Judgment in public Affairs? What a Torrent of Passion did I oppose several years ago, disdaining the protection of the Proprietary Faction, while at the same Instant I brought on myself the utmost Indignation of the ruling Faction in Assembly?... Indeed by that single step, I cast myself out of a certain Income of several Hundreds of pounds a Year, besides losing the promising Prospects that presented themselves of my rising by the Power of the Factions![107]

Despite this political independence, interestingly, because of a passionate temperament and, no doubt, the contentious political culture in which he moved at this early stage of his career, Dickinson's personal deportment was not always in keeping with stated Quakerly principles of peaceful discourse and moderation. Despite his counsel of moderate behavior to the Assembly, he did not practice what he preached; the disagreement with Galloway provoked him to decidedly rash behavior. In his *Reply* to Galloway, for example, he spent little time on the constitutional debate, focusing instead on defending his reputation and criticizing in a taunting and sarcastic tone his opponent's lack of skills in writing and argumentation. More than this, however, after a particularly contentious session of the Assembly, he and Galloway came to blows on the steps of the State House.[108] Over the next two decades however, as Dickinson's faith matured with his politics, he managed to become more of an "orderly walker" and example to others of "peaceable conversation."

[107] Dickinson to unknown, August 25, 1774, Ser. I. a. Correspondence, 1762–1808, RRL/HSP.
[108] Flower, *John Dickinson, Conservative Revolutionary*, 42.

THE POLITICAL QUAKERISM OF JOHN DICKINSON, 1763–1789

6

Turbulent but Pacific

"Dickinsonian Politics" in the American Revolution

With the controversy over royal government decided, Pennsylvania turned its attention to the problems with Britain. In the next decade, the same issues at stake in the provincial debate over the Charter would be writ large in a national debate – how best to unify the polity and preserve rights in the face of an unjust government. This and the following chapter form a pair as they describe how the three factions of Quakerism persisted and exerted a tremendous influence on the course of national events. The traditional faction, supported by the withdrawers – who were hardly withdrawn at this point – dominated the Assembly until days before independence and infuriated the Revolutionary leaders. After the royal government controversy was decided, the radical faction temporarily lost all influence in the Assembly, and instead merged with other radical groups. As in this earlier controversy, the coming Revolution raised the question of which constitution Quakers of all sorts and their followers ultimately preferred – their local and peculiarly Quaker constitution or the remote and non-Quakerly constitution of the British Empire, or neither.[1] Throughout it all, Dickinson would remain a mediator and counsel the same course for America as he had for Pennsylvania, adherence to the constitution and peaceful advocacy of rights.

The story of Dickinson's *via media* between the extremes of withdrawing Quaker pacifism and revolutionary radicalism unfolds in five main episodes: The first is the period of the Stamp Act Controversy in 1765. The second is from the Townshend Acts and the publication of his *Letters from a Farmer in Pennsylvania* in 1767–68 until 1774. The third is the pivotal years just prior to independence, 1774 and 1775. The fourth is the spring months of 1776, immediately preceding the Declaration of Independence. The final phase, treated in Chapter 7, is the Critical Period, when Pennsylvania suffered its own revolution. At various points, Dickinson was embraced and rejected by

---

[1] "Non-Quakerly," as opposed to "un-Quakerly." The British constitution, while no longer hostile to Quakers, did not, as Dickinson argued, secure their liberties *as* Quakers.

all factions. Ultimately, without deviation, he ended up where he began, a Quakerly Patriot. As he explained it, "My Principles were formed very early in the Course of this unhappy Controversy. I have not yet found Cause to change a single Iota of my political Creed."[2] This and the next chapter will describe what his opponents would call "Dickinsonian Politics," noting especially the position of the Quaker community and his stance in relation to it.[3]

The Stamp Act Controversy, 1765

Contemporaneous with the campaign for royal government in which Dickinson was embroiled was the Stamp Act controversy, into which he entered with equal vigor. The peaceful resistance to the Act began not in Philadelphia, but in Boston. After days of almost-uncontrolled rioting, destruction of property, and other civil misconduct, Bostonians finally realized that violent protest was achieving nothing and was, in fact, counterproductive. They were compelled by their own extremism to reexamine their use of violence and force as a political tool. In this way they happened upon the use of nonviolent protest techniques such as boycott and nonimportation. But their abandonment of violence was also prompted by the demise of the Grenville ministry, which seemed to lessen the tyrannical inclinations of the British government.[4] Their peaceful techniques, in other words, were born of necessity and convenience, not principle. They did not disavow their earlier violent acts. Neither, as some scholarship would have it, did they engage in civil disobedience.[5]

At this point in the controversy with Britain, the Quaker position was generally unified in favor of resistance. The Pennsylvania Assembly resolved that it was their duty "to remonstrate to the Crown against the Stamp Act, and other late Acts of Parliament, by which heavy Burdens have been laid on the Colonies" and that they would send a committee to the Stamp Act Congress in New York.[6] Dickinson was nominated to be on the committee, and they were "strictly required to take Care that such Addresses, in which you join, are drawn up in the most decent and respectful Terms, so as to avoid every Expression that can give the least occasion of Offense to his Majesty, or to either House of Parliament."[7]

In New York, Dickinson served as the de facto leader of the Stamp Act Congress and the draftsman of the Resolutions of the Congress. He then began

---

[2] John Dickinson, "Notes for a Speech in Congress," May 23, 1775, *Delegates*, 1: 378.

[3] William Whipple to Josiah Bartlett, February 7, 1777, *Delegates*, 6: 236.

[4] See Maier, *From Resistance to Revolution*, 53–70.

[5] The less violent activities of Bostonians, such as the Boston Tea Party, are often noted as examples of civil disobedience. See, for example, Harry W. Jones, "Civil Disobedience," *Proceedings of the American Philosophical Society* vol. 111, no. 4 (1967), 195–98, 196; William G. McLoughlin, "Massive Civil Disobedience as a Baptist Tactic in 1773," *American Quarterly* vol. 21, no. 4 (1969), 710–727, 710; Michael Couzens, "Reflections on Violence," *Law & Society Review* vol. 5, no. 4 (1971), 583–604, 597.

[6] *PA*, 7: 5767.

[7] Ibid., 5769.

a campaign to publicize Quaker resistance tactics through a number of publications. Although Bostonians had realized that peaceful protest would get them farther than violence, they still had not mastered the subtleties of their technique. They resigned themselves to avoiding business that required the use of stamps.[8] Dickinson proposed a remedy to this passivity. There were two modes of peaceful resistance that he advocated, both of which were at the core of Quaker political behavior. One was the "business-as-usual" model; the other was economic sanctions. Both were tactics Quakers had been using in a variety of situations for years to resist unjust laws and customs. Indeed, the business-as-usual model of resistance was as old as Quakerism itself, and almost synonymous with it.

In an address on the Stamp Act to "Friends and Countrymen" (1765), Dickinson called for immediate resistance. His concern was that after all the initial violence, the new passivity was extremely hazardous. In continuation of the theme of the danger of precedent he expressed in the royal government controversy, he wrote, "They will have a Precedent furnished by yourselves, and a Demonstration that the Spirit of *Americans*, after great Clamour and Bluster, is a *most submissive servile spirit.*"[9] He reiterated that "Your compliance with this Act will save future Ministers the Trouble of reasoning on this head, and your Tameness will free them from any Kind of Moderation when they shall hereafter mediate any other Tax upon you."[10] Insofar as precedents established the constitutionality – and hence the permanence – of an act, Englishmen were generally wary of them. In this regard, Quakers were similar to their countrymen, though not identical. To Englishmen, legal "innovations" were potentially dangerous because they were measures that had never been tried before and did not have the weight of custom behind them. Precedents, on the other hand, had constitutionality because they were accepted and put to use.[11] To Friends, suspicious of human traditions, both innovations and precedents were dangerous because neither determined definitively the constitutionality of an act.[12]

Rather than risk the entrenchment of unconstitutional laws, then, Dickinson counseled civil disobedience by simply ignoring the act and continuing publicly about their business. "It appears to me the wisest and the safest course for you," he explained, "to proceed in all Business as usual, without taking the least

[8] Maier, *From Resistance to Revolution*, 71.

[9] John Dickinson, "Friends and Countrymen" [Address on the Stamp Act], (Philadelphia, 1765), 1.

[10] Ibid. On the doctrine of precedent during the conflict with Britain, see John Phillip Reid, *Constitutional History of the American Revolution: The Authority to Tax* (Madison: University of Wisconsin Press, 1987), 122–34.

[11] According to Reid, "The doctrine of innovation warned that an action was legally dubious because it had not been done before. Precedent was evidence of legality or constitutionality because something had been done before" (*Authority to Tax*, 123).

[12] Dickinson wrote, "Another argument for the extravagant power of internal legislation over us remains. It has been urged with great warmth against us, that '*precedents*' shew this power is rightfully vested in parliament." *Essay on the constitutional power*, 105.

Notice of the Stamp Act." In a Quakerly plea to the denizens of Pennsylvania, he suggested the salutary consequences of this course of action. "If you behave in this spirited Manner, you may be assured, that every colony on the Continent will follow the Example of a Province so justly celebrated for its Liberty." It had always been the goal of Quakers to set an example to others – whether in religious belief, personal deportment, or political action – as a form of proselytizing. The end result, reasoned Dickinson, could not be anything but favorable for the colonists. He calculated carefully the degree of resistance necessary to achieve their ends without too much disruption. "Your Conduct will convince *Great-Britain*, that the Stamp Act will never be carried into execution, but by Force of Arms; and this one Moment's Reflection must demonstrate, that she will never attempt."[13]

Dickinson's pamphlet *Late Regulations Respecting the British Colonies on the Continent of America Considered* (1765) took a slightly different approach. It also departed from other publications on British policy at the time that focused on the theories of republican government and the injustice of taxation without representation.[14] The purpose of this pamphlet was not to discuss rights in the abstract or what constituted proper parliamentary representation, although these too concerned him. Rather, he laid out the issues – the sufferings – and then a plan of action. Quaker theory was, as we have seen, a theory of action. In all his writings on the controversy, Dickinson stopped short of calling for an outright economic boycott of British goods by all the colonies in unison. This was something that Friends generally considered too harmful and disruptive to the polity when conducted en masse. Rather, the best choice seemed to Dickinson to be more subtle, "to promote manufacturers among ourselves, with a habit of conomy, and thereby remove the necessity we are now under of being supplied by *Great-Britain*."[15] He elaborated by suggesting that the colonists "keep the *British* manufactures we purchase longer in use or wear than we have been accustomed to do" and "supply their place by manufactures of our own."[16] Frugality and industriousness were far from being disruptive or illegal; they were republican virtues. They were also Quaker testimonies. In issuing this call for peaceful resistance through economic sanctions, Dickinson was drawing on Quaker practice, following in the footsteps of ministers such as John Woolman who boycotted products made by slave labor. A few scholars have appropriately noted that the nonimportation of the pre-Revolutionary period "appeared to be a Quaker method of resistance."[17]

---

[13] Dickinson, "Friends and Countrymen," 2.

[14] See James Otis, *Rights of the British Colonies Asserted and Proved* (Boston, 1764); Daniel Dulaney, *Considerations on the Propriety of Imposing Taxes on the British Colonies* (New York, 1765).

[15] John Dickinson, *Late Regulations Respecting the British Colonies on the Continent of America Considered* (1765), 25.

[16] Ibid., 26.

[17] Arthur M. Schlesinger, *Colonial Merchants and the American Revolution, 1763–1776* (New York: Atheneum, 1968), 191. Arthur J. Mekeel finds that over eighty Quaker merchants signed (*The Relation of the Quakers to the American Revolution*, 20). Bauman's and Sharpless's

The main concern of Friends was that resistance activities seemed close to being out of control. "In hopes to prevent the ill Effects" of riots in Philadelphia, Joseph Galloway reported that "near 800 of the sober Inhabitants [were] posted in different Places, ready to prevent any Mischief that should be attempted by the Mob, which effectively intimidated them, and kept all tolerably quiet." He was careful to note, however, that this Friendly intimidation was "not by any Order of the Government of the City."[18] This same concern for peace likely accounts for why Dickinson downplayed the not-insignificant violence in much of the protest, dismissing the destruction of property and assaults against British officials as isolated incidents perpetrated by "mobs composed of the lower ranks of people in some *few* of the colonies."[19] Although the resistance may have ended on a peaceful note, the reality was that the violence likely had much to do with the ultimate repeal of the Act in February of 1766. Nonetheless, Dickinson would later emphasize the civil disobedience, praising his countrymen for persisting in their "usual business" and effectively repealing the act themselves.

Dickinson's role in the Stamp Act controversy was merely a prelude for his much greater part in the disputes to come. With the passage of the Townshend Acts, he would step beyond his sphere as a Pennsylvania politician to become a recognizable American figure. He would also come to be seen as a radical.

The Townshend Acts and *Letters from a Farmer in Pennsylvania*, 1767–1768

Dickinson's *Farmer's Letters* have been heralded by his contemporaries and by historians as one of the greatest pieces of writing in the Revolutionary era and the one that served to unite the colonists against Britain as never before. With its publication, he became America's first political hero – her "best son"[20] – and one of the most powerful political leaders in the colonies. With his publication of America's first hit song, "The Liberty Song," at the same time, he was indeed a "popular idol."[21] In the *Letters*, he articulated the fullest expression of his constitutionalism to date and with that became the most eloquent spokesman

findings concur with Schlesinger's that their resistance "accorded fairly well with the Quaker tradition." See Sharpless, *A Quaker Experiment in Government*, 2: 77; and Bauman, *For the Reputation of Truth*, 128. Robert M. Calhoon finds that "[t]he Quakers conducted the most strenuous and conscientious and the only truly collective pursuit of reconciliation in the pre-Revolutionary period." Calhoon, *The Loyalists in the American Revolution, 1760–1781* (New York: Harcourt, Brace, Jovanovich, 1973), 170.

[18] Joseph Galloway to unknown, Sept. 20, 1765. Treasury Papers, Class I, Bundle 439, Public Record Office, Library of Congress Transcripts. My thanks to Josh Beatty for bringing this document to my attention.

[19] John Dickinson [as "A North-American"], *An Address to the Committee of Correspondence in Barbados* (Philadelphia, 1766), 16.

[20] "Son of Liberty," *Pennsylvania Journal*, January 7, 1768.

[21] Arthur M. Schlesinger, *Prelude to Independence: The Newspaper War on Britain, 1764–1776* (New York: Alfred A. Knopf, 1958), 42. This term was no doubt taken from Stillé and Ford,

for the traditional Quaker theologico-political process – one's opinion voiced in a calm demeanor, advocacy of the people's rights, peaceful resistance to oppression, and reform to preserve the sanctity and unity of the constituted polity. The *Letters* proceeded from a sense of duty to testify. As Dickinson proclaimed, "the Dictates of my Conscience command Me boldly to speak on the naked Sentiments of my Soul."[22] This refrain of not remaining silent when obliged to speak – a Quaker injunction that applied to all people in the religious polity – recurs throughout Dickinson's writings, speeches, and personal correspondence. Despite the way these *Letters* have been interpreted by contemporaries and historians, they were not a call for revolution; they were written to *prevent* revolution by giving Americans a peaceful and productive outlet for their frustrations with British policy.

Thinking within the framework of Quaker constitutionalism, Dickinson treated the civil polity like the religious polity writ large. In the first place, he cast America in the same role in relation to the rest of the world as Quakers did their meeting. He wrote, "Let us consider ourselves as MEN – FREEMEN – CHRISTIAN FREEMEN – *separated from the rest of the world, and firmly bound together* by the *same rights, interests and dangers.*"[23] This is very similar to how Friends referred to themselves – as a "peculiar people," a group "hedged off" from the rest of the world, distinguished and united by their unique behaviors, customs, and understanding of God and the world. They were further bound together by their insistence on their rights and their martyrdom for their cause of liberty. In the Quaker understanding of their religious polity, however, the uniqueness and separateness of their body were conditional. These qualities were dependent upon the protection the body received from the British constitution. Therefore, although Quakers and British North Americans may each have been a "separate people" in some ways, Dickinson did not consider the colonies disconnected and autonomous entities from Britain with a special charge to pursue their own interests contrary to the will of the government. Rather, he spoke of the colonies as "parts of a *Whole*," as limbs that must "bleed at every vein" if separated from the body.[24] The colonies and Britain, he repeated, "form *one* political body, of which *each colony is a member*. Their *happiness* is founded on *their constitution*; and is to be promoted by preserving that constitution

Life and Writings, 1: 108. Richard Alan Ryerson calls him "an indispensable symbol of unified resistance to Great Britain" (*The Revolution Is Now Begun: The Radical Committees of Philadelphia, 1765–1776* [Philadelphia: University of Pennsylvania Press, 1978], 51). On the popularity of "The Liberty Song," and it being a "model" for later patriotic songs, see Kenneth Silverman, *A Cultural History of the American Revolution: Paintings, Music, Literature, and the Theatre in the Colonies and the United States from the Treaty of Paris to the Inauguration of George Washington, 1763–1789* (New York: Columbia University Press, 1987), 117, 115.
[22] John Dickinson, "Notes for a Speech in Congress," May 23, 1775, *Delegates*, 1: 378.
[23] John Dickinson, *Letters from a Farmer in Pennsylvania, To the Inhabitants of the British Colonies* (1767–68), in Forrest McDonald, ed., *Empire and Nation: Letters from a Farmer in Pennsylvania (John Dickinson); Letters from a Federal Farmer (Richard Henry Lee)*, 2nd ed. (Indianapolis: The Liberty Fund, 1999), 80.
[24] Ibid., 7, 19.

in unabated vigor, *throughout every part.*"[25] Happiness lay in the security the constitution provided for their rights, a security that could only be preserved through unity. "The legal authority of Great Britain may indeed lay hard restrictions upon us; but, like the spear of Telephus, it will cure as well as wound."[26] In other words, the remedy for their ills was to be found in the same place as the cause – the British government. This understanding of a unique people protected as part of a perpetual constitutional polity is reminiscent of William Penn's vision of religious diversity within the polity. The religious liberty of all should be safeguarded by the "true Principles" of civil government. The preeminent principle was that of liberty of conscience, and union upon this principle protected the religious rights of all. "Men embark'd in the same Vessel," said Penn, "seek the safety of the *Whole* in their *Own*, whatever other differences they may have."[27] Like other thinkers in the Quaker tradition, Dickinson wrote, "Our *vigilance* and our *union* are our *success* and *safety*."[28]

Like Quaker theorists William Penn, Robert Barclay, and Isaac Penington before him, Dickinson clearly argued that although the constitution was perpetual, the power of the government was not unlimited. Similarly, he made a distinction between laws that were constitutional and those that were not. The imperative that Dickinson expressed in the *Letters* was adherence to the first principles of the constitution regardless of subsequent statutes or acts that had misrepresented it in the past, or might do so in the present, and a return to them when necessary.[29] In keeping with the Quaker tradition of following the living spirit of the law as opposed to the dead letter, Dickinson persisted in cautioning against Parliament's legal innovations. He echoed the distinction made by Penn between fundamental immutable laws and superficial, alterable ones. Also like other Quakers thinkers, he differed from most Americans in his attitude toward the law. He was not an unmitigated supporter of the common law tradition. "Custom," he said, "undoubtedly has a mighty force in producing opinion, and reigns in nothing more arbitrarily than in public affairs. It gradually reconciles us to objects even of dread and detestation."[30] It was like ritual in religious practice – a path that *appeared* to lead to salvation, but really took the traveler in the opposite direction. He suspected that many innovations were inspired by false guides and thus departed from the divine spirit. "Nothing is more certain," he explained, "than that the *forms* of liberty may yet be retained, when the *substance* is gone." Repeating the Quaker attitude toward dogma of any kind, he wrote: "In government, as well as in religion, 'The *letter* killeth, but the *spirit* giveth life.'" When the spirit is ignored, there is a great potential for "manifest violation of the constitution, *under the appearance of using legal*

---

[25] Ibid., 80–81.
[26] Ibid., 81.
[27] William Penn, *A Perswasive to Moderation* ... (London, 1686), preface.
[28] *Letters*, 79.
[29] Ibid., 69.
[30] *Letters*, 71. On other Americans' acceptance of custom, see Reid, *Authority to Tax*, 181–93.

prerogative."[31] His sentiments concur with Penn's, who wrote "That Country which is False to its first Principles of Government . . . must Unavoidably Decay."[32]

In a line that would be much quoted in the Constitutional Convention, Dickinson wrote, "A PERPETUAL *jealousy*, respecting liberty, is absolutely requisite in all free states." He then articulated the importance of bringing the polity back to its foundational elements. "*Machiavel*," he wrote, "employs a whole chapter in his discourses, to prove that a state, to be long lived, must be frequently corrected, and reduced to its first principles." Dickinson reiterated throughout the *Letters* that the Townshend Acts were a dangerous legal precedent. But like his Quaker forebears, he was not advocating a return to first principles through violence, which many came to believe was the only way to resist British tyranny. "To talk of 'defending' [the principles], as if they could be no otherwise 'defended' than by arms" was nonsensical to him.[33] Yet some historians have interpreted the ominous statement at the end of his fourth letter, "We have a statute, laid up for future use, like a sword in the scabbard,"[34] as a threat of violence against Britain and indicative of Dickinson's "revolutionary" message.[35] But although it is true that this statement is a threat, it is a threat with a nonviolent weapon, a legal threat. Here Dickinson has secularized the Quaker call for "spiritual" rather than "carnal" weapons and said that the weapon should be on paper and in principle – such as the "American 'bill of rights'" that New York produced to delineate the extent of Britain's right to tax the colonists.[36] To back up these words and principles, Dickinson advocated a plan of nonviolent measures that ranged in severity from humble pleas in petitions, to nonimportation, to open disobedience of the offending laws.[37] But the latter was the furthest extreme Quaker constitutionalism would allow.

In keeping with proper behavior within the Quaker meeting – that is, with the aim to preserve liberty, peace, and constitutional perpetuity – Dickinson very carefully outlined the colonists' rights and obligations in the face of royal oppression. In conducting protest, there was a duty to be upheld and a particular process to be followed. He encouraged his countrymen to action based on the Quaker process of dissent. He suggested that not revolution, but reformed relations with the crown could solve their problems. It seemed to Dickinson, however, that at the early phase of the controversy, the colonists were vulnerable to either total submission to the injustice, on the one hand, or war, on

---

[31] Ibid., 36.

[32] Dunn, *Politics and Conscience*, 49.

[33] *Letters*, 16–17.

[34] Ibid., 26.

[35] Richard M. Gummere calls it a threat against the British government "that rings like the clashing of steel." "John Dickinson, the Classical Penman of the Revolution," *Classical Journal* vol. 52, no. 2 (1956), 81–88, 84.

[36] *Letters*, 23.

[37] See Larry Kramer on the various forms of pressure the people could put on the government for change (*The People Themselves*, 25–29).

the other. A middle ground seemed lacking. He was equally concerned about both extremes of behavior, either of which could destroy the constitutional relationship. Importantly, because the polity belonged to the people, it was their responsibility to behave in a way that would preserve it.

The first danger was that the colonists' passive acceptance of the unjust laws would cause "a dissolution of our constitution."[38] Accordingly, the first ill to be combated was their submissiveness to the new act. Dickinson was surprised that "little notice has been taken of [the Townshend Acts]," although they were "as injurious in principle to the liberties of these colonies, as the Stamp Act."[39] In keeping with the Quaker belief in a popular review of laws, he wrote, "Ought not the people therefore to watch? to observe facts? to search into causes? to investigate designs? And have they not a right of JUDGING from the evidence before them, on no slighter points then their *liberty* and *happiness*?"[40] He concluded that their neglect of this duty was based in the first place on a misunderstanding of the legitimate reach of government. "Millions entertain no other idea of the *legality* of power, than it is founded upon the exercise of power." He continued, "They voluntarily fasten their chains, by adopting the pusillanimous *opinion* 'that there will be too much *danger* in attempting a remedy' – or another *opinion* no less fatal – 'that the government has a right to treat them as it does.'"[41] This opinion was based on the understanding of government as something that cannot be resisted by the people as a whole or individuals. Dickinson's stance was that resistance was not only acceptable, it was a constitutional duty; it was the people's responsibility to keep the government within its proper bounds and preserve the constitution, and if they did not resist unconstitutional laws, the polity would be destroyed by their own negligence.

There was also a second explanation for Americans' submissiveness: a "deplorable poverty of spirit, that prostrates the dignity bestowed by divine providence on our nature."[42] Certainly Dickinson was using the word *spirit* here as we understand it to mean courage or will; however, in the context of his time and culture the meaning was deeper. It was, as he suggests, something related to divinity, a God-given motivating force – in Quaker parlance, the Inner Light. Conformity or submission to ungodly laws was a denial of the spirit of God itself. Immediate resistance against injustice, in other words, was a divine injunction that supersedes human law. It was a spiritual as much as a political act – the two were, in fact, the same. And it was for the good of the country. Dickinson said, "In such cases, it is a submission to *divine authority*, which forbids us to injure our country; not to the *assumed authority*, on which the unjust sentences were founded. But *when* submission becomes inconsistent

[38] Dickinson, *Essay on the constitutional power*, 53.
[39] *Letters*, 4.
[40] Ibid., 37.
[41] Ibid., 72.
[42] Ibid.

with and destructive of the public good, the same veneration for and duty to the *divine authority*, commands us to oppose."[43] He reiterated, "God has given us the right and means of asserting [our freedom]. We may reasonably ask and expect his gracious assistance in the reasonable employment of those means. To look for miracles, while we abusively neglect the powers afforded us by divine goodness, is not only stupid, but criminal."[44] When ignoring the call to defend liberty and protect the country, Americans were *"pusillanimously* deserting the post assigned to us by Divine Providence."[45] Resistance against injustice was thus an act in keeping with a sacred constitution.

Because the Townshend Acts were as unconstitutional as the Stamp Act, he argued in Quakerly language that "we should have born our testimony against it."[46] Because Quakers believed in "publishing" injustices and oppression in order to heighten awareness and encourage reform, Dickinson did not believe that evading the oppression, as Bostonians had done in the Stamp Act crisis, was sufficient for Americans.[47] Certainly it would be possible for a time, he acknowledged, to "elude this act" by inventing other materials to serve in place of the ones taxed by Britain. But, he warned, "[America's] ingenuity would stand her in little stead; for then the parliament would have nothing to do but to prohibit such manufactures."[48] Dickinson's solution was more direct and definitive. The law must be challenged and changed; the demonstration must be public and visible. This approach was rooted in the ancient Quaker practice of bearing public witness to their persecution, testifying openly as martyrs for God's law against corrupted human law.

Dickinson's success in rousing Americans to resistance is well known; but he also anticipated the dangerous enthusiasm of their response. Although there was no serious thought of revolution at this early date, Dickinson looked ahead, keenly aware of the rapidity with which passion could overwhelm prudence. The other threat to the country, therefore, was that the people would destroy the constitutional relationship through their aggression: When "oppressions and dissatisfactions [are] permitted to accumulate," he explained, "if ever the governed throw off the load, they will do more. A people," he warned, "does not reform with moderation."[49] The danger was not simply that Britain would violate American rights, but that Americans would turn violent because of it.

---

[43] Dickinson, *Essay on the constitutional power,* 105.

[44] John Dickinson, "Letters to the Inhabitants of the British Colonies in America" (1774), in Stillé and Ford, *Life and Writings,* 2: 499.

[45] John Dickinson, "Instructions of the Pennsylvania Convention" (1774), in Peter Force, ed., *American Archives,* ser. 4 (Washington, DC, 1837–53), 1: 595.

[46] *Letters,* 7.

[47] Maier describes how Bostonians began with violent resistance, but eventually settled on evasion of the law as the most expedient way to handle the oppression (*From Resistance to Revolution,* 53–70).

[48] *Letters,* 25.

[49] Ibid., 69.

Dickinson's other point, then, articulated with like force, was to convince his countrymen to restrain themselves in their protests. It was a delicate balance to achieve, and a solution that most of Dickinson's readers then and now have overlooked. His remedy to the injustice was pacifism without passivity. "The constitutional modes of obtaining relief," he explained, "are those which I wish to see pursued on the present occasion." Just as there were laws that were constitutional and unconstitutional, so were there actions that are in keeping with the spirit of the constitution and those that departed from it. Working through the established machinery was constitutional. Likewise, civil disobedience and other nonviolent resistance, though illegal, were constitutional. Violent protest and revolution were not. In the spirit of harmony within the polity, therefore, Dickinson presented himself as someone who was "by no means fond of inflammatory measures" and explained that he would be "sorry that anything should be done which might justly displease our sovereign."[50]

Dickinson did not leave it to his readers to guess at, and perhaps misconstrue, his intentions in the heat of their passion for rights. He announced: "I will now tell the gentlemen, what is 'the meaning of these letters.'" "The meaning of them," he continued, "is to convince the people of these colonies, that they are at this moment exposed to the most imminent dangers; and to persuade them immediately, vigorously, and unanimously, to exert themselves, in the most firm, but most peaceable manner for obtaining relief." But this is what most readers today have missed. His aim was to impress upon them that rights were important, but so was the process by which they were asserted. "The cause of liberty," he explained, "is a cause of too much dignity, to be sullied by turbulence and tumult."[51] Those who believe that "riots and tumults" are the only way to solve the problem are, says Dickinson, "much mistaken, if they think that grievances cannot be redressed without such assistance." He reiterated the idea of political obligation that was at the core of Quaker political thought: if a "government at some time or other falls into wrong measure" this nevertheless "does not dissolve the obligation between the governors and the governed." "It is the duty of the governed," he explained, "to endeavor to rectify the mistake."[52] Like Penington and Penn, who argued throughout their lives and works for orderly, yet dramatic constitutional change without revolution, Dickinson suggested that a people "may change their king, or race of kings, and, retaining their ancient form of government, be gainers by changing." Because the colonies were not an independent nation, they had to be especially careful as such change could result in independence, destruction of the fundamental constitution, and the demise of America as it succumbed to external threats and internal chaos.[53]

[50] Ibid., 6.
[51] Ibid., 17
[52] Ibid., 18.
[53] Ibid., 19.

Like other American founders, Dickinson had his eye on history for a guide, but he used it differently from most of his countrymen. While Whig thinkers used the English Civil War as an example of oppression rightly and effectively resisted,[54] Dickinson, following his Quaker predecessors, used it as a negative example. Writing during and after the upheaval of the Civil War, Penington saw not revolution but an orderly process of reform as a "last remedy," and Penn warned that when first principles were not preserved, "the *Civil Government* must receive and suffer a *Revolution*."[55] Likewise, Dickinson admonished against the overt disrespect for the law that the Puritans demonstrated in the revolt against Charles I. They could not, he argued, distinguish between instances of the king's legitimate exercise of the law and an imagined "system of oppression." Furthermore, "It was in vain," he observed, "for prudent and moderate men to insist that there was no necessity to abolish royalty."[56] He agreed with those thinking in the Quaker tradition that it was a "subversion of the constitution."[57] It was precisely this difficulty in delineating the boundaries of *gubernaculum* and *jurisdictio* that made any resistance difficult and peaceful resistance essential.

Dickinson then described several steps that the colonists should take to testify against the British government. First, they must organize themselves for their own protection, to eliminate the "confusion in our laws" that made the colonies vulnerable to oppression by the crown;[58] maintain "a perpetual jealousy" of their liberty; and exercise "utmost vigilance" against new oppressive laws.[59] This was the very purpose for which Quakers organized under the name of the Meeting for Sufferings in 1676 to oppose their persecution, with due respect to the government. They must retain power in themselves in order to resist oppression. At first, however, a people's rights were closely circumscribed in the beginning of a disagreement with the secular authorities. "[The people] have not at first any other right," he explained, "than to represent their grievances, and to pray for redress."[60] Dickinson's method would have

[54] Bernard Bailyn emphasizes that the political thought of the English Civil War and Commonwealth period brought the "disparate strands of thought together" for the Revolutionary leaders (*Ideological Origins of the American Revolution*, 34).
[55] Penington, *Right, Safety and Liberty*, 7; Penn, *One Project*, 1.
[56] *Letters*, 70.
[57] John Jones to John Dickinson, October 15, 1774. Small Manuscript Collection, John Dickinson Letters, DPA.
[58] In this instance, Dickinson was questioning parliamentary authority over the colonial legislatures and arguing that the latter, along with the colonial courts, had the right to determine which aspects of the British common law and statutes ought to apply to them in their particular circumstances. His recommendation in practical terms was to pass laws in America delimiting the extent of English laws in the colonies and allowing the courts to determine rules for their regulation and practice (ibid., 55).
[59] Ibid., 68.
[60] Ibid., 18.

been very familiar to those who had attended a Quaker meeting – to fulfill the obligation to speak when led by God to do so, to "publish" one's dissent:

[W]hile Divine Providence, that gave me existence in a land of freedom, permits my head to think, my lips to speak, and my hand to move, I shall so highly and gratefully value the blessing received, as to take care, that my silence and inactivity shall not give my implied assent to any act, degrading my brethren and myself from the birthright, wherewith heaven itself "hath made us free."[61]

After they were sufficiently organized and in agreement about their grievances, Dickinson then advised speaking through the ancient British tradition of "petitioning of our assemblies."[62] But this was only the beginning of a process that was increasingly informed by Quaker principles.

Should petitioning not be effective, there were other means of a "firm, but modest exertion of a free spirit" on a "public occasion."[63] Only after all the conventional measures had failed did "opposition become justifiable." But by "opposition" Dickinson still did not mean violence or disruptive activities, such as the mob uprisings so common at this time. Rather, he favored opposition "which can be made without breaking the laws, or disturbing the public peace."[64] The course he outlined from there was one of peaceful resistance: "This," he explained, "consists in the prevention of the oppressors reaping advantage from their oppressions, and not in their punishment." Dickinson suggested that "If . . . our applications to his Majesty and the parliament for redress prove ineffectual, let us then take *another step*, by withholding from Great Britain all the advantages she has been used to receive from us."[65] This subtle suggestion would not have been lost on the colonists. It would have been clear to his audience that Dickinson was referring to the boycotts and civil disobedience against the Stamp Act only three years earlier.

They would also exert pressure on Parliament through the power of their own provincial assemblies. With their "purse strings" the people "have a *constitutional check* upon the administration, which may thereby be brought into order *without violence*." Using their own power, he argued, "is the proper and successful way to obtain redress of grievances." He asked, "How often have [kings] been brought to reason, and peaceably obliged to do justice, by the exertion of this constitutional authority of the people?"[66] This is "the gentlest method which human policy has yet been ingenious enough to invent."[67] This is in part what he meant by bearing their testimony against the injustice. Only if all these measures had been exploited and failed should revolution even be

[61] Ibid., 16. Dickinson is citing St. Paul's Letter to the Galatians 5:1.
[62] Ibid., 20.
[63] Ibid., 6.
[64] Ibid., 18.
[65] Ibid., 20.
[66] Ibid., 51.
[67] Ibid., 56.

considered. But these cases, he assured the colonists, are rare.[68] In advocating such peaceful means – passing laws, petitioning, boycotting, engaging in civil disobedience, and using monetary leverage – Dickinson's underlying message was that the power and right are ultimately with the people to limit the government, but that they must do so as members of the constituted polity. Their protest might be extralegal, but it should not be extraconstitutional.

If Dickinson's overall message about resistance was emerging as different from the political thought and methods of his countrymen, so too was his patriotism of another sort. He expressed it as a God-given spirit of loyalty to the British constitution that was not incompatible with a love of rights. It was a "spirit that shall so guide you that it will be impossible to determine whether an *American's* character is most distinguishable for his loyalty to his Sovereign, his duty to his mother country, his love for freedom, or his affection for his native soil."[69] To Dickinson, those who might rush to revolution did so only "under pretenses of patriotism."[70] He agreed with Penn who wrote, "Let us go together as far as our way lies, and Preserve our Unity in those Principles, which maintain our Civil Society . . . [I]t is both Wise and Righteous to admit no Fraction upon this Pact, no violence upon this Concord."[71] In a prophetic moment, Dickinson made a final attempt in his last letter to clarify his position and preempt what would become the accepted interpretation of this work: "I shall be extremely sorry, if any man mistakes my meaning in any thing I have said." "If I am an *Enthusiast* for any thing, it is in my zeal for the *perpetual dependence* of these colonies on their mother country."[72] He closed the *Letters* with the admonition to Americans to

call forth into use the *good sense* and *spirit* of which you are possessed. You have nothing to do, but to conduct your affairs *peaceably – prudently – firmly – jointly*. By *these means* you will support the character of *freemen*, without losing that of *faithful subjects* – a good character in any government – the best under a *British* government. You will *prove*, that *Americans* have that true *magnanimity* of soul, that can resent injuries, without falling into rage.[73]

The *Farmer's Letters* were thus intended for more than simple suggestions on how to resist the British. They advocated change, but they were certainly not intended to foment revolution. Rather, they were intended to do the opposite – to save the constitutional relationship between Britain and America as the best means to protect American liberty. This was clearly recognized by some, as Dickinson was once portrayed leaning on a copy of the Magna Carta (Figure 7). While superficially there is much in Dickinson's argument that looks whiggish,

[68] Ibid., 18.
[69] Ibid.
[70] Ibid., 17.
[71] Penn, *One Project*, 6.
[72] *Letters*, 82.
[73] Ibid., 84.

FIGURE 7. James Smither, "The Patriotic American Farmer" (1768). (LCP)

ultimately Whigs could justify revolution as legitimate; Dickinson, in this case, did not.

Withdrawing Quakers and the Townshend Acts

The publication of the *Farmer's Letters* marks a turning point in Dickinson's relationship with many Philadelphia Quakers. Although the *Letters* mobilized most Americans to undertake economic sanctions, they did not sway many Friends to acquiesce. In fact, while many agreed with the message of the *Letters*, some disapproved of the timing and, as far as they were concerned, "imprudent" tone.[74] Two months after the *Letters* appeared in the newspapers, Dickinson spoke to the reluctant Quaker merchants and appealed to their sense of right and patriotism. He drew a comparison between the Stamp Act and the current policy and urged that economic sanctions were necessary and that the less aggressive measures pursued by the Pennsylvania Assembly, now led by

[74] Mekeel, *The Relation of the Quakers to the American Revolution*, 35.

Dickinson's political enemy, Joseph Galloway, were sure to fail. "Our Assembly," said Dickinson, "has applied for Relief from their Acts of Parliament. But having nothing left to give, they could not enforce their Application by withholding Anything." He continued, "It is, however, in our Power in a peaceable Way, to add Weight, to the Remonstrance and Petition of our Representatives, by stopping the Importation of Goods from Britain, until we obtain Relief and Redress by a Repeal of these unconstitutional Acts."[75]

Although Dickinson was greatly respected among the Quaker merchants, many still were not convinced. Charles Thomson, soon-to-be secretary of the Continental Congress, chastised Quakers for their lack of attention to the public interest by quoting "the Farmer" and reminding them that the eyes of God were upon them.[76] Then ensued a vigorous public debate in the newspapers between Thomson and Galloway, in which Dickinson also joined. Dickinson attacked the merchants for their inconsistent behavior. Whatever religious grounds Friends may have claimed for this new stance, Dickinson would not accept it. He charged them with sacrificing their patriotism to their self-interest. During the Stamp Act, he explained,

Your *Patriotism* and *private Interests* were so intimately connected that you could not prostitute the one, without endangering the other: and you would have been particularly fortunate, if Great-Britain, when she repealed the Stamp-Act, had redressed all your Grievances; and had never thought of imposing new ones – You would, *then*, have been distinguished, in the Annals of America, among her best and most virtuous sons, for a *timely* and *resolute* Defense of her Liberties; . . . But Charles Townshend, with an artful and penetrating Eye, saw clearly to the Bottom of your Hearts . . . To this Gentlemen, you must attribute the Loss of your Reputation.[77]

Although Dickinson himself was a wealthy man and potentially had much to lose from either severing ties with Britain or defeat at her hands, he believed that, insofar as the two could be distinguished, rights were sacred while property was replaceable.[78] In 1775 he wrote to Arthur Lee, "Our Towns are but brick and stone, and mortar and wood; they, perhaps, may be destroyed; they are only the hairs of our heads; if sheared ever so close, they will grow again. We compare them not with our rights and liberties." The "Quaker Reformation" of 1756 was an indication that many Friends believed that, over the course of the eighteenth century, the Society had come to privilege money over otherworldly concerns. But Dickinson clearly thought that they had not reformed enough as a body. He held to an earlier understanding of Quaker priorities

75 Dickinson, "An Address Read to a Meeting of Merchants to Consider Non-Importation" (1768), in Stillé and Ford, *Life and Writings*, 2: 415.
76 Schlesinger, *Colonial Merchants*, 118–19.
77 Dickinson, "Letter to the Philadelphia Merchants Concerning Non-Importation" (1768), in Stillé and Ford, *Life and Writings*, 2: 441.
78 John Phillip Reid, *Constitutional History of the American Revolution: The Authority of Law* (Madison: University of Wisconsin Press, 1993), 214.

and applied them to the current political situation. "We worship as our fathers worshipped," he explained, "not idols which our hands have made."[79]

This dispute highlights the differences between Dickinson's priorities and methods and those that PYM was coming to advocate. Despite Dickinson's charges, many in PYM were interested in protecting liberties – both religious and economic. But these Quakers had a narrower scope in mind than did Dickinson. Thomson complained that "[t]he Quakers oppose from various motives."[80] Although there were Patriots among them, some were primarily concerned with their particular interests in Pennsylvania.[81] What "Loyalism" existed among Quakers was more likely to be loyalty to their 1701 Charter rather than the British constitution. In addition to the unique liberties that the Charter provided them, Pennsylvania was flourishing economically in spite of the new taxes, and Quakers might have reckoned that some taxation was a small price to pay for stability. The alternatives did not look promising. If America should lose a struggle with the British, they might find themselves under Anglican rule. If, on the other hand, America prevailed, Presbyterians and others hostile to Quakerism might overwhelm the province. As it was, the animosity that had been building against Quakers for years and was coming to a head in the current contest boded ill for Friends and their religious liberties. As John Jones put it, "all wise & virtuous men so ardently wish for an accommodation, for if wee come to blows, I must sorely own I shou'd dread a victory almost as much as a defeat."[82] In either case, Quakers would be much worse off than under their own Charter. Other Friends, while they supported the American cause, simply could not take part in resistance they believed would lead to violence.[83] But there were also those Quakers who genuinely wished to remove themselves from the tumult of the world. "They want to do nothing," said Thomson, "& withdraw themselves from the general cause for fear their religious principles may be affected by the struggle."[84] Minister Job Scott confirmed this: "I had no desire to promote the opposition to Great Britain; neither had I any desire on the other hand to promote the measures

---

[79] John Dickinson to Arthur Lee, 29 April 1775, in *American Archives*, 2: 445. Similarly, a Quaker wrote, "God dwelleth not in temples made by hands, neither is worshipped with mens hands." George Bishop, *The Burden of Babylon and the Triumph of Zion as it was seen in the Valley of Vision* (1661), 5.

[80] Charles Thomson Memorandum Book, June 10–11, 1774, Simon Gratz Autograph Collection, HSP. On this occasion, Dickinson proposed a plan for electing delegates to the congress that was the same as how representatives to the Assembly were elected.

[81] For a discussion of the practical concerns of many Quakers, see Thomas M. Doerflinger, "Philadelphia Merchants and the Logic of Moderation, 1760-1775," *WMQ*, 3rd Ser., vol. 40, no. 2 (1983): 197–226.

[82] John Jones to John Dickinson, March 20, 1775, Incoming Correspondence, Sept. 22, 1759–June 23, 1782, JDP/LCP.

[83] See also Anne M. Ousterhout, *A State Divided: Opposition in Pennsylvania to the American Revolution* (New York: Greenwood Press, 1987), 29–32.

[84] Thomson Memorandum Book, June 10–11, 1774, HSP.

or success of Great Britain."[85] The Society as a body thus began to revive its 1756 stance and adopted a more reserved position than Dickinson. By 1769 its official policy was that the increasingly strict economic sanctions should be avoided. Philadelphia Monthly Meeting and Philadelphia Meeting for Sufferings advised against taking part in nonimportation and threatened disownment of those who transgressed the peace testimony.[86]

In his *Letters*, and then in his subsequent efforts to convince Quaker merchants to engage in nonimporation, Dickinson had articulated a position that was consistent with the Quakerism of Pennsylvania politics from the founding of the province until only very recently. "Heaven," he wrote, "seems to have placed in our hands means of an effectual, yet peaceable resistance, if we have the sense and integrity to make proper use of them. A general agreement between these colonies of non-importation and non-exportation faithfully observed would certainly be attended with success."[87] And many Friends still held these views. A good number of the Quaker merchants ultimately sided with Dickinson in thinking that resistance in the form of boycotting was just, but that violence or rebellion was not.[88] And although Quaker merchants as a group were slow to join intercolonial nonimportation committees, they were some of the most active boycotters as individuals.[89] Nonimportation in Philadelphia, however, was never an entire success without the support of PYM, the Assembly, and the whole merchant class.

The differences that were beginning to surface between Dickinson's position and the Society of Friends were indicative of a growing rift in the Society itself. For whatever reason – whether principle or profit – the majority of Friends, or at least the ones who controlled PYM, were becoming increasingly reserved in their protest against Britain. Meanwhile, a significant number were growing more enthusiastic in their resistance. Almost a century after the Revolution, Abraham Lincoln summarized their situation. "On principle and faith, opposed to both war and oppression, they can only practically oppose oppression by war," he wrote. "In this hard dilemma, some [Quakers] have chosen one horn and some another."[90] Lincoln wrote these words in the midst of the Civil War; but this very dilemma for Quakers had always been present to a degree. Until now, however, there had been no incident great enough to endanger the Society seriously. But with so much at stake, and after more than ninety years of cultivated dissent in Pennsylvania, the time was ripe for a change.

---

[85] Scott, *Journal of the Life, Travels, and Gospel Labours*, 53.
[86] Mekeel, *The Relation of the Quakers to the American Revolution*, 34–48; Schlesinger, *Colonial Merchants*, 191–92.
[87] John Dickinson, "Letters to the Inhabitants of the British Colonies" (1774), in Stillé and Ford, *Life and Writings*, 2: 499.
[88] Mekeel, *The Relation of the Quakers to the American Revolution*, 46–47; Schlesinger, *Colonial Merchants*, 192.
[89] Mekeel, *The Relation of the Quakers to the American Revolution*, 36–40.
[90] Abraham Lincoln to Eliza P. Gurney, September 4, 1864, in Roy P. Basler, ed., *The Collected Works of Abraham Lincoln* (New Brunswick, NJ: Rutgers University Press, 1953), 7: 535.

The Pivotal Years, 1774–1775

Since the *Farmer's Letters*, Dickinson's reputation in Pennsylvania had grown exponentially, and by 1774 he could be rightly considered the leader of the resistance movement, not just in that colony but, at least for the moment, in America as a whole.[91] Joseph Reed conveyed that "At this time

> Mr. Dickinson was in the highest point of Reputation, & possessed a vast influence not only over the public at large but among the Quakers in particular... No person in Pennsylvania ever approached as a rival in personal influence. In short he was of that weight, that it seemed to depend on his being present at the meeting whether or not there should be any measures in opposition to Britain in consequence of it.

Moreover, it was "owing to his 'farmer's letters,' and his conduct, that there was a present disposition to dispose the tyranny of Parliament."[92]

The progress and process of the resistance thus depended in large part on him. The meeting to which Reed was referring was on May 20 to decide Philadelphia's response to the Coercive Acts. The triumvirate who planned it, Reed, Thomson, and Thomas Mifflin, knew that they would not have credence without Dickinson's approbation of the proceedings. They proposed in advance, "if necessary that, the conduct should be carried to extremity." Dickinson was reportedly "shocked." He admitted that "opposition ought to be used," but "that the public proceedings could not be too cautious and temperate." Accordingly, in the meeting itself, Dickinson made his appearance after the others had exhorted the audience so passionately that Thomson fainted from his efforts and "moderate[d] that fire, by proposing measures of a more gentle nature." "The contrast between the two measures advised," the report reads, "& Mr. Dickinson's weight precipitated the company into an adoption of the latter; which being so gentle in its appearance, was a great relief against the violence of the first." Following the meeting, amidst turmoil and conflict between Quakers and radicals over how to express support for Boston, Dickinson appealed to the colonists to remember the success of their own peaceful efforts in the Stamp Act controversy. Despite the fact there was great clamor for nonimportation, in a series of letters in late May and early June, he praised his countrymen in their handling of an earlier controversy, writing, "You behaved as you ought... You proceeded in your usual business without any regard to [the Stamp Act]... The act [was] thus revoked by you" before it was formally repealed by Parliament.[93] He called for the same "virtual repeal" that Quakers

---

[91] In "John Dickinson as President of Pennsylvania," *Pennsylvania History* vol. 28, no. 3 (1961), 254–267, J. H. Powell says that he "dominated the Congress" (255). The editors of the *Delegates* speak of "The Farmer's extraordinary fame and influence" (1: 194). It is puzzling how Eric Foner can conclude that in the early 1770s Dickinson "lapsed into political silence as the movement for independence accelerated" (*Tom Paine and Revolutionary America*, 108.).

[92] "Copy of a paper drawn up by Joseph Reed for W. Henry Drayton," n.d., Maria Dickinson Logan Collection, HSP.

[93] John Dickinson, "Letters to the Inhabitants of the British Colonies," in Stillé and Ford, *Life and Writings*, 2: 475, 476, 479.

had always practiced. Their continued success in this vein against the Coercive Acts was not unreasonable.

One of Dickinson's most significant contributions to the resistance cause arose out of Philadelphia's response to the Coercive Acts – the organization of measures that would lead to the convening of the Continental Congress. He proposed a broad-based committee of freeholders representing all segments of society. This committee would then instruct Pennsylvania's congressmen in a colony-wide congress.[94] Interestingly, Dickinson was not a member of the First Continental Congress when it met for the first time on September 5, 1774. He could not become one until he was elected to the Assembly (which, it had been determined, should appoint the delegates) on September 19. John Adams approved, noting "the Change in the elections for this City and County is no small event. Mr. Dickinson and Mr. Thompson, now joined to Mr. Mifflin, will make a great weight in favour of the American Cause."[95] But not being a formal member of that body did not stop him from drafting the several of the first and most important documents.[96]

Congress among the Quakers

Quaker unity was failing rapidly about how to oppose oppression when the delegates convened for the First Continental Congress in Philadelphia. But at first, these differences were by no means clear to outsiders. As the delegates gathered and deliberated in Quaker Philadelphia, they did not yet understand the depths or complexities of the culture with its strong inclinations for both unity and dissent. Neither did they yet see that the Society was dividing on the best course to secure the rights for which they had always aimed. Instead they were impressed with more readily visible things – the Quakerism that permeated the city. They were fascinated, affronted, enticed, and perplexed by Quaker proselytizing – the distinctive dress, speech, and manners of their hosts – and commented frequently and favorably, at least at first, on Quakers being interesting, clever, and pleasing with their politeness and hospitality, informal yet elegant manners, plain dress, and their "Thee's and Thou's."[97]

See "Notes of a meeting of a number of Gentlemen convened on 10 June 1774," in "Memorandum Book, 1754–1774," 159–62, Charles Thomson Papers, Simon Gratz Autograph Collection, HSP; John Dickinson, *Pennsylvania Journal, and the Weekly Advertiser*, June 22, 1774. Also, Ryerson, *The Revolution Is Now Begun*, 47–48.

L. H. Butterfield, ed., *Diary and Autobiography of John Adams* (Cambridge, MA: Belknap Press, Harvard University, 1961), 2: 147.

These include the Bill of Rights [and] a List of Grievances, "Memorial to the Inhabitants of the Colonies," the First Petition to the King, and *An Address from Congress to the Inhabitants of Quebec*. For discussion of the authorship of these documents, some of which had been attributed to other delegates, see James H. Hutson, comp. and ed., *A Decent Respect to the Opinions of Mankind: Congressional State Papers, 1774–1776* (Washington, DC: Library of Congress, 1976), 50–52; and *Delegates*, 1: 194.

Silas Deane to Elizabeth Deane, Aug. 31 and Sept. 3, 10–11, 1774, *Delegates*, 1: 16, 23, and 62; John Adams's Diary, Sept. 7, 1774, *Delegates*, 1: 33.

The influence Friends had on the delegates was both positive and negative, social and personal, but also increasingly and profoundly political.

For some of the delegates, Quakerism was very appealing. Silas Deane of Connecticut was especially taken with Philadelphia and its Quaker culture. He wrote repeatedly to his wife of his positive impressions of the city and people. "The aspect of the Inhabitants, bespeak them, affable & Clever, and the Freind [*sic*] or Quaker habit was always agreeable To me," he admitted.[98] Deane, so charmed by the distinctive Quaker speech, could not refrain from quoting it: "[E]very one of my Quaker Friends I meet tells Me, Thee lookest very well Freind Dean."[99] Living in such close proximity to Friends and finding them so agreeable made Deane consider becoming a convinced Friend himself. "[I] have almost resolved," he wrote Elizabeth, "if I alter To Turn Quaker."[100]

For other delegates, however, the Quaker culture and customs were simply strange. By way of excusing himself for not wishing his correspondent a merry Christmas and happy new year, James Duane wrote, "I am in a Quaker Town. No body has wished me the Compliments of the Season, & I forgot to pay you that Respect."[101] John Adams was clearly fascinated with Friends and, as his opinion about them fluctuated from one extreme to the other, he recorded his thoughts and observations of their peculiarities. "Dined with the whole Congress at the City Tavern, at the Invitation of the House of Representatives of the Province of Pensylvania," he wrote in his diary in October 1774. "[T]he whole House dined with Us, making near 100 Guests in the whole – a most elegant Entertainment. A Sentiment was given, 'May the Sword of the Parent never be Stain'd with the Blood of her Children.'" Adams noted that "Two or 3 broadbrims, over against me at Table – one of em said this is not a Toast but a Prayer, come let us join in it – and they took their Glasses accordingly."[102] It is hard to know precisely Adams's thoughts on this scene. It may be that he was commenting on the antiquated Pennsylvania laws against toasting and, perhaps, the subtle hypocrisy of cloaking a toast in a prayer; or possibly the Quaker support for the Revolutionary cause.

With such eminent men visiting their own city, Philadelphia Quakers were not about to let the opportunity to exert their influence pass them by. The Massachusetts Baptists, who had been undertaking a nonviolent campaign of their own for religious freedom in Massachusetts, appealed to the Quakers to confront the Massachusetts delegates on their behalf about the restriction of their religious freedoms in that colony.[103] After the delegates had convened,

[98] Silas Deane to Elizabeth Deane, August 31, 1774, *Delegates*, 1: 16.

[99] Ibid., September 19, 1774, *Delegates*, 1: 84.

[100] Ibid., September 3, 1774, *Delegates*, 1: 23.

[101] James Duane to Robert Livingston, January 5, 1776, *Delegates*, 3: 34.

[102] John Adams's Diary, October 20, 1774, *Delegates*, 1: 221.

[103] In her study of the rise of Baptists in the South, Christine Leigh Heyrman finds that Baptists were greatly influenced by Quaker practice, to the point of emulating them in dress, deportment, and meeting style. See *Southern Cross: The Beginnings of the Bible Belt* (New York: Alfred A. Knopf, 1997). For more on the Baptists' civil disobedience in Massachusetts, see McLoughlin, "Massive Civil Disobedience."

Adams and a number of other men from Massachusetts were summoned to appear before a committee of Quakers, headed by Israel Pemberton, meeting in Carpenter's Hall. Here Friends took the delegates to task because "the laws of New England, and particularly of Massachusetts, were inconsistent with [liberty of conscience], for they not only compelled men to pay to the building of churches and support of ministers, but to go to some known religious assembly on first days, etc."[104] Bernard Bailyn includes this event in his chapter on the "Contagion of Liberty," calling it "an extraordinary episode, demonstrating vividly the mutual reinforcement that took place in the Revolution between the struggles for civil and religious liberty."[105] But in Pennsylvania history, this episode was nothing very extraordinary. The "great number of Quakers seated at the long table with their broad brimmed beavers on their heads" were simply doing what they had always done – treating in a solemn manner with a person or group whom they hoped to convince of their principles and to persuade to amend their ways to be "as they were in Pennsylvania."[106] It demonstrated to the Revolutionary leaders that the Quakers were persistent and aggressive in exerting what pressure they could to mold society in their image.

As America moved toward civil war with Great Britain, the political leaders were anxious that the colonists unite and show support for the American cause. They were eagerly attentive to the tenor of popular opinion in each colony. At this crucial moment, the delegates looked to the behavior of the Quaker population as a barometer with which to gauge the patriotic sentiment of the whole country. With Quakers known for their caution and desire to preserve peace, the delegates felt they could be sure the colonists were united and ready for resistance when Quakers joined the cause. Indicative of the Quakers' continued ambivalence toward resistance, John Adams observed that there was "a most laudable Zeal, and an excellent Spirit, which every Day increases, especially in this City. The Quakers had a General Meeting here last Sunday, and are deeply affected with the Complexion of the Times. They have recommended it to all their People to renounce Tea."[107] The first battles of the war brought a wave of patriotism and support from even many of the "stiff Quakers" who had earlier opposed the resistance.[108] In June of 1775, the Pennsylvania Assembly, still more than half Quaker, recommended the formation of a Military Association for the protection of the city.[109]

Throughout the spring and summer of that year, one delegate after another remarked incredulously on the general enthusiasm for the coming conflict, with Quaker activity as the chief indicator. Joseph Hewes surely exaggerated when

---

[104] John Adams quoted in Theodore Thayer, *Israel Pemberton, King of the Quakers* (Philadelphia: Historical Society of Pennsylvania, 1943), 209.
[105] Bernard Bailyn, "Contagion of Liberty," in *Ideological Origins of the American Revolution* (Cambridge: Belknap Press, Harvard University, 1967), 268.
[106] John Adams quoted in Thayer, *Israel Pemberton*, 209.
[107] John Adams to William Tudor, September 29, 1774, *Delegates*, 1: 130.
[108] Christopher Marshall quoted in Thayer, *Pennsylvania Politics*, 165.
[109] PA, 8: 7237–7240; Thayer, *Pennsylvania Politics*, 166.

he wrote that "All the Quakers except a few of the old Rigid ones have taken up arms." "[T]here is not one Company," he explained more realistically, "without several of these people in it, and I am told one or two of the Companies are composed entirely of Quakers."[110] Congressman Richard Caswell compared Pennsylvania to other colonies, writing, "Here a Greater Martial Spirit prevails if possible, than I have been describing in Virginia & Maryland." His proof was that "there are Several Companies of Quakers only." Moreover, they were enrolling "promiscuously" in other companies and rumor had it that "they will in a few days have 3000 Men under Arms ready to defend their Liberties."[111] Silas Deane was impressed by the "high Spirits" in the city, evinced by the fact that "the very Quakers have taken Arms, & imbodied themselves, & exercise many of them Twice every Day." "[B]ut," he added cautiously, as though the "fighting Quakers" were the secret weapon of the rebel army, "let no hint of this, get into the public papers."[112]

But if these accounts are to be trusted, it would have been hard indeed to hide the preparations underway. In addition to the large numbers of Quakers forming into militias, several of the most celebrated Revolutionary military and political leaders were either Friends, or had very close ties to them, including, Benjamin Franklin, Thomas Wharton, Jr., Christopher Marshall, Thomas Mifflin, Samuel Meredith, Owen and Clement Biddle, Samuel Morris, Jr., Thomas Paine, Nathanael Greene, and Timothy Matlack. Quakers, together with the rest of the city, "Seem Animated with one soul & Spirit for the most Vigorous defence of American rights & Liberty."[113] With this demonstration of support from Quakers indicating the level of commitment of America as a whole to the cause, the delegates were encouraged that Great Britain would have to acknowledge them as a formidable enemy. Roger Sherman wrote confidently to Joseph Trumbull: "you may be sure we are in earnest, when [Quakers] handle a Musquet."[114]

But more than just serving as a barometer for popular sentiment, Quakers were a concern to the delegates for other and contradictory reasons. In the mid-1770s, Friends still held considerable political, economic, and social influence over Pennsylvania. On the one hand, those fighting against the Americans recognized this influence as a significant force. A spy for the British reported in June of 1775 that "[t]here was a general review of the militia of this City this day... among them there was some Company of Quackers: this example (of the quackers) will have a great effect over all the Country people."[115] Similarly, Hessian officer Johann Heinrichs wrote that "[t]hose true Americans who take

[110] Joseph Hewes to Samuel Johnston, May 11, 1775, *Delegates*, 1: 342.
[111] Richard Caswell to William Caswell, May 11, 1775, *Delegates*, 1: 340.
[112] Silas Deane to John Trumbull, May 12, 1775, *Delegates*, 25: 553.
[113] Eliphalet Dyer to Joseph Trumbull, May 18, 1775, *Delegates*, 1: 357. On the religious affiliation of the radicals, see Ryerson, "Political Mobilization," 578–81.
[114] A Delegate in Congress to a Correspondent in London August 24, 1775, *Delegates*, 1: 705.
[115] Gilbert Barkly to Grey Cooper, June 7, 1775, in Geoffrey Seed, "A British Spy in Philadelphia," *PMHB* vol. 85 (1961), 3–37, 10.

the greatest part [in the Revolution], are the famous Quakers. The most celebrated, the first ones in entire Pennsylvania and Philadelphia and Boston, are,
properly speaking, the heads of the Rebellion."[116] The rebel army, in both its
good and bad attributes, was seemingly influenced by Quaker behavior that
Heinrichs found distasteful. The soldiers' "bravery is surprisingly enhanced by
the enthusiasm engendered by falsehood and vagaries, which are drilled into
them, so that it requires but time and leadership to make them formidable."
But their weakness was also a Quaker by-product: "[T]he great thing wanting
with them is subordination; for their very spirit of independence is detrimental to them; as Hans cannot concede that Peter, who is his neighbour should
command him."[117]

This spirit of independence that Heinrichs observed was native to Pennsylvania. Gordon Wood notes the interesting development within the Pennsylvania political culture in the years leading to the Revolution. "It is ironic,"
he writes, "that both the Revolution and the rhetoric should have been so
violently extreme in Pennsylvania." But as Wood hints at last, it was not so
very ironic that the freedoms of Pennsylvania would result in a heightened
revolutionary sentiment in that province. "By its blend of natural rusticity and
Quaker simplicity," writes Wood, "Pennsylvania had become the epitome of
all that was good in the New World;... it was to America what America was
to the rest of the world – a peculiar "land of freedom." "Its very elements
of freedom," Wood concludes, "bred a revolutionary situation."[118] The "very
elements" of Pennsylvania to which Wood is referring were endemic in Pennsylvania political culture. In the first seventy years of the colony's life, Quakers
had cultivated a culture of dissent and resistance to what they perceived to
be arbitrary authority that spread well beyond the bounds of their immediate Society and party to permeate the entire political culture of the colony. It
was this radical dissenting culture that led to Benjamin Franklin's campaign
for royal government, and which was now manifesting itself *against* the royal
government. It is no surprise, considering the extreme culture of dissent and
resistance that the Quakers fostered in their government, that many of the
most radical Revolutionaries would emerge from Pennsylvania. What Quakers
had wanted to instill was Christian morality, unity, fidelity to government, and
peaceful dissent. What they wanted were John Dickinsons; what they got were
Benjamin Franklins and Thomas Paines.[119]

This oppositional energy could and did work in favor of the American cause,
but, despite the highly visible military demonstrations of some Quakers and

[116] Johann Heinrichs, "Extracts from the Letter-Book of Captain Johann Heinrichs of the Hessian
Jäger Corps, 1778–1780," *PMHB* vol. 22, no. 2 (1898), 137–70, 137–38.
[117] Ibid., 139.
[118] Wood, *Creation of the American Republic*, 85–86.
[119] See also R. R. Palmer, who writes: "Quaker individualism and rational abstraction combined to produce in [Paine] the pure type of cosmopolitan revolutionary," in "Tom Paine:
Victim of the Rights of Man," *PMHB* vol. 66, no 2 (1942), 161–175, 169. It should be
noted, however, that Palmer conflates Quakerism and Puritanism. See also fn. 145 in this
chapter.

their apparent unanimity in the Assembly, it was clear to none yet exactly where Friends as a body stood on the question of war and independence. Nor was it clear to supporters of the war exactly how Quakers might use their substantial power of influence in this complicated political struggle. While most of the delegates celebrated the Quakers' example and leadership in the early preparations for the conflict, others, such as Joseph Hewes, were leery that Quakers were the leaders of a capricious oppositional fervor that might easily turn in any direction. "A military spirit has diffused itself in an extraordinary manner thro' this Province," wrote Hewes. "[I]t is said a Majority of the Quakers have taken up Arms certain it is that many in this City have done it, some of which are Officers and appear in Uniform. This strong current of opposition to ministerial measures in some instances bordering on licentiousness calls for the most prudent and temperate deliberations of the Congress."[120]

In the early phase of the conflict during the taxation controversies when the imbalance seemed to favor the crown and weight needed to be thrown behind American rights, economic sanctions and other protests seemed reasonable and appropriate to Friends. At this point, Quaker protest appeared to be a species of Whiggism. By the mid-1770s, PYM, led by those who were inclined to withdraw, was enacting its role as trimmer and shifting its weight to the other side of the ship, away from resistance to preserve constitutional status quo. The result was the first real separation in the history of Quakerism, based on the divisions that began in the 1750s. A radical group calling themselves "Free Quakers" discarded the peace testimony by taking up arms and broke with PYM. Also known as the "Fighting Quakers," it was these Friends whose military preparations the delegates were watching with such interest. Philadelphia Yearly Meeting declared in 1776: "Under affliction and sorrow we painfully feel, for the deviation of some, who have made profession with us, from our peaceable principles."[121] Accordingly, the Free Quakers were read out of PYM, and they formed their own society in 1781.[122] Several members then went on to earn distinguished records in military leadership.

Because of PYM's resistance to violence, eventually people articulated the distinction between Quakers and Whigs that hinged on their pacifism. Across the Atlantic in 1780, Horace Walpole said, "I am a settled Whig; for if one thinks, one must before my age have fixed one's creed by the lamp of one's own reason: but I have much Quakerism in my composition, and prefer peace to doctrines."[123] As the conflict advanced, the Revolutionary leaders ceased to

---

[120] Joseph Hewes to Samuel Johnston, May 23, 1775, *Delegates*, 397.

[121] Philadelphia Yearly Meeting, Minutes, 21st of the 9th mo. 1776, HQC.

[122] Isaac Sharpless, *The Quakers in the Revolution* (1902); Facsimile (Honolulu: University Press of the Pacific, 2002), 209.

[123] Horace Walpole to Sir Horace Mann, April 17, 1780, in W. S. Lewis et al., eds., *Horace Walpole's Correspondence* (New Haven, CT: Yale University Press, 1971), 25: 40. In a letter to Alexander Hamilton, Gouverneur Morris makes a similar, though less charitable distinction, identifying Samuel Howel[l?], a powerful merchant, as "A Quaker who would have been a Whig, if he had not been afraid" (Morris to Hamilton, January 27, 1784. *The Papers of Alexander Hamilton*, Harold C. Syrett, et al., eds. [New York: Colombia University Press, 1967], 3: 498–503. 500).

generalize Friends by the example of those who would fight and began characterizing them by the ones who would not. Indeed, it was the case that most Quakers were now more concerned with preserving their province of Pennsylvania than resisting British policy, and they attempted to quell the growing radicalism among their countrymen.[124] Since the early 1770s, PYM had begun to publicize its concerns much more broadly and forcefully than before. For example, leaders sent an epistle to New York Friends encouraging them to maintain their peaceful principles, "since by doing so might influence others to follow a more peaceful course."[125] And they sent epistles and testimonies in the same vein to the other colonies.[126]

One of the most notable Quaker-informed products of the period was written by Joseph Galloway. His 1774 Plan of Union seems to represent a traditional Quaker stance on the conflict. Galloway, like Dickinson and PYM Quakers, was intent on preserving the relationship with Britain. In his Plan, he proposed a new governmental structure for the colonies that would unite it more firmly with Britain. Among other features of this new government, it would give Americans representation in Parliament, but it would also make the colonies clearly subordinate to Britain. Although the colonists would retain some authority over local matters, the executive and upper house appointed by the king would keep them firmly under British control. After Galloway's proposal was rejected by Congress, he soon left Pennsylvania to support the British in New York. This would seem to be the most likely path for conscientious Quakers to take.

There were remaining Quakers and their ilk who, thinking like Dickinson, were neither reluctant to defend their rights as Americans, nor, like the Free Quakers, quick to take up arms. John Jones, a New York physician and John Dickinson's cousin, was one of these.[127] Jones expressed his opinion to Dickinson on the proper course to pursue during the conflict. He desired "the reconciliation between England & her Colonies, upon . . . constitutional principles," because those "uninfluenced by party or selfish views" know that "preserve[ing] that union . . . alone must constitute our political salvation." At the moment, however, he felt "an equal mixture of shame & indignation at the contemptible part which our own Province has exhibited to the world." Accordingly, he laid out to Dickinson "the thing which is right." Sending delegates to Congress and

---

[124] Mekeel, *The Relation of the Quakers to the American Revolution*, 85.

[125] Ibid., 47.

[126] Philadelphia Yearly Meeting, Meeting for Sufferings Minutes, 1771–80, FHL.

[127] Dr. John Jones was the preeminent American surgeon in the colonies and early Republic, instrumental in organizing the medical department of the Continental Army during the Revolution, attended to Washington, and was at Franklin's deathbed. Charles A. Gliozzo, "John Jones," *American National Biography* (New York: Oxford University Press, 1999), 12: 214–16. He is described as a "pious, almost a primitive Quaker" by J. H. Powell, and also as a Quaker in Gliosso's entry, but the *Dictionary of Quaker Biography* in the Haverford College Quaker Collection notes without elaboration that he was disowned. See also J. H. Powell, finding aid, item 360, JDP/LCP.

"strictly adher[ing] to" nonimportation was right; obstructing these measures was not. Equally wrong, however, were the "ignorant hotheaded Demagogues, whose highest views extended no farther than leading a mob round the City." All parties should unite, he said, "in opposing such shameful violence." He looked to Dickinson to solve the problem: "[H]appy the man who cou'd chalk out a system of Legislative policy which would preserve to England her just Authority, & secure to Americans the rights of Englishmen. Labour at it my Dear Sir!"[128]

The year 1775 was a pivotal one for the cause – as Dickinson's stance remained the same, the world around him turned. As he put it himself, his principles and creed had not changed "a single Iota" since the conflict began. "I have never had & now have not any Idea of Happiness for these Colonies for several ages to come, but in a State of Dependence upon & subordination to our Parent State."[129] He was still in fundamental, though not total agreement with most Friends. In February, congressional delegate and speaker of the Pennsylvania Assembly Edward Biddle wrote, "We are all in Confusion. The Quakers are moving Heaven & Earth to defeat the Measures of the Congress & introduce a Submission to Parliamt."[130] In this year, as the nation and Philadelphia were precariously balanced between peace and war, Dickinson's job as trimmer was the most delicate it would be.

Perhaps the best example of Dickinson's political philosophy and his stance as trimmer during this period is his authorship of two apparently opposing documents that appeared on consecutive days in 1775 – The Olive Branch Petition, issued by Congress on July 5, and the Declaration for the Causes and Necessity of Taking up Arms, issued the sixth. The Olive Branch Petition is the best known of his efforts at reconciliation. A reluctant and impatient Congress appointed a committee to draft a plea to the crown. John Jay produced a draft with harsh language and threats of rebellion, but it was Dickinson's version, proclaiming the colonies' suffering and their loyalty to the king and placing the blame for the controversy with the king's ministers, that was adopted and submitted.[131] The king, of course, dismissed the petition, and the war proceeded.

We must not forget, however, that Dickinson was not a Quaker; he was not a rigid pacifist in the most basic sense of rejecting all violence in every circumstance. He believed in the "lawfulness of defensive war." He strove for the best outcome, but prepared for the worst, continuing to press for reconciliation, even as he prepared for war. In June he had become the chairman of the Committee on Public Safety and in that capacity organized a company

[128] John Jones to John Dickinson, March 20, 1775, Incoming Correspondence, Sept. 22, 1759 – June 23, 1782, JDP/LCP.

[129] John Dickinson, "Notes for a Speech in Congress," May 23, 1775, *Delegates*, 1: 378.

[130] Edward Biddle to Jonathan Pott, February 25, 1775, *Delegates*, 1: 315.

[131] John Jay, draft of the Olive Branch Petition, 1775, in Government Documents, Revolution and Early National Period, 1765–1788, JDP/LCP.

of Associators, the first battalion of troops raised in Philadelphia, of which he was the colonel.[132]

Accordingly, the next day, after approving the Olive Branch Petition, Congress issued A Declaration for Taking Up Arms. Various drafts were produced in a tense collaboration between Thomas Jefferson and Dickinson. One added fiery and aggressive tones, promising a formidable threat from America and a prolonged war. The other used language that was mild and conciliatory. While logic would seem to suggest that Jefferson would have penned the more bellicose lines and, indeed, he later claimed to have written them, the historical record proved him wrong when the draft with the harsher language was found in Dickinson's papers in Dickinson's own hand.[133] And on closer inspection, Dickinson's authorship of these portions actually makes more sense. Dickinson was trying to avert war; Jefferson was, if not in favor of it, then at least not opposed. Thus Dickinson, unlike Jefferson, had a motive to write a declaration that would give the British pause. His tack was to produce such "apprehensions" in England that they might "procure Relief of all our Grievances."[134] There is thus a continuity of purpose between the Olive Branch Petition and the Declaration that belies the superficial impression either that Jefferson wrote the Declaration or Dickinson had come to support rebellion.

Probably with the Olive Branch Petition in mind, some of his colleagues began to murmur unfavorably. "Mr Dickinson the Pensylvania farmer as he is Called in his Writings," said Congressman Eliphalet Dyer, "is lately most bitter against us & Indeavours to make every ill Impression upon the Congress against us but I may say he is not very highly Esteemd in Congress."[135] In the same vein as the Petition, on November 9 Dickinson wrote the document that would become the single biggest hindrance to the Revolutionary movement – the Instructions of the Pennsylvania Assembly to the Delegates in Congress, which restricted this central-most colony to pursuing reconciliation and no more.[136] "He has taken," observed Dyer, "a part very different from what I believe was expected from the Country in general or from his Constituents."[137] Misunderstanding Dickinson's principles, he would later write, "tho' a whig in principle . . . his nerves were weak."[138]

---

[132] "John Dickinson," in *Soldier-Statesmen of the Constitution* (Washington, DC: Center of Military History, U.S. Army, 1987), 82–84, 83.

[133] It does not appear that Dickinson and Jefferson sat down together to write this, as the term collaboration would imply. Rather they seem to have only reviewed one another's drafts. For a fuller discussion of the genesis of this document, see Julian P. Boyd, "The Disputed Authorship of The Declaration on the Causes and Necessity of Taking up Arms, 1775," *PMHB* vol. 74 (1950), 51–73. A close comparison of the drafts can be found in Julian P. Boyd et al., eds., *The Papers of Thomas Jefferson* (Princeton, NJ: Princeton University Press, 1950), 1: 187–219.

[134] Dickinson, "Notes for a Speech in Congress," May 23, 1775, *Delegates*, 1: 372.

[135] Eliphalet Dyer to William Judd, July 23, 1775, *Delegates*, 1: 654.

[136] "John Dickinson's Proposed Instructions of Pennsylvania Assembly to the Delegates in Congress," Nov. 9, 1775, *Delegates*, 2: 319–21.

[137] Eliphalet Dyer to William Judd, July 23, 1775, *Delegates*, 1: 654.

[138] "Copy of a paper drawn up by Joseph Reed for W. Henry Drayton" (1774), Maria Dickinson Logan Collection, HSP.

Last Resistance to Revolution, 1776

By the advent of 1776, Pennsylvania was the locus of the American Revolution. Although there were other colonies uncertain about the decision to revolt, it was in great part this colony on which a declaration of independence and success of the Revolution depended. The year began with a flurry of activity. In Congress, Dickinson authored a myriad of instructions, proposals, and speeches for negotiations with Britain.[139] The delegates to Congress were soon abuzz about Dickinson, "the eldest Colonel" in Pennsylvania who "cheerfully" stepped forward and "insisted on his right to command" a detachment being sent to New York to meet the British.[140] As Dickinson had said in 1775, preparations for war "must go pari passu with Measure of Reconciliation."[141]

At the same time, a print war that would have major implications for the progress of the cause was taking place in Pennsylvania. First, on January 8, Thomas Paine published *Common Sense*. Within days, on January 20, PYM responded with a testimony addressed to the "people in general" of America.[142] If there were any lingering doubt about where Quakers as a body stood on the issue of war and independence, this resolved it. The purpose of the *Testimony* was for Friends to explain their position on religious duty, government, and revolution, to present a model for non-Friends to follow and to absolve themselves of any complicity with one side or another. Quoting from *The History of the Rise, Increase, and Progress, of the Christian People Called Quakers* (1722) by William Sewell, they explained their understanding of the government as a sacred institution and how man ought therefore to relate to it:

It hath ever been our judgment and principle, since we were called to profess the Light of Christ Jesus, manifested in our consciences unto this day that the setting up, and putting down kings and governments, is God's peculiar prerogative; for causes best known to himself: and that it is not our business, to have any hand or contrivance therein; nor to be busybodies above our station, much less to plot and contrive the ruin, or overturn of any of them, but to pray for the king, and safety of our nation, and good of all men; that we may live a peaceable and quiet life, in all godliness and honesty; under the government which God is pleased to set over us.[143]

---

[139] These include the Grievances and Resolves of Congress, the first Petition to the King, and the *Letter to the Inhabitants of Quebec*.

[140] Joseph Hewes to Samuel Johnston, February 13, 1776, *Delegates*, 3: 247; and John Hancock to George Washington, Feb. 12, 1776, *Delegates*, 3: 236. Others to comment on or soon after February 13 were John Adams to John Trumbull; John Adams to Abigail Adams; Josiah Bartlett to John Langdon; John Hancock to Thomas Cushing; Robert Morris to Charles Lee, *Delegates*, 3: 241–44, 267.

[141] John Dickinson, undated notes, John Dickinson Correspondence, 1775–98. Simon Gratz Autograph Collection, HSP.

[142] The Religious Society of Friends, *The Ancient Testimony and Principles of the People Called Quakers; Renewed, with respect to the King and Government; Touching the Commotions now prevailing in these and other Parts of America, addressed to the People in General* (Philadelphia, 1776).

[143] Ibid., 4.

So problematic was this statement for the Revolutionary leadership that it provoked a number of responses. The most notable of these is Paine's often-ignored appendix to *Common Sense*, published in April with his third edition, that executed a biting attack on the Quakers.[144] And he was perhaps the most qualified person to do so. If Dickinson was the representative of traditional Quaker political philosophy that emphasized peace, reconciliation, and individual rights within a unified polity, Paine, drawing on the same heritage, was his radical counterpart. Raised by a Quaker father and given a "guarded" Quaker education, Paine was intimately familiar with the theology of Friends. Moreover, his revolutionary zeal was no doubt fueled by the sense of rights and dissent instilled in him in his upbringing. Paine's father was likely a strong influence on his egalitarianism and his rejection of practices ranging from slavery to dueling.[145] Clearly Paine's firsthand knowledge of Quakerism is what allowed him to challenge Friends on their own beliefs and principles and effectively preach Quakerism to the Quakers, even going so far as to quote Barclay's *Apology* to them. "We do not complain against you because ye are *Quakers*," he wrote, "but because ye pretend to be and are not Quakers."[146]

Paine focused on the heart of the PYM *Testimony* as evidence of the hypocrisy of Quaker withdrawal. He asked, "If these are *really* your principles why do ye not abide by them?" Although the *Testimony* does not categorically deny the efficacy and propriety of human agency in affairs of state, or the Quakers' own role in Pennsylvania government, they probably intended it to be read as such. How much familiarity Paine had with Quaker political history in Pennsylvania is uncertain; yet, insofar as their position on the *Testimony* could work to his advantage, he was certainly willing to exploit any vagueness in it. "The principles of Quakerism," said Paine, reiterating the Quakers' claim of neutrality, "have a direct tendency to make a man the quiet and inoffensive subject of any, and every government *which is set over him.*" Logically, then, Friends should simply stand passively by and "approve of every thing, which

---

[144] Some of his sentiments echo those expressed earlier by Samuel Adams, writing as "Candidus," February 3, 1776, in William V. Wells, *The Life and Public Services of Samuel Adams: Being a Narrative of His Acts and Opinions, and of His Agency in Producing and Forwarding the American Revolution, with Extracts From His Correspondence, State Papers, and Political Essays* (Boston: Little, Brown and Company, 1865), 2: 360–63.

[145] Foner, *Tom Paine and Revolutionary America*, 3. Although it is clear that Paine had a close affiliation with Quakers and was undoubtedly influenced in no small degree by Quakerism, it is clearly going much too far, as some have done, to say that Paine was a "Quaker Revolutionary" or that *Common Sense* is the "product of a 'dyed-in-the-wool-Quaker'" (William Kashatus III, "Thomas Paine: A Quaker Revolutionary," *Quaker History* vol. 73, no. 2 [1984]: 38–61, 61). Paine himself wrote of his attitudes toward war and peace: "I am thus far a Quaker, that I would gladly agree with all the world to lay aside the use of arms, and settle matters by negotiations; but, unless the whole world wills, the matter ends, and I take up my musket, and thank heaven he has put it in my power" (quoted in Moncure Daniel Conway, ed., *The Life of Thomas Paine* [New York: G. P. Putnam's Sons, 1893], 1: 44). Thus, anything in *Common Sense* that is specifically Quaker is virtually lost when it was blurred with the Calvinist revolutionary theory, which alone disqualifies it from being a Quaker tract.

[146] Thomas Paine, *Common Sense* (1776), 142.

ever happened, or may happen to kings as being [God's] work." For the Revolutionary leadership, it would have been most preferable if PYM Quakers had adhered to their stated principle. The inconsistency of Quakers, of all people, writing a political pamphlet to disavow their political involvement was not lost on Paine. His point, then, was apt: "[W]hat occasion is there for your political testimony if you fully believe what it contains: And the very publishing of it proves, that either ye do not believe what ye profess, or have not virtue enough to practice what ye believe." The bottom line for Paine was that "[w]herefore, as ye refuse to be the means on one side, ye ought not to be meddlers on the other; but to wait the issue in silence." It was apparent to non-Friends that PYM was not as neutral as it would like to seem. "Ye appear to us," he concludes, "to have mistaken party for conscience." He exclaimed, "O ye partial ministers of your own acknowledged principles."[147] Not surprisingly, Paine aligned himself with the Free Quakers.

Dickinson, meanwhile, had a decidedly different view of Friends and their politics – different both from Paine's and their own – and one that was more historically accurate. According to him, the Quakers' enemies objected, not unrealistically, that their insistence on pacifism created factional differences in Pennsylvania so great that they would give the British the impression of American "disunity." This, in turn, would encourage Great Britain to attack the colonies and thereby make Pennsylvania liable for "all the Bloodshed & Calamities, that may follow." In his "answer to these Objectors," in the clearest terms, Dickinson implored Pennsylvanians to look to the Quakers and their history of peaceful protest in the province for guidance. He explained

that the good men who have promoted the pacific Measures of this Province, have no doubt duly considered their Objections; & as it appears to have had no weight with them, we may fairly conclude from the great Proofs they have given of their wisdom in this Affair, that it did not deserve the least regard.

We may therefore now justly rejoice, that we have reached the most consummate Degree of virtue and Prudence in Politics. It is true, that those who have gone before Us, in settling & constructing this Province, did tolerably well for the Times in which they lived: but every impartial Reader of our public Transactions, that from the very Beginning of the settlement, there was a certain turbulent Spirit in our Forefathers, which never would suffer them to sit down in Silence and submission under any Attack upon their Privileges or Liberties: Nor do I believe that the History of any People upon Earth can shew Instances of a more steady attention to their Rights, or of quicker Alarms, on any affront or Injury being offered to them.

However, tho they had their turbulent Disposition for maintaining their Rights, as they were called, yet in Justice to their Memory we must acknowledge, that their Turbulence was of such a kind, that no other turbulence can be compared with it. It was the Turbulence of Sense, Spirit, Virtue, Meekness, Piety, employed – Mistaken Men! as they thought, in Defence of publick Happiness. It was cautious: it was firm: it was noble: it was gentle: it was ~~religious~~ devout:

[147] Ibid., 53–58.

In short, their Policy was like the Religion they professed; and it would not have been Turbulence, if it had not been employed – Mistaken Men! as they thought, in Defence of publick Happiness.

How must they be delighted, if Heaven permits them to take Notice of these worldly Things, to observe their wiser, more virtuous Posterity, preserving the <u>public Tranquility</u> by taking care of it.[148]

This account of the Quakers clearly comports better with their actual history than either PYM's *Testimony* or Paine's diatribe. Though historically many devout Quakers were reluctant to enter politics, aware of the spiritual pitfalls that abound, until the Revolution, they always considered it an obligation. In *Some Fruits of Solitude* (1693), Penn mused about the fine line between acceptable retreat and necessary engagement. "Neutrality," he said, "is something else than Indifferency; and yet of kin to it too." It meant "not to meddle at all." "A Neuter," he continued, "only has room to be a Peace-Maker: For being of neither side, he has the Means of mediating a Reconciliation of both."[149] We have seen this claim about *meddling* before as Quakers defended their government in early Pennsylvania.[150] They parsed their words carefully, defining meddling as partisanship, yet allowing interference in politics for the right "Causes." In the same way, Penn qualified his remarks by saying, "tho' Meddling is a Fault, Helping is a duty."[151] While the private life was preferable, still, "the Publick must and will be served."[152] Thus, while Penn seemed to urge Quakers towards the neutral position that they adopted during the Revolution, he ultimately gave them not just permission to engage, but a pointed directive not to remain on the sidelines. Interestingly, Penn might well have sided with Paine in his assessment of PYM. "[W]here Right or Religion gives a Call," Penn said, "a Neuter must be a Coward or a Hypocrite."[153]

With Dickinson's statement, there can be no doubt as to his position advocating traditional Quaker action – "turbulent" but "pacific." It is perhaps this very idea that he had in mind when he scribbled cryptically in his notes, "A peaceable War."[154] And with such sympathies, Dickinson did not emerge unscathed in his efforts to balance "our *little vessel*."[155] As tensions rose and he showed more signs of dissent from the increasingly bellicose attitude of his countrymen, his reputation among those in favor of independence began to falter. John Adams infamously called him a "piddling genius," someone who was

---

[148] John Dickinson, untitled document, n.d., Ser. I. b. Political, 1774–1708, n.d. RRL/HSP.

[149] Penn, *Some Fruits of Solitude*, 61. By *indifferency* Penn meant *disinterestedness*.

[150] See Chapter 4, page 245.

[151] Penn, *Some Fruits of Solitude*, 60–62.

[152] Ibid., 55.

[153] Ibid., 61.

[154] John Dickinson, untitled fragment, n.d., Ser. I. b. Political, 1774–1708, n.d. RRL/HSP.

[155] Wrongly cited in Colbourn, "John Dickinson, Historical Revolutionary," 272, as appearing in Stillé and Ford, *Life and Writings*, 2:326.

"warped by the Quaker interest."[156] Others suspected that he might have been unduly influenced in matters of governmental policy by the Quakerism of his immediate family. Charles Thomson claimed that Dickinson's Quaker mother and wife "were continually distressing him with their remonstrances."[157] And, indeed, Dickinson later said, "I took it for granted, that my Behaviour would be supposed to be influenced by too strong an addiction to the [Society of Friends], ~~if that Society would approve my Conduct~~."[158]

In a significant sense, the final contest over revolution came down to a struggle between Dickinson and Adams. It was Dickinson who had almost single-handedly stalled the Revolution for months with his instructions to the Pennsylvania delegates. "To them," said Elbridge Gerry, "is owing the delay of Congress in agitating questions of the greatest importance, which long ere now must have terminated in a separation from Great Britain."[159] John Adams added more bluntly that the government in Pennsylvania is "incumbered with a large Body of Quakers," which "clogg[s its] operations a little."[160] It was Adams, then, long critical of the Quakers in general and Dickinson in particular, who had the greatest hand in bringing down the Pennsylvania Assembly. In order to revoke and replace Dickinson's instructions with something more agreeable to his designs, on May 10 Adams motioned in Congress to dissolve all proprietary governments and replace them with ones friendly to the Revolutionary cause; it passed and was published on the fifteenth.[161] "It was a measure," he confessed, "which I had invariably pursued for a whole year."[162] When the radicals succeeded in supplanting the Quaker Assembly over the course of only a few weeks, on May 29, John Adams wrote with what must have been great satisfaction, "these [Quaker] cloggs are falling off, as you will Soon see" (Figure 8).[163]

[156] John Adams to James Warren, July 24, 1776, *Delegates*, 1: 658; and John Adams's Diary, Sept. 24, 1775, *Delegates*, 2: 50.

[157] Thomson cited in Mekeel, *The Relation of the Quakers to the American Revolution*, 136.

[158] John Dickinson to unknown, August, 25, 1776, Ser. I. a. Correspondence, 1762–1808, RRL/HSP.

[159] James T. Austin, *Life of Elbridge Gerry* (New York: Da Capo, 1970), 1: 179.

[160] For a fuller account of this episode see Jack N. Rakove, *The Beginnings of National Politics: An Interpretive History of the Continental Congress* (New York: Alfred A. Knopf, 1979), 69–97.

[161] Steven Rosswurm claims that "[e]ven Dickinson supported it" and cites an unpublished manuscript by [Jerrilyn Greene?] Marston entitled "Congress Grants Authority for Government." Yet neither the *JCC* or *Delegates* give any indication of individuals' support or dissent of the motion and, as we shall see in the next chapter, Dickinson later protested the illegality of the displacement of the Assembly and fought against the new government (*Arms, Country, and Class: The Philadelphia Militia and the "Lower Sort" during the American Revolution, 1776–1783* [New Brunswick, NJ: Rutgers University Press, 1987], 94).

[162] John Adams, *The Works of John Adams, Second President of the United States: with a Life of the Author, Notes and Illustrations* Charles Francis Adams (Boston: Little, Brown and Co., 1856), 3: 45.

[163] John Adams to Benjamin Hichborn, May 29, 1776, *Delegates*, 4: 96.

FIGURE 8. "Quakerism Drooping." An early eighteenth-century depiction of an ailing Quaker, propped up by "Sinless Perfection" and "Infallibility." (Francis Bugg, *Quakerism Drooping, and its cause sinking*... [London, 1703], 75. (FHL)

What the radicals and their representatives in Congress wanted were new instructions that would cause Pennsylvania to support independence. Compelled by the turn of events in his province, Dickinson obliged – partly. With a committee, he drew up a new set of instructions that removed the restrictions of the previous ones. But the instructions were not as clear cut as radicals wanted. Putting his lawyerly skills to use, he did not prevent the delegates from voting for independence, but neither did the language of the instructions give them the express instructions to vote for it.[164] This ambiguity was Dickinson's final procedural attempt to avert revolution, and the greatest extent to which he would obstruct – as some saw it[165] – the popular will. It was a subtle strategy, but obstruction it was not. On the contrary, this wording gave the delegates a

---

[164] John Paul Selsam, *The Pennsylvania Constitution of 1776: A Study in Revolutionary Democracy* (Philadelphia: University of Pennsylvania Press, 1936), 132–33. See the Instructions in the *Pennsylvania Evening Post*, June 8, 1776.

[165] Robert Whitehall to friends, June 10, 1776 in "Delegates' Certification of James Wilson's Conduct in Congress," June 20, 1776, *Delegates*, 4: 274.

freedom that was heavy with responsibility. Rather than *instruct* them to vote for independence, which he knew some of them and many of their constituents were against, his intent, no doubt, was to lay the weighty decision on the consciences of the individual delegates. Their true instructions would thus come from God.

A matter of days after the new instructions were published, Dickinson began preparing the country not just for war, but for independence. In spite of the rising animosity toward him – one commentator observed that "Dickinson, Wilson, and the others, have Rendered them selves obnoctious to Every Whig in town, and Every Day of theyr Existance are losing the Confidence of the people"[166] – he headed a committee to write the nation's first constitution.

Independence

On July 1, 1776, the day before the vote on independence, John Adams wrote that "[t]his morning is assigned for the greatest Debate of all."[167] It was the day Adams and Dickinson would confront one another directly in Congress to convince their colleagues for or against Revolution. Dickinson began. Exemplifying the Quaker conviction that "whatsoever tendeth to break that Bond of Peace and Love, must be testified against,"[168] and in full awareness of the consequences of his actions, he opened with the admission that "My Conduct, this Day, I expect will give the finishing blow to my once too great, and my Integrity considered, now too diminish'd Popularity." Becoming a political martyr to testify for "a Truth known in Heaven," he said, "I might indeed, practise an artful, an advantageous Reserve upon this Occasion [but] Silence would be guilt. I despise its Arts – I detest its Advantages. I must speak, tho I should lose my Life, tho I should lose the Affections of my C[ountrymen]." Prefacing his speech with a prayer, he then passionately reiterated his previous objections. He was even more concerned than he had been in 1765 that independence would result in "a multitude of Commonwealths, crimes and Calamities – centuries of mutual Jealousies, Hatreds, Wars and Devastations, until at last the exhausted Provinces shall sink into Slavery under the yoke of some fortunate conqueror."[169] This common Quaker fear of disunion was ultimately what differentiated Dickinson from his compatriots – he adhered to the meaning of liberty that was synonymous with safety through union under the British constitution. Those who pressed for independence effectively argued that "[w]e ought to brave the Storm in a Skiff made of Paper."[170]

---

[166] Ibid.

[167] Adams to Archibald Bulloch, July 1, 1776, *Delegates*, 4: 345.

[168] Barclay, *Apology*, 57.

[169] John Dickinson to William Pitt, 21 December 1765, from Jack P. Greene, "The Background of the Articles of Confederation," *Publius* vol. 12, no. 4, The Continuing Legacy of the Articles of Confederation (1982), 15–44, 35.

[170] John Dickinson, "Notes for a Speech in Congress," July 1, 1776, John Dickinson Correspondence, 1775–1798, Simon Gratz Autograph Collection, HSP.

When Dickinson finished, the room remained silent. "No Member rose to answer him," said John Adams, until he himself took up the task.[171] With the general sentiment favoring Adams, his argument won the day. Accordingly, on July 2, Dickinson absented himself from the vote on independence. By such an act, he knew from a poll taken the evening before that the vote would be nearly unanimous and the Revolution would proceed. Of the seven Pennsylvania delegates, one other absented himself, two voted against independence, and three voted for it.[172] This moment signaled a shift in American thinking from defining liberty as security to it being freedom from authority, with the corresponding release of democratic impulses.

What Dickinson did next compounded the enigma for his contemporaries and historians. From this point on, they wanted very much for him to fulfill their expectations of a "loser" in the debate, to see him defect to the British, and to be able to call him a Loyalist. John Adams spoke with contempt of "the timid and trimming Politicks of some Men" who would not approve independence.[173] But immediately after the Declaration was passed, Dickinson took up arms and led his battalion to Elizabethtown. Meanwhile, Adams hoped to "leave the War to be conducted by others" and return home to Massachusetts.[174]

Disappointed, those in favor of independence persisted in attributing Dickinson's stance to timidity or other self-interested motives. To this he said:

What can be more evident than that I have acted on Principle? Was there a Man in Pennsylvania, that possessed a larger share of the public Confidence . . . than I did? Or that had a more certain Prospect of personal advantages from Independency, or of a smaller chance of advantages from Reconciliation? . . . I knew most assuredly & publicly declared in Congress that I should lose a great Part of my popularity and all the benefits of an artful, or what some would call a prudent Man, might coin it into – I despised them, when to be purchased only by violation of my Conscience – I should have been a Villain, if I had spoken and voted differently from what I did – for I should have spoken & voted differently from what I judged to be for the Interest of my Country . . . While I was there voluntarily & deliberately, step by step, sacrificing my Popularity . . . what would be my object & whom was I trying to please? The proprietary People are known to be & to have been uniformly my deadly foes throughout my Life. Was it to please the People called Quakers? Allow it – What was I to obtain by pleasing them? All things were converging to a Revolution in which they would have little Power. Besides, I had as much displeased quieted them by other measures I took as I did others by opposing the Declaration of Independence.[175]

[171] Adams to Archibald Bulloch, July 1, 1776, *Delegates*, 4: 346.

[172] Dickinson and Morris did not appear; Franklin, Wilson, and Morton voted in favor; and Humphreys and Willing opposed (Ryerson, *The Revolution Is Now Begun*, 329).

[173] John Adams to William Tudor, June 24, 1776, *Delegates*, 4: 306. There is no doubt Adams is referring in particular to Dickinson as one of these "Men of large Property [in Pennsylvania who], have almost done their Business for [the Quakers and Proprietarians]. They have lost their Influence and grown obnoxious."

[174] John Adams to John Winthrop, June 23, 1776, *Delegates*, 4: 299.

[175] John Dickinson to unknown, August, 25, 1776, Ser. I. a. Correspondence, 1762–1808, RRL/HSP.

Through all the turmoil, John Dickinson's political actions at the moment of independence were complex, but hardly as enigmatic as many have suggested. They are comprehensible when understood in the light of Quaker theologico-politics. In a Quaker meeting, individual dissent was tolerated, and even encouraged, provided it followed a specific process. Those with minority viewpoints were allowed and expected to try to convince their brethren that theirs was the correct understanding of God's will; but only to a certain extent. If an interpretation or "leading" was disavowed by the meeting as a whole, the individual was obliged to submit his will to the meeting and not undermine its mission. Since Dickinson, as a traditional "Quaker" politician, was acting consistently with the idea of the civil polity as the meeting writ large, his actions were not only consistent but perfectly in keeping with appropriate Quaker political behavior. In his description of the Quaker decision-making process, Michael Sheeran explains how a Quaker may take the position of disagreement without obstructionism: "The meeting is left aware of the dissenter's opinion, yet the dissenter has indicated a wish not to keep the matter from moving forward. Equivalently, the objector has thus endorsed the action of the group by implying that in his or her own judgment the objection is not serious enough to prevent action."[176] Therefore, after Dickinson spoke his mind, rather than continue to dissent from the Declaration, which he knew was going to win majority approval, he abstained from the vote in Congress and allowed Pennsylvania to support the Declaration. Sheeran describes the interesting position in which this act places the individual. It shifts him from a position of dissent to one of tacit endorsement: "[He] tends to take some responsibility for the decision, even to feel some obligation for making it work out well in practice."[177] Accordingly, after the passage of the Declaration, Dickinson supported his country fully by taking up arms and working to perfect an American constitution. As Dickinson himself explained it: "Although I spoke my sentiments freely, – as an honest man ought to do, – yet when a determination was reached upon the question against my opinion, I regarded that determination as the voice of my country. That voice proclaimed her destiny, in which I was resolved by every impulse of my soul to share, and to stand or fall with her in that scheme of freedom which she had chosen."[178] Sheeran calls this technique of withdrawing one's opposition, though not one's disagreement, "virtually an art form of graciousness."[179]

Reflecting on political obligation and resistance in the next century, Quaker theorist Jonathan Dymond confirmed the propriety of Dickinson's actions. "If I had lived in America fifty years ago," he said,

and had thought the disobedience of the colonies wrong, and that the whole empire would be injured by their separation from England, I should have thought myself at

---

[176] Michael Sheeran, *Beyond Majority Rule*, 66. See also The Religious Society of Friends, *Faith and Practice: A Book of Christian Discipline* (Philadelphia: Philadelphia Yearly Meeting, 1997), 28.

[177] Sheeeran, *Beyond Majority Rule*, 67.

[178] Stillé and Ford, *Life and Writings*, 1: 204.

[179] Sheeran, 67.

liberty to urge these considerations upon other men, and otherwise to exert myself (always within the limits of Christian conduct) to support the British cause.

He then described the course of peaceful resistance Americans could have pursued and the results it would have brought:

Imagine America to have acted upon Christian principles, and to have refused to pay [the tax], but without those acts of exasperation and violence which they committed...Does any man...believe that England...would have gone on destroying them...if the Americans continually reasoned coolly and honorably with the other party, and manifested, by the unequivocal language of conduct, that they were actuated by reason and by Christian rectitude?...They would have attained the same advantage with more virtue, and at less cost.

And finally, he explained the position that the dissenter should take when the people decide on their course:

But when the colonies were actually separated from Britain, and it was manifestly the general will to be independent, I should have readily transferred my obedience to the United States, convinced that the new government was preferred by the people; that, therefore, it was the rightful government; and, being such, that it was my Christian duty to obey it.[180]

Dickinson was not a perfect example of Quaker constitutionalism. He did eventually take up arms. But for that one exception, Dymond would have done what Dickinson did. And, indeed, that was also how most other Quakers at the time proceeded, in support of the Federal government.[181]

---

[180] Jonathan Dymond, *Essays on the Principles of Morality, and on the Private and Political Rights and Obligations of Mankind* (New York: Collins Brothers and Co., 1845), 327–29.

[181] The behavior of the Society of Friends in the Revolution is undoubtedly problematic within the context of their theories both of political engagement and constitutional perpetuity. If traditional Quaker thinkers were concerned with upholding the extant fundamental constitution, why did they not all chose a path similar to Galloway's and become Loyalists? How could they justify ultimately supporting the new American constitution, which they did overwhelmingly, rather than the British? If they did indeed favor one side, why did they not continue their political advocacy for the cause that they believed was more likely to preserve liberty? There are no easy answers to these questions. The possible reasons are ideological and practical: First, and most likely, is that, because of the lack of security for dissenters' rights in the British constitution, and the nonexistence of an American constitution, there was more of an incentive to adhere to the only trustworthy constitution at hand, their Charter of Privileges. We will see in the next chapter that, in this rough transitional period, localism prevailed over nationalism. One might expect that they would have leaned toward a proposal by one of the leaders of their Assembly, Joseph Galloway with his 1774 Plan of Union. But this would have been a disturbing prospect. Although Galloway exemplified some traditional Quaker concerns, most notably preserving the ancient constitution, he actually departed from other principles that were very important to Friends. His proposal for a hierarchical restructuring of the government proved that he was less concerned with liberty of conscience and productive dissent within the polity than most Friends. Most Quakers were evidently less troubled about establishing a new American constitution than they were with being oppressed under a hierarchical and intolerant one.

Conclusion

For Dickinson, as for the Quakers, a central constitution was a tool with which to safeguard American liberties. When that tool was no longer accepted by his countrymen, he went to work creating a new one, the Articles of Confederation. His priority was always the preservation of American liberties by the surest means. Dickinson's record, when situated in the context of his culture, reflects not hesitancy, indecisiveness, or pessimism, but unambiguous resolve in favor of peace, liberty, and unity – and caution lest these things be lost in the heat of passion. Neither was his caution indicative of negativity, but rather the opposite – while some "despair[ed] of seeing the [British] constitution recover its former vigor," Dickinson did not give up hope until his entire country had spoken.[182] He has also been painted as a traitor or a lukewarm patriot, but if patriotism is defined by a denial of self for the good of one's country, then his absence from the vote on independence should be seen as one of the greatest patriotic acts of the Revolution. Furthermore, as the religious dissenters he followed, he chose derision and infamy rather than admiration and popularity. Very much in the Quaker mentality, he reflected on July 25, 1776, "I have so much of the spirit of Martyrdom in me, that I have been conscientiously compelled to endure in my political Capacity the Fires & Faggots of persecution."[183]

Dickinson's contribution to American political thought is therefore both different from and more significant than what scholars have claimed. Advocate of rights though he was, he was no intentional "Penman of the Revolution." In the 1760s and 1770s Dickinson was expressing an idea that most Americans would not articulate until after the Revolution when they were faced with creating their own state and national constitutions – the idea of the perpetuity of a fundamental constitution along with an internal process of amendment.

In short, when Friends were forced to choose between a flawed British constitution (that might get worse if Galloway had his way) and the possibility of preserving their unique Quaker constitution under a *potentially* perfect American constitution, they chose the what appeared to be a safer course in the long run, and one that respected the voice of the "meeting" with which they were most intimately bound, the American one.

A second possible reason for their acceptance of a new American constitution was practical: Once independence had been declared and there was no return to the British constitution, it was not difficult for Friends to change course because of the federal system they were used to in their meeting structure. As discussed in Chapters 1 and 8, it was a natural part of the Quaker ecclesiastical structure that when a far-flung group became too physically remote from the center, it would itself establish a new central government. It was also clearly in their interest to support the new government and advocate their liberties under it. But none of these explanations addresses their reluctance during the early years of the war to engage politically to support either constitution. This is a problem that will be addressed in the next chapter.

[182] Charles Caroll quoted in Bailyn, *The Ideological Origins of the American Revolution*, 131.
[183] John Dickinson to Charles Lee, July 25, 1776, quoted in Martha Calvert Slotten, "John Dickinson on Independence, July 25, 1776," *Manuscripts* 28 (1976), 189. Like Quakers who believed persecution was a sign of divine chosenness, in the margins of his notes for his July 1 speech before Congress he wrote: "Drawing Resentment one proof of Virtue," *Delegates*, 4: 356.

These were ideas basic to Quaker political thought. Historians who have seen the significance of Dickinson's work as preparing the country for revolution have been interpreting it both with the benefit of hindsight – that America did eventually revolt – and without understanding the context of Dickinson's thought. Despite the fact that his writings did lead to the Revolution and he was compelled to abandon his conciliatory stance, his place in history is not among the leaders of revolutions, but rather, to the extent Americans used nonviolence, as the first leader of a national peaceful protest movement. In this capacity, he actually did make a significant contribution to the Revolution – John Adams noted that "the delay of the Declaration to [1776] has many great advantages attending it," not the least of which was that it served to "cement the union."[184] But, as we shall see in the following chapter, his judgment in this case was premature as the cement of the Union was not quite cured.

[184] John Adams to Abigail Adams, July 3, 1776, *Delegates*, 4: 376.

7

"The Worthy Against the Licentious"

The Critical Period in Pennsylvania

If the progress toward the Revolution in Pennsylvania was untidy, the realization of it was decidedly ugly. This chapter examines the extremely troubled period between the Revolution and the Constitutional Convention in order to shed light on John Dickinson's hopes for the new state and nation and his fears as national problems were magnified in Pennsylvania.[1] Earlier arguments both in this study and elsewhere maintain that party lines were drawn based on religion and that theology has a significant "explanatory potential" that needs to be elucidated.[2] We have already seen that, since the campaign for royal

---

[1] See Woody Holton, *Unruly Americans and the Origins of the Constitution* (New York: Hill and Wang, 2007). Holton claims that because they did not include a Bill of Rights, the Framers of the Constitution were not genuinely concerned with preserving rights and justice. He finds that their complaints about the violations of rights and justice were empty, and they had no actual cause for seeking a strong central government except for expanding their own economic power. Likewise, there was no democratic excess, and historians mistakenly compare popular action during this period to real tragedies such as slavery and the persecution of religious minorities (16). What he fails to consider, however, is that there was, in fact, religious persecution and denial of the civil rights of many Pennsylvanians. It was these things, this chapter will show, that proved the claims of at least one Framer: that a strong central government was necessary to control and unify the states.

[2] Much has been written on this complex time in Pennsylvania, specifically the conflict between the radical "Constitutionalists" – those who supported the Pennsylvania constitution of 1776 – and the "Republicans" – those who sought to reform it. Most recently, see Terry S. Bouton, *Taming Democracy: "The People," The Founders and the Troubled Ending of the American Revolution* (New York: Oxford University Press, 2007). This chapter follows Owen S. Ireland's interpretation in "The Crux of Politics: Religion and Party in Pennsylvania, 1778–1789," *WMQ* 3rd ser., vol. 42, no. 4 (1985), 453–75. 474; and Douglas Arnold's in *A Republican Revolution: Ideology and Politics in Pennsylvania, 1776–1790* (New York: Garland Publishing, 1989). Before these studies on religion, assessments of party politics assumed the priority of class and region as determining factors of factional alliance. The standard works on the period are John Paul Selsam, *The Pennsylvania Constitution of 1776* (Philadelphia: University of Pennsylvania Press, 1936); Robert L. Brunhouse, *The Counter-Revolution in Pennsylvania, 1776–1790* (Harrisburg: Pennsylvania Historical and Museum Commission, 1971); Jackson Turner Main, *The Sovereign States, 1775–1783* (New York: New Viewpoints: A Division of Franklin Watts,

government in 1764, three Quaker-informed factions existed in Pennsylvania. Influenced by the conflict with Britain, two of them were gradually moving away from traditional Quaker theologico-politics – one toward individualistic, democratic, and armed radicalism; the other toward a withdrawn, passive stance, based on a new, narrower interpretation of the peace testimony. These factions were now set against one another with resistance to the British the apparent point of conflict. The radical group, in its beginnings hostile to Presbyterians in the campaign for royal government, now united with them, ostensibly to further the American cause. The withdrawing group of Quakers retreated from civic engagement and adopted a neutrality that was historically uncharacteristic of their Society when rights were threatened.

As the previous chapter demonstrated, a few Quakerly types, such as John Dickinson, maintained a stance more in keeping with traditional Quaker behavior than either of these two strains – rights advocacy and peaceful protest for reform. Now that the break with Britain was formalized, he could in good conscience (not being a convinced Quaker) take up arms and defend America against her attacks. But also, because of the alliance between radical Presbyterians and former Quakers, he found himself fighting a battle at home as challenging as extracting Americans from British rule – securing the fundamental rights of Pennsylvanians and Americans against the "patriotism" of the new governors.[3] Indeed, the localism of all parties often obscured the larger conflict.

In the spring of 1776 John Adams commented that Dickinson was both an "Advocate for Colony Governments, and Continental Confederation."[4] During this period, he struggled to establish constitutions for the state and nation that would preserve the unique liberties that Quakers had enjoyed in colonial Pennsylvania, as well as their traditional English liberties. Now, at a time when there was no central constitution and only a weak and defective state constitution, his fears for dissenters' rights before independence were realized as he, members of the Society of Friends, and others perceived as hostile to the regime fell through a constitutional gap that left them without protection from overly enthusiastic Patriots. At issue was the fact that the

---

Inc. 1973); Adams, *The First American Constitutions*; Anne M. Ousterhout, "Controlling the Opposition in Pennsylvania during the American Revolution," *PMHB* vol. 105 (1981), 3–34; Rosswurm, *Arms, Country, and Class*; Ousterhout, *A State Divided*; Marc W. Kruman, *Between Authority and Liberty: State Constitution-Making in Revolutionary America* (Chapel Hill: University of North Carolina Press, 1997). My argument will only touch lightly on the theological and constitutional motives of the radicals, focusing instead on the priorities of Quakers and their supporters during this period.

[3] The argument here differs in some fundamental ways from that put forth by Bouton in *Taming Democracy*. It agrees that the Revolutionary elites sought to limit the new popular power in Pennsylvania; however, it disputes the claim that Pennsylvania during the Critical Period was the "healthy" or "expansive" democracy Bouton portrays, or that it could be seen as enlightened exemplar for other states (6, 7).

[4] John Adams to John Winthrop, May 12, 1776, *Delegates*, 3: 663.

national and state constitutions depended upon the stability of one another. His attempts to prevent the problems began before independence with his draft of the Articles of Confederation. Immediately after independence was declared, he fought for a just and balanced constitution for Pennsylvania, which culminated in his presidency toward the end of the period. The ideals he espoused in his version of the Articles of Confederation and in Pennsylvania government represented Quaker concerns, and his constant equation of liberty with safety led to his presidency of the Annapolis Convention that met to amend the national constitution. The following pages will highlight his ideals within the context of the clash between withdrawn and traditional Quakers and their supporters on the one hand, and radical Revolutionaries on the other, many of whom had learned from radicalized Quakerism that had grown over the last decades.

The 1776 Articles of Confederation

Although Dickinson wrote the Articles of Confederation for the nation, he did so with an eye toward the increasing anti-Quaker sentiment in Pennsylvania. The coup of the Pennsylvania government by the radicals and his recognition of the reality that America would probably – though not "inexorably" – revolt instigated his attempt to secure the Quakers' constitutional rights.[5] His fear at this point was that the patriotic furor of the radicals, combined with their deep-seated resentment of nonradical Quakers, would overrun any regard for dissenters' rights that had existed under the now-incapacitated 1701 Charter. Not wanting independence, but in preparation for it, he took the lead immediately before the Declaration in writing the Articles.[6] Although there were several attempts at an American constitution before Dickinson's draft, none of these had a significant influence on Dickinson's document.[7] Earlier authors were limited by their desire for reconciliation. They thought not in terms of confederation but of disparate colonies essentially independent from one another and bound only by a distant and oppressive (or happily negligent) imperial government.[8] Dickinson on the other hand, despite his fervent hope for continued unity with Britain, did not let this wish interfere with his vision for the future and what was necessary for an independent America. In fact, it was his conviction that independence was dangerous and likely that prompted him to

---

[5] Rakove, *Beginnings*, 152.

[6] He was one of a committee of thirteen that included, among others, Josiah Bartlett, Edward Rutledge, Samuel Adams, and Thomas McKean. The document that was submitted to Congress on July 12 was originally written by Dickinson, and then revised by him according to the critiques of his colleagues. This version was then debated and amended by Congress before it was approved in late August. Rakove, *Beginnings*, 139.

[7] Ibid., 138. Adams describes the a few points that resemble Franklin's version (*The First American Constitutions*, 281).

[8] Ibid., 138–39.

write it as he did and create a document that would bear a strong resemblance to the 1787 Constitution.[9]

There are several proposals in the Dickinson Plan that scholars consider "innovative."[10] Among the most notable of his contributions are the provisions for a powerful central government and religious liberty.[11] These may have been exceptional when compared to the work and thought of other Founders, but most were standard in the context of Quaker political thought and practice. Because there have been several competent analyses of the Dickinson Plan, what follows is not exhaustive.[12] Rather, as a preface to a deeper treatment of the Constitution in Chapter 8, this discussion will only touch some of Dickinson's ideas.

The main issue in framing an American constitution was similar to the question of the relation of the colonies to the British constitution – the power of the states in relation to the central government. Dickinson was not alone in his concern for such a power, but he was one of the most consistent advocates of it, so much so that he has drawn suspicion from colleagues and historians alike that he was an "ardent nationalist."[13] The editors of the *Letters from Delegates* consider his efforts in this regard to be "radical."[14] Such a perception is unbalanced, however; as we shall see, he was no less concerned with state's

[9] Jack N. Rakove, "Legacy of the Articles of Confederation," *Publius* vol. 12, no. 4, The Continuing Legacy of the Articles of Confederation (1982), 45–66; Harry W. Jones, "The Articles of Confederation and the Creation of a Federal System," in George W. Corner, ed., *Aspects of American Liberty: Philosophical, Historical, and Political* (Memoirs of the American Philosophical Society) (Philadelphia, 1977), 126–145; Robert W. Hoffert, *A Politics of Tensions: The Articles of Confederation and American Political Ideas* (Niwot: University of Colorado Press, 1992), 85.

[10] Rakove, *Beginnings*, 139.

[11] Not directly related to the topic of this chapter is Indian relations, which drew Dickinson's attention more than the other Founders. As we have seen, while most Americans regarded Indians little or with hostility, Quakers had a long history of intimate and amicable relations with them. Accordingly, Dickinson addressed his fourteenth and fifteenth articles to Indian relations. The former restricts attacks against Indian nations to defense in the face of imminent danger of invasion. The latter is concerned with peaceful dealings. It establishes in the first instance a "perpetual alliance" between the entire Union and all other Indian nations. From there, provisions were made for "their Lands to be secured, and not to be encroached on" and an ambassador from the United States to "reside among the Indians" to "take Care to prevent Injustice in the Trade with them." Finally, the United States would establish a fund to provide "occasional Supplies to relieve their personal Wants & Distresses." Isolated points concerning Indians appeared in the final version of the Articles and in the Constitution; however, none consider their welfare.

[12] For his draft, annotated with inclusion of his marginalia and edits on the final product, see *Delegates*, 4: 233–55. For analyses of the Dickinson Plan, see Merrill Jensen, *The Articles of Confederation: An Interpretation of the Social-Constitutional History of the American Revolution, 1774–1781* (Madison: University of Wisconsin Press, 1940), 126–39; Jones, "The Articles of Confederation"; Rakove, *Beginnings*, 151–58.

[13] James H. Hutson, "John Dickinson at the Federal Constitutional Convention," *WMQ* 3rd ser., vol. 40, no. 2 (1983), 256–82, 258.

[14] *Delegates*, 4: 253.

rights. Even at this early point, Dickinson had a sense for the relationship between state and nation that eluded most of his colleagues. Others, too, worried about the "mutual Jealousies, Hatreds, Wars and Devastations" that might ensue with independence, but many were unconcerned, and none had much to say, about how to address the potential for democratic problems in America, which were already becoming reality in Pennsylvania.[15] Dickinson's priority was to create a primary central structure that would resolve problems both in and between states and impose a coercive power that would compel them to defer their own interests to that of the Union. The ultimate effect would be twofold: A central power would protect the states and allow them to flourish in their own unique ways. Conversely, stable states would ensure a secure and perpetual union.

According to Dickinson, there were three primary ways to accomplish the preservation of the Union. First, the states must submit to the Union and promote its good. To this end, he drafted articles that restricted the power of states and secured the powers of the central confederation in negotiating war and peace, regulating foreign and domestic trade, and regulating the states' relations with one another. The states would retain their discrete rights provided that these did "not interfere with the Articles of this Confederation."[16] Significantly, however, the directives from the central government were not necessarily negative. States should actively contribute to the common good. Article Twelve, for example, stipulates that "all Expences that shall be incurr'd for the general Wellfare . . . shall be defrayed out of a Common Treasury." Second, the Union could not survive without peace between the states. Individual states must therefore be restrained from wantonly exercising their own wills and Congress empowered to mediate conflicts. Dickinson wrote that the central government would have the right of "[s]ettling all Disputes and Differences now subsisting, or that hereafter may arise between two or more Colonies." One area in particular in which Dickinson anticipated conflict was over the Western lands, over which multiple states laid claim. Congress would regulate their boundaries. As scholars of the Articles have noted, Dickinson was laying the groundwork for a federal system.[17] To do so, he drew on his experiences with Quakerism, specifically, their history of mediating conflicts and the structure of their church government.

A third way in which the central government should regulate involves individuals, specifically, protecting their rights. Jack Rakove implicitly acknowledges the Quaker influence when he discusses what he considers to be the most innovative aspect of Dickinson's Articles – religious liberty. As we have seen, Quakers believed that civil union and liberty depended on civil safety, which

---

[15] John Dickinson to William Pitt, 21 December 1765, quoted in Greene, "The Background of the Articles of Confederation," 35.

[16] All quotations from the Dickinson draft are from "John Dickinson's Draft Articles of Confederation," *Delegates*, 4: 233–55.

[17] Jones, "The Articles of Confederation," 130–31. Hoffert, *Politics of Tensions*, 84.

they believed would be achieved by state-protected religious liberty. Dickinson was focused on the sectarian problems in Pennsylvania at this time and worried that they would – as they did already – create problems in forming and stabilizing the state governments that would be so essential to the survival of the Union.[18] His third article, therefore, preserved laws in the states exactly as they had existed under the colonial governments. What he had in mind is clear from the fourth article. There he enumerated the unique liberties Pennsylvania Quakers had under their 1701 Charter, such as that individuals should not be compelled "to maintain any religious Worship, Place of Worship, or Ministry contrary to his or her Mind," and, significantly, "whenever on Election or Appointment to any Offices, or on any other occasions, the Affirmation of persons conscientiously taking an Oath hath been admitted in any Colony or Colonies, no Oath shall in any such Cases be imposed by any Law or Ordinance." Both of these provisions were, of course, based on long-standing Quaker testimonies and did not necessarily exist elsewhere in the colonies. They were the same ones that he worried Pennsylvanians would give up by changing to a royal government in 1764, and, with the hostility to Quakers in Philadelphia palpable as he wrote, it was these he feared would evaporate under the revolutionary government.

But Americans were not ready for this constitution. Edward Rutledge, one of Dickinson's colleagues on the committee, believed that the Dickinson Plan would destroy "all Provincial Distinctions"[19] and consolidate the states "into one unitary polity."[20] Accordingly, after it was submitted to Congress on July 12, it was reworked over the next months to remove all of the offending passages, namely those that empowered the central government, restricted the power of the states, and, most significant to the purposes here, the article on religious liberty.[21] If the latter would have passed, observes John Witte, "it would have been a remarkable step on the path toward creating a law on national religious liberty."[22] Indeed, in his notes on a later version, Dickinson questioned the absence of an article on religion. Anticipating the First and Fourteenth Amendments, he asked, "Should not the first Article provide for a Toleration and agt. Establishments hereafter to be made?"[23] Having joined his battalion days after independence, and having been voted out of Congress by

---

[18] See also Rakove, *Beginnings*, 153.

[19] Edward Rutledge to John Jay, June 29, 1776, *Delegates*, 4: 338. Interestingly, Rutledge seemed to fear that Dickinson's Plan would make the nation too democratic. He worried that it would unleash the "leveling Principles" and "occasion such a fluctuation of Property as to introduce the greatest disorder."

[20] Greene, "The Background of the Articles of Confederation," 41. Also Rakove, *Beginnings*, 155–57.

[21] For the revisions that were made, see Rakove, *Beginnings*, 158–62; Rakove, "Legacy," 45–53; Jensen, *The Articles of Confederation*, esp. 177–84.

[22] John Witte, Jr., *Religion and the American Constitutional Experiment*, 2nd ed. (Boulder, CO: Westview Press, 2005), 75.

[23] "John Dickinson's Draft Articles of Confederation," *Delegates*, 4: 253, n, 3.

the new Pennsylvania Assembly, he was not present to defend his provisions. A much weaker version emerged, the only sort that could win approval.

Rutledge complained famously that Dickinson's draft "has the Vice of all his Productions to a considerable Degree; I mean the Vice of Refining too much."[24] But clearly, considering how events unfolded in Pennsylvania, the excise of these portions of the draft had grave implications for certain segments of society. As they were being written, John Adams was sanguine that with these Articles, "the last finishing Stroke will be given to the Politicks of this Revolution."[25] He might have been right, had the articles been implemented as Dickinson wrote them; some scholars muse that if they had, the 1787 Constitution might not have been necessary.[26] But in reality, the politics had only just begun. More prophetically, Abraham Clark of New Jersey remarked to Elias Dayton, "We are now Sir embarked on a most Tempestious Sea."[27]

The Revolutionary Convention and the 1776 Pennsylvania Constitution

As soon as independence was declared, the radicals moved to establish formally the new Pennsylvania government.[28] Elections were held July 8 and the first meeting of the Convention was July 15. If it had not been clear before, the tone of the proceedings was extreme – only fervent radicals were elected. Moderate members of the Assembly were unceremoniously turned out, "all fallen, like Grass before the Scythe."[29] Dickinson got the news on the front. "While I was exposing my person to every hazard, and lodging within half a mile from the enemy," he explained, "the members of the Convention at Philadelphia, resting in quiet and safety, ignominiously voted me, as unworthy of my seat, out of the National Senate."[30] But no sooner had the election taken place than onlookers began to have doubts about the competency of the new government and regret that a tone of moderation had not been preserved. Particularly, they lamented Dickinson's absence. Charles Thomson wrote to him in the field saying, "I wish they had chosen better; & that you could have headed them."[31] Even John Adams was inclined "to wish that [Dickinson and others] may be restored, at a fresh Election."[32]

---

[24] Edward Rutledge to John Jay, June 29, 1776, *Delegates*, 4: 338.

[25] John Adams to John Winthrop, June 23, 1776, *Delegates*, 4: 299.

[26] Forrest McDonald and Ellen Shapiro McDonald, *Requiem: Variations on Eighteenth-Century Themes* (Lawrence: University Press of Kansas, 1988), 90.

[27] Abraham Clark to Elias Dayton, July 4, 1776, *Delegates*, 4: 378.

[28] For a concise narrative of the establishment and functioning of the new government and constitution, see *Guide to the Microfilm of the Records of Pennsylvania's Revolutionary Governments, 1776–1790* (Harrisburg: Pennsylvania Historical and Museum Commission, 1978), 1–6.

[29] John Adams to Abigail Adams, July 10, 1776, *Delegates*, 4: 243.

[30] Dickinson quoted in Stillé and Ford, *Life and Writings*, 1: 206. He did not resign, as Rakove claims (*Beginnings*, 151).

[31] Charles Thomson to John Dickinson, Aug. 16, 1776, quoted in Flower, *John Dickinson, Conservative Revolutionary*, 174.

[32] John Adams to Abigail Adams, July 10, 1776, *Delegates*, 4: 423.

The radicals' first job was to write a new constitution. The document was the offspring of two men with Quaker-informed radicalism in their blood – Benjamin Franklin and Thomas Paine. While Franklin was the president of the Convention, he was busy with national affairs and did not devote much time to the proceedings. Perhaps the real leader – in spirit if not in body – was erstwhile Quaker Paine. His partisans, James Cannon and George Bryan, crafted a document that generally followed the guide laid out in *Common Sense*.[33] The delegates to Congress who had orchestrated and approved the coup of the Assembly looked on as though they had not quite anticipated the turn of events. They observed in horror as the "numsculs" who were "intirely unacquainted with such high matters" took up their pens. Even some of the members of the Convention themselves agreed that they were "hardly equal to ye Task to form a new plan of Government."[34] Thomas Smith reported that they were wholly uneducated on the matter of law. They "might have prevented [themselves] from being ridiculous in the eyes of the world" had some members not prostituted themselves to the popular democratic sentiment. "They would go to the devil for popularity," he said.[35] They were farmers, artisans, and mechanics, and they garnered their support from the same ranks and lower.

The constitution that the Convention produced was an anomaly among state constitutions, but not for the reasons some scholars have claimed. It was at once the legacy of Quakerism and hostile to it; it originated as a response to hegemonic Quaker rule, but it drew some of its defining features from the very constitution it replaced – the 1701 Quaker Charter of Privileges. Commentators on the 1776 constitution often mention two supposedly unique qualities.[36] The first is the unicameral legislature. But of course, this was one of the distinguishing aspects of the colonial government. As we have seen, the Charter of Privileges was created specifically to abolish the upper house of the Assembly and nullify the powers of the proprietor.[37] While the radicals claimed to want to "reject everything" from the old constitution, "to clear every part of the old rubbish out of the way and begin upon a clean foundation," they were actually preserving what had already existed in Pennsylvania for seventy-five years.[38] The other notable provision, one that scholars almost universally

[33] Selsam, *Pennsylvania Constitution of 1776*, 49–50; Wood, *The Americanization of Benjamin Franklin*, 164; Foner, *Tom Paine and Revolutionary America*, 131.

[34] Peter Grubb quoted in Selsam, *The Pennsylvania Constitution of 1776*, 149; Francis Alison to Cozen Robert, Aug. 20, 1776, "Notes and Queries," *PMHB* vol. 28, no. 3 (1904), 375–84, 379.

[35] Thomas Smith to Arthur St. Clair, quoted in Burton A. Konkle, *Life and Times of Thomas Smith, 1754–1809* (Philadelphia: Campion & Company, 1904), 75.

[36] Kruman presents a fairly sanitized version of this process (*Between Authority and Liberty*, 24–27).

[37] *American Archives*, ser. 5, 2: 1149.

[38] Thomas Smith to Arthur St. Clair, quoted in Selsam, *Pennsylvania Constitution of 1776*, 205. Bouton seems to have accepted this claim uncritically. He finds that the "solution" that the Radicals found to the undemocratic Quaker constitution was to implement exactly the same

laud, is its democratic quality.[39] And indeed it was the first constitution – and the only one at this time – to abolish property qualifications for voting. Pennsylvania had always had a relatively liberal franchise because of the liberty of conscience clause in the Charter, and the radicals expanded it even further. But, as will become apparent, this democratic quality was not all it appears to be on the surface.

Other provisions of the constitution stipulated the basic rights Pennsylvanians had long enjoyed. It specified trial by jury and the inviolability of one's house and papers from seizure without warrant. There was also a clause protecting religious liberty that grew directly out of Quakerism – Section Two provides for freedom of worship and the right not to be compelled to support any church or ministry. Significantly, it also provided for civil liberties connected with religion, including a provision for those principled against taking an oath to take an affirmation. The test would be whether these fundamental laws would be upheld.

Protesting the Constitution

The 1776 constitution took effect on September 28. That autumn, having resigned his commission in the militia to move his family out of the path of the British Army, Dickinson returned to Philadelphia to oppose the constitution and, he hoped, restrain the radicals. He wrote, spoke, and agitated strenuously against both the process by which the constitution came into being, as well as the specific provisions it enumerated, which he considered "confused, inconsistent, and dangerous."[40] Dickinson expressed his constitutional priorities for Pennsylvania in three main places. In the autumn of 1776 he published *An Essay of a Frame of Government for Pennsylvania* and on October 21–22, he spoke at a public meeting about the constitution, out of which were published thirty-one resolutions.[41] He also made edits in his printed copy of the Pennsylvania Declaration of Rights.[42] Each of these instances shows both continuity and evolution of thought as new problems became apparent. As one might expect, each also shares many provisions with his Articles of Confederation.

features as that constitution – a unicameral legislature and a weak executive (*Taming Democracy,* 55). By contrast, Selsam is clear that there was "preponderant influence in favor of the old constitution" (*Pennsylvania Constitution of 1776,* 151).

[39] Bouton is only the latest to argue that the 1776 constitution would "remove the barriers that had kept their voices from being heard" (*Taming Democracy,* 55).

[40] Resolutions from the "Meeting in the State-House Yard," in *American Archives,* ser. 5 (Washington, DC, 1837–53), 1149–52. Published in the *Pennsylvania Gazette,* Oct 23, 1776. (Hereafter referred to as *Resolutions.*)

[41] It is unknown who penned the *Resolutions;* however, given his expertise and his history of authoring most of the publications of Congress, it is probable that Dickinson took the lead in writing these as well.

[42] John Dickinson, handwritten notes on his copy of *The Constitution of the Common-Wealth of Pennsylvania* (Philadelphia, 1776), 5–9, LCP. (Hereafter referred to as "Notes.")

As the October *Resolutions* state, the most fundamental objection to the new constitution of the Republicans, as they would be called, was that the proceedings of the Convention were illegitimate. The Convention, they said, "assumed and exercised powers with which they were not entrusted by the people." Although it was a legal truism that, as Dickinson wrote in his notes, "no Laws can bind the People but what they assent to by themselves or by their legal Representatives,"[43] the Convention ignored it. That body had grown out of the coup of the old government and was representative of the will of only some people. Also, the constitution was not voted on by the people – it was proclaimed as a fait accompli. Beyond this, however, the document was troubling to Dickinson on many levels.

Four main criteria for an effective and legitimate constitution recur throughout Dickinson's criticisms. The order in which they appear varies; thus it is difficult to tell which, if any, he thought should take precedence. One is that the laws and structure of the new government should not "[deviate] from all resemblance to the former Government of this state, to which the people have been accustomed,"[44] and, looking as far back in the state's history as possible, he stipulated that they ought not subvert the basic constitution given William Penn by Charles II in 1681.[45] But his references tend toward the more recent 1701 Charter. Many of his calls for constitutional continuity came in the context of another top priority – civil rights and liberties for religious dissenters. Like his fourth section of the Articles, he stipulated that the people of Pennsylvania "shall for ever enjoy the same rights, privileges, and immunities, and exemptions, unchanged, unrestrained, and altogether undiminished by any law or ordinance whatever, for or on account of any religious persuasion, profession or practice, which they now enjoy, or have been accustomed to the charter and laws of this colony."[46] With every mention of religion, special attention was given to the matter of oaths – that no "person conscientiously scrupulous of taking an oath [shall] be obliged or required by any law whatsoever . . . in order to be admitted into any office whatever" but "shall be permitted to take an affirmation, according to the ancient, legal and laudable usage in this colony."[47] It is interesting that Dickinson and other Republicans felt compelled to emphasize these provisions; after all, they were enumerated in the new constitution. It suggests that they were not secured well enough in their language to preserve them against the current climate in the state.

Another recurring point in Dickinson's writings is the separation of powers – or lack of it. On this matter, the *Resolutions* are somewhat contradictory. They demand continuity with the ancient laws of Pennsylvania, but they also deride the new constitution for establishing a unicameral legislature, with the judicial

---

[43] "Notes," 6.
[44] *Resolutions,* 1149.
[45] "Notes," 6.
[46] John Dickinson, *Essay of a Frame of Government for Pennsylvania* (1776), 13.
[47] Dickinson, *Essay of a Frame,* 13.

and executive branches dependent on the legislative. This is a clear point where we can see an important evolution in Dickinson's constitutional thought. During the 1764 campaign for royal government, he argued for the preservation of the 1701 Charter by touting its distinctive unicameralism and legislation unchecked by "a council instituted, in fancied imitation of the House of Lords."[48] But by now, Dickinson had undergone a similar "striking change of mind" to that of other Founders, though perhaps earlier – he turned away from the idea that the popular branch should bear the preponderance of power.[49] But it did not take ten years of turmoil under the new Articles for him to realize it. Although he had been in favor of a more egalitarian or democratic structure before, he now advocated one that was more hierarchical, or at least placed new checks on the popular branch.

Dickinson's change of mind in this regard could be traced to a variety of factors – the fractiousness of the Pennsylvania government under Quakers and the fact that this is what almost led to a drastic and potentially damaging change of government in 1764; the current difficulties with parliamentary supremacy in England; or the current democratic despotism in Pennsylvania. Regardless of the impetus, it is important to remember that Quakers had never – or not since their earliest years – advocated a pure democracy that would make unicameralism so dangerous. As we have seen, their government, while more "liberal" than some, was premised upon the idea of a spiritual aristocracy that would result in a sort of representative democracy and a check on the people. They believed in egalitarianism of a sort, but we might consider it as equal opportunity rather than equal liberties and privileges by default. In other words, individuals might all potentially speak publicly (i.e., vote and hold office), but each must prove that his voice was worthy of being heard, and only those whose did would lead. For the government to function otherwise would lead to licentiousness. On the other hand, because of this fundamental sense of the *possibility* of equality, Quakers tried to bring individuals along with education to the point where all voices had weight. However, they ultimately believed that a government conducted by men who were in power solely on the basis of their earthly equality with others as human beings rather than on spiritual merit was a dangerous and unacceptable foundation. In recent years and in various ways, Dickinson had likewise seen problems with an immoderate popular voice. And he saw it now.

Excessive popular power notwithstanding, in their arguments for separation of powers, the Republicans' greatest concern was the service of judges at the pleasure of the Assembly. This was actually an important difference from the colonial government, which had given judges more independence.[50] The *Resolutions* cite two of Dickinson's earlier writings for the Continental

---

[48] John Dickinson, *A Speech*, 18.

[49] Lance Banning, *The Jeffersonian Persuasion: Evolution of a Party Ideology* (Ithaca, NY: Cornell University Press, 1978), 89.

[50] Justices of the peace could only be removed after being found guilty in a trial. See Marietta and Rowe, *Troubled Experiment*, 166–67.

Congress, the First Petition to the King and the *Letter to the Inhabitants of Quebec*, to show how America had long disagreed with such an arrangement. Dickinson's *Essay of a Frame* spends considerable time explaining how "vesting the Supreme Legislature in three different bodies, has a great tendency to give maturity and precision to acts of legislation, as also stability to the state, by preventing measures from being too much influenced by sudden passions."[51] In this regard, the Republicans were unhappy with the constitution because it was an anomaly among state constitutions. "[I]t differs," they complained, "from others lately formed."[52]

A final repeating theme of Dickinson's criticisms was that the new constitution had no provision for amendment. He would have had the Declaration of Rights read "the People have a Right and ought to establish a new or reform the old Government in such Manner as shall by the Community be judged most conducive to the public Weal."[53] What the Convention did instead was to mandate that it was to be accepted in toto by the people without a vote, that it was not to be changed for the first seven years, and then not by the people, but rather by a Council of Censors established for that purpose. What was worse, it demanded that all inhabitants of Pennsylvania take an oath or affirmation so that they could not "directly or indirectly do any act or thing prejudicial or injurious to the constitution or government thereof, as established by the Convention."[54] Accordingly, the Republicans resolved that no one should swear to or affirm any such thing and urged resistance.

These were the consistent arguments that appeared in all Dickinson's constitutional writings.[55] But there were some that were unique to a particular document. For example, he ended his *Essay of a Frame* by suggesting some provisions that might eventually be added to the Frame. Two deserve special note. The first is "[t]o prohibit the punishing of any crime but murder, or military offences with Death."[56] Such a law would revive one of the oldest laws in Pennsylvania from the days when the Quaker colony stood out as the most gentle to criminals of all British governments. The other law would stipulate that "[n]o person coming into, or born in this country, to be held in Slavery under any pretense whatever."[57] With the abolition movement beginning among Quakers in

---

[51] Dickinson, *Essay of a Frame*, 3 (page unnumbered).

[52] *Resolutions*, 1150.

[53] "Notes," 6.

[54] *The Proceedings Relative to Calling the Convention of 1776 and 1790* (Harrisburg, 1825), 54.

[55] The one exception to this is that, oddly enough, a provision for amendment does not appear in Dickinson's draft of the Articles. The very fact that this omission is so out of keeping with all his other writings on the subject, we must assume its absence here is due to some other reason than that he did not consider it important. Indeed, is clear that he was thinking about the issue of change. In his notes on the draft, he wrote, "The Power of Congress interf[ering] in any Change of the Const[ituti]on? Also the Propeity of guaranteeing the respective Constitutions & Frames of Government." ("John Dickinson's Draft Articles of Confederation," *Delegates*, 4: 252, n. 2.)

[56] Dickinson, *Essay of a Frame*, 16.

[57] Ibid.

Pennsylvania, it was the first state to outlaw slavery in 1780. Dickinson would continue to express his objection to slavery in the Constitutional Convention.

The majority of Dickinson's notes on his copy of the Declaration of Rights suggest that he wrote them later than the autumn of 1776. They highlight potential problems that were not yet in existence or not clearly apparent at the time the constitution was proclaimed. It is likely that, as events unfolded and Dickinson witnessed or learned of the infringement on individual liberties in Pennsylvania, his criticisms of the constitution became more refined.

During the last months of 1776, Pennsylvania spiraled into chaos. There was no clear leadership in Philadelphia as the Constitutionalists and Republicans contested for power. It was very much a dispute over who should rule at home.[58] The ultimate source of the confusion was that there was no clear preference for one party or the other by the people; the state was split virtually down the middle. On the traditional election day, October 1, some counties held elections to support the old government. When the new election day approached, these resisters made plans to undermine the proceedings on November 5 by strategic voting and attempting to persuade electors not to take the oath. The Constitutionalists, meanwhile, allowed the Associators to control elections in some areas; they conducted the voting by battalion and did not allow others to cast a ballot. Also, it was, in general, difficult for those unwilling to take the oath to vote. Although the Republicans won heavily Quaker Philadelphia overwhelmingly, the Constitutionalists carried the election with the support of the Presbyterian Western counties.[59]

By this time, Pennsylvania not only had crippling internal difficulties, it was under direct threat from the British. In an attempt to remedy the political situation, on November 27 Dickinson offered a compromise to the Constitutionalists. They would cooperate if the radicals "will agree to call a free Convention for a full & fair Representation of the Freemen of Pennsylvania." The purpose would be for "reversing the Constitution form'd by the late Convention and making such Alterations & Amendments therein as shall by [the Freemen] be thought proper." The offer was rejected.[60] Unable to give allegiance to a flawed constitution, Dickinson left the Assembly, taking many Republicans with him. Clearly even the most devoted traditionalists struggled with the urge to withdraw when their theologico-political purity was threatened. Remaining members of the party hoped for his return. "The eyes of the whole city are fixed upon you," said Benjamin Rush. "[T]he whole city *waits* only to see what part you will take."[61] At this point, however he resolved to return to Delaware and enlist in the militia as a private. Thus, with no hope of a quorum, the government was paralyzed.

[58] Carl Becker, *History of Political Parties in the Province of New York* (Madison: University of Wisconsin Press, 1909), 22.

[59] Selsam, *Pennsylvania Constitution of 1776*, 226–30.

[60] John Dickinson, note on constitutional revisions in Pennsylvania, Nov. 27, 1776, Government Documents, Revolutionary and Early National Periods, 1765–1788, n .d., JDP/LCP.

[61] Benjamin Rush to John Dickinson, December 1, 1776, in Butterfield, *Letters of Rush*, 1: 119.

With the danger to the state from the British increasing, Congress demanded that the Council of Safety, now the state's acting government, call out the militia to protect the city. Though calls went out, they were of little effect because the Associators were now too complacent to fight, and they ran rampant in the city with little or no accountability to their officers. One historian has argued that the apathy of the Associators toward the invasion of the British was because they had a more immediate concern in mind – gaining power in the Pennsylvania government. Once that was achieved, they did not look beyond their own state to the national situation and had little interest in fighting a revolution.[62] Their grievances were not against England; they were against the Quaker government. In early December, Congress placed Pennsylvania under martial law.[63]

Although the alliance between radical Presbyterians and radicalized Quakers seems counterintuitive, at this point it was logical. The Presbyterians had long railed against Quaker power. "You are the persons who have made us slaves," they claimed in 1764, "you have depriv'd us of charter-privileges; have made laws for us; and have offer'd to deprive us of juries, so that you might have the power to spare our lives, or take them away, at pleasure"[64] Likewise, the radicalized Quakers bristled at the restrictions withdrawing Friends sought to impose on their revolutionary activities. The split between Quakers followed a similar fault line that existed since their origins and once again appeared in the early 1760s: One side, including withdrawing and traditional Quakerism – with Dickinson at the head – favored unity, security, and a sort of hierarchy; the other side – guided by Paine's ethos – favored individual leadings, democracy, and dangerous innovation. Paine claimed that "[w]hen I turned my thoughts towards matters of government, I had to form a system for myself, that accorded with the moral and philosophical principles in which I had been educated."[65] But former Quakers such as he rejected not just the representational quality of their religion's democracy that had been established by Fox, Barclay, and others in favor of pure democracy but also the pacifism that had restrained many members for years. Presbyterians were experiencing similar problems with factionalism in the church. Radical Presbyterians, acting perhaps out of the enthusiasm of the First Great Awakening, rejected the hierarchy by which their church had been organized and then attempted to democratize the state accordingly.[66] With Presbyterians and radicalized Quaker

---

[62] Selsam, *Pennsylvania Constitution of 1776*, 258–59. For an extensive discussion of the lack of commitment of militiamen, see James Kirby Martin and Mark Edward Lender, *A Respectiable Army: The Military Origins of the Republic, 1763–1789* (Arlington Heights, IL: Harlan Davidson, 1982).

[63] *JCC*, 5: 1017.

[64] Williamson, *Plain Dealer*, 1: 14.

[65] Thomas Paine, "The Age of Reason," in Moncure Daniel Conway, ed., *The Writings of Thomas Paine* (New York: G. P. Putnam and Sons, 1896), 4: 63.

[66] It is well known that radical Presbyterians took the lead in the Revolution. Peter C. Messer attempts to explain the radical behavior in terms of evangelical millenarianism in "'A Species of

types all alienated from or disillusioned with the reticence of traditional and withdrawing Quakerism, they could find common ground both politically and theologically.

Now armed, the Quaker element in the new government looked and acted much like reformed and democratized Calvinism. In the constitutional priorities that Paine expressed, we see what radicalized Quakerism devoid of the peace testimony and allied with reformed Calvinism could do in opposition to traditional Quaker constitutionalism. In wartime, historic rights and liberties were obliterated. The February before independence was declared, Samuel Adams scoffed at the fear that "Presbyterians, if freed from the restraining power of Great Britain, would overrun the peaceable Quakers in government."[67] Over the next few years, however, the radical leaders of Pennsylvania proceeded to violate every provision of their constitution named here.

"Torism is dum": The Constitutional Gap in Pennsylvania and Persecution of Dissenters

Although the sentiment in this heading was expressed by a learned Delawarian,[68] it is representative of the lack of nuance with which the uneducated radicals who crafted the Pennsylvania constitution perceived resistance to their cause. There is no doubt that some Quakers were Tories actively aiding the British – "just enough to taint the neutrality of the whole sect," says Robert M. Calhoon.[69] Thus anything less than patriotic enthusiasm was suspect, and neutrality, or even moderation, became the blank canvass for all the radicals' fears. George Savile's 1688 characterization of a trimmer summarized well the attitude of the Revolutionaries toward Quakers: "But it so happens, that the poor *Trimmer* hath all the Powder spent on him alone...there is no danger now to the state...but from the Beast called a *Trimmer*."[70] And it is clear that what provoked the Patriots was as much Quakers' trimming as their perceived Toryism. The seventeenth-century Trimmer faction was known for fence sitting and opportunism. And when the political situation became heated and revolution broke out, they stood passively by, letting others take the risks for liberty.

Treason & Not the Least Dangerous Kind': The Treason Trials of Abraham Carlisle and John Roberts," *PMHB* vol. 128, no. 4 (1999), 303–32. See also fn. 113, this chapter.

[67] Samuel Adams, February 3, 1776, in William V. Wells, *The Life and Public Services of Samuel Adams*, 2: 363.

[68] Thomas Rodney to Caesar Rodney, May 19, 1776, *Delegates*, 4: 62. On Toryism, see, among others, Leonard W. Larabee, *Conservatism in Early American History*, (New York: New York University Press, 1948); William H. Nelson, *The American Tory* (New York: Oxford University Press, 1961); the special issue of *Pennsylvania History* devoted to exploring the varieties of Loyalism, vol. 62, no. 3 (1995); work by Calhoon, including *The Loyalists in the American Revolution*.

[69] Calhoon, *The Loyalists in the American Revolution*, 388. He finds that only "[a] very few Friends were forthright apologists for British policy" and that "the great majority of the sect and virtually all its leadership were genuine pacifists" (170).

[70] Savile, *The Character of a Trimmer*, preface.

Although Quakers had never been trimmers in this sense, always being willing to take a stand and accept punishment for their beliefs, they now appeared to be so, adopting a more cautious stance that seemed to many to be cowardice or economic self-interest.

In 1768 Dickinson proclaimed that "[w]ise and good men in vain oppose the storm" of violent resistance. He anticipated the suffering he and Friends would ultimately experience, writing that they "may think themselves fortunate, if, endeavouring to preserve their ungrateful fellow citizens, they do not ruin themselves." He prophesied, "Their prudence will be called baseness; their moderation guilt" and "their virtue" may "lead them to destruction."[71] Speaking in 1775 of the "ignorant hotheaded Demagogues" leading mobs around New York, physician John Jones echoed his cousin's fears. "Nothing less than death or banishment will satisfy the resentment of these raging Patriots," he said. It was this "popular fury" that in large part made Quakers dread the "victory" of these Americans.[72]

Dickinson's and Quakers' worst fears came to pass as the basic rights they had had under the Charter vanished and were replaced with a degree of persecution they had not known since the seventeenth century, then also at the hands of reformed Calvinists in Massachusetts. Many of the most important civil liberties that Dickinson outlined in his *Essay of a Frame* and elsewhere were repeatedly violated – religious liberty, no tests or oaths, trial by jury, habeas corpus, no capital punishment except for murder and military crimes.[73] As in Restoration England under the Anglicans, the persecution took place both formally and informally, by thugs and government officials alike, often indistinguishable in Revolutionary Pennsylvania. It ranged from petty name calling, to libel, slander, and false charges, to destruction of property, deprivation of personal liberty without due process, and ultimately, for some, loss of life. Dickinson, being the most public and outspoken of the radicals' adversaries and the most visible of the Quakers' leaders, was the first target.

The majority of Dickinson's troubles occurred during the eight-month period when there was no constitution firmly in place in either Pennsylvania or the United States. An indication of growing problems came after he refused to sign the Declaration. "I had not been ten days in camp at Elizabethtown [New Jersey]," he said, "when I was by my persecutors turned out of Congress."[74] When he returned to fight for historic constitutional liberties, he presented such a problem for his opponents, speaking and acting against the unconstitutionality of their laws and proceedings, that he made more enemies than he ever

---

[71] Dickinson, *Letters*, 19.

[72] John Jones to John Dickinson, March 20, 1775. Incoming Correspondence, Sept. 22, 1759–June 23, 1782, JDP/LCP.

[73] While Bouton acknowledges many of these violations took places, he elides their import by referring to them in passing as mere "limits" that did minimize the "transformation" that had taken place in the government (*Taming Democracy*, 55–57). But indeed, the transformation was in important ways from a freer system to a more tyrannical one.

[74] Stillé and Ford, *Life and Writings*, 1: 206.

had before. Samuel Adams, who could be as vitriolic as his cousin, articulated a sentiment that must have been prevalent among the struggling radicals. On December 12, he decried Dickinson's power in that state, claiming that he "has poisond the Minds of the People, the Effect of which is a total Stagnation of the Power of Resentment, the utter Loss of every manly Sentiment of Liberty & Virtue. I give up [Philadelphia] & [Pennsylvania] for lost until recover['d] by other Americans."[75]

What happened next was the radicals' attempt to "recover" their state – retribution against Dickinson for interfering with their revolution. On December 15, Dickinson unwittingly provided the acting government, the Council of Safety, the excuse it needed to pursue him as an enemy to the cause. He sent a letter to his brother, the commanding officer of the Delaware militia, advising him not to accept Continental currency.[76] Without reasonable suspicion as to the contents of the letter, the Council apprehended Dickinson's servant, confiscated the letter, and opened it. They also seized his house in Philadelphia for a hospital. Within days, on the twenty-first, Benjamin Rush wrote to Richard Henry Lee, "Gen Putnam sent a guard to apprehend Mr Dick-n yesterday; you will soon hear of the cause of it. He has escaped."[77]

At this time, there was so much inflammatory gossip about Dickinson swirling around Philadelphia that it is hard to know how accurate Rush's statement was. Congressman William Hooper complained that "Dickinsons Apostatization" was so complete in that city that little said of him was to be believed, including the rumor that he had defected to the British.[78] Even if arrested, it is unlikely that he would have fled. On the contrary, Dickinson, who, like other gentlemen, had moved his family out of the city to safety, returned for the express purpose of facing the Council and refuting the accusations levied against him.[79] With a verdict of treason as the clear goal, the charges were, in addition to advising his brother against accepting Continental currency, that he had refused to sign the Declaration of Independence; he opposed the Convention and constitution; he deserted his military post; and he had not taken a seat in the Delaware assembly, as the people there had requested.

Dickinson put a good amount of effort into responding to these charges and would be required to continue his defense over the next several years. In addition to writing lengthy addresses to the public and the Council, in January, he appeared daily at its meeting place for almost a week seeking a satisfactory explanation for the interception of his mail, seizure and retention of £10,000 worth of his property, and slanderous remarks against his character.[80] In each

[75] Samuel Adams to James Warren, Dec. 12, 1776, *Delegates*, 5: 601.
[76] Flower, *John Dickinson, Conservative Revolutionary*, 213.
[77] Benjamin Rush to Richard Henry Lee, Dec. 21, 1776, *Delegates*, 5: 628.
[78] William Hooper to Robert Morris, Dec. 28, 1776, *Delegates*, 5: 689.
[79] His own departure from the city does not appear to have been entirely voluntary. Flower explains that his wife refused to leave without him (*John Dickinson, Conservative Revolutionary*, 181).
[80] Flower, *John Dickinson, Conservative Revolutionary*, 284; John Dickinson, "Defense of Actions Before the Council of Safety," 1777, Ser. 1. b. Political, 1774–1807, n.d., RRL/HSP.

instance, the explanation he offered the Council demonstrated the vacuity of the charges. Regarding the currency, the advice to his brother meant that he should not accept it in the field, having no safe place to keep it. He then provided affidavits from tenants that he himself had accepted American money.[81] As for refusing to sign the Declaration and support the Pennsylvania government, that was certainly no secret, and he reiterated that he was only doing what his conscience told him was best for the country. "The Council of Safety knows," he wrote, "that I might have reign'd with them, if I had been so false to my Countrymen, as to have concealed my real Sentiments for fear of displeasing them." Proof of his patriotism was that "there was not one Man at that Time in Philadelphia, who had acted as publicly in the Common Cause as I had done." But precisely because of this, "[f]or some time past I have been incessantly attacked on every side."[82] The great irony of Dickinson's situation, of course, was that he was seen by the British, according to John Adams, as "the ruler of America"[83] and one of the primary leaders of the Revolution, the "Penman." Thus, as his countrymen were harrying him, the British and American Tories were burning and looting his homes.[84] Aware that "the part I had taken from the very Beginning of the present Controversy, and my having born Arms, might have drawn peculiar Insults and Injuries on those who were connected with me," he officially resigned his commission in the militia to protect his family. Unapologetic, he announced, "I owe it to my Country, to involve [my family] in such a Danger, I also owe it to them, to make a reasonable provision for their Safety." Finally, as to the charge he had not sat in the Delaware assembly, a post he had declined for health reasons, he said, simply, that was "a matter in which they have no business."[85] He ended his defense with steadfast opposition to the bullying: "[C]onfiding in my Innocence, I defy your power, and if any of you bear me Malice, I would have you assuredly know, I equally defy that."[86]

Dickinson received no satisfaction from the confrontation. There was no apology or withdrawal of the accusations; yet neither were the charges pursued. There was no restitution for his stolen and damaged property; in short, there was no sign that the Council had been serious or had intended to do anything more than harass an adversary and ruin his reputation.[87] That spring

---

[81] Alexander Douglas, affidavit that Dickinson did not refuse to take Continental money in payment for rent, March 6, 1777, Ser. 1. b. Political, 1774–1807, n.d., RRL/HSP.

[82] John Dickinson, untitled ms, January 21, 1777, Ser. 1. b. Political, 1774–1807, n.d., RRL/HSP.

[83] John Adams, *Twenty-Six Letters, upon Interesting Subjects, Respecting the Revolution of America* (New York, 1780), 32.

[84] John Adams's Diary, Sept. 20, 1777, *Delegates*, 8: 5.

[85] Dickinson, "Defense of Actions Before the Council of Safety," 1777, Ser. 1. b. Political, 1774–1807, n.d. RRL/HSP. He explained his reasons – ill health and the care of his family – in a letter to George Read, Jan. 20, 1777, Small Manuscript Collection, John Dickinson Letters, DPA.

[86] John Dickinson, untitled document, Jan. 21, 1777, Ser. 1. b. Political, 1774–1807, n.d., RRL/HSP.

[87] On the seminal importance of reputation in this period, see Joanne Freeman, *Affairs of Honor: National Politics in the New Republic* (New Haven, CT: Yale University Press, 2002) Andrew Trees, *The Founding Fathers and the Politics of Character* (Princeton, NJ: Princeton University Press, 2004).

Dickinson was abused in the papers, as he was called the "compromising farmer," "piddling politician," "summer soldier," and a "procrastinating delegate, whose chilling breath b[l]ackened all measures of Congress." Addressing his diatribe to "Phocion," the author claimed that "[y]ou ransacked the Constitution through every page and paragraph, to find some real flaw in it that might expose it to contempt, but drove to the shameful shift of irritating religious spleen, your low art persuaded people that the *church*, and indeed our *land* was *in danger*."[88] Now that Dickinson had left for Delaware, in Congress, William Whipple seemed gleeful that "Dickinsonian Politics are Banish'd."[89]

The Virginia Exiles

At roughly the same time the radicals began with Dickinson, they also turned their attention toward the Society of Friends.[90] The October *Resolutions* against the constitution began rather cryptically with the point that "the Christian religion is not treated with the proper respect."[91] There was no further elaboration. The Constitutionalists, however, found the speeches of the "velvet mouthed gentlemen" worthy of satire. "Some of these men were lawyers," they said, "but they talked just like ministers, so devoutly and piously, there was no standing it." The simple cooper John Trusshoop was thoroughly duped. He explained in the *Pennsylvania Gazette* that "I am sure lawyer ----- made it so clear, and was so distressed about it, that I was ready to cry."[92] Although the resolution was, perhaps, more of a prognostication than a reality at that point, the tone of the response was indicative of its accuracy.

After the punishment Quakers received in *Common Sense*, they had restrained themselves from addressing the general public. Now they addressed only their meetings, but this enraged the radicals as well. In November 1776,

---

[88] "Demophilus," in *Pennsylvania Gazette*, March 19, 1777. Phocion was a Greek statesman who, according to Plutarch's *Lives*, tried to save the people from their own foolishness and was thus slandered for his virtue rather than revered.

[89] William Whipple to Josiah Bartlett, February 7, 1777, *Delegates*, 6: 236.

[90] There is surprisingly little written on this episode in the Revolution. See Isaac Sharpless, *The Quakers in the Revolution*, 145–206; Mekeel, *Relation of the Quakers to the American Revolution*, 173–88; Calhoon, *The Loyalists in the American Revolution*, 387–90; Robert F. Oaks, "Philadelphians in Exile: The Problem of Loyalty during the American Revolution." *PMHB* vol. 96 (1972), 298.

[91] *Resolutions*, 1149. John K. Wilson acknowledges that many state constitutions had provisions for religious liberty, but that they were often not enforced. He contends, however, that the Pennsylvania constitution contained strong protections for religious freedom. "Religion under the State Constitutions, 1776–1800," *Journal of Church and State* vol. 32, no. 4 (1990), 753–774, 762.

[92] John Trusshoop, Nov. 13, 1776, *Pennsylvania Gazette*. In this and Demophilus, cited earlier, the Constitutionalists make dubious claims about the Republicans' demands. Here Trusshoop claims the unnamed lawyer was advocating that adherence to the belief in the Trinity needed to be enforced, and Demophilus claims that Dickinson wanted the "Athanasian Creed, Heidelberg Catechism, Westminster Confession of Faith, or some other such esteemed *form of sound words*" written into the constitution and an oath to it sworn before anyone "could enjoy the rights of a citizen."

Congressman Oliver Wolcott warned that "[t]he Quakers may not be expected to take any open Active part in any political matter in these Times, but their secret Influence I fear is to Embarrass our measures. They dread to lose that Predominancy which they have heretofore held."[93] One epistle in particular instigated a new phase of persecution. As Philadelphia devolved into chaos in early December, the Meeting for Sufferings urged Friends to "with Christian firmness and fortitude withstand and refuse to submit to the arbitrary injunctions and ordinances of men, who assume to themselves the power of compelling others, either in person or by assistance, to join in carrying on war, and of prescribing modes of determining concerning our religious principles." What they were most concerned about was that the radicals were "imposing tests not warranted by the precepts of Christ." Like Dickinson, they were distressed that the new government refused to observe *"the laws of the happy constitution, under which we and others long enjoyed tranquility and peace."*[94]

In their admiration of what they think is the democratization of Pennsylvania, some scholars forget – or dismiss as unimportant – the motives behind the radical movement and the simultaneous restrictions they put on the rights of a significant segment of society. Their motives were not civil liberty for all, but only for some. Their aim was to secure the overthrow of the Quaker government and block any dissent to the new rule. And in order to do this, they would not only have to broaden the franchise to include the propertyless lower sorts but also restrict the voting and other civic activities of their opponents. They did so in the only way they could – to stop a religious opponent, they imposed tests and oaths to the revolutionary government that they knew Quakers could not take. They proclaimed that anyone "refusing or neglecting to take and subscribe the said oath or affirmation, shall, during the time of such neglect or refusal, be incapable of holding any office in this State, serving on juries, suing for any debts, electing or being elected, buying, selling, or transferring any lands, tenements, or hereditaments."[95] They insisted that Quakers renounce their allegiance to the crown. The irony was, of course, that Quakers had never sworn an oath of allegiance to the crown. And neither could they swear to the Convention, even had they been inclined to support it. In this way the Constitutionalists barred Friends from civic participation exactly as they had been barred in seventeenth-century England. Justifications for the oaths from radical supporters rang hollow. One asked, "Is an oath that bars an inveterate enemy who would enter a garrison on purpose to throw open its gates to the besiegers of tyrannie, [a] cruel and unreasonable thing?" He rationalized the oath by claiming that "these wonderful sticklers for free election" had themselves restricted the franchise by, among other things, property requirements. Then, in a perplexing statement grossly ignorant of republican political theory,

[93] Oliver Wolcott to Matthew Griswold, November 18, 1776, *Delegates*, 5: 514.
[94] Religious Society of Friends, *An Epistle . . . To Our Friends and Brethren in Religious Profession, in These and the Adjacent Provinces* (Philadelphia, 1776).
[95] *Statutes*, 5: 9, 75–94.

the author concluded that "I care not how free our future elections may be, provided the persons we elect be not impowered to subvert our legal freedom when elected."[96]

Like Dickinson, the Quakers' troubles began during the constitutional hiatus when there was neither a state nor a national structure to protect them. Although in 1775 Congress issued a resolution to protect conscientious objectors, it seems to have been forgotten by 1776.[97] There is no doubt that some Quakers considered themselves Tories and actively supported the British cause. But even those Friends who were Patriots were restrained by conscience from expressing themselves. They could not light their windows, aid troops, or join in any patriotic celebrations. Their refusal to participate in these things was both civil and social disobedience. The oaths soon became the least of their troubles as the harassment turned to persecution, and Quakers went from simply having their civic voice silenced to enduring the overt violations of their most basic civil rights – the precise rights for which Americans claimed to be fighting.

Because of Dickinson's agitations against the constitution and the immediate threat from the British, the new year opened as badly for Friends as for him. In late January the Council of Safety issued a resolve that ordered soldiers to be quartered in the homes of Non-Associators. Quaker Sarah Fisher knew that "[t]his wicked resolve is particularly levied against Friends, as the violent people were much enraged at the last publication of the Meeting of Sufferings." In this and other ways, the Convention turned the table on the Quakers. Radicals believed that, under the Quaker government, Non-Associators had received preferential treatment to the detriment of the colony.[98] Now they exacted retribution by compelling Quakers to do their part for the cause. Fisher considered the new resolve "an act of violence almost too great to bear."[99]

The treatment of Quakers evolved in proportion to the problems in Pennsylvania. It was relatively mild when the difficulties were internal and political; it turned most severe when the war was going badly. In August of 1777 as the British were approaching the state, Associators were not reporting for duty;

[96] Consideration, "In the Day of Adversity consider," *Pennsylvania Gazette*, Oct. 30, 1776. This article was a response to the *Resolutions*.

[97] *JCC*, 2: 220; See also Derek H. Davis, *Religion and the Continental Congress, 1774–1789: Contributions to Original Intent* (New York: Oxford University Press, 2000), 164–66; John Witte, Jr., *Religion and the American Constitutional Experiment*, 2nd ed. (Boulder, CO: Westview Press, 2005), 73.

[98] Under Quaker rule, Non-Associators had exemptions for "Pretenders" (7406) that the Associators believed unfair and detrimental to the country. *PA* 8th ser., 8: 7399–7400, 7402–07.

[99] Nicholas B. Wainwright, "'A Diary of Trifling Occurrences': Philadelphia, 1776–1778," *PMHB* vol. 82, no. 4 (1958), 411–65, 425–26. See Judy Van Buskirk, who also focuses on Quaker women, one of whom is Fisher, in "They Didn't Join the Band: Disaffected Woman in Revolutionary Philadelphia," *Pennsylvania History* vol. 62, no. 3 (1995), 306–29. For other women's accounts, see Elaine Forman Craine, *The Diary of Elizabeth Drinker: The Life Cycle of an Eighteenth-Century Woman* (Boston: Northeastern University Press, 1994); Kenneth A. Radbill, "The Ordeal of Elizabeth Drinker," *Pennsylvania History* vol. 47, no. 2 (1980), 146–72.

they were deserting. Pennsylvania, the state that should have been the country's biggest asset, had, as Charles Caroll put it, "become rather a burthen than strength to the Union."[100] Rather than look to the Associators as the problem, Congress and the Pennsylvania Executive Council identified the Quakers as the main cause, to the exclusion of most others. "There is not such a Collection of disaffected people on the Continent, as of the quakers inhabiting [eastern] Pennsylvania," wrote Elbridge Gerry. "The Disputes about the Constitution of this State," he continued, "have produced such a Division & Torpor thro out the same, as renders it at present an inactive, lifeless, unwieldy, Mass."[101] Accordingly, on August 26, a congressional committee composed of John Adams and Richard Henry Lee, among others, recommended to the Council "to cause a diligent search to be made in the houses of the inhabitants...who have not manifested their attachment to the American cause, *for firearms, swords, bayonets, &c.*"[102]

The absurdity and fruitlessness of searching pacifists' homes for weapons must have occurred to someone because, before the Council carried out the recommendation, new "evidence" surfaced to justify – in the minds of the radicals if not by any law – more than a mere search for weapons they knew did not exist. Some papers appeared from an alleged Friends meeting at Spanktown, New Jersey, indicating that Friends knew of British movements and were aiding them. These papers from a fictitious meeting, whose dates did not correspond with the events to which they were supposed to relate, were the excuse for a citywide round-up of forty-one Philadelphians, twenty of whom were Friends, the unwarranted search of their homes, and the confiscation of their papers. The most prominent Quaker in Pennsylvania, John Pemberton, Dickinson's cousin, recalled his arrest. "I told them, that as they had nothing justly to lay to my Charge, & my House was my Own & I a freeman, I could not consent to Comply with their Unreasonable demand." In a scene that cannot but remind us of the civil disobedience of the 1960s, he informed the men, "I could not leave my house without being forced." One of them then "took me by the arm & said he would force me to go, but I would not move from my seat...So I was lifted by two of them off my seat & led to the Door."[103] Pemberton and others were conveyed to the Free Masons' Lodge.

Over the next few days, from September 2 through 5, the deficiencies of both the state and national constitutions became strikingly apparent as Friends tested them. The Quaker community and those arrested began what would be a seven-month long appeals process to two governments, neither of which would

[100] Charles Carroll to Charles Carroll, Sr. September 29, 1777, *Delegates*, 8: 26.
[101] Elbridge Gerry to James Warren, October 6, 1777, *Delegates*, 8: 66.
[102] Thomas Gilpin, *Exiles in Virginia: With Observations on the Conduct of the Society of Friends During the Revolutionary War Comprising the Official Papers of the Government Relating to that Period. 1777–1778* [1848] (facsimile rpt. Bowie, MD: Heritage Books, Inc. 2002), 35. Gilpin's collection of documents pertaining to the Exiles is the best source on the episode and the one from which much of this discussion is drawn.
[103] *Diaries of John Pemberton, 1777–1781*, 2nd of the 9th mo. 1777, 3, HSP.

bear responsibility for the arrest or detention of the men, who, not having been charged with a crime, were not officially traitors. They petitioned for a hearing before the Council and were denied because, said the Council, it was Congress who had ordered them arrested. They then petitioned Congress, which said that the matter was out of their jurisdiction because these Quakers were inhabitants of Pennsylvania. On the fifth of the month, the Council offered that if Quakers would simply take the oath to the government, they would be released.

Henry Laurens, writing to John Lewis Gervais, expressed the majority opinion in Congress and the Council. "If the Quakers pretend to claim protection of the Laws of the Land," he said, "it should be remembered they refuse to obey those Laws & deny allegiance to the State[.]" Of course, Quakers had few illusions that they would get the "protection" of the state and wanted the security of their ancient constitution. Laurens continued to justify the governments' actions not by America's professed principles but by its enemy's behavior during the war. Because "the British powers Seize & confine the persons of our Subjects or friends upon Suspicion," he said, Americans ought to do the same to Friends. But instead, he complained, "we suffer [England's] professed friends to be at large & to go through all the Ceremonies & chicanery of Courts of Law in their defense, we proceed upon very unequal terms." He intimated that Quakers were guilty of worse than some men who had already been put to death for treason, yet they were spared. As to the unwarranted arrest and detention of Quakers and other alleged traitors, he said: "A dangerous Rule I confess this would be in days of tranquility," but the "present Circumstances" made it "absolutely necessary." This was from a man who claimed that "[n]o Man has more Love for the Society of Quakers than I have." After protesting that he did not "mean to condemn the whole Society of Quakers," he proceeded to mock them. "To Speak in their Style," he said, "'my mind being deeply impressed with a fervent & anxious concern for . . . the true Spirit of Liberty & Independence," the "Crafty Men" ought to be sent "to a place where they will be deprived of the means of doing harm."[104]

On September 9, 1777, the Council resolved that the prisoners should be sent away. In a moment of conscience, Chief Justice Thomas McKean finally issued writs of habeas corpus. But no sooner had he done that than the Council passed an act forbidding the writs.[105] Accordingly, the Quakers were sent into exile in Virginia. In the next months, as they became ill or died and their families suffered financial hardships, members of the Society, demonstrating their characteristic – and offensive – unity, launched a vigorous petitioning, letter writing, and publicity campaign.

Richard Henry Lee remarked to Patrick Henry in clear disgust that "[t]he Quaker m[otto] ought to be 'Nos turba sumus' for if you attack one, the whole

---

[104] Henry Laurens to John Lewis Gervais, September 5, 1777, *Delegates*, 7: 606–19, 13–14.
[105] Gail S. Rowe, *Thomas McKean: The Shaping of an American Republicanism* (Boulder: Colorado Associated University Press, 1978), 106.

Society is roused."[106] But their success was not greater than before. They continued to be foisted to and fro between Congress and Council, Congress saying that it could not interfere because these were prisoners of Pennsylvania. Quakers were out of everyone's jurisdiction with no recourse to any of the fundamental laws stated in the constitutions – America's, Pennsylvania's, or, for that matter, Virginia's, in which rights of the accused were carefully described.

On March 15, 1778, Congress finally stepped up and ordered the prisoners released. But come April when they were still detained, Israel Pemberton wrote to Secretary of Congress Charles Thomson to discover what was to become of them. Thomson responded and described more deferral of responsibility. He had asked the Board of War about the matter, which said it was waiting for an application from the Council of Pennsylvania. Because it had not received one, "they had not taken any steps in pursuance of the Act of Congress." He closed with the sentiment, "I am sorry for the Death & sickness of your friends," he said. "Inclination and humanity easily lead me to do you any service in my power."[107] Thomson's regret must have been genuine and his actions effective. The Quakers were released later that month. In all, two had died, two had escaped behind enemy lines, and the rest, a good deal impoverished, were restored to their families. As in Dickinson's case, there were never any charges pressed, no apology or explanation issued, and no restitution for property lost, damaged, or confiscated.

Even after the Virginia Exiles were released, Quakers were still widely seen as traitors to the American cause. Indeed, the perceptions of them remained as negative as before. Congressman Josiah Bartlett believed that "[t]he majority of the Quakers remain the same dark, hidden, designing hypocrites as formerly."[108] Pennsylvania president Joseph Reed was still convinced months after their release that "[t]he Designs of a Tory, Proprietary Quaker Party are too obvious; & if not crushed in the Bud will produce a plentiful Crop of Mixing & Dissension thro this State."[109] Quakers continued to be maligned and harassed, their property destroyed and stolen into the 1780s. Their shops were forcibly closed, and other penalties were imposed – the seizure of property, fines in court for failure to appear for military duty, and the quartering of soldiers in their homes. Still if they did not swear the oath of allegiance they were forbidden from "holding any public office or place of trust" including "serving on juries, sueing for any debts, electing or being elected, buying, selling or transferring any lands, tenements, or hereditaments."[110] There were also continued acts of spontaneous public violence against them, such as having their businesses and homes vandalized and being harassed by mobs for not observing

[106] Richard Henry Lee to Patrick Henry, September 8, 1777, *Delegates*, 7: 637.
[107] Israel Pemberton to Charles Thomson, April 8, 1778, Letters of Charles Thomson, Miscellaneous Personal Autographs, Simon Gratz Autograph Collection (250A), HSP.
[108] Josiah Bartlett to William Whipple, August 18, 1778, *Delegates*, 10: 472.
[109] Joseph Reed to John Armstrong, October 5, 1778, *Delegates*, 11: 26.
[110] *Statutes*, 5: 9, 75–94.

public fasting days or lighting their windows.[111] Moreover, the suspicion that non-Quakers would use the peace testimony as an excuse to evade military service persisted into the early Republic, with some Congressmen wondering during the 1790 debates over an official policy for conscientious objectors that exemptions based on a person's religion would tempt people to "wear the mask of Quakerism."[112] Ultimately, were a Quaker Tory to confess and turn himself in as a traitor, he could expect markedly worse treatment than others similarly guilty. In 1778 two Quakers gave themselves up under the Act of Attainder. They were among 130-some men who surrendered to authorities, but they were the only two executed for their crimes.[113]

One scholar says that the Pennsylvania constitution must have looked like a "cruel hoax" to those who were denied its protection, yet she, like the radicals, excused the actions of the Constitutionalists as necessary. But in fact, it was they themselves who made the legal proceedings in Pennsylvania truly little more than "Ceremonies & chicanery."[114] In 1779 the man primarily responsible for laying the groundwork for the abolition of the 1701 Charter of Privileges and the rise of the revolutionary government wrote in disgust at the happenings in that state: "The people of Pennsylvania in two years," said John Adams, "will be glad to petition the crown of Britain for reconciliation in order to be delivered from the tyranny of their Constitution."[115]

The Quakers' uncharacteristic neutrality during the Revolution, the cause of their persecution, was a stance with no single or uncomplicated reason behind it. And it could be that there is no satisfying explanation. We, like the Revolutionaries and traditional Quaker thinkers, want the Quakers to have chosen one side or the other. From a modern perspective, it is not hard to imagine what pushed some Quakers away from their peace testimony and toward Revolution. We have more difficulty understanding neutrality and Loyalism. There is only one scenario in which neutrality would fit with traditional Quaker

[111] Philadelphia Yearly Meeting, Meeting for Sufferings, miscellaneous papers, 1771–80, FHL; Mekeel, *The Relation of the Quakers to the American Revolution*, 160–69; Sharpless, *The Quakers in the Revolution*, 200–03.
[112] William Charles diGiacomantonio, et al., eds. *Documentary History of the First Federal Congress of the United States of America*, vol. XIV: *Debates in the House of Representatives, Third Session: December 1790–March 1791* (Baltimore: The Johns Hopkins University Press, 1995), 138. My thanks to Chuck diGiacomantonio for suggesting this quotation. See also, Richard Wilson Renner, "Conscientious Objection and the Federal Government, 1787–1792," *Military Affairs* vol. 38, no. 4 (1974), 142–45, 143.
[113] For a discussion of this incident, see Rosswurm, *Arms, Country, and Class,* 156–58. Messer's interpretation of this incident justifies the actions of the Council by couching its decision in terms of Old Light versus New Light evangelicalism. He argues that the Old Light presence on the Council desired to quell the increasing New Light inclination in the masses to be more tolerant to dissent and belief in rebirth through repentance. The Old Lights, he argued, were not unjustly singling out Friends, but simply doing what they thought "necessary for the safety of the state" and that they were not "misguided" in their decision (305).
[114] Anne Ousterhout goes on to excuse the radicals, saying that "the number of persons denied that document's guarantees was relatively small" ("Controlling the Opposition," 33–34).
[115] John Adams to Benjamin Rush, October 12, 1779, in Butterfield, *Letters of Rush*, 1: 240.

theologico-politics, and that is, if they truly believed that neither side was completely in the right or wrong. Traditionally, of course, the Quakers' peace testimony had never prevented them from protesting unjust governmental practices; on the contrary, they felt obliged to protest. But the evidence in the case of the conflict with Britain suggests that the matter was not that simple for Friends. While it was clear that many Quakers believed Britain was behaving unjustly, there was also the sense that Americans might deserve it, that tyranny might be punishment for the sins of luxury and slavery, in which case, harsh taxation would be appropriate. If this were the case, then the correct response would be introspection and reformation, which they urged of their compatriots. If, on the other hand, British policy were overly harsh, then peaceful resistance would be appropriate, which they also did, to a point. Perhaps because both of these things seemed to be true, Quakers attempted their traditional role of mediators, which entailed, as Paine noted, unfairly rebuking only the Americans for their rash behavior. From the Quaker perspective, they could be neutral in this case because they were not the sinners, having reformed their Society to abolish both luxury and slavery. As the conflict progressed, however, most Quakers believed that there was "no opportunity offering where we can be instrumental to promote the peace, & good of our Country."[116] This could be one explanation.

But a clear-eyed view of their situation demands recognition not just of their abstract theologico-political principles but also of the reticence they had toward the American cause that was based on practical concerns. It was because some feared the Patriots abandoning their own principles more than they feared the British, who had not threatened their religious liberty for decades. Less honorably, they did not fear financial hardship the way other Americans did. Nonetheless, many Quakers favored the American cause, just not the way it was being executed. Some actively turned to the British for relief and protection; for others, neutrality and faith in their own constitution may have seemed the most prudent option both practically and theologically.[117]

There is little record of what John Dickinson thought about the persecution of his friends and relatives. His edits on the Pennsylvania Declaration of Rights might be a clue. It is impossible to know exactly when he made them, but considering their substance, it seems clear that they were written in anticipation of or response to the Quakers' ordeal in 1777 and 1778. He emphasized equal rights under the law for Christians who refuse to take oaths and added a number of other provisions – some of them seemingly copied verbatim from

[116] John Pemberton to John Fothergill, October 25, 1776, quoted in Mekeel, *The Relation of the Quakers to the American Revolution*, 164. Fothergill, a Quaker, was himself a "secret negotiator" between Benjamin Franklin and Lord Dartmouth in 1774–75 (Bailyn, *The Ideological Origins of the American Revolution*, 149).

[117] For the likelihood of better treatment under the British, compare Van Buskirk's description of Sarah Fisher's and Elizabeth Drinker's handling by the Americans with Darlene Emmert Fisher's description of their experiences with the British in "Social Life in Philadelphia under the British Occupation," *Pennsylvania History* vol. 37, no. 3 (1970), 237–60. She describes it as generally "cordial" (239). See also Nelson, *American Tory*.

other constitutions[118] and others in his own language not enumerated in his earlier writings. These additions and changes reflect a clear concern for the protection of the rights of life, liberty, and property of religious dissenters and alleged criminals. These, along with other Quaker principles of peaceful reconciliation and strong central government, were the ones that he would try to put into effect as president of the state.

President of Pennsylvania, 1782–1785

After his departure from Pennsylvania and worn from his ordeal, Dickinson exclaimed in 1777 that "no Temptation, except that of serving my Country, America, could engage Me ever again to take any share in Pennsylvanian Affairs."[119] His experience at the hands of the Pennsylvania radicals had a profound effect on him that was similar to what Quakers as a body experienced. It caused an inward retreat – into himself and his immediate family. It was during this period, in between 1777 and 1782, as he spent time at home to recover his health, that he began to awaken to Quakerism as more than just a political philosophy. Over these years we see the beginnings of a more overt and personal expression of Quaker concerns and testimonies – subtle at first, but increasing in frequency and strength until his death.

When the 1782 presidential election in Pennsylvania approached and Dickinson's name was put forward, Benjamin Rush proclaimed, "There is no other member of Council that can with decency be raised up as a competitor." To John Montgomery he wrote, "His enemies (who are enemies of virtue and public justice) tremble and sicken at this name."[120] Like Joseph Reed before him and Benjamin Franklin after, Dickinson served the maximum of three one-year terms. His behavior as he accepted the presidency was highly significant in understanding the policy he would pursue. In assuming office on November 7, 1782, he did not take the oath but instead took an affirmation.[121] With this action he broadcast his political position throughout the state: It announced that, although anti-Quaker sentiment was still high, he would be sympathetic to Friends and pursue an agenda that would aim at restoring the basic rights that Pennsylvanians had once enjoyed under

---

[118] One of these is the Maryland constitution. It is hard to know, however, which came first, Dickinson's ideas or the printed constitution. For example, before the Maryland constitution was ratified on November 11, 1776, in September Dickinson had sent his comments on it and its bill of rights to Samuel Chase. In his response to Dickinson, Chase did not mention Dickinson's particular suggestions. Samuel Chase to John Dickinson, September 29 and October 19, 1776, Ser. 1. a. Correspondence, RRL/HSP.

[119] John Dickinson to Benjamin Rush, June 14, 1777, Small Manuscript Collection, John Dickinson Letters, DPA.

[120] Benjamin Rush to John Montgomery, November 5, 1782, in Butterfield, *Letters of Rush*, 1: 291–93, 292.

[121] Dickinson had been taking an affirmation instead of an oath at least as early as 1778. Copies of his affirmations are in Ser. 1. b. Political, 1774–1807, n.d., RRL/HSP. Also, it is important to note that the oath/affirmation had changed since Dickinson was last in the Pennsylvania government. Now it no longer demanded allegiance to an unchangeable constitution.

the Charter of Privileges. His first act as president was to issue a *Proclamation Against Vice and Immorality* (1783).

Not surprisingly, the initial response to his election was polarized. Before his term had begun, a disgruntled Pennsylvanian published a series of scathing attacks on Dickinson's character in the papers. "Valerius" revived all the same accusations that the Convention had levied at him seven years prior, hingeing mainly on his qualifications as a patriot. Dickinson responded with a lengthy defense, also in the papers. His first term thus opened in controversy.[122]

Despite a hostile reception from some quarters, naturally Quakers and their supporters were sanguine about the turn of events. Congressional delegate David Howell, a frequent attender at the Philadelphia Friends Meeting, wrote expectantly to Quaker Moses Brown of Rhode Island, "[T]here is about to be a change of men & measure I am told in this State."[123] He enclosed a newspaper clipping with "noble Sentiments" from the president-elect "in regard to personal Liberty," specifying a few "very considerable amendments" that need to be made in the laws. The first two were "securing the inestimable benefits of the writ of Habeas Corpus; and for fixing the trial by jury on such a solid basis, as will guard as much as possible against its being shaken by the dreadful efforts of party rage." Then, wrote Dickinson, "[a]nother amendment [which] humanity compels me to propose" concerned the "contest" for the freedom of slaves and "laws for alleviating the afflictions of this helpless, and too often abused part of their fellow creatures."[124] A few months later, English Quaker David Barclay wrote to Dickinson, adding protection for Quakers to his list:

I trust, you will ever keep in view the liberality of Sentiment & Conduct of your Founder William Penn, whose memory & example must ever be venerated by wise & good men … As the Society of Friends will doubtless be considered a Body of useful Subjects, I shall expect to find their known religious Scruples provided for, in a degree not less than in this country, where the Legislature has been kindly disposed towards them.[125]

Such optimism notwithstanding, by most accounts, Dickinson's presidency was a failure.[126] Even a favorable assessment must find it at least anticlimactic after the drama of the ensuing years. One might hope that Dickinson would

---

[122] For Dickinson's "Vindication" of himself, see Stillé and Ford, *Life and Writings*, 1: 364–414.

[123] David Howell to Moses Brown, Nov 6 1782, *Delegates*, 19: 356–59

[124] John Dickinson's address to the Delaware Assembly, *Pennsylvania Journal*, October 29, 1782. Although this address was made to the Delaware Assembly, it must be inferred from the date that the amendments he mentions should be to the Pennsylvania constitution and also that the need for them serves as the explanation for why he was leaving Delaware for Pennsylvania.

[125] David Barclay to John Dickinson, 10th of 2nd mo. 1783, Ser. 1 a. Correspondence, 1762–1808, RRL/HSP.

[126] J. H. Powell bemoans Dickinson's entire performance in "John Dickinson as President of Pennsylvania." Flower agrees (*John Dickinson, Conservative Revolutionary*, 233) but finds a bit more to condone. Alexander Graydon remembers the era as charitably as Powell. See Graydon, *Memoirs of a Life Chiefly Passed in Pennsylvania within the Last Sixty Years* (Harrisburg, 1811), esp. 311.

have swept into office and effected the legal and political changes he had long advocated. But owing to several factors, few of his goals were accomplished, or they did not turn out as he hoped. One of these factors was the climate and circumstances in the state when he took office. Although some Pennsylvanians hoped that, with Dickinson's election, "the Malignant, and Envideous Spirit, which too much Possessed the Opposition is nearly Silenced, and in a Short time . . . will be intirely extirpated," Dickinson's terms in office can be characterized by constant partisan bickering about the distribution and enactment of power in the government. So troublesome were they that John Jay believed "[i]t will not be [Dickinson's] fault if Pennsylvania does not derive advantages from his administration."[127] But the "Dickinson administration" is a bit of a misnomer, which speaks to another obstacle to his leadership. The president of the state was merely the head of an executive body, itself at the mercy of the powerful popular assembly, and limited in the changes it could implement by a Council of Censors. Usually, the most the president could do was to side with the faction whose position he preferred.

Although the Republicans retained control over the executive and the representative branches, the Council of Censors, the body that alone could determine whether there would be constitutional amendment, was still controlled by the Constitutionalists. That faction also continued to wield enough power in the Assembly to obstruct reform efforts that their opponents might attempt. When issues arose such as jurisdiction in criminal proceedings, managing disputes on the frontier, and changing offensive laws in the state, the president and Executive Council, the Assembly, and the Censors hurled accusations at one another based on differing interpretations of the constitution, or, in some cases, they simply tried to circumvent the faulty process of amendment.[128] They charged one another with instituting "innovations," "deviations," and presuming to prescribe laws and practices "where the constitution does not."[129] In most instances, Dickinson was caught in the middle, powerless to effect change, and his long-time goal to amend the constitution remained unfulfilled. From this experience, his views about a properly balanced government must have been confirmed.

The stagnant situation was similar with regard to the relations between the state and the central government. With the relative power of the two governments undetermined and their jurisdictions unclear, disputes of various sorts were difficult to resolve. Two incidents demonstrate the weaknesses of the 1777 version of the Articles of Confederation. First, the Wyoming Controversy raised two issues – the management of Western lands and mediation

---

[127] John Jay to John Vaughn, February 15, 1783, quoted in Flower, *John Dickinson, Conservative Revolutionary*, 211.

[128] See, for example, Brunhouse's description of the Assembly's failed attempt to bypass the Censors by passing a law to repeal the test act (*The Counter-Revolution in Pennsylvania*, 154).

[129] For a litany of constitutional disputes, see Dickinson's "Reply to the Censors," January–June 1784, Pennsylvania Government Documents, 1764–84, JDP/LCP, and "Minutes of the Council of Censors, 1783–1784" in *PA* 3rd ser., vol. 10: 787–809.

of disputes between states, both matters the Dickinson Plan had addressed. The controversy had begun before independence was declared and involved disputed lands on the frontier. At different points, settlers from Pennsylvania and Connecticut contested violently for the right to settle the western lands. In question was to which state the lands belonged and therefore whether land titles purchased in other states were valid. The Pennsylvania Assembly, sympathetic to the speculators, wanted to send troops to remove the settlers and confiscate their corn, thus leaving them destitute. Dickinson denounced such a plan and struggled on the settlers' behalf with the Assembly. When the matter was decided by a congressional committee in 1782 in favor of Pennsylvania, many settlers from other states lost the land they had bought. The settlers also petitioned their representatives in Congress, who declined to act further. The episode confirmed Dickinson's early concerns addressed in his Plan.[130]

A second incident was one of the defining moments of Dickinson's presidency, an event little discussed by scholars, but with enormous national implications.[131] The Mutiny of 1783 highlights two themes – the relative power of the national and state governments when in conflict and Dickinson's preferences for peaceful over violent resolution of conflicts. The incident, simply described, was that after the war, Congress had proposed to disband the Continental Army and send the men home without pay. With most of these men dependent on this pay to satisfy immediate needs for food and clothing, they angered and threatened Congress and the Pennsylvania government. Congress looked to Dickinson to solve the problem; but their solution was not his. They demanded that he call out the Pennsylvania militia to intimidate the Continentals and put down any action by them through force of arms. Dickinson refused, believing that if troops "come into this Place, or very near to it, there will be Danger of the public Peace being again disturbed."[132] Instead Dickinson preferred to negotiate with the men. He traveled to the camp and, in dramatic fashion, leapt upon a table and, as he described, "I then addressed them, reminded them of their fault, – unprecedented and heinous, – approved the evidence of

---

[130] Stillé and Ford, *Life and Writings*, 1: 247–51; Flower, *John Dickinson, Conservative Revolutionary*, 215–17. Merrill Jensen, *The New Nation: A history of the United States during the Confederation, 1781–1789* (New York: Alfred A. Knopf, 1950), 335–36; Lester J. Cappon, et al., eds., *The Atlas of Early American History: The Revolutionary Era, 1760–1790* (Princeton, NJ: Princeton University Press, 1976), 62, 131. Kenneth R. Bowling, "Biography of William Maclay," Bowling and Helen E. Veit, eds. *The Diary of William Maclay* (Baltimore: The Johns Hopkins University Press, 1988), 435–36

[131] The following discussion draws from and agrees with Kenneth R. Bowling's interpretation of the incident in "New Light on the Philadelphia Mutiny of 1783: Federal-State Confrontation at the Close of the War for Independence," *PMHB* vol. 101 (1977), 446–49. Other works that treat it include Stillé and Ford, *Life and Writings*, 1: 243–47; Powell, "John Dickinson as President," 266; Flower, *John Dickinson, Conservative Revolutionary*, 217–25; Varnum Lansing Collins, *Continental Congress at Princeton* (Princeton, NJ: University Library, 1908), Chapters 1–3; *JCC*, Chapter 24.

[132] John Dickinson, June 24, 1783, Government Documents, Revolutionary and Early National Periods, 1765–1788, n.d., JDP/LCP.

their dutiful disposition, insisted on their instantly putting themselves under the command of their officers and yielding to them a proper obedience."[133]

His sense of the situation proved accurate and his methods effectual; the men acquiesced and the mutiny was averted. But the damage, as some have portrayed it, had been done.[134] Most of Congress was furious with Dickinson for his alleged lack of firmness and decisiveness. The final result was a significant change in the nation: Congress, feeling vulnerable both in body and reputation, removed to Princeton, and then New York, and ultimately the District of Columbia. Being in a district that it could control rather than a state with a stubbornly peaceful governor would, they believed, allowed Congress to protect itself better.

While some historians have seen this move as a loss for Philadelphia and Dickinson's failure to manage the situation effectively, others have interpreted it as an instance of Dickinson's resolve not to be cowed by the more hawkish members of Congress. More importantly, however, the incident and its outcome points to larger issues beyond Dickinson's resolve for peace. It demonstrated the need for a strong central government to which the people could look for resolution of their difficulties, and one that would honor its obligations. In the midst of this controversy, Dickinson wrote to Charles Thomson, "We anxiously desire, that instead of being satisfied with *partial* provisions, [a strong Federal Council] may lead to as *perfect* an establishment of the Union as the wisdom of *America* can desire."[135] In his last term of office, he spoke plainly to the Assembly, saying, "It has been demonstrated, that, in order that [Congress] may provide in the best Manner for the Honor, the Defence, the Harmony, and Welfare of these States, their Hands ought rather to be strengthened, than weakened."[136]

The Annapolis Convention of 1786

Over the last few years, Dickinson had hardly been the only one who perceived the need for drastic change in the central government. By the autumn of 1786, it was clear to many that the Articles of Confederation as they had been passed were failing to cement the Union. The events in Pennsylvania, as well as similar and worse incidents in other states, proved that the concerns about union and safety that had prompted Dickinson to write the initial draft of the Articles as he did were justified. Trade was not regulated effectively, foreign affairs were not managed properly, many disputes between states were not mediated, and civil liberties were not protected. The leaders in other states were gradually awakening to the same concerns. They declared that the Articles

[133] Dickinson quoted in Stillé and Ford, *Life and Writings*, 1: 246.
[134] See Powell, "John Dickinson as President," 266.
[135] John Dickinson to Charles Thomson, July 12, 1783, quoted in Flower, *John Dickinson, Conservative Revolutionary*, 237.
[136] John Dickinson, Message to the General Assembly, February 1, 1785, Pennsylvania Government Documents, 1764–84, JDP/LCP.

were "imbecile"[137] and the cause of "the embarrassments which Characterize the present State of our National Affairs, foreign and domestic."[138] When the delegates from five states met in Annapolis, their first point of business was to elect a chairman. In what can only be considered a tacit recognition of Dickinson's earlier foresight, he was elected unanimously. In the report from the Convention to the states and Congress, he "decline[d] an enumeration of those national Circumstances" that prompted the convention, citing that "it would be an useless intrusion of facts and observations" that would more appropriately be discussed elsewhere. The report therefore recommended that "speedy measures may be taken to effect a general Meeting of the States in a future Convention."[139]

[137] Rakove, "Legacy," 45–66, 45.
[138] John Dickinson, "Report of the Annapolis Convention." Sept 14, 1786, Simon Gratz Autograph Collection, HSP.
[139] Ibid.

8

"The Political Rock of Our Salvation"

The U.S. Constitution According to John Dickinson

Historians have not considered the Quaker presence at the creation of the U.S. Constitution, although there is good reason for doing so. As we have seen, Quakers were a powerful force in Pennsylvania, and they disseminated their theologico-political thought aggressively and, in some regards, successfully. Although at the Revolution, the Society of Friends as a body had withdrawn from formal politics, they remained active on a grassroots level, and they retained a significant measure of political influence. In debates over the ratification of the Constitution, delegates to the Convention speculated on the position of Friends, their views on such specifics as liberty of conscience, slavery, and religious tests for office; their past influence in Pennsylvania; and their future influence on the state and the federal governments.[1] Moreover, because of their strong presence as the governors of provincial Pennsylvania, there remained a residual influence even at the highest level of government.

As far as religious influences on the Constitution are concerned, historians have given most of their attention to reformed Calvinism.[2] But there is more evidence of a direct, albeit limited Quaker influence on this important moment in history than there is of a Puritan, deistic, or Evangelical one. John Dickinson, with his strengthening Quaker convictions, was among the most important participants at the Convention. He was part of what Jack Rakove calls the "crucial nucleus" of Framers.[3] Forrest McDonald suggests that Dickinson's thought "may well be regarded as [a model] for the American political tradition."[4] The argument here agrees with both assertions and seeks to elaborate on them.

---

[1] For a discussion and documentary history of the Quakers' position on the Constitution with a focus on the slavery question, see "Appendix III" in John Kaminski and Gaspare J. Saldino, et al., eds., *The Documentary History of the Ratification of the Constitution*, vol. 14, *Commentaries on the Constitution Public and Private* (Madison: State Historical Society of Wisconsin, 1983), 503–30.

[2] See Chapter 2, fn. 4.

[3] Rakove, *Beginnings*, 377.

[4] Forrest McDonald, "Introduction," in *Letters*, x.

Because of Dickinson's stature as elder statesman in the Convention, Rakove notes that "his views would have to be taken seriously [by other Framers], for he was one of only a handful of colonial leaders whose personal position could substantially affect public opinion."[5] Importantly, Dickinson's personal position had evolved over the Revolutionary years to be a more overt expression of traditional political Quakerism than before. In the foregoing chapters, we have seen that according to Quaker political theory, God ordained the civil polity, and it functioned as the ecclesiastical polity writ large. When studying Scripture, Friends followed an interpretation of the Greek *ekklēsia* that meant political assembly as well as church.[6] The way the two establishments were ordered and the processes and principles by which they operated were, according to Quakers, fundamentally the same. They could be separated and the political theory secularized, but for most Quaker thinkers, they were not. Although Dickinson's language and ideas can be and were translated into a secular context, by this time in his life he thought of them in terms similar to those of his Quaker forebears – as realms overlapping. He wrote,

> There is a Relation between the Principles of Religion and the Principles of Civil Society – and it is very observable that many prophets of the New Testament, that in their primary sense referr to the Church, with equal propriety referr to political constitutional Establishments – and those Maxims of Religion will ever be formed by Experience to be Maxims of the [government?] Policy – such as these "Be ye obedient one to another." "Submit yourselves one to another." "Ye are members one of another." All of them directly pointing to that benignant Communion of Rights and Benefits, that is the soul of true Republicanism. In short, Christianity is a system formed by Divine Wisdom, and communicated to us by Divine Goodness, for teaching and enabling us to do the least thing with the best affections. Our Savior lived and died for this End.[7]

He thought that adherence to these republican–Christian principles "bind those who believe them to one another in a kind of sacred union."[8] Dickinson would have agreed with Quakers of his time who equated "undevout" behavior with "incivility."[9]

The following analysis of Dickinson's theologico-political thought is not meant to supplant, but merely supplement, several earlier studies of the secular interpretations of his ideas.[10] Clearly, Quakerism was not the only tradition

---

[5] Rakove, *Beginnings* 28.

[6] Barclay *Anarchy*, 32. See also Nancy Isenberg, "'Pillars in the Same Temple and Priests of the Same Worship': Women's Rights and the Politics of Church and State in Antebellum America," *The Journal of American History* vol. 85, no. 1 (1998), 98–128, 98, 101–02.

[7] John Dickinson, untitled document, n.d., in John Dickinson, 1681–1882, n.d., Ser. 1. b. Political, 1774–1807, n.d., RRL/HSP.

[8] John Dickinson to R. R. Livingston, n.d., American Prose Writers, Roberts Autograph Collection, HQC.

[9] Scott, *Journal of the Life, Travels, and Gospel Labours*, 228.

[10] A few brief works that deal with Dickinson's constitutional thought and his role during the convention are M. Susan Power, "John Dickinson after 1776: The Fabius Letters"; J. H. Powell, "John Dickinson and the Constitution"; Leon deValinger, Jr., "John Dickinson and the Federal Constitution," *Delaware History* vol. 22, no. 4 (1987), 299-308; Forrest McDonald and

on which he drew. His language exhibits a mixture of some, though not all of those strains of thought that were current among his peers in politics – classic republicanism, liberalism, Scottish Enlightenment thought, and the common law tradition. And although some have speculated that his religious language was simply a "rhetorical strategy," implying, perhaps, a lack of genuine feeling. His sincerity in this regard was not less than when he used secular political language. Dickinson believed that political principles were derived from and undergirded by religious ones. The following discussion of Dickinson's philosophy will be presented as a transparency imposed upon the template of the Quaker theory laid out in Chapters 1 and 2. In other words, it will be structured according to the same political creation myth and, through some repetition of the major points in those initial chapters, will show how Dickinson's constitutionalism comported with traditional Quaker ideas of the form and function of a constitution.

In 1676 Robert Barclay wrote *The Anarchy of the Ranters* to convince recalcitrant Quakers to accept the new church government that leading Friends were establishing. The way to know a rightly constituted *ekklēsia*, he wrote, "is by considering the Principles, & Grounds upon which [the people] are gathered together, the Nature of that Hierarchy & Order they have among themselves, the Way and Method they take to uphold it, and the Bottom upon which it standeth."[11] These were also the issues Dickinson addressed when convincing Americans to accept the Constitution, most notably in the *Fabius Letters*, on which this discussion will largely draw.[12] But more than simply addressing these issues, we will see how through the style of his argument Dickinson was modeling a Quakerly mode of civic engagement.

Constituting the People

For Dickinson, a polity must be and, in the case of America, was constituted otherwise than merely on paper. And his understanding of how man entered political society was largely the same as the way most Americans understood it, but with subtle differences in process and emphases. While most political thinkers of the day agreed that joining society, forming a union, was "primarily a matter of reason,"[13] Dickinson believed that to unite was to obey a divine

---

Ellen Shapiro McDonald, "John Dickinson and the Constitution," in *Requiem: Variations on Eighteenth-Century Themes* (Lawrence: University Press of Kansas, 1988), 85-103; Gregory S. Ahern, "The Spirit of American Constitutionalism: John Dickinson's *Fabius Letters*," *Humanitas* vol. 11, no. 2 (1998), 57–76. Most recently, see Robert G. Natelson, "The Constitutional Contributions of John Dickinson," *Penn State Law Review* vol. 108 (2004), 415–77.

[11] Barclay, *Anarchy*, 33.

[12] For a general discussion of the publication of the *Letters*, see John Kaminski and Gaspare J. Saldino, eds. *The Documentary History of the Ratification of the Constitution*, vol. 17, *Commentaries on the Constitution Public and Private* (Madison: State Historical Society of Wisconsin, 1995), 74–80.

[13] John C. Ranney, "The Bases of American Federalism," *WMQ* 3rd ser., vol. 3, no. 1 (1946), 1–35, 1.

command, a "sacred law."[14] Like Locke, he held that society was first occasioned "by the command of our *Creator*."[15] God, said Dickinson, "designed
men for society, because otherwise they cannot be happy."[16] But more than
that, God "demands that we should seek for happiness in his way, and not
our own," which meant joining one another on specific terms and with a
particular mode of engagement.[17] Moreover, reason was not man's primary
impetus for joining; the "common sense of mankind," Dickinson explained,
merely "agrees."[18] This original constitution ordained by God was prior to and
independent of any written documents codifying that union. "[T]hose corner
stones of liberty," he wrote, "were not obtained by a bill of rights, or any other
records, and have not been made and cannot be preserved by them."[19] Rather,
ten years before Jefferson wrote that "all men are endowed by their Creator
with certain unalienable rights," Dickinson asserted that "Rights are created
in us by the decrees of Providence."[20]

On the surface, Jefferson and Dickinson seem to agree, but as we have seen
from our earlier discussion, Quaker thinkers did not usually speak of *natural*
rights. While many thinkers of all persuasions, including Penn and Dickinson
on occasion, conflated the languages of rights and referred interchangeably
to natural or God-given rights, for Quakers, who more often spoke in terms
of providence, there was ultimately a difference. If the divine and the natural
were the same (an idea many Quakers rejected outright), they were much more
closely related in Quaker thought than in Jefferson's, with nature not over-
shadowing divinity. Dickinson clearly did not subscribe to the deist theology
of other Founders. He explained that "[w]e claim [rights] from a higher source,
from the King of kings, and Lord of all the earth ... They are born within us;
exist with us; and cannot be taken from us by any human power, without
taking our lives."[21] Because they came from God rather than nature, man, or
his history of established institutions, "rights must be preserved by *soundness
of sense and honesty of heart*. Compared with these, what are a bill of rights,
or any characters drawn upon parchment, those frail rememberances?"[22] If

---

[14] John Dickinson, *The Letters of Fabius in 1788 on the Federal Constitution* (Kila, MT: Kessinger
Publishing, 2004), 114. For the sake of accessibility of this work to others, I have chosen to use
a facsimile reprint published by a modern press.
[15] Ibid., 13. On the religious underpinnings of Locke's thought, see Dunn, *The Political Thought
of John Locke*.
[16] Ibid.
[17] Ibid.
[18] Ibid., 17.
[19] Ibid., 24.
[20] John Dickinson, *Address to ... Barbados*, 4.
[21] Ibid.
[22] Dickinson, *Letters of Fabius*, 24. This attitude toward written documents does not, however,
as Powell has argued, translate into a fundamental distrust of written constitutions. As we have
seen, Quakers argued for the importance of written laws, but that the spirit, rather than the
letter, was the essence of them ("John Dickinson and the Constitution," 7).

this seems to us an overly fine distinction, that Dickinson made it was in keeping with Quaker thinking about rights. Such subtleties caused contemporary and historical criticism that his work consisted of "fine-spun theories and hair-splitting distinctions"[23] and that he had the "Vice of Refining too much."[24] But if his thought has been misunderstood, it is because his critics did not care to understand these distinctions or the complex theories and arrangement to which they gave rise. It is mainly this difference between the natural or human and the divine that distinguished the Quaker theory of government and their process of legal discernment from others.

Discernment of the Fundamental Law

Once men have come together, their first task is to determine the fundamental law by which they will live. Quakers believed that God's law could only be known through a process of collective discernment of his will. All individuals must come together and worship (or, in secular terms, deliberate) as a group – to combine their individual understandings of God's Light – to know what direction to move in the world. This process worked the same way whether the polity was ecclesiastical or civil. Everyone had a role to play. Dickinson wrote, "*What concerns us all should be considered by all.*"[25] But there are difficulties with such a process of discernment; the people may be misled by false guides. "Men," says Dickinson, "have suffered so severely by being deceived upon subjects of the highest import, those of religion and freedom, that *truth* becomes infinitely valuable to them, not as a matter of curious speculation, but of beneficial practice – A spirit of inquiry is excited, information diffused, judgment strengthened."[26] There were several reliable ways of knowing the fundamental principles of government. It was not necessarily formal education, although this too was important. Rather, Dickinson put them in this order: "divine Goodness, common sense, experience, and some acquaintance with the constitution." These, he said, "teach us a few salutary truths on this important subject."[27]

For Quakers, the primary guide was God's Light in the conscience, the "divine Goodness" of revelation and Scripture. In the political realm, the process of knowing God's law in the conscience was *synteresis*. Dickinson, however, did not use this word. Nor did he refer much to the idea of "the Light" as a way of knowing. He hoped that the nation would be animated by an "enlightened spirit" and that the "body will be enabled with the clearest light that can

---

[23] John C. Miller, *Origins of the American Revolution* (Boston: Little, Brown and Company, 1943), 259. An explicit discussion from a Quaker theorist of the distinction between natural law and divine law can be found in the work of Jonathan Dymond, *Essays on the Principles of Morality*, 322–33.

[24] Edward Rutledge to John Jay, June 29, 1776, *Delegates*, 4: 338.

[25] Dickinson, *Letters of Fabius*, 3.

[26] Ibid., 4.

[27] John Dickinson, *Essay on the constitutional power*, 34.

be afforded every part of it" to make the right decisions for the nation.[28] But these were vague references and might be taken for ordinary usage of the word. They would likely not have alerted anyone to Dickinson's Quaker sympathies. And that would have been a wise political move. In 1788 when Dickinson wrote as Fabius, many people still despised and distrusted Quakers as loyalists and traitors to the American cause. Additionally, even though Dickinson was a trusted patriot to some, he was still under suspicion by many. Had he expressed his sentiments in characteristically Quaker language, recognizable to anyone who had spent time in Pennsylvania, he might not have been heard as widely. But more than that, he was concerned not to overemphasize revelation – a concern that was no doubt heightened by the recent rise of pietism with its rejection of rationalism and encouragement of enthusiasm, something of which Quakers disapproved.[29] Moreover, there had always been different strands of Quakerism that emphasized either Scripture or the Light.[30] It is clear, as evinced in the following discussion, that Dickinson believed that inward revelation was a key to knowing, but he did not privilege it over the Bible. "[N]o divine or inward Communication at this Day," he said, "do or can contradict that testimony."[31] He focused therefore on the other guides that Quakers had always used to know God's will, and ones that all Americans would accept, especially the Bible. It was safe and would speak loudly to the ordinary people he was trying to reach. The Bible, he proclaimed, was an *"Inestimable truth!* which our Maker in his providence, enables us, not only to talk and write about, but to adopt in practice of vast extent, and of instructive example."[32] He counseled that it "would do much more, if duly regarded; and might lead the objectors against it to happiness, if they would value it as they should."[33] "The Bible," he wrote in his notes, "is the most republican Book that ever was written."[34]

As we might expect of a political thinker in the Age of Enlightenment, history and reason were important tools in the search for Truth. But these things were not disconnected from God for Dickinson. "It is our duty," he said, "humbly, constantly, fervently, to implore the protection of our most gracious maker . . . and incessantly strive, as we are commanded, to recommend our selves to that protection, by 'doing his will,' diligently exercising our reason in

---

[28] Dickinson, *Letters of Fabius*, 51, 48.

[29] Frederick Tolles, "Enthusiasm versus Quietism: The Philadelphia Quakers and the Great Awakening," *PMHB* vol. 69 (1945), 26–49.

[30] Recall, for example, the Wilkinson-Story Controversy discussed in Chapter 1 and the Keithian Controversy in Chapter 3.

[31] John Dickinson, "An Essay Towards the Religious Instruction of Youth," n.d., Ser. 1. e. Miscellaneous, 1761–1804, n.d., RRL/HSP.

[32] Dickinson, *Letters of Fabius*, 13.

[33] Ibid., 25.

[34] John Dickinson, notes, n.d., Ser. 1. e. Miscellaneous, 1761–1804, n.d., RRL/HSP. Robert W. Hoffert claims that there was minimal, if any, influence of religion on the Founders' ideas of virtue and that "it is debatable whether or not there even is an active, positive form of political virtue available within biblical Christianity" (*Politics of Tensions*, 69).

fulfilling the purposes for which that and our existence were given to us."[35] But neither was reason a failsafe of good government, as many Enlightenment figures and common lawyers held. The Light Dickinson referred to was not the light of reason. Like all Quaker thinkers, he believed that reason was suspect; it was of man, and therefore it was corrupt or corruptible. As he famously said in the Constitutional Convention:

Experience must be our only guide. Reason may mislead us. It was not Reason that discovered the singular & admirable mechanism of the English Constitution. It was not Reason that discovered or even could have discovered the odd & in the eye of those who are governed by reason, the absurd mode of trial by Jury. Accidents probably produced these discoveries, and experience has given sanction to them. This is then our guide.[36]

This quotation has been used repeatedly by those seeking to explain Dickinson's thought and the thought of the Founding generation in general. But *we* might be misled here if we took Dickinson's use of the words "experience" and "accident" at face value. Experience for Dickinson was similar, though not identical, to how most lawyers understood it.[37] It was generally understood to mean the customs of the common law proven reasonable and valid through induction or practice. The common law was largely the history of reasonable practice that had become custom. This is certainly a part of what Dickinson meant by "experience." Experience was history, and Dickinson advocated reliance on "history sacred and profane."[38] But while Quakers did use secular history as a guide for their political direction, Scripture was the most important history book. They considered it "[a] faithful Historical Account of the Actings of God's People in divers Ages."[39] Dickinson likewise believed that "wise admired Instructors of the World have modestly cloathed their Lessons in the Language of Fables."[40]

Apart from physical experiences that are recorded in human history, however, we should also consider that Dickinson included spiritual experience as well – revelation, or the experience of God in one's conscience. This, contrary to common law theory, would be nonrational induction and a divine basis for legal developments. Dickinson wrote, "The great question as to reason is this –

---

[35] Dickinson, *Letters of Fabius*, 28.

[36] Max Farrand, ed., *The Records of the Federal Convention of 1787* (New Haven, CT: Yale University Press, 1937), 2: 278.

[37] Forrest and Ellen Shapiro McDonald give a good account of Dickinson's understanding of history and experience in "John Dickinson, Founding Father." My analysis does not disagree with theirs, it merely deepens it. See also H. Trevor Colbourn, "John Dickinson, Historical Revolutionary."

[38] Dickinson, *Letters of Fabius*, 18.

[39] Barclay, *Apology*, 4.

[40] John Dickinson, "Notes for a Speech (III)," in James H. Hutson, ed., *Supplement to Max Farrand's* The Records of the Federal Convention of 1787 (New Haven, CT: Yale University Press, 1987), 137–38. The example he gives in these notes is the biblical fable of the lamb lying down with the lion.

whether reason since the introduction of sin into the world is sufficient to discover our duty and incline us to enforce its performance. Denied." It must be paired with "revelation."[41] This is in clear contrast to other deeply religious men such as John Adams, who derided the idea that in making a constitution men "were in any degree under the inspiration of heaven."[42] Therefore, Dickinson departed from other common law thinkers in his interpretation of experience.[43] In keeping with this understanding of it, if Dickinson's use of the word "accident" to describe the advent of trial by jury here is confusing, Fabius clarified when he said that trial by jury is a "Heaven-taught institution."[44] It was then merely supported by reasonable practice.

Insofar as reasonable experience or custom was the foundation of the common law, then, Dickinson distrusted it. For Quakers, experience and custom were not necessarily the same thing. Friends could and often did make a distinction between custom as it was based on reasonable experimentation on the one hand, and experience, as being primarily revelation, on the other. If the reasonable customs established through worldly experience were valid, they should comport with revelation. Customs based solely on practical reason were dangerous in that they led to the establishment of pernicious traditions – the

---

[41] John Dickinson, notes, n.d., Ser. 1. e. Miscellaneous, 1761–1804, n.d., RRL/HSP. Elsewhere he wrote, "Revelation is positive," and "Reason" is used only after "matured Meditation." John Dickinson to his cousin, Senator George Logan of Pennsylvania, 10th of the 9th mo. 1806, Maria Dickinson Logan Collection, HSP.

[42] John Adams, *Defense of the Constitutions of Government in the United States of America* (1788) cited in John Witte, Jr., "'A Most Mild and Equitable Establishment of Religion': John Adams and the Massachusetts Experiment," in J. Hutson, ed., *Religion and the New Republic: Faith in the Founding of America* (Lanham, MD: Rowman & Littlefield, 2000), 1–40, 16.

[43] An interesting comparison might be made with Dickinson's understanding of experience or tradition and history and Edmund Burke's. Their thinking looks very similar – a sort of conservatism, a suspicion of reason, and a respect for history – but there are subtle differences. On Burke's position, see J. G. A. Pocock, "Burke and the Ancient Constitution," in his *Politics, Language, & Time: Essays on Political Thought and History* (Chicago: The University of Chicago Press, 1989), 202–32. It would seem the most important factor that accounts for the divergences between the two men's thought is Dickinson's inclusion of revelation as part of his legal epistemology. In a private dialogue with Locke, Dickinson wrote, "If, as seems to be agreed by the advocates for the Powers of Reason, the soul be furnished with all the Ideas it can naturally have, by the senses – and, by reflecting on its own operations about the Ideas thus furnished – or, 'in one Word, by Experience' [cites Locke's *Essay on Understanding*] – its Knowledge must be proportioned to its 'Experience.' But, before this 'Experience' could be extended to the farthest Limits in the Discovery of Truth, the mind might rest satisfied with an inferior 'Experience,' as imagining it to be the most that could be attained. Reason is not infallible.

"Reason is not infallible. Such errors once adopted, the its progress of Reason would thenceforward be obstructed by the Embarrassments of Prejudices. In Reality, by Mistakes of this kind, Men have extremely injured themselves, without a probability of ever recovering from their Delusions. Therefore, it is highly improbable that God would have left Men to this fallible Guide for finding Mistakes and discovering his Duties. All Religion is revealed." John Dickinson, religious notes, n.d., Ser. 2. Miscellaneous, 1761–1801, n.d., RRL/HSP.

[44] Dickinson, *Letters of Fabius*, 22.

blind acceptance of practices that were enemies of the truth. Quakers equated custom with ritual – the sort of ritual that followed the letter of the law, but killed the spirit, much like sacraments in the high church. It was a form without function and with harmful consequences. Over the course of decades of persecution, they had proven that religious dissent and toleration – things that seemed irrational and dangerous to many Englishmen and therefore not a part of custom or law – were actually not only salutary in a polity, but also constitutional. As the Farmer, Dickinson wrote, "Custom undoubtedly has a mighty force in producing opinion, and reigns in nothing more arbitrarily than in public affairs. It gradually reconciles us to objects even of dread and detestation."[45] Because of this, Quakers distrusted the common law, much of which had no basis in the Light, apostolic history, or, necessarily, reason.

These guides were meant to facilitate a process of collective deliberation that would encourage accurate discernment of the fundamental law. After studying these guides and coming to their understanding of the law, there was an obligation on every individual to speak should God require it. Barclay said that man must speak if "by his Master he were commanded and allowed to do so."[46] Moreover, they had the obligation to be "Discerners of Evils" who "reprove and warn" their brethren of transgressions from the law.[47] "[I]ndividuals," explained Dickinson, "may injure a whole society, by not declaring their sentiments. It is therefore not only their right, but their duty, to declare them."[48] This injunction holds true regardless of how unwelcome the words may be to the recipient – even ministers religious and civil – however much the individual himself does not want to express them, or the unpleasant consequences he might face because of them. There is a duty, said Dickinson, "to testify of [God's] Truth even against those whom he made instruments in preserving them."[49] He had repeatedly upheld his duty in this regard through the major controversies of which he was a part – the campaign for royal government, the Revolution, and the constitutional turmoil in postindependence Pennsylvania – and endured harsh treatment from his countrymen as a result. Now, in the debates over the Constitution, he was once again giving his own "imperfect testimony."[50] Speaking, however, was not the only obligation; as we shall see momentarily, it is important to note that if man were not commanded by his Master to speak, he "ought not to open his mouth."[51]

In order that all might participate in the discernment process, Dickinson believed that all needed to be able to understand the issues at hand. Therefore, one important Quaker testimony was plainness – clarity, simplicity, and

[45] Ibid., 71. On other Americans' acceptance of custom, see Reid, *Authority to Tax*, 181–93.
[46] Barclay, *Apology*, 365–66.
[47] Barclay, *Anarchy*, 56–57.
[48] Dickinson, *Letters of Fabius*, 3.
[49] Dickinson, "Religious Instruction of Youth."
[50] Dickinson, *Letters of Fabius*, 54.
[51] Barclay, *Apology*, 365.

honesty in all things, including speech. They wore plain clothing; used *thee* and *thou*; and refused to swear oaths, engage in haggling over prices, or use frivolous greetings such as "good day." They demanded that laws and other official political proceedings be conducted and written down in English so all could have knowledge of them.[52] In this important matter of the ratification of the Constitution – this "plain-dealing work"[53] – Dickinson thought it important that everyone in the nation, not only the elite, be conversant with the issues under consideration. "What he wishes," wrote Fabius of himself, "is to simplify the subject, so as to facilitate the inquiries of his fellow citizens."[54] Where the *Federalist Papers* described and defended the Constitution in sophisticated detail, Dickinson took on the task, as he did in his *Farmer's Letters*, of addressing the "unpolished but honest-hearted" Americans.[55] Where the elite were concerned, another sort of plainness must be used. In his *Apology*, Barclay had written to King Charles II that Quakers had "faithfully discharged their consciences towards thee without flattering words."[56] Fabius now went farther to say that "flattery is treason" in the momentous affairs of state.[57]

This popular decision-making process was as important as the ends for which it was used. It determined whether or not the discernment was accurate and, therefore, whether the decisions reached by the body were binding. In a Quaker meeting, when the discernment process was functioning correctly, the meeting was led directly by the "infallible spirit" of God. In this way, God had sovereignty by proxy through the people. In secular terms, we think of this simply as popular sovereignty. If the process functioned correctly and the discernment was accurate, the people were bound by the decisions made by the group. If, on the other hand, the process were flawed, the people would not be bound, and the meeting should not move forward. It was only recently that other Americans began thinking of popular sovereignty as the Quakers did, as the "voice of God."[58]

---

[52] All of these practices were for the same end. Not swearing oaths had to do with not taking God's name in vain, but also was a testimony for their honesty. Similarly, as merchants, Quakers set prices and refused to haggle on the principle that it was dishonest – not plain speaking about the true cost – and caused goods to be either under- or overvalued. On honesty in business, see Tolles, *Meeting House and Counting House*, 58–61.

[53] Dickinson, *Letters of Fabius*, 12.

[54] Ibid., 4.

[55] Ibid., 18. See also the second of his *Farmer's Letters*, which he addresses particularly to those "whose employments in life may have prevented your attending to the consideration of some points that are of great public importance" (*Letters*, 38). Dickinson's concern for the participation of the lower sort in the polity, evinced here and later in this chapter, defies Holton's generalization in *Unruly Americans* that the Founders were entirely antidemocratic. While Dickinson certainly was concerned to stem the excesses of democracy that had led to the abuses of rights in Pennsylvania, he had no desire to silence the people or to pronounce a "slur on the capacities of ordinary citizens" (278).

[56] Barclay, *Apology*, v.

[57] Dickinson, *Letters of Fabius*, 13.

[58] Morgan, *Inventing the People*, 13; and Jensen, *The Articles of Confederation*, 4.

Political Unity

Although unity of the political body was an ideal commonly expressed in the seventeenth and eighteenth centuries, for Quakers it was more than an expedient measure for the defense of property, the defensibility of policy, or even as assurance of spiritual chosenness. It was, rather, an organizing principle that expressed a commitment to the inclusive spiritual process that should animate the polity. Legal discernment could come only through the unity of the body. Quakers call this unity "corporate witness."[59] Because unity was so important, how individuals conducted themselves in the discernment process was crucial. Beyond simply being obliged to speak plainly and honestly, one's mode of delivery was equally important. To find the true fundamental law, Dickinson said, "Before this tribunal of *the People*, let every one freely speak, what he really thinks, but with so sincere a reverence for the cause he ventures to discuss, as to use the utmost caution, lest he should lead into any errors, upon a point of such sacred concern as the public happiness."[60] One of the greatest errors man could commit was intemperance in public discourse. "Hot, rash, disorderly proceedings," Dickinson warned in his *Farmer's Letters*, "injure the reputation of the people as to wisdom, valor, and virtue, without procuring the least benefit."[61] It could disrupt the very means by which the law was discerned. The goal was twofold – accuracy in determining the law and preservation of concord in the group. Dickinson therefore counseled, "May our national character be – an animated moderation."[62] His Quakerly moderation was a means of gentle persuasion to preserve unity. It was neither coercive nor a way to disengage for the sake of merely conserving the existing system. Rather it was a way to engage more intimately with the community in order to facilitate greater understanding and avoid oppression of one faction by another. In this process, there would be more security for the rights they would achieve and less risk of losing everything in a schism or revolution. Barclay wrote that one must not "break that Bond of Love and Peace" that held the meeting together.[63] Thus agreement and harmony should take precedence over dissent if it threatens to disunite the body. "In political affairs," wrote Fabius, "is it not more safe and advantageous, for all to agree in measures that may not be the best, than to quarrel among themselves, what are best?"[64] As Barclay asserted, "The Honor of Truth [is] prostrated by Divisions."[65] Dickinson thus chose to speak to Americans as "Fabius," the Roman politician who was known for

---

59 Braithwaite, *The Second Period of Quakerism*, 345.
60 *Letters*, 4.
61 Ibid., 17.
62 Dickinson, *Letters of Fabius*, 53.
63 Barclay, *Anarchy*, 57.
64 Dickinson, *Letters of Fabius*, 25.
65 Barclay, *Anarchy*, 20.

preserving the state through his cautious methods, with the intention to act as a model for the process he advocated.[66]

Significantly, this emphasis on unity did not preclude dissent. Dissent within the body was desirable, but a matter to be handled very delicately. The onus was on the dissenter first to deliver his message, to express his understanding of the law or the correct decision to make concerning the polity. Second, he must deliver it in a way that was as inoffensive as possible. And third, even if the body chose another path against his counsel, he must submit his will to that of the collective rather than try to obstruct it. Finally, he must support the body in its goals. Barclay explained that the speaker must have "Forbearance in Things, wherein [the others] have not yet attained; yet... [the dissenter] must walk so, as they have him for an Example." Although some individuals may have a more advanced understanding than the group, in time, Quakers believed, God would eventually reveal the Truth to all.[67] Dissent thus should be a process of persuasion and convincement through speech-acts, not coercion through threatening or disruptive behavior. On several occasions, Dickinson expressed clearly his sense of how to achieve the balance between speaking as one is moved and expressing one's dissent without disrupting the unity of the body. He demonstrated this sort of moderation in action during the Revolution and in words:

> Two Rules I have laid down for myself throughout this Contest [with Britain], to which I have constantly adhered, and still design to adhere – First – on all occasions where I am called upon, as a Trustee for my Countrymen, to deliberate on Questions important to their Happiness, disdaining all personal advantages to be derived from a Suppression of my real Sentiments, and defying all Dangers to be risked by a Declaration of them, openly to avow them; and secondly – after thus discharging this Duty, whenever the public Resolutions are taken, to regard them, tho opposite to my opinion, as sacred, because they lead to public Measures in which the Common Weal must be interested, and to join in supporting them as if my voice had been given for them.[68]

Dickinson followed Penn, who said, "Nor is there any Interest so inconsistent with *Peace* and *Unity*, as that which dare not rely upon the Power of *Persuasion*."[69] There is in this theory of civic engagement a sense of humility, peace, and self-sacrifice that is alien to modern republicanism.

Constituting a Polity and the Purpose of Government

In the interest of clarity and openness in legal matters, the unity that the people achieved through the collective discernment process must eventually be

---

[66] Dickinson may have had further and more personal reasons for choosing "Fabius." The Roman, while ridiculed at first for his tactics, was later vindicated as a hero for them. This choice may have been Dickinson's subtle way of suggesting that his initial approach to an American constitution in the Articles was the appropriate one and that this fact should be widely recognized.

[67] Ibid., 55–56.

[68] John Dickinson to president of Congress [John Jay] on peace negotiations with Britain, July 22, 1779, Ser. 1. b. Political, 1774–1807, n.d., RRL/HSP.

[69] Penn, *England's Present Interest Discovered*, 32.

codified in a written document. Insofar as the people have been led by the correct guides – higher authorities and not their own selfish interests – the written constitution was valid and binding. Insofar as it represented the polity, it too was sacred. This was by no means a ubiquitous understanding of a constitution. Some Framers, in fact, derided this notion of the Constitution as sacrosanct. In 1816 Thomas Jefferson wrote, "Some men look at Constitutions with sanctimonious reverence, and deem them, like the ark of the covenant, too sacred to be touched."[70] Dickinson, like other Quaker political thinkers before him, would have agreed with some of this sentiment, but not all. In 1682 William Penn wrote that "Government is sacred in its institution and end." In 1788, Dickinson agreed that "[Government] is founded on the nature of man, that is, on the will of his Maker, and is therefore sacred. It is then an offence against Heaven, to violate that trust."[71] He emphasized, "*It is* [the people's] *duty to watch, and their right to take care, that the constitution be preserved.*"[72]

Part of constructing a written constitution involved the creation and establishment of governmental structures. While most political theory held that the institution of government was necessary primarily because of man's propensity for evil, Quakers believed that just as political society was designed to facilitate good works, so was their government designed for benevolence more than punishment. It was not, as it was to Thomas Paine and many other Americans then and since, a "necessary evil."[73] Rather, for Dickinson and other Quaker thinkers, it was a "sacred obligation" designed to produce "public Affections," "Universal Benevolence," and "Infinite Kindness."[74]

Because of the understanding Quakers had of the relationship of individuals to one another and their government, Dickinson did not often speak of government or constitution in terms of a contract, as did Puritan-informed thinkers in the covenant tradition.[75] Rather, he spoke of it as a "trust" given by Heaven,[76]

---

[70] Thomas Jefferson to Samuel Kerchival, July 12, 1816, quoted in Charles Warren, *The Making of the Constitution* (Boston: Little, Brown and Company, 1937), 781.

[71] Dickinson, *Letters of Fabius*, 19.

[72] Ibid., 21.

[73] Garry Wills points out that it is a "vulgarization" of Lockean theory to believe that no good can come from government (*A Necessary Evil*, 299–308). Nevertheless, he says, this has been the dominant understanding Americans have had of government. The issue here is not so much whether government is good or evil, but whether man himself is and what the government's role is in regulating man's behavior.

[74] John Dickinson, notes, n.d., Ser. 1. e. Miscellaneous, 1761–1804, n.d., RRL/HSP.

[75] This is not to say he never referred to the relationship of the governed to the governors as a contract. See Dickinson, *An Essay on the constitutional power*, 10–11. We might understand this change of language and concept arising from the different purposes for which Dickinson was writing. In urging colonists to resist encroachments on their liberties by the British government, breach of contract is a straightforward way to convey the idea of injustice done. On the other hand, in attempting to encourage submission to the authorities, the metaphor of a trust connotes an irresistible quality of the institution as a whole. Earlier Quaker thinkers also used the idea of contract sparingly. Barclay referred to contract in regards to the obligations of members of a civil society, but not their rights (*Anarchy*, 42). In his political treatises, Penn used the idea more frequently than the other two.

[76] Dickinson, *Letters of Fabius*, 19.

and himself, as a politician, "a Trustee for my Countrymen."[77] The concept of government – or, more specifically, the legislature – as a trust was a common theory, especially in the second half of the eighteenth century. But there was a difference between Dickinson's trust theory and those of his contemporaries.

There were two main trust theories in circulation, which have their origins in the ancient and modern understandings of a constitution discussed in Chapter 2. Many Englishmen adhered to a theory that we might call an "irrevocable trust." Such a model imposed a duty on the governed to entrust their welfare to their legislators because, as their betters, they were inherently trustworthy. To change the terms of this trust was problematic, and neither could the relationship be abolished because the governors were placed in the Great Chain to lead. The strictures within this theory are on the governed to obey. The second theory, to which most American Revolutionaries adhered, we might call a "contract" or "fiduciary trust." It imposed limitations on the government that were negotiated at the advent of the system. If the government overstepped its bounds, the trust was broken. A breach of the trust would dissolve the obligations of the governed to the governors because there was no internal means to repair the relationship, to renegotiate the terms of the contract.[78]

Dickinson's Quaker theory borrowed from both of these understandings of "trust." At first glance, however, it appears to bear a stronger resemblance to an irrevocable trust. Along with other Quaker thinkers, he believed that God ordains government itself as the steward of the people, and the people must honor it. When the liberty of the people is in jeopardy, said the Farmer, "it is our duty, humbly, constantly, fervently, to implore the protection of our most gracious maker."[79] The trust was irrevocable. For Dickinson, a trust was a term of possession and protection. His vision for the American government was that it "will bear the remarkable resemblance to the mild features of patriarchal government."[80] He described the relationship of the states to the central government in almost Filmerian terms as "A Father surrounded by a Family of hearty, affectionate strong sons... attached to him and each other not by fear or servile dependence but by a generous tender participation of Blessings and a Reciprocity of Kindness and Advantages."[81]

Dickinson's understanding of the negative and positive legal implications for man in this irrevocable trust are in keeping with Quaker thought on the

---

[77] John Dickinson to president of Congress [John Jay] on peace negotiations with Britain, July 22, 1779, Ser. 1. b. Political, 1774–1807, n.d., RRL/HSP.

[78] On trust theories in the eighteenth century, see John Phillip Reid, *Constitutional History of the American Revolution: The Authority to Legislate* (Madison: The University of Wisconsin Press, 1991), 87–96. On Dickinson's trust theory, see also Natelson, "The Constitutional Contributions of John Dickinson," 432–36. He rightly emphasizes the importance of impartiality, the idea that the trust was above faction in Dickinson's thinking.

[79] Dickinson, *Letters of Fabius*, 38.

[80] Ibid., 46.

[81] John Dickinson, "Notes on a Speech (IV)," in Hutson, *Supplement*, 139.

paternal benignity of government. On the surface, it is much like contract theory of government; but with emphases on different aspects, the theories played out quite differently in practice. Dickinson argued that when God constitutes society, he commands two things of man: the contribution of his rights and submission of his will to society. For Dickinson, rights and will were related but different things. The language he uses is important. First, man "contributes" his rights. *Contribution* is a term with positive connotations. Unlike the Lockean language that man "hath quitted [his] natural power," that he loses something when he enters into political society, Dickinson's is a term of enablement.[82] When man "contributes" or "delegates" rights to the "common stock," he enables himself to be a benefit to society, to participate in it, to contribute to it. Where rights are concerned, political society is not created merely to give man negative liberty, although there is an important way in which it does, so much as it is for positive liberty. By contributing, Dickinson said, man gains

[T]he aid of those associated with him, for his relief from the incommodities of mental or bodily weakness – the pleasure for which his heart is formed – of doing good – *protection* against injuries – a capacity of enjoying his undelegated rights to the best advantage – a repeal of his fears – and tranquility of mind – or, in other words, that perfect liberty better described in the Holy Scriptures, than any where else, in these expressions – "When every man shall sit under his vine and his fig-tree, and *none shall make him afraid.*"[83]

The idea of entering society to do good is, of course, one of the fundamental bases of all Christian communities. Contributing his rights to society thus "prompts [man] to a *participated* happiness."[84] This understanding of rights and happiness are significantly different from how Jefferson articulated them in the Declaration of Independence. Although Jefferson undoubtedly had the welfare of the whole in mind, the "pursuit of happiness" is an individual right that may take an ambitious person in any direction.[85] "Participated happiness," by contrast, is an explicit link of the individual to the collective, a drawing of individuals together, not a protection of their right to separate and solitary quests. *Participated* means active engagement in the polity for the good of all.[86]

---

[82] Locke, *Second Treatise*, sec. 87.

[83] Dickinson, *Letters of Fabius*, 14.

[84] Ibid. Emphasis added.

[85] John Patrick Diggins mistakenly generalizes this individualistic impulse to all Americans when he writes that "[i]ndividualism provided the means by which Americans could pursue their interests, pluralism the means by which they could protect them." *The Lost Soul of American Politics: Virtue, Self-Interest, and the Foundations of Liberalism* (New York: Basic Books, 1984), 5. In his interpretation, community thus becomes nothing more than a useful tool for the satisfaction of individual desires.

[86] In secular terms, Dickinson's sense of rights and liberty seem to be something in between Jefferson's and an Old Whig's understanding of them as public things. Dickinson certainly saw the right to participate and liberty in individualistic terms, but there was a regard for the public as a whole, the collective that was falling out of use. Specifically, see Gordon Wood on liberty (*The Creation of the American Republic*, 609). On changes in this and other political terms at

And, as we can see in each instance in which he uses the word, *happiness* for Dickinson was not a secular good as it was for Jefferson. An example Dickinson used is trial by jury. While we normally understand trial by jury to aid the defendant in a trial, Dickinson was as concerned with the right of men to sit on a jury. This right to unfettered participation on a jury was a concern that was at the top of the Quakers' list of reforms in the seventeenth century, and they were at the forefront of a movement to protect that right and the ability of the jurymen to exercise it. In *Bushell's Case*, the trial of William Penn and William Mead for public preaching, they asked, as Dickinson did, "Can freedom be preserved, by keeping twelve men closely confined without meat, drink, fire, or candle, until they unanimously agree ... until under duress they speak as they are ordered?"[87] Dickinson held that serving on a jury was a "blessing" that would lead to the security of other liberties.[88] Throughout his unpublished papers, he repeated incessantly the primacy of man's duty to do good and the godly unity this creates in a society. "As every Duty is allied to a Benefit (Blessing), so every Right is allied to a Duty – there is a [social?] sacred Relationship that binds mankind together in a system consistently merging (drawing them) nearer & nearer to the Divine Author, all the powers, faculties, Functions, and Enjoyments, which they possess or can exercise."[89]

Of course, joining political society also necessitated that man give something up. Man "submits" his will to society: "He must submit his will *in what concerns all*, to the will of all, that is of the whole society." *Submission*, of course, is a negative term. Dickinson devotes only one line to describing what he gives up: "The power of doing injury to others – and the dread of suffering injuries from him."[90] While this idea of the "will of society" sounds much like Rousseau's "general will" with its ominous potential for democratic despotism, as we will see later, it is not exactly the same. Dickinson's vehement arguments against submission to the injustices of the British before the Revolution clearly indicate that there are limits to man's acquiescence to government in specific instances. When man submits his will, he is not necessarily depriving himself of rights, he is depriving himself of a certain kind of agency, in this case unlimited autonomous decision making. To submit one's will to the whole, therefore, also means to subject oneself to a process of deliberation. The difference between an oppressive general will and one that is liberating lies in how the government is structured and how the decision-making process is undertaken. It is not directed by man, but by God.

---

this time, see Terrence Ball, "A Republic – If You Can Keep It," in Terrence Ball and J. G. A. Pocock, eds., *Conceptual Change and the Constitution* (Lawrence: University Press of Kansas, 1988), 137–64.

[87] Dickinson, *Letters of Fabius*, 22–23.

[88] Ibid., 23.

[89] John Dickinson, "Government," n.d., Ser. 1. b. Political, 1774–1807, n.d., RRL/HSP. The words I have put in parentheses Dickinson wrote above the preceding word.

[90] Dickinson, *Letters of Fabius*, 14.

With God working through the community practicing synteresis, the ultimate will to be obeyed was not man's, even embodied in the entire community, but God's discerned by man, both by the individual and the whole. There were thus limits to man's control over man. For example, as we have seen, an individual may or may not have the legal right (according to man) to dissent. But for Quaker thinkers, how and when a person dissents is regulated by no human law: speech – both content and mode – is regulated by God for the benefit of the polity. As Dickinson exclaimed, "O Ye people of United America, I embrace and love you; but I will obey God rather than you; and if my Life was exposed to Danger and you would save it or if you would bestow on Me all that you can give; on Condition that I should not address to my Fellow citizens my present sentiments, I would rather dye than accept the proposal."[91]

The system that would ensure this God-given right to speak involved both a constitution (first in a sense of solidarity among the people and then also a written document) and a governmental structure. The construction of these related things by man was a "labour of public love."[92] As Dickinson explained, "If it be considered separately, a *constitution* is the *organization* of the contributed rights in society. *Government* is the *exercise* of them."[93] It was in similar terms that Barclay described the form and function of the Quaker church government – the "order" and "method." These categories explain the structures and decision-making process of the constituted polity. It was not just any kind of government that Dickinson and Quakers had in mind. The way the constitution was ordered and the way the government exercised rights were "offered to us by our Creator."[94] There was a particular mode, as Dickinson put it, of "holy conversation."[95] He explained further that "we never consult our own happiness more effectually, than when we most endeavor to correspond with *the divine designs.*"[96]

"A More Perfect Union" – Creating the Constitution

When contemplating a new constitution, the Framers disagreed whether the Union existed in spite of the demise of the Articles of Confederation. The question at hand was, if the Articles constituted a perpetual union, then was not the Union destroyed with the Articles? Some believed that it had existed before the Articles and would continue to exist without them. But others held that the Union had been abolished and needed to be reconstituted.[97] The latter was a

---

[91] John Dickinson, notes, n.d., Ser. II, Miscellaneous, 1671–1801, n.d., RRL/HSP.
[92] Dickinson, *Letters of Fabius*, 22.
[93] Ibid., 19.
[94] Ibid., 46.
[95] John Dickinson, notes, n.d., Ser. II, Miscellaneous, 1671–1801, n.d., RRL/HSP.
[96] Dickinson, *Letters of Fabius*, 13.
[97] See Kenneth M. Stampp, "The Concept of a Perpetual Union," *The Journal of American History* vol. 65, no. 1 (1978), 5–33. Stampp makes clear that these issues were not resolved in the minds of most Framers.

problematic argument since, without a polity that was previously constituted in spirit, the perpetuity of the Union would always be in doubt.[98] And so it was for many years until after the Civil War. But Dickinson was certain on this point. "Did not our Hearts dictate our Words[?] Our Hands confirm the stipulation by subscription for perpetual Remembrance[?]" he asked. "Did we not call the Nations of the Earth and Heaven itself to witness our agreement with each other?" The agreement for union may no longer be convenient to some, he explained, who wished to pursue their economic interests unfettered, "[b]ut does this [in]convenience outweigh the Considerations for an adherence to sacred Obligations?"[99]

For Dickinson and the Quakers, constituting a polity was not a discrete event with a beginning and an end. There was not a stark separation between man in the "state of nature" and man under government, between prelapsarian man and fallen man. The formation of government (as the spiritual progress of man) was rather an on-going providential process; man answering the call to enter society was only the first step. The process was one of continual improvement of society with the possibility of a perfect union. As Barclay put it, God "hath also gathered and *is gathering* us into the good Order, Discipline, and Government" of Christ.[100] The way toward perfection was to order the polity correctly. Dickinson thought of it in the same terms. "Herein there is a progression," he explained. "As a *man*, he becomes a citizen; as a citizen he becomes a federalist."[101] Because America had been constituted as a people before the Articles of Confederation were written, that document was simply an attempt to codify that unity. But, as ratified, they turned out to be an incomplete and insufficient structure of government. The government was failing, and the written constitution was therefore abandoned. But in the Quaker view, the abandonment of the written constitution did not dissolve the constituted polity. As Penn said, the paper constitution is "not the *Original* Establishment, but a *Declaration and Confirmation* of that Establishment."[102] The fundamental constitution, the Union, and the processes that animated it, still existed, although imperfectly. The written expression of it, the formal organization of the Union, simply needed to be made more perfect.

Some Americans considered the actions of the Annapolis Convention and the Constitutional Convention to be illegal in that they met to amend the Articles

[98] Rakove notes that "the idea that the confederation was essentially only a league of sovereign states was ultimately a fiction. Congress was in fact a national government, burdened with legislative and administrative responsibilities unprecedented in the colonial past" (*Beginnings*, 184–85). It is probable that this was how Dickinson perceived it.
[99] John Dickinson, "Notes on a Speech (II), in Hutson, *Supplement*, 136.
[100] Barclay, *Anarchy*, 9. Emphasis added.
[101] Dickinson, *Letters of Fabius*, 15.
[102] Penn, *England's Present Interest Discovered*, 29. If Michael Warner is correct in arguing that Americans considered themselves rightly constituted only through a written document, then the Quaker theory was a significant departure from the norm. For Quakers, textuality was for the purpose of reference, not legitimation of the union. See Warner, "Textuality and Legitimacy in the Printed Constitution," 97–117.

but ended up abandoning them entirely. But this was to take a fairly narrow view of the constitutional process. How the U.S. Constitution was created was very similar to the Quaker process that brought the 1701 Pennsylvania Charter of Privileges into being. The polity was already constituted, but the first few written constitutions and the governments they established did not meet the needs of the polity. This was in keeping with how Barclay described the evolution of the Quaker ecclesiastical government:

Things commanded and practiced at certain times and seasons fall of themselves, whenas the Cause and Ground for which they were commanded is removed . . . We confess we are against such, as from the bare Letter of the Scripture seek to uphold *Customs*, *Forms, or Shadows*, when the Use for which they were appointed, is removed, or the Substance itself known and witnessed.[103]

But Quakers did not overthrow the Pennsylvania government. Rather, they retained the unity of their polity, rewrote the constitution from a better understanding of what they needed, and restructured the government accordingly. At no time did they consider that their union or unwritten constitution was abolished. This was how Dickinson saw the situation in America. The creation of a "more perfect union," presumed the existence of a union in the first place. It also presumed the idea of change toward perfection.

The mechanism by which change could happen – whether in the case of Pennsylvania or America – was premised on the idea that the people were already constituted regardless of what paper documents did or did not exist, and that the power to discern the law lay with the people as a body. Samuel Beer explains, however, that Western political thought had historically rejected popular rule in favor of hierarchy. "Classical philosophy had taught the rule of the wise," he says, "Christianity taught the rule of the holy."[104] The latter was also true of Quaker political thought. The crucial difference was that, in the Quaker view, all could be holy. Divine competence was in the people. They had what Beer calls a "constituent sovereignty"; that is, when a government dissolves and must be renewed, the people do not return to a state of nature, a state of anarchy.[105] Rather, the power that they invested in the law-making body reverts to them and they can recreate – reconstitute – their political arrangements.

In this way, we see that Dickinson's trust theory of government, although similar to the "irrevocable" model, was not identical to it. It bore an important resemblance to the contract trust in that negotiation was possible. The main difference here was that the negotiations were not finished at the Founding – they were continual. Dickinson therefore knew that the conventional contract trust theory of government, as articulated by Locke, in which revolution was rightful when the contract was violated by the government, was neither an

---

[103] Barclay, *Anarchy*, 29.
[104] Beer, *To Make a Nation*, 139.
[105] Ibid., 171.

appropriate nor a legitimate basis on which to found the American government. In the first place, Americans were no longer represented by a parliament
that was distant from them in both interests and geography. In the second, they
had a theory of a constitutional change that was absent from British constitutionalism. They had what their British counterparts did not – both constituent
and governmental sovereignty. In other words, the government and governors
were no longer something separate from the people. The people *were* the government and they could change themselves, their laws and institutions, as they
willed.

This had always been the Quaker way of addressing the problem of the
origin of governmental authority in relation to the people. And later it was the
theoretical and practical problem Americans needed to solve in constituting
the federal government. Quaker theory, and what Americans would discover,
was that, as Michael Warner explains, "[t]he legal-political order would be
transcendent in its authority but immanent in its source. The trick was to see
how law could be given to the people transcendently and received from it
immanently at the same time."[106] Quakers dealt with this problem by claiming
that those who were already the de facto leaders of the informally constituted
polity ("such whom [God] hath made use of in gathering of his Church") were
to be the ones who wrote the constitution and laws (to whom God "commu-
nicat[ed] his Will under his Gospel").[107] The people, who remained part of
the legal-political process after the initial "gathering," had consented to this
arrangement by obeying God's command to come together and follow his des-
ignated leaders. In this way, Quakers employed the same process that Gordon
Wood describes legitimated the constitutional conventions of the Founding
period – the conventions were legitimate precisely because their legality was
in a specific sense inferior to that of the provincial assemblies – they had no
ordinary legislative powers; but in other ways superior – they had the power
to create.[108]

As in the pre-Revolutionary American Congresses, Quaker meetings were
illegal under civil law as well as contrary to the Church of England. But
although they were illegal by man-made standards, Quakers believed that they
actually were sanctioned by a higher authority, and thus had greater legitimacy
if not positive legality. Thus for Dickinson and his fellow Quaker thinkers, the
"bizarre new American project of writing charters as fundamental law for all
government [that] aimed at removing the circular legitimation of representative
assemblies" was not actually bizarre at all.[109] The idea of popular sovereignty
thus allowed the creation of the Constitution. But it did more than that. It
prepared the way for the American system of government, federalism.

---

[106] Warner, "Textuality and Legitimacy in the Printed Constitution," 101.
[107] Barclay, *Anarchy*, 68.
[108] Wood, *Creation*, 337–38.
[109] Warner, "Textuality and Legitimacy in the Printed Constitution," 102.

The Order and Method of the Polity: Popular Sovereignty in a Federal System

In the early years of Quakerism, there was the sense that all individuals should have a direct role in the decision-making process of the meeting. Before the establishment of London Yearly Meeting and its subsidiary meetings, Friends generally believed that if there were unity and consensus at the local level, the decisions they produced were infallible and binding. This arrangement did not work, and neither did the American experience with democracy and weak central government in the Critical Period. Dickinson therefore asked, "How are the contributed rights to be managed?" His purpose in the *Letters of Fabius* was precisely the same as Barclay's in *The Anarchy of the Ranters* – to answer this question by explaining the concept of a balanced polity and persuade them to accept it. Barclay hoped Quakers would be "vindicated from those that accuse them of Disorder and Confusion on the one Hand, and from such as Calumniate them with Tyranny and Imposition on the other."[110] Both Barclay and Dickinson had to prove to their readers that there was a way to maintain order in a democratic system that did not result in tyranny. For Quaker thinkers, order, union, safety, and liberty had always been inextricably intertwined.[111] The solution for Barclay and Dickinson was the same – a strong central government made up of a quasi-aristocratic element in a federal system. Dickinson's plan would "melt tyrants into men, and . . . soothe inflamed minds of a multitude into mildness."[112]

The Quaker ecclesiastical polity was founded for four primary reasons: to allow the collective process of discerning God's will to function properly; to facilitate good works; to prevent encroachments on the Society from the outside; and to keep the centrifugal forces inherent in the doctrine of the Inward Light from atomizing the Society. A strong central power for America seemed a necessity to Dickinson for similar reasons. The most challenging issues of the moment were the latter two. The nation had to deal with these first in order to facilitate the former two. America was young and vulnerable, especially with regards to Britain. His fears after the Revolution were the same as before – factionalism, strife, disunity. As Fabius, however, his purpose was to emphasize the commonalities Americans shared. He described them as a "people who were so drawn together by religion, blood, language, manners and customs, undisturbed by former feuds and prejudices."[113] Dickinson was not opposed to a large republic, but in such an expansive geographical area as America, it was not realistic to suppose that Americans would cohere without

---

[110] Barclay, *Anarchy*, title page.

[111] In *Spheres of Liberty: Changing Perceptions of Liberty in American Culture* (Madison: University of Wisconsin Press, 1986), Michael Kammen finds that the American equation of liberty and order did not arise until the nineteenth century ("Ordered Liberty and Law in Nineteenth-Century America," 65–126).

[112] Dickinson, *Letters of Fabius*, 13.

[113] Ibid., 43.

a centralizing force. And with such a danger of "licentiousness" in democracy, neither was it realistic to think that everyone necessarily should have a direct role to play in the government. Anything short of a system that managed both the great size of the country and the passions of its people, Dickinson believed, would result in the downfall of the country. He therefore saw the central government as a "superintending sovereign will" over the states and individuals.[114] The method and the structure of the government would settle the question of the locus of authority – individual or group; local unit or central – and facilitate the deliberative decision-making process.

The federal structure that Dickinson advocated shared some distinctive features with the Quaker church government, which was itself unique among church governments. The Quaker polity was organized on the dual bases of geography and the calendar. There were local meetings at the county level that met on a weekly and monthly basis. The monthly meetings sent representatives to quarterly meetings. Then, once a year, representatives met at the yearly meeting. The yearly meeting was the central governing body for all the subsidiary meetings. The Discipline, then, was the constitution that governed the whole region.

Although other religious groups in the seventeenth and eighteenth centuries also used systems of representatives, none had the same kind of geographically based structure. Unlike other churches, such as the Congregationalist, which did not have a central organizing structure for multiple bodies and tried in vain to keep members from settling too far away to attend meeting regularly, the Quaker arrangement allowed Friends to expand their church and its influence across great distances and remain unified.[115] When Quakers moved to the frontiers, they simply established new meetings whenever a few of them were together.[116] Eventually, when there were enough members and meetings, the government would reproduce itself in that region with a central structure that was separate, yet still in close contact with the others. London Yearly Meeting was established first, then New England, Philadelphia, Baltimore, North Carolina, Indiana, and Western Yearly Meetings followed. This system encouraged Friends to maintain a corporate identity primarily as members of a central body as they spanned geographic boundaries, rather than as members of a particular local or monthly meeting.[117] Quakers thus solved the problem of "peripheries

---

[114] Ibid., 17.

[115] For a case study that exemplifies the difficulties of expanding Congregationalist churches in New England, see Kenneth A. Lockridge, A New England Town: The First Hundred Years, Dedham, Massachusetts, 1637–1736 (New York: W. W. Norton & Co., 1970).

[116] A case study that follows one frontier meeting is Karen Guenther, "Rememb'ring our Time and Work is the Lords": The Experiences of Quakers on the Eighteenth-Century Pennsylvania Frontier (Selinsgrove: Susquehanna University Press, 2005).

[117] The other churches that also spread and established themselves around the colonies, most especially the Catholic and Anglican, had the least amount of egalitarianism and popular participation in the church government. Moreover, as a result of having the governing authority so far away, the distant branches were less unified as they depended on all their order coming

and center" quite easily with "a network of societies in a federated system similar to the United States government."[118]

Part of establishing the central governing structure in the Quaker meeting was creating a system of representation to replace the pure democracy that had tyrannized their early church. Although all had a measure of the Light of God in his or her conscience, and thus a voice in the meeting, it had become clear that all voices did not carry equal weight.[119] There were those who had a greater measure of the Light, and it was they who had a greater power and responsibility to determine the direction of the meeting. Barclay wrote, "That God hath ordinarily, in the communicating of his Will under his Gospel, imployed such whom he hath made use of in gathering of his Church, and in feeding and watching over them; though not excluding others."[120] Neither did any of the Framers envision America as a pure democracy. It should be, many of them agreed, a natural aristocracy in which the leaders should have, as Dickinson said, "wisdom and integrity," and "genius."[121] In the Quaker hierarchy, Barclay said, everyone has a place "and so in this there ought to be a mutual Forbearance, that there may neither be a coveting nor aspiring spirit on the one hand, nor yet a despising or condemning on the other."[122] Likewise, Dickinson believed that there were some people who were more suitable to be leaders, while others ought to be primarily followers. He argued that the "worthy" should prevail "against the licentious."[123] It would be the duty of the people not to make the critical decisions of government directly, but rather to choose their betters to do it for them. This was their voice, and it was vital that they discern the proper person for the job. They should be, as Dickinson explained to Americans, "religiously attentive" in choosing their representatives.[124]

The hierarchical and representational structure of the government would act as a sieve, as Gordon Wood has described the Constitution, or a "refining process," as Dickinson put it, to let only the most worthy individuals – the most "virtuous" in republican language, the most "weighty" in the Quaker – into

---

from the top. Michael Sheeran explains that "[the Quaker founders'] action opened the door for Friends to metamorphose from a sect of locally sovereign communities to a church with a central polity. The transition involved a substitution of central for local divine guidance" (*Beyond Majority Rule*, 15).

[118] Jack. P. Greene, *Peripheries and Center: Constitutional Development in the Extended Polities of the British Empire and the United States, 1607–1788*, (New York: W. W. Norton and Co., 1990); Isenberg, "Pillars in the Same Temple," 109. Barbara Allen describes Quaker ideas of federalism as "'federal liberty' without reference to federal theology" (*Tocqueville, Covenant, and the Democratic Revolution*, 59).

[119] And, it should be noted that although women did have a voice in the ecclesiastical polity, they did not in the civil. This, however, would change. See the Epilogue for further discussion.

[120] Barclay, *Anarchy*, 69.

[121] Dickinson, *Letters of Fabius*, 33, 53.

[122] Barclay, *Anarchy*, 63.

[123] Dickinson, *Letters of Fabius*, 12.

[124] Ibid., 7.

positions of leadership.[125] There would, therefore, be an element of the government that would, as Dickinson said in the Convention, "consist of the most distinguished characters, distinguished for the rank in life and their weight of property, and bearing as strong a likeness to the British House of Lords as possible."[126] Later, however, he reconsidered the property qualification for office holding. Madison reported,

[Dickinson] doubted the policy of interweaving into a Republican constitution a veneration for wealth. He had always understood that a veneration for poverty & virtue, were the objects of republican encouragement. It seemed improper that any man of merit should be subjected to disabilities in a Republic where merit was understood to form the great title to public trust, honors & rewards.[127]

On the other hand, he held fast to a property qualification for voting, arguing that the freeholders were "the best guardians of liberty" and the restriction of suffrage to them was "a necessary defence agst. the dangerous influence of those multitudes without property & without principle." But, he reminded the Convention, "the great mass of our Citizens is composed at this time of freeholders."[128]

Despite the spiritual aristocracy in the Quaker meeting, there was still a democratic component and egalitarianism based on the idea of the universality of the Inward Light. Each member of the meeting had the potential to contribute to the process that members of other religious bodies did not necessarily have in their churches. In keeping with this popular model of governance, Dickinson saw the people, endowed as they were with the capacity to discern the law, as the key to the order, strength, and safety of the American polity. He "detest[ed] the position, that different ranks are necessary for our welfare. It is an idea, borrowed from the errors or vices of other centuries," he said. "It is a rank high enough for a mortal, to be a trustee for his fellow citizens."[129]

In keeping with this egalitarian principle, Dickinson had a firmer stance on the immorality of slavery than any member of the Constitutional Convention.[130] Having manumitted his own slaves ten years prior, he reiterated the sentiments he expressed in his *Essay of a Frame of Government for Pennsylvania* that he "considered it inadmissible on every principle of honor and safety that the importation of slaves should be authorized by the Constitution."[131] He worried that American hypocrisy on the slavery issue would compromise

---

[125] Wood, *The Creation of the American Republic*, 512; and Farrand, *Records of the Federal Convention*, 1: 136.
[126] Farrand, *Records of the Federal Convention*, 1: 150.
[127] Ibid., 2: 123.
[128] Ibid., 2: 202. We should note here Dickinson's use of the term "mass" here as contradistinct from his use of "weight" earlier.
[129] John Dickinson to Benjamin Rush, February 14, 1791 John Dickinson Materials, John Harvey Powell Papers, APS.
[130] Rakove, *Original Meanings*, 88.
[131] Farrand, *Records of the Federal Convention*, 2: 378. He freed them conditionally in 1777, unconditionally in 1786. In 1800, he also paid some slaveholders to manumit their slaves. See Miscellaneous Notes, John Harvey Powell Papers, APS.

the national reputation. "Acting before the World," he wrote, "What will be said of this new principle of founding a right to Freemen on a power derived from Slaves," who were "themselves incapable of governing yet giving to other what they have not. The omitting the Word will be regarded as an Endeavor to conceal a principle of which we are ashamed."[132] In the Convention he proposed a motion that would allow the national government to determine when intervention on the slavery issue was necessary. It was defeated.[133]

For Dickinson, the popular principle extended to the highest level of government. There was no executive in the Quaker polity. With no formal ministry, the leadership was collective and fluid. There was a clerk of every meeting, who had a great deal of weight, but he was as much a bureaucrat as a leader, and his leadership was not autonomous. Moreover, there were elders and overseers, who, along with the clerk, could come from any rank of society. Dickinson was therefore the most vocal critic of the proposed executive office. In the Convention he again expressed his opinion that "the business is so important that no man ought to be silent or reserved." He expressed his belief that "such an Executive as some seem to have in contemplation was not consistent with a republic." He went on to compare the office of a single executive to that of a monarch and warned that it was not the office that people would revere, but rather the person. Such an attachment, of course, could eventually undermine the liberty of the people if they allowed a single individual to hold too much sway over the affairs of the state. "In place of these attachments," he counseled, "we must look out for something else." The proper place for loyalty was not in a single figure, but in the legislature, the individual states, and in "one great Republic." He preferred an executive council to an individual; but this idea was not on the table long. He called for the executive to be removable by a national legislature at the request of a majority of the states. The motion was rejected.[134] He later opposed the election of the executive by a national legislature and instead "leaned towards an election by the people, which he regarded as the best and purest source."[135]

Because a strong central authority was a feature of every Quaker government, ecclesiastical or civil, it is no surprise that Quakers generally favored the proposed system. In the debates over the Constitution, Benjamin Rush observed that Friends were "all (with an exception of three or four persons only) highly fœderal."[136] The question was: How would the representational structure function on a practical level? Where would the preponderance of

---

[132] Hutson, *Supplement*, 158.
[133] Paul Finkelman, "Slavery and the Constitutional Convention: Making a Covenant with Death," in Richard R. Beeman, ed., *Beyond Confederation: Origins of the Constitution and American National Identity* (Chapel Hill: University of North Carolina Press, 1987), 188–225, 222.
[134] Farrand, *Records of the Federal Convention*, 1: 86–87.
[135] Ibid., 2: 114.
[136] Benjamin Rush to Jeremy Belknap, 28 February 1788; John Kaminski and Gaspare J. Saldino, eds., *The Documentary History of the Ratification of the Constitution*, vol. 16, *Commentaries on the Constitution Public and Private* (Madison: State Historical Society of Wisconsin, 1986),

power lie and how would it be organized? In this regard, Dickinson has been described both as an "ardent nationalist" and a champion of states' rights.[137] But to consider him one or the other supposes a stark distinction in his thinking between federalism and nationalism. Merrill Jensen articulates the difference: true Federalists "believed that a federal government was one created by equal and independent states who delegated to it sharply limited authority and who remained superior to it in every way." On the other hand, "a national government was a central organization with coercive authority over both the states and its citizens."[138] Dickinson, characteristically uncategorizable, was advocating a bit of both and neither in its entirety – a hybrid system. For the sake of unity and process, he wanted a national authority with a degree of coercive power over the states. But, as we will see later, he also wanted a federal system that would preserve a significant degree of liberty and give protection for all states; he believed among the most "Dangerous symptoms to America" were "Attempts to consolidate the states into one power." "This," he said, "is a favorite Measure of the large States," which wanted "the aggrand[izement] of some states at the Expense of others."[139]

Dickinson was therefore not an extreme nationalist without any regard for states' or individual rights. He did not want an authoritarian government.[140] Liberty, he wrote, is a "sacred, salutary principle."[141] This is why we find Dickinson on both sides of the debate – to preserve states' and individual rights but also to secure a strong central government. Not just liberty, but directed and moderated liberty was Dickinson's aim. In spite of this aristocratic check on the people, weight should be with the democratic side of the equation. The benefits of British government, Dickinson reminded his skeptics, "are derived from a single democratical branch."[142] In America as well, the strength of the polity came from the democratic element: "[The people] have held, and now hold *the true balance* in their government. While they retain their enlightened spirit, they will continue to hold it."[143] In his personal notes he reiterated that "there never was upon Earth a Body of Nobility, who had such a Regard for the Rights and welfare of their fellow Citizens, as the Nobility of G.B. and

250–52. When Quakers did oppose the Constitution it was mainly because it did not prohibit slavery. See also 403–04.

[137] James H. Hutson refutes earlier claims that Dickinson was an advocate of states' rights over nationalism. He attributed this to Dickinson being "too much a student of Blackstone" to have thought otherwise. "John Dickinson at the Federal Constitutional Convention," 258.

[138] Merrill Jensen, "The Idea of a National Government during the American Revolution," *Political Science Quarterly* vol. 58, no. 3 (1943), 356–379, 357.

[139] John Dickinson, notes, n.d., Ser. II, Miscellaneous, 1671–1801, n.d., RRL/HSP; and John Dickinson, notes, n.d., Government Documents, Revolutionary and Early National Periods, 1765–1788, JDP/LCP.

[140] It is worth noting in this regard that after the ratification of the Constitution and despite his dislike of parties, Dickinson sympathized with the Democratic-Republicans.

[141] John Dickinson to Thomas McKean, 4th of the 3rd mo., 1801, in Stillé and Ford, *Life and Writings*, 1: 286.

[142] Dickinson, *Letters of Fabius*, 49.

[143] Ibid., 51.

yet it would be better for us to encounter all the Calamities of a Civil War, than that a Nobility should be established among us."[144] Dickinson's thought exemplifies what Beer calls "the national theory of American federalism."[145] This is the balanced theory that eventually animated the Constitution.

Few ideas of the Convention can be traced solely to one individual; the creation of the Constitution was a collaborative effort, and ideas put forth by one man were often held simultaneously or were developed beyond their infancy by the body. But there were some notable instances in which a delegate proposed an idea that was not initially approved by the rest of the Convention, but that was ultimately persuasive. At a pivotal moment early on, Dickinson provided what Forrest McDonald calls "one of the crucial conceptual breakthroughs" of the Convention.[146] As the delegates stalled in their discussion about the form and function of the government – whether and how to move away from a confederation and to a national government, Dickinson provided the solution that is the essence of the national-federal system. He advocated a structure in which "one Branch of the Legislature shd. be drawn immediately from the people" and "the other shd. be chosen by the Legislatures of the states."[147] In this system, the states would have equal representation in the senate. This was the first suggestion of the kind.[148] His proposal arose out of a concern for the welfare of the small states. In his notes he wrote, "What will be the situation of the smaller, if in both branches, the Representation is in the apportionment? They will [be] deliver'd up into the absolute power of the larger." And "Repre[sentation] in both Branches founded on numbers – unreasonable & dangerous."[149]

While his insistence on the election of senators through the state legislatures was accepted and implemented, this structure, of course, only lasted until the early twentieth century.[150] But the fundamentals of his system that would preserve the agency of the states while also representing the people in a strong national government prevailed over the opposition of a number of other prominent Framers, including Madison, who at first advocated a purely national system.[151] Later, however, Madison and others such as Wilson adopted Dickinson's metaphor of the national-federal plan as a solar system, "in which the States were the planets, and ought to be left to move freely in

[144] John Dickinson, "Government," Ser. 1. b. Political, 1774–1807, n.d., RRL/HSP.

[145] Beer, *To Make a Nation*, 21.

[146] Forrest McDonald, *Novus Ordo Seclorum: The Intellectual Origins of the Constitution* (Lawrence: University of Kansas Press, 1985), 260. The other was Pierce Butler's idea of the Electoral College.

[147] Farrand, *Records of the Federal Convention*, 1: 136.

[148] M. E. Bradford, *Founding Fathers: Brief Lives of the Framers of the United States Constitution* (Lawrence: University of Kansas Press, 1994), 102.

[149] John Dickinson, notes, n.d, Government Documents, Revolutionary and Early National Periods, 1765–1788, LCP.

[150] It was repealed by the Seventeenth Amendment.

[151] On Madison, see McDonald, *Novus Ordo Seclorum*, 276–77. For a fuller discussion of the debates on Dickinson's role in this debate, and from which this summary is drawn, see 212–15, 230–32, 233, 260, 277.

their proper orbits" around the central government.[152] Dickinson argued that "a government thus established would harmonize the whole."[153]

Dickinson also had a divergent conception of factions from others. While Madison is usually the figure historians look to for the advent of this theory, Dickinson held to a similar idea – pressing it further in some cases than did Madison. Like Penn, Dickinson believed that diversity within the polity was a salutary thing. Penn believed that a diversity of interests would "[b]allance factions, not...Irritate or give Strength to them."[154] Likewise, Dickinson thought the Senate would be better off with more and diverse members, something Madison found too dangerous.[155] But more importantly, the two men supported their theories on different bases. On the surface, both men saw the need to balance competing interests and let them check one another. They also believed that the Senate should be a body composed of the "better sorts" to check the excesses of democracy. One way they differed, however, was where and how this checking by faction should take place. Dickinson wanted it throughout the system, both among the people and in both houses of Congress; Madison, by contrast, wanted it among the people, but not in the Senate. Dickinson therefore advocated a Senate that was elected through the state legislatures – to ensure the "Talent" of the senators; and, to provide for the interests of the small states, he did not object to a large number of senators. Madison, on the other hand, did not care to have the states represented, or, if so, thought the numbers must be very low, so as to imitate the Roman Tribunes. "When they multiplied," he argued, "they divided, were weak, and ceased to be that Guard to the people which was expected in their institution." Dickinson responded in two ways. He argued that "[w]e cannot abandon the states" and reiterated his solar system metaphor. He also replied that if they used the model of the Tribunes, there would be no logical limit to how small the Senate should be. Finally, he said that a complete unity of interests was not desirable. "The objection is that you attempt to unite distinct Interests," he replied to Madison. "I do not consider this an objection, Safety may flow from this variety of Interests."[156] This system, he explained, "will produce that collision between the different authorities which should be wished for in order to check each other."[157]

Thus, although Madison and Dickinson shared the theory of competitive factions, it is clear that they had different ideas of how they should function. Although "collision" is a more violent image than we are used to seeing from Dickinson, it is tempered by his many other comments on the importance of peaceful deliberation in political process. He saw civic engagement as ideally a

---

[152] Farrand, *Records of the Federal Convention*, 1: 153, 157.

[153] Ibid., 1: 157.

[154] William Penn quoted in Schwartz, "A Mixed Multitude," 39.

[155] Farrand, *Records of the Federal Convention*, 1: 153.

[156] Ibid., 1: 158–59.

[157] Ibid., 1: 153. Ultimately, of course, Dickinson was compelled to make the greater compromise and did so with his proposal of equal representation in the Senate.

cooperative, disinterested, and persuasive endeavor – one motivated by a sense of love and obligation. Dickinson later lamented the development of the Party System and reiterated his concern for "participated happiness." "I do hope," he elaborated, "that a Disposition to Reconciliation, and mutual Kindness, & just Attentions will prevail, and that the chief Contest among Us will be, who shall most strenuously exert himself in doing Good to all. I wish, We were well rid of the Words Federalists and Republicans as Titles of Opposition."[158]

On the other hand, Madison's hope for the competitive system, as articulated in *Federalist* nos. 10 and 56, lay not in the populace possessing republican virtue enough to engage disinterestedly in policy making but rather in their exercising sufficient reason to recognize that the welfare of the individual was bound up with the welfare of the whole, what Tocqueville would later call "self-interest properly understood."[159] As we have seen, Dickinson suspected reason as the sole guide for determining the public welfare. He believed that individuals might well *rationalize* their motives to pursue ends that would benefit only themselves rather than the public. He would have been skeptical of the claim that individual and factional competition alone and with ambition unchecked could prevent the atomization of the polity. It ultimately could not be a reliable unifying force.[160] As we have seen, he held that individuals' behavior must be regulated by multiple guides – foremost "divine Goodness," in concert with a balanced federal system that encourages a kind of consensus.

Thus, in the American system, neither Rousseau's general will nor Locke's majority would prevail; both could lead to democratic despotism. The system of national federalism included a measure of consensus based on "contributed rights" that would prevent it. Of course, the decision-making process was not the pure consensus – the "sense of the meeting," as Friends said, without voting – that Quakers used in their ecclesiastical polity. In a body so large and diverse as the United States, complete unanimity is never possible and voting must take place. The representational model that Dickinson proposed based the general will neither on a majority vote system nor a pure consensus, but rather a mixture of both. His system is one in which all voices were heard and all views represented as much as possible. This way, as he put it, the "sense of

---

[158] John Dickinson, untitled document [1802?], Government Documents, Revolutionary and Early National Period, 1765–1788, n.d., JDP/LCP.

[159] See Beer, *To Make a Nation,* for example: "For Madison, although men differed greatly in their 'faculties,' they all had 'reason' sufficient to enable and to entitle them to live a free, republican life" (365).

[160] Dickinson would not have been alone in his concerns on this point. Beer notes that the shortcomings of this very rational theory were widely recognized at the time and tempered by the theories of others, such as James Wilson (Dickinson's former law student), on public "affections" that would reconcile citizens to a common interest (*To Make a Nation,* 363–77). Wilson's theories look much like secular versions of Dickinson's. Beer notes, for example, Wilson's belief in an inward moral "guide" (366); that "the heart of the political process" for Wilson "was individual reflection and collective deliberation" (370); and the "danger of perfectionism" that "lurk[ed]" in Wilson's exalted view of social passion" (367).

the people"[161] as a whole, and the "sense of the states" were used to determine the direction of the polity, rather than merely a count of individual opinions. "In this way of proceeding," he said,

[T]he undoubted sense of every state, collected in the coolest manner, not the sense of individuals, will be laid before the whole union in congress, and that body will be enabled with the clearest light that can be afforded every part of it...forthwith to adopt such alterations as are recommended by the general unanimity; by degrees to devise modes of conciliation upon contradictory propositions.[162]

America would be protected from the natural aristocracy turning into tyranny, Fabius explained, by "*the power of the people* pervading the proposed system, together with the *strong confederation of the states*, [which] forms an adequate security against every danger that has been apprehended" – anarchy, democratic despotism, or tyranny by a nobility or an executive.[163]

There were three factors that made Dickinson the natural leader on the subject of a national-federal government. First, he was one of the few framers, if not the only one, who had been studying and writing about constitutionalism since the days of Empire and struggling with how federalism could work under this model. His colleagues had come of age politically in an era that sought to destroy a central government; Dickinson, by contrast, had always been concerned with preservation. Second, he was the only delegate who had interests in both one of the largest states (Pennsylvania) and one of the smallest (Delaware), thus giving him a unique perspective on the debate. Third, his life in the Quaker community made him intimately familiar with a workable federal system.[164] This model was perhaps the best from which to formulate the solution to the problem of majority and minority expressions.[165] Within this context, then, he was not as innovative as some have claimed. He was not "rebelling" against earlier traditions of hierarchical thought, as American republicans were.[166] He was doing what he recommended to other politicians of the time – drawing on history and experience. There was not, therefore, as some have claimed, an entire "absence of positive examples" of a federal system.[167] As conversant as Dickinson was with ancient history and philosophy, the Quaker system was a tangible example close at hand.[168]

---

[161] Dickinson, *Letters of Fabius*, 20.

[162] Ibid., 47–48.

[163] Ibid., 6.

[164] Beer acknowledges that the origins of the "delegate convention model of political organization" can be traced back to "certain Protestant sects." He does not, however, mention which ones (197).

[165] With Dickinson's close ties to Delaware, it is not likely a coincidence that it was the first state to ratify the Constitution.

[166] Beer, *To Make a Nation*, 22.

[167] Greene, *Peripheries and Center*, 161.

[168] J. C. D. Clark in *The Language of Liberty, 1660–1832: Political Discourse and Social Dynamics in the Anglo-American World* (Cambridge: Cambridge University Press, 1994) suggests that Americans might have drawn on the Holy Roman Empire as a model, but anti-Catholicism

Yet Dickinson did not advocate a Quaker model in its entirety or indiscriminately. When he wrote that "[t]he best Philo[sophy] is drawn from Experiments[;] The best Policy from Experience," he had the "Holy Experiment" in mind.[169] He seems to have learned from both the mistakes and the salutary principles and practices of Pennsylvania Quaker government and church. The Pennsylvania Charter was decidedly unbalanced in favor of the popular branch, yet the government was controlled by the powerful hand of the Quaker spiritual aristocracy, which, many inhabitants of Pennsylvania argued, had become an oligarchy not just of spirit but of wealth. If we remember, in the controversy over royal government, Dickinson lauded the lop-sided Pennsylvania constitution. "Our legislation," he said, "suffers no checks, from a council instituted, in fancied imitation of the House of Lords."[170] But this system created a population that was restless under the supervision of the Quaker church in part, ironically enough, because of the antiauthoritarianism of its teachings, which in turn necessitated more control from above. In other words, because the democratic and aristocratic elements of the government converged in one house, although Pennsylvania's government had been stable for decades, it was increasingly unsteady because there was not a system of real popular control that had checks and balances. Then when the Pennsylvania Convention adopted the same governmental structure, but without the Quaker check, disorder ensued. Nevertheless, at one time, the elements of popular sovereignty and aristocratic representation were there, and insofar as they worked – or had potential to work – Dickinson drew on them.[171]

"prevented colonists from exploring the federal implications of Roman-law traditions: federalism was not a common topic of American speculation before 1776" (103). If we remember Dickinson's thought in the *Farmer's Letters*, however, specifically his argument concerning internal and external taxation (101), we see that he was already working toward this concept. He revived his old argument in the Constitutional Convention (132).

[169] John Dickinson, notes, n.d., Government Documents, Revolutionary and Early National Periods, 1765–1788, LCP.

[170] Dickinson, *A Speech*, 16.

[171] Also, when considering Dickinson's concern to control democratic impulses, one should not make the mistake of assuming that he shared the oligarchic inclinations of some Quakers. With their privileged position in society, Friends were sometimes willing to engage in heavy-handed tactics to achieve their theologico-political aims – tactics that, while not necessarily illegal, could involve flouting conventions of civil or legal process and honorable behavior. As we have seen, in England they obstructed the courts by overattention to legal technicalities; and in Pennsylvania they subverted the governor by petitioning the king in secret, and they imposed the affirmation on non-Friends in courts rather than the oath. Although Dickinson shared most of the theologico-political aims, he paid greater heed to civil processes and conventional ethics than Friends. A notable example of the differences between them was when Dickinson and Quakers were suing a man for establishing a theater on land Dickinson sold him, in violation of an agreement to the contrary. In order to prevail, the Quakers encouraged Dickinson to use his greater wealth either to bribe the defendant or to prolong the trial and win by draining his opponent's purse. But Dickinson refused to use his wealth and abuse the judicial system in this way, even though it meant losing this particular battle. A series of letters over the course of 1791 on this matter between Dickinson, Charles Jervis, Henry Hill, and George Read can be found in Ser. 1. a. Correspondence, 1762–1808, RRL/HSP.

When the Constitution was in the process of being ratified in 1788, and when the Quaker 1669 Discipline was instituted, neither the Framers nor the Quaker leaders sought consensus or complete popular approval. Had they done so, they knew that no constitution would ever have been implemented. When Quakers created their ecclesiastical Discipline, some individuals who considered themselves good Quakers opposed it bitterly. Therefore, after Barclay wrote his treatise explaining and defending the creation of the Discipline, it was imposed on the entire body over the objections of some. Likewise, after the *Federalist Papers* and the *Fabius Letters*, as well as other popular appeals on behalf of the Constitution were published, when it was ratified, there was mixture of persuasion and coercion as Anti-Federalists were made to accept a framework that seemed to them un-American. The Framers of both constitutions expected that those who disagreed would abstain from obstructionism and agree to support the new government, regardless of their disapproval. Of course, such graceful acquiescence was not always forthcoming, and in both polities, the threat of schism has always lurked where unity was weak.

Conclusion: The Flexible and Perfectible Constitution

Some scholars deny that Dickinson was after a "theoretical perfection" in the Constitution.[172] On the contrary, he did believe that perfection was theoretically possible. But he was also willing to accept momentary imperfection that would allow the polity to move forward to its goals. Temporary imperfection was acceptable and theoretical perfection possible for the same reason. Dickinson explained the on-going process of constitution making:

If all the wise men of ancient and modern times could be collected together for deliberation on the subject, they could not form a Constitution or system of government that would not require future improvements. The British government which some persons so much celebrate is a collection of innovations. There is a continual tide in human affairs, a progression still towards something better than what is possessed. The unceasing reason has carried man to delightful discoveries, greatly ameliorating his condition. There are other discoveries yet to be made and perhaps more favorable to his condition.[173]

The U.S. Constitution was thus designed to be a living, flexible document that would change as the polity matured to reflect "the living Elasticity within Man."[174] The delegates, he said, "not only laboured from the best plan they could, but, *provided for making at any time amendments on the authority of the people,* without shaking the stability of the government."[175] Beer calls Edmund Burke "one of the first political thinkers to recommend prudent, gradual, but continual adaptation and improvement."[176] This attribution is perhaps more

[172] Ahern, "The Spirit of American Constitutionalism," 57–76, 75.
[173] John Dickinson, notes, n.d., Ser. 1. b. Political, 1774–1807, n.d., RRL/HSP.
[174] Ibid.
[175] Dickinson, *Letters of Fabius*, 47.
[176] Beer, *To Make a Nation*, 141.

applicable to Dickinson and other Quakerly thinkers and politicians since the seventeenth century. Likewise, while Americans in general had finally come to see a "distinction between a constitution and ordinary law," it had existed for over a century in Quaker theory and practice.[177] "Thus, by a gradual process," said Dickinson, "we may from time to time *introduce every improvement in our constitution*, that shall be suitable to our situation."[178] He believed that the United States would eventually be a "perfect body" that "corresponds with the gracious intentions of our maker towards us his creations."[179] This idea allows Americans to continue the on-going process of constitutional "gathering." The polity would be, Dickinson explained, "ever new, and always the same."[180]

[177] Rakove, *Original Meanings*, 130.
[178] Dickinson, *Letters of Fabius*, 47.
[179] Ibid., 45.
[180] Ibid., 23.

EPILOGUE

The Persistence of Quaker Constitutionalism, 1789–1963

In undertaking a study of the origins of ideas and the influence of groups and individuals on movements and events, definitive evidence is often difficult to come by. Moreover, parallel strains of thought often arise from similar sources and develop independently from one another, allowing individuals moving in different circles to come to similar conclusions without knowledge of one another. Unless the historian finds solid evidence, such as well-used books in a personal library or that rare explicit statement bestowing credit, much of the influence must be deduced through the practical expression of a strain of thought and the ubiquity of the culture it created. It is clear, for example, that despite the absence of a succinctly articulated theory of civil disobedience in the early modern period, Quakers were the first practitioners of it. By the late-eighteenth century, this language and tradition was concrete enough that it could be recognized and explicitly referenced as an example, as Dickinson did during the Revolution.

To the extent American resistance to Britain remained peaceful, inspired by Quakerism, Dickinson became the first leader of a national peaceful protest movement, a position that would later be held by Gandhi and Martin Luther King, Jr. But because until now he has not been recognized as such, we cannot properly consider him the "founder" of this tradition of leadership. He was not their model; he was merely the first. Some might object that this designation is inaccurate because the cause he led ultimately resulted in war. But we should not forget that both Gandhi's and King's peaceful protests had the same unintended effect of encouraging violence among their followers. Moreover, although he did admit the necessity of defensive war in rare cases, and although he ultimately joined the cause by fighting, at no point did Dickinson ever advocate war or revolution for America. And as to the question of going to war compromising his pacifist principles, even Gandhi admitted the necessity of defensive violence to stop certain kinds of assailants.[1] The pacifist stance need not be an absolute

---

[1] Namely snipers and rapists. See Mark Juergensmeyer, "Nonviolence," *The Encyclopedia of Religion*, 2nd ed. (Detroit: Macmillan Reference USA, 2005), 6645–49, 6646.

one, and Dickinson's happened to be more pragmatic, though no less sincere, than that of his Quaker brethren.[2]

But although Dickinson led the peaceful protest against Britain, and it is clear that he exerted strong and direct influence early in the conflict, because the violence continued to escalate, and the Revolutionary War did eventually take place, his influence was short-lived and circumscribed. When we consider that even in the twenty-first century, when Quaker dissent and pacifism are still mistaken for disloyalty to the country, it is not surprising that his pacifism diminished his reputation considerably and cost him his place in American history.[3] Before the Constitution, Americans were simply not ready – and perhaps had little pragmatic need – for peaceful protest. As Josiah Quincy, Jr., told Dickinson in 1774, "those maxims of discipline are not universally known in this early period of Continental warfare."[4] But this would change.

When Americans came to the understanding that a constitution needs to be permanent, but changeable through peaceful measures, John Dickinson's thought and the Quaker tradition out of which he was writing immediately became vitally relevant. A political theory such as Whiggism that allows constitutional change through revolution is a fine idea if a people wants to start completely anew. But a different approach is needed if the object is to preserve the fundamental constitution and achieve reform within the existing structure of government. As Herbert Storing notes, after the Revolution the Federalists became acutely aware of the need for moderation in reforming the new Republic. Quoting Dickinson to the effect that "'a people does not reform with moderation,'" Storing explains that "[i]t is necessary that every precaution be taken not to upset that original patriotic act and to preserve and foster reverence for the laws, and particularly for the highest law."[5] An anonymous newspaper article occasioned by the Whiskey Rebellion, found among Dickinson's papers, proclaimed:

If our Constitution should prove either deficient or oppressive, it contains within itself the seeds of its own reformation; if laws are either impolitic or unjust, a complaint

---

[2] See Jane E. Calvert, "Pacifism," in Gary L. Anderson and Kathryn G. Herr, eds., *The Encyclopedia of Activism and Social Justice* (Thousand Oaks, CA: Sage Publications, 2007), 3: 1075–78.

[3] Shortly after September 11, 2001, but before the commencement of the Iraq War, the government began illegal surveillance of Quaker meetings, individuals, and organizations in various parts of the country for their peaceful protest activities. See American Civil Liberties Union, "ACLU of Colorado Seeks to Close Denver Police 'Spy Files' on Peaceful Protesters, Including Quakers and 73-Year-Old Nun," March 28, 2002, http://www.aclu.org/freespeech/protest/11056prs20020328.html. Accessed February 19, 2008. For later reports in addition to those from the ACLU, see, for example, Lisa Myers, Douglas Pasternak, Rich Gardella, and the NBC Investigative Unit, "Is the Pentagon spying on Americans? Secret database obtained by NBC News tracks 'suspicious' domestic groups," December 14, 2005. http://www.msnbc.msn.com/id/10454316/. Accessed January 12, 2008.

[4] Josiah Quincy, Jr., to John Dickinson, August 20, 1774, Ser. 1. a. Correspondence, 1762–1808, RRL/HSP.

[5] Herbert J. Storing, *What the Anti-Federalists Were For* (Chicago: University of Chicago Press, 1981), 74.

of our grievances or change of our representation, open the path to every desirable amendment. In countries where the interest and authority of government are distinct and independent from the interests and will of the people, insurrection may have been ranked among the most sacred of duties; in ours who can hesitate to regard it as the most pernicious of crimes?[6]

Thomas Jefferson's theory that "a little rebellion now and then is a good thing" was quickly becoming obsolete.[7] Indeed, Paul Douglas Newman's work on the 1798–99 Fries's Rebellion, with its peaceful, constitutional protest, indicates that there was an important change in attitude and behavior that was due in large part to Quaker influence.[8]

Despite Dickinson's considerable presence at the Constitutional Convention, it is difficult to ascertain the influence of his Quakerism on the proceedings. By this time, many of the delegates had similar ideas. About the concept of the perpetual and amendable constitution, for example, one can only argue that the idea originally developed in Quaker thought. That it came to be expressed by other Americans at the Founding may or may not have been coincidental. With a few exceptions, such as his original proposal for state and national representation, Dickinson's role may only have been to reinforce and encourage the direction to which his countrymen were already inclined. Because illness took him from the Convention early, we cannot know what more he might have contributed.

Quaker Influence beyond the Founding

Whereas in the seventeenth and eighteenth centuries hard evidence of direct Quaker influence on the polity is limited, in the nineteenth century it is abundant. Despite their claims of rejecting politics, not only did Quakers themselves step to the fore on the national scene to advocate their traditional causes, but there also appeared explicit statements by non-Friends of how Quakers and Quakerism shaped their thought and action. In fact, in significant ways, Quakers became more, not less, political after their withdrawals from politics in 1756 and 1776: Where early on their stated cause had been spiritual equality of the poor, women, blacks, and other oppressed groups, it had now evolved

[6] Ser. 1. b. Political, 1774–1807, n.d., RRL/HSP. The language and message are indicative enough of his writings that we have reason to suspect his authorship. The clipping included no title or indication of the paper in which it was published.

[7] Thomas Jefferson to James Madison, January 30, 1787, in Julian P. Boyd and Barbara B. Oberg, et al., eds., *The Papers of Thomas Jefferson* (Princeton, NJ: Princeton University Press, 2001), 29: 280. This is not to say that violence as a tool for change was no longer used. We know that it has been used even through the twentieth century, but now, few would justify it. One might also argue that the Civil War complicates this conclusion. Certainly it demonstrates that the question of unity and how to dissent was not unanimous (if it ever has been) until after the mid-nineteenth century. But we must remember that although revolution of a sort and separation seemed acceptable to half the country, the other half disagreed. And the view of the latter prevailed.

[8] Paul Douglas Newman, *Fries's Rebellion: The Enduring Struggle for the American Revolution* (Philadelphia: University of Pennsylvania Press, 2005).

into a conscious struggle for civil equality for these same groups. Quakers were the founders and among the most active leaders of the movements for civil rights in the nineteenth and twentieth centuries.[9]

Not only were Quakers continuing their grassroots activism with renewed fervor, their efforts were facilitated and their influence deepened by a new public image. By the early nineteenth century, the public had forgotten their ranting enthusiasm of the seventeenth century, and even the memory of their alleged Loyalism in the Revolution had faded considerably. Much to the contrary, a new image of the virtuous Quaker began to take a wide hold. Their moral uprightness was interpreted by some as priggishness, and jokes and cartoons surfaced that poked fun at Quakers' rigidity and linguistic idiosyncrasies, not to mention their religious dilemma in the Civil War. By most, however, the Quaker was now seen as a paragon of virtue. As the language of republicanism became diffuse through the new nation, Americans came around to the French understanding of Friends as representing all that republican citizens ought to be – simple and plain, frugal, industrious, trustworthy, honest, concerned with the rights of man, and patriotic. One might look to the popular literature of the nineteenth and early twentieth centuries to see the American fascination with Friends. It is replete with Quaker intonations such as "The Quaker Settlement" in Harriet Beecher Stowe's *Uncle Tom's Cabin*, Meg as pretty as a Quakeress in Louisa May Alcott's *Little Women* (1869), Melville's Nantucket Quakers in *Moby Dick* (1851), and characters such as Old Broadbrim and Young Broadbrim in the dime detective novels at the turn of the century.[10] By the time of the Civil War, Quakers were once again used as a barometer, not, this time, to gauge popular sentiment so much as to indicate the righteousness of the Northern cause. As the "New Quaker Bonnet" indicates, Americans had come to recognize – at least intuitively – that the Quakers' twin concerns were liberty and union (Figure 9). Far from being subversive of government, in the popular mind, they now represented the core values of American political culture.[11]

Another powerful indicator of the American fascination with Quakerism is found in commerce and popular culture. Since the Quakers' ascent into respectability, Americans have capitalized on their name and image, using it to sell everything imaginable: clothing of all sorts, firefighters' protective

---

[9] Lest one is inclined to associate Quaker activism too closely and simply with modern liberal social activism, Howell John Harris has offered a caution in "War in the Social Order: The Great War and the Liberalization of American Quakerism," in David K. Adams and Cornelis A. Van Minnen, eds., *Religious and Secular Reform in America: Ideas, Belief, and Social Change* (New York: New York University Press, 1999), 179–203.

[10] For more instances of Quakers in popular literature, see Anna Breiner Caulfield, *Quakers in Fiction: An Annotated Bibliography* (Northhampton, MA: Pittenbruach Press, 1993).

[11] The Quaker image was hardly as uncomplicated as I have represented it here. Not surprisingly, because of their peace testimony, their advocacy of the Northern cause and participation in the war was problematic and heavily qualified. This led to substantial public ridicule by non-Quakers. For a rich discussion of the Quaker image in the popular mind that deals with this and other topics, see Jennifer Connerley, "Friendly Americans: Representing Quakers in the United States, 1850–1920" (Ph.D. Thesis, University of North Carolina, 2006).

FIGURE 9. "The New Quaker Bonnet, 1861." Covers such as this were sent through the mail as envelopes or postcards during the Civil War era. A similar image is also represented by Quaker poet John Greenleaf Whittier in "Barbara Frietchie." After Frietchie protects the American flag from Confederate invaders, he writes, "Over Barbara Frietchie's grave,/ Flag of Freedom and Union, wave!/ Peace and order and beauty draw/ Round thy symbol of light and law[.]"

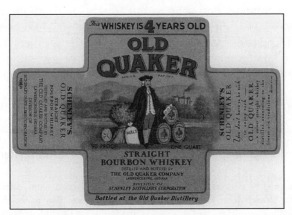

FIGURE 10. Old Quaker Whiskey label, n.d. No doubt related to this brand is "An Old Quaker 'Health': Here's to thee and thy folks/ From me and my folks./ Sure there never was folks,/ Since folks was folks,/ Ever loved any folks,/ Half as much as me and my folks,/ Love thee and thy folks" (postcard, 1910). One must suspect that the irony on the part of the Schenley Corporation and this health was intentional, considering the close association of Quakers with the temperance movement.

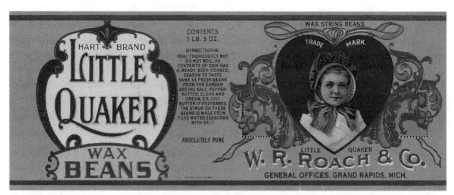

FIGURE 11. Hart Brand Little Quaker Wax Beans can label, n.d.

gear, table cloths, silver, heaters, canned vegetables, insurance, beer, doors and windows, cornmeal, rubber, Coca-Cola, pottery and tableware, pens, wall paper, bird calls, brake fluid, macaroni, cocoa, anti-freeze, scissors, model airplanes, cooking ranges, birdseed, rugs, pet food, bitters, postcards, oil and grease, milk, safety matches, bread, handbags, knives, coffee, and chili powder, among other things. Of course, the best-known Quaker logo is the Quaker Oats man, the very picture of the honest and trustworthy citizen, framed, of course, in red, white, and blue.[12] And then there are less wholesome products, such as cigars and whiskey. Some of these items bear the image of a steady "Old Quaker" or an innocent and blushing "Quaker maid" (Figures 10–13). "Pure" and "honest" are adjectives that often accompany the images, as seen in the advertisements for Little Quaker Wax Beans and Armstrong's Quaker Rugs (Figures 11 and 12). There are also plays, a flower, a color, a moth, restaurants, popular songs, "silent guns,"[13] and a breed of parakeet that carry the name of Quaker. No other religious group has held such a sway over the national imagination. Although this fascination has waned considerably since the mid-twentieth century, there are still vestiges of an idea of Quakerly purity. The rock band the Red Hot Chili Peppers depicts this purity sullied with their lyrics, "Pushing dirt into a Quaker."[14] And a Quaker Oats television commercial shows a statue of an eighteenth-century Quaker with a tray of presumably wholesome granola bars, accompanying children to school and

[12] It is interesting to note that Quakers themselves were profoundly unhappy with their name and image being represented and used in this way. In 1910 they sued the Quaker Oats Company and lost. See ibid. on the Quakers' frustration with the use of their image (226–27).

[13] "Quaker Guns" were logs painted to look like canons that the Confederate Army used in the Civil War to give the impression of a strongly fortified position. See Jane Chapman Whitt, *Elephants and Quaker Guns . . . A History of Civil War and Circus Days* (New York: Vantage Press, 1966).

[14] Red Hot Chili Peppers (Michael Balzary. John Fruscianti, Anthony Kiedis, Chad Smith), "We Believe," *Stadium Arcadium* Disc 2: *Mars* (Burbank, CA: Warner Bros. Records, Inc., 2006).

FIGURE 12. Armstrong's Quaker Rugs advertisement. (*The Saturday Evening Post*, 1934.) Used with permission from Armstrong World Industries, Inc.

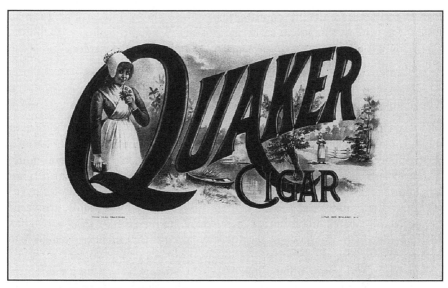

FIGURE 13. Quaker Cigar label, n.d.

play while singing a jolly tune. On the other hand, today many people think Quakers live in Utah and build nice furniture.[15]

The main difficulty in dealing with Quakerism from the nineteenth century forward is not lack of evidence of their influence on American popular and political culture, but rather, because of an event in Quaker history known as the Hicksite Separation of 1827–29, exactly what the range and quality of that influence was.[16] Before this, Quakerism, while not homogenous, had at least been able to strike that delicate balance between unity and dissent; or, if the balance was off, the dissent was never strong enough to challenge the unity seriously or permanently, and the Society remained whole. The Separation was the loss of this balance.

The remaining pages will touch on the thought of a few of the most influential Quaker reformers in the nineteenth and twentieth centuries, with an overview of some of the changes and continuities in political or "civil" Quakerism.[17] To unravel the complexities of modern Quakerism and its influences

[15] Dickinson, when remembered, has not fared as well in contemporary popular culture. He serves mainly as foil to John Adams in the Broadway musical and film *1776* (1969, 1972). More recently he has appeared in cartoon form on PBS's *Liberty's Kids* and on Comedy Central's *South Park* as a "soft pussy [war] protester" (Episode 701: "I'm a Little Bit Country," April 9, 2003). Most recently, he is cast as the villain opposite hero John Adams in the HBO mini-series based on David McCullough's biography, *John Adams* (New York: Simon and Schuster, 2001).

[16] The two works that form a pair in dealing with this topic are H. Larry Ingle, *Quakers in Conflict: The Hicksite Reformation* (Knoxville: University of Tennessee Press, 1986); and Hamm, *The Transformation of American Quakerism.*

[17] Once again, I am intentionally neglecting mention of the myriad Quaker reform organizations that existed during these periods. As in the seventeenth and eighteenth centuries, they were established or maintained for giving aid to various unfortunate and disenfranchised groups, such as blacks, alcoholics, women, Indians, and the poor. In addition to carrying on many

on American culture would require at least another book and certainly more to
follow the various threads to their conclusions. With this epilogue, therefore,
I hope only to give a sense of the import of Quakerism for modern American
political culture and suggest further avenues for thought.

The Transformation of Quaker Political Thought in Antebellum America

In 1764 Quaker minister George Churchman proclaimed, "Let none neither
male nor female be discouraged, who may feel an engagement for Israel's
welfare: Let not your Lights be hidden under any bed of ease, nor under
Mammon's bushel, but let them be set up on the candlestick in sight of your
neighbors, that others may be thereby incited to look at their own indolence."[18]
Lucretia Mott, prominent women's rights advocate and abolitionist, answered
Churchman's call eighty-six years later when she preached, "[L]et our lights
so shine that men may see our good works and glorify our father which is in
heaven."[19]

But Mott and many other Quaker reformers of this age had a different
understanding of the Light, as well as many other theological principles, than
did Churchman.[20] The activism of Quakers is usually at least mentioned by
historians of Antebellum reform movements, but an in-depth treatment is often
lacking. Although scholars have explored the lives and works of figures such
as Lucretia Mott, Susan B. Anthony, and fellow travelers such as William
Lloyd Garrison and Elizabeth Cady Stanton, few have analyzed the theologico-
political philosophy that drove them into the public sphere and conditioned
their mode of civic engagement.[21] Likewise, there is little mention in the
literature of the fact that the inspiration for the Seneca Falls Convention grew
from the Junius Friends Meeting in New York.[22]

of these concerns, they also organized to face new ones such as the Vietnam and Gulf Wars,
nuclear proliferation, environmental issues, and the death penalty.
[18] Journal of George Churchman, 1764, 2: 46, HQC.
[19] Lucretia Mott, "Keep yourselves from Idols," in Dana Greene, ed., *Lucretia Mott: Her Complete
Sermons and Speeches* (New York: The Edwin Mellen Press, 1980), 178–79.
[20] The following argument challenges conventional interpretations of Quaker history that agrees
with Mott and finds that her Quakerism corresponded with that of earlier Friends. See Margaret
Hope Bacon, *Valiant Friend: The Life of Lucretia Mott* (New York: Walker and Company,
1980), 115.
[21] See, for example, Nancy A. Hewitt, *Women's Activism and Social Change: Rochester, New
York, 1822–1872* (Ithaca, NY: Cornell University Press, 1984); and Zigler, *Advocates of Peace
in Antebellum America*. Exceptions include Thomas D. Hamm, *God's Government Begun:
The Society for Universal Inquiry and Reform, 1842–1846* (Bloomington: Indiana University
Press, 1995); and Nancy Isenberg, "Pillars in the Same Temple." Likewise, Anna M. Speicher
provides a model for how such analysis might be undertaken in greater depth in *The Religious
World of Antislavery Women: Spirituality in the Lives of Five Abolitionist Lecturers* (New
York: Syracuse University Press, 2000). For Stanton's religious convictions as they pertained
specifically to women, see Kathi Kern, *Mrs. Stanton's Bible* (Ithaca, NY: Cornell University
Press, 2001).
[22] My thanks to Christopher Densmore of Friends Historical Library, Swarthmore College, for
bringing this fact to my attention. For a recent study of the Convention and its origins, see

When the Society split for theological reasons, the Hicksites took some aspects of the theology and political theory with them, the Orthodox took others, and yet more splinter groups did the same. It is impossible to discuss all the variations here. I will instead restrict the discussion to the strain that had the most influence on the reform movements – the radical Hicksite Quakerism of Mott and her followers – and compare it with the traditional theory.[23]

When Friends separated, at issue was the locus of divine authority and, by extension, the seat of authority in the ecclesiastical polity. To describe it very simply, those who followed Elias Hicks came to believe that power was in the Light (now becoming indistinguishable from reason) and the individual conscience, while the Orthodox held that it was found in dogma, Scripture, and the church government. Hicksites accused the Orthodox of tyranny; the Orthodox accused the Hicksites of anarchy. The dissenters no longer sought to convince, and the Orthodox no longer let themselves be convinced. For the former, individual conscience took precedence over unity; for the latter, conformity to existing ideas and structures prevailed over expression of the individual conscience. There was no longer a *via media*.

Lucretia Mott was clearly the leading proponent of this brand of Hicksite Quakerism. Her understanding of the Light, like those of most Hicksites, emphasized individual interpretations and opposed coercion of the conscience by the church. If Mott was not as radical as conservative Friends painted her, her sermons were sometimes vague and suggestive in such a way that could easily lead to extremist interpretations. A case in point is William Lloyd Garrison, whose thought was shaped by Mott's teachings. He wrote, "If my mind has... become liberalized to any degree, (and I think it has burst every sectarian trammel) – if theological dogmas which I once regarded as essential to Christianity, I now repudiate as absurd and pernicious – I am largely indebted to [James and Lucretia Mott] for the change."[24] He and others picked up on Mott's strain of theologico-political thought and developed it into the nonresistance and come-outerism movements. Not only was Mott the mentor for radical reformers such as Garrison, she also approved of their actions. "I care not," she said, "how radical the true inquirer may become, if a regard for *true* religion is preserved."[25]

Judith Wellman, *The Road to Seneca Falls: Elizabeth Cady Stanton and the First Woman's Rights Convention* (Urbana and Chicago: University of Illinois Press, 2004).

[23] Orthodox Friends represented the withdrawing extreme of Quaker behavior. While they were also in favor of abolition, for example, they did not openly advocate the cause, preferring instead to undertake any efforts surreptitiously, if at all. The result was that they were accused by some of contributing to the problem. See Ryan Jordan, *Slavery and the Meetinghouse: The Quakers and the Abolitionist Dilemma, 1820–1865* (Bloomington: Indiana University Press, 2007).

[24] William Lloyd Garrison, *The Liberator*, November 9, 1849. See also William L. van Deberg, "William Lloyd Garrison and the 'Pro-Slavery Priesthood': The Changing Beliefs of an Evangelical Reformer, 1830–1840," *Journal of the American Academy of Religion* vol. 43, no. 2 (1975), 224–37.

[25] Lucretia Mott to Sister, 1st mo. 3rd, 1865, in Anna Davis Hallowell, ed., *James and Lucretia Mott: Life and Letters* (Boston: Houghton Mifflin and Co., 1884), 415.

Nonresistance and come-outerism were seminal to the radical activism on abolitionism and women's rights. And both of them were extreme interpretations of some Quaker theological tenets. Come-outerism was the idea that people should remove themselves from the corrupt institutions of society, namely the church and the state.[26] This, of course, is a legacy of Quaker quietism that caused some Friends to remove themselves from the civil government of Pennsylvania. Nonresistance was an extreme pacifist position that held that these institutions had no right to coerce the consciences of individuals, yet they must not be resisted by force. As Thomas Hamm has noted, this was a logical extension of the peace testimony.[27] In essence, these movements denied the legitimacy of government and the engagement of the individual with it. Both were based on the idea of the perfection of the individual and the notion that when man was perfect, and under the government of God directly, he would need no earthly government.

The advocates of these theologico-political philosophies were very conscious of the Quaker roots of their beliefs and argued for their own continuity with the faith and practice of early Friends and notable eighteenth-century activists. James and Lucretia Mott proclaimed their beliefs were "in accordance with Fox, Penn, and Barclay."[28] Mott seemed to be trying to revive the practices of early Friends in defiance of how Orthodox Quakers were now portraying the same principles – accurately or not. "'Our principles,'" she quoted an early source, "'lead us to reject and to intreat the oppressed to reject all carnal weapons, relying solely on those which are mighty through God to the pulling down of strongholds.'"[29] Garrison and others also thought of themselves as the heirs of these early Friends, as did Edward Burrough and, later, John Woolman. Then in a statement that many Quakers would consider heretical, Mott declared, "I am no advocate of passivity." But she did not mean to sanction overt violence. To clarify, she continued by making the distinction that has eluded most historians for decades: "Quakerism, as I understand it, does not mean quietism. The early Friends were agitators; disturbers of the peace; and were more obnoxious in their day to charges which are now so freely made than we are."[30]

While Mott was correct in her interpretation of early Quaker activism, ironically, in spite of their rhetoric of peace and salvation, there was something quite violent and unforgiving about the pacifism of nonresisters. Their beliefs were an expression of the peace testimony in one way, but, in another way, they violated it. The philosophy of government and civic engagement that Mott,

---

[26] Isenberg, "Pillars in the Same Temple," 101–02; and Lewis Perry, *Radical Abolitionism: Anarchy and the Government of God in Antislavery Thought* (Ithaca, NY: Cornell University Press, 1973), passim.

[27] Thomas D. Hamm, "Hicksite Quakerism and the Antebellum Non-resistance Movement," *Church History* vol. 63, no. 4 (1994), 557–69. See also, Hamm, *God's Government Begun.*

[28] James Mott to Wiliam Smeal, 8th mo. 24th, 1840, in Hallowell, *Life and Letters,* 178.

[29] Mott, "I am no advocate of passivity," in Greene, *Lucretia Mott,* 261–62, 261.

[30] Ibid., 262.

Garrison, Stanton, and others advocated was decidedly contrary to traditional Quaker theologico-political thought in several ways. Although Mott was also correct that there had always been a powerful individualistic component of the Inward Light, early Quakers believed that it was precisely to restrict the "scattering" tendency of the Light that God ordained the government. As we have seen, Fox wrote the first constitution of the Quaker church to control wayward Friends, and Barclay wrote the *Anarchy of the Ranters* in its defense to explain to radical Friends why they were about to be coerced by the new church government, and why this was part of God's plan for them. Subsequent Quakers in the Society and Pennsylvania government advocated a measure of coercion to achieve unity. By contrast, Mott preached that "we are perhaps too much taught to venerate... the government... more than is consistent with true Quakerism or true Christianity."[31] Famously, Garrison went so far as to burn the Constitution in public, call it "a covenant with Death and an agreement with Hell," and advocate its abolition.[32] Such language and behavior is clearly contrary to the peaceable conversation and walking of earlier Quakerism. Moreover, politicians thinking in the Quaker tradition, such as William Penn and John Dickinson, referred to the constitution and government as sacred institutions. Nevertheless, Mott responded to Garrisonian hostility to the Constitution by saying, "[The abolitionists] have found it their duty to come out against the Constitution and Government of the country, as it is at present construed... I am glad... of the progress evident in this."[33] Therefore, while they crusaded for individual rights and rejected institutional coercion, radical Quakers and their followers applied their own coercion to the polity with the intent to disrupt it as much as need be to achieve their ends – to abolish it along with civil injustice.

What Quakers had always striven for, and what Mott, Garrison, and their followers abandoned to one degree or another in their pursuit of individual liberties, was the security for liberty that a balanced system would ensure. Barclay wrote *Anarchy of the Ranters* (renamed blandly in 1822 *A Treatise on Church Government*) in hopes that Quakers could avoid both tyranny and anarchy in their ecclesiastical government. There was no aspect of traditional Quaker politics that would have supported Elizabeth Cady Stanton's goal to "Educate women into rebellion."[34] For many, if not most Quakers, the question had never been *whether* slaves should be freed or women given equal rights, but *how*. In traditional Quakerism, the ends did not justify the means because the wrong means might destroy the polity. And when the polity is destroyed, the freedom of all is lost. As president of Delaware, John Dickinson

[31] Mott, "Keep Yourselves from Idols," in Greene, *Lucretia Mott*, 173–74.
[32] Perry, *Radical Abolitionism*, 189; James H. Hutson, "The Creation of the Constitution: Scholarship at a Standstill," *Reviews in American History* vol. 12, no. 4 (1984), 463–477, 465.
[33] Mott, "Law of Progress," in Greene, *Lucretia Mott*, 77–78.
[34] Elizabeth Cady Stanton quoted in Sandra Stanley Holton, "'To Educate Women into Rebellion': Elizabeth Cady Stanton and the Creation of a Transatlantic Network of Suffragists," *American Historical Review* vol. 99, no. 4 (1994), 1112–36.

drafted a bill for the *gradual* abolition of slavery in that state.[35] Slavery was abhorrent to him, yet he believed that cautious, measured manumission was the only way to do it without risking the polity. Freedoms should be introduced into society slowly in order that both individuals and the established order can have time to adjust to adjust to it properly. Nonresisters, for their part, abandoned the political and ecclesiastical process that in many ways defined Quakerism.

Even as Garrison and others protested that they were following in the steps of great reformers such as John Woolman, they rejected the conciliatory language that more moderate Friends used to preach against slavery while also preserving the harmony and perpetuity of the Union. Garrison wrote to Mott that "there seems to be something like an attempt to propitiate the spirit of these cruel and ungodly oppressors, in a way which I do not like."[36] Unlike Woolman, Garrison had apparently given up on the possibility of salvation for these "ungodly" people.

For nonresisters and come-outers, perfectionism was possible for individuals – or rather, for some individuals. For traditional Quakers, perfectionism also applied to the civil constitution. This idea was exemplified in how Friends actualized their ecclesiastical and civil constitutions and governments. Despite tremendous convulsions in the early Society and in Pennsylvania government, Friends never separated as a Society, except briefly during the Keithian Controversy and during the Revolution, or resorted to the overthrow of the government to achieve the liberties they sought. Instead, as we have seen, they worked through peaceful extralegal means or within the system for reform rather than revolution.

Early Quakers had a theory and practice of civil disobedience that would gradually lead to constitutional perfection, but we cannot say the same for the most noteworthy of Quaker reformers in the nineteenth century, who abandoned the key element that defined civil disobedience – political obligation. Although seventeenth- and eighteenth-century Quaker politicians demonstrated in their theory and practice that profound reforms could be achieved peacefully within the political system, prior to the Civil War, many Americans seemed not yet to have learned this lesson. The radical Hicksites and their followers articulated the question clearly on the minds of many Americans in the Antebellum period: Could a constitution be amended peacefully, or must it be abandoned when it or the union it symbolizes is imperfect?

With such a vigorous public campaign for the rights of the individual over the collective, it is interesting to speculate about the long-term effects that radical Hicksites and their followers had on the rise of what Tocqueville, observing Americans during this period, called *individualism*. Today the popular connotation of this word is positive, and it is used as a synonym for *individuality*;

---

[35] John Dickinson, "An Act for the Gradual Abolition of Slavery," Logan Family Papers, vol. 30, HSP.
[36] William Lloyd Garrison to Lucretia Mott, April 28, 1840, in Hallowell, *Life and Letters*, 140.

but for Tocqueville, it was a particularly detrimental development in American culture. He described it as a focus on the individual to the exclusion of the rest of society that "dams the spring of public virtues" and eventually "attacks and destroys all the others too and finally merges in egoism."[37] As we have seen, Quakers were always concerned that many within their meeting might develop a "libertine spirit" that was difficult to keep in check. And they recognized that non-Quakers also took this spirit away from their meetings instead of "bearing the cross" of membership. This was most certainly at issue with the Quaker-infused political culture in Pennsylvania before the Revolution and the disproportionate number of radical Revolutionaries that emerged from the colony. And as certainly, if they looked, scholars would find a connection between Quakerly libertinism and the rise of American individualism. Radical Quakers and their followers left it instead to their more moderate and more obscure brethren to show them how to advocate both rights and political obligation at the same time.

Traditional Quaker Thought in the Nineteenth Century

Despite the dominance of radical Hicksite Quakerism in the reform movements, the traditional strain of Quaker theologico-political thought remained in a few thinkers and actors. Their mark was, however, relatively faint, and they have largely disappeared from Anglo-American historical consciousness. Thomas Clarkson and Jonathan Dymond were among the traditionalists who made an impression both within and without the Society of Friends.[38] What we see for the first time during this period are explicit expressions of many of the principles of Quaker theologico-politics that in the seventeenth and eighteenth centuries must be deduced mainly from their practice and theology. They articulated the same priorities – a strong central government with a divinely ordained constitution, and the imperative to resist it peacefully by breaking unjust laws with the aim of reform.

Thomas Clarkson (1760–1846) was an abolitionist and president of the British and Foreign Anti-Slavery Society, which still exists today as Anti-Slavery International. What is most significant about Clarkson's writing is his near-complete articulation of the definition of civil disobedience. Following almost exactly Edward Burrough's statement in 1661, Clarkson wrote in 1806, "As the governed in [the case of an unjust law] ought in obedience to God . . . refuse a compliance with the law of their own governors, so they ought to be prepared to submit to the penalties which are annexed to such a refusal, and on no account, if just representations made in the quiet spirit of their religion, are not

---

37 Tocqueville, *Democracy in America*, 507.

38 Although Clarkson and Dymond were British Friends, with the strong transatlantic Quaker network, their influence would not have been markedly less in America than that of American Friends. On this network, which persisted long after the American Revolution and still exists to some extent today, see Alison Olson, "The Lobbying of London Quakers for Pennsylvania Friends," *PMHB* vol. 117, no. 3 (1993), 131–52.

likely to be effectual, to take up arms or resist them by force."[39] This statement lacks only two components to make it complete. The first is the condition that the breaking of the law must be public. At this time, publicity was still understood by all to be the Quaker way. The other is that it should be for change and not merely to appease the conscience. A statement of this principle was forthcoming.

Jonathan Dymond (1796–1828), a British linen draper and political theorist, gives us perhaps the most explicit discussion of civil disobedience by any Quaker until the twentieth century.[40] In *Essays on the Principles of Morality and on the Private and Political Rights and Obligations of Mankind* (1829) he lays out the tenets that have defined Quaker civic engagement since nearly the beginning and, in doing so, comes tantalizingly close to using the very phrase in question. First, he identifies the imperative for political obligation to the divinely ordained constitution. "[T]he general duty of Civil obedience," he writes, is "*because* government is an institution sanctioned by the Deity."[41] Dymond went on to articulate even more aspects typical of Quaker philosophy than did Clarkson, including the reason–revelation dilemma, the perpetuity and mutability of the constitution, and the popular sovereignty that could change it. In an interesting mixture of the language of reason and progressive revelation, he described the changeable constitution:

The science of government ... acquires a constant accession of light. ... Forms of Government should be capable of admitting, without disturbance, those improvements which experience may dictate, or the advancing conditions may require. Upon these grounds no constitution should be regarded as absolutely and sacredly fixed, so that none ought and none have the right to alter it.

And he continued with a statement of what Quakers had known and practiced since the establishment of their ecclesiastical polity, and which they continued in their civil polity – the principle of constituent sovereignty. "The question of right," he explained, "is easily settled. It is inherent in the community, or in the legislature as their agents."[42]

Although for some Quakers the difference between reason and the Light was becoming negligible, a few such as Dymond still maintained the distinction, at least when it came to civil resistance. He adhered to the traditional understanding put forth by the early Quakers that reason might allow various courses of action, but divine revelation only one. When following the law of nature – the law of reason – all means are permitted to resist government.

---

[39] Thomas Clarkson, *A Portraiture of Quakerism*, 3: 7. On Clarkson, see Ellen Gibson Wilson, *Thomas Clarkson: A Biography* (New York: St. Martin's Press, 1990).

[40] There is no extant biography of Dymond. For a brief discussion of his life and work, see Jones, *The Later Periods of Quakerism*, 716–17.

[41] Dymond, *Essays on the Principles of Morality*, 323, 324.

[42] Ibid., 337.

But, said Dymond, "When we turn from the law of nature to *Christianity*, we find, as we are wont, that the moral cord is tightened, and that *not every* means of opposing government for the public good is permitted to us."[43] The government, he wrote, "should be susceptible to *peaceable* change"; "Christianity forbids an armed resistance to the civil power."[44] Finally, Dymond added one of the missing components of Clarkson's description: Disobedience must generally be undertaken with the "view to an alteration of the existing institutions."[45] At least one scholar of the period has found that Dymond's work not only prefigured the work of important nineteenth-century dissenters but also likely shaped it.[46]

If non-Quakers have heard of Dymond, it is likely because he was read and noted by Henry David Thoreau (1817–62). While at Harvard, Thoreau wrote that he undertook an "examination of Mr. Dymond's opinions."[47] But although he read this Quaker theorist, who was very clear in his explanation of civil disobedience, and although during his life he was surrounded by social reform movements that had grown out of and were in large part led by Quakers, he did not espouse or practice their teachings in their entirety. It is one of the biggest misconceptions in American scholarship that Thoreau was a civil disobedient. Only a few scholars have noted that his famous work, which they call *On Civil Disobedience* (1866), was actually originally entitled *On Resistance to Civil Government*; and this was not merely because the term *civil disobedience* was not yet in use. If we adhere to the definition used in this study, Thoreau did not advocate it. Nor did he practice it in his own resistance. He does not make acceptance of legal punishment a condition of resistance, nor must resistance necessarily be peaceful. Further, his resistance was not undertaken publicly. He was imprisoned for not paying taxes to support the Mexican-American War, but he did not announce his intentions, and was not even arrested until years later. At the time, he did it to appease his own conscience, not to convince the world of the injustice of the war. Neither should we overlook the fact that he openly supported violent rebellion. He was a champion and sympathizer of John Brown's bloody raid on Harper's Ferry.[48] As important as Thoreau's influence was on later reformers, we must look elsewhere for a theory and practice of true civil disobedience.

---

[43] Ibid., 323.

[44] Ibid., 337 and 326.

[45] Ibid., 330. He qualifies statement by saying that one ought to resist orders to commit crimes without a view to changing the system.

[46] James Duban, "Thoreau, Garrison, and Dymond: Unbending Firmness of Mind," *American Literature* vol. 57, no. 2 (1985), 309–17, 310–11.

[47] Thoreau quoted in Duban, "Thoreau, Garrison, and Dymond," 312.

[48] See William H. Herr, "Thoreau: A Civil Disobedient?" *Ethics* vol. 85, no. 1 (1974), 87–91; and Daniel Walker Howe, *Henry David Thoreau on the Duty of Civil Disobedience: An Inaugural Lecture delivered before the University of Oxford on 21 may 1990* (Oxford: Clarendon Press, 1990).

Quaker Activism in the Twentieth Century

As in the nineteenth century, Quakers and Quaker organizations in the twentieth century were among the seminal actors in the reform movements, most notably women's suffrage and civil rights. Yet most of the individuals are unknown except to scholars in the fields of civil rights or peace studies, or to activists themselves.

Alice Paul (1885–1977), president of the National American Woman Suffrage Association, was the most important woman in the suffrage movement. The passage of the Nineteenth Amendment was a direct result of her organization of one of the largest protest campaigns in American history. Under Paul's direction, thousands of women calling themselves the "Silent Sentinels" picketed the White House for eighteen months from January 1917 until June 1919 when the "Susan B. Anthony Amendment" passed both houses. In spite of the progressive reforms underway in other areas, the political climate was not friendly to such disruption. With the country at war, to dissent from the government on any issue was tantamount to treason in the eyes of many. Over the months, dozens of women were arrested, imprisoned, and some of them beaten and tortured psychologically. They demanded political prisoner status to secure humane treatment. Paul herself went on a hunger strike and was force fed.[49] Though her tactics were extremely disruptive, they were submissive, and never violent or destructive.

Paul's Quaker credentials are impressive. A descendant of William Penn, she explained that "I don't know whether I had *any* [ancestor] who wasn't a Quaker."[50] She was raised by devout Quaker parents in "a little Quaker village" in New Jersey and attended Quakers schools, including Swarthmore College, which was "purely Quaker" at this time, and a school for training Friends in social work in Woodbridge, England.[51] As she was growing up, she said that "I never met anybody who wasn't a Quaker, and I never heard of anybody who wasn't a Quaker."[52] To be a suffragist was a natural (or rather, a divine) step for Paul. In her community of Friends, the right of women to vote was taken for granted; this was just one of the "many things in which the world hadn't yet come along."[53] She followed early Quaker women's rights activists Susan B. Anthony and Elizabeth Cady Stanton and was a colleague of Jane Addams, herself raised by a Hicksite father. Paul's biographer, Christine A. Lunardini, describes her as "perhaps the single truly charismatic figure in the twentieth-century suffrage movement" and adds that "Max Weber might have used Alice Paul as his model in developing the concept of the charismatic

---

[49] Christine A. Lunardini, *From Equal Suffrage to Equal Rights: Alice Paul and the National Women's Party, 1910–1928* (New York: New York University Press, 1986), 123–49.

[50] *Conversations with Alice Paul: Woman Suffrage and the Equal Rights Amendment.* An interview conducted by Amelia Fry (Regents of the University of California, 1976), 6.

[51] Ibid., 5.

[52] Ibid., 15.

[53] Ibid., 33.

leader."[54] Her personality and ethic were quintessentially Quaker. She was a polarizing figure who elicited extreme comments from her followers and detractors. By some she was considered charitable, patient, well-intentioned, and conscientious.[55] The response of her followers, suggests Lunardini, "can be understood as a symbol of their search for balance and equality in a world they perceived to be disorderly."[56] She was, according to her fellow suffragists, "a genius for organization."[57] On the other hand, she was also perceived to be abrasive, a "fanatic," and a "martyr" for the women's cause.[58] Her efforts to secure women's rights continued into the 1970s as she fought for the passage of the Equal Rights Amendment, a measure she helped create.

None would dispute the claim that Martin Luther King, Jr., was the pre-eminent leader of civil rights reform in the nation's history. Few, however, know about his intellectual and spiritual mentors. Because of the disjuncture between Quaker history and mainstream American history, most scholars have assumed that King drew his inspiration primarily from Thoreau and Gandhi. And, to be sure, these men were important teachers for him. Similarly, some King scholars assume that his drive for reform came from his Baptist tradition. Reasonable though these assumptions are, they are misguided if taken as the main source of his thought. For reasons discussed previously, he could not have gotten a full-fledged theory of civil disobedience from Thoreau. Also, although King had been exposed to the teachings of Gandhi in college, learning about them theoretically had not caused him to internalize the ethic and strategy of nonviolent resistance. Finally, the imperative for social activism was not strong in the black ministers with whom King associated; they were more concerned with bringing people to Jesus than effecting change.[59] A little-documented fact is that Quakers were a major impulsion behind the Civil Rights Movement. Two Friends who were crucial to it were Richard Gregg (1885–1974) and Bayard Rustin (1912–87). Although they were activists in their own right and engaged in civil disobedience, they have been overshadowed by their more famous successor and protégé.

No doubt Gandhi was a powerful influence on King, but this assertion should be qualified and amended in some important ways. First, it was Gregg who brought Gandhian philosophy to America. In addition to publishing several early works with a Quaker press, in 1934 he produced the first major work in the United States on Gandhi's peaceful resistance, *The Power of Nonviolence*, with an introduction written by Rufus Jones, a foremost Quaker historian and theologian. This work enumerates the same principles as those that appeared

54 Lunardini, *From Equal Suffrage to Equal Rights*, xiv–xv.
55 Ibid., 9.
56 Ibid., xvi.
57 Lucy Berns quoted in ibid., 10.
58 Ibid., 9, 10.
59 John D'Emilio, *Lost Prophet: The Life and Times of Bayard Rustin* (Chicago: University of Chicago Press, 2003), 226.

later in *An Introduction to the American Friends Service Committee* (1962).[60]
Scholars agree that Gregg's work "more than any source helped to popularize
Gandhi's teachings in America."[61] As a group that believes in the universality
of the Light, Quakers were likewise ecumenical in their use of sources to support their teachings. Gregg's use of Gandhian principles was hardly a stretch,
considering Gandhi's own philosophy was shaped in large part by the Sermon
on the Mount.[62] In his forward to a 1959 edition of *The Power of Nonviolence*,
King calls the book "a classic."[63]

Second, Gregg did not merely popularize Gandhi; he also added his own
concepts to the theory of nonviolent resistance and made an original contribution to King's thinking. In addition to Gandhi's *satyagraha*, Gregg put forth
his own interpretation of peaceful resistance, calling it "moral jiu jitsu" – the
method of knocking one's opponent off balance with love. This is in the same
tradition as Dymond, who wrote, "He that resists by force, may be overcome
by greater force," but "nothing can overcome a calm and fixed determination
not to obey."[64] Gregg's aim and his method of disobedience fit the mold of
the Quaker bureaucratic libertine of the seventeenth and eighteenth centuries;
it centered on Quaker process. "The process," said Gregg, "is sure and, if the
method is faithfully adhered to, the result is certain."[65] His end, liberty and
unity through peaceful means, was explicit: "War also acts to unify nations
engaged in it. But the unity engendered by non-violent resistance is deeper,
more closely knit and more permanent than that produced by war."[66] Ignoring
even Thoreau, not to mention the centuries of Quakerism before Gregg, one
historian has called him "the first American to develop a substantial theory of
nonviolent resistance."[67]

It is hardly an exaggeration to say that Bayard Rustin was the single most
important influence on the thought and practice of King. Rustin was a birthright
Quaker, attended a Quaker-founded school for black children, and was a
member of a meeting in Manhattan. His biographer John D'Emilio writes that

[60] Judith Hicks Stiehm, "Contemporary Theories of Nonviolent Resistance" (Ph.D. Diss.,
Columbia University, 1969), 64.

[61] Maurice Isserman, *If I Had a Hammer*, 132. See also Richard G. Fox, "Passage from India,"
in R. Fox and O. Starn, eds., *Between Resistance and Revolution: Cultural Politics and Social
Protest* (New Brunswick, NJ: Rutgers University Press, 1997), 65–82.

[62] V. V. Ramana Murti, "Influence of the Western Tradition on Gandhian Doctrine," *Philosophy
East and West* vol. 18, no. 1/2 (1968), 55–65; A. L. Herman, "Satyagraha: A New Indian Word
for Some Old Ways of Western Thinking," *Philosophy East and West* vol. 19, no. 2 (1968),
123–42.

[63] Martin Luther King, Jr., Forward to *The Power of Nonviolence*, Richard Gregg (Nyack, NY:
Fellowship Publications, 1959).

[64] Dymond, *Essays on the Principles of Morality*, 110.

[65] Richard Gregg, *The Power of Nonviolence* (Philadelphia: J.B. Lippincott Company, 1934), 108.

[66] Ibid.

[67] Joseph Kip Kosek, "Richard Gregg, Mohandas Gandhi, and the Strategy of Nonviolent Resistance," *The Journal of American History* vol. 91, no. 4 (2005), 1318–48, 1318.

Rustin left a profound mark – on the unfolding of the Montgomery bus boycott as a national story, on the evolution of King's role as a national leader, on the particular association of nonviolence with Montgomery and King. Rustin was as responsible as anyone else for the insinuation of nonviolence into the very heart of what became the most powerful social movement in twentieth-century America.[68]

Like Gregg, Rustin drew on Gandhi. He also looked to Marx for his inspiration, and Gregg's *The Power of Nonviolence* was an "essential primer" for him.[69] Like other Quaker activists, the tradition in which he was raised provided the foundation for his principles, and he passed it self-consciously on to King. D'Emilio explains that "the Quaker inflection to his faith, with its pacifist tradition and nonconforming stance, made social activism his gospel."[70] Rustin handed these traditional principles down to King: universality of the Light, peaceful process, and activism. It would not be difficult to convince a Baptist minister that "the spark of God is in each of us"; by this time, Quakers were hardly the only people to reject predestination or retain hope for the regeneration of man.[71] But the other principles were not native to King's tradition, nor had he acquired them by 1955 when he met Rustin. He was not a pacifist. In fact, when Rustin visited King's home for the first time, there were guns lying about the house. Nor was he an activist.[72] For Quakers, of course, pacifism and activism were intimately connected.

In the first place, Rustin said in his schooling of King, "We cannot remain honest unless we are opposed to injustice wherever it occurs."[73] This meant that there was an imperative to enter the public sphere to challenge the dominant culture. But it also meant that they must do so in a way that would convince, not coerce. "We pacifists urge nonviolence," he said, "because if change toward justice is to take place, it must be in an atmosphere where creative conflict and debate are possible."[74] In an assertion of Quaker process, he wrote, "We pacifists maintain that the law of ends and means does, in fact operate."[75] As an indication of the nonexplicit way – by example as opposed to overt instruction – in which Quakers generally transmit their tradition, it is interesting to see that Rustin had to study Quaker process and apply the traditional principles himself to learn through experience. He learned that peaceful

---

[68] D'Emilio, *Lost Prophet*, 237. The reason Rustin's name is not more closely associated with King's would seem to be because of the former's homosexuality. As D'Emilio explains it, Rustin was reticent about being too public a figure for this reason (237), and, for a period he and King became estranged as an opponent of King's threatened to levy charges against him of a sexual affair with Rustin (298). On Rustin, see also Jervis Anderson, *Bayard Rustin: The Troubles I've Seen: A Biography* (New York: Harper-Collins, 1997).

[69] Ibid., 52.

[70] Ibid., 236.

[71] Rustin in ibid., 459.

[72] Ibid., 230.

[73] Rustin in ibid., 459.

[74] Bayard Rustin, "Nonviolence on Trial," in Staughton Lynd, ed., *Nonviolence in America: A Documentary History* (Indianapolis: Bobbs-Merrill, 1966), 496.

[75] Ibid., 495.

dissent is not easy, and neither is balancing dissent and unity, while still making progress toward the Truth. "As a Quaker," he explained, "I started out
by saying that I thought we had to make all decisions by consensus." But he
eventually realized that "[c]onsensus does not mean that everybody agrees. It
means that the person who disagrees must disagree so vigorously that he is
prepared to fight with everybody else."[76] Of course, we must understand that
"to fight" in this context means "creative conflict" or "positive confrontation"
rather than hostility. Robert Barclay wrote that it is "unlawful to do Evil, that
Good may come of it... it is far better to suffer Loss."[77] King again echoed
this fundamental Quaker process. "Constructive ends," he said, "can never
give absolute moral justification to destructive means, because in the final analysis the end is preëxistent in the mean."[78] Moreover, he recognized the same
imperative for balance between the individual and community that Quakers
had struggled with in their process for centuries. He wrote, "The Kingdom of
God is neither the thesis of individual enterprise not the antithesis of collective
enterprise, but a synthesis which reconciles the truths of both."[79]

This "creative conflict" is the way in which Rustin counseled King toward
activism. For Quakers, looking for "God's spark" inside and then peacefully,
but firmly disagreeing with those who would sanction injustice was a duty.
Jonathan Dymond explained that "the business of man is to act as the Christian
citizen – not merely to prepare himself for another world, but to do such good
as he may, political as well as social, in the present."[80] Rustin believed that this
was what he bequeathed to King. Rather than saving souls for the next world,
Rustin taught him "to save souls in this life by making it simpler for people to
be good." He gave him "a socialist education" and taught him the importance
of modeling the process.[81]

Not just his teachings, but Rustin himself launched King into the public
sphere. He was not only the inspiration behind much of King's work, but, at
first, he was actually King's voice. The first publication under King's name was
Rustin's work – "Our Struggle," published in 1956 in *Liberation*.[82] Reflecting
on King's relationship with Rustin, one contemporary asked: "How would it
have been possible for King not to have become a protégé of Bayard? Not how
did he, but how could he not have been?"[83]

We need not hunt through King's papers or his more obscure publications
to find only a smattering of statements that prove Quaker influence. He wrote
it all in one place as he sat in a jail cell in Birmingham. He presented himself
as one of the primitive Christian apostles who roamed the land proclaiming

[76] Rustin quoted in D'Emilio, *Lost Prophet*, 342.
[77] Barclay, *Anarchy*, 41.
[78] Martin Luther King, Jr., "Pilgrimage to Nonviolence," in *Nonviolence in America*, 211.
[79] Ibid., 213.
[80] Dymond, *Essays on the Principles of Morality*, 326.
[81] D'Emilio, *Lost Prophet*, 238, 231.
[82] Ibid., 239.
[83] David McReynolds quoted in D'Emilio, *Lost Prophet*, 236.

the "gospel of freedom."[84] He described the process, the steps, one must take to bring one's case before the people: "(1) collection of the facts to determine whether injustices are alive; (2) negotiation; (3) self-purification; and (4) direct action." Their "very bodies" would be presented "as a means of laying our case before the conscience of the local and the national community."[85] Recognizing the performative aspect of this sort of protest, he explained that the disobedience "seeks to dramatize the issue." The resulting "constructive, nonviolent tension," he continued, "is necessary for growth" within the community.[86] He addressed the usual misconception by outsiders that had attended all Quaker civil disobedience – that this behavior was a sort of antinomianism, a rejection of civil law in favor of some internal, private law. "At first glance," he acknowledged, "it may seem rather paradoxical for us consciously to break laws." He explained to his readers how to distinguish between just and unjust laws.[87] Following Barclay, who assured King Charles II of his fidelity to the government, he continued, "In no sense do I advocate evading or defying the law" clandestinely. "That would lead to anarchy. One who breaks an unjust law must do so *openly, lovingly*... and with a willingness to accept the penalty. I submit that an individual who breaks a law that conscience tells him is unjust and who willingly accepts the penalty of imprisonment in order to arouse the conscience of the community over its injustice, is in reality expressing the highest respect for law."[88]

The American Friends Service Committee found this letter to be "an eloquent statement of the nonviolent approach to the restructuring of our social order" and linked it with early Quakers, who were "led by conscience to practice civil disobedience as a witness to the supremacy of God's commands over the dictates of men."[89] The Society of Friends could not have written a better statement of their traditional theologico-political philosophy themselves. Thus, in May of 1963, Quakers once again became the "First Publishers of Truth" when they released the first 50,000 copies of King's letter to the world.[90]

---

[84] Martin Luther King, Jr., *Letter from a Birmingham City Jail*, 3

[85] Ibid., 4.

[86] Ibid., 5.

[87] Ibid., 6–7.

[88] Ibid., 7

[89] Colin W. Bell, preface to ibid.

[90] S. Jonathan Bass, *Blessed Are the Peacemakers: Martin Luther King, Jr., Eight White Religious Leaders, and the "Letter from Birmingham Jail"* (Baton Rouge: Louisiana State University Press, 2001), 141.

Bibliography

Primary Sources—Manuscripts

American Philosophical Society
John Harvey Powell Papers.

Delaware Public Archives
Small Manuscript Collection, John Dickinson Letters.

Friends Historical Library, Swarthmore (PA) College
John Alston Papers, 1797–1847.
Elizabeth Ashbridge. "Some Account of the forepart of the life of Elizabeth Ashbridge," 1713–55.
Association of Friends for the Free Instruction of Adult Colored Persons, 1795–1905.
Bringhurst Papers, 1732–1819. (transcribed)
Journal of Joshua Brown, 1717–98.
Journal of Margaret Ellis, 1752.
Journal of Joshua Evans, 1731–98.
Journal of Benjamin Ferris, 1740–71.
Fisher Warner Family Papers, Miers Fisher, 1748–1819.
Journal of John Kinsey, 1693–1750.
Lindley Murray Papers, 1785–1830.
Journal of Ann Moore,1756–62 (transcribed).
Mary Pennington, A Brief Account of some of my exercises from my Childhood, 1680.
Philadelphia Yearly Meeting, Minutes,1682–1746, 1747–79.
———, Miscellaneous papers, 1662–1790.
———, Meeting for Suffering, Minutes, miscellaneous papers, 1755–1800.
Journal of Charles Williams, 1785–87.
Miscellaneous Letters, Richardson Manuscripts, 1773–1862.

Historical Society of Pennsylvania

American Society for Promoting Useful Knowledge, 1790.
Cox-Parrish-Wharton Papers, 1600–1900.
John Dickinson, Commonplace Book.
Logan Family Papers, 1664–1871.
Maria Dickinson Logan Collection, 1671–1890.
R. R. Logan Collection, 1671–1882.
Isaac Norris Letterbook, 1719–56.
Norris Family Papers, 1742–1860.
Pemberton Papers, Letters.
Diaries of John Pemberton, 1777–81.
William Penn Papers, Domestic and Miscellaneous Letters, 1654–1735.
Richard Peters Letterbook, 1739–43.
Peter Stephen Du Ponceau Papers, 1760–1864.
Philadelphia Society for Alleviating the Miseries of Public Prisons, 1787–1793.

Library Company of Philadelphia

John Dickinson Papers.
Powell, J. H., Finding Aid for John Dickinson Papers.

Library of Congress

Public Records Office Transcripts, Treasury Papers.

Quaker Collection, Haverford (PA) College

Allinson Family Papers, 1698–1939.
American Friends Letters, c. 1676–1986.
Associated Executive Committee of Friends on Indian Affairs, 1758–1929.
Journal of George Churchman, 1759–1813.
Dictionary of Quaker Biography
Henry Drinker Correspondence, 1777–1778.
Thomas Pym Cope Collection, 1768–1854.
Female Society for the Relief of the Distressed and Employment of the Poor, 1795–
    ca.1900.
Pemberton Papers, 1741–89.
Philadelphia Yearly Meeting, Books of Discipline,1689, 1704, 1719, 1761, 1797, 1806,
    1997.
———, Minutes, 1739–41.
Henry Simmons, Jr., Papers, 1796–1800.
Journal of Ann Cooper Whitall, 1716–97.
Roberts Autograph Collection.
Nicholas Waln Family Papers, 1742–1813.

Primary Sources—Published

Adams, John. *Twenty-Six Letters, upon Interesting Subjects, Respecting the Revolution
    of America.* New York, 1780.

_____. *The Works of John Adams, Second President of the United States: with a Life of the Author, Notes and Illustrations.* Charles Francis Adams, ed. Boston: Little, Brown and Co., 1856.

The Address of some of the Peaceable and Well Affected Freeholders and Inhabitants of the Town and County of Philadelphia. Philadelphia, 1693.

An Address to the Rev. Alison, the Rev. Mr. Ewing, and others, Trustees of the Corporation for the Relief of Presbyterian Ministers, their Widows and Children: Being a Vindication of the Quakers from the Aspersions of the said Trustees in their Letter published in the London Chronicle, No. 1223. By a Lover of Truth, Philadelphia, 1765.

An Answer to an Invidious Pamphlet, intituled, A Brief State.... London, 1755.

Armstrong, Edward, ed. *Correspondence between William Penn and James Logan, Secretary of the Province and Others.* 2 vols. Philadelphia: The Historical Society of Pennsylvania, 1870–72.

Barclay, Robert. *The Anarchy of the Ranters and other Libertines.* London, 1676.

_____. *An Apology for the True Christian Divinity* [1675]. New York, 1827.

Basler, Roy P., ed. *The Collected Works of Abraham Lincoln*, New Brunswick, NJ: Rutgers University Press, 1953.

Bellers, John. *Essays about the poor, manufactures, trade, plantations, & immorality.* London, 1699.

Benezet, Anthony. *Memoirs of the Life of Anthony Benezet.* Roberts Vaux, ed. Philadelphia, 1817.

Besse, Joseph. *A Collection of Sufferings of the People Called Quakers for the Testimony of a Good Conscience.* London, 1753.

Bishop, George. *The Burden of Babylon and the Triumph of Zion as it was seen in the Valley of Vision.* London, 1661.

Boyd, Julian P., Barbara B. Oberg, et al., eds. *The Papers of Thomas Jefferson*, 34 vols. + Princeton, NJ: Princeton University Press, 1950.

Brissot de Warville, Jean-Paul. *A Critical Examination of the Marquis de Chatellux's Travels in North America in a Letter Addressed to the Marquis; principally intended as a Refutation of his Opinions Concerning the Quakers, the Negroes, the People, and Mankind.* Philadelphia, 1788.

Bugg, Francis. *Hidden Things brought to Light. Whereby The Fox is Unkennel'd: And the Bowells of Quakerism Ript up, laid open, and expos'd to Publick View; by a Dialogue Tripartite. Whereby the Quakers Inside (to speak Figuratively) is turn'd Outward; and the Great Mystery of the Little Whore Farther Unfolded.* London, 1707.

_____. *The Pilgrim's Progress from Quakerism to Christianity.* London, 1698.

_____. *Quakerism Anatomized, and Finally Dissected: Shewing, from Plain Fact, that a Rigid Quaker is a Cruel Persecutor.* London, 1709.

_____. *A Retrospective-Glass for the Quakers*, (1710) republished in *A Finishing Stroke: Or, Some Gleanings, Collected out of the Quakers Books... Whereby The Great Mystery of the Little Whore is farther Unfolded.* London, 1712.

Burnaby, Andrew. *Travels Through the Middle Settlements in North-America in the years 1759 and 1760 with Observations upon the State of the Colonies.* Ithaca, NY: Cornell University Press, 1963.

Burrough, Edward. *A Message for Instruction to all the Rulers, Judges, and Magistrates...* London, 1658.

Butterfield, L. H., ed. *Diary and Autobiography of John Adams.* Cambridge, MA: Belknap Press, Harvard University, 1961.

————, ed. *The Letters of Benjamin Rush*. Princeton, NJ: Princeton University Press, 1951.

Byllynge, Edward. *A Mite of Affection*. London, 1659.

————. *A Word of Reproof, and Advice*. London, 1659.

Chew, Samuel. *The Speech of Samuel Chew, Esq. Chief Judge of the Counties of Newcastle, Kent, and Sussex on Delaware. On the Lawfulness of Defence against an Armed Enemy. Delivered from the Bench to the Grand Jury of the County of Newcastle, Nov. 21. 1741*. Philadelphia, 1775.

Churchman, John. *An Account of the Gospel Labours and Christian Experiences of a Faithful Minister of Christ*. Philadelphia, 1779.

Clarkson, Thomas. *A Portraiture of Quakerism. Taken from a view of the Education and Discipline, Social Manners, Civil and Political Economy, Religious Principles and Character of the Society of Friends*. 3 vols. New York, 1806.

Cockson, Edward. *Rigid Quaker, Cruel Persecutor*. London, 1705.

Conference Between a Parish-Priest and a Quaker; Published for the preventing (if possible) the vile deceits of priestcraft in America. Philadelphia, 1725.

Conversations with Alice Paul: Woman Suffrage and the Equal Rights Amendment. An interview conducted by Amelia Fry. Regents of the University of California, 1976.

Conway, Moncure Daniel, ed. *The Writings of Thomas Paine*. New York: G. P. Putnam and Sons, 1896.

Crèvecœur, J. Hector St. John de. *Letters from an American Farmer*. New York: Oxford University Press, 1997.

G. D., of the Inner-Temple. *The Quaker No Occasional Conformist, but a Sincere Christian in his Life*. London, 1703.

Dickinson, John. *An Address to the Committee of Correspondence in Barbados*. Philadelphia, 1766.

————. "Friends and Countrymen" [Address on the Stamp Act]. Philadelphia, 1765.

————. *An Essay of a Frame of Government for Pennsylvania*. Philadelphia, 1776.

————. *An Essay on the Constitutional Power of Great-Britain over the Colonies in America*. Philadelphia, 1774.

————. *Late Regulations Respecting the British Colonies on the Continent of America Considered*. Philadelphia, 1765.

————. *A Reply to a piece called The speech of Joseph Galloway, Esquire*. Philadelphia, 1764.

————. *A Speech Delivered in the House of Assembly of the Province of Pennsylvania*. Philadelphia, 1764.

————. *Letters from a Farmer in Pennsylvania, To the Inhabitants of the British Colonies* (Boston, 1768) in *Empire and Nation*, 2nd ed. Forrest McDonald, ed. Indianapolis: Liberty Fund, 1999.

————. *The Letters of Fabius in 1788 on the Federal Constitution*. facsimile rpt. Kila, MT: Kessinger Publishing, 2004.

————. "Notes for a Speech (III)," in James H. Hutson, ed. *Supplement to Max Farrand's* The Records of the Federal Convention of 1787. New Haven, 1987; 137–38.

Dickinson, John, and Thomas Jefferson. *A Declaration by the Representatives of the United Colonies of North-America, Now Met in Congress at Philadelphia, Setting Forth the Causes and Necessity of Their Taking Up Arms*. Philadelphia, 1775.

diGiacomantonio, William Charles, et al., eds. *Documentary History of the First Federal Congress of the United States of America*, vol. XIV: *Debates in the House of*

Representatives, Third Session: December 1790–March 1791. Baltimore: The Johns Hopkins University Press, 1995.

Dulaney, Daniel. *Considerations on the Propriety of Imposing Taxes on the British Colonies.* New York, 1765.

Dunn, Richard S., and Mary Maples Dunn, eds. *The Papers of William Penn.* 5 vols. Philadelphia: University of Pennsylvania Press, 1981–87.

Dymond, Jonathan. *Essays on the Principles of Morality and on the Private and Political Rights and Obligations of Mankind.* New York, 1845.

Ellwood, Thomas. *A discourse concerning riots: occasioned by some of the people called Quakers, being imprisoned and indicted for a riot, for only being at a peaceable meeting to worship God.* London, 1683.

_____. *The History of the Life of Thomas Ellwood.* London, 1714.

Evans, William, and Thomas Evans, eds. *The Friends' Library: comprises journals, doctrinal treatises, and other writings of the Religious Society of Friends.* 16 vols. Philadelphia, 1837–50.

Faldo, John. *Quakerism no Christianity: Or, a Thorow Quaker no Christian proved by the Quakers Principles, detected out of their chief Writers . . . with . . . an Account of their Foundation laid in Popery.* London, 1675.

Farrand, Max, ed. *The Records of the Federal Convention of 1787.* 3 vols. New Haven, CT: Yale University Press, 1937.

Force, Peter, ed. *American Archives,* ser. 4. 9 vols. Washington, DC, 1837–53.

Ford, Paul Leicester, ed. *The Writings of Thomas Jefferson.* 10 vols. New York: G.P. Putnam, 1892–99.

Fox, George. *A Declaration from the Harmles & Innocent People of GOD called Quakers. Against all Plotters and Fighters in the World.* London, 1660.

_____. *A Few Plain Words to be considered by those of the Army, or others that would have a parliament that is chosen by the voices of the people, to govern three nations. Wherein is shewn unto them according to the Scripture of Truth, that a parliament so chosen are not likely to govern for God and the good of his people.* London, 1660.

Gilpin, Thomas. *Exiles in Virginia: With Observations on the Conduct of the Society of Friends During the Revolutionary War Comprising the Official Papers of the Government Relating to that Period. 1777–1778.* (1848). facsimile rpt. Bowie, MD: Heritage Books, 2002.

Graydon, Alexander. *Memoirs of a Life Chiefly Passed in Pennsylvania within the Last Sixty Years.* Harrisburg, PA, 1811.

Greene, Dana, ed. *Lucretia Mott: Her Complete Sermons and Speeches.* New York: Edwin Mellen Press, 1980.

Gregg, Richard. *The Power of Nonviolence.* Introduction by Rufus Jones. Philadelphia: J. B. Lippincott Company, 1934.

Hallowell, Anna Davis, ed. *James and Lucretia Mott: Life and Letters.* Boston: Houghton Mifflin and Co., 1884.

Heinrichs, Johann. "Extracts form the Letter-Book of Captain Johann Heinrichs of the Hessian Jäger Corps, 1778–1780," *PMHB* vol. 22, no. 2 (1898): 137–70.

Hunt, Isaac. *A Looking-Glass for Presbyterians. Or A brief examination of their loyalty, merit, and other qualifications for government. With some animadversions on the Quaker unmask'd. Humbly addres'd to the consideration of the loyal freemen of Pennsylvania.* Philadelphia, 1764.

Hutson, James H. comp. and ed. *A Decent Respect to the Opinions of Mankind: Congressional State Papers, 1774–1776.* Washington, DC: Library of Congress, 1976.

———, ed. *Supplement to Max Farrand's* The Records of the Federal Convention of 1787. New Haven, CT: Yale University Press, 1987.

Janney, Samuel Macpherson. *Memoirs of Samuel M. Janney*. Philadelphia: Friends' Book Association, 1881.

Jennings, Samuel. *Truth Rescued from Falsehood, being and answer to a Late Scurrilous Piece Entituled*. The Case Put and Decided . . . London, 1699.

Kaminski, John, and Gaspare J. Saldino, et al., eds. *The Documentary History of the Ratification of the Constitution*, vols. 14, 16, 17. *Commentaries on the Constitution: Public and Private*. Madison: State Historical Society of Wisconsin, 1983, 1986, 1995.

Keith, George. *An Appeal from the Twenty Eight Judges to the Spirit of Truth & True Judgment in all Faithful Friends, called Quakers*. Philadelphia, 1692.

———. *The plea of the innocent against the false judgment of the guilty. . . .* Philadelphia, 1692.

King, Martin Luther, Jr. *Letter from a Birmingham City Jail*. Philadelphia: American Friends Service Committee, 1963.

———. Forward to *The Power of Nonviolence*, by Richard Gregg. Nyack, NY: Fellowship Publications, 1959.

Lay, Benjamin. *All Slave-Keepers That Keep the Innocent in Bondage, Apostates Pretending to lay Claim to the Pure & Holy Christian Religion*. Philadelphia, 1738.

Lewis, W. S., et al., eds. *Horace Walpole's Correspondence*. New Haven, CT: Yale University Press, 1971.

The Liberties of the Massachusetts Collonie in New England [1641]. *Old South Leaflets*. Boston: Directors of the Old South Work, 1896-1900s, 7: 261–267.

Lloyd, David. *A Defence of the Legislative Constitution of the Province of Pennsylvania as it now stands Confirmed and Established, by Law and Charter*. Philadelphia, 1728.

Locke, John. *A Letter Concerning Toleration*. London, 1689.

———. *On the Reasonableness of Christianity*. London, 1695.

———. *The Second Treatise of Government* in *The Selected Writings of John Locke*, Paul E. Sigmund, ed. New York: W. W. Norton & Co., 2005.

———. *Two Tracts of Government*. London, 1660–c.1662.

Logan, James. *The Antidote to A Vindication of the Legislative Power*. Philadelphia, 1725.

MacKinney, Gertrude, ed. *Pennsylvania Archives, Eighth Series: Votes and Proceedings of the House of Representatives of the Province of Pennsylvania*. 8 vols. Philadelphia: Franklin and Hall, 1931–35.

Minutes of the Provincial Council of the Province of Pennsylvania from the Organization to the Termination of the Proprietary Government. Vols. 1–4. Philadelphia: Jo. Severn, 1852.

Mitchell, James T., and Henry Flanders, eds. *Statutes-at-Large of Pennsylvania from 1682–1801*. 15 vols. Harrisburg, PA: Clarence M. Busch, State Printer of Pennsylvania, 1896–1911.

Moulton, Phillips P., ed. *The Journal and Major Essays of John Woolman*. Richmond, IN: Friends United Press, 1989.

"New York and Philadelphia in 1787," *PMHB* vol. 12, no. 1, (1888): 97–115.

Otis, James. *Rights of the British Colonies Asserted and Proved*. Boston, 1764.

Paine, Thomas. *Common Sense*. Philadelphia, 1776.

Pearson, John. *Anti-Christian Treachery Discover'd and Its Way Block'd Up....* London, 1686.

Penington, Isaac. "A Brief Account of What the People Called Quakers Desire in Reference to Civil Government" (1661) in *Penington's Works.* London, 1680.

———. *Concerning Persecution....* London, 1661.

———. *A Considerable Question About Government.* London, 1653.

———. *The Consideration of a Position Concerning the Book of Prayer....* London, 1660.

———. *The Fundamental Right, Safety and Liberty of the People.* London, 1651.

———. *Three Queries Propounded to the King and Parliament.* London, 1662.

———. *The Way of Life and Death Made Manifest, and Set Before Men.* London, 1680.

Penn, William. *The Continued Cry of the Oppressed for Justice....* London, 1675.

———. *A Discourse of the General Rule of Faith and Practice.* London, 1699.

———. *England's Great Interest in the Choice of this New Parliament.* London, 1678/79.

———. *England's Present Interest Discovered.* London, 1675.

———. *An Essay Towards the Present and Future Peace of Europe.* London, 1693.

———. *The Great Case of Liberty of Conscience.* London, 1670.

———. To James Logan. [Notes and Queries.] *PMHB* vol. 7 (1883): 228–36.

———. *No Cross, No Crown.* London, 1669.

———. *One Project for the Good of England: That is, Our Civil Union is Our Civil Safety.* London, 1679.

———. *A Persuasive to Moderation.* London, 1686.

———. *Some Fruits of Solitude.* London, 1693; rpt. Richmond, IN: Friends United Press, 1978.

The Pennsylvania Chronicle; and Universal Advertiser. Philadelphia, 1767–74.

The Pennsylvania Gazette. Philadelphia, 1728–89.

Pennsylvania Journal, and the Weekly Advertiser. Philadelphia, 1766–77.

The Peoples Ancient and Just Liberties Asserted in the Tryal of William Penn, *and* William Mead. London, 1670.

The Proceedings Relative to Calling the Convention of 1776 and 1790. Harrisburg, PA, 1825.

Quaker Tracts. 9 vols. London, 1658–76.

Ramsay, David. *The History of the American Revolution.* 2 vols. Philadelphia, 1789.

Red Hot Chili Peppers (Michael Balzary, John Fruscianti, Anthony Kiedis, Chad Smith). *Stadium Arcadium* 2 CDs. Burbank, CA: Warner Bros. Records, Inc., 2006.

The Religious Society of Friends. *The Address of the People call'd Quakers, In the Province of Pennsylvania, To John Penn, Esquire, Lieutenant Governor of the said Province, &c.* Philadelphia, 1764.

———. *The Ancient Testimony and Principles of the People Called Quakers; Renewed, with Respect to the King and Government; Touching the Commotions now prevailing in these and other Parts of America, addressed to the People in General.* Philadelphia, 1776.

———. *An Epistle of Caution and Advice, &c.* Philadelphia, 1754.

———. *An Epistle... To Our Friends and Brethren in Religious Profession, in These and the Adjacent Provinces.* Philadelphia, 1776.

———. *Faith and Practice: A Book of Christian Discipline*. Philadelphia: Philadelphia Yearly Meeting, 1997.

———. *A Representation on Behalf of the People called Quakers, to the President and Executive Council, and the General Assembly of Pennsylvania, &c. Reasons why Friends do not illuminate their Houses at the Time of public rejoicing, nor shut their Shops for the public Fasts, Feasts and Thanksgivings*. Dublin, 1782.

———. *The Testimony of the People called Quakers, given forth by a Meeting of the Representatives of said People, in Pennsylvania and New-Jersey, held at Philadelphia the twenty-fourth Day of the first Month*. Philadelphia, 1775.

———. *To Our Fellow Citizens of the United States of North America and others whom it may concern*. Philadelphia, 1799.

———. *To the General Assembly of Pennsylvania. The Representation of a Number of the Citizens of Philadelphia, Members of the Religious Society of the People called Quakers*. Philadelphia, 1784.

Roberts, Kenneth, and Anna M. Roberts, trans. and eds. *Moreau de St. Méry's American Journey, 1793–98*, Garden City, NJ: Doubleday, 1947.

Rogers, William. *The Christian-Quaker, Distinguished from the Apostate & Innovator*. London, 1680.

Savile, George, Marquis of Halifax. *The Character of a Trimmer*. London, 1688.

Scott, Job. *Journal of the Life, Travels, and Gospel Labours of that Faithful Servant and Minister of Christ, Job Scott*. London, 1815.

Smith, Paul Hubert, ed. *Letters from the Delegates to Congress, 1774–1789*. 25 vols. Summerfield, FL: Historical Database, 1995.

Smith, William. *A Brief State of the Province of Pennsylvania... In a Letter from a Gentleman who has resided many Years in Pennsylvania to his Friend in London*. London, 1755.

———. *A Brief View of the Conduct of Pennsylvania*. Philadelphia, 1755.

Soderlund, Jean R. ed. *William Penn and the Founding of Pennsylvania, 1680–1684: A Documentary History*. Philadelphia: University of Pennsylvania Press, 1983.

Sparks, Jared, ed. *The Writings of George Washington*. 2 vols. Boston, 1838.

Stillé Charles J. and Paul Leicester Ford, eds., *The Life and Writings of John Dickinson*. 2 vols. Volume 1: *The Life and Times of John Dickinson, 1732 –1808*, Charles J. Stillé, ed.; Volume 2: *The Writings of John Dickinson: Volume 1: The Political Writings*, Paul Leicester Ford, ed. Philadelphia: The Historical Society of Pennsylvania, 1891–95.

Syrett, Harold C., et al., eds. *The Papers of Alexander Hamilton*. 27 vols. New York: Colombia University Press, 1961–87.

Tatham, John, Thomas Revell, and Nathaniel Westland. *The Case Put and Decided by George Fox, George Whitehead, Stephen Crisp, and other [of] the most Ancient & Eminent Quakers, between Edward Billing on the One Part, and some West-Jersians, headed by Samuell Jennings on the other Part.... London, 1699.*

Tocqueville, Alexis de. *Democracy in America*. J. P. Mayer, ed. New York: Harper-Perennial, 1988.

Trimmer, Tim. *Now in the Press, and will be speedily published, The Life and Adventures of a Certain Quaker Presbyterian Indian Colonel. To which will be added, The Qualifications necessary to entitle a Man to the dignified Name of a "modern moderate Quaker.'"* Philadelphia, 1766.

Turnbull, Robert. *A Visit to the Philadelphia Prison; Being an accurate and particular account of the wise and humane administration adopted in every part of that building.* . . . Philadelphia, 1796.

Voltaire, Francis de. *Letters Concerning the English Nation.* London, 1733.

Warville, Jean-Paul Brissot de. *A Critical Examination of the Marquis de Chatellux's Travels in North America in a Letter Addressed to the Marquis; principally intended as a Refutation of his Opinions Concerning the Quakers, the Negroes, the People, and Mankind.* Philadelphia, 1788.

Williamson, Hugh. *The Plain Dealer: Or, a Few Remarks upon Quaker-Politicks, and their Attempts to Change the Government of Pennsylvania. With some Observations on the false and abusive Papers which they have lately published.* No. 1 & 3. Philadelphia, 1764.

Winstanley, Gerard. *The Law of Freedom and other writings.* Christopher Hill, ed. Cambridge: Cambridge University Press, 1973.

Secondary Sources—Books

Adams, Willi Paul. *The First American Constitutions: Republican Ideology and the Making of State Constitutions in Revolutionary America.* Chapel Hill: University of North Carolina Press, 1979.

Ahlstrom, Sydney E. *A Religious History of the American People.* New Haven, CT: Yale University Press, 1972.

Aldridge, Alfred Owen. *Franklin and His Contemporaries.* New York: New York University Press, 1957.

Alexander, Howard Wright. *George Fox and the Early Quakers.* Richmond, IN: Friends United Press, 1986.

Allen, Barbara. *Tocqueville, Covenant, and the Democratic Revolution: Harmonizing Earth with Heaven.* Lanham, MD: Lexington Books of Rowman & Littlefield Publishers, 2005.

Allen, Devere, ed., *Pacifism in the Modern World.* New York: Garland Publishing, 1972.

Anderson, Fred, and Andrew Cayton. *The Dominion of War: Empire and Liberty in North America, 1500–2000.* New York: Viking, 2005.

Anderson, Jervis. *Bayard Rustin: The Troubles I've Seen: A Biography,* New York: Harper-Collins, 1997.

Arnold, Douglas. *A Republican Revolution: Ideology and Politics in Pennsylvania, 1776–1790.* New York: Garland Publishing, 1989.

Ashcraft, Richard. *Revolutionary Politics and Locke's 'Two Treatises of Government.'* Princeton, NJ: Princeton University Press, 1986.

Austin, J. L. *How To Do Things with Words,* 2nd ed. Cambridge: Harvard University Press, 1975.

Austin, James T. *Life of Elbridge Gerry.* 2 vols. Boston, 1828–29; rpt. New York: Da Capo, 1970.

Bacon, Margaret Hope. *Valiant Friend: The Life of Lucretia Mott.* New York: Walker and Company, 1980.

Bailyn, Bernard. *The Ideological Origins of the American Revolution.* Cambridge, MA: Belknap Press, Harvard University, 1967.

———, ed. *Pamphlets of the American Revolution, 1750–1776.* Vol. 1. Cambridge, MA: Belknap Press, Harvard University, 1965.

Baltzell, E. Digby. *Puritan Boston and Quaker Philadelphia: Two Protestant Ethics and the Spirit of Class Authority and Leadership.* New York: The Free Press, 1979.

Bancroft, George. *History of the United States from the Discovery of the Continent.* New York: D. Appleton and Co. 1912.

Banning, Lance. *The Jeffersonian Persuasion: Evolution of a Party Ideology.* Ithaca, NY: Cornell University Press, 1978.

Barbour, Hugh. *The Quakers in Puritan England.* New Haven, CT: Yale University Press, 1964.

Barbour, Hugh, and J. William Frost. *The Quakers.* New York: Greenwood Press, 1988.

Barnes, Harry Elmer. *The Evolution of Penology in Pennsylvania.* Indianapolis: Bobbs-Merrill, 1927.

Barton, David. *Original Intent: The Courts, the Constitution and Religion.* Aledo, TX: WallBuilder Press, 2004.

Bass, S. Jonathan. *Blessed Are the Peacemakers: Martin Luther King, Jr., Eight White Religious Leaders, and the "Letter from a Birmingham Jail."* Baton Rouge: Louisiana State University Press, 2001.

Bauman, Richard. *Let Your Words Be Few: Symbolism of Speaking and Silence among Seventeenth-Century Quakers.* Cambridge: Cambridge University Press, 1983.

_____. *For the Reputation of Truth: Politics, Religion, and Conflict among the Pennsylvania Quakers, 1750–1800.* Baltimore: Johns Hopkins University Press, 1971.

Baylor, Michael C. *Action and Person: Conscience in Late Scholasticism and the Young Luther.* Leiden: E. J. Brill, 1977.

Beatty, Edwin Corbyn Obert. *William Penn as Social Philosopher.* New York: Columbia University Press, 1939.

Becker, Carl. *History of Political Parties in the Province of New York.* Madison: University of Wisconsin Press, 1909.

Bedau, Hugo Adam. *Civil Disobedience in Focus.* New York: Routledge, 1991.

_____, ed. *Civil Disobedience: Theory and Practice.* New York: Pegasus, 1969.

Beeman, R. Richard. *The Varieties of Political Experience in Eighteenth-Century America.* Philadelphia: University of Pennsylvania Press, 2005.

Beer, Samuel H. *To Make a Nation: The Rediscovery of American Federalism.* Cambridge, MA: Belknap Press, Harvard University, 1993.

Bloch, Maurice, ed. *Political Language and Oratory in Traditional Society.* New York: Academic Press, 1975.

Bonomi, Patricia U. *Under the Cope of Heaven: Religion, Society, and Politics in Colonial America.* New York: Oxford University Press, 1986.

Boorstin, Daniel. *The Americans: The Colonial Experience.* New York: Vintage Books, 1958.

Bouton, Terry. *Taming Democracy: "The People," the Founders, and the Troubled Ending of the American Revolution.* New York: Oxford University Press, 2007.

Boyd, Julian P. *Anglo-American Union: Joseph Galloway's Plans to Preserve the British Empire, 1774–1788.* Philadelphia: University of Pennsylvania Press, 1941.

Bradford, M. E. *Founding Fathers: Brief Lives of the Framers of the United States Constitution.* Lawrence: University of Kansas Press, 1994.

Braithwaite, W. C. *The Beginnings of Quakerism.* Cambridge: Cambridge University Press, 1955.

_____. *The Second Period of Quakerism.* London: Macmillan and Co., 1919.

Bridenbaugh, Carl, and Jessica Bridenbaugh. *Rebels and Gentlemen: Philadelphia in the Age of Franklin.* New York: Oxford University Press, 1962.

Brinton, Howard, H., ed. *Children of Light, in Honor of Rufus Jones*. New York: Macmillan, 1938.

_____. *Friends for 300 Years: History and Beliefs of the Society of Friends Since George Fox Started the Movement*. New York: Harper & Brothers, 1952.

_____. *Quaker Education in Theory and Practice*. Wallingford, PA: Pendle Hill, 1940.

_____. *Quaker Journals: Varieties of Religious Experience among Friends*. Wallingford, PA: Pendle Hill, 1972.

_____. *The Religious Philosophy of Quakerism: The Beliefs of Fox, Barclay, and Penn as Based on the Gospel of John*. Wallingford, PA: Pendle Hill, 1973.

Brinton, Anna Cox. *Then and Now: Quaker Essays: Historical and Contemporary*. Philadelphia: University of Pennsylvania Press, 1960.

Brock, Peter. *Pacifism in Europe to 1914*. Princeton, NJ: Princeton University Press, 1972.

_____. *Pioneers of the Peaceable Kingdom*. Princeton, NJ: Princeton University Press, 1970.

_____. *The Quaker Peace Testimony 1660 to 1914*. Syracuse, NY: Syracuse University Press, 1990.

_____. *Radical Pacifists in Antebellum America*. Princeton, NJ: Princeton University Press, 1968.

Bronner, Edwin B. *William Penn's Holy Experiment: The Founding of Pennsylvania, 1681–1701*. New York: Temple University Publications; distributed by Columbia University Press, 1962.

Brunhouse, Robert L. *The Counter-Revolution in Pennsylvania, 1776–1790*. Harrisburg: Pennsylvania Historical and Museum Commission, 1971.

Burgess, Glenn. *The Politics of the Ancient Constitution: An Introduction to English Political Thought, 1603–1642*. University Park: Pennsylvania State University Press, 1993.

Bury, J. B. *The Idea of Progress: An Inquiry into Its Growth and Origin*. New York: Dover Publications, 1932.

Calhoon, Robert M. *The Loyalists in the American Revolution, 1760–1781*. New York: Harcourt, Brace, Jovanovich, 1973.

_____. *The Loyalist Persuasion and Other Essays*. Columbia: University of South Carolina Press, 1989.

_____. *Political Moderation in America's First Two Centuries*. New York: Cambridge University Press, 2008.

Cantor, Geoffrey. *Quakers, Jews, and Science: Religious Responses to Modernity and the Sciences, 1650–1900*. Oxford: Oxford University Press, 2005.

Cappon, Lester J., et al., eds. *The Atlas of Early American History: The Revolutionary Era, 1760–1790*. Princeton, NJ: Princeton University Press, 1976.

Caulfield, Anna Breiner. *Quakers in Fiction: An Annotated Bibliography*. Northampton, MA: Pittenbruach Press, 1993.

Childress, James F. *Civil Disobedience and Political Obligation: A Study in Christian Social Ethics*. New Haven: Yale University Press, 1971.

Chu, Jonathan. *Neighbors, Friends, or Madmen: The Puritan Adjustment to Quakerism in Seventeenth-Century Massachusetts Bay*. Westport, CT: Greenwood Press, 1985.

Clark, J. C. D. *The Language of Liberty, 1660–1832: Political Discourse and Social Dynamics in the Anglo-American World*. Cambridge: Cambridge University Press, 1994.

Colbourn, H. Trevor. *The Lamp of Experience: Whig History and the Intellectual Origins of the American Revolution.* Chapel Hill: University of North Carolina Press, 1965.

Collins, Varnum Lansing. *Continental Congress at Princeton.* Princeton, NJ: University Library, 1908.

Como, David R. *Blown by the Spirit: Puritanism and the Emergence of an Antinomian Underground in Pre-Civil War England.* Stanford, CA: Stanford University Press, 2004.

Conway, Moncure Daniel. *The Life of Thomas Paine.* New York: G. P. Putnam's Sons, 1893.

Cooney, Robert, and Helen Michalowski, eds. *The Power of the People: Active Non-Violence in the United States.* Philadelphia: New Society, 1987.

Cowie, John, and William Hammond. *Alliterative Anomalies for Infants and Invalids.* New York: Dodd, Mead & Co., 1913.

Craine, Elaine Forman. *The Diary of Elizabeth Drinker: The Life Cycle of an Eighteenth-Century Woman.* Boston: Northeastern University Press, 1994.

Crane, Verner W. *Benjamin Franklin and a Rising People.* Boston: Little, Brown, 1954.

Curry, Thomas. *The First Freedoms: Church and State in America to the Passage of the First Amendment.* New York: Oxford University Press, 1986.

Damrosch, Leo. *The Sorrows of the Quaker Jesus: James Nayler and the Puritan Crackdown on the Free Spirit.* Cambridge, MA: Harvard University Press, 1996.

Dandelion, Pink. *The Creation of Quaker Theory: Insider Perspectives.* Burlington, VT: Ashgate, 2004.

Daniels, Bruce C., ed. *Power and Status: Office Holding in Colonial America.* Middletown, CT: Wesleyan University Press, 1986.

Daniels, Bruce C. *Puritans at Play: Leisure and Recreation in Colonial New England.* New York: St. Martin's Press, 1995.

Davis, David Brion. *The Problem of Slavery in Western Culture.* Ithaca, NY: Cornell University Press, 1966.

D'Emilio, John. *Lost Prophet: The Life and Times of Bayard Rustin.* Chicago: University of Chicago Press, 2003.

Diggins, John Patrick. *The Lost Soul of American Politics: Virtue, Self-Interest, and the Foundations of American Liberalism.* New York: Basic Books, 1984.

Drake, Thomas E. *Quakers and Slavery in America.* New Haven, CT: Yale University Press, 1950.

Dunn, John. *The Political Thought of John Locke: An Historical Account of the Argument of "The Two Treatises of Government."* Cambridge: Cambridge University Press, 1969; rpt. 1995.

Dunn, Mary Maples. *William Penn: Politics and Conscience.* Princeton, NJ: Princeton University Press, 1967.

Echeverria, Durand. *Mirage in the West: A History of the French View of American Society to 1815.* Princeton, NJ: Princeton University Press, 1968.

Elazar, Daniel J. *American Federalism: A View from the States,* 3rd ed., New York: Harper and Row, 1984.

Endy, Melvin B. *William Penn and Early Quakerism.* Princeton, NJ: Princeton University Press, 1973.

Eshleman, H. Frank. *The Constructive Genius of David Lloyd in Early Colonial Pennsylvania Legislation and Jurisprudence, 1686–1731.* Philadelphia: Pennsylvania Bar Association, 1910.

Ewen, David. *Songs of America: A Cavalcade of Popular Songs.* Chicago: Ziff-David Publishing Co., 1947.

Faÿ, Bernard. *The Revolutionary Spirit in France and America.* Ramon Guthrie, trans. New York: Harcourt, 1927.

Ferling, John E. *A Leap in the Dark: The Struggle to Create the American Republic.* New York: Oxford University Press, 2003.

_____. *The Loyalist Mind: Joseph Galloway and the American Revolution.* University Park: Pennsylvania State University Press, 1977.

Flower, Milton E. *John Dickinson, Conservative Revolutionary.* Charlottesville: University Press of Virginia, 1983.

Foner, Eric. *Tom Paine and Revolutionary America.* New York: Oxford University Press, 1976.

Fredman, Lionel. *John Dickinson: American Revolutionary Statesman.* Charlottesville, NY: SamHar Press, 1974.

Freeman, Joanne. *Affairs of Honor: National Politics in the New Republic.* New Haven, CT: Yale University Press, 2002.

Frost, J. William. *The Keithian Controversy in Early Pennsylvania.* Norwood, PA: Norwood, 1980.

_____. *A Perfect Freedom: Religious Liberty in Pennsylvania.* New York: Cambridge University Press, 1990.

Gallagher, Lowell. *Medusa's Gaze: Casuistry and Conscience in the Renaissance.* Stanford: Stanford University Press, 1991.

Garraty, John Arthur, and Mark C. Carnes. *American National Biography.* New York: Oxford University Press, 1999.

Gaustad, Edwin Scott. *Historical Atlas of Religion in America.* New York: Harper and Row, 1962.

Gerona, Carla. *Night Journeys: The Power of Dreams in Transatlantic Quaker Culture.* Charlottesville: University of Virginia Press, 2004.

Gilje, Paul A. *Rioting in America.* Interdisciplinary Studies in History. Bloomington and Indianapolis: Indiana University Press, 1996.

Gough, J. W. *Fundamental Law in English Constitutional History.* Oxford: Oxford University Press, 1955.

Green, Thomas Andrew. *Verdict according to Conscience: Perspectives on the English Criminal Trial Jury, 1200–1800.* Chicago: University of Chicago Press, 1985.

Greene, Jack P. *Negotiated Authorities: Essays in Colonial Political and Constitutional History.* Charlottesville: University Press of Virginia, 1994.

_____. *Peripheries and Center: Constitutional Development in the Extended Polities of the British Empire and the United States, 1607–1788.* New York: W. W. Norton and Co., 1990.

Guenther, Karen. *"Rememb'ring our Time and Work is the Lords": The Experiences of Quakers on the Eighteenth-Century Pennsylvania Frontier.* Selinsgrove, PA: Susquehanna University Press, 2005.

Guide to the Microfilm of the Records of Pennsylvania's Revolutionary Governments, 1776–1790. Harrisburg: Pennsylvania Historical and Museum Commission, 1978.

Hale, Edward Everett. *Franklin in France.* Boston: Roberts Bros., 1887–88.

Hamburger, Philip. *Separation of Church and State.* Cambridge, MA: Harvard University Press, 2002.

Hamm, Thomas D. *God's Government Begun: The Society for Universal Inquiry and Reform, 1842–1846.* Bloomington: Indiana University Press, 1995.

———. *The Transformation of American Quakerism: Orthodox Friends, 1800–1907.* Bloomington: Indiana University Press, 1988.

Harris, Tim. *Politics under the Later Stuarts: Party Conflict in a Divided Society, 1660–1715.* New York: Longman, 1993.

Hart, Benjamin. *Faith and Freedom: The Christian Roots of American Liberty.* San Bernardino: Here's Life Publishers, 1988.

Hatton, Jean. *George Fox: A Biography of the Founder of the Quakers.* Oxford: Monarch, 2007.

Heffner, William Clinton. *The History of Poor Relief Legislation in Pennsylvania, 1682–1913.* Cleona, PA: Holzapfel, 1913.

Herndon, Ruth Wallis. *Unwelcome Americans: Living on the Margin in Early New England.* Philadelphia: University of Pennsylvania Press, 2001.

Hewitt, Nancy A. *Women's Activism and Social Change: Rochester, New York, 1822–1872.* Ithaca, NY: Cornell University Press, 1984.

Heyrman, Christine Leigh. *Southern Cross: The Beginnings of the Bible Belt.* New York: Alfred A. Knopf, 1997.

Hill, Christopher. *Experience of Defeat: Milton and Some Contemporaries.* New York: Viking, 1984.

———. *The Religion of Gerrard Winstanley.* Oxford: The Past and Present Society, 1978.

———. *The World Turned Upside Down: Radical Ideas during the English Revolution.* New York: Viking Press, 1972.

Hinshaw, William Wade. *The Encyclopedia of American Quaker Genealogy.* Ann Arbor, MI: Edwards Brothers, 1938.

Hoffert, Robert W. *A Politics of Tensions: The Articles of Confederation and American Political Ideas.* Niwot, CO: University of Colorado Press, 1992.

Holton, Woody. *Unruly Americans and the Origins of the Constitution.* New York: Hill and Wang, 2007.

Horle, Craig W., et al., eds. *Lawmaking and Legislators: A Biographical Dictionary.* 3 vols. Philadelphia: University of Pennsylvania Press, 1991–97.

———. *Quakers and the English Legal System, 1660–1688.* Philadelphia: University of Pennsylvania Press, 1988.

Howe, Daniel Walker. *Henry David Thoreau on the Duty of Civil Disobedience: An Inaugural Lecture Delivered before the University of Oxford on 21 May 1990.* Oxford: Clarendon Press, 1990.

Hull, William I. *William Penn: A Topical Biography.* London: Oxford University Press, 1937.

Hutson, James H. *The Founders on Religion: A Book of Quotations.* Princeton, NJ: Princeton University Press, 2005.

———. *Pennsylvania Politics, 1740–1770: The Movement for Royal Government and Its Consequences.* Princeton, NJ: Princeton University Press, 1972.

Ingle, H. Larry. *Quakers in Conflict: The Hicksite Reformation.* Knoxville: University of Tennessee Press, 1986.

Ireland, Owen S. *Religion, Ethnicity, and Politics: Ratifying the Constitution in Pennsylvania.* University Park: Pennsylvania State University Press, 1995.

Isserman, Maurice. *If I Had a Hammer . . . The Death of the Old Left and the Birth of the New Left.* New York: Basic Books, 1987.

Jacobson, David L. *John Dickinson and the Revolution in Pennsylvania, 1764–1776.* Berkeley: University of California Press, 1965.

James, Coy Hilton. *Silas Deane: Patriot or Traitor?* East Lansing: Michigan State University Press, 1975.

James, Sydney V. *A People among Peoples: Quaker Benevolence in Eighteenth-Century America.* Cambridge, MA: Harvard University Press, 1963.

James, William. *Varieties of Religious Experience.* New York: Modern Library, 1936.

Jensen, Merrill. *The Articles of Confederation: An Interpretation of the Social-Constitutional History of the American Revolution, 1774–1781.* Madison: University of Wisconsin Press, 1940.

_____. *The New Nation: A History of the United States during the Confederation, 1781–1789.* New York: Knopf, 1950.

Jervis, Anderson. *Bayard Rustin: The Troubles I've Seen: A Biography.* New York: HarperCollins Publishers, 1997.

Jones, J. R. *The First Whigs: The Politics of the Exclusion Crisis, 1678–1683.* New York: Oxford University Press, 1961.

Jones, Rufus M. *The Later Periods of Quakerism.* Westwood, CT: Greenwood Press, 1970.

_____. *The Quakers in the American Colonies.* New York: W. W. Norton and Co., 1966.

Jordan, Ryan. *Slavery and the Meetinghouse: The Quakers and the Abolitionist Dilemma, 1820–1865.* Bloomington: Indiana University Press, 2007.

Kamensky, Jane. *Governing the Tongue: The Politics of Speech in Early New England.* New York: Oxford University Press, 1997.

Kammen, Michael. *Spheres of Liberty: Changing Perceptions of Liberty in American Culture.* Madison: University of Wisconsin Press, 1986.

Kashatus, William C. *Conflict of Conviction: A Reappraisal of Quaker Involvement in the American Revolution.* Lanham, MD: University Press of America, 1990.

Kern, Kathi. *Mrs. Stanton's Bible.* Ithaca, NY: Cornell University Press, 2001.

Kirby, Ethyl Williams. *George Keith, 1636–1716.* New York: D. Appleton-Century Company, 1942.

Konkle, Burton. *Life and Times of Thomas Smith, 1754–1809.* Philadelphia: Campion & Company, 1904.

Korey, Marie Elena. *The Books of Isaac Norris at Dickinson College.* Carlisle, PA: Dickinson College, 1976.

Kramer, Larry. *The People Themselves: Popular Constitutionalism and Judicial Review.* New York: Oxford University Press, 2004.

Kruman, Marc W. *Between Authority and Liberty: State Constitution-Making in Revolutionary America.* Chapel Hill: University of North Carolina Press, 1997.

Kunze, Bonnelyn Young. *Margaret Fell and the Rise of Quakerism.* Stanford, CA: Stanford University Press, 1994.

Lambert, Frank. *The Founding Fathers and the Place of Religion in America.* Princeton, NJ: Princeton University Press, 2003.

Lapsansky, Emma Jones, and Anne A. Verplanck. *Quaker Aesthetics: Reflections on a Quaker Ethic in Design and Consumption.* Philadelphia: University of Pennsylvania Press, 2003.

Larabee, Leonard. *Conservatism in Early American History.* New York: New York University Press, 1948.

Larkin, Edward. *Thomas Paine and the Literature of Revolution.* New York: Cambridge University Press, 2005.

Larson, Rebecca. *Daughters of Light: Quaker Women Preaching and Prophesying in the Colonies and Abroad, 1700–1775.* New York: Alfred A. Knopf, 1999.

Lee, Wayne E. *Crowds and Soldiers in Revolutionary North Carolina: The Culture of Violence in Riot and War.* Gainesville: University Press of Florida, 2001.

Levine, Daniel. *Bayard Rustin and the Civil Rights Movement.* New Brunswick, NJ: Rutgers University Press, 2000.

Levy, Leonard. *Original Intent and the Framer's Constitution.* New York: Macmillan, 1988.

Lockridge, Kenneth A. *A New England Town: The First Hunred Years, Dedham, Massachusetts, 1636–1736.* New York: W. W. Norton & Co., 1970.

Lokken, Roy N. *David Lloyd: Colonial Lawmaker.* Seattle: University of Washington Press, 1959.

Lunardini, Christine A. *From Equal Suffrage to Equal Rights: Alice Paul and the National Women's Party, 1910–1928.* New York: New York University Press, 1986.

Lutz, Donald S. *The Origins of the American Constitutionalism.* Baton Rouge: University of Louisiana Press, 1988.

Lynd, Straughton, ed. *Intellectual Origins of American Radicalism.* New York: Pantheon Books, 1968.

_____. *Nonviolence in America: A Documentary History.* Indianapolis: Bobbs-Merrill, 1966.

Mack, Phyllis. *Visionary Women: Ecstatic Prophesy in Seventeenth-Century England.* Berkeley: University of California Press, 1992.

MacPherson, C. B. *The Political Theory of Possessive Individualism: Hobbes to Locke.* Oxford: Clarendon Press, 1962.

Maier, Pauline. *American Scripture: Making the Declaration of Independence.* New York: Alfred A. Knopf, 1997.

_____. *From Resistance to Revolution: Colonial Radicals and the Development of American Opposition to Britain, 1765–1776.* New York: W. W. Norton & Co., 1991.

Main, Jackson Turner. *The Sovereign States, 1775–1783.* New York: New Veiwpoints: A Division of Franklin Watts, 1973.

Marietta, Jack D. *The Reformation of American Quakerism, 1748–1783.* Philadelphia: University of Pennsylvania Press, 1984.

Marietta, Jack D., and G. S. Rowe. *A Troubled Experiment: Crime and Justice in Pennsylvania, 1682–1800.* Philadelphia: University of Pennsylvania Press, 2006.

Martin, James Kirby, and Mark Edward Lender. *A Respectiable Army: The Military Origins of the Republic, 1763–1789.* Arlington Heights, IL: Harlan Davidson, 1982.

Masson, David. *The Life of John Milton: Narrated in Connexion with the Political, Ecclesiastical, and Literary History of his Time.* 1896; rpt. New York: Peter Smith, 1945.

McCullough, David. *John Adams.* New York: Simon and Schuster, 2001.

McDonald, Forrest. *Novus Ordo Seclorum: The Intellectual Origins of the Constitution.* Lawrence: University of Kansas Press, 1985.

McDonald, Forrest, and Ellen Shapiro McDonald. *Requiem: Variations on Eighteenth-Century Themes.* Lawrence: University Press of Kansas, 1988.

McIlwain, Charles Howard. *The American Revolution: A Constitutional Interpretation.* Ithaca, NY: Cornell University Press, 1966.

_____. *Constitutionalism Ancient and Modern.* Ithaca, NY: Cornell University Press, 1947.

_____. *The High Court of Parliament and Its Supremacy*. New Haven, CT: Yale University Press, 1910.

Mekeel, Arthur J. *The Relation of the Quakers to the American Revolution*. Washington, DC: University Press of America, 1979.

Middlekauff, Robert. *Glorious Cause: The American Revolution, 1763–1789*. New York: Oxford University Press, 1982.

Miller, Glenn T. *Religious Liberty in America: History and Prospects*. Philadelphia: Westminster Press, 1976.

Miller, John C. *Origins of the American Revolution*. Boston: Little, Brown and Company, 1943.

Minda, Gary. *Boycott in America: How Imagination and Ideology Shape the Legal Mind*. Carbondale: Southern Illinois University Press, 1999.

Morgan, Edmund S. *Inventing the People: The Rise of Popular Sovereignty in England and America*. New York: W. W. Norton & Company, 1988.

_____. *The Puritan Dilemma: The Story of John Winthrop*. New York: HarperCollins Publisher, 1958.

_____. *Visible Saints: The History of a Puritan Idea*. Ithaca, NY: Cornell University Press, 1963.

Morris, Richard B. *The Forging of the Union, 1781–1789*. New York: Harper and Row, 1987.

Munroe, John. *History of Delaware*. Newark: University of Delaware Press, 1979.

Murphy, Andrew R. *Conscience and Community: Revisiting Toleration and Religious Dissent in Early Modern England and America*. University Park: Pennsylvania State University Press, 2001.

Nash, Gary B. *Quakers and Politics: Pennsylvania, 1681–1726*. Princeton, 1968; rpt. Boston: Northeastern University Press, 1993.

Nash, Gary B., and Jean Soderlund. *Freedom by Degrees: Emancipation in Pennsylvania and Its Aftermath*. New York: Oxford University Press, 1991.

Nelson, William H. *The American Tory*. New York: Oxford University Press, 1961.

Newcomb, Benjamin. *Franklin and Galloway: A Political Partnership*. New Haven, CT: Yale University Press, 1972.

Newman, Paul Douglas. *Fries's Rebellion: The Enduring Struggle for the American Revolution*. Philadelphia: University of Pennsylvania Press, 2005.

Odell, George C. D. *Annals of the New York Stage*. 15 vols. New York: Columbia University, 1927–49.

Ogg, David. *England in the Reign of Charles II*. Oxford: Oxford University Press, 1955.

Ousterhout, Anne M. *A State Divided: Opposition in Pennsylvania to the American Revolution*. New York: Greenwood Press, 1987.

Pangle, Thomas. *The Spirit of Modern Republicanism: The Moral Vision of the Founding Fathers and the Philosophy of John Locke*. Chicago: University of Chicago Press, 1988.

Pencak, William, Matthew Dennis, and Simon P. Newman, eds. *Riot and Revelry in Early America*. University Park: Penn State University Press, 2003.

Perry, Lewis. *Radical Abolitionism: Anarchy and the Government of God in Antislavery Thought*. Ithaca, NY: Cornell University Press, 1973.

Peters, Kate. *Print Culture and the Early Quakers*. Cambridge: Cambridge University Press, 2005.

Philips, Edith. *The Good Quaker in French Legend*. Philadelphia: University of Pennsylvania Press, 1932.

Pocock, J. G. A. _The Ancient Constitution and the Feudal Law: A Study of English Historical Thought in the Seventeenth Century_. Cambridge: Cambridge University Press, 1957.

_____. _Politics, Language, and Time: Essays on Political Thought and History_. Chicago: The University of Chicago Press, 1992.

Pollock, Thomas Clark. _The Philadelphia Theatre in the Eighteenth Century_. Philadelphia: University of Pennsylvania Press, 1933.

Pomfret, John E. _Colonial New Jersey: A History_. New York: Scribner, 1973.

_____. _The New Jersey Proprietors and their Lands, 1634–1776_. Princeton, NJ: Van Nostrand, 1964.

_____. _The Province of West New Jersey, 1609–1702: A History of the Origins of an American Colony_. New York: Octagon Books, 1976.

_____, ed. _West New Jersey and The West Jersey Concessions and Agreements of 1676/77: A Roundtable of Historians_. Occasional Papers, no 1. Trenton: New Jersey Historical Commission, 1979.

Potts, Timothy C. _Conscience in Medieval Philosophy_. Cambridge: Cambridge University Press, 1980.

Rahe, Paul A. _Republics Ancient and Modern: Volume Two: New Modes & Orders in Early Modern Political Thought; Volume Three: Inventions of Prudence: Constituting the American Regime_. Chapel Hill: University of North Carolina Press, 1994.

Rakove, Jack N. _The Beginnings of National Politics: An Interpretive History of the Continental Congress_. New York: Alfred A. Knopf, 1979.

_____. _Original Meanings: Politics and Ideas in the Making of the Constitution_. New York: _Vintage Books_, 1997.

Rawls, John. _A Theory of Justice_. Cambridge, MA: Harvard University Press, 1971.

_____. _Constitutional History of the American Revolution: The Authority to Tax_. Madison: University of Wisconsin Press, 1987.

_____. _The Concept of Liberty in the Age of the American Revolution_. Chicago: University of Chicago Press, 1988.

_____. _Constitutional History of the American Revolution: The Authority to Legislate_. Madison: University of Wisconsin Press, 1991.

_____. _Constitutional History of the American Revolution: The Authority of Law_. Madison: University of Wisconsin Press, 1993.

Reid, John Phillip. _In a Rebellious Spirit: The Argument of Facts, the Liberty Riot, and the Coming of the American Revolution_. University Park: Penn State University Press, 1979.

Reimherr, E. Otto. _Quest for Freedom: Aspects of Pennsylvania's Religious Experience_. Selinsgrove: Susquehanna University, 1987.

Robbins, Caroline. _The Eighteenth-Century Commonwealthman: Studies in the Transmission, Development and Circumstance of English Liberal Thought from the Restoration of Charles II until the War with the Thirteen Colonies_. Cambridge, MA: Harvard University Press, 1961.

Ross, Isabel. _Margaret Fell, Mother of Quakerism_. 2nd ed. York: William Sessions Book Trust, 1984.

Rossiter, Clinton. _1787: The Grand Convention_. New York: W. W. Norton & Company, 1966.

Rosswurm, Steven. _Arms, Country, and Class: The Philadelphia Militia and the "Lower Sort" during the American Revolution, 1776–1783_. New Brunswick, NJ: Rutgers University Press, 1987.

Rowe, Gail S. *Thomas McKean: The Shaping of an American Republicanism.* Boulder: Colorado Associated University Press, 1978.

Ryerson, Richard Alan. *The Revolution Is Now Begun: The Radical Committees of Philadelphia, 1765–1776.* Philadelphia: University of Pennsylvania Press, 1978.

Sandoz, Ellis. *A Government of Laws: Political Theory, Religion, and the American Founding.* Baton Rouge: Louisiana State University Press, 1990.

Schlesinger, Arthur M. *Colonial Merchants and the American Revolution, 1763–1776.* New York: Atheneum, 1968.

———. *Prelude to Independence: The Newspaper War on Britain, 1764–1776.* New York: Alfred A. Knopf, 1958.

Schoenbrun, David. *Triumph in Paris: The Exploits of Benjamin Franklin.* New York: Harper & Row, 1976.

Schwartz, Sally. *"A Mixed Multitude": The Struggle for Toleration in Colonial Pennsylvania.* New York: New York University Press, 1987.

Selleck, George A. *The Quakers in Boston, 1656–1964: Three Centuries of Friends in Boston and Cambridge.* Cambridge, MA: Friends Meeting at Cambridge, 1976.

Selsam, John Paul. *The Pennsylvania Constitution of 1776: A Study in Revolutionary Democracy.* Philadelphia: University of Pennsylvania Press, 1936.

Sharpless, Isaac. *Political Leaders of Provincial Pennsylvania.* New York: Macmillan, 1919.

———. *Quakerism and Politics.* Philadelphia: Ferris & Leach, 1905.

———. *A Quaker Experiment in Government: History of Quaker Government in Pennsylvania, 1682–1783.* Philadelphia: Ferris and Leach, 1902.

———. *The Quakers in the Revolution* (1902); facsimile rpt. Honolulu: University Press of the Pacific, 2002.

Sheeran, Michael J. *Beyond Majority Rule: Voteless Decisions in the Religious Society of Friends.* Philadelphia: Philadelphia Yearly Meeting of the Religious Society of Friends, 1996.

Silverman, Kenneth. *A Cultural History of the American Revolution: Paintings, Music, Literature, and the Theatre in the Colonies and the United States from the Treaty of Paris to the Inauguration of George Washington, 1763–1789.* New York: Columbia University Press, 1987.

Skemp, J.B., trans. *Statesman: A Translation of the Politicus of Plato.* New Haven, CT: Yale University Press, 1952.

Skinner, Quentin. *The Foundations of Modern Political Thought: Volume Two: The Age of Reformation.* Cambridge: Cambridge University Press, 1978.

Slonim, Schlomo, ed. *The Constitutional Bases of Political and Social Change in the United States.* New York: Praeger Publishers, 1990.

Smith, Joseph. *Bibliotheca Anti-Quakeriana: A Catalogue of Books Adverse to the Society of Friends.* London, 1873; rpt. New York: Kraus, 1963.

Soderlund, Jean. *Quakers and Slavery: A Divided Spirit.* Princeton, NJ: Princeton University Press, 1985.

Speicher, Anna M. *The Religious World of Antislavery Women: Spirituality in the Lives of Five Abolitionist Lecturers.* New York: Syracuse University Press, 2000.

Stanley, Matthew. *Practical Mystic: Religion, Science, and A. S. Eddington.* Chicago: University of Chicago Press, 2007.

Stoner, James R. *Common-Law Liberty: Rethinking American Constitutionalism.* Lawrence: University Press of Kansas, 2003.

_____. *Common Law & Liberal Theory: Coke, Hobbes, & the Origins of American Constitutionalism*. Lawrence: University Press of Kansas, 1992.

Storing, Herbert J. *What the Anti-Federalists Were For*. Chicago: University of Chicago Press, 1981.

Thayer, Theodore. *Israel Pemberton, King of the Quakers*. Philadelphia: Historical Society of Pennsylvania, 1943.

_____. *Pennsylvania Politics and the Growth of Democracy: 1740–1776*. Harrisburg: Pennsylvania Historical and Museum Commission, 1953.

Thompson, Peter. *Rum Punch and Revolution: Taverngoing & Public Life in Eighteenth-Century Philadelphia*. Philadelphia: University of Pennsylvania Press, 1999.

Toll, Jean Barth, and Mildred S. Gillam, eds. *Invisible Philadelphia: Community Through Voluntary Organizations*. Philadelphia: Atwater Kent Museum, 1995.

Tolles, Frederick B. *James Logan and the Culture of Provincial America*. Boston: Little, Brown, 1957.

_____. *Meeting House and Counting House: The Quaker Merchants of Colonial Pennsylvania, 1682–1763*. New York: W. W. Norton, 1948.

_____. *Quakers and the Atlantic Culture*. New York: Macmillan, 1960.

Trees, Andrew. *The Founding Fathers and the Politics of Character*. Princeton, NJ: Princeton University Press, 2004.

Trenchard, John, and Thomas Gordon. *Cato's Letters, or Essays on Liberty, Civil and Religious, and Other Important Subjects*. Indianapolis: Liberty Fund Press, 1995.

Trevett, Christine. *Women and Quakerism in the 17th Century*. York: Sessions Book Trust, The Ebor Press, 1991.

Tuck, Richard. *Natural Rights Theories: Their Origin and Development*. New York: Cambridge University Press, 1979.

Tully, Alan. *Forming American Politics: Ideals, Interests, and Institutions in Colonial New York and Pennsylvania*. Baltimore: John Hopkins University Press, 1994.

_____. *William Penn's Legacy: Politics and Social Structure in Provincial Pennsylvania, 1726–1755*. Baltimore: Johns Hopkins University Press, 1977.

Tyler, Moses Coit. *The Literary History of the American Revolution, 1763–1783*. New York: Barnes & Noble, 1941.

Walzer, Michael. *Obligations: Essays on Disobedience, War, and Citizenship*. New York: Simon and Schuster, 1971.

_____. *Revolution of the Saints: A Study in the Origins of Radical Politics*. New York: Atheneum, 1976.

Warren, Charles. *The Making of the Constitution*. Boston: Little, Brown and Company, 1937.

Weber, Max. *Economy and Society: An Outline of Interpretive Sociology*, G. Roth and C. Wittich, eds., 2 vols. Berkeley: University of California Press, 1978.

_____. *The Protestant Ethic and the Spirit of Capitalism*. New York: Charles Scribner's Sons, 1958.

Weddle, Meredith Baldwin. *Walking in the Way of Peace: Quaker Pacifism in the Seventeenth Century*. New York: Oxford University Press, 2001.

Weisen Cook, Blanche, et al., eds. *Peace Projects of the Seventeenth Century*. New York: Garland Publishing, Inc., 1972.

Wellenreuther, Herman. *Glaube und Politik in Pennsylvania, 1681–1776: Die Wandlungen der Obrigkeitsdoktrin und des Peace Testimony der Quäker*. Köln: Böhlau, 1972.

Wellman, Judith. *The Road to Seneca Falls: Elizabeth Cady Stanton and the First Woman's Rights Convention.* Urbana and Chicago: University of Illinois Press, 2004.

Wells, William V. *The Life and Public Services of Samuel Adams: Being a Narrative of His Acts and Opinions, and of His Agency in Producing and Forwarding the American Revolution, with Extracts From His Correspondence, State Papers, and Political Essays.* 3 vols. Boston: Little, Brown and Company, 1865.

Whitt, Jane Chapman. *Elephants and Quaker Guns... A History of Civil War and Circus Days.* New York: Vantage Press, 1966.

Wills, Garry. *A Necessary Evil: A History of the American Distrust of Government.* New York: Simon & Schuster, 1999.

Wilson, Ellen Gibson. *Thomas Clarkson: A Biography.* New York: St. Martin's Press, 1990.

Witte, John, Jr. *Religion and the American Constitutional Experiment.* 2nd ed. Boulder, CO: Westview Press, 2005.

Wolf, Edwin, 2nd. *John Dickinson: Forgotten Patriot.* Wilmington: n. p., 1967.

Wood, Gordon S. *The Americanization of Benjamin Franklin.* New York: Penguin, 2004.

_____. *The Creation of the American Republic: 1776–1787.* New York: W. W Norton, 1972.

_____. *The Radicalism of the American Revolution.* New York: Random House, 1991.

Yount, David. *How Quakers Invented America.* Lanham, MD: Rowman & Littlefield Publishers, 2007.

Zigler, Valeri. *Advocates of Peace in Antebellum America.* Bloomington: Indiana University Press, 1992.

Zinn, Howard. *Disobedience and Democracy: Nine Fallacies on Law and Order.* New York: Vintage Books, 1968.

Zuckert, Michael. *Natural Rights and the New Republicanism.* Princeton, NJ: Princeton University Press, 1994.

Secondary Sources—Articles and Book Chapters

Ahern, Gregory S. "The Spirit of American Constitutionalism: John Dickinson's *Fabius Letters,*" *Humanitas* vol. 11, no. 2 (1998): 57–76.

Alsop, James. "Gerrard Winstanley's Later Life," *Past and Present* no. 82 (1979): 73–81.

Bailyn, Bernard. "Contagion of Liberty," in *Ideological Origins of the American Revolution.* Cambridge: Belknap Press, Harvard University, 1967: 230–319.

Ball, Terrence. "A Republic – If You Can Keep It," in Terrence Ball and J.G. A. Pocock, eds. *Conceptual Change and the Constitution.* Lawrence: University Press of Kansas, 1988: 137–64.

Banner, Lois W. "Religious Benevolence as Social Control: A Critique of an Interpretation," *Journal of American History* vol. 60, no. 1 (1973): 23–41.

Bedau, Hugo A. "On Civil Disobedience," *The Journal of Philosophy* vol. 58, no. 21 (1961): 653–65.

Behrens, B. "The Whig Theory of the Constitution in the Reign of Charles II," *Cambridge Historical Journal* vol. 7, no. 1 (1941): 42–71.

Black, William. "The Journal of William Black," *PMHB* vol. 1, no. 3, (1877): 233–49.

Boughton, Lynne Courter. "Choice and Action: William Ames's Conception of the Mind's Operation in Moral Decisions," *Church History* vol. 56, no. 2 (1987): 188–203.

Bowling, Kenneth R. "Biography of William Maclay," Bowling and Helen E. Veit, eds. *The Diary of William Maclay.* Baltimore: The Johns Hopkins University Press, 1988.

――――. "New Light on the Philadelphia Mutiny of 1783: Federal-State Confrontation at the Close of the War for Independence," *PMHB* 101 (1977): 446–49.

Boyd, Julian P. "The Disputed Authorship of The Declaration on the Causes and Necessity of Taking up Arms, 1775," *PMHB* 74 (1950): 51–73.

Bradford, M. E. "A Better Guide than Reason: The Politics of John Dickinson," *Modern Age* vol. 21, no. 1 (1977): 39–49.

Breen, T. H. "Narrative of Commercial Life: Consumption, Ideology, and Community on the Eve of the American Revolution," *WMQ* 3rd ser. vol. 50, no. 3 (1993): 471–501.

Breen, Timothy H., and Stephen Foster. "The Puritans' Greatest Achievement: A Study of Social Cohesion in Seventeenth-Century Massachusetts," *Journal of American History* vol. 60, no. 1 (1973): 5–22.

Bridenbaugh, Carl. "The Press and the Book in Eighteenth-Century Philadelphia," *PMHB* vol. 65, no. 1 (1941): 1–30.

Brinton, Howard H. "Stages in Spiritual Development as Exemplified in Quaker Journals," in H. Brinton, ed. *Children of Light, in Honor of Rufus M. Jones.* New York: Macmillan, 1938: 383–406.

Bronner, Edwin B. "The Failure of the 'Holy Experiment' in Pennsylvania, 1684–1699," *Pennsylvania History* vol. 21 (1954): 93–108.

Brooks, Lynn Matluck. "Emblem of Gaiety, Love, and Legislation: Dance in Eighteenth-Century Philadelphia," *PMHB* vol. 115 (1991): 63–87.

Brown, Stuart M., Jr., "Civil Disobedience," *The Journal of Philosophy* vol. 58, no. 22 (1961): 669–81.

Butler, Jon. "'Gospel Order Improved': The Keithian Schism and the Exercise of Quaker Ministerial Authority in Pennsylvania," *WMQ* vol. 31 no. 3 (1974): 431–52.

――――. "Into Pennsylvania's Spiritual Abyss: The Rise and Fall of the Later Keithians, 1693–1703," *PMHB* vol. 101 (1977): 151–70.

Calhoon, Robert M. "On Political Moderation," *The Journal of the Historical Society* vol. 6, no. 2 (2006): 275–95.

Calvert, Jane E. "Pacifism," in Gary L. Anderson and Kathryn G. Herr, eds. *The Encyclopedia of Activism and Social Justice* vol. 3. Thousand Oaks, CA: Sage Publications, 2007: 1075–78.

Caroll, Kenneth. "Early Quakers and 'Going Naked as a Sign,'" *Quaker History* 67 (1978): 69–87.

――――. "Singing in the Spirit in Early Quakerism," *Quaker History* vol. 73 (Spring 1984): 1–13.

Chapin, Bradley. "Written Rights: Puritan and Quaker Procedural Guarantees," *PMHB* vol. 114, no.3 (1990): 323–48.

Clemmens, Paul G. E. "The *Concessions* in Relation to Other Seventeenth-Century Colonial Charters," in *West New Jersey and The West Jersey Concessions and Agreements of 1676/77: A Roundtable of Historians.* Occasional Papers, no. 1. Trenton, NJ: New Jersey Historical Commission, 1979: 29–33.

Cohen, Marshall. "Liberalism and Civil disobedience," *Philosophy and Public Affairs* vol. 1, no. 3 (1972): 283–314.

Colbourn, H. Trevor. "John Dickinson, Historical Revolutionary," *PMHB* vol. 83 (1959): 271–92.

_____. "A Pennsylvania Farmer at the Court of King George: John Dickinson's London Letters, 1754–1756," *PMHB* vol. 83, no 3 (1959): 417–53.

Conniff, James. "The Politics of Trimming: Halifax and the Acceptance of Political Controversy," *The Journal of Politics* vol. 34, no. 4 (1972): 1172–1202.

Corwin, Edward S. "'Higher Law' Background of American Constitutional Law," in *Corwin on the Constitution: Volume One: The Foundations of American Constitutional Political Thought, the Powers of Congress, and the President's Power of Removal.* Ithaca, NY: Cornell University Press, 1981: 79–139.

Couzens, Michael. "Reflections on Violence," *Law & Society Review* vol. 5, no. 4 (1971): 583–604.

Davis, David Brion. "Reflections on Abolitionism and Ideological Hegemony," *American Historical Review* vol. 92, no. 4 (1987): 797–812.

Deberg, William L. van "William Lloyd Garrison and the 'Pro-Slavery Priesthood': The Changing Beliefs of an Evangelical Reformer, 1830–1840," *Journal of the American Academy of Religion* vol. 43, no. 2 (1975): 224–37.

deValinger, Leon, Jr., "John Dickinson and the Federal Constitution," *Delaware History* vol. 22, no. 4 (1987): 299–308.

Doerflinger, Thomas M. "Philadelphia Merchants and the Logic of Moderation, 1760–1775," *WMQ* 3rd ser., vol. 40, no. 2. (April 1983): 197–226.

Duban, James. "Thoreau, Garrison, and Dymond: Unbending Firmness of Mind," *American Literature* vol. 57, no. 2 (1985): 309–17.

Dunn, Mary Maples. "Did Penn Write the Concessions," in *West New Jersey and The West Jersey Concessions and Agreements of 1676/77: A Roundtable of Historians.* Occasional Papers, no.1. Trenton, NJ: New Jersey Historical Commission, 1979: 24–28.

_____. "William Penn, Classical Republican," *PMHB* vol. 81 (1957): 138–56.

Eberlein, Harold D., and Cortlandt Van Dyke Hubbard. "Music in the Early Federal Era," *PMHB* vol. 69, no 2 (1945): 103–127.

Endy, Melvin B. "Puritanism, Spiritualism, and Quakerism," in Mary Maples Dunn and Richard Dunn, eds. *The World of William Penn.* Philadelphia: University of Pennsylvania Press, 1986: 281–301.

Falk, Robert P. "Thomas Paine and the Attitude of the Quakers to the American Revolution," *PMHB* vol. 61 (1939): 302–10.

Finkelman, Paul. "Slavery and the Constitutional Convention: Making a Covenant with Death," in Richard R. Beeman, ed. *Beyond Confederation: Origins of the Constitution and American National Identity.* Chapel Hill: University of North Carolina Press, 1987: 188–225.

Fisher, Darlene Emmert. "Social Life in Philadelphia Under the British Occupation," *Pennsylvania History* vol. 37, no. 3 (1970): 237–60.

Fitzroy, Herbert William Keith. "The Punishment of Crime in Provincial Pennsylvania," *PMHB* vol. 60, no. 3 (1936): 242–69.

Fox, Richard G. "Passage from India," in R. Fox and O. Starn, eds. *Between Resistance and Revolution: Cultural Politics and Social Protest.* New Brunswick, NJ: Rutgers University Press, 1997: 65–82.

Fradkin, Hillel G. "The 'Separation' of Religion and Politics: The Paradoxes of Spinoza," *The Review of Politics* vol. 50, no. 4, Fiftieth Anniversary Issue: Religion and Politics (1988): 603–27.

Gliozzo, Charles A. "John Jones," *American National Biography* vol. 12. New York: Oxford University Press, 1999: 214–16.

Greene, Jack P. "The Background of the Articles of Confederation," *Publius* vol. 12, no. 4, The Continuing Legacy of the Articles of Confederation (1982): 15–44.

———. "The Role of the Lower Houses of Assembly in Eighteenth-Century Politics," *The Journal of Southern History* vol. 27, no. 4 (1961): 451–74.

Greene, Robert A. "Instinct of Nature: Natural Law, Synderesis, and the Moral Sense," *Journal of the History of Ideas* vol. 58, no. 2 (1997): 173–98.

———. "Synderesis, the Spark of Conscience, in the English Renaissance," *Journal of the History of Ideas* vol. 52, no.2 (1991): 195–219.

Grey, Thomas C. "Origins of the Unwritten Constitution: Fundamental Law in American Revolutionary Thought," *Stanford Law Review* vol. 30 no. 5 (1978): 843–93.

Gummere, Richard M. "John Dickinson: Classical Penman of the Revolution," *The Classical Journal* vol. 52, no. 2 (1956): 81–88.

Hamm, Thomas D. "Hicksite Quakerism and the Antebellum Non-resistance Movement," *Church History* vol. 63, no. 4 (1994): 557–69.

———. "The Problem of the Inner Light in Nineteenth-Century Quakerism," in *The Lamb's War: Quaker Essays to Honor of Hugh Barbour.* M. L. Birkel and J. W. Newman, eds. Richmond, IN: Earlham College Press, 1992: 101–17.

Harris, Howell John. "War in the Social Order: The Great War and the Liberalization of American Quakerism," in David K. Adams and Cornelis A. Van Minnen, eds., *Religious and Secular Reform in America: Ideas, Belief, and Social Change.* New York: New York University Press, 1999: 179–203.

Herman, A. L. "Satyagraha: A New Indian Word for Some Old Ways of Western Thinking," *Philosophy East and West* vol. 19, no. 2 (1968): 123–42.

Herr, William H. "Thoreau: A Civil Disobedient?" *Ethics* vol. 85, no. 1 (1974): 87–91.

Hindle, Brooke. "The March of the Paxton Boys," *WMQ* 3rd ser., vol. 3, no. 4 (1946): 461–86.

———. "The Quaker Background and Science in Colonial Philadelphia," *Isis* vol. 46, no. 3 (1955): 243–50.

Holton, Sandra Stanley. "'To Educate Women into Rebellion': Elizabeth Cady Stanton and the Creation of a Transatlantic Network of Radical Suffragists," *American Historical Review* vol. 99, no. 4 (Oct. 1994): 1112–36.

Hooker, Richard J. "John Dickinson on Church and State," *American Literature* vol. 16, no. 2 (May, 1944): 82–98.

Hudson, Winthrop. "William Penn's English Liberties: Tract for Several Times," *William and Mary Quarterly* 3rd ser., vol. 12, no 4 (1969): 578–85.

Hutson, James. "The Birth of the Bill of Rights," *Prologue* vol. XX (1988): 143–61.

———. "The Campaign to Make Pennsylvania a Royal Province, 1764–1770, Part I," *PMHB* vol. 94 (1970): 427–63.

———. "The Creation of the Constitution: Scholarship at a Standstill," *Reviews in American History* vol. 12, no. 4. (1984): 463–77.

———. "John Dickinson at the Federal Constitutional Convention," *WMQ* 3rd ser., vol. 40, no. 2 (1983): 256–82.

Ingle, Larry H. "Richard Hubberthorne and History: The Crisis of 1659," *Journal of the Friends' Historical Society* vol. 56, no. 3 (1992): 189–200.

Ireland, Owen S. "The Crux of Politics: Religion and Party in Pennsylvania, 1778–1789," *WMQ* 3rd ser., vol. 42, no. 4 (1985): 453–75.

Isenberg, Nancy. "'Pillars in the Same Temple and Priests of the Same Worship': Women's Rights and the Politics of Church and State in Antebellum America," *The Journal of American History* vol. 85, no. 1 (1998): 98–128.

Jacobson, David L. "John Dickinson's Fight against Royal Government, 1964," *WMQ* 3rd ser., vol. 19, no. 1 (1962): 64–85.

Jensen, Merrill. "The Idea of a National Government during the American Revolution," *Political Science Quarterly* vol. 58, no. 3 (1943): 356–79.

Johnson, Karen. "Perspectives on Political Obligation: A Critique and a Proposal," *The Western Political Quarterly* vol. 27, no. 3. (1974): 520–35.

Jones, Harry W. "The Articles of Confederation and the Creation of a Federal System," in George W. Corner, ed., *Aspects of American Liberty: Philosophical, Historical, and Political* (Memoirs of the American Philosophical Society). Philadelphia: American Philosophical Society, 1977: 126–45.

———. "Civil Disobedience," *Proceedings of the American Philosophical Society* vol. 111, no. 4 (1967): 195–98.

Juergensmeyer, Mark. "Nonviolence," *The Encyclopedia of Religion*, 2nd ed. Detroit: Macmillan Reference USA, 2005: 6645–49.

Kashatus, III, William. "Thomas Paine: A Quaker Revolutionary," *Quaker History* vol. 73, no. 2 (1984): 38–61.

Kelsey, Rayner Wickersham. "Early Books of Discipline of Philadelphia Yearly Meeting," *Bulletin of the Friends Historical Association* vol. 24, no. 1 (1935): 12–23.

———. *Friends and the Indians, 1655–1917*. Philadelphia: Associated Executive Committee of Friends on Indian Affairs, 1917.

Kent, Stephen A., and James V. Spickerd. "The 'Other' Civil Religion and the Tradition of Radical Quaker Politics," *Journal of Church and State* vol. 36, no. 2 (1994): 374–87.

Kirby, Ethyn Williams. "The Quakers' Efforts to Secure Civil and Religious Liberty, 1660–96," *The Journal of Modern History* vol. 7, no. 4 (1935): 401–21.

Knollenberg, Bernard. "John Dickinson vs. John Adams," *Proceedings of the American Philosophical Society* vol. 107, no. 2 (1963): 138–44.

Konkle, Burton Alva. "David Lloyd, Penn's Great Lawmaker," *Pennsylvania History* vol. 4 no. 3 (1937): 153–56.

Kosek, Joseph Kip. "Richard Gregg, Mohandas Gandhi, and the Strategy of Nonviolent Resistance," *The Journal of American History* vol. 91, no. 4 (2005): 1318–48.

LeBaron, Bently. "Three Components of Political Obligation," *Canadian Journal of Political Science / Revue canadienne de science politique* vol. 6, no. 3 (1973): 478–93.

Leonard, Sister Joan deLourdes. "The Organization and Procedure of the Pennsylvania Assembly," Parts I & II *PMHB* vol. 72 (1948): 215–39; 376–412.

Levy, Barry. "'Tender Plants': Quaker Farmers and Children in the Delaware Valley, 1681–1735," *Journal of Family History* vol. 3 no. 2 (1978): 116–35.

Lewis, John Underwood. "Sir Edward Coke (1552–1633): His Theory of 'Artificial Reason' as a Context for Modern Basic Legal Theory," *Law Quarterly Review* vol. 84 (1968): 330–42.

Lutz, Donald S. "Religious Dimensions in the Development of American Constitutionalism," *Emory Law Journal* vol. 31, no. 1 (1990): 21–40.

Maclear, James F. "Quakerism and the End of the Interregnum: A Chapter in the Domestication of Radical Puritanism," *Church History* vol. 19 (1950): 240–70.

Marietta, Jack D. "Conscience, the Quaker Community, and the French and Indian War," *PMHB* vol. 95 (1971): 3–27.

McDonald, Forrest. "Introduction," in *Empire and Nation. Letters from a Farmer in Pennsylvania (John Dickinson); Letters from a Federal Farmer (Richard Henry Lee)*, 2nd ed. Indianapolis: Liberty Fund, 1999, ix–xvi.

McDonald, Forrest, and Ellen Shapiro McDonald. "John Dickinson and the Constitution," in *Requiem: Variations on Eighteenth-Century Themes*. Lawrence: University Press of Kansas, 1988: 85–103.

———. "John Dickinson, Founding Father," *Delaware History* vol. 23, no. 1 (1988): 24–38.

McLoughlin, William G. "Massive Civil Disobedience as a Baptist Tactic in 1773," *American Quarterly* vol. 21, no. 4 (1969): 710–27.

McWilliams, Wilson Carey. "Civil Disobedience and Contemporary Constitutionalism: The American Case," *Comparative Politics* vol. 1, no. 2 (1969): 211–27.

Messer, Peter C. "'A Species of Treason & Not the Least Dangerous Kind': The Treason Trials of Abraham Carlisle and John Roberts," *PMHB* vol. 128, no. 4 (1999): 303–32.

Miller, Perry. "Errand into the Wilderness," in *Errand into the Wilderness*. Cambridge, MA: Belknap Press, Harvard University, 1956: 1–15.

———. "The Marrow of Puritan Divinity," in *Errand into the Wilderness*. Cambridge, MA: Belknap Press, Harvard University, 1956: 48–98.

———. "The Puritan State and Puritan Society," in *Errand into the Wilderness*. Cambridge, MA; Belknap Press, Harvard University, 1956: 141–52.

Murrin, John M. "Religion and Politics from the First Settlements to the Civil War," in Mark A. Noll, ed. *Religion and American Politics: From the Colonial Period to the 1980s*. New York: Oxford University Press, 1990: 19–43.

Murti, V. V. Ramana. "Influence of the Western Tradition on Gandhian Doctrine," *Philosophy East and West* vol. 18, no.1/2 (1968): 55–65.

Natelson, Robert G. "The Constitutional Contributions of John Dickinson," *Penn State Law Review* vol. 108 (2004): 415–77.

Oaks, Robert F. "Philadelphians in Exile: The Problem of Loyalty during the American Revolution," *PMHB* vol. 96 (1972): 298–325.

Olson, Alison. "The Lobbying of London Quakers for Pennsylvania Friends," *PMHB* vol. 117, no. 3 (1993): 131–52.

———. "The Pamphlet War over the Paxton Boys," *PMHB* vol. 123, nos. 1/2 (1999): 31–55.

Ousterhout, Anne M. "Controlling the Opposition in Pennsylvania during the American Revolution," *PMHB* vol. 105 (1981): 3–34.

Paine, Tom, and Robin West. "Tom Paine's Constitutionalism," *Virginia Law Review* vol. 89, no. 6, *Marbury v. Madison*: A Bicentennial Symposium (2003): 1413–61.

Palmer, R. R. "Tom Paine: Victim of the Rights of Man," *PMHB* vol. 66, no 2 (1942): 161–75.

Parkin-Speer, Diane, "John Lilburne: A Revolutionary Interprets Statute and Common Law Due Process," *Law and History Review* vol. 1, no.2 (1983): 276–96.

Pencak, William. "In Search of the American Character: French Travelers in Eighteenth-Century Pennsylvania," *Pennsylvania History* vol. 55 no. 1 (1988): 2–30.

Pennington, Edgar L. "The Work of the Bray Associates in Pennsylvania," *PMHB* vol. 58, no 1 (1934): 1–25.

Pestana, Carla Gardina. "The City upon a Hill under Siege: The Puritan Perception of the Quaker Threat to Massachusetts Bay, 1656–1661," *The New England Quarterly* vol. 56, no. 3 (1983): 323–53.

Pocock, J. G. A. "Interregnum and Restoration," in *The Varieties of British Political Thought, 1500–1800*. New York: Cambridge University Press, 1993: 146–79.

_____. "Radical Criticisms of the Whig Order in the Age between Revolutions," in Margaret Jacobs and James Jacobs, eds. *The Origins of Anglo-American Radicalism*. London: George Allen & Unwin, 1984: 33–57.

Pomfret, John E. "The Proprietors of the Province of West New Jersey, 1674–1702," *PMHB* vol. 75 (1951): 117–46.

Powell, J. H. "John Dickinson and the Constitution," *PMHB* vol. 60, no. 1 (1936): 1–14.

_____. "John Dickinson as President of Pennsylvania," *Pennsylvania History* vol. 28, no. 3 (1961): 254–67.

Power, M. Susan. "John Dickinson after 1776: The Fabius Letters," *Modern Age* vol. 16, no. 4 (1972): 387–97.

_____. "John Dickinson: Freedom, Protest, and Change," *Susquehanna Studies* vol. 9, no. 2 (1972): 99–121.

Prosch, Harry. "Toward an Ethic of Civil Disobedience," *Ethics* vol. 77, no. 3 (1967): 176–92.

Radbill, Kenneth A. "The Ordeal of Elizabeth Drinker," *Pennsylvania History* vol. 47, no. 2 (1980): 146–72.

Rakove, Jack N. "Legacy of the Articles of Confederation," *Publius* vol. 12, no. 4, The Continuing Legacy of the Articles of Confederation (1982): 45–66.

Ranney, John C. "The Bases of American Federalism," *WMQ* 3rd ser., vol. 3, no. 1 (1946): 1–35.

Renner, Richard Wilson. "Conscientious Objection and the Federal Government, 1787–1792," *Military Affairs* vol. 38, no. 4 (1974): 142–45.

Robbins, Caroline. "Algernon Sidney's *Discourses on Government*: A Textbook of Revolution," *WMQ* 3rd ser., vol. 4, no. 3 (1947): 267–96.

_____. "William Penn, Edward Byllynge and the Concessions of 1677," in *The West Jersey Concessions and Agreements of 1676/77: A Roundtable of Historians*, Occasional Papers, no. 1. Trenton, NJ: New Jersey Historical Commission, 1979: 17–23.

Rustin, Bayard. "Nonviolence on Trial," in Straughton Lynd, ed. *Nonviolence in America: A Documentary History*. Indianapolis: Bobbs-Merrill, 1966: 485–97.

Ryerson, Richard Alan. "Political Mobilization and the American Revolution: The Resistance Movement in Philadelphia, 1765–1776," *WMQ* 3rd ser., vol. 31, no. 4 (1974): 556–88.

_____. "Portrait of a Colonial Oligarchy: The Quaker Elite in the Pennsylvania Assembly, 1729–1776," in Bruce C. Daniels, ed. *Power and Status: Office Holding in Colonial America*, Middletown, CT: Wesleyan University Press, 1986: 106–35.

_____. "William Penn's Gentry Commonwealth: An Interpretation of the Constitutional History of Early Pennsylvania," *Pennsylvania History* vol. 61, no. 4 (1994): 393–428.

Seed, Geoffrey. "A British Spy in Philadelphia," *PMHB* vol. 85 (1961): 3–37.

Sheldon, John P. "A Description of Philadelphia in 1825," *PMHB* vol. 60, no 1 (1936): 74–76.

Shideler, Emerson. "The Concept of the Church in Seventeenth-Century Quakerism (Part I)," *The Bulletin of Friends Historical Association* vol. 45 no. 2 (1965): 67–81.

Slotten, Martha Calvert. "John Dickinson on Independence, July 25, 1776," *Manuscripts* vol. 28, no. 3 (1976): 188–94.

Stampp, Kenneth M. "The Concept of a Perpetual Union," *The Journal of American History* vol. 65, no. 1 (1978): 5–33.

Stern, Simon. "Between Local Knowledge and National Politics: Debating Rationales for Jury Nullification after *Bushell's Case*," *Yale Law Journal* vol. 111, no. 7 (2002): 1815–59.

Stourzh, Gerald. "*Constitution*: Changing Meaning of the Term," in Terrence Ball and J. G. A. Pocock, eds. *Conceptual Change and the Constitution*. Lawrence: University Press of Kansas, 1988: 35–54.

Tachau, Mary K. Bonsteel. "The Whiskey Rebellion in Kentucky: A Forgotten Episode of Civil Disobedience," *Journal of the Early Republic* vol. 2, no. 3 (1982): 239–59.

Thompson, Martyn P. "The History of Fundamental Law in Political Thought from the French Wars of Religion to the American Revolution," *The American Historical Review* vol. 91, no. 5 (1986): 1103–28.

———. "A Note on 'Reason' and 'History' in Late Seventeenth Century Political Thought," *Political Theory* vol. 4, no. 4 (1976): 491–504.

Thompson, Peter. "'The Friendly Glass': Drink and Gentility in Colonial Philadelphia," *PMHB* vol. 113, no. 4 (1989): 549–73.

———. *Rum Punch and Revolution: Taverngoing & Public Life in Eighteenth-Century Philadelphia*. Philadelphia: University of Pennsylvania Press, 1999.

Tolles, Frederick B. "Enthusiasm versus Quietism: The Philadelphia Quakers and the Great Awakening," *PMHB* vol. 69 (1945): 26–49.

———. "John Dickinson and the Quakers," *"John and Mary's College"*: The Boyd Lee Spahr Lectures in Americana. Carlisle, PA: Fleming H. Revell Co., 1951–56: 67–88.

Tully, Alan. "Ethnicity, Religion, and Politics in Early America," *PMHB* vol. 107, no. 4 (1983): 491–536.

Van Buskirk, Judith. "Social Life in Philadelphia under the British Occupation," *Pennsylvania History* vol. 37, no. 3 (1970): 237–60.

———. "They Didn't Join the Band: Disaffected Women in Revolutionary Philadelphia," *Pennsylvania History* vol. 62, no. 3 (1995): 306–39.

Wainwright, Nicholas B. "'A Diary of Trifling Occurrences': Philadelphia, 1776–1778," *PMHB* vol. 82, no. 4 (1958): 411–65.

Warden, G. B. "The Proprietary Group in Pennsylvania, 1754–1764," *WMQ* 3rd ser., vol. 21, no. 3 (1964): 367–89.

Warner, Michael. "Textuality and Legitimacy in the Printed Constitution," in *The Letters of the Republic: Publication and the Public Sphere in Eighteenth-Century America*. Cambridge: Harvard University Press, 1990: 97–117.

Wasserstrom, Richard A. "Disobeying the Law," *The Journal of Philosophy* vol. 58, no. 21 (1961): 641–53.

Weber, Max. "The Genesis and Transformation of Charismatic Authority," in *Economy and Society: An Outline of Interpretive Sociology*. Berkeley: University of California Press, 1978: 1121–57.

Wellenreuther, Herman. "The Political Dilemma of the Quakers in Pennsylvania, 1681–1748," *PMHB* vol. 94 (1970): 135–72.

———. "The Quest for Harmony in a Turbulent World: The Principle of 'Love and Unity' in Colonial Pennsylvania Politics," *PMHB* vol. 108 (1983): 537–76.

Williams, Robert F. "The Influence of Pennsylvania's 1776 Constitution on American Constitutionalism during the Founding Decade," *PMHB* vol. 112, no. 1 (1988): 25–48.

Wilson, John K. "Religion under the State Constitutions, 1776–1800," *Journal of Church and State* vol. 32, no. 4 (1990): 753–74.

Witte, John J. "A Most Mild and Equitable Establishment of Religion': John Adams and the Massachusetts Experiment," in J. Hutson, ed. *Religion and the New Republic.* Lanham, MD: Rowman & Littlefield, 2000: 1–40.

Wolf, 2nd, Edwin. "The Authorship of the 1774 Address to the King Restudied," *WMQ* vol. 22, no. 2 (1965): 189–224.

Wolin, Sheldon. "Political Theory as a Vocation," *The American Political Science Review* vol. 63, no. 4 (1969): 1062–82.

Wood, Gordon "State Constitution-Making in the American Revolution," *Rutgers Law Journal*, vol. 24 (1993): 911–26.

Wright, Benjamin F., Jr., "The History of Written Constitutions in America," in *Essays in History and Political Theory in Honor of Charles Howard McIlwain.* New York: Russell & Russell, 1964: 344–71.

Wright, Robert K. and Morris J. MacGregor. "John Dickinson," in *Soldier-Statesmen of the Constitution.* Washington, DC: Center of Military History, U.S. Army, 1987.

Secondary Sources—Dissertations

Abend, Rosemary. "Constant Samaritans: Quaker Philanthropy in Philadelphia, 1680–1799." Ph.D. Diss., University of California, Los Angeles, 1988.

Brady, Marilyn Dell. "'The Friendly Band': Quaker Women's Benevolence and the Poor in Late Eighteenth-Century Philadelphia." M.A. Thesis, Texas Christian University, 1978.

Connerley, Jennifer. "Friendly Americans: Representing Quakers in the United States, 1850–1920." Ph.D. Diss., University of North Carolina, 2006.

Heller, Michael Alan. "Soft Persuasion: A Rhetorical Analysis of John Woolman's Essays and 'Journal'". Ph.D. Diss., Arizona State University, 1989.

Hohwald, Robert S. "The Structure of Pennsylvania Politics, 1739–1966." Ph.D. Diss., Princeton University, 1978

Powell, J. H. "John Dickinson, Penman of the Revolution." Ph.D. Diss., University of Iowa, 1938.

Stiehm, Judith Hicks. "Contemporary Theories of Nonviolent Resistance." Ph.D. Diss., Columbia University, 1969.

White, Stephen Jay. "Early American Quakers and the Transatlantic Community, 1700–1756." Ph.D. Diss., University of Illinois at Urbana–Champaign, 1990.

Secondary Sources—Unpublished Manuscripts

McKenzie, D. F. *The London Book Trade in the Later Seventeenth Century.* Unpublished manuscript, Cambridge: Sandars Lectures, 1976.

Index